WEBSTER'S NEW WORLD™

Pocket French Dictionary

WILEY

Wiley Publishing, Inc.

Contents

Free Audio Content
Go to www.wiley.com/go/wnwpocketfrench to
access free audio downloads featuring pronunciation of
twenty-five key French verbs. You will hear three regular
verbs given in their full conjugations in all tenses and the
remaining twenty-two in their full conjugations in the
most common tenses.

Preface

This revised *Pocket French Dictionary* offers wide coverage of both French and English, in a portable format with a clear, user-friendly design. With more than 25,000 words and expressions and a focus on American English, it is an accurate, reliable tool for learners of French.

This new edition provides a wide-ranging selection of the most useful and up-to-date vocabulary, including colloquial language and terms from the ever-expanding fields of information technology and telecommunications. All English headwords have been syllabified to further assist the user.

The dictionary has been designed for easy navigation through the entries. Different senses of the headword are shown by source-language indicating material in brackets, as in **chance** *(luck)* hasard *m*; *(opportunity)* chances *fpl*. Further contextualization is provided by target-language indicators which are given after the translation in cases where its sense is ambiguous, eg **scrapbook** album *m (pour collages etc)*. Finally, source-language labels such as *Grammar, Sports, Cartes* and so on are provided for items belonging to specific fields of vocabulary.

The different grammatical divisions of an entry (such as noun, verb or adjective) are easily identified by bold numbers **1, 2, 3** and so on. Similarly, sense divisions within longer entries are clearly indicated by a ▪ symbol.

For added clarity, English phrasal verbs (such as **go ahead**), many French pronominal verbs (such as **se laver**) and the most common English compound nouns (such as **heat wave**) are all presented as separate entries.

Various space-saving devices help to maximize the content of this pocket-sized book. A headword is represented by its first letter when it appears as an example within the entry, for example **on the h.** in the entry **horizon**. In addition, a slash (/) within an entry is used both to separate non-interchangeable parts of a phrase matched exactly in English and in French, such as **qui/quoi encore?** who/what else? and to show productive expressions such as **how many apples/etc?** combien de pommes/*etc*?.

Finally, the book contains helpful supplementary material to aid communication. In the centre, the user will find information on French verbs as well as names of countries, regions and nationalities. And in an exciting new feature, ten conversation panels have been added throughout the text, with useful phrases for situations like meeting people, expressing opinions and using the telephone.

French grammar notes

In French, the feminine of an adjective is formed, when regular, by adding **e** to the masculine form (eg grand, grande; carré, carrée; fin, fine). If the masculine already ends in **e**, the feminine is the same as the masculine (eg utile). Both regular and irregular feminine forms of adjectives (eg généreux, généreuse; léger, légère; doux, douce) are given on the French-English side of the dictionary. On the English-French side, French adjectives are shown in the masculine, but highly irregular feminine forms (eg frais, fraîche; faux, fausse) have also been included to help the user.

To form the plural of a French noun or adjective **s** is usually added to the singular (eg arbre, arbres; taxi, taxis; petit, petits). The plural form of a noun ending in **s, x** or **z** (eg pois, croix, nez) is the same as that of the singular. Plurals of nouns and adjectives which do not follow these general rules (eg where **x** or **aux** is added in the plural, or where there is a highly irregular plural such as œil, yeux) are listed in the French section. Also included are the plurals of French compounds where the formation of the plural involves a change other than the addition of final **s** (eg chou-fleur, choux-fleurs; arc-en-ciel, arcs-en-ciel). The irregular plurals of French nouns (and irregular masculine plurals of French adjectives) ending in **al, eau, eu, au, ail** and **ou** are listed on the French-English side (eg cerveau, -x; général, -aux). Included on the English-French side, to help the user, are the plurals of French nouns (and adjectives) ending in **al, eu** and **au** where **s**, and not the usual **x**, forms the plural (eg pneu, pneus; naval, navals) and of those nouns in **ail** and **ou** where the plural is formed with **x**, and not the usual **s** (eg travail, travaux; chou, choux).

Pronunciation of French

Table of phonetic symbols

Vowels

[i] vite, cygne, sortie
[e] été, donner, légal
[ɛ] elle, mais, père, prêt
[a] chat, fameux, toit [twa]
[ɑ] pas, âge, tâche
[ɔ] donne, fort, album
[o] dos, chaud, peau, dôme
[u] tout, cour, roue, goût

[y] cru, sûr, rue
[ø] feu, meule, nœud
[œ] œuf, jeune, cueillir [kœjir]
[ə] le, refaire, entre
[ɛ̃] vin, plein, faim, saint
[ɑ̃] enfant, temps, paon
[ɔ̃] mon, nombre, honte
[œ̃] lundi, humble, un

Consonants

[p] pain, absolu, taper, frapper
[b] beau, abbé, robe
[t] table, nette, vite
[d] donner, sud, raide
[k] camp, képi, qui, taxe [taks], accès [aksɛ]
[g] garde, guerre, second, exister [ɛgziste]
[f] feu, siffler, phase
[v] voir, trouver, wagon

[s] son, cire, ça, chasse, nation
[z] cousin, zéro, rose
[ʃ] chose, hache, schéma
[ʒ] gilet, jeter, âge
[l] lait, facile, elle
[r] rare, rhume, sortir, barreau
[m] mon, flamme, aimer
[n] né, canne, animal
[ɲ] campagne, agneau
[ŋ] jogging

Semi-consonants

[j] piano, voyage, fille, yeux
[w] ouest, noir [nwar], tramway
[ɥ] muet, lui, huile

Abbreviations

abbreviation	*abbr, abrév*	abréviation
adjective	*adj*	adjectif
adverb	*adv*	adverbe
article	*art*	article
auxiliary	*aux*	auxiliaire
Canadian	*Can*	canadien
conjunction	*conj*	conjonction
definite	*def, déf*	défini
demonstrative	*dem, dém*	démonstratif
et cetera	*etc*	et cetera
feminine	*f*	féminin
familiar	*Fam*	familier
feminine plural	*fpl*	féminin pluriel
French	*Fr*	français
indefinite	*indef, indéf*	indéfini
interjection	*int*	interjection
invariable	*inv*	invariable
masculine	*m*	masculin
masculine and feminine	*mf*	masculin et féminin
masculine plural	*mpl*	masculin pluriel
noun	*n*	nom
plural	*pl*	pluriel
possessive	*poss*	possessif
past participle	*pp*	participe passé
preposition	*prep, prép*	préposition
present participle	*pres p*	participe présent
pronoun	*pron*	pronom
	qch	quelque chose
	qn	quelqu'un
registered trademark	®	marque déposée
relative	*rel*	relatif
somebody	*sb*	
singular	*sing*	singulier
something	*sth*	
United States	*US*	États-Unis
auxiliary verb	*v aux*	verbe auxiliare
intransitive verb	*vi*	verbe intransitif
pronominal verb	*vpr*	verbe pronominal
transitive verb	*vt*	verbe transitif
transitive and intransitive verb	*vti*	verbe transitif et intransitif

English – French
Anglais – Français

A

a (*before vowel or mute h* **an**) *indef art* un, une; **a man** un homme; **an apple** une pomme; **two dollars a pound** deux dollars la livre; **30 miles an hour** 50 km à l'heure; **he's a doctor** il est médecin; **twice a month** deux fois par mois.

a·ban·don *vt* abandonner.

ab·bey abbaye *f.*

ab·bre·vi·a·tion abréviation *f.*

a·bil·i·ty capacité *f* (**to do** pour faire); **to the best of my a.** de mon mieux.

a·ble *adj* capable; **to be a. to do** être capable de faire, pouvoir faire; **to be a. to swim/drive** savoir nager/conduire.

a·ble-bod·ied *adj* robuste.

ab·nor·mal *adj* anormal.

a·board **1** *adv* (*on ship*) à bord; **all a.** (*on train*) en voiture. **2** *prep* **a. the ship** à bord du navire; **a. the train** dans le train.

a·bol·ish *vt* supprimer.

a·bor·tion avortement *m*; **to have an a.** se faire avorter.

a·bout **1** *adv* (*approximately*) à peu près, environ; **(at) a. two o'clock** vers deux heures; **out and a.** (*after illness*) sur pied; **up and a.** (*out of bed*) levé, debout. **2** *prep* (*concerning*) au sujet de; **to talk a.** parler de; **a book a.** un livre sur; **what's it (all) a.?** de quoi s'agit-il?; **what** *or* **how a. me?** et moi?; **what** *or* **how a. a drink?** que dirais-tu de prendre un verre? ▪ (+ *infinitive*) **a. to do** sur le point de faire.

a·bove **1** *adv* au-dessus; **from a.** d'en haut; **floor a.** étage *m* supérieur. **2** *prep* au-dessus de; **a. all** par-dessus tout; **he's a. me** (*in rank*) c'est mon supérieur.

a·bove-men·tioned *adj* susmentionné.

a·breast *adv* **four a.** par rangs de quatre; **to keep a. of** se tenir au courant de.

a·broad *adv* à l'étranger; **from a.** de l'étranger.

a·brupt *adj* (*sudden, rude*) brusque.

ab·scess abcès *m.*

ab·sence absence *f.*

ab·sent *adj* absent (**from** de).

ab·sent-mind·ed *adj* distrait.

ab·so·lute *adj* absolu; (*coward etc*) parfait.

ab·so·lute·ly *adv* absolument.

ab·sorb *vt* (*liquid*) absorber; **absorbed in one's work** absorbé dans *or* par son travail.

ab·surd *adj* absurde.

a·buse **1** *n* abus *m* (**of** de); (*of child etc*) mauvais traitements *mpl*; (*insults*) injures *fpl*. **2** *vt* (*use badly or wrongly*) abuser de; (*ill-treat*) maltraiter; (*insult*) injurier.

a·bu·sive *adj* grossier.

ac·a·dem·ic **1** *adj* (*year, diploma etc*) universitaire. **2** *n* (*teacher*) universitaire *mf.*

ac·cel·er·ate *vi* (*in vehicle*) accélérer.

ac·cel·er·a·tor accélérateur *m.*

ac·cent accent *m.*

ac·cept *vt* accepter.

ac·cept·a·ble *adj* acceptable.

ac·cess accès *m* (**to sth** à qch; **to sb** auprès de qn).

ac·ces·si·ble *adj* accessible.

ac·ces·so·ries *npl* (*objects*) accessoires *mpl.*

ac·ci·dent accident *m*; **by a.** (*without meaning to*) accidentellement; (*by chance*) par hasard.

ac·ci·den·tal *adj* accidentel.

ac·ci·den·tal·ly *adv* accidentellement.

ac·com·mo·date *vt* (*of house*) loger; (*oblige*) rendre service à.

ac·com·mo·da·tion(s) logement *m*

ac·com·pa·ny *vt* accompagner.

ac·com·plish *vt* accomplir; *(aim)* réaliser.

ac·cord of my own a. volontairement.

ac·cor·dance in a. with conformément à.

ac·cord·ing·ly *adv* en conséquence.

ac·cord·ing to *prep* selon.

ac·cor·di·on accordéon *m*.

ac·count *(with bank or firm)* compte *m*; *(report)* compte rendu *m*; **accounts** *(of firm)* comptabilité *f*; **to take into a.** tenir compte de; **on a. of** à cause de.

ac·count·ant comptable *mf*.

▶ **account for** *vt (explain)* expliquer; *(represent)* représenter.

ac·count·ing comptabilité *f*.

ac·cu·mu·late 1 *vt* accumuler. 2 *vi* s'accumuler.

ac·cu·ra·te *adj* exact, précis.

ac·cu·rate·ly *adv* avec précision.

ac·cu·sa·tion accusation *f*.

ac·cuse *vt* accuser *(of de)*.

ac·cused the a. l'accusé, -ée *mf*.

ac·cus·tomed *adj* habitué *(to sth* à qch; *to doing* à faire); **to get a. to** s'habituer à.

ace *(card, person)* as *m*.

ache 1 *n* douleur *f*; **to have an a.** in one's arm avoir mal au bras. 2 *vi* faire mal; **my head aches** ma tête me fait mal; **I'm aching all over** j'ai mal partout.

a·chieve *vt* réaliser; *(success, result)* obtenir; *(victory)* remporter.

a·chieve·ment *(success)* réussite *f*.

ach·ing *adj* douloureux.

ac·id *adj & n* acide *(m)*.

ac·knowl·edge *vt* reconnaître *(as* pour); **to a.** *(receipt of)* accuser réception de.

ac·ne acné *f*.

a·corn gland *m*.

ac·quaint *vt* **to be acquainted with sb** connaître qn; **we are acquainted** on se connaît.

ac·quain·tance connaissance *f*.

ac·quire *vt* acquérir.

a·cre acre *f (= 0,4 hectare)*.

ac·ro·bat acrobate *mf*.

ac·ro·bat·ic *adj* acrobatique.

a·cross *adv & prep (from side to side (of))* d'un côté à l'autre *(de)*; *(on the other side (of))* de l'autre côté *(de)*; *(so as to cross, diagonally)* en travers *(de)*; **to be half a mile a.** *(wide)* avoir un kilomètre de large; **to walk** or **go a.** *(street)* traverser.

a·cryl·ic acrylique *m*; **a. sweater/** *etc* pull *m/etc* en acrylique.

act 1 *n (deed, part of play)* acte *m*; *(in circus)* numéro *m*; **caught in the a.** pris sur le fait. 2 *vt (role in play or film)* jouer. 3 *vi (do sth, behave)* agir; **to a. as** *(secretary etc)* faire office de; *(of object)* servir de.

▶ **act for** *vt* représenter.

ac·tion action *f*; *(military)* combat *m*; **to take a.** prendre des mesures; **to put into a.** *(plan)* exécuter; **out of a.** hors d'usage; *(person)* hors *(de)* combat.

ac·tive 1 *adj* actif; *(interest, dislike)* vif. 2 *n Grammar* actif *m*.

ac·tiv·i·ty activité *f*; *(in street)* animation *f*.

▶ **act (up)on** *vt (affect)* agir sur; *(advice)* suivre.

ac·tor acteur *m*.

ac·tress actrice *f*.

ac·tu·al *adj* réel; **the a. book** le livre même.

ac·tu·al·ly *adv (truly)* réellement; *(in fact)* en réalité.

a·cute *adj* aigu *(f* -uë); *(emotion)* vif; *(shortage)* grave.

AD *abbr (anno Domini)* après Jésus-Christ.

ad *Fam* pub *f*; *(private, in newspaper)* annonce *f*; **want ad** petite annonce.

a·dapt *vt* adapter *(to* à); **to a.** *(oneself)* s'adapter.

a·dapt·a·ble *adj (person)* souple.

a·dap·ter, a·dap·tor *(plug)* prise *f* multiple.

add *vt* ajouter (**to** à; **that** que); *(total)* additionner.

ad·dict TV **a.** fana *mf* de la télé; **drug a.** drogué, -ée *mf*.

ad·dict·ed *adj* to be a. to *(TV)* se passionner pour; **a. to alcohol** alcoolique; **to be a. to cocaine** avoir une dépendance à la cocaïne, être cocaïnomane.

ad·dic·tion drug a. toxicomanie *f*.

▸ **add in** *vt (include)* inclure.

ad·di·tion addition *f*; **in a.** de plus; **in a. to** en plus de.

ad·di·tion·al *adj* supplémentaire.

ad·di·tive additif *m*.

ad·dress 1 *n (on letter etc)* adresse *f*; *(speech)* allocution *f*. **2** *vt (person)* s'adresser à; *(audience)* parler devant; *(letter)* mettre l'adresse sur.

▸ **add to** *vt (increase)* augmenter.

▸ **add together** *vt (numbers)* additionner.

▸ **add up 1** *vt (numbers)* additionner. **2** *vi* to a. up to *(total)* s'élever à; *(mean)* signifier; *(represent)* constituer.

ad·e·noids *npl* végétations *fpl* (adénoïdes).

ad·e·quate *adj (quantity etc)* suffisant; *(acceptable)* convenable; *(person)* compétent.

ad·e·quate·ly *adv* suffisamment; convenablement.

▸ **ad·here to** *vt* adhérer à; *(decision, rule)* tenir à.

ad·he·sive *adj & n* adhésif *(m)*.

ad·ja·cent *adj (building, angle)* adjacent (**to** à).

ad·jec·tive adjectif *m*.

ad·just *vt (machine)* régler; *(salaries)* ajuster; **to a. (oneself) to** s'adapter à.

ad·just·a·ble *adj (seat)* réglable.

ad·just·ment réglage *m*; *(of person)* adaptation *f*.

ad lib *vi* improviser.

ad·min·is·ter *vt* administrer.

ad·min·is·tra·tion administration *f*; *(government)* gouvernement *m*.

ad·min·is·tra·tive *adj* administratif.

ad·min·is·tra·tor directeur, -trice *mf*, administrateur, -trice *mf*.

ad·mi·ral amiral *m*.

ad·mi·ra·tion admiration *f*.

ad·mire *vt* admirer (**for** pour; **for doing** de faire).

ad·mis·sion *(to movies etc)* entrée *f*; **a. charge** prix *m* d'entrée.

ad·mit *vt (let in)* laisser entrer, admettre; *(acknowledge)* reconnaître, admettre (**that** que).

ad·mit·tance entrée *f*; **'no a.'** 'entrée interdite'.

▸ **admit to** *vt (confess)* avouer.

ad·o·les·cent adolescent, -ente *mf*.

a·dopt *vt (child, attitude)* adopter.

a·dopt·ed *adj (child)* adoptif.

a·dop·tion adoption *f*.

a·dor·a·ble *adj* adorable.

a·dore *vt* adorer (**doing** faire).

a·dult 1 *n* adulte *mf*. **2** *adj (animal etc)* adulte; **a. class/film/etc** classe *f*/film *m*/etc pour adultes.

ad·vance 1 *n (movement, money)* avance *f*; **advances** *(sexual)* avances *fpl*; **in a.** à l'avance, d'avance. **2** *adj (payment)* anticipé; **a. reservation** réservation *f*. **3** *vt (put forward, lend)* avancer. **4** *vi (go forward, progress)* avancer.

ad·vanced *adj* avancé; *(studies, level)* supérieur; *(course)* de niveau supérieur.

ad·van·tage avantage *m* (**over** sur); **to take a. of** profiter de; *(person)* exploiter.

ad·ven·ture aventure *f*.

ad·ven·tur·ous *adj* aventureux.

ad·verb adverbe *m*.

ad·ver·tise 1 *vt (commercially)* faire de la publicité pour; *(pri-*

vately) passer une annonce pour vendre; *(make known)* annoncer. **2** *vi* faire de la publicité; *(privately)* passer une annonce (**for** pour trouver).

ad·ver·tise·ment publicité *f*, *(private, in newspaper)* annonce *f*, *(poster)* affiche *f*, **classified a.** petite annonce.

ad·vice conseil(s) *m(pl)*; **a piece of a.** un conseil.

ad·vis·a·ble *adj (wise)* prudent (**to do** de faire).

ad·vise *vt* conseiller; *(recommend)* recommander; **to a. sb to do** conseiller à qn de faire.

▶ **advise against** *vt* déconseiller.

ad·vis·er conseiller, -ère *mf*.

ad·vo·cate 1 *n (supporter)* défenseur *m*. **2** *vt* préconiser.

aer·i·al antenne *f*.

aer·o·bics *npl* aérobic *m*.

aer·o·sol aérosol *m*.

aes·thet·ic *adj* esthétique.

af·fair affaire *f*, **(love) a.** liaison *f*.

af·fect *vt (concern, move)* toucher, affecter; *(harm)* nuire à.

af·fec·tion affection *f* (**for** pour).

af·fec·tion·ate *adj* affectueux.

af·flu·ent *adj* riche.

af·ford *vt (be able to pay for)* avoir les moyens d'acheter; *(time)* pouvoir trouver.

af·ford·a·ble *adj (price etc)* abordable.

a·float *adv (ship, swimmer, business)* à flot.

a·fraid *adj* **to be a.** avoir peur (**of**, **to do**); **he's a. (that) she may be sick** il a peur qu'elle (ne) soit malade; **I'm a. he's out** *(I regret to say)* je regrette, il est sorti.

Af·ri·can 1 *n* Africain, -aine *mf*. **2** *adj* africain.

af·ter 1 *adv* après; **the month a.** le mois suivant. **2** *prep* après; **a. all** après tout; **a. eating** après avoir mangé; **a. you!** je vous en prie!; **ten a. four** quatre heures dix; **to**

be a. sth/sb *(seek)* chercher qch/qn. **3** *conj* après que.

af·ter·ef·fects *npl* suites *fpl*.

af·ter·noon après-midi *m or f inv*; **in the a.** l'après-midi; **good a.!** *(hello)* bonjour!

af·ter·noons *adv* l'après-midi.

af·ter·shave après-rasage *m*.

af·ter·ward(s) *adv* après, plus tard.

a·gain *adv* de nouveau, encore une fois; **never a.** plus jamais; **a. and a., time and (time) a.** bien des fois, maintes fois.

a·gainst *prep* contre; **a. the law** illégal.

age 1 *n* âge *m*; **(old) a.** vieillesse *f*, **the Middle Ages** le Moyen Âge; **five years of a.** âgé de cinq ans; **under a.** trop jeune. **2** *vti* vieillir.

aged *adj* **a. ten** âgé de dix ans.

a·gen·cy *(office)* agence *f*.

a·gen·da ordre *m* du jour.

a·gent agent *m*; *(dealer)* concessionnaire *mf*.

ag·gra·vate *vt (make worse)* aggraver; *(annoy)* Fam exaspérer.

ag·gra·va·tion *(annoyance)* ennui(s) *m(pl)*.

ag·gres·sion agression *f*.

ag·gres·sive *adj* agressif.

ag·ile *adj* agile.

ag·i·tat·ed *adj* agité.

a·go *adv* **a year a.** il y a un an; **how long a.?** il y a combien de temps (de cela)?

ag·o·ny **to be in a.** souffrir horriblement.

a·gree 1 *vi (come to an agreement)* se mettre d'accord; *(be in agreement)* être d'accord (**with** avec); *(of facts, dates)* concorder; *Grammar* s'accorder; **to a. to sth/to doing** consentir à qch/à faire; **it doesn't a. with me** *(food, climate)* ça ne me réussit pas. **2** *vt* **to a. to do** accepter de faire; **to a. that** admettre que.

a·gree·a·ble *adj (pleasant)* agréable.

a·greed *adj (time, place)* convenu; **we are a.** nous sommes d'accord; **a.!** entendu!

a·gree·ment accord *m*; **in a. with** d'accord avec; **to reach an a.** tomber d'accord.

▶ **agree (up)on** *vt* convenir de.

ag·ri·cul·tur·al *adj* agricole.

ag·ri·cul·ture agriculture *f*.

a·head *adv (in space)* en avant; *(leading)* en tête; *(in the future)* dans l'avenir; **a. (of time)** en avance (sur l'horaire); **to be one hour a.** avoir une heure d'avance (**of** sur); **a. of** *(space)* devant; *(time)* en avance sur; **straight a.** *(to walk)* tout droit; *(to look)* droit devant soi.

aid aide *f*, *(device)* accessoire *m*, support *m*; **with the a. of** *(a stick etc)* à l'aide de; **in a. of** *(charity)* au profit de.

AIDS *abrev (acquired immune deficiency syndrome)* SIDA *m*.

aim **1** *n* but *m*; **with the a. of** dans le but de. **2** *vt (gun)* braquer (**at** sur); **aimed at children**/*etc (product)* destiné aux enfants/*etc*. **3** *vi* viser; **to a. at sb** viser qn; **to a. to do** *or* **at doing** avoir l'intention de faire.

air **1** *n* air *m*; **in the open a.** en plein air; **by a.** *(to travel, send)* par avion; **(up) in(to) the a.** en l'air. **2** *adj (raid, base)* aérien. **3** *vt (room)* aérer.

air-con·di·tioned *adj* climatisé.

air con·di·tion·ing climatisation *f*.

air·craft *inv* avion(s) *m(pl)*.

air·craft car·ri·er porte-avions *m inv*

air·fare prix *m* du billet d'avion.

air force armée *f* de l'air.

air·line ligne *f* aérienne.

air·line tick·et billet *m* d'avion.

air·mail poste *f* aérienne; **by a.** par avion.

air·plane avion *m*.

air·port aéroport *m*.

air·sick·ness mal *m* de l'air.

air ter·mi·nal aérogare *f*.

air·tight *adj* hermétique.

air traf·fic con·trol·ler aiguilleur *m* du ciel.

aisle *(walkway in plane, theater)* allée *f*, *(in church)* nef *f* latérale; *(row of seats)* rangée *f*, *(section of supermarket)* rayon *m*.

a·jar *adj (door)* entrouvert.

a·larm **1** *n (warning, device in house or car)* alarme *f*, *(mechanism)* sonnerie *f* (d'alarme); **a. (clock)** réveil *m*. **2** *vt* alarmer.

al·bum *(book, record)* album *m*.

al·co·hol alcool *m*.

al·co·hol·ic **1** *adj (drink)* alcoolisé. **2** *n (person)* alcoolique *mf*.

a·lert *adj (watching carefully)* vigilant.

al·ge·bra algèbre *f*.

a·li·as **1** *n (pl* **aliases)** nom *m* d'emprunt. **2** *adv* alias.

al·i·bi alibi *m*.

a·li·en étranger, -ère *mf*.

a·light *adj (fire)* allumé; **to set a.** mettre le feu à.

a·like *adj (people, things)* semblables; **to look** *or* **be a.** se ressembler. **2** *adv* de la même manière.

a·live *adj* vivant, en vie.

all **1** *adj* tout, toute, *pl* tous, toutes; **a. day** toute la journée; **a. (the) men** tous les hommes. **2** *pron* tous *mpl*, toutes *fpl*; *(everything)* tout; **my sisters are a. here** toutes mes sœurs sont ici; **he ate it a., he ate a. of it** il a tout mangé; **a. (that) he has** tout ce qu'il a; **a. of us** nous tous; **in a., a. told** en tout; **a. but** *(almost)* presque; **if there's any wind at a.** s'il y a le moindre vent; **not at a.** pas de tout; *(after 'thank you')* pas de quoi. **3** *adv* tout; **a. alone** tout seul; six **a.** *Sport* six buts partout.

al·le·giance fidélité *f* (**to** à).

al·ler·gic *adj* allergique (**to** à).

al·ley ruelle *f*, *(in park)* allée *f*.

al·li·ance alliance *f*.

al·lied *adj (country)* allié; *(matters)* lié.

al·li·ga·tor alligator *m*.

al·lo·cate *vt* allouer (**to** à); *(distribute)* répartir.

al·lot·ment *(land)* lopin *m* de terre *(loué pour la culture)*.

all-out *adj (effort)* énergique.

al·low *vt* permettre; *(give)* accorder; *(as discount)* déduire; **to a. sb to do** permettre à qn de faire; **you're not allowed to go** on vous interdit de partir.

al·low·ance allocation *f*, *(for travel, housing, food)* indemnité *f*, *(for duty-free goods)* tolérance *f*, *(for children)* argent *m* de poche; **to make allowances for sb** être indulgent envers qn.

▸ **allow for** *vt* tenir compte de.

all-pur·pose *adj (tool)* universel.

all-right 1 *adj (satisfactory)* bien *inv*; *(unharmed)* sain et sauf; *(undamaged)* intact; *(without worries)* tranquille; **it's a.** ça va; **I'm a.** *(healthy)* je vais bien. **2** *adv (well)* bien; **a.!** *(agreement)* d'accord!; **I got your letter a.** *(emphatic)* j'ai bien reçu votre lettre.

all-round *adj* complet.

al·ly allié, -ée *mf*.

al·mond amande *f*.

al·most *adv* presque; **he a. fell/etc** il a failli tomber/*etc*.

a·lone *adj & adv* seul; **to leave a.** *(person)* laisser tranquille; *(thing)* ne pas toucher à.

a·long 1 *prep (all)* **a.** (tout) le long de; **to go** *or* **walk a.** *(street)* passer par; **a. with** avec. **2** *adv* **all a.** *(time)* dès le début.

a·long·side *prep & adv* à côté (de).

a·loud *adv* à haute voix.

al·pha·bet alphabet *m*.

al·pha·bet·i·cal *adj* alphabétique.

Alps *npl* **the A.** les Alpes *fpl*.

al·read·y *adv* déjà.

al·right *adv Fam* = **all-right**.

al·so *adv* aussi.

al·tar autel *m*.

al·ter **1** *vt* changer; *(clothing)* retoucher. **2** *vi* changer.

al·ter·a·tion changement *m*; *(of clothing)* retouche *f*.

al·ter·nate 1 *adj* alterné; **on a. days** tous les deux jours. **2** *vi* alterner (**with** avec).

al·ter·na·tive 1 *adj (other)* autre. **2** *n* alternative *f*.

al·ter·na·tive·ly *adv* comme alternative.

al·though *adv* bien que (+ *subjunctive*).

al·to·geth·er *adv (completely)* tout à fait; *(on the whole)* somme toute; **how much a.?** combien en tout?

a·lu·mi·num aluminium *m*.

al·ways *adv* toujours.

am *see* **be**.

a.m. *adv* du matin.

am·a·teur 1 *n* amateur *m*. **2** *adj* **a. painter/etc** peintre/*etc* amateur.

a·maze *vt* étonner.

a·mazed *adj* stupéfait (**at sth** de qch; **at seeing** de voir); *(filled with wonder)* émerveillé.

a·maz·ing *adj* stupéfiant; *(incredible)* extraordinaire.

am·bas·sa·dor ambassadeur *m*; *(woman)* ambassadrice *f*.

am·ber **a. (light)** *(of traffic signal)* (feu *m*) orange *m*.

am·big·u·ous *adj* ambigu *(f* -uë).

am·bi·tion ambition *f*.

am·bi·tious *adj* ambitieux.

am·bu·lance ambulance *f*.

am·bu·lance driv·er ambulancier, -ière *mf*.

a·mend *vt (text)* modifier; *(law)* amender.

A·mer·i·can 1 *n* Américain, -aine *mf*. **2** *adj* américain.

a·mid(st) *prep* au milieu de, parmi.

am·mu·ni·tion munitions *fpl*.

a·mong(st) *prep* parmi, entre; **a. the crowd/books** parmi la foule/ les livres; **a. themselves/friends** entre eux/amis.

a·mount quantité *f*, *(sum of money)* somme *f*, *(total of bill etc)* montant *m*.

▸ **amount to** *vt* s'élever à; *(mean)* signifier; *(represent)* représenter.

am·ple *adj (enough)* largement assez de; **you have a. time** tu as largement le temps.

am·pli·fi·er amplificateur *m*.

am·pu·tate *vt* amputer.

a·muse *vt* amuser.

a·muse·ment amusement *m*.

a·mus·ing *adj* amusant.

an *see* **a**.

an·al·y·sis, *pl* **-ses** analyse *f*.

an·a·lyst analyste *mf*; *(psycho-analyst)* (psych)analyste *mf*.

an·a·lyze *vt* analyser.

an·ar·chy anarchie *f*.

a·nat·o·my anatomie *f*.

an·ces·tor ancêtre *m*.

an·chor ancre *f*.

an·chored *adj* ancré.

an·cho·vy anchois *m*.

an·cient *adj* ancien; *(pre-medie-val)* antique.

and *conj* et; **two hundred a.** two deux cent deux; **better a. better** de mieux en mieux; **go a. see** va voir.

an·es·thet·ic anesthésie *f*, *(sub-stance)* anesthésique *m*; **general a.** anesthésie générale.

an·gel ange *m*.

an·ger colère *f*.

an·gle angle *m*; **at an a.** en biais.

an·gler pêcheur, -euse *mf* à la ligne.

an·gri·ly *adv (to speak etc)* avec colère.

an·gry *adj* fâché; *(letter)* indigné; **to get a.** se fâcher (**with** contre).

an·i·mal *n & adj* animal *(m)*.

an·kle cheville *f*.

an·kle sock socquette *f*.

an·nex *(building)* annexe *f*.

an·ni·ver·sa·ry *(of event)* anniversaire *m*.

an·nounce *vt* annoncer; *(birth, marriage)* faire part de.

an·nounce·ment *(statement)* annonce *f*, *(notice)* avis *m*.

an·nounc·er *(on TV)* speaker *m*, speakerine *f*.

an·noy *vt (inconvenience)* ennuyer; *(irritate)* agacer.

an·noyed *adj* fâché; **to get a.** se fâcher (**with** contre).

an·noy·ing *adj* ennuyeux.

an·nu·al 1 *adj* annuel. **2** *n (book)* annuaire *m*.

an·nu·al·ly *adv* annuellement.

a·non·y·mous *adj* anonyme.

an·oth·er *adj & pron* un(e) autre; **a. man** un autre homme; **a. month** *(additional)* encore un mois; **a. ten** encore dix; **one a.** l'un(e) l'autre, *pl* les un(e)s les autres; **they love one a.** ils s'aiment (l'un l'autre).

an·swer 1 *n* réponse *f*, *(to pro-blem)* solution *f* (**to** de). **2** *vt (per-son, question, phone)* répondre à; *(prayer, wish)* exaucer; **to a. the door** ouvrir la porte. **3** *vi* répondre.

▸ **answer back** *vt* répondre à.

▸ **answer for** *vt* répondre de.

an·swer·ing ma·chine répondeur *m*.

ant fourmi *f*.

an·te·lope antilope *f*.

an·ten·na antenne *f*.

an·them national **a.** hymne *m* national.

an·thol·o·gy recueil *m*.

an·ti- *prefix* anti-.

an·ti·bi·ot·ic antibiotique *m*.

an·ti·bod·y anticorps *m*.

an·ti·ci·pate *vt (foresee)* prévoir; *(expect)* s'attendre à.

an·tic·i·pa·tion **in a. of** en prévision de.

an·tics *npl* singeries *fpl*.

an·ti·freeze antigel *m*.

an·ti·his·ta·mine antihistaminique *m*.

an·tique 1 *adj (furniture etc)* ancien. **2** *n* antiquité *f*.
an·tique deal·er antiquaire *mf*.
an·tique shop magasin *m* d'antiquités.
an·ti·sep·tic *adj & n* antiseptique *(m)*.
anx·i·e·ty *(worry)* inquiétude *f*, *(fear)* anxiété *f*.
anx·ious *adj (worried)* inquiet (**about** de, pour); *(afraid)* anxieux; *(eager)* impatient (**to do** de faire).
anx·ious·ly *adv (to wait)* impatiemment.
an·y 1 *adj (with question)* du, de la, des; **do you have a. milk/tickets?** avez-vous du lait/des billets? ▪ *(negative)* de; **he hasn't got a. milk/tickets** il n'a pas de lait/de billets. ▪ *(no matter which)* n'importe quel. ▪ *(every)* tout; **in a. case, at a. rate** de toute façon. **2** *pron (no matter which one)* n'importe lequel; *(somebody)* quelqu'un; **if a. of you** si l'un d'entre vous. ▪ *(quantity)* en; **do you have a.?** en as-tu? **3** *adv* **(not) a. happier/etc** (pas) plus heureux/etc; **I don't see him a. more** je ne le vois plus; **a. more tea?** encore du thé?; **a. better?** c'est mieux?
an·y·bod·y *pron (somebody)* quelqu'un; **do you see a.?** vois-tu quelqu'un? ▪ *(negative)* personne; **he doesn't know a.** il ne connaît personne. ▪ *(no matter who)* n'importe qui.
an·y·how *adv (at any rate)* de toute façon; *(badly)* n'importe comment.
an·y·one *pron* = **anybody**.
an·y·place *adv* = **anywhere**.
an·y·thing *pron (something)* quelque chose. ▪ *(negative)* rien; **he doesn't do a.** il ne fait rien. ▪ *(everything)* tout; **a. you like** *(tout)* ce que tu veux. ▪ *(no matter what)* **a. (at all)** n'importe quoi.
an·y·way *adv (at any rate)* de toute façon.

an·y·where *adv (no matter where)* n'importe où. ▪ *(everywhere)* partout; **a. you go** partout où vous allez; **a. you like** là où tu veux. ▪ *(negative)* nulle part; **he doesn't go a.** il ne va nulle part.
a·part *adv* **we kept them a.** *(separate)* on les tenait séparés; **with legs a.** les jambes écartées; **they are three feet a.** ils se trouvent à un mètre l'un de l'autre; **a. from** *(except for)* à part.
a·part·ment appartement *m*; **a. house** *or* **building** immeuble *m* (d'habitation).
ape singe *m*.
a·pé·ri·tif apéritif *m*.
a·pol·o·get·ic *adj* **to be a.** s'excuser (**about** de).
a·pol·o·gize *vi* s'excuser (**for** de); **to a. to sb** faire ses excuses à qn (**for** pour).
a·pol·o·gy excuses *fpl*.
a·pos·tro·phe apostrophe *f*.
ap·pall *vt* consterner.
ap·pall·ing *adj* épouvantable.
ap·pa·ra·tus appareil *m*; *(in gym)* agrès *mpl*.
ap·par·el vêtements *mpl*.
ap·par·ent *adj* apparent; **it's a. that** il est évident que.
ap·par·ent·ly *adv* apparemment.
ap·peal¹ *(charm)* attrait *m*; *(interest)* intérêt *m*.
ap·peal² **1** *n (in court)* appel *m*. **2** *vi* faire appel.
▸ **appeal to** *vt (attract)* plaire à; *(interest)* intéresser.
ap·pear *vi (become visible)* apparaître; *(present oneself)* se présenter; *(seem, be published)* paraître; *(in court)* comparaître; **it appears that** il semble que *(+ subjunctive or indicative)*.
ap·pear·ance *(act)* apparition *f*; *(look)* apparence *f*.
ap·pen·di·ci·tis appendicite *f*.
ap·pen·dix, *pl* **-ixes** *or* **-ices** *(in book, body)* appendice *m*.

ap·pe·tite appétit *m*.

ap·pe·tiz·ing *adj* appétissant.

ap·plaud *vti (clap)* applaudir.

ap·plause applaudissements *mpl*.

ap·ple pomme *f*; **cooking a.** pomme *f* à cuire; **a. pie** tarte *f* aux pommes.

ap·pli·ance appareil *m*.

ap·pli·ca·ble *adj* applicable (**to** à).

ap·pli·cant candidat, -ate *mf* (**for** à).

ap·pli·ca·tion *(for job)* candidature *f*; *(for membership)* demande *f* d'adhésion; **a. (form)** *(for job)* formulaire *m* de candidature.

ap·ply 1 *vt* appliquer; *(brake)* appuyer sur; **to a. oneself to** s'appliquer à. **2** *vi (be relevant)* s'appliquer (**to** à).

▶**apply for** *vt (job)* poser sa candidature à.

ap·point *vt (person)* nommer (**to sth** à qch; **to do** pour faire).

ap·point·ment nomination *f*; *(meeting)* rendez-vous *m inv*.

ap·point·ment book agenda *m*.

ap·prais·al évaluation *f*.

ap·praise *vt* évaluer.

ap·pre·ci·ate *vt (enjoy, value)* apprécier; *(understand)* comprendre; *(be grateful for)* être reconnaissant de.

ap·pre·ci·a·tion *(gratitude)* reconnaissance *f*.

ap·pren·tice apprenti, -ie *mf*.

ap·pren·tice·ship apprentissage *m*.

ap·proach 1 *vt (person, door etc)* s'approcher de; *(age, result, town)* approcher de; *(subject)* aborder. **2** *vi (of person, vehicle)* s'approcher; *(of date)* approcher. **3** *n (method)* façon *f* de s'y prendre.

ap·pro·pri·ate *adj* convenable.

ap·prov·al approbation *f*; **on a.** *(goods)* à l'essai.

▶**ap·prove of** *vt (conduct etc)* approuver; **I don't a. of him** il ne me

plaît pas; **I a. of his going** je trouve bon qu'il y aille.

ap·prox·i·mate *adj* approximatif.

ap·prox·i·mate·ly *adv* à peu près.

a·pri·cot abricot *m*.

A·pril avril *m*.

a·pron tablier *m*.

apt *adj (remark, reply)* juste, convenable; **to be a. to** avoir tendance à.

ap·ti·tude aptitude *f* (**for** à, pour).

a·quar·i·um aquarium *m*.

Ar·ab *adj & n* arabe *(mf)*.

Ar·a·bic *adj & n (language)* arabe *(m)*; **A. numerals** chiffres *mpl* arabes.

ar·bi·trar·y *adj* arbitraire.

arc *(of circle)* arc *m*.

arch *(of bridge)* arche *f*; *(of building)* voûte *f*.

arch·er archer *m*.

arch·e·ry tir *m* à l'arc.

ar·chi·tect architecte *mf*.

ar·chi·tec·ture architecture *f*.

Arc·tic the A. l'Arctique *f*.

are *see* **be**.

ar·e·a *(in geometry)* superficie *f*; *(of country)* région *f*; *(of town)* quartier *m*; **parking a.** aire *f* de stationnement.

ar·e·a code *(phone number)* indicatif *m*.

a·re·na arène *f*.

ar·gue 1 *vi (quarrel)* se disputer (**with** avec; **about** au sujet de); *(reason)* raisonner (**with** avec, **about** sur). **2** *vt* **to a. that** *(maintain)* soutenir que.

ar·gu·ment *(quarrel)* dispute *f*; *(reasoning)* argument *m*; **to have an a.** se disputer.

a·rise* *vi (of problem, opportunity)* se présenter; *(result)* résulter (**from** de).

a·rith·me·tic arithmétique *f*.

arm 1 *n* bras *m*; *(weapon)* arme *f*. **2** *vt* armer (**with** de).

arm·band brassard *m*.

arm·chair fauteuil m.

ar·mor (of knight) armure f, (of tank etc) blindage m.

ar·mored adj (car etc) blindé.

arm·pit aisselle f.

ar·my 1 n armée f. **2** adj militaire.

a·round 1 prep autour de; (approximately) environ. **2** adv autour; **a. here** par ici; **he's still a.** il est encore là; **there's a lot of flu a.** il y a pas mal de grippes dans l'air; **there's a rumor going a.** il y a un bruit qui court; **up and a.** (after illness) sur pied.

a·rouse vt éveiller.

ar·range vt arranger; (time, meeting) fixer; **to a. to do** s'arranger pour faire.

ar·range·ment (layout, agreement) arrangement m; **arrangements** préparatifs mpl; (plans) projets mpl.

ar·rears npl in a. en retard dans ses paiements.

ar·rest 1 vt arrêter. **2** n arrestation f; **under a.** en état d'arrestation.

ar·ri·val arrivée f.

ar·rive vi arriver.

ar·row flèche f.

art art m; **work of a.** œuvre f d'art.

ar·te·ry artère f.

ar·thri·tis arthrite f.

ar·ti·cle (object, in newspaper, in grammar) article m.

ar·tic·u·late¹ adj (speech) clair; (person) qui s'exprime clairement.

ar·tic·u·late² vti articuler.

ar·ti·fi·cial adj artificiel.

ar·tist (actor, painter etc) artiste mf.

ar·tis·tic adj artistique; (person) artiste.

as adv & conj (manner etc) comme; **as you like** comme tu veux; **as much or as hard as I can** (au)tant que je peux; **as (it) is** (to leave sth) comme ça, tel quel; **as if, as though** comme si. ▪ (comparison) **as tall as you** aussi grand que vous; **as white as a sheet** blanc comme un linge; **as much or as hard as you** autant que vous; **twice as big as** deux fois plus grand que. ▪ (though) **(as) smart as he is** si intelligent qu'il soit. ▪ (capacity) **as a teacher** comme professeur; **to act as a father** agir en père. ▪ (reason) puisque; **as it's late** puisqu'il est tard. ▪ (time) **as I was leaving** comme je partais; **as he slept** pendant qu'il dormait; **as from, as of** (time) à partir de. ▪ (concerning) **as for that** quant à cela. ▪ (+ infinitive) **so as to** de manière à; **so stupid as to** assez bête pour.

asap abbr (as soon as possible) le plut tôt possible.

as·cer·tain vt établir, déterminer.

ash cendre f.

a·shamed adj **to be a.** avoir honte (of de).

a·shore adv **to go a.** débarquer.

ash·tray cendrier m.

A·sian 1 n Asiatique mf. **2** adj asiatique.

a·side adv de côté; **a. from** en dehors de.

ask 1 vt demander; (a question) poser; (invite) inviter; **to a. sb (for) sth** demander qch à qn; **to a. sb to do** demander à qn de faire. **2** vi demander; **to a. for sth/sb** demander qch/qn; **to a. about sth** se renseigner sur qch; **to a. about sb** demander des nouvelles de qn; **to a. sb about** interroger qn sur.

a·sleep adj **to be a.** dormir; **to fall a.** s'endormir.

as·par·a·gus asperges fpl.

as·pect aspect m.

as·pi·rin aspirine f.

as·sault 1 n (crime) agression f. **2** vt (attack) agresser.

as·sem·ble 1 vt assembler; (people) rassembler; (machine) monter. **2** vi se rassembler.

as·sem·bly (meeting) assemblée f, (in school) rassemblement m.

as·sert vt affirmer; **to a. oneself**

s'affirmer; **to a. one's rights** faire valoir ses droits.

as·sess vt (estimate) évaluer; (decide amount of) fixer le montant de.

as·set (advantage) atout m; **assets** (of business) actif m.

as·sign vt (give) attribuer (**to** à).

as·sign·ment (task) mission f.

as·sist vti aider (**in doing, to do** à faire).

as·sis·tance aide f; **to be of a. to sb** aider qn.

as·sis·tant 1 n assistant, -ante mf; (in shop) vendeur, -euse mf. **2** adj adjoint.

as·so·ci·ate 1 vt associer; **associated with sth/sb** associé à qch/avec qn. **2** n & adj associé, -ée (mf).

as·so·ci·a·tion association f.

as·sort·ed adj variés; (foods) assortis.

as·sort·ment assortiment m.

as·sume vt (suppose) présumer (**that** que); (take on) prendre; (responsibility, role) assumer.

as·sur·ance assurance f.

as·sure vt assurer (**sb that** à qn que; **sb of** qn de).

as·ter·isk astérisque m.

asth·ma asthme m.

asth·mat·ic adj & n asthmatique (mf).

a·ston·ish vt étonner; **to be astonished** s'étonner (**at sth** de qch).

a·ston·ish·ing adj étonnant.

a·stray adv **to go a.** s'égarer.

as·trol·o·gy astrologie f.

as·tro·naut astronaute mf.

as·tron·o·my astronomie f.

a·sy·lum asile m; **to seek a.** chercher asile; (**mental) a.** asile m (d'aliénés).

at prep à; **at work** au travail; **at six (o'clock)** à six heures; **at sign** (in e-mail address) arrobas m, arobase f. ▪ **chez**; **at the doctor's** chez le médecin. ▪ **en**; **at sea** en mer. ▪ **contre**; **angry at** fâché contre. ▪ **sur**; **to shoot at** tirer sur. ▪ **de**; **to**

laugh at rire de. ▪ (au)près de; **at the window** (au)près de la fenêtre. ▪ **par**; **six at a time** six par six.

ath·lete athlète mf.

ath·let·ic adj athlétique.

ath·let·ics npl athlétisme m.

At·lan·tic 1 adj atlantique. **2** n **the A.** l'Atlantique m.

at·las atlas m.

ATM abbr (automatic teller machine) DAB m.

at·mos·phere atmosphère f.

at·om atome m.

a·tom·ic adj (bomb etc) atomique.

at·tach vt attacher (**to** à); (document) joindre (**to** à); **attached to** (fond of) attaché à.

at·ta·ché case attaché-case m, mallette f.

at·tach·ment (tool) accessoire m; (to e-mail) fichier m joint.

at·tack 1 n attaque f. **2** vti attaquer.

at·tack·er agresseur m.

at·tain vt (aim) atteindre; (goal, ambition) réaliser; (rank) parvenir à.

at·tempt 1 n tentative f; **to make an a.** to tenter de. **2** vt tenter; (task) entreprendre; **to a. to do** tenter de faire.

at·tend 1 vt (meeting etc) assister à; (course) suivre; (school, church) aller à. **2** vi assister.

at·ten·dance présence f (**at** à); (school) a. scolarité f.

at·ten·dant employé, -ée mf, (in gas station) pompiste mf, (in museum) gardien, -ienne mf.

▸**attend to** vt (customer, task) s'occuper de.

at·ten·tion attention f; **to pay a.** faire attention (**to** à).

at·ten·tive adj attentif (**to** à).

at·tic grenier m.

at·ti·tude attitude f.

at·tor·ney avocat, -e mf.

at·tract vt attirer.

at·trac·tion (charm) attrait m.

at·trac·tive adj (price, offer etc) intéressant; (person) attirant, séduisant.

at·trib·ute 1 *n (quality)* attribut *m*.
2 *vt* attribuer (**to**) à.

auc·tion (off) *vt* vendre (aux enchères).

auc·tion·eer commissaire-priseur *m*.

au·di·ble *adj* perceptible.

au·di·ence *(of speaker, musician)* auditoire *m; (in theater)* spectateurs *mpl; (of radio broadcast)* auditeurs *mpl;* **TV** &. téléspectateurs *mpl*.

au·di·o *adj* audio *inv*.

au·di·o·vi·su·al *adj* audiovisuel.

au·dit 1 *n* audit *m*. 2 *vt* vérifier.

Au·gust août *m*.

aunt tante *f*.

aunt·ie, aunt·y *Fam* tata *f*.

au pair 1 *adv* au pair. 2 *n* **au p. (girl)** jeune fille *f* au pair.

Aus·tra·li·an 1 *n* Australien, -ienne *mf*. 2 *adj* australien.

Aus·tri·an 1 *n* Autrichien, -ienne *mf*. 2 *adj* autrichien.

au·then·tic *adj* authentique.

au·thor auteur *m*.

au·thor·i·ty autorité *f, (permission)* autorisation *f* (**to do** à faire).

au·thor·i·za·tion autorisation *f* (**to do** à faire).

au·to·bi·og·ra·phy autobiographie *f*.

au·to·graph 1 *n* autographe *m*. 2 *vt* dédicacer (**for** à).

au·to·mat·ic *adj* automatique.

au·to·mat·i·cal·ly *adv* automatiquement.

au·to·mo·bile auto(mobile) *f*.

au·ton·o·mous *adj* autonome.

au·tumn automne *m*.

aux·il·ia·ry *adj & n* **a. (verb)** (verbe *m*) auxiliaire *m*.

a·vail·a·bil·i·ty disponibilité *f*.

a·vail·a·ble *adj* disponible; **a. to all** accessible à tous.

av·a·lanche avalanche *f*.

av·e·nue avenue *f*.

av·er·age 1 *n* moyenne *f,* **on a.** en moyenne. 2 *adj* moyen.

a·vi·a·tion aviation *f*.

av·o·ca·do, *pl* -os avocat *m*.

a·void *vt* éviter; **to a. doing** éviter de faire.

a·void·a·ble *adj* évitable.

a·wake 1 *vi** se réveiller. 2 *adj* éveillé; **to keep sb a.** empêcher qn de dormir; **he's (still) a.** il ne dort pas (encore).

a·ward 1 *vt (money, prize)* attribuer. 2 *n (prize)* prix *m; (scholarship)* bourse *f;* **awards ceremony** distribution *f* des prix.

a·ware *adj* **a. of** *(conscious)* conscient de; *(informed)* au courant de; **to become a. of** prendre conscience de.

a·way *adv (distant)* loin; **far a.** au loin; **3 miles a.** à 5km (de distance); **to play a.** *(of team)* jouer à l'extérieur. ■ *(in time)* **ten days a.** dans dix jours. ■ *(absent)* parti. ■ *(continuously)* **to work/talk/etc a.** travailler/parler/etc sans relâche.

aw·ful *adj* affreux; *(terrifying)* épouvantable; **an a. lot of** *Fam* un nombre incroyable de.

aw·ful·ly *adv (very) Fam* affreusement.

awk·ward *adj (clumsy)* maladroit; *(difficult)* difficile; *(tool)* peu commode; *(time)* inopportun.

awn·ing *(over shop)* store *m*.

ax 1 *n* hache *f*. 2 *vt (job etc)* supprimer.

ax·is, *pl* -es axe *m*.

ax·le essieu *m*.

B

BA *abbr* = **Bachelor of Arts**.

ba·by bébé *m;* **b. boy** petit garçon *m;* **b. girl** petite fille *f*.

ba·by car·riage landau *m (pl* -aus).

ba·by clothes vêtements *mpl* de bébé.

ba·by·sit *vi* garder les enfants.

ba·by·sit·ter baby-sitter *mf*.

bach·e·lor célibataire *m*; **B. of Arts/of Science** licencié, -ée *mf* ès lettres/ès sciences.

back¹ 1 *n* dos *m*; *(of chair)* dossier *m*; *(of hand)* revers *m*; *(of house)* derrière *m*, arrière *m*; *(of room)* fond *m*; *(of vehicle)* arrière *m*; *(of page)* verso *m*; **at the b. of the book** à la fin du livre; **b. to front** devant derrière; **in b. of** derrière. **2** *adj* arrière *inv*; de derrière; **b. door** porte *f* de derrière; **b. tooth** molaire *f*. **3** *adv (behind)* en arrière; **to come b.** revenir; **he's b.** il est de retour, il est revenu.

back² *vt (support)* appuyer; *(with money)* financer; *(horse etc)* parier sur.

back·ache mal *m* de dos; **to have a b.** avoir mal au dos.

back·fire *vi (of vehicle)* pétarader.

back·ground fond *m*; *(events)* antécédents *mpl*; *(education)* formation *f*; *(environment)* milieu *m*; **b. music** musique *f* de fond.

back·ing *(aid)* soutien *m*; *(material)* support *m*.

back·log *(of work)* arriéré *m*.

▶ **back out** *vi (withdraw)* se retirer.

back·pack sac *m* à dos.

back·side *(buttocks) Fam* derrière *m*.

back·stage *adv* dans les coulisses.

▶ **back up** *vt (support)* appuyer qn.

back·ward *adj (retarded)* arriéré; *(glance)* en arrière.

back·wards *adv* en arrière; *(to walk)* à reculons; *(to put on garment)* à l'envers.

back·yard jardin *m*.

ba·con bacon *m*.

bac·te·ri·a *npl* bactéries *fpl*.

bad *adj* mauvais; *(wicked)* méchant; *(accident, wound)* grave; *(arm, leg)* malade; *(pain)* violent; **to feel b.** *(ill)* se sentir mal; **things**

are b. ça va mal; **not b.!** pas mal!

badge *(plastic)* badge *m*; *(metal)* pin's *m*; *(of policeman etc)* plaque *f*.

badg·er blaireau *m*.

bad·ly *adv* mal; *(hurt)* grièvement; **b. affected** très touché; **to want b.** avoir grande envie de.

bad-man·nered *adj* mal élevé.

bad·min·ton badminton *m*.

bad-tem·pered *adj* grincheux.

baf·fle *vt* déconcerter.

bag sac *m*; **bags** *(baggage)* valises *fpl*; *(under eyes)* poches *fpl*.

bag·gage bagages *mpl*.

bag·gage check consigne *f*.

bag·gy *adj (out of shape)* déformé; *(by design)* large.

bag·pipes *npl* cornemuse *f*.

bail *(in court)* caution *f*; **on b.** en liberté provisoire.

bait amorce *f*, appât *m*.

bake 1 *vt (faire) cuire (au four)*. **2** *vi (of cook) (make cakes)* faire de la pâtisserie; *(make bread)* faire du pain; *(of cake etc)* cuire (au four).

baked beans *npl* haricots *mpl* blancs (à la tomate).

bak·er boulanger, -ère *mf*.

bak·e·ry boulangerie *f*.

bal·ance 1 *n* équilibre *m*; *(of account)* solde *m*; *(remainder)* reste *m*; **to lose one's b.** perdre l'équilibre. **2** *vt* tenir en équilibre (**on** sur); *(account)* équilibrer. **3** *vi (of person)* se tenir en équilibre; *(of accounts)* être en équilibre.

bal·ance sheet bilan *m*.

bald *adj* chauve.

bald-head·ed *adj* chauve.

bald·ness calvitie *f*.

ball¹ *(round object)* balle *f*; *(inflated) (for sports)* ballon *m*; *(of string, wool)* pelote *f*; *(any round shape)* boule *f*; *(of meat or fish)* boulette *f*; **on the b.** *Fam (alert)* éveillé; *(efficient)* au point.

ball² *(dance)* bal *m (pl* bals).

bal·le·ri·na ballerine *f*.

bal·let ballet *m*.

bal·loon ballon *m*.

bal·lot *(voting)* scrutin *m*.

ball·park stade *m* de base-ball; **a b. figure** une estimation.

ball·point stylo *m* à bille, bic® *m*.

ball·room salle *f* de danse.

ban 1 *n* interdiction *f*. 2 *vt* interdire (**sb from doing** à qn de faire); *(exclude)* exclure (**from** de).

ba·na·na banane *f*.

band *(strip)* bande *f*; *(musicians)* (petit) orchestre *m*; *(pop group)* groupe *m*; **rubber b.** élastique *m*.

band·age bande *f*.

▸**bandage up** *vt (arm, wound)* bander.

Band-Aid® pansement *m* adhésif.

bang 1 *n* coup *m (violent); (of door)* claquement *m*. 2 *vt* cogner; *(door)* (faire) claquer. 3 *vi* cogner; *(of door)* claquer.

▸**bang down** *vt (lid)* rabattre (violemment).

▸**bang into** *vt* heurter.

ban·gle bracelet *m* (rigide).

bangs *npl (of hair)* frange *f*.

ban·is·ter(s) *n(pl)* rampe *f* (d'escalier).

bank *(of river)* bord *m*; *(for money)* banque *f*.

bank ac·count compte *m* en banque.

bank·er banquier *m*.

bank·ing *(activity)* la banque.

▸**bank on** *vt* compter sur.

bank·rupt *adj* **to go b.** faire faillite.

bank·rupt·cy faillite *f*.

ban·ner *(at rallies, on two poles)* banderole *f*.

bar 1 *n* barre *f*; *(of gold)* lingot *m*; *(of chocolate)* tablette *f*; *(on window)* barreau *m*; *(pub, counter)* bar *m*. 2 *vt (way)* bloquer; *(prohibit)* interdire (**sb from doing** à qn de faire); *(exclude)* exclure (**from** de).

bar·be·cue barbecue *m*.

barbed *adj* **b. wire** fil *m* de fer barbelé.

bar·ber coiffeur *m*.

bare *adj* nu; *(tree)* dénudé; **with his b. hands** mains nues.

bare·foot *adv* nu-pieds.

bare·ly *adv (scarcely)* à peine.

bar·gain 1 *n (deal)* marché *m*; **a b.** *(cheap buy)* une affaire; **b. price** prix *m* exceptionnel. 2 *vi* négocier.

▸**bargain for** *vt (expect)* s'attendre à.

barge chaland *m*.

▸**barge in** *vi (enter a room)* faire irruption; *(interrupt sb)* interrompre.

bark 1 *n (of tree)* écorce *f*. 2 *vi (of dog)* aboyer.

bark·ing aboiements *mpl*.

bar·ley orge *f*.

bar·maid serveuse *f* de bar.

bar·man barman *m*.

barn *(for crops)* grange *f*.

ba·rom·e·ter baromètre *m*.

bar·racks *npl* caserne *f*.

bar·rage *(barrier)* barrage *m*.

bar·rel *(cask)* tonneau *m*; *(of oil)* baril *m*; *(of gun)* canon *m*.

bar·ren *adj* stérile.

bar·rette barrette *f*.

bar·ri·cade 1 *n* barricade *f*. 2 *vt* barricader.

bar·ri·er barrière *f*.

bar·tend·er barman *m*.

base 1 *n* base *f*; *(of tree, lamp)* pied *m*. 2 *vt* baser.

base·ball base-ball *m*.

base·board plinthe *f*.

base·ment sous-sol *m*.

bash 1 *n (bang)* coup *m*. 2 *vt (hit)* cogner.

▸**bash up** *vt* **to b. sb up** tabasser qn.

ba·sic 1 *adj* essentiel, de base; *(elementary)* élémentaire; *(pay)* de base. 2 *n* **the basics** l'essentiel *m*.

ba·si·cal·ly *adv* au fond.

ba·sin bassin *m*; *(sink)* lavabo *m*.

ba·sis *(of agreement etc)* bases *fpl*; **on the b. of** d'après; **on that b.** dans ces conditions; **on a weekly b.** chaque semaine.

bask *vi* se chauffer.

bas·ket panier *m*; *(for bread, laundry, litter)* corbeille *f*.

bass 1 *n (singer)* basse *f*, *(notes)* graves *mpl*; **b. drum** grosse caisse *f*, **b. (guitar)** (guitare *f*) basse *f*. **2** *adj* grave, bas *(f* basse).

bat 1 *n (animal)* chauve-souris *f*, *Sports* batte *f*. **2** *vt* **she didn't b. an eyelid** elle n'a pas sourcillé.

batch *(of people)* groupe *m*; *(of letters)* paquet *m*; *(of papers)* liasse *f*.

bath 1 *n* bain *m*; *(tub)* baignoire *f*; **to take a b.** prendre un bain. **2** *vt* baigner.

bathe 1 *vt* baigner. **2** *vi (swim)* se baigner; *(take a bath)* prendre un bain. **3** *n* bain *m* (de mer).

bath·ing suit maillot *m* de bain.

bath·robe robe *f* de chambre.

bath·room salle *f* de bain(s); *(toilet)* toilettes *fpl*.

bath·tub baignoire *f*.

bat·ter 1 *n* pâte *f* à frire. **2** *vt (child)* martyriser.

▶**batter down** *vt (door)* défoncer.

bat·tered *adj (car)* cabossé.

bat·te·ry batterie *f*, *(in radio, appliance)* pile *f*.

bat·tle 1 *n* bataille *f*, *(struggle)* lutte *f*. **2** *vi* se battre.

bat·tle·ship cuirassé *m*.

bawl (out) *vti* beugler; **to b. sb out** *Fam* engueuler qn.

bay *(part of coastline)* baie *f*, *(for loading)* aire *f*.

BC *abbr (before Christ)* avant Jésus-Christ.

be* *vi* être; **she's a doctor** elle est médecin; **it's 3 o'clock** il est trois heures. ■ avoir; **to be hot/right/lucky** avoir chaud/raison/de la chance; **he's 20** il a 20 ans; **to be 7 feet high** avoir 2 mètres de haut. ■ *(health)* aller; **how are you?** comment vas-tu? ■ *(go, come)* **I've been to see her** je suis allé *or* j'ai été la voir; **he's (already) been here** il est (déjà) venu. ■ *(weather, cal-*

culations) faire; **it's sunny** il fait beau; **2 and 2 are 4** 2 et 2 font 4. ■ *(cost)* faire; **how much is it?** ça fait combien? ■ *(auxiliary)* **I am/was doing** je fais/faisais; **he was killed** il a été tué; **I've been waiting (for) two hours** j'attends depuis deux heures; **isn't it?/aren't you?/***etc* n'est-ce pas?, non? ■ *(+ infinitive)* **he is to come** il doit venir. ■ **there is** *or* **are** il y a; *(pointing)* voilà!; **here is** *or* **are** voici.

beach plage *f*.

bea·con balise *f*.

bead perle *f*, *(of sweat)* goutte *f*; **(string of) beads** collier *m*.

beak bec *m*.

beak·er *(for drinking)* gobelet *m*; *(in laboratory)* vase *m* à bec.

beam *(of wood)* poutre *f*, *(of light)* rayon *m*; *(of headlight)* faisceau *m*.

beam·ing *adj (radiant)* radieux.

bean haricot *m*; *(of coffee)* grain *m*; **(broad) b.** fève *f*.

bean·sprouts *npl* germes *mpl* de soja.

bear¹ *(animal)* ours *m*.

bear²* 1 *vt (carry, show)* porter; *(endure)* supporter; *(responsibility)* assumer; **to b. in mind** tenir compte de. **2** *vi* **to b. left/right** tourner à gauche/droite.

bear·a·ble *adj* supportable.

beard barbe *f*.

beard·ed *adj* barbu.

bear·ing *(relevance)* relation *f* (**on** avec); **to get one's bearings** s'orienter.

▶**bear out** *vt* corroborer.

beast bête *f*, *(person)* brute *f*.

beast·ly *adj (bad) Fam* vilain.

beat 1 *n (of heart, drum)* battement *m*; *(of policeman)* ronde *f*. **2** *vt** battre.

▶**beat down 1** *vt (door)* défoncer. **2** *vi (of rain)* tomber à verse; *(of sun)* taper.

beat·ing *(blows, defeat)* raclée *f*.

▶**beat off** *vt* repousser.

▶**beat up** vt tabasser.
beau·ti·ful adj (très) beau (f belle).
beau·ty (quality, woman) beauté f.
beau·ty mark (on skin) grain m de beauté.
beau·ty par·lor institut m de beauté.
beau·ty spot (on skin) grain m de beauté.
bea·ver castor m.
be·cause conj parce que; **b. of** à cause de.
be·come* vi devenir; **to b. a pain·ter** devenir peintre; **what has b. of her?** qu'est-elle devenue?
bed lit m; **to go to b.** (aller) se coucher; **in b.** couché; **to get out of b.** se lever; **b. and breakfast** chambre f avec petit déjeuner.
bed·clothes npl couvertures fpl et draps mpl.
bed·room chambre f à coucher.
bed·side chevet m; **b. lamp/book** lampe f/livre m de chevet.
bed·time heure f de coucher.
bee abeille f.
beech (tree, wood) hêtre m.
beef bœuf m.
bee·hive ruche f.
been pp de be.
beep 1 n bip m; (on answering machine) bip m sonore. **2** vt biper.
bee·per récepteur m d'appels, bip m.
beer bière f; **b. glass** chope f.
beet betterave f (potagère).
bee·tle scarabée m.
be·fore 1 adv avant; (already) déjà; (in front) devant; **the day b.** la veille. **2** prep (time) avant; (place) devant; **the year b. last** il y a deux ans. **3** conj avant que (+ ne + subjunctive), avant de (+ infinitive); **b. he goes** avant qu'il (ne) parte; **b. going** avant de partir.
be·friend vt prendre en amitié, prendre d'amitié pour.
beg 1 vt **to b. (for)** solliciter;

(bread, money) mendier; **to b. sb to do** supplier qn de faire. **2** vi mendier.
beg·gar mendiant, -ante mf.
be·gin* 1 vt commencer; (campaign) lancer; **to b. doing** or **to do** commencer or se mettre à faire. **2** vi commencer (**with** par; **by doing** par faire); **to b. with** (first) d'abord.
be·gin·ner débutant, -ante mf.
be·gin·ning commencement m, début m.
be·grudge vt (envy) envier (**sb sth** qch à qn); **to b. doing sth** faire qch à contrecœur.
be·half on b. of (to act) pour le compte de; (to call, write) de la part de.
be·have vi se conduire; (of machine) fonctionner; **to b. (oneself)** se tenir bien; (of child) être sage.
be·hav·ior conduite f.
be·hind 1 prep derrière; (in making progress) en retard sur. **2** adv derrière; (late) en retard. **3** n (buttocks) Fam derrière m.
beige adj & n beige (m).
belch 1 vi faire un renvoi. **2** n renvoi m.
Bel·gian 1 n Belge mf. **2** adj belge.
be·lief croyance f (**in** en); (trust) confiance f, foi f; (opinion) opinion f.
be·liev·a·ble adj croyable.
be·lieve vti croire (**in sth** à qch; **in God** en Dieu); **I b. so** je crois que oui; **to b. in doing** croire qu'il faut faire.
be·liev·er (religious) croyant, -ante mf.
be·lit·tle vt dénigrer.
bell cloche f, (small) clochette f; (in phone) sonnerie f, (on door, bicycle) sonnette f.
bell·boy groom m.
bel·ly ventre m; **b. button** Fam nombril m.
bel·ly·ache mal m au ventre.
be·long vi appartenir (**to** à); **to b.**

to (club) être membre de.

be·long·ings npl affaires fpl.

be·low 1 prep au-dessous de. 2 adv en dessous.

belt ceinture f; (in machine) courroie f.

belt·way périphérique m.

bench (seat) banc m; (work table) établi m.

bend 1 n courbe f; (in river) coude m; (in road) virage m; (of arm, knee) pli m. 2 vt* courber; (leg, arm) plier. 3 vi (of road) tourner.

bend (down) vi se baisser.

bend (over) vi se pencher.

be·neath 1 prep au-dessous de. 2 adv (au-)dessous.

ben·e·fi·cial adj bénéfique.

ben·e·fit 1 n avantage m; (money) allocation f; child b. allocations familiales; for your (own) b. pour vous. 2 vt faire du bien à; (be useful to) profiter à. 3 vi you'll b. from it ça vous fera du bien.

bent adj (nail) tordu; b. on doing résolu à faire.

be·reave·ment deuil m.

ber·ry baie f.

ber·serk adj to go b. devenir fou.

berth (in ship, train) couchette f.

be·side prep à côté de; that's b. the point ça n'a rien à voir.

be·sides 1 prep en plus de; (except) excepté. 2 adv de plus; (moreover) d'ailleurs.

best 1 adj meilleur (in de); the b. part of (most) la plus grande partie de. 2 n the b. le meilleur, la meilleure; at b. au mieux; to do one's b. faire de son mieux; to make the b. of s'accommoder de. 3 adv (the) b. (to play, sing etc) le mieux; the b. loved le plus aimé.

best man (at wedding) garçon m d'honneur.

best·sell·er best-seller m.

bet 1 n pari m. 2 vti* parier (on sur; that que).

be·tray vt trahir.

be·tray·al trahison f.

bet·ter 1 adj meilleur (than que); she's (much) b. (in health) elle va (beaucoup) mieux; that's b. c'est mieux; to get b. (recover) se remettre; (improve) s'améliorer; it's b. to go il vaut mieux partir. 2 adv mieux; I had b. go il vaut mieux que je parte. 3 vt to b. oneself améliorer sa condition.

betting pari(s) m(pl).

be·tween 1 prep entre; in b. sth and sth/two things entre qch et qch/deux choses. 2 adv in b. au milieu; (time) dans l'intervalle.

bev·er·age boisson f.

be·ware vi to b. of se méfier de; b.! méfiez-vous!

be·wil·der vt dérouter.

be·yond 1 prep au-delà de; (reach, doubt) hors de; b. my means au dessus de mes moyens; it's b. me ça me dépasse. 2 adv au-delà.

bi·as penchant m (towards pour); (prejudice) préjugé m.

bi·as(s)ed adj partial; to be b. against avoir des préjugés contre.

bib (baby's) bavoir m.

Bi·ble bible f; the B. la Bible.

bi·cy·cle bicyclette f.

bid* 1 vt (money) offrir. 2 vi faire une offre (for pour). 3 n (at auction) offre f; (for job) tentative f.

big adj grand, gros (f grosse); (in age, generous) grand; (in bulk, amount) gros; b. deal! Fam (bon) et alors!

big·head Fam (conceited) prétentieux, -euse mf; (boasting) vantard, -arde mf.

big·shot Fam gros bonnet m.

bike Fam vélo m.

bike path Fam piste f cyclable.

bi·ki·ni deux-pièces m inv; b. briefs mini-slip m.

bile bile f.

bi·lin·gual adj bilingue.

bill 1 n (invoice) facture f, note f; (in restaurant) addition f; (in hotel)

note f; *(money)* billet m; *(proposed law)* projet m de loi. **2** vt to **b. sb** envoyer la facture à qn.
bill·board panneau m d'affichage.
bill·fold portefeuille m.
bil·liards npl *(jeu* m de) billiard m.
bil·lion milliard m.
bin boîte f; *(for trash)* poubelle f.
bind vt* lier; *(book)* relier.
bind·er *(for papers)* classeur m.
bind·ing *(of book)* reliure f.
bin·go loto m.
bin·oc·u·lars npl jumelles fpl.
bi·o·log·i·cal adj biologique.
bi·ol·o·gy biologie f.
bi·o·tech·nol·o·gy biotechnologie f.
birch (silver) b. *(tree)* bouleau m.
bird oiseau m; *(fowl)* volaille f; **b.'s-eye view** vue f d'ensemble.
birth naissance f; **to give b. to** donner naissance à.
birth cer·tif·i·cate acte m de naissance.
birth·day anniversaire m; **happy b.!** bon anniversaire!
birth·mark tache f de naissance.
bis·cuit petit pain m.
bish·op évêque m.
bit morceau m; **a b.** *(a little)* un peu; **quite a b.** *(very)* très; *(a lot)* beaucoup; **not a b.** pas du tout; **b. by b.** petit à petit.
bitch **1** n *(dog)* chienne f; *(spiteful woman)* Fam garce f. **2** vi to **b.** (about) Fam *(criticize)* déblatérer (contre).
bite **1** n *(wound)* morsure f; *(from insect)* piqûre f; **a b. to eat** quelque chose à manger. **2** vti* mordre; **to b. one's nails** se ronger les ongles.
bit·ter adj amer; *(cold, wind)* glacial; *(conflict)* violent.
bit·ter·ness amertume f; *(of conflict)* violence f.
bi·zarre adj bizarre.
black **1** adj noir; **b. eye** œil m poché; **to give sb a b. eye** pocher

l'œil à qn; **b. and blue** *(bruised)* couvert de bleus. **2** n *(color)* noir m; *(person)* Noir, -e mf.
black·ber·ry mûre f.
black·bird merle m.
black·board tableau m (noir); **on the b.** au tableau.
black·cur·rant cassis m.
black·list **1** n liste f noire. **2** vt mettre sur la liste noire.
black·mail **1** n chantage m. **2** vt faire chanter.
black·mail·er maître-chanteur m.
black·out panne f d'électricité; *(fainting fit)* syncope f.
▶ **black out** vi *(faint)* s'évanouir.
blad·der vessie f.
blade lame f; *(of grass)* brin m.
blame **1** vt accuser; **to b. sb for sth** reprocher qch à qn; **you're to b.** c'est ta faute. **2** n faute f.
blame·less adj irréprochable.
bland adj *(food)* fade.
blank **1** adj *(paper, page)* blanc (f blanche); *(check)* en blanc. **2** adj & n **b.** (space) blanc m.
blan·ket couverture f.
blare (out) vi *(of radio)* beugler; *(of music)* retentir.
blast **1** n explosion f; *(air from explosion)* souffle m. **2** int Fam zut!
blast·ed adj Fam fichu.
blast-off *(of spacecraft)* mise f à feu.
blaze **1** n *(fire)* flamme f; *(large)* incendie m. **2** vi *(of fire)* flamber; *(of sun)* flamboyer.
blaz·er blazer m.
blaz·ing adj en feu; *(sun)* brûlant.
bleach *(household)* eau f de Javel.
bleak adj morne.
bleed* vti saigner.
blem·ish *(fault)* défaut m; *(mark)* tache f.
blend **1** n mélange m. **2** vt mélanger. **3** vi se mélanger.
blend·er *(for food)* mixer m.
bless vt bénir; **b. you!** *(after sneeze)* à tes souhaits!

bles·sing bénédiction *f*; *(benefit)* bienfait *m*.

blew *pt de* **blow**[1].

blind 1 *adj* aveugle; **b. person** aveugle *mf*. **2** *n (on window)* store *m*; **the b.** les aveugles *mpl*.

blind·fold 1 *n* bandeau *m*. **2** *vt* bander les yeux à.

blind·ly *adv* aveuglément.

blind·ness cécité *f*.

blink 1 *vi (of person)* cligner des yeux; *(of eyes)* cligner. **2** *n* clignement *m*.

bliss félicité *f*.

blis·ter *(on skin)* ampoule *f*.

bliz·zard tempête *f* de neige.

bloat *vt* gonfler.

blob goutte *f*; *(of ink)* tache *f*.

block 1 *n (of stone)* bloc *m*; *(of buildings)* pâté *m* (de maisons); *(child's toy)* cube *m*. **2** *vt (obstruct)* bloquer.

block·age obstruction *f*.

▸**block off** *vt (road)* barrer.

▸**block up** *vt (pipe, hole)* bloquer.

blog *no m*.

blog·ger blogueur, -euse *mf*.

blond *adj & n* blond (*m*).

blonde *adj & n* blonde (*f*).

blood sang *m*; **b. donor** donneur, -euse *mf* de sang; **b. group** groupe *m* sanguin; **b. pressure** tension *f* (artérielle); **to have high b. pressure** avoir de la tension.

blood·shed effusion *f* de sang.

blood·shot *adj (eye)* injecté de sang.

blood·y *adj* sanglant.

bloom 1 *n* fleur *f*; **in b.** en fleur(s). **2** *vi* fleurir.

blos·som 1 *n* fleur(s) *f(pl)*. **2** *vi* fleurir.

blot tache *f*.

blotch·y *adj* couvert de taches.

blot·ting pa·per buvard *m*.

blouse chemisier *m*.

blow[1]* **1** *vt (of wind)* pousser (*un navire*), chasser (*la pluie*); *(of person)* (*smoke*) souffler; *(bubbles)*

faire; *(trumpet)* souffler dans; **to b. one's nose** se moucher; **to b. a whistle** siffler. **2** *vi (of wind, person)* souffler.

blow[2] *(with fist, tool etc)* coup *m*.

▸**blow away 1** *vt (of wind)* emporter. **2** *vi (of hat, newspaper etc)* s'envoler.

▸**blow down, blow over 1** *vt (chimney etc)* faire tomber. **2** *vi* tomber.

blow-dry Brushing® *m*.

blow-dry·er sèche-cheveux *m*.

▸**blow off 1** *vt (hat etc)* emporter. **2** *vi* s'envoler.

▸**blow out** *(candle)* souffler.

blow·torch chalumeau *m*.

▸**blow up 1** *vt (building)* faire sauter; *(tire, balloon)* gonfler. **2** *vi* exploser.

blue 1 *adj* bleu (*mpl* bleus). **2** *n* bleu *m* (*pl* bleus).

blue·ber·ry myrtille *f*.

blue·print bleu *m*; *(plan)* plan *m*, projet *m*.

bluff 1 *vti* bluffer. **2** *n* bluff *m*.

blun·der 1 *n (mistake)* bévue *f*. **2** *vi* faire une bévue.

blunt *adj (edge)* émoussé; *(person, speech)* franc, brusque.

blur 1 *n* tache *f* floue. **2** *vt* rendre flou.

blurred *adj* flou.

blush *vi* rougir (**with** de).

blus·te·ry *adj (weather)* de grand vent.

board[1] **1** *n (piece of wood)* planche *f*; *(for notices)* tableau *m*; *(cardboard)* carton *m*; **b. (of directors)** conseil *m* d'administration; **on b.** *(ship, aircraft)* à bord (de). **2** *vt* monter à bord de; *(bus, train)* monter dans.

board[2] *(food)* pension *f*; **room and b.** pension *f* (complète).

board·er pensionnaire *mf*.

board·ing *(of passengers)* embarquement *m*.

board·ing house pension *f* (de famille).

board·ing school pensionnat m.

board·walk promenade f (de planches).

boast vi se vanter (**about, of** de).

boat bateau m; (small) barque f, canot m; (liner) paquebot m.

bob·by pin pince f à cheveux.

bob·by socks, bob·by sox npl socquettes fpl (de fille).

bod·i·ly adj (need) physique.

bod·y corps m; (institution) organisme m.

bod·y·guard garde m du corps.

bod·y·work carrosserie f.

bogged down adj to get b. s'enliser.

bo·gus adj faux (f fausse).

boil[1] (pimple) furoncle m.

boil[2] **1** n to come to the b. bouillir. **2** vt faire bouillir. **3** vi bouillir.

boiled adj bouilli; (potato) à l'eau; **b. egg** œuf m à la coque; **hard-b. egg** œuf m dur.

boil·er chaudière f.

boil·ing adj b. (hot) bouillant; it's **b. (hot)** (weather) il fait une chaleur infernale.

▶ **boil over** vi (of milk) déborder.

▶ **boil up** vt faire bouillir.

bold adj hardi.

bold·ness hardiesse f.

bolt 1 n (on door) verrou m; (for nut) boulon m. **2** vt (door) fermer au verrou. **3** vi (dash) se précipiter.

bomb 1 n bombe f. **2** vt bombarder.

bomb·er (aircraft) bombardier m.

bomb·ing bombardement m.

bond (link) lien m; (investment certificate) bon m.

bone os m; (of fish) arête f.

bon·fire (celebration) feu m de joie; (for dead leaves) feu m (de jardin).

bon·net (hat) bonnet m; (of car) capot m.

bo·nus prime f.

bon·y adj (thin) osseux; (fish) plein d'arêtes.

boo 1 vti siffler. **2** n **boos** sifflets mpl.

boo·by-trap vt piéger.

book 1 n livre m; (of tickets) carnet m; (exercise) **b.** cahier m (de brouillon); **books** (accounts) comptes mpl. **2** vt (room etc) réserver.

book·case bibliothèque f.

booked up adj (hotel) complet.

book·ing réservation f.

book·keep·er comptable mf.

book·keep·ing comptabilité f.

book·let (pamphlet) brochure f.

book·mak·er bookmaker m.

book·sell·er libraire mf.

book·shelf rayon m.

book·store librairie f.

boom (economic) expansion f.

boost vt (increase) augmenter; (product) faire de la réclame pour; (economy) stimuler.

boot (footwear) botte f; (ankle) **b.** bottillon m; **to get the b.** Fam être mis à la porte; (Denver) **b.** (on car) sabot m (de Denver).

booth (for phone) cabine f.

▶ **boot out** vt mettre à la porte.

booze Fam **1** n alcool m. **2** vi picoler.

bor·der (of country) frontière f; (edge) bord m.

bor·der (on) vt (country) toucher à.

bor·der·line case cas m limite.

bore 1 vt ennuyer; **to be bored** s'ennuyer. **2** n (person) raseur, -euse mf; (thing) ennui m.

bore·dom ennui m.

bor·ing adj ennuyeux.

born adj né; **to be b.** naître; **he was b.** il est né.

bor·ough municipalité f.

bor·row vt emprunter (**from** à).

boss patron, -onne mf, chef m.

▶ **boss around** vt donner des ordres à.

boss·y adj Fam autoritaire.

botch (up) vt (ruin) bâcler.

both 1 adj les deux. **2** pron tous/ toutes (les) deux; **b. of us** nous deux. **3** adv (at the same time) à la fois; **b. you and I** vous et moi.

both·er 1 vt (annoy, worry) ennuyer; (disturb) déranger; (pester) importuner; **to b. doing** or **to do** se donner la peine de faire; **I can't be bothered** je n'en ai pas envie. **2** n (trouble) ennui m; (effort) peine f, (inconvenience) dérangement m.

▶ **bother about** vt (worry about) se préoccuper de.

bot·tle bouteille f, (small) flacon m; (for baby) biberon m; **hot-water b.** bouillotte f.

bot·tle o·pen·er ouvre-bouteilles m inv.

bot·tom 1 n (of sea, box) fond m; (of page, hill) bas m; (buttocks) Fam derrière m; **to be at the b. of the class** être le dernier de la classe. **2** adj (part, shelf) inférieur, du bas; **b. floor** rez-de-chaussée m.

boul·der rocher m.

bounce 1 vi (of ball) rebondir; (of check) Fam être sans provision. **2** vt faire rebondir. **3** n (re)bond m.

bound adj (**b. to do** (obliged) obligé de faire; (certain) sûr de faire; **it's b. to happen/snow**/etc ça arrivera/il neigera/etc sûrement; **b. for** en route pour.

bound·a·ry limite f.

bounds npl out of b. (place) interdit.

bou·quet (of flowers) bouquet m.

bou·tique boxe f (de mode).

bow¹ (weapon) arc m, (knot) nœud m.

bow² **1** n révérence f, (nod) salut m. **2** vi s'incliner (**to** devant); (nod) incliner la tête (**to** devant).

bow·els npl intestins mpl.

bowl (for food) bol m; (for sugar) sucrier m; (for salad) saladier m; (for fruit) coupe f.

bowl·ing (tenpin) b. bowling m.

bowl·ing al·ley bowling m.

bow tie nœud m papillon.

box 1 n boîte f, (large) caisse f. **2** vi (of boxer) boxer.

box·er boxeur m.

box·er shorts caleçon m.

▶ **box in** vt (enclose) enfermer.

box·ing boxe f; **b. ring** ring m.

box of·fice guichet m (pour spectacles).

boy garçon m; **American b.** jeune Américain m; **oh b.!** mon Dieu!

boy·cott 1 vt boycotter. **2** n boycottage m.

boy·friend petit ami m.

bra soutien-gorge m.

brace·let bracelet m.

brack·et (in typography) crochet m; (for shelf etc) équerre f.

brag vi se vanter (**about, of** de).

brag·ging vantardise f.

braid 1 n (of hair) tresse f. **2** vt tresser.

brain cerveau m; **to have brains** avoir de l'intelligence.

brain·storm (brilliant idea) idée f géniale.

brain·wash vt faire un lavage de cerveau à.

brain·y adj Fam intelligent.

brake 1 n frein m. **2** vi freiner.

brake light (signal m de) stop m.

branch branche f, (of road) embranchement m; (of store, office) succursale f.

▶ **branch off** vi (of road) bifurquer.

▶ **branch out** vi (of firm, person) étendre ses activités (**into** à).

brand (trademark) marque f.

brand-new adj tout neuf (f toute neuve).

bran·dy cognac m.

brass cuivre m.

brave adj courageux, brave.

brav·e·ry courage m.

brawl bagarre f.

brawn·y adj musclé.

bread inv pain m; **loaf of b.** pain m; **(slice** or **piece of) b. and butter** tartine f.

bread·box coffre m à pain.

bread·crumb miette f (de pain); **breadcrumbs** (in cooking) chapelure f.

breadth largeur *f.*

bread·win·ner soutien *m* de famille.

break 1 *vt** casser; *(into pieces)* briser; *(silence, spell)* rompre; *(strike, heart, ice)* briser; *(sports record)* battre; *(law)* violer; *(one's word, promise)* manquer à; *(journey)* interrompre; *(news)* révéler (to à). **2** *vi(se)* casser; *(into pieces)* se rompre; *(of news)* éclater; *(stop work)* faire la pause. **3** *n* cassure *f*, *(in bone)* fracture *f*, *(with person, group)* rupture *f*, *(in journey)* interruption *f*, *(rest)* repos *m*; *(in activity, for tea etc)* pause *f*, *(in school)* récréation *f*, **a lucky b.** une chance.

break·a·ble *adj* fragile.

▸ **break away** *vi* se détacher.

break·down *(of vehicle, machine)* panne *f*, *(in talks)* rupture *f*, *(nervous)* dépression *f.*

▸ **break down 1** *vt (door)* enfoncer. **2** *vi(of vehicle, machine)* tomber en panne; *(of talks)* échouer; *(collapse) (of person)* s'effondrer.

break·fast petit déjeuner *m.*

▸ **break in 1** *vi (of burglar)* entrer par effraction. **2** *vt (door)* enfoncer; *(vehicle)* roder.

break-in cambriolage *m.*

▸ **break into** *vt (house)* cambrioler; *(safe)* forcer.

▸ **break loose** *vi* s'échapper.

▸ **break off 1** *vt* détacher; *(relations)* rompre. **2** *vi* se détacher; *(stop)* s'arrêter; **to b. off with sb** rompre avec qn.

▸ **break out** *vi (of war, fire)* éclater; *(escape)* s'échapper.

break·through percée *f*, découverte *f.*

break·up *(of marriage)* rupture *f.*

▸ **break up 1** *vt* mettre en morceaux; *(fight)* mettre fin à. **2** *vi(of group)* se disperser; *(of marriage)* se briser.

breast sein *m*; *(of chicken)* blanc *m.*

breast·feed *vt* allaiter.

breast·stroke brasse *f.*

breath haleine *f*, souffle *m*; **out of b.** (tout) essoufflé.

Breath·a·lyz·er® alcootest® *m.*

breathe *vti* respirer; **to b. in** aspirer; **to b. out** expirer.

breath·ing respiration *f*, **b. space** moment *m* de repos.

breath·tak·ing *adj* époustouflant.

breed 1 *vt** *(animals)* élever. **2** *vi (of animals)* se reproduire. **3** *n* race *f.*

breed·er éleveur, -euse *mf.*

breed·ing *(of animals)* élevage *m*; *(good manners)* éducation *f*, **b. ground** foyer *m*, terrain *m* propice.

breeze brise *f.*

breez·y *adj (weather)* frais.

brew *vi (storm)* se préparer; *(of tea)* infuser; **something is brewing** il se prépare quelque chose.

brew·e·ry brasserie *f.*

bribe 1 *n* pot-de-vin *m.* **2** *vt (person)* acheter.

brick brique *f.*

brick·lay·er maçon *m.*

bride mariée *f*, **the b. and groom** les mariés *mpl.*

bride·groom marié *m.*

brides·maid demoiselle *f* d'honneur.

bridge pont *m.*

brief 1 *adj* bref (*f* brève). **2** *vt (inform)* mettre au courant (on de). **3** *n briefs (underpants)* slip *m.*

brief·case serviette *f.*

brief·ing instructions *fpl.*

brief·ly *adv (quickly)* en vitesse.

bright 1 *adj* brillant; *(weather, room)* clair; *(clever)* intelligent; *(idea)* génial. **2** *adv* **b. and early** de bonne heure.

bright·en (up) 1 *vt (room)* égayer. **2** *vi (of weather)* s'éclaircir.

bright·ly *adv* avec éclat.

bright·ness éclat *m.*

bril·liance éclat *m*; *(of person)* grande intelligence *f.*

bril·liant *adj (light)* éclatant; *(clever)* brillant.

bring* *vt (person, vehicle)* amener; *(thing)* apporter; *(to cause)* amener; **to b. to an end** mettre fin à; **to b. to mind** rappeler.

▸**bring about** *vt* provoquer.

▸**bring along** *vt (object)* emporter; *(person)* emmener.

▸**bring around** *vt* ranimer.

▸**bring back** *vt (person)* ramener; *(object)* rapporter; *(memories)* rappeler.

▸**bring down** *vt (object)* descendre; *(overthrow)* faire tomber; *(reduce)* réduire.

▸**bring in** *vt (object)* rentrer; *(person)* faire entrer; *(introduce)* introduire.

▸**bring out** *vt (object)* sortir; *(person)* faire sortir; *(meaning)* faire ressortir; *(book)* publier; *(product)* lancer.

▸**bring to** *vt* ranimer.

▸**bring together** *vt (reconcile)* réconcilier.

▸**bring up** *vt (object)* monter; *(child)* élever; *(subject)* mentionner.

brink bord *m.*

brisk *adj* vif.

brisk·ly *adv (to walk)* vite.

bris·tle poil *m.*

Brit·ish 1 *adj* britannique. **2** *n* **the B.** les Britanniques *mpl.*

Brit·ish Isles îles *fpl* Britanniques.

Brit·on Britannique *mf.*

brit·tle *adj* fragile.

broad *adj (wide)* large; *(outline)* général; **in b. daylight** en plein jour.

broad·band ADSL *m.*

broad·cast 1 *vt** diffuser, retransmettre. **2** *n* émission *f.*

broad·en *vt* élargir.

broc·co·li *inv* brocolis *mpl.*

bro·chure brochure *f.*

broke 1 *pt de* break. **2** *adj (penniless)* fauché.

bro·ken *pp de* break.

bro·ken-down *adj (machine)* délingué.

bron·chi·tis bronchite *f.*

bronze bronze *m.*

brooch broche *f.*

brood 1 *n* couvée *f.* **2** *vi* méditer tristement (**over** sur).

brook ruisseau *m.*

broom balai *m.*

broom·stick manche *m* à balai.

broth·er frère *m.*

broth·er-in-law, *pl* brothers-in-law beau-frère *m.*

brought *pt & pp de* bring.

brow *(forehead)* front *m; (eyebrow)* sourcil *m; (of hill)* sommet *m.*

brown 1 *adj* marron; *(hair)* châtain; *(tanned)* bronzé. **2** *n* marron *m.*

brown·ie brownie *m.*

browse *vi (in bookstore)* feuilleter des livres; *(in store)* regarder.

bruise 1 *vt* **to b. one's knee**/*etc* se faire un bleu au genou/*etc.* **2** *n* bleu *m (pl* bleus), contusion *f.*

bruised *adj* couvert de bleus.

brunch brunch *m.*

bru·nette brunette *f.*

brush 1 *n* brosse *f, (for painting)* pinceau *m.* **2** *vt (teeth, hair)* (se) brosser.

▸**brush aside** *vt* écarter.

▸**brush away, brush off** *vt* enlever.

▸**brush up (on)** *vt (language)* se remettre à.

bru·tal *adj* brutal.

bru·tal·i·ty brutalité *f.*

brute brute *f.*

BS, BSc *abbr* = **Bachelor of Science.**

bub·ble 1 *n* bulle *f.* **2** *vi* bouillonner.

▸**bubble over** *vi* déborder.

buck *Fam* dollar *m.*

buck·et seau *m.*

buck·le 1 *n* boucle *f.* **2** *vt* boucler. **3** *vti (warp)* voiler.

▸**buck up 1** *vt (person)* remonter le moral à. **2** *vi (become livelier)* reprendre du poil de la bête.

bud 1 n (of tree) bourgeon m; (of flower) bouton m. **2** vi (of tree) bourgeonner; (of flower) pousser des boutons.

Bud·dhist adj & n bouddhiste (mf).

bud·dy Fam copain, -ine mf.

budge vi bouger.

budg·et budget m.

▶ **budget for** vt inscrire au budget.

buf·fa·lo, pl -oes or -os buffle m; (American) b. bison m.

buff·er (device) tampon m; (in computer) tampon, mémoire f intermédiaire.

buf·fet (table, meal) buffet m.

bug[1] punaise f; (any insect) bestiole f; (germ) microbe m, virus m; (in machine) défaut m; (in computer program) erreur f; (listening device) micro m clandestin.

bug[2] vt (annoy) Fam embêter.

bu·gle clairon m.

build 1 n (of person) carrure f. **2** vt* construire; (house) construire, bâtir.

build·er maçon m; (contractor) entrepreneur m.

build·ing bâtiment m; (of apartments, offices) immeuble m.

▶ **build up 1** vt (increase) augmenter; (collection) constituer; (business) monter; (speed) prendre. **2** vt (of tension, pressure) augmenter.

built-in adj (closet) encastré; (part of machine) incorporé.

built-up a·re·a agglomération f.

bulb (of plant) oignon m; (of lamp) ampoule f.

bulge renflement m.

bulge (out) vi se renfler.

bulg·ing adj renflé.

bulk inv grosseur f; the b. of (most) la majeure partie de.

bulk·y adj gros (f grosse).

bull taureau m.

bull·dog bouledogue m.

bull·doz·er bulldozer m.

bul·let boule f (de révolver etc).

bul·le·tin bulletin m.

bul·le·tin board tableau m d'affichage.

bull·fight corrida f.

bul·ly 1 n (grosse) brute f. **2** vt brutaliser.

bum Fam (tramp) clochard, -arde mf; (good-for-nothing) propre mf à rien.

bum·ble·bee bourdon m.

bump 1 vt (of car) heurter; **to b. one's head/knee** se cogner la tête/le genou. **2** n (impact) choc m; (jerk) cahot m; (on road, body) bosse f.

bump·er pare-chocs m inv.

▶ **bump into** vt se cogner contre; (of car) rentrer dans; (meet) tomber sur.

bump·y adj (road, ride) cahoteux.

bun (roll) petit pain m au lait.

bunch (of flowers) bouquet m; (of keys) trousseau m; (of people) bande f; **b. of grapes** grappe f de raisin.

bun·dle 1 n paquet m; (of papers) liasse f. **2** vt (put) fourrer; (push) pousser (into dans).

▶ **bundle up** vi (dress warmly) se couvrir.

bun·ga·low bungalow m.

bunk couchette f; **b. beds** lits mpl superposés.

bun·ny Fam Jeannot m lapin.

buoy bouée f.

bur·den 1 n fardeau m; (of tax) poids m. **2** vt accabler (with de).

bu·reau, pl bureaux (office) service m, office m; (chest of drawers) commode f.

bu·reau·cra·cy bureaucratie f.

bu·reau·crat bureaucrate mf.

burg·er hamburger m.

bur·glar cambrioleur, -euse mf.

bur·glar a·larm alarme f antivol.

bur·glar·ize vt cambrioler.

bur·gla·ry cambriolage *m.*

bur·gle *vt* cambrioler.

bur·i·al enterrement *m.*

burn 1 *n* brûlure *f.* **2** *vti** brûler; **burnt alive** brûlé vif.

▸**burn down 1** *vt* détruire par le feu. **2** *vi* être détruit par le feu.

burn·er *(of stove)* brûleur *m.*

burn·ing *adj* en feu; *(fire, light)* allumé.

burp 1 *n* rot *m.* **2** *vi* roter.

burst 1 *n (of laughter)* éclat *m;* *(of thunder)* coup *m.* **2** *vi* (with force)* éclater; *(of bubble, balloon, boil, tire)* crever.

burst·ing *adj (full)* plein à craquer.

▸**burst into** *vt (room)* faire irruption dans; **to b. into tears** fondre en larmes.

▸**burst out** *vi* **to b. out laughing** éclater de rire.

bur·y *vt* enterrer; *(hide)* enfouir; *(plunge, absorb)* plonger.

bus *(auto)* bus *m;* *(long-distance)* (auto)car *m.*

bush buisson *m.*

bush·y *adj* broussailleux.

busi·ness 1 *n* affaires *fpl,* commerce *m;* *(shop)* commerce *m;* *(task, concern, matter)* affaire *f;* **on b.** pour affaires; **it's your b. to…** c'est à vous de…; **that's none of your b.!, mind your own b.!** ça ne vous regarde pas! **2** *adj* commercial; *(meeting, trip)* d'affaires; **b. hours** heures *fpl* de bureau; **b. card** carte *f* de visite.

busi·ness·man, *pl* **-men** homme *m* d'affaires.

busi·ness·wom·an, *pl* **-women** femme *f* d'affaires.

bus shel·ter abribus *m.*

bus sta·tion gare *f* routière.

bus stop arrêt *m* d'autobus.

bust 1 *n (sculpture)* buste *m;* *(woman's breasts)* poitrine *f.* **2** *adj* **to go b.** *Fam (bankrupt)* faire faillite.

bus·tle 1 *vi* s'affairer. **2** *n* activité *f.*

bus·tling *adj (street, town)* bruyant.

bus·y *adj* occupé *(doing* à faire); *(active)* actif; *(day)* chargé; *(street)* animé; *(phone)* occupé; **to be b. doing** *(in the process of)* être en train de faire; **b. signal** sonnerie *f* occupé.

bus·y·bod·y *Fam* fouineur, -euse *mf.*

but 1 *conj* mais. **2** *prep (except)* sauf; **b. for that/him** sans cela/lui. **3** *adv (only)* seulement.

butch·er boucher, -ère *mf;* **b.'s shop** boucherie *f.*

but·ler maître *m* d'hôtel.

butt *(of cigarette)* mégot *m;* *(buttocks) Fam* cul *m.*

but·ter 1 *n* beurre *m.* **2** *vt* beurrer.

but·ter·cup bouton-d'or *m.*

but·ter·fly papillon *m.*

▸**butt in** *vi* interrompre.

but·tock fesse *f.*

but·ton bouton *m;* *(of phone etc)* touche *f;* *(bearing slogan)* pin's *m.*

button (up) *vt (garment)* boutonner.

but·ton·hole boutonnière *f.*

buy 1 *vt** acheter *(from sb* à qn; *for sb* à *or* pour qn). **2** *n* **a good b.** une bonne affaire.

buy·er acheteur, -euse *mf.*

buzz 1 *vi* bourdonner. **2** *n* bourdonnement *m.*

▸**buzz off** *vi Fam* décamper.

by 1 *prep (agent, manner)* par; **hit/ etc by** frappé/*etc* par; **surrounded/ etc by** entouré/*etc* de; **by doing** en faisant; **by sea** par mer; **by car** en voiture; **by bicycle** à bicyclette; **by day** de jour; **by oneself** tout seul. ▪ *(next to)* à côté de; *(near)* près de; **by the lake** au bord du lac. ▪ *(before in time)* avant; **by Monday** avant lundi; **by now** à cette heureci. ▪ *(amount)* à; **by weight** au poids; **paid by the hour** payé à l'heure. **2** *adv* close by tout près; **to go by, pass by** passer; **by and large** en gros.

bye(-bye)! *int Fam* salut!

by·pass 1 *n* (of highway) bretelle *f* (de contournement); (heart surgery) pontage *m*. **2** *vt* contourner.

by·stand·er spectateur, -trice *mf*.

C

cab taxi *m*.

cab·bage chou *m* (*pl* choux).

cab·in (on ship) cabine *f*, (hut) cabane *f*.

cab·i·net¹ armoire *f*, (for display) vitrine *f*, **(filing) c.** classeur *m* (de bureau).

cab·i·net² (in politics) gouvernement *m*; **c. meeting** conseil *m* des ministres.

ca·ble câble *m*; **c. television** la télévision par câble.

ca·ble car téléphérique *m*; (on tracks) funiculaire *m*.

cac·tus, *pl* -ti or -tuses cactus *m*.

caf·e·te·ri·a cafétéria *f*.

caf·feine caféine *f*.

cage cage *f*.

cake gâteau *m*.

cal·cu·late *vti* calculer.

cal·cu·la·tion calcul *m*.

cal·cu·la·tor calculatrice *f*.

cal·en·dar calendrier *m*.

calf, *pl* calves (animal) veau *m*; (part of leg) mollet *m*.

call 1 *n* appel *m*; (shout) cri *m*; (visit) visite *f*, **(telephone) c.** communication *f*; **to make a c.** (phone) téléphoner (**to** à). **2** *vt* appeler; (shout) crier; (attention) attirer (**to** sur); **he's called David** il s'appelle David; **to c. a meeting** convoquer une assemblée; **to c. sb a liar/etc** qualifier

qn de menteur/etc. **3** *vi* appeler; (cry out) crier; (visit) passer.

▶ **call back** *vti* rappeler.

call·er visiteur, -euse *mf*, (on phone) correspondant, -ante *mf*.

▶ **call for** *vt* (require) demander; (summon) appeler; (collect) passer prendre.

▶ **call in** *vt* (into room etc) faire entrer.

call·ing card (for telephone) télécarte *f*.

▶ **call off** *vt* (cancel) annuler.

▶ **call on** *vt* (visit) passer voir; **to c. on sb to do** inviter qn à faire; (urge) presser qn de faire.

▶ **call out 1** *vt* (shout) crier; (doctor) appeler. **2** *vi* crier; **to c. out for** demander à haute voix.

▶ **call up** *vt* (phone) appeler.

calm 1 *adj* calme; **keep c.!** du calme! **2** *n* calme *m*. **3** *vt* calmer.

▶ **calm down 1** *vi* se calmer. **2** *vt* calmer.

calm·ly *adv* calmement.

cal·o·rie calorie *f*.

cam·cord·er caméscope *m*.

came *pt de* come.

cam·el chameau *m*.

cam·er·a appareil photo *m*; **(TV or film) c.** caméra *f*.

camp camp *m*.

camp (out) *vi* camper.

camp·er (person) campeur, -euse *mf*, (recreational vehicle) camping-car *m*; (trailer) caravane *f*.

camp·fire feu *m* de camp.

camp·ing camping *m*; **c. site** camping *m*.

camp·site camping *m*.

cam·pus campus *m*, complexe *m* universitaire.

can¹ *v aux* (*pt* could) pouvoir; (know how to) savoir; **he couldn't help me** il ne pouvait pas m'aider; **she c. swim** elle sait nager; **you could be wrong** (possibility) tu as peut-être tort; **he can't be old**

(probability) il ne doit pas être vieux; **c. I come in?** puis-je entrer?

can² *(for food)* boîte *f*; *(for drinks)* cannette *f*.

Ca·na·di·an 1 *n* Canadien, -ienne *mf*. **2** *adj* canadien.

ca·nal canal *m*.

ca·nar·y canari *m*.

can·cel *vt (flight, appointment etc)* annuler; *(goods, taxi)* décommander; *(train)* supprimer.

can·cel·la·tion *(of flight, appointment etc)* annulation *f*; *(of train)* suppression *f*.

can·cer cancer *m*.

can·did *adj* franc *(f* franche*)*.

can·di·date candidat, -ate *mf*.

can·dle bougie *f*; *(in church)* cierge *m*.

can·dle·stick bougeoir *m*; *(tall)* chandelier *m*.

can·dy bonbon(s) *m(pl)*.

can·dy·store confiserie *f*.

cane 1 *n (stick)* canne *f*; *(for punishment)* baguette *f*. **2** *vt (punish)* fouetter.

can·na·bis *(drug)* haschisch *m*.

canned *adj* en boîte; **c. food** conserves *fpl*.

can·ni·bal cannibale *mf*.

ca·noe canoë *m*.

ca·noe·ing to go c. faire du canoë.

can·o·la colza *m*.

can·o·pen·er ouvre-boîtes *m inv.*

can·o·py *(hood of baby carriage)* capote *f*; *(small roof)* auvent *m*.

can·ta·loup(e) *(melon)* cantaloup *m*.

can·teen *(place)* cantine *f*; *(flask)* gourde *f*.

can·vas toile *f*.

can·yon canyon *m*.

cap *(hat)* casquette *f*; *(for shower)* bonnet *m*; *(of soldier)* képi *m*; *(of bottle, tube)* bouchon *m*; *(of milk or beer bottle)* capsule *f*; *(of pen)* capuchon *m*; *(of child's gun)* amorce *f*.

ca·pa·bil·i·ty capacité *f*.

ca·pa·ble *adj (person)* capable *(* **of sth** de qch; **of doing** de faire*)*.

ca·pac·i·ty *(of container)* capacité *f*; *(ability)* aptitude *f*; **in my c. as** en ma qualité de.

cape *(cloak)* cape *f*; *(of cyclist)* pèlerine *f*.

cap·i·tal *(money)* capital *m*; **c. (city)** capitale *f*; **c. (letter)** majuscule *f*.

cap·size *vti* chavirer.

cap·sule capsule *f*.

cap·tain capitaine *m*.

cap·ture *vt (of person, town)* prendre.

car voiture *f*, auto *f*; *(of train)* wagon *m*; **c. radio** autoradio *m*.

car·a·mel caramel *m*.

car·a·van caravane *f*; *(horse-drawn)* roulotte *f*.

car·bon carbone *m*; **c. copy** double *m* (au carbone).

car·bon pa·per (papier *m*) carbone *m*.

car·bu·re·tor carburateur *m*.

card carte *f*; *(cardboard)* carton *m*; **(index) c.** fiche *f*; **to play cards** jouer aux cartes.

card·board carton *m*.

car·di·gan gilet *m*.

car·di·nal *adj (number, point)* cardinal.

card in·dex fichier *m*.

care 1 *vi (like)* aimer; **would you c. to try?** aimeriez-vous essayer?; **I don't c.** ça m'est égal; **who cares?** qu'est-ce que ça fait? **2** *n (attention)* soin(s) *m(pl)*; *(protection)* garde *f*; *(anxiety)* souci *m*; **to take c. not to do** faire attention à ne pas faire; **to take c. to do** veiller à faire; **to take c. of** s'occuper de; *(keep safely)* garder; *(* **for sb** pour qn*)*; *(sick person)* prendre soin de; **to take c. of oneself** *(manage)* se débrouiller; *(keep healthy)* faire bien attention à soi.

▸**care about** *vt* se soucier de.

ca·reer carrière *f*.

► **care for** vt (want) avoir envie de; **to c. for sb** (look after) s'occuper de qn; (sick person) soigner qn; (like) avoir de la sympathie pour qn; **I don't c. for it** je n'aime pas beaucoup ça.

care·free adj insouciant.

care·ful adj (exact, thorough) soigneux (about de); (cautious) prudent; **to be c. of** or **with** faire attention à.

care·ful·ly adv avec soin; (cautiously) prudemment.

care·giv·er (professional) aide mf à domicile; (relative) = personne s'occupant d'un parent malade ou âgé.

care·less adj négligent; (absentminded) étourdi.

care·tak·er gardien, -ienne mf.

car fer·ry ferry-boat m.

car·go, pl -os cargaison f.

car·ing adj (loving) aimant; (understanding) très humain.

car·na·tion œillet m.

car·ni·val carnaval m (pl -als).

car·ol chant m (de Noël).

carp (fish) carpe f.

car·pen·ter charpentier m; (for light woodwork) menuisier m.

car·pen·try charpenterie f; menuiserie f.

car·pet tapis m, (fitted) moquette f.

car·pet·ing (wall-to-wall) c. moquette f.

car·pet sweep·er balai m mécanique.

car·riage (of train, horse-drawn) voiture f.

car·ri·er (company) entreprise f de transport; (of disease) porteur, -euse mf.

car·rot carotte f.

car·ry vt porter; (goods) transporter; (sell) stocker; (in calculation) retenir.

car·ry·all fourre-tout m inv.

► **carry away** vt emporter; **to get carried away** (excited) s'emballer.

► **carry back** vt rapporter; (person) ramener.

► **carry off** vt emporter; (prize) remporter; **to c. it off** réussir.

► **carry on 1** vt continuer; (conduct) diriger; (sustain) soutenir. **2** vi continuer (**doing** à faire).

► **carry out** vt (plan, order, promise) exécuter; (repair, reform) effectuer; (duty) accomplir; (meal) emporter.

► **carry through** vt (plan) mener à bien.

cart (horse-drawn) charrette f, (in supermarket) caddie® m; (serving) **c.** table f roulante.

cart (a·round) vt Fam trimbal(l)er.

► **cart away** vt emporter.

car·ton (box) carton m; (of milk etc) brique f, (of cigarettes) cartouche f, (of cream) pot m.

car·toon dessin m (humoristique); (film) dessin m animé; (strip) bande f dessinée.

car·tridge cartouche f.

carve vt tailler (**out of** dans); (initials etc) graver.

carve (up) vt (meat) découper.

car wash (machine) lave-auto m.

case¹ (instance, in hospital) cas m; (in court) affaire f; **in any c.** en tout cas; **in c. it rains** pour le cas où il pleuvrait; **in c. of** en cas de; (**just**) **in c.** à tout hasard.

case² (bag) valise f, (crate) caisse f, (for pen, glasses, camera, cigarettes) étui m; (for jewels) coffret m.

cash 1 n argent m; **to pay (in) c.** payer en espèces. **2** vt **to c. a check** encaisser un chèque; (of bank) payer un chèque.

cash·box caisse f.

cash·ier caissier, -ière mf.

cash ma·chine distributeur m de billets.

cash price prix m (au comptant).

cash re·gis·ter caisse f enregistreuse.

ca·si·no, pl -os casino m.

cas·se·role cocotte f; (stew) ragoût m en cocotte.

cas·sette (audio, video) cassette f; (film) cartouche f.

cas·sette play·er lecteur m de cassettes.

cas·sette re·cord·er magnétophone m à cassettes.

cast[1] (actors) acteurs mpl; (list of actors) distribution f; (for broken bone) plâtre m.

cast[2]* vt jeter; (light, shadow) projeter; (doubt) exprimer; **to c. a vote** voter.

cast-i·ron adj (pan) en fonte; (alibi) inattaquable, en béton.

cas·tle château m; Chess tour f.

cas·tor (wheel) roulette f.

ca·su·al adj (remark) fait en passant; (stroll) sans but; (offhand) désinvolte; (worker) temporaire; (work) irrégulier; **c. clothes** vêtements mpl sport.

ca·su·al·ty (dead) mort m, morte f; (wounded) blessé, -ée mf.

cat chat m; (female) chatte f; **c. food** pâtée f.

cat·a·log catalogue m.

cat·a·pult catapulte f.

ca·tas·tro·phe catastrophe f.

catch[1]* vt (ball, thief, illness, train etc) attraper; (grab, surprise) prendre; (understand) saisir; (attention) attirer; (on nail etc) accrocher (**on** à); (finger etc) se prendre (**in** dans); **to c. fire** prendre feu; **to c. one's breath** (rest) reprendre haleine. **2** vi **her skirt (got) caught in the door** sa jupe s'est prise dans la porte; **to c. on fire** prendre feu. **3** n (trick) piège m; (on door) loquet m.

catch·ing adj contagieux.

▸**catch on** vi (become popular) prendre; (understand) saisir.

▸**catch out** vt prendre en défaut.

▸**catch up 1** vt **to c. sb up** rattraper qn. **2** vi se rattraper; **to c. up with sb** rattraper qn.

cat·e·go·ry catégorie f.

▸**cater for, cater to** vt (need, taste) satisfaire.

cat·er·pil·lar chenille f.

ca·the·dral cathédrale f.

Cath·o·lic adj & n catholique (mf).

cau·li·flow·er chou-fleur m.

cause 1 n cause f. **2** vt causer; **to c. sth to move/etc** faire bouger/etc qch.

cau·tion (care) prudence f; (warning) avertissement m.

cau·tious adj prudent.

cau·tious·ly adv prudemment.

cave caverne f.

▸**cave in** vi (fall in) s'effondrer.

cav·i·ty cavité f.

CCTV (closed-circuit television) télévision f en circuit fermé.

CD abbr (compact disc) CD m; **CD player** lecteur m de CD.

cease vti cesser (**doing** de faire).

cease-fire cessez-le-feu m inv.

ceil·ing plafond m.

cel·e·brate 1 vt fêter; (mass) célébrer. **2** vi faire la fête.

cel·e·bra·tion fête f.

ce·leb·ri·ty (person) célébrité f.

cel·er·y céleri m.

cell cellule f.

cel·lar cave f.

cel·lo·phane® cellophane® f.

cell·phone (téléphone m) portable m.

ce·ment 1 n ciment m. **2** vt cimenter.

ce·ment mix·er bétonnière f.

cem·e·ter·y cimetière f.

cen·sus recensement m.

cent (coin) cent m.

cen·ter 1 n centre m. **2** vt centrer.

cen·ti·grade adj centigrade.

cen·ti·me·ter centimètre m.

cen·ti·pede mille-pattes m inv.

cen·tral adj central.

cen·tral·ize vt centraliser.

cen·tu·ry siècle m.

ce·ram·ic adj (tile) de céramique.

ce·re·al céréale f.

cer·e·mo·ny cérémonie f.

cer·tain adj (sure, particular) certain; she's c. to come c'est certain qu'elle viendra; I'm not c. what to do je ne sais pas très bien ce qu'il faut faire; to be c. of sth/that être certain de qch/que; to make c. of (fact) s'assurer de; (seat etc) s'assurer.

cer·tain·ly adv certainement; (yes) bien sûr.

cer·tain·ty certitude f.

cer·tif·i·cate certificat m; (from university) diplôme m.

cer·ti·fied adj certifié, agréé; C. Public Accountant expert-comptable m.

cer·ti·fy vt (document etc) certifier.

chain (of rings, mountains) chaîne f.

chain (up) vt (dog) mettre à l'attache; (person) enchaîner.

chain saw tronçonneuse f.

chain store magasin m à succursales multiples.

chair chaise f; (armchair) fauteuil m.

chair lift télésiège m.

chair·man, pl -men président, -ente mf.

cha·let chalet m.

chalk 1 n craie f. 2 vti écrire à la craie.

chal·lenge 1 n défi m; (task) challenge m, gageure f. 2 vt défier (sb to do qn de faire); (dispute) contester.

chal·leng·ing adj (job) exigeant.

cham·ber c. of commerce chambre f de commerce.

cham·ois (leather) peau f de chamois.

cham·pagne champagne m.

cham·pi·on champion, -onne mf.

cham·pi·on·ship championnat m.

chance 1 n (luck) hasard m; (possibility) chances fpl; (opportunity) occasion f; by c. par hasard. 2 vt to c. it risquer le coup.

chan·cel·lor (head of state, in embassy) chancelier m.

chan·de·lier lustre m.

change 1 n changement m; (money) monnaie f; for a c. pour changer; it makes a c. from ça change de; a c. of clothes des vêtements de rechange. 2 vt changer; (exchange) échanger (for contre); (money) changer; to c. trains/one's skirt/etc changer de train/de jupe/etc; to c. the subject changer de sujet. 3 vi changer; (change clothes) se changer.

change·a·ble adj changeant.

▸ **change over** vi passer (from de; to à).

change·o·ver passage m (from de; to à).

chang·ing room vestiaire m.

chan·nel (on television) chaîne f; (for inquiry etc) voie f; the English C. la Manche; to go through the normal channels passer par la voie normale.

chant 1 vt (slogan) scander. 2 vi (of demonstrators) scander des slogans.

cha·os chaos m.

cha·ot·ic adj sens dessus dessous.

chap·el chapelle f.

chapped adj gercé.

chap·ter chapitre m.

char vt carboniser; (scorch) brûler légèrement.

char·ac·ter caractère m; (in book, film) personnage m; (strange person) numéro m.

char·ac·ter·is·tic adj & n caractéristique (f).

charge[1] 1 n (cost) prix m; charges (expenses) frais mpl; there's a c. (for it) c'est payant; free of c. gratuit. 2 vt (amount) demander (for pour); (person) faire payer.

charge[2] 1 n (in court) accusation f; (care) garde f; to take c. of prendre en charge; to be in c. of (child) avoir la garde de; (office) être responsable de. **2** vt (battery, soldiers) charger; (accuse) accuser (**with** de). **3** vi (rush) se précipiter.

char·ger (for battery, phone) chargeur m.

char·i·ty (society) fondation f charitable; **to give to c.** faire la charité.

charm 1 n charme m; (trinket) amulette f. **2** vt charmer.

charm·ing adj charmant.

chart (map) carte f, (graph) graphique m; (**pop**) **charts** hit-parade m.

char·ter 1 n (of institution) statuts mpl. **2** vt (plane, boat) affréter.

char·ter flight charter m.

chase 1 n poursuite f. **2** vt poursuivre.

▶**chase after** vt courir après, poursuivre.

▶**chase away** or **off** vt chasser.

chasm abîme m, gouffre m.

chas·sis (of vehicle) châssis m.

chat 1 n petite conversation f; **to have a c.** bavarder. **2** vi causer.

chat·ter 1 vi (of person) bavarder; **his teeth are chattering** il claque des dents. **2** n bavardage m.

chat·ter·box bavard, -arde mf.

chat·ty adj bavard.

chauf·feur chauffeur m.

cheap 1 adj bon marché inv; (rate) réduit; (worthless) sans valeur; **cheaper** meilleur marché. **2** adv (to buy) (à) bon marché.

cheap·ly adv (à) bon marché.

cheat 1 vt tromper; **to c. sb out of sth** escroquer qch à qn. **2** vi (at games etc) tricher.

cheat·er tricheur, -euse mf.

check 1 vt (examine) vérifier; (inspect) contrôler; (stop) arrêter; (baggage) mettre à la consigne. **2** vi vérifier. **3** n vérification f, (inspection) contrôle m; Chess échec m; (mark) = coche f, (receipt) reçu m; (bill in restaurant) addition f, (in banking) chèque m.

check·book carnet m de chèques.

checked, check·ered adj à carreaux.

check·ers npl jeu m de dames.

check-in enregistrement m (des bagages).

▶**check in 1** vt (luggage) enregistrer. **2** vi (at hotel) signer le registre; (arrive) arriver; (at airport) se présenter (à l'enregistrement).

check·ing ac·count compte m courant.

check·mate Chess échec et mat m.

▶**check off** vt (names on list etc) cocher.

▶**check on** vt vérifier.

check-out (in supermarket) caisse f.

▶**check out 1** vt confirmer. **2** vi (at hotel) régler sa note.

check-up bilan m de santé.

▶**check up** vi vérifier.

ched·dar (cheese) cheddar m.

cheek (impudence) culot m.

cheek·y adj effronté.

cheer 1 n cheers acclamations fpl, **cheers!** Fam à votre santé! **2** vt (applaud) acclamer. **3** vi applaudir.

cheer·ful adj gai.

cheer·ing acclamations fpl.

▶**cheer up 1** vt donner du courage à; (amuse) égayer. **2** vi prendre courage; (become happier) s'égayer; **c. up!** (du) courage!

cheese fromage m.

cheese·burg·er cheeseburger m.

cheese·cake tarte f au fromage blanc, cheesecake m.

chef (cook) chef m.

chem·i·cal 1 adj chimique. **2** n produit m chimique.

chem·ist chimiste mf.

chem·is·try chimie f.

cher·ry cerise f.

cher·ry bran·dy cherry m.

chess échecs mpl.

chess·board échiquier m.

chest (part of body) poitrine f, (box) coffre m; **c. of drawers** commode f.

chest·nut châtaigne f.

chew 1 vt to c. (up) mâcher. **2** vi mastiquer.

chew·ing gum chewing-gum m.

chick poussin m.

chick·en 1 n poulet m. **2** adj (cowardly) Fam froussard.

▸ **chicken out** vi Fam se dégonfler.

chick·en·pox varicelle f.

chick·pea pois m chiche.

chic·o·ry (for salad) endive f.

chief 1 n chef m; **in c.** en chef. **2** adj principal.

chief·ly adv principalement.

chil·blain engelure f.

child, pl **children** enfant mf.

child care (for working parents) crèches fpl et garderies fpl.

child·hood enfance f.

child·ish adj puéril.

chil·i, pl **-ies** piment m (de Cayenne).

chill 1 n froid m; (illness) refroidissement m; **to catch a c.** prendre froid. **2** vt (wine, melon) faire rafraîchir; (meat) réfrigérer.

chilled adj (wine) frais.

chill·y adj froid; **it's c.** il fait (un peu) froid.

chime vi (of clock) sonner.

chim·ney cheminée f.

chim·ney·pot tuyau m de cheminée.

chim·pan·zee chimpanzé m.

chin menton m.

chi·na 1 n inv porcelaine f. **2** adj en porcelaine.

Chi·nese 1 n inv Chinois, -oise (mf); (language) chinois m. **2** adj chinois.

chip 1 vt (cup etc) ébrécher; (paint) écailler. **2** n (break) ébréchure f; (microchip) puce f, (counter) jeton m; (potato) **chips** chips mpl.

chi·ro·po·dist pédicure mf.

chis·el ciseau m.

chives ciboulette f.

chock-a-block adj Fam archiplein.

choc·o·late 1 n chocolat m; **milk c.** chocolat m au lait; **bittersweet c.** chocolat m à croquer. **2** adj (cake) au chocolat.

choice choix m.

choir chœur m.

choke 1 vt (person) étrangler; (clog) boucher. **2** vi s'étrangler (on avec).

cho·les·ter·ol cholestérol m.

choose* 1 vt choisir; **to c. to do** (decide) juger bon de faire. **2** vi choisir.

choos·(e)y adj difficile.

chop 1 n (of lamb, pork) côtelette f. **2** vt couper (à la hache); (food) hacher.

▸ **chop down** vt (tree) abattre.

▸ **chop off** vt (branch, finger etc) couper.

chop·per hachoir m.

chop·sticks npl baguettes fpl.

▸ **chop up** vt couper en morceaux.

chord (in music) accord m.

chore travail m (routinier); (unpleasant) corvée f; **chores** travaux mpl ménagers.

cho·rus (of song) refrain m.

chris·ten vt baptiser.

chris·ten·ing baptême m.

Chris·tian adj & n chrétien, -ienne (mf).

Christ·mas 1 n Noël m; **Merry C.** Joyeux Noël; **C. Eve** la veille de Noël. **2** adj de Noël.

chrome Fam chrome m.

chron·ic adj chronique.

chry·san·the·mum chrysanthème m.

chub·by adj potelé.

chuck vt Fam (throw) jeter; (job etc) laisser tomber.

▸ **chuck out** vt (old clothes etc) Fam balancer.

chum Fam copain m, copine f.

chunk (gros) morceau m.

church église f.

chute (for refuse) vide-ordures m inv; (in pool) toboggan m.

ci·der cidre *m*.

ci·gar cigare *m*.

cig·a·rette cigarette *f*.

cig·a·rette butt mégot *m*.

cig·a·rette light·er briquet *m*.

cin·e·ma cinéma *m*.

cin·na·mon cannelle *f*.

cir·cle 1 *n* cercle *m*; **circles** *(political etc)* milieux *mpl*. **2** *vt* faire le tour de; *(word)* encadrer. **3** *vi (of aircraft etc)* décrire des cercles.

cir·cuit *(electrical path, in sports etc)* circuit *m*.

cir·cu·lar 1 *adj* circulaire. **2** *n (letter)* circulaire *f*; *(advertisement)* prospectus *m*.

cir·cu·late 1 *vi (of blood etc)* circuler. **2** *vt (pass around)* faire circuler.

cir·cu·la·tion *(of newspaper)* tirage *m*.

cir·cum·fer·ence circonférence *f*.

cir·cum·stance circonstance *f*; **in** *or* **under no circumstances** en aucun cas.

cir·cus cirque *m*.

cite *(quote)* citer.

cit·i·zen citoyen, -enne *mf*; *(of town)* habitant, -ante *mf*.

cit·y (grande) ville *f*.

cit·y coun·cil conseil *m* municipal.

cit·y hall hôtel *m* de ville.

civ·ic *adj (authority, building)* municipal; *(duty, rights)* civique.

civ·il *adj* civil.

ci·vil·ian *adj & n* civil, -ile (*mf*).

civ·i·li·za·tion civilisation *f*.

civ·il ser·vant fonctionnaire *mf*.

civ·il ser·vice fonction *f* publique.

claim 1 *vt* réclamer; **to c. that** prétendre que. **2** *n (demand)* revendication *f*; *(statement)* affirmation *f*; *(right)* droit *m* (**to** à); *(insurance)* c. demande *f* d'indemnité.

clam *(shellfish)* palourde *f*.

clap *vti* applaudir; **to c. (one's hands)** battre des mains.

clap·ping applaudissements *mpl*.

clar·i·fy *vt* clarifier.

clar·i·net clarinette *f*.

clash 1 *vi (of plates)* s'entrechoquer; *(of interests)* se heurter; *(of colors)* jurer (**with** avec); *(of people)* se bagarrer; *(coincide)* tomber en même temps (**with** que). **2** *n (noise)* choc *m*; *(of interests)* conflit *m*.

clasp 1 *vt* serrer. **2** *n (fastener)* fermoir *m*; *(of belt)* boucle *f*.

class 1 *n* classe *f*; *(lesson)* cours *m*. **2** *vt* classer.

clas·sic 1 *adj* classique. **2** *n (work etc)* classique *m*.

clas·si·cal *adj* classique.

clas·si·fy *vt* classer.

class·mate camarade *mf* de classe.

class·room (salle *f* de) classe *f*.

clause *(in sentence)* proposition *f*.

claw griffe *f*; *(of lobster)* pince *f*.

clay argile *f*.

clean 1 *adj (not dirty)* propre; *(clearcut)* net (*f* nette). **2** *adv (utterly)* complètement; *(to break, cut)* net. **3** *vt* nettoyer; *(wash)* laver; *(wipe)* essuyer. **4** *vi* faire le nettoyage.

clean cop·y copie *f* au propre.

clean·er (dry) c. teinturier, -ière *mf*.

clean·ing nettoyage *m*; *(housework)* ménage *m*.

clean·ing la·dy femme *f* de ménage.

clean·ly *adv (to break, cut)* net.

▸ **clean out** *vt (room etc)* nettoyer; *(empty)* vider.

cleans·ing cream crème *f* démaquillante.

▸ **clean up 1** *vt* nettoyer. **2** *vi* faire le nettoyage.

clear 1 *adj (sky, outline, sound, thought etc)* clair; *(glass)* transparent; *(road)* libre; *(profit)* net; *(obvious)* évident, clair; **to be c. of** *(free of)* être libre de; **to make one-**

self c. se faire comprendre. **2** *adv* **to keep** *or* **steer c. of** se tenir à l'écart de; **to get c. of** s'éloigner de. **3** *vt (path, table)* débarrasser; *(fence)* franchir; *(accused person)* disculper; *(check)* faire passer (sur un compte); *(through customs)* dédouaner; **to c. one's throat** s'éclaircir la gorge. **4** *vi (of weather)* s'éclaircir; *(of fog)* se dissiper.

clear·ance *(sale)* soldes *mpl*; *(space)* dégagement *m*.

▶ **clear away** *vt (remove)* enlever.

clear-cut *adj* net (*f* nette).

clear·ing *(in wood)* clairière *f*.

clear·ly *adv* clairement; *(obviously)* évidemment.

▶ **clear out 1** *vt* vider; *(clean)* nettoyer; *(remove)* enlever. **2** *vi (go)* *Fam* décamper.

▶ **clear up 1** *vt (room)* ranger; *(mystery)* éclaircir. **2** *vi (tidy)* ranger.

cleat *(sports shoe)* crampon *m*.

clem·en·tine clémentine *f*.

clench *vt (fist)* serrer.

cler·gy clergé *m*.

cler·i·cal *adj (job)* d'employé; *(work)* de bureau.

clerk employé, -ée *mf* (de bureau); *(in store)* vendeur, -euse *mf*.

clev·er *adj* intelligent; *(smart)* astucieux; *(skillful)* habile; *(machine, book etc)* ingénieux.

click 1 *n (noise)* petit bruit *m* sec; *(with mouse)* clic *m*. **2** *vi (make noise)* faire un bruit sec; *(with mouse)* cliquer (**on** sur).

cli·ent client, -ente *mf*.

cliff falaise *f*.

cli·mate climat *m*.

cli·max point *m* culminant.

climb (o·ver) *vt (wall)* escalader.

climb (up) 1 *vt (stairs, steps)* monter; *(hill, mountain)* gravir; *(tree, ladder)* monter à. **2** *vi* monter.

▶ **climb down 1** *vt (wall, tree, hill)* descendre de. **2** *vi* descendre (**from** de).

climb·er *(mountaineer)* alpiniste *mf*.

cling* *vi* se cramponner; *(stick)* adhérer (**to** à).

clin·ic *(private)* clinique *f*; *(public)* centre *m* médical.

clip 1 *vt* couper; *(hedge)* tailler; *(ticket)* poinçonner; *(attach)* attacher. **2** *n (paper)* trombone *m*; *(of brooch, of cyclist, for hair)* pince *f*.

▶ **clip on** *vt* attacher (**to** à).

clip·pers *npl (for hair)* tondeuse *f*; *(for nails)* coupe-ongles *m inv*.

clip·ping *(newspaper article)* coupure *f*.

cloak *(grande)* cape *f*.

cloak·room vestiaire *m*.

clock horloge *f*; *(small)* pendule *f*; **around the c.** vingt-quatre heures sur vingt-quatre.

clock·wise *adv* dans le sens des aiguilles d'une montre.

clone 1 *n* clone *m*. **2** *vt* cloner.

close¹ 1 *adj (place, relative etc)* proche (**to** de); *(collaboration, connection)* étroit; *(friend)* intime; *(atmosphere)* lourd. **2** *adv* **c. (by)** (tout) près; **c. to** près de; **c. behind** juste derrière.

close² 1 *n (end)* fin *f*. **2** *vt (door, shop etc)* fermer; *(road)* barrer; *(deal)* conclure. **3** *vi* se fermer; *(of shop)* fermer.

closed *adj* fermé; **c.-circuit television** télévision *f* en circuit fermé.

▶ **close down** *vti (for good)* fermer (définitivement).

▶ **close in** *vi* approcher.

close·ly *adv (to follow, guard)* de près; *(to listen)* attentivement.

clos·et *(for linens, clothes etc)* placard *m*; *(for clothing only)* penderie *f*.

▶ **close up 1** *vt* fermer. **2** *vi (of shopkeeper)* fermer; *(of line of people)* se rapprocher.

clos·ing time heure *f* de fermeture.

clo·sure fermeture *f*.

clot 1 *n (of blood)* caillot *m*. **2** *vi* se coaguler.

cloth tissu *m*; *(for dusting)* chiffon *m*; *(for dishes)* torchon *m*; *(table-cloth)* nappe *f*.

clothes *npl* vêtements *mpl*; **to put one's c. on** s'habiller.

clothes brush brosse *f* à habits.

clothes-line corde *f* à linge.

clothes-pin pince *f* à linge.

cloth·ing vêtements *mpl*; **an article of c.** un vêtement.

cloth·ing store magasin *m* d'habillement.

cloud nuage *m*.

▸ **cloud over** *vi (of sky)* se couvrir.

cloud·y *adj (weather)* couvert.

clove c. of garlic gousse *f* d'ail.

clown clown *m*.

club *(society, stick for golf)* club *m*; **club(s)** *(at cards)* trèfle *m*.

club so·da eau *f* gazeuse.

clue indice *m*; *(of crossword)* définition *f*, **I don't have a c.** *Fam* je n'en ai pas la moindre idée.

clum·sy *adj* maladroit; *(tool)* peu commode.

clunk·er *(car) Fam* tacot *m*.

clus·ter 1 *n* groupe *m*. **2** *vi* se grouper.

clutch 1 *vt (hold)* serrer; *(grasp)* saisir. **2** *n (in vehicle)* embrayage *m*; *(pedal)* pédale *f* d'embrayage.

▸ **clut·ter up** *vt (room etc)* encombrer (**with** de).

cm *abbr (centimeter)* cm.

Co *abbr (company)* Cie.

coach 1 *n (part of train)* voiture *f*; *(bus)* autocar *m*. **2** *vt (pupil)* donner des leçons (particulières) à.

coal charbon *m*.

coal·mine mine *f* de charbon.

coarse *adj (person, fabric)* grossier.

coast côte *f*.

coat 1 *n* manteau *m*; *(jacket)* veste *f*; *(of animal)* pelage *m*; *(of paint)* couche *f*. **2** *vt* couvrir (**with** de).

coat·hang·er cintre *m*.

coat·ing couche *f*.

cob corn on the c. épi *m* de maïs.

cob·bled *adj* pavé.

cob·web toile *f* d'araignée.

co·caine cocaïne *f*.

cock *(fowl)* coq *m*.

cock·le *(shellfish)* coque *f*.

cock·pit poste *m* de pilotage.

cock·roach *(insect)* cafard *m*.

cock·tail cocktail *m*; **fruit c.** macédoine *f* (de fruits); **shrimp c.** crevettes *fpl* à la mayonnaise.

cock·tail par·ty cocktail *m*.

co·coa cacao *m*.

co·co·nut noix *f* de coco.

cod morue *f*.

code code *m*.

cod-liv·er oil huile *f* de foie de morue.

co·ed·u·ca·tion·al *adj (school etc)* mixte.

cof·fee café *m*; **c. with milk** café *m* au lait; *(in restaurant)* (café *m*) crème *m*.

cof·fee bar café *m*.

cof·fee break pause-café *f*.

cof·fee·pot cafetière *f*.

cof·fee ta·ble table *f* basse.

cof·fin cercueil *m*.

co·gnac cognac *m*.

co·her·ent *adj* cohérent.

coil 1 *n (of wire, rope etc)* rouleau *m*. **2** *vt* enrouler.

coin pièce *f* (de monnaie).

coin bank tirelire *f*.

co·in·cide *vi* coïncider (**with** avec).

co·in·ci·dence coïncidence *f*.

coke *(Coca-Cola®)* coca *m*.

col·an·der passoire *f*.

cold 1 *n* froid *m*; *(illness)* rhume *m*; **to catch c.** prendre froid. **2** *adj* froid; **to be or feel c.** avoir froid; **my hands are c.** j'ai froid aux mains; **it's c.** *(of weather)* il fait froid; **to get c.** *(of weather)* se refroidir; *(of food)* refroidir.

cold cuts assiette *f* anglaise.

cold·ness froideur *f*.

cole·slaw salade *f* de chou cru.

col·lab·o·rate *vi* collaborer (**on** à).

col·lab·o·ra·tion collaboration f.

col·lapse 1 vi (of person, building) s'effondrer. **2** n effondrement m.

col·lar col m; (of dog) collier m.

col·lar·bone clavicule f.

col·league collègue mf.

col·lect 1 vt (pick up) ramasser; (gather) rassembler; (taxes) percevoir; (rent) encaisser; (stamps etc) collectionner; (fetch) (passer) prendre; **to c. (money)** (in street, church) quêter. **2** vi (of dust) s'accumuler. **3** adv **to call c.** téléphoner en PCV.

col·lec·tion (group of objects) collection f; (of poems etc) recueil m; (of mail) levée f.

col·lec·tor (of stamps etc) collectionneur, -euse mf.

col·lege université f.

col·lide vi entrer en collision (with avec).

col·li·sion collision f.

col·lo·qui·al adj familier.

co·logne eau f de Cologne.

co·lon Grammar deux-points m inv.

colo·nel colonel m.

co·lo·ni·al adj colonial.

col·o·ny colonie f.

col·or 1 n couleur f. **2** adj (photo, TV set) en couleurs. **3** vt colorer.

col·ored adj (pencil) de couleur.

col·or·ful adj coloré; (person) pittoresque.

▸ **col·or in** vt (drawing) colorier.

col·or·ing book album m de coloriages.

col·umn colonne f; (newspaper feature) chronique f.

co·ma coma m; **in a c.** dans le coma.

comb 1 n peigne m. **2** vt **to c. one's hair** se peigner.

com·bi·na·tion combinaison f.

com·bine 1 vt joindre (**with** à); **our combined efforts achieved a result** en joignant nos efforts nous

avons obtenu un résultat. **2** vi s'unir.

come* vi venir (**from** de; **to** à); **to c. first** (in race) arriver premier; (in exam) être le premier; **to c. close to doing** faillir faire.

▸ **come about** vi (happen) se faire, arriver.

▸ **come across** vt (thing, person) tomber sur.

▸ **come along** vi venir (**with** avec); (progress) avancer; **c. along!** allons!

▸ **come apart** vi (of two objects) se séparer.

▸ **come around** vi (visit) venir; (of date) revenir; (regain consciousness) revenir à soi.

▸ **come away** vi (leave, come off) partir.

come·back to make a c. faire un come-back.

▸ **come back** vi revenir; (return home) rentrer.

▸ **come by** vt obtenir; (find) trouver.

co·me·di·an (acteur m) comique m, actrice f comique.

▸ **come down** vi descendre; (of rain, price) tomber.

▸ **come down with** vt attraper.

com·e·dy comédie f.

▸ **come for** vt venir chercher.

▸ **come forward** vi s'avancer; (volunteer) se présenter; **to c. forward with sth** offrir qch.

▸ **come in** vi entrer; (of tide) monter; (of train) arriver.

▸ **come into** vt (room etc) entrer dans; (money) hériter de.

▸ **come off 1** vi (of button etc) se détacher; (succeed) réussir. **2** vt (fall from) tomber de; (get down from) descendre de.

▸ **come on** vi (progress) avancer; **c. on!** (reproving, encouraging) allons!, allez!

▸ **come out** vi sortir; (of sun, book) paraître; (of stain) partir.

▸ **come over 1** vi (visit) venir. **2** vt (of feeling) saisir.

▶**come through 1** vi (survive) s'en tirer. **2** vt (crisis etc) se tirer indemne de.

▶**come to 1** vt (amount to) revenir à; (a decision) parvenir à. **2** vi (regain consciousness) revenir à soi.

▶**come under** vt (heading) être classé sous; (sb's influence) tomber sous.

▶**come up** vi (rise) monter; (of plant) sortir; (of question, job) se présenter.

▶**come up against** vt (wall, problem) se heurter à.

▶**come up to** vt (reach) arriver jusqu'à.

▶**come up with** vt (idea, money) trouver.

com·fort 1 n confort m; (consolation) réconfort m. **2** vt consoler.

com·fort·a·ble adj (chair etc) confortable; (rich) aisé; **he's c.** (in chair etc) il est à l'aise; **make yourself c.** mets-toi à l'aise.

com·fort·er (quilt) édredon m, couette f.

com·ic 1 adj comique. **2** n (magazine) bande f dessinée.

com·ings npl c. and goings allées fpl et venues.

com·ma virgule f.

com·mand 1 vt (order) commander (**sb to do** à qn de faire). **2** n (order) ordre m; (mastery) maîtrise f (of de); **to be in c. (of)** (army etc) commander; (situation) être maître (de).

com·mand·er commandant m.

com·mem·o·rate vt commémorer.

com·mence vti commencer (**doing** à faire).

com·ment commentaire m.

com·men·tar·y commentaire m; (**live**) **c.** reportage m.

com·men·ta·tor reporter m.

▶**comment on** vt (event etc) commenter.

com·merce commerce m.

com·mer·cial 1 adj commercial.

2 n commercial(s) (on television) publicité f.

com·mis·sion (fee, group) commission f.

com·mit vt (crime) commettre; **to c. suicide** se suicider.

com·mit·ment (promise) engagement m.

com·mit·tee comité m.

com·mod·i·ty produit m.

com·mon adj (shared, frequent etc) commun; **in c.** (shared) en commun (**with** avec); **in c. with** (like) comme.

com·mon·ly adv (generally) en général.

com·mon·place adj banal (mpl banals).

com·mon room salle f commune.

com·mon sense sens m commun.

com·mo·tion agitation f.

com·mu·nal adj (bathroom etc) commun.

com·mu·ni·cate vti communiquer.

com·mu·ni·ca·tion communication f.

com·mun·ion communion f.

com·mu·ni·ty communauté f.

com·mu·ni·ty cen·ter centre m socio-culturel.

com·mute vi faire la navette (**to work** pour se rendre à son travail).

com·mut·er banlieusard, -arde mf.

com·mut·ing trajets mpl journaliers.

com·pact 1 adj compact. **2** n (for face powder) poudrier m.

com·pact disc or **disk** disque m compact.

com·pan·ion compagnon m.

com·pa·ny (being with others, firm) compagnie f; (guests) invités, -ées mfpl; **to keep sb c.** tenir compagnie à qn.

com·pa·ra·ble adj comparable (**to, with** à).

com·pa·ra·tive·ly adv relativement.

com·pare *vt* comparer (**with, to** à); **compared to** *or* **with** en comparaison de.

com·par·i·son comparaison *f* (**with** avec).

com·part·ment compartiment *m*.

com·pass *(for direction)* boussole *f*; *(on ship)* compas *m*; **(pair of) compasses** *(for drawing etc)* compas *m*.

com·pat·i·ble *adj* compatible.

com·pel *vt* forcer, contraindre (**to do** à faire).

com·pen·sate 1 *vt* **to c. sb** dédommager qn (**for** de). **2** *vi* compenser (**for sth** qch).

com·pen·sa·tion dédommagement *m*.

com·pete *vi (take part)* concourir (**in** à; **for** pour); **to c. (with sb)** rivaliser (avec qn); *(in business)* faire concurrence (à qn).

com·pe·tent *adj* compétent (**to do** pour faire).

com·pe·tent·ly *adv* avec compétence.

com·pe·ti·tion *(rivalry)* compétition *f*, **a c.** *(contest)* un concours; *(in sports)* une compétition.

com·pet·i·tive *adj (price etc)* compétitif; *(person)* aimant la compétition.

com·pet·i·tor concurrent, -ente *mf*.

com·pile *vt (dictionary)* rédiger; *(list)* dresser.

com·plain *vi* se plaindre (**of, about** de; **that** que).

com·plaint plainte *f*, *(in shop etc)* réclamation *f*, *(illness)* maladie *f*.

com·ple·ment 1 *n* complément *m*. **2** *vt* compléter.

com·plete 1 *adj (total)* complet; *(finished)* achevé; **a c. idiot** un parfait imbécile. **2** *vt* compléter; *(finish)* achever; *(a form)* remplir.

com·plete·ly *adv* complètement.

com·plex 1 *adj* complexe. **2** *n* *(feeling, buildings)* complexe *m*.

com·plex·ion *(of face)* teint *m*.

com·pli·cate *vt* compliquer.

com·pli·cat·ed *adj* compliqué.

com·pli·ca·tion complication *f*.

com·pli·ment compliment *m*.

com·pli·men·ta·ry *adj (praising)* flatteur; *(free)* gratuit.

com·ply *vi* obéir (**with** à).

com·pose *vt* composer; **to c. oneself** se calmer.

com·posed *adj* calme.

com·pos·er compositeur, -trice *mf*.

com·po·si·tion *(school essay)* rédaction *f*.

com·pound *(substance, word)* composé *m*.

com·pre·hen·sive *adj* complet; *(insurance)* tous risques.

com·prise *vt* comprendre.

com·pro·mise compromis *m*.

com·pul·sive *adj (smoker etc)* invétéré; **c. liar** mythomane *mf*.

com·pul·so·ry *adj* obligatoire.

com·put·er ordinateur *m*; **c. technician** informaticien, -enne *mf*.

com·put·er·ized *adj* informatisé.

com·put·er sci·ence informatique *f*.

com·put·ing informatique *f*.

con *vt (deceive) Fam* escroquer.

con·ceal *vt* dissimuler (**from sb** à qn); *(plan)* tenir secret.

con·cede *vt* concéder (**to** à).

con·ceit·ed *adj* vaniteux.

con·ceiv·a·ble *adj* concevable.

con·ceive *vti* concevoir.

con·cen·trate 1 *vt* concentrer. **2** *vi* se concentrer (**on** sur); **to c. on doing** s'appliquer à faire.

con·cen·tra·tion concentration *f*.

con·cern 1 *vt* concerner; **to be concerned with/about** s'occuper de/s'inquiéter de; **2** *n (matter)* affaire *f*, *(anxiety)* inquiétude *f*; **his c. for** son souci de; *(business)* **c.** entreprise *f*.

con·cerned adj (anxious) inquiet.

con·cern·ing prep en ce qui concerne.

con·cert concert m.

con·ces·sion concession f.

con·cise adj concis.

con·clude 1 vt conclure; **to c. that** conclure que. **2** vi se terminer (**with** par); (of speaker) conclure.

con·clu·sion conclusion f.

con·crete 1 n béton m. **2** adj en béton; (real) concret.

con·demn vt condamner (**to** à).

con·den·sa·tion (mist) buée f.

con·di·tion condition f; **on c. that one does** à condition de faire, à condition que l'on fasse.

con·di·tion·er (hair) c. après-shampooing m.

con·do, pl -os abbr = **condominium**.

con·dom préservatif m.

con·do·min·i·um (building) copropriété f; (apartment) appartement m dans une copropriété.

con·duct 1 vt conduite f. **2** vt conduire; (orchestra) diriger.

con·duct·ed tour excursion f accompagnée.

con·duc·tor (of orchestra) chef m d'orchestre; (on bus) receveur, -euse mf; (on train) chef m de train.

cone cône m; (of ice cream) cornet m.

con·fer 1 vt (title) conférer, accorder (**on** à). **2** vi (discuss) se consulter (**on, about** sur).

con·fer·ence conférence f; (scientific, etc) congrès m.

con·fess 1 vt avouer (**that** que). **2** vi **to c.** (**to**) avouer.

con·fes·sion aveu(x) m(pl).

con·fet·ti confettis mpl.

con·fi·dence (trust) confiance f; (**self-**)c. confiance f en soi; **in c.** en confidence.

con·fi·dent adj sûr; (**self-**)c. sûr de soi.

con·fi·den·tial adj confidentiel.

con·fi·dent·ly adv avec confiance.

con·fine vt limiter (**to** à); **to c. oneself to doing** se limiter à faire.

con·fined adj (space) réduit; **c. to bed** cloué au lit.

con·firm vt confirmer (**that** que).

con·fir·ma·tion confirmation f.

con·firmed adj (bachelor) endurci.

con·fis·cate vt confisquer (**from sb** à qn).

con·flict 1 n conflit m. **2** vi être en contradiction (**with** avec).

con·flict·ing adj (views etc) contradictoires; (dates) incompatibles.

con·form vi (of person) se conformer (**to** à).

con·front vt (problems, danger) faire face à; **to c. sb** (be face to face with) se trouver en face de qn; (oppose) affronter qn.

con·fron·ta·tion confrontation f.

con·fuse vt (make unsure) embrouiller; **to c. with** (mistake for) confondre avec.

con·fused adj (situation) confus; **to be c.** (of person) s'y perdre; **to get c.** s'embrouiller.

con·fus·ing adj déroutant.

con·fu·sion confusion f.

con·gest·ed adj (street) encombré.

con·ges·tion (traffic) encombrement(s) m(pl).

con·grat·u·late vt féliciter (**sb on sth** qn de qch).

con·grat·u·la·tions félicitations fpl (**on** pour).

con·gre·gate vi se rassembler.

con·gress congrès m; **C.** (political body) le Congrès.

Con·gress·man, pl -men membre m du Congrès.

con·ju·gate vt (verb) conjuguer.

con·ju·ga·tion conjugaison f.

con·junc·tion Grammar conjonction f.

con·jur·er prestidigitateur, -trice mf.

con·jur·ing trick tour m de prestidigitation.

con man Fam escroc m.

con·nect 1 vt relier (**with, to** à); (telephone etc) brancher; **to c. sb with sb** (by phone) mettre qn en communication avec qn. **2** vi **to c. with** (of train, bus) assurer la correspondance avec.

con·nect·ed adj (facts) liés; **to be c. with** (have dealings with, relate to) être lié à.

con·nec·tion (link) rapport m (**with** avec); (train etc) correspondance f; (phone call) communication f; **connections** (contacts) relations fpl; **in c. with** à propos de.

con·quer vt (country) conquérir; (enemy, habit) vaincre.

con·quest conquête f.

con·science conscience f.

con·sci·en·tious adj consciencieux.

con·scious adj (awake) conscient; **c. of sth** (aware) conscient de qch; **to be c. of doing** avoir conscience de faire.

con·sen·sus consensus m.

con·sent 1 vi consentir (**to** à). **2** n consentement m.

con·se·quence (result) conséquence f.

con·se·quent·ly adv par conséquent.

con·ser·va·tion (of energy) économies fpl; d'énergie; (of nature) protection f de l'environnement.

con·ser·va·tive adj & n conservateur, -trice (mf).

con·ser·va·to·ry (room) véranda f.

con·serve vt **to c. energy** faire des économies d'énergie.

con·sid·er vt considérer (**that** que); (take into account) tenir compte f de; **to c. doing** envisager de faire.

con·sid·er·a·ble adj (large) considérable; (much) beaucoup de.

con·sid·er·ate adj plein d'égards (**to** pour).

con·sid·er·a·tion considération f; **to take into c.** prendre en considération.

con·sid·er·ing prep compte tenu de.

con·sign·ment (goods) arrivage m.

con·sis·ten·cy consistance f.

con·sis·tent adj (unchanging) constant; (ideas) logique; **c. with** compatible avec.

con·sis·tent·ly adv (always) constamment.

▶ **con·sist in** vt consister dans; **to c. in doing** consister à faire.

▶ **con·sist of** vt consister en.

con·so·la·tion consolation f; **c. prize** lot m de consolation.

con·sole¹ vt consoler.

con·sole² (control desk) console f.

con·so·nant consonne f.

con·spic·u·ous adj visible; (striking) remarquable.

con·spir·a·cy conspiration f.

con·stant adj (frequent) incessant; (unchanging) constant.

con·stant·ly adv constamment.

con·sti·pat·ed adj constipé.

con·sti·tu·tion constitution f.

con·straint contrainte f.

con·struct vt construire.

con·struc·tion construction f; **under c.** en construction.

con·struc·tive adj constructif.

con·sul consul m.

con·su·late consulat m.

con·sult 1 vt consulter. **2** vi **to c. with** discuter avec.

con·sult·ant (doctor) spécialiste mf; (financial, legal) expert-conseil m.

con·sul·ta·tion consultation f.

con·sult·ing firm cabinet m d'experts-conseils.

con·sume vt (food, supplies) consommer.

con·sum·er consommateur, -trice mf.

con·sump·tion consommation f (of de).

con·tact 1 n contact m; (person) contact m, relation f; **in c. with** en contact avec. **2** vt contacter.

con·tact lens·es lentilles fpl or verres mpl de contact.

con·ta·gious adj contagieux.

con·tain vt contenir.

con·tain·er récipient m; (for goods) conteneur m.

con·tem·po·rar·y adj & n contemporain, -aine (mf).

con·tempt mépris m.

▸ **con·tend with** vt (problem) faire face à; (person) avoir affaire à.

con·tent¹ adj satisfait (**with** de).

con·tent² (of text etc) contenu m; **contents** (of container) contenu m; **(table of) contents** (of book) table f des matières.

con·tent·ed adj satisfait.

con·test concours m; (fight) lutte f.

con·tes·tant concurrent, -ente mf; (in fight) adversaire mf.

con·text contexte m.

con·ti·nent continent m.

con·ti·nen·tal adj continental; **c. breakfast** petit déjeuner m à la française.

con·tin·u·al adj continuel.

con·tin·ual·ly adv continuellement.

con·tin·ue 1 vt continuer (**to do** or **doing** à or de faire); **to c. (with)** (work etc) poursuivre; (resume) reprendre. **2** vi continuer; (resume) reprendre.

con·tin·u·ous adj continu.

con·tin·u·ous·ly adv sans interruption.

con·tra·cep·tion contraception f.

con·tra·cep·tive adj & n contraceptif (m).

con·tract contrat m.

con·trac·tor entrepreneur m.

con·tra·dict vt contredire.

con·tra·dic·tion contradiction f.

con·tra·ry 1 adv c. to contrairement à. **2** n on the c. au contraire.

con·trast contraste m; **in c. to** par opposition à.

con·trast·ing adj (colors, opinions) opposés.

con·trib·ute 1 vt donner (**to** à); (article) écrire (**to** pour); **to c. money** to contribuer à. **2** vi **to c. to** contribuer à; (publication) collaborer à.

con·tri·bu·tion contribution f, (to fund etc) cotisation(s) f(pl).

con·trive vt **to c. to do** trouver moyen de faire.

con·trived adj artificiel.

con·trol 1 vt (organization) diriger; (traffic) régler; (prices, quality, situation, emotion) contrôler; **to c. oneself** se contrôler. **2** n autorité f (**over** sur); (over prices, quality) contrôle m; **controls** (of train etc) commandes fpl; (of TV set etc) boutons mpl; **everything is under c.** tout est en ordre; **in c. of** maître de; **to lose c. of** perdre le contrôle de.

con·trol tow·er tour f de contrôle.

con·va·lesce vi être en convalescence.

con·va·les·cence convalescence f.

conva·les·cent home maison f de convalescence.

con·ven·ience commodité f; **c. foods** plats mpl tout préparés; (public) **conveniences** toilettes fpl.

con·ven·ient adj commode; (well-situated) bien situé (**to shopping/etc**) par rapport aux magasins/etc); (moment) convenable; **to be c. (for)** (suit) convenir (à).

con·vent couvent m.

con·ver·sa·tion conversation f.

con·verse vi s'entretenir (**with** avec).

con·ver·sion conversion f; (of building) aménagement m.

con·vert vt convertir (**into** en; **to** à); (building) aménager (**into** en).

con·vert·i·ble (car) (voiture f) décapotable f.

con·vey vt (goods, people) transporter; (sound, message) transmettre; (idea) communiquer.

con·vey·or belt tapis m roulant.

con·vict vt déclarer coupable.

con·vic·tion (for crime) condamnation f; (belief) conviction f.

con·vince vt convaincre (**of** de).

con·vinc·ing adj convaincant.

con·voy (cars) convoi m.

cook 1 vt (food) (faire) cuire. 2 vi (of food) cuire; (of person) faire la cuisine. 3 n cuisinier, -ière mf.

cook·book livre m de cuisine.

cook·ie biscuit m.

cook·ing cuisine f.

cook·ing ap·ple pomme f à cuire.

cool 1 adj (weather, place, drink etc) frais (f fraîche); (manner) calme; (unfriendly) froid; (fashionable, good) cool inv; **to keep sth c.** tenir qch au frais. 2 n (of evening) fraîcheur f; **to lose one's c.** perdre son sang-froid.

cool (down) 1 vi (of angry person) se calmer; (of hot liquid) refroidir. 2 vt refroidir.

cool·er (for food) glacière f.

cool-head·ed adj calme.

cool·ness fraîcheur f; (unfriendliness) froideur f.

▶ **cool off** vi (refresh oneself) se rafraîchir.

co-op appartement m en copropriété.

co·op·er·ate vi coopérer (**in** à; **with** avec).

co·op·er·a·tion coopération f.

▶ **coop up** vt (person) enfermer.

co·or·di·nate 1 vt coordonner. 2

n **coordinates** (clothes) coordonnés mpl.

cop (policeman) Fam flic m.

cope vi **to c. with** s'occuper de; (problem) faire face à; **(to be able) to c.** (savoir) se débrouiller.

cop·per (metal) cuivre m.

cop·y 1 n copie f; (of book, magazine etc) exemplaire m. 2 vti copier.

▶ **copy up, copy down** vt (address etc) (re)copier.

cord cordon m; (electrical) cordon m électrique.

cor·dial (fruit) c. sirop m.

▶ **cor·don off** vt (of police etc) interdire l'accès de.

cor·du·roy velours m côtelé; **corduroys** pantalon m en velours (côtelé).

core (of apple etc) trognon m.

cork liège m; (for bottle) bouchon m.

cork (up) vt (bottle) boucher.

cork·screw tire-bouchon m.

corn maïs m; (on foot) cor m.

corn·bread pain m à la farine de maïs.

corned beef corned-beef m.

cor·ner 1 n coin m; (bend in road) virage m. 2 vt (person in corridor etc) coincer; (market) monopoliser.

corn·flakes céréales fpl.

corn·starch fécule f de maïs.

corn·y adj (joke) rebattu.

cor·o·nar·y infarctus m.

cor·po·ral caporal(-chef) m.

corps inv corps m.

corpse cadavre m.

cor·rect 1 adj exact, correct; (proper) correct; **he's c.** (right) il a raison. 2 vt corriger.

cor·rec·tion correction f.

cor·rect·ly adv correctement.

cor·re·spond correspondre (**to, with** à); (by letter) correspondre (**with** avec).

cor·re·spon·dence correspondance f; **c. course** cours m par correspondance.

cor·re·spond·ing adj (matching) correspondant.

cor·ri·dor couloir m.

cor·ru·gat·ed adj c. iron tôle f ondulée.

cor·rupt adj corrompu.

cor·rup·tion corruption f.

cos·met·ic produit m de beauté.

cost 1 vti coûter; **how much does it c.?** ça coûte combien? **2** n prix m; **at all costs** à tout prix.

cost·ly adj coûteux.

cos·tume costume m.

cos·tume ball bal m masqué.

cos·tume jew·el·ry bijoux mpl de fantaisie.

cot lit m d'enfant; (camp bed) lit m de camp.

cot·tage petite maison f de campagne; **(thatched) c.** chaumière f.

cot·tage cheese fromage m blanc (maigre).

cot·ton coton m; (yarn) fil m (de coton); **c. wool** coton m hydrophile.

couch canapé m.

cou·chette (on train) couchette f.

cough 1 n toux f; **c. syrup** sirop m contre la toux. **2** vi tousser.

cough up 1 vt (blood) cracher. **2** vti (pay) Fam casquer.

could see **can**[1].

coun·cil conseil m; **(city) c.** conseil m municipal, municipalité f.

coun·cil·man (city) c. conseiller m municipal.

coun·sel·ing aide f psychologique.

count[1] **1** vt compter. **2** vi (calculate, be important) compter. **3** n **he's lost c.** of the books he has il ne sait plus combien il a de livres.

count[2] (title) comte m.

count·down compte m à rebours.

coun·ter (in shop, bar etc) comptoir m; (in bank etc) guichet m; (in games) jeton m.

coun·ter- prefix contre-.

coun·ter·at·tack contre-attaque f.

coun·ter·clock·wise adj & adv dans le sens inverse des aiguilles d'une montre.

coun·ter·part (thing) équivalent m; (person) homologue mf.

▸ **count in** vt inclure.

▸ **count on** vt (rely on) compter sur; **to c. on doing** compter faire.

▸ **count out** vt exclure; (money) compter.

coun·try pays m; (regarded with affection) patrie f; (opposed to town) campagne f; **c. house** maison f de campagne.

coun·try·side campagne f.

coun·ty comté m.

coup coup m d'état.

cou·ple (of people) couple m; **a c. of** deux ou trois; (a few) quelques.

cou·pon (voucher) bon m.

cour·age courage m.

cou·ra·geous adj courageux.

cou·ri·er (messenger) messager m.

course 1 n (duration, movement) cours m; **c. (of action)** ligne f de conduite; (option) parti m; **in the c. of** au cours de. ▪ (lessons) cours m; **c. of lectures** série f de conférences. ▪ **c. (of treatment)** traitement m. ▪ (of meal) plat m; **first c.** entrée f. ▪ **(golf) c.** terrain m de golf. **2** adv **of c.!** bien sûr!; **of c. not!** bien sûr que non!

court (of king etc, for trials) cour f; **(tennis) c.** court m (de tennis); **to take sb to c.** poursuivre qn en justice.

cour·te·ous adj poli.

cour·te·sy politesse f, courtoisie f.

court·room salle f du tribunal.

court·yard cour f.

cous·in cousin, -ine mf.

cov·er 1 n (lid) couvercle m; (of book) couverture f; (for furniture etc) housse f; **the covers** (on bed) les couvertures fpl et les draps mpl; **to take c.** se mettre à l'abri. **2** vt couvrir (**with** de); (insure) assurer.

cov·er·age couverture f.

cov·er·alls bleu *m* (de travail).

cov·er charge *(in restaurant)* couvert *m*.

cov·er·ing *(wrapping)* enveloppe *f*; *(layer)* couche *f*.

cov·er let·ter lettre *f* jointe (à un document); *(seeking job)* lettre *f* de motivation.

▸ **cover over** *vt (floor etc)* recouvrir.

▸ **cover up** 1 *vt* recouvrir; *(truth, tracks)* dissimuler; *(scandal)* étouffer. 2 *vi (wrap up)* se couvrir.

▸ **cover up for** *vt* couvrir.

cow vache *f*.

cow·ard lâche *mf*.

cow·ard·ice lâcheté *f*.

cow·ard·ly *adj* lâche.

cow·boy cow-boy *m*.

co·zy *adj* douillet.

CPA *abbr* = **Certified Public Accountant**

crab crabe *m*.

crack 1 *n* fente *f*; *(in glass, china, bone)* fêlure *f*; *(noise)* craquement *m*; *(of whip)* claquement *m*; *(joke)* Fam plaisanterie *f*. 2 *vt (glass, ice)* fêler; *(nut)* casser; *(whip)* faire claquer; *(joke)* lancer. 3 *vi* se fêler; *(of branch, wood)* craquer; **to get cracking** *(get to work)* Fam s'y mettre.

crack·er *(biscuit)* biscuit *m* (salé).

crack·pot Fam cinglé, -ée *mf*.

▸ **crack up** *vi (mentally)* Fam craquer.

cra·dle berceau *m*.

craft *(skill)* art *m*; *(job)* métier *m* (artisanal).

crafts·man, *pl* -men artisan *m*.

craft·y *adj* astucieux.

cram 1 *vt* **to c. into** *(force)* fourrer dans; **to c. with** *(fill)* bourrer de. 2 *vi* **to c. into** *(of people)* s'entasser dans; **to c. (for an exam)** banchoter.

cramp *(muscle pain)* crampe *f* (in à).

cramped *adj* à l'étroit.

crane *(machine, bird)* grue *f*.

crank¹ *(handle)* manivelle *f*.

crank² Fam *(person)* excentrique *mf*.

crash 1 *n* accident *m*; *(of firm)* faillite *f*; *(noise)* fracas *m*. 2 *int (of fallen object)* patatras! 3 *vt (car)* avoir un accident avec; **to c. one's car into** faire rentrer sa voiture dans. 4 *vi (of car, plane)* s'écraser; **to c. into** rentrer dans.

crash course cours *m* intensif.

crash di·et régime *m* intensif.

▸ **crash down** *vi (fall)* tomber; *(break)* se casser.

crash hel·met casque *m* (anti-choc).

crash-land *vi* atterrir en catastrophe.

crash land·ing atterrissage *m* en catastrophe.

crate caisse *f*.

crav·ing désir *m* (for de).

crawl 1 *vi* ramper; *(of child)* marcher à quatre pattes; *(of vehicle)* avancer au pas; **to be crawling with** grouiller de. 2 *n (swimming stroke)* crawl *m*.

cray·on crayon *m* de couleur *(en cire)*.

craze manie *f* (for de).

cra·zy *adj* fou *(f* folle); **c. about sth** fana de qch; **c. about sb** fou de qn.

creak *vi (of hinge)* grincer.

cream crème *f*; **c. cake** gâteau *m* à la crème.

cream cheese fromage *m* blanc.

cream·y *adj* crémeux.

crease 1 *vt (wrinkle)* froisser. 2 *vi* se froisser. 3 *n (in trousers)* pli *m*.

cre·ate *vt* créer; *(impression, noise)* faire.

cre·a·tion création *f*.

cre·a·tive *adj* créatif.

crea·ture animal *m*; *(person)* créature *f*.

crèche *(nursery)* crèche *f*.

cred·i·bil·i·ty crédibilité *f*.

cred·i·ble *adj* croyable; *(politician etc)* crédible.

cred·it 1 n (financial) crédit m; (merit) mérite m; (from university) unité f de valeur; **to be a c. to** faire honneur à; **on c.** à crédit; **my account shows a c. balance of** mon compte est créditeur de. **2** vt (of bank) créditer (**sb with sth** qn de qch).

cred·it card carte f de crédit.

cred·it terms facilités fpl de paiement.

cred·it·wor·thy adj solvable.

creek (stream) ruisseau m.

creep* vi ramper; (silently) se glisser; (slowly) avancer lentement.

creep·y adj (causing fear) Fam terrifiant.

cre·mate vt incinérer.

cre·ma·tion crémation f.

cre·ma·to·ri·um, **cre·ma·to·ry** crématorium m.

crêpe pa·per papier m crêpon.

cress cresson m.

crest (of wave etc) crête f, (of hill) sommet m.

crew (of ship, plane) équipage m.

crew cut (coupe f en) brosse f.

crib (cot) lit m d'enfant; (list of answers) pompe f, anti-sèche f.

crick·et (insect) grillon m.

crime crime m; (not serious) délit m; (criminal practice) criminalité f.

crim·i·nal adj & n criminel, -elle (mf).

cri·sis, pl -ses crise f.

crisp adj (cookie) croustillant; (apple) croquant.

cri·te·ri·on, pl criteria critère m.

crit·ic critique m.

crit·i·cal adj critique.

crit·i·cal·ly adv (ill) gravement.

crit·i·cism critique f.

crit·i·cize vti critiquer.

cro·chet 1 vt faire au crochet. **2** vi faire du crochet. **3** n (travail m au) crochet m.

croc·o·dile crocodile m.

cro·cus crocus m.

crook (thief) escroc m.

crook·ed adj (stick) courbé; (path) tortueux; (hat, picture) de travers.

crop (harvest) récolte f, (produce) culture f.

▶ **crop up** vi se présenter.

cro·quet croquet m.

cross¹ 1 n croix f, **a c. between** (animal) un croisement entre or de. **2** vt (street, room etc) traverser; (barrier) franchir; (legs) croiser. **3** vi (paths) se croiser.

cross² adj (angry) fâché (**with** contre).

cross-coun·try race cross(-country) m.

cross-eyed adj qui louche.

cross·ing (by ship) traversée f.

▶ **cross off** or **out** vt (word, name etc) rayer.

▶ **cross over** vti traverser.

cross-ref·er·ence renvoi m.

cross·roads carrefour m.

cross-sec·tion coupe f transversale; (sample) échantillon n.

cross·walk passage m clouté.

cross·word (puz·zle) mots mpl croisés.

crouch (down) vi s'accroupir.

crow corbeau m.

crow·bar levier m, pied m de biche.

crowd foule f, (particular group) bande f.

crowd·ed adj plein (**with** de).

▶ **crowd into** vt (of people) s'entasser dans.

▶ **crowd round** vt se presser autour de.

crown couronne f.

cru·cial adj crucial.

crude adj (manners, language) grossier; (work) rudimentaire.

cru·el adj cruel.

cru·el·ty cruauté f, **an act of c.** une cruauté.

cru·et petit flacon m; (for oil and vinegar) huilier m.

cruise 1 vi (of ship) croiser; (of car

rouler; *(of plane)* voler. **2** *n* croisière *f*; **to take a c.** faire une croisière.

crumb miette *f*.

crum·ble 1 *vt (bread)* émietter. **2** *vi (in small pieces)* s'effriter; *(of bread)* s'émietter; *(become ruined)* tomber en ruine.

crum·bly *adj* friable.

crum·my *adj Fam* moche.

crum·ple *vt* froisser.

crunch *vt (food)* croquer.

crunch·y *adj (apple etc)* croquant; *(bread, cookie)* croustillant.

crush 1 *n (crowd)* cohue *f*; *(rush)* bousculade *f*. **2** *vt* écraser; *(clothes)* froisser; *(cram)* entasser (**into** dans).

crust croûte *f*.

crust·y *adj (bread)* croustillant.

crutch *(of invalid)* béquille *f*.

cry 1 *n (shout)* cri *m*; **to have a c.** *Fam* pleurer. **2** *vi* pleurer; *(shout)* pousser un cri.

cry·ing *(weeping)* pleurs *mpl*.

▸ **cry off** *vi* se décommander.

▸ **cry out 1** *vi* pousser un cri; *(exclaim)* s'écrier. **2** *vt* crier.

▸ **cry out for** *vt* demander (à grands cris); **to be crying out for sth** avoir grand besoin de qch.

▸ **cry over** *vt* pleurer (sur).

crys·tal cristal *m*.

cub *(scout)* louveteau *m*.

cube cube *m*; *(of meat etc)* dé *m*.

cu·bic *adj (meter etc)* cube.

cu·bi·cle *(in office building)* box *m*.

cuck·oo *(bird)* coucou *m*.

cu·cum·ber concombre *m*.

cud·dle 1 *vt (hug)* serrer; *(caress)* câliner. **2** *vi* se serrer contre. **3** *n* caresse *f*.

▸ **cuddle up to** *vt* se serrer contre.

cud·dly *adj* câlin; *(toy)* doux (*f* douce).

cue *(in theatre)* réplique *f*; *(signal)* signal *m*.

cuff *(of shirt)* poignet *m*; *(of trousers)* revers *m*.

cuff link bouton *m* de manchette.

cul-de-sac impasse *f*.

cul·prit coupable *mf*.

cult culte *m*; **c. film** film *m* culte.

cul·ti·vate *vt* cultiver.

cul·ti·vat·ed *adj* cultivé.

cul·tur·al *adj* culturel.

cul·ture culture *f*.

cul·tured *adj* cultivé.

cum·ber·some *adj* encombrant.

cun·ning 1 *adj* astucieux. **2** *n* astuce *f*.

cup tasse *f*; *(prize)* coupe *f*.

cup·board armoire *f*; *(built-in)* placard *m*.

cup·cake petit gâteau *m*.

cup·ful tasse *f*.

cur·a·ble *adj* guérissable.

curb bord *m* du trottoir.

cure 1 *vt* guérir (*qn*) (**of** de). **2** *n* remède *m* (**for** contre); **rest c.** cure *f* de repos.

cu·ri·os·i·ty curiosité *f*.

cu·ri·ous *adj (odd)* curieux; *(inquisitive)* curieux (**about** de).

curl 1 *vti (hair)* boucler. **2** *n* boucle *f*.

curl·er bigoudi *m*.

▸ **curl up** *vi* se pelotonner.

curl·y *adj (hair)* bouclé.

cur·rant *(dried grape)* raisin *m* de Corinthe.

cur·ren·cy monnaie *f*; *(foreign)* devises *fpl* (étrangères).

cur·rent 1 *adj* actuel; *(opinion)* courant; *(year)* courant. **2** *n (of river, electric)* courant *m*.

cur·rent af·fairs questions *fpl* d'actualité.

cur·rent·ly *adv* actuellement.

cur·ric·u·lum programme *m* (scolaire).

cur·ry curry *m*.

curse *vi (swear)* jurer.

cur·sor *(of computer)* curseur *m*.

cur·tain rideau *m*.

curt·s(e)y 1 *n* révérence *f*. **2** *vi* faire une révérence.

curve 1 *n* courbe *f*; *(in road)* virage *m*. **2** *vi* se courber; *(of road)* faire une courbe.

cush·ion coussin *m.*

cus·tard crème *f* anglaise; *(when set)* crème *f* renversée.

cus·to·dy garde *f.*

cus·tom coutume *f*, *(customers)* clientèle *f.*

cus·tom·ar·y *adj* habituel.

cus·tom·er client, -ente *mf.*

cus·tom·er ser·vice service *m* après-vente.

cus·toms la douane; **c. (duty)** droits *mpl* de douane; **c. officer** douanier *m.*

cut 1 *n (mark)* coupure *f*, *(stroke)* coup *m*; *(of clothes, hair)* coupe *f*, *(in salary, prices etc)* réduction *f*, *(of meat)* morceau *m*. **2** *vt** couper; *(meat)* découper; *(glass, tree)* tailler; *(salary etc)* réduire; **to c. open** ouvrir *(au couteau etc)*. **3** *vi (of person, scissors)* couper; **to c. in line** passer avant son tour.

▸ **cut away** *vt (remove)* enlever.

cut·back réduction *f.*

▸ **cut back (on)** *vti* réduire.

▸ **cut down** *vt (tree)* abattre; *(reduce)* réduire.

▸ **cut down on** *vt* réduire.

cute *adj Fam (pretty)* mignon *(f* mignonne).

▸ **cut into** *vt (cake)* entamer.

cut·ler·y couverts *mpl.*

cut·let côtelette *f.*

▸ **cut off** *vt* couper; *(isolate)* isoler.

cut·out *(picture)* découpage *m.*

▸ **cut out 1** *vi (of engine)* caler. **2** *vt (article)* découper; *(remove)* enlever; **to c. out drinking** s'arrêter de boire; **c. it out!** *Fam* ça suffit!; **c. out to be a doctor/etc** fait pour être médecin/*etc.*

cut·ting 1 *n (from newspaper)* coupure *m*; *(plant)* bouture *f.* **2** *adj (wind, remark)* cinglant.

▸ **cut up** *vt* couper (en morceaux).

cy·cle 1 *n (bicycle)* bicyclette *f*, *(series, period)* cycle *m.* **2** *vi* aller à bicyclette *(to à).*

cy·cling cyclisme *m.*

cy·clist cycliste *mf.*

cyl·in·der cylindre *m.*

cym·bal cymbale *f.*

cyn·i·cal *adj* cynique.

D

dab *vt (wound)* tamponner; **to d. sth on sth** appliquer qch sur qch.

Da·cron® tergal® *m.*

dad·dy *Fam* papa *m.*

daf·fo·dil jonquille *f.*

daft *adj Fam* idiot, bête.

dai·ly 1 *adj* quotidien. **2** *adv* quotidiennement. **3** *n* **d. (paper)** quotidien *m.*

dair·y *adj (product)* laitier.

dai·sy pâquerette *f.*

dam barrage *m.*

dam·age 1 *n* dégâts *mpl*, *(harm)* préjudice *m.* **2** *vt (spoil)* abîmer; *(harm)* nuire à.

dam·ag·ing *adj* préjudiciable.

damn *Fam* **1** *int* **d. (it)!** merde!; **d. him!** qu'il aille au diable! **2** *adj (awful)* fichu. **3** *adv (very)* vachement.

damp 1 *adj* humide. **2** *n* humidité *f.*

damp·en *vt* humecter.

damp·ness humidité *f.*

dance 1 *n* danse *f*, *(social event)* bal *m (pl* bals). **2** *vti* danser.

dance hall salle *f* de danse.

danc·er danseur, -euse *mf.*

danc·ing danse *f.*

dan·de·li·on pissenlit *m.*

dan·druff pellicules *fpl.*

Dane Danois, -oise *mf.*

dan·ger danger *m (to pour)*; **in d.** en danger; **to be in d. of falling/etc** risquer de tomber/*etc.*

dan·ger·ous *adj* dangereux **(to pour).**

Dan·ish 1 *adj* danois. **2** *n* (*language*) danois *m*.

dare *vt* oser (**do** faire); **to d. sb to do** défier qn de faire.

dar·ing *adj* audacieux.

dark 1 *adj* obscur, noir; (*color, eyes*) foncé; (*skin, hair*) brun; **it's d.** il fait nuit *or* noir; **d. glasses** lunettes *fpl* noires. **2** *n* noir *m*, obscurité *f*.

dark-haired *adj* aux cheveux bruns.

dark·ness obscurité *f*, noir *m*.

dark-skinned *adj* brun.

dar·ling (**my**) **d.** (mon) chéri, (ma) chérie.

dart fléchette *f*, **darts** (*game*) fléchettes *fpl*.

dart·board cible *f*.

dash 1 *vi* se précipiter. **2** *n* (*stroke*) trait *m*.

▸ **dash away, dash off** *vi* partir en vitesse.

dash·board tableau *m* de bord.

da·ta *npl* données *fpl*.

dat·a bank banque *f* de données.

dat·a pro·cess·ing informatique *f*.

date¹ 1 *n* (*time*) date *f*, (*meeting*) *Fam* rendez-vous *m inv* (galant); (*person*) *Fam* copain, -ine *mf*; **up to d.** moderne; (*information*) à jour; (*well-informed*) au courant (**on** de); **out of d.** (*old-fashioned*) démodé; (*expired*) périmé. **2** *vt* (*letter etc*) dater; (*girl, boy*) *Fam* sortir avec.

date² (*fruit*) datte *f*.

dat·ed *adj* démodé.

date stamp (tampon *m*) dateur *m*; (*mark*) cachet *m*.

daugh·ter fille *f*.

daugh·ter-in-law, *pl* **daughters-in-law** belle-fille *f*.

daw·dle *vi* traîner.

dawn aube *f*.

day jour *m*; (*whole day long*) journée *f*, **all d. (long)** toute la journée; **the following** *or* **next d.** le lendemain; **the day before** la veille; **the**

d. before yesterday avant-hier; **the d. after tomorrow** après-demain.

day·break point *m* du jour.

day·care (*for ages 3 and below*) crèche *f*, (*for older children*) garderie *f*.

day·light (lumière *f* du) jour *m*.

day·time journée *f*, jour *m*.

dead 1 *adj* mort; (*battery*) à plat. **2** *adv* (*completely*) absolument; (*very*) très.

dead-end (*street*) impasse *f*.

dead·line date *f* limite; (*time*) heure *f* limite.

dead·ly 1 *adj* mortel; **d. weapon** arme *f* meurtrière. **2** *adv* (*very*) mortellement.

deaf *adj* sourd; **d. and dumb** sourd-muet (*f* sourde-muette).

deaf·ness surdité *f*.

deal¹ a good *or* **great d.** (a lot) beaucoup (**of** de).

deal² 1 *n* (*in business*) marché *m*, affaire *f*, **it's a d.** d'accord. **2** *vi** (*trade*) traiter (**with sb** avec qn); **to d. in** faire le commerce de; **to d. with** s'occuper de; (*concern*) traiter de. **3** *vt* (*cards*) donner.

deal·er marchand, -ande *mf* (**in** de); (*agent*) dépositaire *mf*, (*for cars*) concessionnaire *mf*.

deal·ings *npl* relations *fpl* (**with** avec); (*in business*) transactions *fpl*.

dear 1 *adj* (*loved, expensive*) cher; **D. Sir** (*in letter*) Monsieur; **oh d.!** oh là là! **2** *n* (**my**) **d.** (*darling*) (mon) chéri, (ma) chérie; (*friend*) mon cher, ma chère.

death mort *f*.

death cer·tif·i·cate acte *m* de décès.

de·bate 1 *vti* discuter. **2** *n* débat *m*, discussion *f*.

deb·it 1 *n* débit *m*; **my account shows a d. balance of** mon compte est débiteur de. **2** *vt* débiter (**sb with sth** qn de qch).

DATE AND TIME

Days of the week
lundi; mardi; mercredi; jeudi; vendredi; samedi; dimanche

Months of the year
janvier; février; mars; avril; mai; juin; juillet; août; septembre; octobre; novembre; décembre

Days and months are written without a capital letter in French. The first of the month is *le premier*; other dates are expressed in cardinal numbers (**March 3rd** *le trois mars*).

What day is it today?
On est quel jour aujourd'hui ?

It's Friday.
On est vendredi.

What's today's date?
On est le combien aujourd'hui ?

It's April 15th, 2008.
On est le quinze avril deux mille huit.

It's Wednesday April 12th.
On est le mercredi douze avril.

It's Thursday tomorrow.
Demain c'est jeudi.

I was born in 1980.
Je suis né(e) en mille neuf cent quatre-vingt.

I came to Paris a few years ago.
Je suis venu(e) à Paris il y a quelques années.

How long are you staying?
Vous restez jusqu'à quand ?

We leave on Sunday/the 8th.
Nous partons dimanche/le huit.

We got here last weekend.
Nous sommes arrivés le weekend dernier.

I waited all day.
J'ai attendu toute la journée.

See you on Saturday!
À samedi !

See you next week!
À la semaine prochaine !

> Use the masculine words an, jour, matin, soir when talking about time in general. Use the feminine année, journée, matinée, soirée to express duration.

Take it three times a day.
Prenez-le trois fois par jour.

I see them every two weeks.
Je les vois toutes les deux semaines.

The French commonly use the 24-hour clock and write times with an *h* for *heure(s)*, eg 7.30 a.m. = 7h30 (*sept heures trente*), 7.30 p.m. = 19h30 (*dix-neuf heures trente*).

What's the time?
Quelle heure est-il ?

It's 2 o'clock.
Il est deux heures.

It's nearly midday/midnight.
Il est presque midi/minuit.

It's half four/four-thirty.
Il est quatre heures et demie/quatre heures trente.

It's a quarter to seven.
Il est sept heures moins le quart.

It's twenty after seven.
Il est sept heures vingt.

I'll be there about eight.
Je serai là vers huit heures.

I'll meet you in half an hour.
On se retrouve dans une demi-heure.

My plane was two hours late.
Mon avion a eu deux heures de retard.

I'm early/late/on time.
Je suis en avance/en retard/à l'heure.

I don't have time (to...).
Je n'ai pas le temps (de...).

It's time to go.
C'est l'heure de partir.

debt dette f; **to be in d.** avoir des dettes.

debt·or débiteur, -trice mf.

de·but début m; **to make one's d.** faire ses débuts.

dec·ade décennie f.

de·caf·fein·at·ed adj décaféiné.

de·cal décalcomanie f.

de·cay (of tooth) carie(s) f(pl).

de·ceive vti tromper.

De·cem·ber décembre m.

de·cent adj (respectable) convenable, décent; (good) Fam bon; (kind) Fam gentil.

de·cep·tion tromperie f.

de·cide 1 vt (question etc) décider; **to d. to do** décider de faire; **to d. that** décider que. **2** vi (make decisions) décider (on de); (make up one's mind) se décider (on doing à faire); (choose) se décider (on pour).

dec·i·mal 1 adj d. **point** virgule f. **2** n décimale f.

de·ci·sion décision f.

de·ci·sive adj décisif; (victory) net (f nette).

deck (of ship) pont m; (of cards) jeu m; (of house) terrasse f.

deck·chair transat m.

de·clare vt déclarer (**that** que); (verdict, result) proclamer.

de·cline 1 vi (become less) (of popularity etc) être en baisse. **2** vt (invitation) refuser.

dec·o·rate vt (cake, house, soldier) décorer (**with** de); (hat, skirt etc) orner (**with** de); (paint etc) peindre (et tapisser).

dec·o·ra·tion décoration f.

dec·o·ra·tive adj décoratif.

dec·o·ra·tor peintre m décorateur; **(interior)** d. décorateur, -trice mf.

de·crease 1 vti diminuer. **2** n diminution f (**in** de).

de·cree 1 n (by court) jugement m. **2** vt décréter.

ded·i·cate vt consacrer (**to** à); (book) dédier (**to** à).

ded·i·cat·ed adj (teacher etc) consciencieux.

de·duct vt déduire (**from** de); (from wage, account) prélever (**from** sur).

de·duc·tion déduction f.

deed action f, acte m; (document) acte m (notarié).

deep adj profond; (voice) grave; **to be 20 feet/etc d.** avoir six mètres/etc de profondeur; **the d. end** (in pool) le grand bain.

deep-freeze 1 vt surgeler. **2** n congélateur m.

deer inv cerf m.

de·fault vt **by d.** par défaut; **to win by d.** gagner par forfait.

de·feat 1 vt battre. **2** n défaite f.

de·fect défaut m.

de·fec·tive adj défectueux.

de·fend vt défendre.

de·fend·ant (accused) prévenu, -ue mf.

de·fense défense f.

de·fen·sive adj défensif; **to be d.** être sur la défensive. **2** n **to be on the d.** être sur la défensive.

de·fi·ant adj (tone, attitude) de défi; (person) rebelle.

de·fi·cien·cy manque m; (of vitamins etc) carence f.

de·fi·cient adj insuffisant; **to be d. in** manquer de.

def·i·cit déficit m.

de·fine vt définir.

def·i·nite adj (date, plan) précis; (reply, improvement) net (f nette); (order, offer) ferme; (certain) certain; **d. article** Grammar article m défini.

def·i·nite·ly adv certainement; (considerably) nettement; (to say) catégoriquement.

def·i·ni·tion définition f.

de·formed adj (body) difforme.

de·frost vt (fridge) dégivrer; (food) décongeler.

de·fy vt défier (qn); **to d. sb to do** défier qn de faire.

de·gen·er·ate vi dégénérer (**into** en).

de·gree (angle, temperature) degré m; (from university) diplôme m; (Bachelor's) licence f; (Master's) maîtrise f; (PhD) doctorat m; **to such a d.** à tel point (**that** que).

de·ice vt (car window etc) dégivrer.

de·ic·er (substance) dégivreur m.

de·ject·ed adj abattu.

de·lay 1 vt retarder; (payment) différer. 2 vi (be slow) tarder (**doing** à faire); (linger) s'attarder. 3 n retard m; (waiting period) délai m; **without d.** sans tarder.

del·e·gate 1 vt déléguer (**to** à). 2 n délégué, -ée mf.

del·e·ga·tion délégation f.

de·lete vt rayer.

de·lib·er·ate adj (intentional) intentionnel.

de·liber·ate·ly adv (intentionally) exprès.

del·i·ca·cy (food) mets m délicat.

del·i·cate adj délicat.

del·i·ca·tes·sen traiteur m, épicerie f fine.

de·li·cious adj délicieux.

de·light 1 n délice m; **to take d. in sth/in doing** se délecter de qch/à faire. 2 vt réjouir. 3 vi **to d. in doing** se délecter à faire.

de·light·ed adj ravi (**with** sth de qch; **to do** de faire; **that** que).

de·light·ful adj charmant; (meal) délicieux.

de·lin·quent délinquant, -ante mf.

de·liv·er vt (goods etc) livrer; (letters) distribuer; (hand over) remettre (**to** à); (speech) prononcer; (warning) lancer.

de·liv·er·y livraison f, (of letters) distribution f; (handing over) remise f; (birth) accouchement m.

de·lude vt tromper; **to d. oneself** se faire des illusions.

de·lu·sion illusion f.

de·luxe adj de luxe.

de·mand 1 vt exiger (sth from sb qch de qn); (rights, more pay) revendiquer; **to d. that** exiger que. 2 n exigence f, (claim) revendication f; (for goods) demande f; **in great d.** très demandé.

de·mand·ing adj exigeant.

dem·o Fam (demonstration) manif f, **d. tape** cassette f de démonstration.

de·moc·ra·cy démocratie f.

dem·o·crat·ic adj démocratique; (person) démocrate.

de·mol·ish vt démolir.

dem·o·li·tion démolition f.

de·mon démon m.

dem·on·strate 1 vt démontrer; (machine) faire une démonstration de. 2 vi manifester.

dem·on·stra·tion démonstration f, (protest) manifestation f.

dem·on·stra·tive adj & n Grammar démonstratif (m).

dem·on·stra·tor (protester) manifestant, -ante mf.

de·mor·al·ize vt démoraliser.

den tanière f.

de·ni·al (of rumor) démenti m.

den·im (toile f de) coton m.

de·nounce vt (person, injustice etc) dénoncer (**to** à).

dense adj dense; (stupid) Fam lourd, bête.

dent 1 n (in car etc) bosse f. 2 vt cabosser.

den·tal adj dentaire.

den·tist dentiste mf.

den·tures npl dentier m.

de·ny vt nier (**doing** avoir fait; **that** que); (rumor) démentir; **to d. sb sth** refuser qch à qn.

de·o·dor·ant déodorant m.

de·part vi partir; (deviate) s'écarter (**from** de).

de·part·ment département m; (in office) service m; (in shop) rayon m; (of government) = ministère m;

D. of State Ministère des Affaires Etrangères.

de·part·ment store grand magasin m.

de·par·ture départ m; **a d. from** (rule) un écart par rapport à.

de·pend vi dépendre (**on, upon** de); **to d. (up)on** (rely on) compter sur (**for sth** pour qch).

de·pend·a·ble adj sûr.

de·pen·dant personne f à charge.

de·pen·dent adj dépendant; **to be d. on sth** dépendre de qch.

de·pict vt (describe) dépeindre; (in pictures) représenter.

de·plor·a·ble adj déplorable.

de·plore adj déplorer.

de·pos·it 1 vt déposer; **to d.** (check) verser (**to one's account** sur son compte). 2 n dépôt m; (part payment) acompte m, arrhes fpl; (against damage) caution f; (on bottle) consigne f.

de·pot (railroad station) gare f, bus d. gare f routière.

de·press vt (discourage) déprimer.

de·pressed adj déprimé; **to get d.** se décourager.

de·pres·sion dépression f.

de·prive vt priver (**of** de).

de·prived adj (child etc) déshérité.

depth profondeur f.

dep·u·ty (replacement) remplaçant, -ante mf, (assistant) adjoint, -ointe mf.

de·rail·ment déraillement m.

der·e·lict adj abandonné.

de·rive vt to d. **from sth** (pleasure etc) tirer de qch; **to be derived from** (of word etc) dériver de.

de·scend 1 vi descendre (**from** de). 2 vt (stairs) descendre.

de·scen·dant descendant, -ante mf.

▶ **descend upon** vt (of tourists) envahir.

de·scent (of aircraft etc) descente f.

de·scribe vt décrire.

de·scrip·tion description f; (on passport) signalement m; **of every d.** de toutes sortes.

des·ert[1] désert m; **d. island** île f déserte.

de·sert[2] vt abandonner.

de·sert·ed adj (place) désert.

de·serve vt mériter (**to do** de faire).

de·sign 1 vt (car etc) dessiner; **designed to do/for sb** conçu pour faire/pour qn; **well designed** bien conçu. 2 n (pattern) motif m; (sketch) plan m, dessin m; (type of dress or car) modèle m.

des·ig·nate vt désigner.

de·sign·er dessinateur, -trice mf.

de·sign·er clothes vêtements mpl griffés.

de·sir·a·ble adj désirable.

de·sire 1 n désir m; **I have no d. to** je n'ai aucune envie de. 2 vt désirer (**to do** faire).

desk (in school) pupitre m; (in office) bureau m; (in shop) caisse f; (reception) d. réception f.

desk clerk (in hotel) réceptionniste mf.

desk·top bureau m; **d. publishing** publication f assistée par ordinateur.

de·spair 1 n désespoir m; **to be in d.** être au désespoir. 2 vi désespérer (**of sb** de qn; **of doing** de faire).

des·per·ate adj désespéré; **to be d. for** avoir désespérément besoin de; (cigarette, baby) mourir d'envie d'avoir.

des·pi·ca·ble adj méprisable.

de·spise vt mépriser.

de·spite prep malgré.

des·sert dessert m.

des·sert·spoon cuillère f à dessert.

des·ti·na·tion destination f.

des·ti·tute adj indigent.

de·stroy vt détruire.

de·struc·tion destruction f.

de·struc·tive adj destructeur.

de·tach vt détacher (**from** de).

de·tach·a·ble adj (lining) amovible.

de·tached house maison f individuelle.

de·tail détail m; **in d.** en détail.

de·tailed adj détaillé.

de·tain vt retenir; (prisoner) détenir.

de·tect (find) découvrir; (see, hear) distinguer.

de·tec·tive inspecteur m de police; (private) détective m.

de·tec·tor détecteur m.

de·ten·tion (school punishment) retenue f.

de·ter vt **to d. sb** dissuader qn (**from doing** de faire; **from sth** de qch).

de·ter·gent détergent m.

de·te·ri·o·rate vi se détériorer.

de·te·ri·o·ra·tion détérioration f.

de·ter·mi·na·tion (intention) ferme intention f.

de·ter·mine vt déterminer; (price) fixer.

de·ter·mined adj déterminé; **d. to do** or **on doing** décidé à faire.

de·ter·rent **to be a d.** être dissuasif.

de·test vt détester (**doing** faire).

de·tour déviation f.

dev·as·tat·ing adj (news, results) accablant.

de·vel·op 1 vt développer; (area, land) mettre en valeur; (habit, illness) contracter. 2 vi se développer.

▸ **develop into** vt devenir.

de·vel·op·ment développement m; housing d. lotissement m; (large) grand ensemble m; **a (new) d.** (in situation) un fait nouveau.

de·vi·ate vi dévier (**from** de).

de·vice dispositif m; left to one's own devices livré à soi-même.

dev·il diable m; what/where/why the d.? que/où/pourquoi diable?

de·vise vt (a plan) combiner; (invent) inventer.

de·vote vt consacrer (**to** à).

de·vot·ed adj dévoué.

de·vo·tion dévouement m (**to sb** à qn).

dew rosée f.

di·a·be·tes diabète m.

di·a·bet·ic diabétique mf.

di·ag·nose vt diagnostiquer.

di·ag·no·sis, pl **-oses** diagnostic m.

di·ag·o·nal 1 adj diagonal. 2 n **d.** (line) diagonale f.

di·ag·o·nal·ly adv en diagonale.

di·a·gram schéma m.

di·al 1 n cadran m. 2 vt (phone number) faire; (person) appeler.

di·a·lect dialecte m.

di·al tone tonalité f.

di·a·log dialogue m.

di·am·e·ter diamètre m.

di·a·mond diamant m; (shape) losange m; Baseball terrain m; diamond(s) Cards carreau m; **d. necklace** collier m de diamants.

di·a·per couche f.

di·ar·rhe·a diarrhée f.

di·a·ry journal m (intime).

dice 1 n inv dé m (à jouer). 2 vt (food) couper en dés.

dic·tate vti dicter (**to** à).

dic·ta·tion dictée f.

dic·tion·ar·y dictionnaire m.

did pt de **do.**

die* vi mourir (**of, from** de); **to be dying to do** mourir d'envie de faire; **to be dying for sth** avoir une envie folle de qch.

▸ **die away** vi (of noise) mourir.

▸ **die down** vi (of storm) se calmer.

▸ **die out** vi (of custom) mourir.

die·sel adj & n **d.** (engine) (moteur m) diesel m; **d.** (oil) gazole m.

di·et 1 n (to lose weight) régime m; (usual food) alimentation f; **to go on a d.** faire un régime. 2 vi suivre un régime.

dif·fer vi différer (**from** de); (dis-

agree) ne pas être d'accord (**from** avec).

dif·fer·ence différence *f* (**in** de); **d. (of opinion)** différend *m*; **it makes no d.** ça n'a pas d'importance; **it makes no d. to me** ça m'est égal.

dif·fer·ent *adj* différent (**from, to** de); (*another*) autre; (*various*) divers.

differ·ent·ly *adv* autrement (**from, to** que).

dif·fi·cult *adj* difficile (**to do** à faire); **it's d. for us to** il nous est difficile de.

dif·fi·cul·ty difficulté *f*; **to have d. doing** avoir du mal à faire.

dig* **1** *vt* (*ground*) bêcher; (*hole*) creuser. **2** *vi* creuser.

di·gest *vti* digérer.

di·ges·tion digestion *f*.

dig·ger (*machine*) pelleteuse *f*.

dig·it (*number*) chiffre *m*.

dig·i·tal *adj* numérique.

dig·ni·ty dignité *f*.

▸ **dig out** *vt* (*from ground*) déterrer; (*accident victim*) dégager; (*find*) dénicher.

▸ **dig up** *vt* (*from ground*) déterrer; (*weed*) arracher; (*earth*) retourner; (*street*) piocher.

di·lap·i·dat·ed *adj* délabré.

di·lem·ma dilemme *f*.

di·lute *vt* diluer.

dim **1** *adj* (*light*) faible; (*room*) sombre; (*memory, outline*) vague; (*person*) stupide. **2** *vt* (*light*) baisser; **to d. one's headlights** se mettre en code.

dime (*pièce f de*) dix cents *mpl*; **d. store** magasin *m* à prix unique.

di·men·sion dimension *f*.

di·min·ish *vti* diminuer.

dimmed head·lights codes *mpl*.

din vacarme *m*.

dine *vi* dîner (**on** de).

▸ **dine out** *vi* dîner en ville.

din·er dîneur, -euse *mf*; (*restaurant*) petit restaurant *m*.

din·ghy petit canot *m*; (*rubber*) **d.** canot *m* pneumatique.

din·gy *adj* (*room etc*) minable; (*color*) sombre.

din·ing car wagon-restaurant *m*.

din·ing room salle *f* à manger.

din·ner dîner *m*; (*lunch*) déjeuner *m*; **to have d.** dîner.

din·ner jack·et smoking *m*.

din·ner par·ty dîner *m* (à la maison).

din·ner ser·vice *or* **set** service *m* de table.

di·no·saur dinosaure *m*.

dip **1** *vt* plonger. **2** *vi* (*of road*) plonger; **to d. into** (*pocket, savings*) puiser dans. **3** *n* (*in road*) petit creux *m*; **to go for a d.** (*swim*) faire trempette.

diph·thong diphtongue *f*.

di·plo·ma diplôme *m*.

dip·lo·mat diplomate *mf*.

dip·lo·mat·ic *adj* Pol diplomatique; (*tactful*) diplomate.

di·rect **1** *adj* direct. **2** *adv* directement. **3** *vt* diriger; (*remark*) adresser (**to** à); **to d. sb to** (*place*) indiquer à qn le chemin de.

di·rec·tion direction *f*; **directions (for use)** mode *m* d'emploi; **in the opposite d.** en sens inverse.

di·rect·ly **1** *adv* directement; (*at once*) tout de suite. **2** *conj* aussitôt que (+ *indicative*).

di·rec·tor directeur, -trice *mf*; (*board member in firm*) administrateur, -trice *mf*; (*of film*) metteur *m* en scène.

di·rec·to·ry (*telephone*) **d.** annuaire *m* (téléphonique).

di·rec·to·ry as·sis·tance renseignements *mpl*.

dirt saleté *f*; (*earth*) terre *f*; **d. cheap** *Fam* très bon marché.

dirt·y **1** *adj* sale; (*job*) salissant; (*word*) grossier; **to get d.** se salir; **to get sth d.** salir qch; **a d. joke** une histoire cochonne. **2** *vt* salir.

dis- *prefix* dé-, dés-.

dis·a·bil·i·ty infirmité f.

dis·a·bled 1 adj handicapé. **2** n **the d.** les handicapés mpl.

dis·ad·van·tage désavantage m.

dis·a·gree vi ne pas être d'accord (**with** avec); **to d. with sb** (of food etc) ne pas réussir à qn.

dis·a·gree·a·ble adj désagréable.

dis·a·gree·ment désaccord m; (quarrel) différend m.

dis·ap·pear vi disparaître.

dis·ap·pear·ance disparition f.

dis·ap·point vt décevoir; **I'm disappointed with it** ça m'a déçu.

dis·ap·point·ing adj décevant.

dis·ap·point·ment déception f.

dis·ap·prov·al désapprobation f.

dis·ap·prove vi **to d. of sb/sth** désapprouver qn/qch; **I d.** je suis contre.

dis·arm vt désarmer.

dis·as·ter désastre m.

dis·as·trous adj désastreux.

dis·card vt se débarrasser de.

dis·charge vt (patient, employee) renvoyer; (soldier) libérer.

dis·ci·pline 1 n discipline f. **2** vt discipliner; (punish) punir.

disc jock·ey disc-jockey m.

dis·close vt révéler.

dis·co, pl **-os** disco f.

dis·com·fort douleur f; **I have d. in my wrist** mon poignet me gêne.

dis·con·nect vt détacher; (unplug) débrancher; (wires) déconnecter; (gas, telephone) couper.

dis·con·tent·ed adj mécontent.

dis·con·tin·ued adj (article) qui ne se fait plus.

dis·co·theque (club) discothèque f.

dis·count (on article) remise f, réduction f; **at a d.** à prix réduit.

dis·count store solderie f.

dis·cour·age vt décourager; **to get discouraged** se décourager.

dis·cov·er vt découvrir (**that** que).

dis·cov·e·ry découverte f.

dis·creet adj discret.

dis·crim·i·nate vi **to d. against** faire de la discrimination contre.

dis·crim·i·na·tion (against sb) discrimination f.

dis·cuss vt discuter de; (plan, question, price) discuter.

dis·cus·sion discussion f.

dis·ease maladie f.

dis·em·bark vti débarquer.

dis·fig·ured adj défiguré.

dis·grace 1 n (shame) honte f (**to** à). **2** vt déshonorer.

dis·grace·ful adj honteux.

dis·guise 1 vt déguiser (**as** en). **2** n déguisement m; **in d.** déguisé.

dis·gust 1 n dégoût m (**for, at, with** de); **in d.** dégoûté. **2** vt dégoûter.

dis·gust·ed adj dégoûté (**at, by, with** de); **d. with sb** (annoyed) fâché contre qn.

dis·gust·ing adj dégoûtant.

dish (container, food) plat m; **the dishes** la vaisselle; **to do the dishes** faire la vaisselle.

dish·cloth (for washing) lavette f; (for drying) torchon m.

di·shev·eled adj débraillé.

dis·hon·est adj malhonnête.

dis·hon·es·ty malhonnêteté f.

▸ **dish out, dish up** vt (food) servir.

dish tow·el torchon m.

dish·wash·er (machine) lave-vaisselle m inv.

dis·il·lu·sioned adj déçu (**with** de).

dis·in·cen·tive mesure f dissuasive.

dis·in·fect vt désinfecter.

dis·in·fec·tant désinfectant m.

disk disque m.

dis·like 1 vt ne pas aimer (**doing** faire). **2** n aversion f (**for, of** pour); **to take a d. to sb/sth** prendre qn/ qch en grippe.

dis·lo·cate vt (limb) démettre.

dis·mal adj morne.

dis·man·tle vt (machine) démonter.

dis·may vt consterner.

dis·miss vt (from job) renvoyer (from de).

dis·miss·al renvoi m.

dis·o·be·di·ence désobéissance f.

dis·o·be·di·ent adj désobéissant.

dis·o·bey 1 vt désobéir à. 2 vi désobéir.

dis·or·der (confusion) désordre m; (illness) troubles mpl.

dis·or·gan·ized adj désorganisé.

dis·patch vt expédier; (troops, messenger) envoyer.

dis·pel vt dissiper.

dis·pens·er (device) distributeur m; cash d. distributeur m de billets.

dis·perse 1 vt disperser. 2 vi se disperser.

dis·play 1 vt montrer; (notice, electronic data) afficher; (painting, goods) exposer; (courage etc) faire preuve de. 2 n (in shop) étalage m; (of data) affichage m; on d. exposé.

dis·pleased adj mécontent (with de).

dis·pos·a·ble adj (plate etc) à jeter, jetable.

dis·pos·al at the d. of à la disposition de.

dis·pose vi to d. of (get rid of) se débarrasser de; (sell) vendre.

dis·pute 1 n (quarrel) dispute f; (industrial) conflit m. 2 vt contester.

dis·qual·i·fy vt rendre inapte (from à); (in sport) disqualifier.

dis·re·gard vt ne tenir aucun compte de.

dis·re·spect·ful adj irrespectueux.

dis·rupt vt (traffic, class etc) perturber; (plan etc) déranger.

dis·rup·tion perturbation f; (of plan etc) dérangement m.

dis·rup·tive adj (child) turbulent.

dis·sat·is·fac·tion mécontentement m.

dis·sat·is·fied adj mécontent (with de).

dis·sent 1 n désaccord m. 2 vi être en désaccord (from avec).

dis·solve 1 vt dissoudre. 2 vi se dissoudre.

dis·suade vt dissuader (from doing de faire).

dis·tance distance f; in the d. au loin; from a d. de loin; it's within walking d. on peut y aller à pied; to keep one's d. garder ses distances.

dis·tant adj éloigné; (reserved) distant.

dis·taste aversion f (for pour).

dis·taste·ful adj désagréable.

dis·tinct adj (voice, light) distinct; (difference, improvement) net (f nette); (different) distinct (from de).

dis·tinc·tion distinction f; (at graduation) with d. avec mention f.

dis·tinc·tive adj distinctif.

dis·tinct·ly adv distinctement; (definitely) sensiblement.

dis·tin·guish vti distinguer (from de; between entre).

dis·tin·guished adj distingué.

dis·tort vt déformer.

dis·tract vt distraire (from de).

dis·trac·tion distraction f.

dis·tress (pain) douleur f; (anguish) détresse f; in d. (ship) en détresse.

dis·tress·ing adj affligeant.

dis·trib·ute vt distribuer; (spread evenly) répartir.

dis·tri·bu·tion distribution f.

dis·trib·u·tor (in car) distributeur m; (of goods) concessionnaire mf.

dis·trict région f; (of town) quartier m; d. attorney = procureur m (de la République).

dis·trust vt se méfier de.

dis·turb vt (sleep) troubler; (pa-

pers, belongings) déranger; **to d. sb** *(bother)* déranger qn; *(worry)* troubler qn.

dis·tur·bance *(noise)* tapage *m*; **disturbances** *(riots)* troubles *mpl*.

dis·turb·ing *adj (worrying)* inquiétant.

ditch fossé *m*.

dit·to *adv* idem.

di·van divan *m*.

dive* 1 *vi* plonger; *(rush)* se précipiter. **2** *n (of swimmer, goalkeeper)* plongeon *m*; *(of aircraft)* piqué *m*.

div·er plongeur, -euse *mf*.

di·ver·sion *(on road)* déviation *f*; *(distraction)* diversion *f*.

di·vert *vt (traffic)* dévier; *(aircraft)* dérouter.

di·vide *vt* diviser *(into* en); *(share out)* partager; *(separate)* séparer *(from* de).

▶ **divide off** *vt* séparer *(from sth de* qch).

▶ **divide up** *vt (share out)* partager.

di·vid·ed high·way route *f* à quatre voies.

div·i·dend dividende *m*.

div·ing plongée *f* sous-marine.

div·ing board plongeoir *m*.

di·vi·sion division *f*.

di·vorce 1 *n* divorce *m*. **2** *vt (husband, wife)* divorcer d'avec.

di·vorced *adj* divorcé *(from* d'avec); **to get d.** divorcer.

DIY *abbr (do-it-yourself)* bricolage *m*.

diz·zi·ness vertige *m*.

diz·zy *adj* **to be** or **feel d.** avoir le vertige; **to make sb (feel) d.** donner le vertige à qn.

DJ *abbr* = **disc jockey**.

do* 1 *v aux* **do you know?** savez-vous?, est-ce que vous savez?; **I do not** or **don't see** je ne vois pas; **he did** say so *(emphasis)* il l'a bien dit; **do** stay reste donc; **you know him, don't you?** tu le connais, n'est-ce pas?; **neither do I** moi non plus; **so do I** moi aussi. **2** *vt* faire; **what does**

she do? *(in general)*, **what is she doing?** *(now)* qu'est-ce qu'elle fait?; **what have you done (with)…?** qu'as-tu fait (de)…?; **well done** *(congratulations)* bravo!; *(steak)* bien cuit; **to do sb out of sth** escroquer qch à qn; **he's done for** *Fam* il est fichu. **3** *vi (get along)* aller; *(suit)* faire l'affaire; *(be enough)* suffire; *(finish)* finir; **how do you do?** *(introduction)* enchanté; **he did well** or **right to leave** il a bien fait de partir; **do as I do** fais comme moi; **to have to do with** *(relate to)* avoir à voir avec; *(concern)* concerner.

▶ **do away with** *vt* supprimer.

dock 1 *n (for ship)* dock *m*. **2** *vi (at pier)* se mettre à quai.

dock·er docker *m*.

dock·yard chantier *m* naval.

doc·tor médecin *m*; *(academic)* docteur *m*.

doc·tor·ate doctorat *m*.

doc·trine doctrine *f*.

doc·u·ment document *m*.

doc·u·men·ta·ry *(film)* documentaire *m*.

dodge 1 *vt* esquiver; *(pursuer)* échapper à; *(tax)* éviter de payer. **2** *vi* **to d. through** *(crowd)* se faufiler dans.

does *see* **do**.

dog chien *m*; *(female)* chienne *f*; **d. food** pâtée *f*.

dog·gy bag *(in restaurant)* petit sac *m* pour emporter les restes.

dog·house niche *f*.

dog tags plaque *f* d'identité.

do·ing **that's your d.** c'est toi qui as fait ça.

do-it-your·self 1 *n* bricolage *m*. **2** *adj (store, book)* de bricolage.

doll poupée *f*.

dol·lar dollar *m*.

doll·house maison *f* de poupée.

dol·phin dauphin *m*.

do·main domaine *m*; **d. name** nom *m* de domaine.

dome dôme *m*.

do·mes·tic *adj* domestique; *(trade, flight)* intérieur.

dom·i·nant *adj* dominant; *(person)* dominateur.

dom·i·nate *vti* dominer.

dom·i·no domino *m*; **dominoes** *(game)* dominos *mpl*.

do·nate 1 *vt* faire don de; *(blood)* donner. **2** *vi* donner.

do·na·tion don *m*.

done *pp de* **do**.

don·key âne *m*.

do·nor *(to charity)* donateur, -trice *mf*, *(of organ, blood)* donneur, -euse *mf*.

door porte *f*.

door·bell sonnette *f*.

door·knob poignée *f* de porte.

door·knock·er marteau *m*.

door·man, *pl* -men *(of hotel)* portier *m*.

door·mat paillasson *m*.

door·step seuil *m*.

door·stop butoir *m* (de porte).

door·way in the d. dans l'encadrement de la porte.

▸**do over** *vt (redecorate)* refaire.

dope *(drugs) Fam* drogue *f*.

dor·mi·to·ry dortoir *m*; *(at university)* résidence *f* (universitaire).

dos·age *(amount)* dose *f*.

dose dose *f*.

dot point *m*.

dot·ted line pointillé *m*.

dou·ble 1 *adj* double; **a d. bed** un grand lit; **a d. room** une chambre pour deux personnes. **2** *adv (twice)* deux fois, le double; *(to fold)* en deux. **3** *n* double *m*. **4** *vti* doubler.

▸**double back** *vi (of person)* revenir en arrière.

dou·ble-breast·ed *adj (jacket)* croisé.

dou·ble-cross *vt* trahir, doubler.

dou·ble-deck·er (bus) autobus *m* à impériale.

dou·ble-glaz·ing double vitrage *m*.

▸**double up** *vi (with pain, laughter)* être plié en deux.

doubt 1 *n* doute *m*; **no d.** *(probably)* sans doute. **2** *vt* douter de; **to d. whether** *or* **that** *or* **if** douter que (+ *subjunctive*).

doubt·ful *adj* **to be d. (about sth)** avoir des doutes (sur qch); **it's d. whether** *or* **that** *or* **if** ce n'est pas sûr que (+ *subjunctive*).

doubt·less *adj* sans doute.

dough pâte *f*, *(money) Fam* fric *m*.

dough·nut beignet *m* (rond).

▸**do up** *vt (coat, button)* boutonner; *(zipper)* fermer; *(house)* refaire, décorer; *(goods)* emballer.

dove colombe *f*.

▸**do with** *vt* **I could do with that** j'aimerais bien ça.

▸**do without** *vt* se passer de.

down 1 *adv* en bas; *(to the ground)* par terre; *(of curtain, temperature)* baissé; *(in writing)* inscrit; *(out of bed)* descendu; **to come** *or* **go d.** descendre; **d. there** *or* **here** en bas; **d. with flu** grippé; **to feel d.** avoir le cafard. **2** *prep (at bottom of)* en bas de; *(from top to bottom of)* du haut en bas de; *(along)* le long de; **to go d.** *(hill, street, stairs)* descendre.

down-and-out *adj* **to be d.** être sur le pavé.

down·fall chute *f*.

down·hill *adv* **to go d.** descendre; *(of sick person, business)* aller de plus en plus mal.

down·load 1 *n* téléchargement *m*. **2** *vt* télécharger.

down pay·ment acompte *m*, arrhes *fpl*.

down·pour averse *f*.

down·right 1 *adj (rogue etc)* véritable; *(refusal)* catégorique. **2** *adv (rude etc)* franchement.

down·stairs 1 *adj (room, neighbors)* d'en bas. **2** *adv* en bas; **to come** *or* **go d.** descendre l'escalier.

down-to-earth *adj* terre-à-terre.

down·town *adj* au centre-ville; **d. Chicago** le centre de Chicago.

down·ward(s) *adv* vers le bas.

doze 1 *n* petit somme *m*. **2** *vi* sommeiller.

doz·en douzaine *f*; **a d.** *(books etc)* une douzaine de.

▸ **doze off** *vi* s'assoupir.

Dr *abbr (Doctor)* Docteur.

drab *adj* terne; *(weather)* gris.

draft courant *m* d'air.

draft beer bière *f* pression.

draft·y *adj (room)* plein de courants d'air.

drag *vti* traîner.

▸ **drag along** *vt* (en)traîner.

▸ **drag away** arracher *(from* à).

drag·on dragon *m*.

▸ **drag on, drag out** *vi (last a long time)* se prolonger, s'éterniser.

drain 1 *n (sewer)* égout *m*; *(outside house)* puisard *m*; *(in street)* bouche *f* d'égout. **2** *vt (tank)* vider; *(vegetables)* égoutter.

drain (off) 1 *vt (liquid)* faire écouler. **2** *vi (of liquid)* s'écouler.

drain·board paillasse *f*.

drain·er *(board)* paillasse *f*; *(rack, basket)* égouttoir *m*.

drain·pipe tuyau *m* d'évacuation.

dra·ma *(event)* drame *m*; *(dramatic art)* théâtre *m*.

dra·mat·ic *adj* dramatique; *(very great, striking)* spectaculaire.

dra·mat·i·cal·ly *adv (to change etc)* de façon spectaculaire.

drapes *npl (heavy curtains)* rideaux *mpl*.

dras·tic *adj* radical.

dras·ti·cal·ly *adv* radicalement.

draw¹* **1** *n (in sports, games)* match *m* nul. **2** *vt* (pull)* tirer; *(attract)* attirer.

draw²* *vt (picture)* dessiner; *(circle)* tracer. **2** *vi* dessiner.

draw·back inconvénient *m*.

draw·er tiroir *m*.

draw·ing dessin *m*.

draw·ing room salon *m*.

▸ **draw near** *vi* s'approcher; *(of time)* approcher.

▸ **draw near to** *vt* s'approcher de; *(of time)* approcher de.

▸ **draw on** *vt (savings)* puiser dans.

▸ **draw up 1** *vt (list, plan)* dresser. **2** *vi (of vehicle)* s'arrêter.

dread 1 *vt (exam etc)* appréhender; **to d. doing** appréhender de faire. **2** *n* crainte *f*.

dread·ful *adj* épouvantable; *(child)* insupportable; *(ill)* malade.

dread·ful·ly *adv* terriblement; **to be d. sorry** regretter infiniment.

dream 1 *vi** rêver *(of* de; *of going* de faire). **2** *vt* rêver *(that* que). **3** *n* rêve *m*; **to have a d.** faire un rêve *(about* de); **a d. house** /*etc* une maison/*etc* de rêve.

▸ **dream up** *vt* imaginer.

drea·ry *adj (gloomy)* morne; *(boring)* ennuyeux.

drench *vt* tremper; **to get drenched** se faire tremper.

dress 1 *n (woman's)* robe *f*; *(style of dressing)* tenue *f*. **2** *vt (person)* habiller; *(wound)* panser; **to get dressed** s'habiller. **3** *vi* s'habiller.

dress·er *(furniture)* coiffeuse *f*.

dress·mak·er couturière *f*.

▸ **dress up** *vi (smartly)* bien s'habiller; *(in disguise)* se déguiser *(as* en).

drew *pt* de **draw¹,²**.

drib·ble 1 *vi (of liquids)* couler lentement. **2** *vti (in sports)* dribbler.

dried *adj (fruit)* sec *(f* sèche); *(flowers)* séché.

drift *vi* être emporté par le vent *or* le courant, dériver.

drill 1 *n (tool)* perceuse *f*; *(bit)* mèche *f*; *(dentist's)* roulette *f*. **2** *vt (hole)* percer.

drink 1 *n* boisson *f*; *(glass of sth)* verre *m*; **to give sb a d.** donner (quelque chose) à boire à qn. **2** *vt** boire *(out of* dans); **to d. to sb** boire à la santé de qn.

drink·a·ble *adj* potable; *(not unpleasant)* buvable.

▸**drink down** *vt* boire.

drink·ing wa·ter eau *f* potable.

▸**drink up 1** *vt* boire. **2** *vi* finir son verre.

drip 1 *vi* dégouliner; *(of laundry, vegetables)* s'égoutter; *(of faucet)* fuir. **2** *vt (paint etc)* laisser couler. **3** *n* goutte *f*; *(fool)* Fam nouille *f*.

drip-dry *adj (shirt etc)* sans repassage.

drip·ping *adj & adv* d. (wet) dégoulinant.

drive 1 *n* promenade *f* en voiture; *(energy)* énergie *f*; *(road to house)* allée *f*, **an hour's d.** une heure de voiture; **four-wheel d. (vehicle)** quatre-quatre *m*. **2** *vt* *(vehicle, train, passenger)* conduire; *(machine)* actionner; *(chase away)* chasser; **to d. sb to do** pousser qn à faire; **to d. sb mad** *or* **crazy** rendre qn fou. **3** *vi (drive a car)* conduire; *(go by car)* rouler.

▸**drive along** *vi (in car)* rouler.

▸**drive away 1** *vt (chase)* chasser. **2** *vi* partir (en voiture).

▸**drive back 1** *vt (enemy)* repousser; *(passenger)* ramener (en voiture). **2** *vi* revenir (en voiture).

▸**drive in** *vt (nail)* enfoncer.

▸**driv·el** idioties *fpl*.

▸**drive off** *vi* partir (en voiture).

▸**drive on** *vi (in car)* continuer.

▸**drive out** *vt (chase away)* chasser.

driv·er conducteur, -trice *mf*; **(train** *or* **engine) d.** mécanicien *m*; **she's a good d.** elle conduit bien.

driv·er's li·cense permis *m* de conduire.

▸**drive up** *vi* arriver (en voiture).

driv·ing conduite *f*.

driv·ing les·son leçon *f* de conduite.

driv·ing school auto-école *f*.

driv·ing test examen *m* du permis de conduire.

driz·zle 1 *n* bruine *f*. **2** *vi* bruiner.

drool *vi* baver.

droop *vi (of flower)* se faner.

drop 1 *n (of liquid)* goutte *f*; *(fall)* baisse *f* (**in** de). **2** *vt* laisser tomber; *(price, voice)* baisser; *(passenger, goods from vehicle)* déposer; *(put)* mettre; *(leave out)* omettre; **to d. a line to** écrire un mot à. **3** *vi* tomber; *(of price)* baisser.

▸**drop back, drop behind** *vi* rester en arrière.

▸**drop in** *vi (visit)* passer (**to sb's house** chez qn).

▸**drop off 1** *vi (fall asleep)* s'endormir; *(fall off)* tomber; *(of sales)* diminuer. **2** *vt (passenger)* déposer.

▸**drop out** *vi (withdraw)* se retirer.

drought sécheresse *f*.

drown 1 *vi* se noyer. **2** *vt* **to d. oneself, to be drowned** se noyer.

drows·y *adj* **to be** *or* **feel d.** avoir sommeil.

drug 1 *n* médicament *m*; *(narcotic)* stupéfiant *m*; **drugs** *(narcotics in general)* la drogue; **to be on drugs, to take drugs** se droguer. **2** *vt* droguer *(qn)*.

drug ad·dict drogué, -ée *mf*.

drug deal·er trafiquant *m* de drogue.

drug·gist pharmacien, -ienne *mf*.

drug·store drugstore *m*.

drum tambour *m*; *(for oil)* bidon *m*; **the drums** *(in pop or jazz group)* la batterie.

drum·mer (joueur, -euse *mf* de) tambour *m*; *(in pop or jazz group)* batteur *m*.

drum·stick baguette *f* (de tambour); *(of chicken)* pilon *m*.

drunk *(pp of drink)* **1** *adj* ivre; **to get d.** s'enivrer; **d. driving** conduite *f* en état d'ivresse. **2** *n* ivrogne *mf*.

drunk·ard ivrogne *mf*.

dry 1 *adj* sec (*f* sèche); *(well, river)* à sec; *(day)* sans pluie; *(book)* aride; **to feel** *or* **be d.** *(thirsty)* avoir soif. **2** *vt* sécher; *(by wiping)* essuyer.

dry-clean *vt* nettoyer à sec.

dry clean·er teinturier, -ière *mf*.

dry clean·ing nettoyage *m* à sec.
dry·er séchoir *m*; *(helmet-style for hair)* casque *m*; *(for laundry)* sèche-linge *m*.
▸**dry off** *vti* sécher.
▸**dry up 1** *vt* sécher. **2** *vi* sécher; *(dry the dishes)* essuyer la vaisselle.
du·al *adj* double.
dub *vt (film)* doubler.
du·bi·ous *adj* douteux; **I'm d. about going** je me demande si je dois y aller.
duch·ess duchesse *f*.
duck 1 *n* canard *m*. **2** *vi* se baisser (vivement).
due *adj (money)* dû *(f* due); *(* to à); *(rent, bill)* à payer; **to fall d.** échoir; **he's d. (to arrive)** il doit arriver; **in d. course** en temps utile; *(finally)* à la longue; **d. to** dû à; *(because of)* à cause de.
du·el duel *m*.
duf·fel coat, duf·fle coat duffel-coat *m*.
duke duc *m*.
dull *adj (boring)* ennuyeux; *(color)* terne; *(weather)* maussade; *(sound, ache)* sourd.
dull·ness *(of life, town)* monotonie *f*.
du·ly *adv (properly)* dûment; *(as expected)* commme prévu.
dumb *adj* muet *(f* muette); *(stupid)* idiot.
dum·my *(for clothes)* mannequin *m*; *(person) Fam* idiot *m*.
dump 1 *vt (garbage)* déposer. **2** *n (dull town) Fam* trou *m*; **(garbage) d.** tas *m* d'ordures; *(place)* dépôt *m* d'ordures; *(room)* dépotoir *m*.
dump truck camion *m* à benne basculante.
du·plex *(apartment)* duplex *m*.
du·pli·cate double *m*; **in d.** en deux exemplaires; **a d. copy** une copie en double.
du·ra·ble *adj (material)* résistant.
du·ra·tion durée *f*.
dur·ing *prep* pendant.

dusk crépuscule *m*.
dust 1 *n* poussière *f*. **2** *vt (furniture etc)* essuyer (la poussière de). **3** *vi* faire la poussière.
dust cloth chiffon *m* (à poussière).
dust jack·et *(for book)* jaquette *f*.
dust·y *adj* poussiéreux.
Dutch 1 *adj* hollandais, néerlandais. **2** *n (language)* hollandais *m*, néerlandais *m*; **the D.** les Hollandais *mpl*, les Néerlandais *mpl*.
Dutch·man, *pl* **-men** Hollandais *m*, Néerlandais *m*.
Dutch·wom·an, *pl* **-women** Hollandaise *f*, Néerlandaise *f*.
du·ty devoir *m*; *(tax)* droit *m*; **duties** *(responsibilities)* fonctions *fpl*; **on d.** *(policeman, teacher)* de service; *(doctor)* de garde; **off d.** libre.
du·ty-free *adj (goods, shop)* hors-taxe *inv*.
du·vet couette *f*.
DVD *abbr (digital versatile disk, digital video disk)* DVD *m*; **D. player** lecteur *m* (de) DVD.
dwarf nain *m*, naine *f*.
dye 1 *n* teinture *f*. **2** *vt* teindre; **to d. green** teindre en vert.
dy·nam·ic *adj* dynamique.
dy·na·mite dynamite *f*.
dy·na·mo, *pl* **-os** dynamo *f*.
dys·lex·ic *adj & n* dyslexique *(mf)*.

E

each 1 *adj* chaque. **2** *pron* **e. (one)** chacun, -une; **e. other** l'un(e) l'autre, *pl* les un(e)s les autres; **e. of us** chacun, -une d'entre nous.
ea·ger *adj* impatient (**to do** de faire); *(enthusiastic)* plein d'enthousiasme; **to be e. to do** *(want)* tenir (beaucoup) à faire.

ea·ger·ly adv avec enthousiasme; (to await) avec impatience.

ea·ger·ness impatience f (to do de faire).

ea·gle aigle m.

ear oreille f.

ear·ache mal m d'oreille; **to have an e.** avoir mal à l'oreille.

ear·ly 1 adj (first) premier; (age) jeune; **it's e.** (on clock) il est tôt; (referring to meeting) c'est tôt; **it's too e. to get up** il est trop tôt pour se lever; **to be e.** (ahead of time) être en avance; **to have an e. meal/ night** manger/se coucher de bonne heure; **in e. summer** au début de l'été. **2** adv tôt, de bonne heure; (ahead of time) en avance; **as e. as possible** le plus tôt possible; **earlier (on)** plus tôt.

earn vt gagner; (interest) rapporter.

ear·nest 1 adj sérieux, -euse. **2 in e.** sérieusement.

earn·ings npl (wages) rémunérations fpl.

ear·phones npl casque m.

ear·plug boule f Quiès®.

ear·ring boucle f d'oreille.

earth (world, ground) terre f; **where/what on e.?** où/que diable?

earth·quake tremblement m de terre.

ease 1 n facilité f; **with e.** facilement; (ill) **at e.** (mal) à l'aise. **2** vt (pain) soulager; (mind) calmer.

ease (off or **up)** vi (become less) diminuer; (of pain) se calmer; (not work so hard) se relâcher.

ea·sel chevalet m.

▸ **ease off** vti enlever doucement.

eas·i·ly adv facilement; **e. the best/**etc de loin le meilleur/etc.

east 1 n est m; **(to the) e. of** à l'est de. **2** adj (coast) est inv; (wind) d'est. **3** adv à l'est.

east·bound adj en direction de l'est.

Eas·ter Pâques m sing or fpl; **Happy E.!** joyeuses Pâques!

east·ern adj (coast) est inv; **E. Europe** Europe f de l'Est.

east·ward(s) adj & adv vers l'est.

eas·y 1 adj facile; (life) tranquille; **it's e. to do** c'est facile à faire. **2** adv doucement; **go e. on** (sugar etc) vas-y doucement avec; (person) ne sois pas trop dur avec; **take it e.** calme-toi; (rest) repose-toi; (work less) ne te fatigue pas.

eas·y chair fauteuil m.

eas·y·go·ing adj (carefree) insouciant; (easy to get along with) facile à vivre.

eat* vt manger; (meal) prendre. **2** vi manger.

eat·er big e. gros mangeur m, grosse mangeuse f.

▸ **eat out** vi manger dehors.

▸ **eat up** vt (finish) finir.

e-bank·ing banque f électronique.

ec·cen·tric adj & n excentrique (mf).

ech·o, pl -oes **1** n écho m. **2** vi **the explosion/**etc **echoed** l'écho de l'explosion/etc se répercuta.

ec·o·nom·ic adj économique; (profitable) rentable.

ec·o·nom·i·cal adj économique.

e·con·o·mize vti économiser (on sur).

e·con·o·my class (on aircraft) classe f touriste.

edge bord m; (of forest) lisière f; (of town) abords mpl; (of page) marge f; (of knife) tranchant m; **on e.** énervé; (nerves) tendu.

▸ **edge forward** vi avancer doucement.

ed·i·ble adj comestible; (not unpleasant) mangeable.

ed·it vt (newspaper) diriger; (article) mettre au point; (film) monter; (text) éditer; (compile) rédiger.

e·di·tion édition f.

ed·i·tor (of newspaper) rédacteur m en chef; (compiler) rédacteur, -trice mf.

ed·i·to·ri·al e. staff rédaction f.

ed·u·cate vt éduquer; (pupil, mind) former.

ed·u·cat·ed adj (well-)e. instruit.

ed·u·ca·tion éducation f; (teaching, training) formation f.

ed·u·ca·tion·al adj (establishment) d'enseignement; (game) éducatif.

eel anguille f.

ef·fect effet m (on sur); to put into e. mettre en application; to come into e., to take e. (of law) entrer en vigueur; to take e. (of drug) agir; to have an e. (of medicine) faire de l'effet.

ef·fec·tive adj (efficient) efficace; (striking) frappant.

ef·fec·tive·ly adv effectivement; (in fact) effectivement.

ef·fi·cien·cy efficacité f, (of machine) performances fpl.

ef·fi·cient adj efficace; (machine) performant.

ef·fi·cient·ly adv efficacement; to work e. (of machine) bien fonctionner.

ef·fort effort m; to make an e. faire un effort (to pour); it isn't worth the e. ça ne or n'en vaut pas la peine.

e.g. abbr par exemple.

egg œuf m.

egg·cup coquetier m.

egg·plant aubergine f.

egg tim·er sablier m.

e·go amour-propre m; to have an enormous e. être imbu de soi-même.

E·gyp·tian 1 n Égyptien, -ienne mf. **2** adj égyptien, -ienne.

ei·der·down édredon m.

eight adj & n huit (m).

eight·een adj & n dix-huit (m).

eighth adj & n huitième (mf).

eight·y adj & n quatre-vingts (m); e.-one quatre-vingt-un.

ei·ther 1 adj & pron (one or other) l'un(e) ou l'autre; (with negative) ni l'un(e) ni l'autre; (each) chaque; on e. side de chaque côté. **2** adv she can't swim e. elle ne sait pas nager non plus; I don't e. (ni) moi non plus. **3** conj e...or ou (bien)...ou (bien); (with negative) ni...ni.

e·lab·o·rate 1 vt (work out) élaborer; (explain) décrire en détail. **2** vi donner des détails; to e. on sth développer qch. **3** adj (meal, system) élaboré; (pattern, design) compliqué; (style, costume) recherché.

e·las·tic adj & n élastique (m).

el·bow 1 n coude m. **2** vt to e. one's way se frayer un chemin (à coups de coude) (through à travers).

eld·er adj & n (of two people) aîné, -ée (mf).

eld·er·ly adj âgé.

eld·est adj & n aîné, -ée (mf); his/her e. brother l'aîné de ses frères.

e·lect vt élire (qn) (to à).

e·lec·tion 1 n élection f. **2** adj (campaign) électoral; (day, results) du scrutin.

e·lec·tor·ate électorat m.

e·lec·tric adj électrique; e. blanket couverture f chauffante; e. chair chaise f électrique; e. shock décharge f électrique.

e·lec·tri·cal adj électrique.

e·lec·tri·cian électricien m.

e·lec·tri·cian's tape chatterton m.

e·lec·tric·i·ty électricité f.

e·lec·tro·cute vt électrocuter.

e·lec·tron·ic adj électronique.

e·lec·tron·ics électronique f.

el·e·gance élégance f.

el·e·gant adj élégant.

el·e·gant·ly adv avec élégance.

el·e·ment élément m; (of heater) résistance f.

el·e·men·ta·ry adj élémentaire; (school) primaire.

el·e·phant éléphant m.

el·e·va·tor ascenseur m.

e·lev·en adj & n onze (m).

e·lev·enth adj & n onzième (mf).

el·i·gi·ble adj (for post) admissible (for à); **to be e. for** (entitled to) avoir droit à.

e·lim·i·nate vt supprimer; (applicant, possibility) éliminer.

e·lite élite f.

else adv d'autre; **everybody e.** tous les autres; **somebody/nobody/nothing e.** quelqu'un/personne/rien d'autre; **something e.** autre chose; **anything e.?** encore quelque chose? **somewhere e.** ailleurs; **how e.?** de quelle autre façon?; **or e.** ou bien.

else·where adv ailleurs.

e·lude vt (of word, name) échapper à (qn).

e-mail 1 n e-mail m, Can courriel m; **by e.** par e-mail; **to send sb an e.** envoyer un e-mail à qn. **2** vt (person) envoyer un e-mail à; (document) envoyer par e-mail.

em·bark vi (s')embarquer.

► **embark on** vt (start) commencer.

em·bar·rass vt embarrasser.

em·bar·rass·ing adj embarrassant.

em·bar·rass·ment embarras m.

em·bas·sy ambassade f.

em·blem emblème m.

em·brace 1 vt (hug) étreindre. **2** vi s'étreindre. **3** n étreinte f.

em·broi·der vt (cloth) broder.

em·broi·der·y broderie f.

em·bry·o embryon m.

em·er·ald émeraude f.

e·merge vi apparaître (from de); (from hole) sortir; (of truth, from water) émerger.

e·mer·gen·cy 1 n urgence f; **in an e.** en cas d'urgence. **2** adj (measure) d'urgence; (exit, brake) de secours; **e. room** salle f des urgences; **e. landing** atterrissage m forcé.

em·i·grate vi émigrer.

e·mo·tion (strength of feeling) émotion f, (joy, love etc) sentiment m.

e·mo·tion·al adj (person, reaction) émotif; (story) émouvant.

em·per·or empereur m.

em·pha·sis (in word or phrase) accent m; **to lay** or **put e. on** mettre l'accent sur.

em·pha·size vt souligner (**that** que).

em·pire empire m.

em·ploy vt employer.

em·ploy·ee employé, -ée mf.

em·ploy·er patron, -onne mf.

em·ploy·ment emploi m; **place of e.** lieu m de travail.

em·ploy·ment a·gen·cy bureau m de placement.

emp·ty 1 adj vide; (stomach) creux; (threat, promise) vain; **to return e.-handed** revenir les mains vides. **2** vi (of building, tank etc) se vider.

emp·ty (out) vt (box, liquid etc) vider; (vehicle) décharger; (objects in box etc) sortir (from de).

e·mul·sion émulsion f.

en·a·ble vt **to e. sb to do** permettre à qn de faire.

e·nam·el 1 n émail m (pl émaux). **2** adj en émail.

en·chant·ing adj charmant, enchanteur (f -eresse).

en·close vt (send with letter) joindre (**in, with** à); (fence off) clôturer.

en·closed adj (space) clos; (receipt etc) ci-joint.

en·clo·sure (in letter) pièce f jointe; (place) enceinte f.

en·coun·ter 1 vt rencontrer. **2** n rencontre f.

en·cour·age vt encourager (**to do** à faire).

en·cour·age·ment encouragement m.

en·cy·clo·pe·di·a encyclopédie f.

end 1 n (of street, box etc) bout m; (of meeting, month, book etc) fin f; (purpose) but m; **at an e.** (discussion etc) fini; (patience) à bout; **in the e.** à la fin; **to come to an e.** prendre fin; **to put an e. to, to bring**

to an e. mettre fin à; **no e.** of *Fam* beaucoup de; **for days on e.** pendant des jours et des jours. **2** *vt* finir (**with** par); *(rumor)* mettre fin à. **3** *vi* finir; **to e. in failure** se solder par un échec.

en·dan·ger *vt* mettre en danger.

end·ing fin *f; (of word)* terminaison *f.*

en·dive *(curly)* chicorée *f, (smooth)* endive *f.*

end·less *adj* interminable.

en·dorse *vt (check)* endosser; *(action)* approuver.

en·dorse·ment *(signature)* aval *m; (backing)* appui *m; (on check)* endossement *m.*

▸ **end up** *vi* **to e. up doing** finir par faire; **to e. up in** *(place)* se retrouver à; **he ended up in prison/a doctor** il a fini en prison/par devenir médecin.

en·dur·ance endurance *f.*

en·dure *vt* supporter (**doing** de faire).

en·e·my *n & adj* ennemi, -ie *(mf).*

en·er·get·ic *adj* énergique.

en·er·gy **1** *n* énergie *f.* **2** *adj (crisis, resources etc)* énergétique.

en·force *vt (law)* faire respecter.

en·gaged *adj* **e.** (**to be married**) fiancé; **to get e.** se fiancer.

en·gage·ment *(to marry)* fiançailles *fpl; (meeting)* rendez-vous *m inv;* **e. ring** bague *f* de fiançailles.

en·gine *(of vehicle)* moteur *m; (of train)* locomotive *f, (of jet)* réacteur *m.*

en·gi·neer ingénieur *m; (repairer)* dépanneur, -euse *mf.*

en·gi·neer·ing ingénierie *f,* génie *m.*

Eng·lish **1** *adj* anglais; *(teacher)* d'anglais; **the E. Channel** la Manche. **2** *n (language)* anglais *m;* **the E.** les Anglais *mpl.*

Eng·lish·man, *pl* **-men** Anglais *m.*

Eng·lish-speak·ing *adj* anglophone.

Eng·lish·wom·an, *pl* **-women** Anglaise *f.*

en·grave *vt* graver.

en·grav·ing gravure *f.*

en·joy *vt* aimer (**doing** faire); *(meal)* apprécier; **to e. the evening** passer une bonne soirée; **to e. one-self** s'amuser; **to e. being in Paris** se plaire à Paris.

en·joy·a·ble *adj* agréable.

en·joy·ment plaisir *m.*

en·large *vt* agrandir.

en·light·en *vt* éclairer (**sb on** or **about sth** qn sur qch).

en·list **1** *vt (recruit)* engager; *(supporter)* recruter; *(support, help)* s'assurer. **2** *vi (in the army)* s'engager.

e·nor·mous *adj* énorme.

e·nor·mous·ly *adv (very much)* énormément; *(very)* extrêmement.

e·nough **1** *adj & n* assez (de); **e. time/cups/***etc* assez de temps/de tasses/*etc;* **to have e.** to live on avoir de quoi vivre; **e. to drink** assez à boire; **to have had e. of** en avoir assez de; **that's e.** ça suffit. **2** *adv* assez; **big/good/***etc* **e.** assez grand/bon/*etc* (**to** pour).

en·quire *vi* = **inquire**.

en·quir·y *n* = **inquiry**.

en·roll *vi* s'inscrire (**in, for** à).

en·roll·ment inscription *f.*

en·sure *vt* assurer; **to e. that** s'assurer que.

en·tail *vt (consequence)* entraîner; *(risk)* comporter.

en·ter **1** *vt (room, vehicle etc)* entrer dans; *(university)* s'inscrire à; *(race, competition)* s'inscrire pour; *(write down)* inscrire (**in** dans); **to e. sb/sth in** *(competition)* présenter qn/qch à; **it didn't e. my head** or **mind** ça ne m'est pas venu à l'esprit. **2** *vi* entrer.

▸ **enter into** *vt (conversation)* entrer en; *(career)* entrer dans; *(agreement)* conclure.

en·ter·prise *(undertaking, firm)*

entreprise f. *(spirit)* initiative f.

en·ter·pris·ing *adj* plein d'initiative.

en·ter·tain 1 *vt* amuser; *(guest)* recevoir. **2** *vi (receive guests)* recevoir.

en·ter·tain·er artiste *mf*.

en·ter·tain·ing *adj* amusant.

en·ter·tain·ment amusement *m*; *(show)* spectacle *m*.

en·thu·si·asm enthousiasme *m*.

en·thu·si·ast enthousiaste *mf*; **jazz/**etc e. passionné, -ée *mf* de jazz/etc.

en·thu·si·as·tic *adj* enthousiaste; *(golfer etc)* passionné; **to be e. about** *(hobby)* être passionné de; *(gift)* être emballé par; **to get e.** s'emballer (**about** pour).

en·thu·si·as·ti·cal·ly *adv* avec enthousiasme.

en·tire *adj* entier.

en·tire·ly *adv* tout à fait.

en·ti·tle *vt* **to e. sb to do** donner à qn le droit de faire; **to e. sb to sth** donner à qn (le) droit à qch.

en·ti·tled *adj* **to be e. to do** avoir le droit de faire; **to be e. to sth** avoir droit à qch.

en·trance entrée *f* (**to** de); *(to university)* admission *f* (**to** à); **e. exam** examen *m* d'entrée.

en·trant *(in race)* concurrent, -ente *mf*; *(for exam)* candidat, -ate *mf*.

en·try *(way in, action)* entrée *f*; *(bookkeeping item)* écriture *f*; *(dictionary term)* entrée *f*; *(in competition)* objet *m* *(or* œuvre *f or* projet *m)* soumis au jury; **'no e.'** 'entrée interdite'; *(road sign)* 'sens interdit'.

en·try form feuille *f* d'inscription.

en·ve·lope enveloppe *f*.

en·vi·ous *adj* envieux (**of sth** de qch); **e. of sb** jaloux de qn.

en·vi·ron·ment milieu *m*; *(natural)* environnement *m*.

en·vi·ron·men·tal *adj* du milieu; *(natural)* de l'environnement; *(group)* écologiste; *(issue)* écolo-

gique, lié à l'environnement.

en·vis·age, en·vi·sion *vt (imagine)* envisager; *(foresee)* prévoir.

en·vy 1 *n* envie *f*. **2** *vt* envier (**sb sth** qch à qn).

ep·i·dem·ic épidémie *f*.

ep·i·sode épisode *m*.

e·qual 1 *adj* égal (**to** à); **to be e. to** *(number)* égaler; **she's e. to** *(task)* elle est à la hauteur de. **2** *n (person)* égal, -ale *mf*.

e·qual·i·ty égalité *f*.

e·qual·ize *vi (score)* égaliser.

e·qual·ly *adv* également; *(to divide)* en parts égales.

e·qua·tion équation *f*.

e·qua·tor équateur *m*.

e·quip *vt* équiper (**with** de); **(well-)equipped with** pourvu de; **(well-)equipped to do** compétent pour faire.

e·quip·ment équipement *(m)*.

e·quiv·a·lent *adj & n* équivalent *(m)*.

e·ra époque *f*; *(historical, geological)* ère *f*.

e·rase *vt* effacer.

e·ras·er gomme *f*.

e·rect 1 *adj (upright)* (bien) droit. **2** *vt* construire; *(statue etc)* ériger; *(scaffolding, tent)* monter.

e·ro·sion érosion *f*.

er·rand commission *f*.

er·rat·ic *adj (service, machine etc)* capricieux; *(person)* lunatique.

er·ror erreur *f*; **to do sth in e.** faire qch par erreur.

e·rupt *vi (volcano)* entrer en éruption; *(war, violence)* éclater.

e·rup·tion *(of volcano)* éruption *f*; *(of violence)* flambée *f*.

es·ca·la·tor escalier *m* roulant.

es·cape 1 *vi* s'échapper; **to e. from** *(person)* échapper à; *(place)* s'échapper de. **2** *vt (death)* échapper à; *(punishment)* éviter; **her name escapes me** son nom m'échappe. **3** *n (of gas)* fuite *f*; *(of person)* évasion *f*.

es·cort 1 n (soldiers etc) escorte f. **2** vt escorter.

Es·ki·mo, pl -os Esquimau, -aude mf.

es·pe·cial·ly adv (tout) spécialement; **e. as** d'autant plus que.

es·pres·so, pl -os (café m) express m inv.

es·say (at school) rédaction f.

es·sen·tial adj essentiel.

es·sen·tial·ly adv essentiellement.

es·tab·lish vt établir.

es·tab·lished adj (company) solide; (fact) reconnu; (reputation) établi.

es·tab·lish·ment (institution, firm) établissement m.

es·tate (land) terre(s) f(pl); (property after death) succession f.

es·ti·mate 1 vt estimer (**that** que). **2** n évaluation f, (price for work to be done) devis m.

etch·ing eau-forte f.

e·ter·nal adj éternel.

eth·ics (study) éthique f, (principles) morale f, (of profession) déontologie f.

e-tick·et billet m électronique.

et·i·quette bienséances fpl.

Euro- prefix euro-.

Eu·ro·pe·an 1 adj européen, -éenne. **2** n Européen, -éenne.

Eu·ro·pe·an Un·ion Union f européenne.

e·vac·u·ate vt évacuer.

e·vade vt éviter; (pursuer, tax) échapper à; (law, question) éluder.

e·val·u·ate vt évaluer (at à).

e·vap·o·rat·ed milk lait m concentré.

eve on the e. of à la veille de.

e·ven 1 adj (flat) uni; (equal) égal; (regular) régulier; (number) pair; **to get e. with sb** se venger de qn; **we're e.** nous sommes quittes; (in score) nous sommes à égalité; **to break e.** (financially) s'y retrouver. **2** adv même; **e. better/more** encore mieux/plus; **e. if** or **though** même si; **e. so** quand même.

eve·ning soir m; (whole evening, event) soirée f; **in the e.** le soir; **at seven in the e.** à sept heures du soir; **every Tuesday e.** tous les mardis soir; **all e. (long)** toute la soirée.

eve·ning dress tenue f de soirée.

eve·ning gown robe f du soir.

e·ven·ly adv de manière égale; (regularly) régulièrement.

▶**even out, even up** vt égaliser.

e·vent événement m; (in sport) épreuve f; **in the e. of death** en cas de décès; **in any e.** en tout cas.

e·ven·tu·al adj final.

e·ven·tu·al·ly adv finalement; (some day or other) un jour ou l'autre.

ev·er adv jamais; **more than e.** plus que jamais; **nothing e.** jamais rien; **hardly e.** presque jamais; **the first e.** le tout premier; **e. since** (that event etc) depuis; **e. since then** depuis lors; **for e.** pour toujours; (continually) sans cesse; **e. so happy/** etc vraiment heureux/etc, **why e. not?** et pourquoi pas?

eve·ry adj chaque; **e. one** chacun, -une; **e. single one** tous or toutes (sans exception); **e. other day** tous les deux jours; **e. so often, e. now and then** de temps en temps.

eve·ry·bod·y pron tout le monde; **e. in turn** chacun or chacune à son tour.

eve·ry·day adj (life) de tous les jours; (ordinary) banal (mpl banals); **in e. use** d'usage courant.

eve·ry·one pron = **everybody**.

eve·ry·place adv = **everywhere**.

eve·ry·thing pron tout; **e. I have** tout ce que j'ai.

eve·ry·where adv partout; **e. she goes** où qu'elle aille.

ev·i·dence preuve(s) f(pl); (given by witness etc) témoignage m; **e. of** (wear etc) des signes mpl de.

ev·i·dent *adj* évident (**that** que).

ev·i·dent·ly *adv* évidemment; *(apparently)* apparemment.

e·vil 1 *adj (influence, person)* malfaisant; *(deed, system)* mauvais. 2 *n* mal *m*.

e·voke *vt* évoquer.

ewe brebis *f*.

ex- *prefix* ex-; **ex-wife** ex-femme *f*.

ex·act *adj* exact; **to be e. about** sth préciser qch.

ex·act·ly *adv* exactement.

ex·ag·ger·ate *vti* exagérer.

ex·ag·ger·a·tion exagération *f*.

ex·am examen *m*.

ex·am·i·na·tion *(in school etc)* examen *m*.

ex·am·ine *vt* examiner; *(accounts, luggage)* vérifier; *(passport)* contrôler; *(question)* interroger.

ex·am·in·er examinateur, -trice *mf*.

ex·am·ple exemple *m*; **for e.** par example; **to set an e.** donner l'exemple (**to** à).

ex·ceed *vt* dépasser.

ex·cel *vi* **to e. in** sth être excellent en qch.

ex·cel·lent *adj* excellent.

ex·cept *prep* sauf, excepté; **e. for** à part; **e. that** sauf que.

ex·cep·tion exception *f*; **with the e. of** à l'exception de.

ex·cep·tion·al *adj* exceptionnel.

ex·cep·tion·al·ly *adv* exceptionnellement.

ex·cerpt extrait *m*.

ex·cess 1 *n* excès *m*; *(surplus)* excédent *m*. 2 *adj* **e. fare** supplément *m* (de billet); **e. baggage** excédent *m* de bagages.

ex·ces·sive *adj* excessif.

ex·ces·sive·ly *adv (too, too much)* excessivement; *(very)* extrêmement.

ex·change 1 *vt* échanger (**for** contre). 2 *n* échange *m*; *(of foreign currencies)* change *m*; *(telephone)* **e.** central *m* (téléphonique); **in e.** en échange (**for** de).

ex·cite *vt (enthuse)* passionner.

ex·cit·ed *adj (happy)* surexcité; *(nervous)* énervé; **to get e.** *(nervous, enthusiastic)* s'exciter; **to be e. about** *(new car etc)* se réjouir de.

ex·cite·ment agitation *f*; *(emotion)* vive émotion *f*.

ex·cit·ing *adj (book etc)* passionnant.

ex·claim *vti* s'exclamer (**that** que).

ex·cla·ma·tion point point *m* d'exclamation.

ex·clude *vt* exclure (**from** de).

ex·clu·sive *adj* exclusif; *(club)* fermé; **e. of wine**/*etc* vin/*etc* non compris.

ex·cur·sion excursion *f*.

ex·cuse 1 *vt* excuser (**sb for doing** qn d'avoir fait, qn de faire); *(exempt)* dispenser (**from** de). 2 *n* excuse *f*.

ex·e·cute *vt (criminal)* exécuter.

ex·e·cu·tion exécution *f*.

ex·ec·u·tive 1 *adj (job)* de cadre; *(car, plane)* de direction. 2 *n (person)* cadre *m*; **senior e.** cadre *m* supérieur; **junior e.** jeune cadre *m*; **sales e.** cadre *m* commercial.

ex·empt 1 *adj* dispensé (**from** de). 2 *vt* dispenser (**from** de).

ex·emp·tion dispense *f*.

ex·ert *vt* exercer; **to e. oneself** *(physically)* se dépenser; **don't e. yourself!** ne te fatigue pas!

ex·er·tion effort *m*.

ex·haust 1 *vt* épuiser. 2 *n* **e. (pipe)** tuyau *m* d'échappement.

ex·haust·ed *adj* épuisé; **to become e.** s'épuiser.

ex·haust·ing *adj* épuisant.

ex·hib·it *vt (put on display)* exposer. 2 *n* objet *m* exposé.

ex·hi·bi·tion exposition *f*.

ex·hib·i·tor exposant, -ante *mf*.

ex·ile 1 *n (banishment)* exil *m*; *(person)* exilé, -ée *mf*. 2 *vt* exiler.

ex·ist *vi* exister; *(live)* vivre (**on** de).

ex·is·tence existence *f*; **to be in e.** exister.

ex·ist·ing adj (situation) actuel.
ex·it sortie f.
ex·or·bi·tant adj exorbitant.
ex·pand 1 vt (trade, ideas) développer; (production) augmenter; (gas, metal) dilater. **2** vi se développer; (of production) augmenter; (of gas, metal) se dilater.
ex·panse étendue f.
ex·pan·sion (of trade etc) développement m.
ex·pect vt s'attendre à; (think) penser (that que); (suppose) supposer (that que); (await) attendre; **to e. sth from sb/sth** attendre qch de qn/qch; **to e. to do** compter faire; **to e. that** s'attendre à ce que (+ subjunctive); **I e. you to come** (want) je compte sur votre présence; **it was expected** c'était prévu; **she's expecting (a baby)** elle attend un bébé.
ex·pec·ta·tion attente f.
ex·pe·di·tion expédition f.
ex·pel vt (from school) renvoyer.
ex·pen·di·ture (money) dépenses fpl.
ex·pense frais mpl; **business expenses** frais mpl généraux; **at sb's e.** aux dépens de qn.
ex·pen·sive adj cher.
ex·pe·ri·ence 1 n expérience f; **he's had e. of driving** il a déjà conduit. **2** vt connaître; (difficulty) éprouver.
ex·pe·ri·enced adj expérimenté; **to be e. in** s'y connaître en.
ex·per·i·ment 1 n expérience f. **2** vi faire une expérience or des expériences.
ex·pert expert m (on, in en); **e. advice** le conseil d'un expert.
ex·per·tise compétence f (in en).
ex·pi·ra·tion date date f d'expiration.
ex·pire vi expirer.
ex·pired adj (ticket, passport etc) périmé.

ex·plain vt expliquer (**to** à; **that** que).
▸ **explain away** vt justifier.
ex·pla·na·tion explication f.
ex·plic·it adj explicite.
ex·plode vi exploser.
ex·ploit 1 vt exploiter. **2** n exploit m.
ex·plo·ra·tion exploration f.
ex·plore vt explorer; (causes etc) examiner.
ex·plor·er explorateur, -trice mf.
ex·plo·sion explosion f.
ex·plo·sive adj & n explosif (m).
ex·port 1 n exportation f. **2** vt exporter (**to** vers; **from** de).
ex·pose vt exposer (**to** à); (plot etc) révéler; (crook etc) démasquer.
ex·press 1 vt exprimer; **to e. oneself** s'exprimer. **2** adj (letter, delivery) exprès inv; (train) rapide. **3** adv (to send) par exprès or Chronopost®. **4** n (train) rapide m.
ex·pres·sion (phrase, look) expression f.
ex·press·way autoroute f.
ex·tend 1 vt (arm, business) étendre; (line, visit) prolonger (**by** de); (house) agrandir; (time limit) reculer. **2** vi s'étendre (**to** jusqu'à); (in time) se prolonger.
ex·ten·sion (for table) rallonge f; (to building) agrandissement(s) m(pl); (of phone) appareil m supplémentaire; (of office phone) poste m; **e. cord** rallonge f.
ex·ten·sive adj étendu; (repairs, damage) important.
ex·ten·sive·ly adv (very much) énormément, considérablement.
ex·tent (scope) étendue f, (size) importance f; **to a large/certain e.** dans une large/certaine mesure; **to such an e. that** à tel point que.
ex·te·ri·or adj & n extérieur (m).
ex·ter·nal adj extérieur; **for e. use** (medicine) à usage externe.
ex·tin·guish·er (fire) e. extincteur m.

ex·tra 1 *adj* supplémentaire; **one e. glass** un verre de or en plus; **to be e.** *(spare)* être en trop; *(cost more)* être en supplément; **e. charge** or **portion** supplément *m*. **2** *adv* **to pay e.** payer un supplément; **wine costs** or **is 10 euros e.** il y a un supplément de 10 euros pour le vin. **3** *n* *(perk)* à-côté *m*; **extras** *(expenses)* frais *mpl* supplémentaires.

ex·tra- *prefix* extra-.

ex·tract 1 *vt* extraire *(from* de). **2** *n* extrait *m*.

ex·tra·cur·ric·u·lar *adj* extrascolaire.

ex·traor·di·nar·y *adj* extraordinaire.

ex·tra-spe·cial *adj* *(occasion)* très spécial.

ex·trav·a·gant *adj* *(wasteful with money)* dépenser.

ex·treme 1 *adj* extrême; *(danger, poverty)* très grand. **2** *n* extrême *m*.

ex·treme·ly *adv* extrêmement.

eye œil *m* *(pl* yeux); **to keep an e. on** surveiller; **to lay** or **set eyes on** voir; **to take one's eyes off sb/sth** quitter qn/qch des yeux.

eye·brow sourcil *m*.

eye·glass·es *npl* lunettes *fpl*.

eye·lash cil *m*.

eye·lid paupière *f*.

eye·lin·er eye-liner *m*.

eye shad·ow fard *m* à paupières.

eye·sight vue *f*.

F

fab·ric tissu *m*, étoffe *f*.

fab·u·lous *adj* *(wonderful)* Fam formidable.

face 1 *n* *(of person)* visage *m*, figure *f*; *(of clock)* cadran *m*; **f. down** *(thing)* tourné à l'en-

vers; **f. to f.** face à face; **to make faces** faire des grimaces. **2** *vt* *(danger, problem etc)* faire face à; *(accept)* accepter; *(look in the face)* regarder *(qn)* bien en face; *(be opposite)* être en face de; *(of window)* donner sur; **faced with** *(problem)* confronté à; **he can't f. leaving** il n'a pas le courage de partir. **3** *vi* *(of house)* être orienté *(north/etc* au nord/*etc*); *(be turned)* être tourné *(towards* vers).

face·cloth gant *m* de toilette.

▶ **face up to** *vt* *(danger, problem)* faire face à; *(fact)* accepter.

fa·cil·i·tate *vt* faciliter.

fa·cil·i·ties *npl* *(for sports, cooking etc)* équipements *mpl*; *(in harbor, airport)* installations *fpl*.

fact fait *m*; **as a matter of f., in f.** en fait.

fac·tor facteur *m*.

fac·to·ry usine *f*.

fac·tu·al *adj* basé sur les faits.

fade *vi* *(of flower)* se faner; *(of light)* baisser; *(of color)* passer; *(of fabric)* se décolorer.

fade (a·way) *vi* *(of sound)* s'affaiblir.

fail 1 *vi* échouer; *(of business)* faire faillite; *(of health, sight)* baisser; *(of brakes)* lâcher. **2** *vt* *(exam)* rater, échouer à; *(candidate)* refuser, recaler; **to f. to do** *(forget)* manquer de faire; *(not be able)* ne pas arriver à faire. **3** *n* **without f.** à coup sûr.

failed *adj* *(attempt, poet)* manqué.

fail·ing 1 *n* défaut *m*. **2** *prep* **f. that** à défaut.

fail·ure échec *m*; *(of business)* faillite *f*, *(person)* raté, -ée *mf*; **f. to do** incapacité *f* de faire.

faint 1 *adj* faible; *(color)* pâle; **I haven't got the faintest idea** je n'en ai pas la moindre idée; **to feel f.** se trouver mal. **2** *vi* s'évanouir.

faint·ly *adv* faiblement; *(slightly)* légèrement.

fair¹ *(for trade)* foire *f*, *(for enter-*

tainment) fête *f* foraine, kermesse *f*; *(for charity)* fête *f*.

fair² *adj (just)* juste; *(game, fight)* loyal; **f. enough!** très bien! ▪ *(rather good)* passable; *(weather)* beau; *(price)* raisonnable; **a f. amount (of)** pas mal (de).

fair³ *adj (hair, person)* blond.

fair-haired *adj* blond.

fair·ly *adv (to treat)* équitablement; *(rather)* assez.

fair·ness justice *f*; *(of person)* impartialité *f*.

fair play fair-play *m inv.*

fair-sized *adj* assez grand.

fair·y fée *f*; **f. tale** *or* **story** conte *m* de fées.

faith foi *f*; **to have f. in sb** avoir confiance en qn.

faith·ful *adj* fidèle (**to** à).

fake 1 *n* faux *m*; *(person)* imposteur *m.* **2** *vt (document etc)* falsifier. **3** *vi* faire semblant. **4** *adj* faux (*f* fausse).

fall 1 *n* chute *f*; *(in price etc)* baisse *f* (**in** de); *(season)* automne *m.* **2** *vi* ▪ tomber; **to f. off** *or* **out of** *or* **down sth** tomber de qch; **to f. over** *(chair)* tomber en butant contre; *(balcony)* tomber de; **to f. ill** tomber malade.

▸ **fall apart** *vi (of machine)* tomber en morceaux; *(of group)* se défaire.

▸ **fall back on** *vt (as last resort)* se rabattre sur.

▸ **fall behind** *vi* rester en arrière; *(in work, payments)* prendre du retard.

▸ **fall down** *vi* tomber; *(of building)* s'effondrer.

▸ **fall for** *vt* tomber amoureux de; *(trick)* se laisser prendre à.

▸ **fall in** *vi (collapse)* s'écrouler.

▸ **fall off** *vi (come off)* se détacher; *(of numbers)* diminuer.

▸ **fall out** *vi (quarrel)* se brouiller (**with** avec).

▸ **fall over** *vi* tomber; *(of table, vase)* se renverser.

▸ **fall through** *vi (of plan)* tomber à l'eau.

false *adj* faux (*f* fausse).

fame renommée *f*.

fa·mil·iar *adj* familier (**to** à); **f. with sb** *(too friendly)* familier avec qn; **to be f. with** *(know)* connaître.

fa·mil·iar·i·ty familiarité *f* (**with** avec).

fam·i·ly famille *f*.

fa·mous *adj* célèbre (**for** pour).

fan¹ *(held in hand)* éventail *m*; *(mechanical)* ventilateur *m*.

fan² *(of person)* fan *mf*, *(of team etc)* supporter *m*; **to be a jazz/sports f.** être passionné de jazz/de sport.

fan·cy 1 *n* **I took a f. to it** j'en ai eu envie. **2** *adj (hat, button etc)* fantaisie *inv.* **3** *int* **f. (that)!** tiens (donc)!

fan·tas·tic *adj* fantastique.

fan·ta·sy *(dream)* fantasme *m*; *(imagination)* fantaisie *f*.

FAQ *(frequently asked questions)* FAQ *f*.

far 1 *adv (distance)* loin; **f. bigger/** *etc* beaucoup plus grand/*etc* (**than** que); **how f. is it to?** combien y a-t-il d'ici à?; **so f.** *(time)* jusqu'ici; **as f. as** *(place)* jusqu'à; **as f. as I know** autant que je sache; **as f. as I'm concerned** en ce qui me concerne; **f. from doing** loin de faire; **f. away** *or* **off** au loin; **by f.** de loin. **2** *adj (side, end)* autre.

far·a·way *adj (country)* lointain.

farce farce *f*.

fare *(price)* prix *m* du billet.

fare·well *int* adieu.

far-fetched *adj* tiré par les cheveux.

farm 1 *n* ferme *f*. **2** *adj (worker, produce)* agricole; **f. land** terres *fpl* cultivées. **3** *vt* cultiver.

farm·er fermier, -ière *mf*.

farm·house ferme *f*.

farm·ing agriculture *f*.

farm·yard basse-cour *f*, cour *f* de ferme.

far-off *adj* lointain.

far-reach·ing *adj* de grande portée.

far·ther adv plus loin; **to get f. away** s'éloigner.

far·thest 1 adj le plus éloigné. **2** adv le plus loin.

fas·ci·nate vt fasciner.

fas·ci·nat·ing adj fascinant.

fas·ci·na·tion fascination f.

fash·ion (style in clothes) mode f; (manner) façon f; **in f.** à la mode; **out of f.** démodé.

fash·ion·a·ble adj à la mode; (place) chic inv.

fash·ion show présentation f de collections.

fast 1 adj rapide; **to be f.** (of clock) avancer (**by** de). **2** adv (quickly) vite; **f. asleep** profondément endormi.

fas·ten vt attacher (**to** à); (door, window) fermer (bien).

fas·ten·er (clip) attache f; (of garment) fermeture f; (of bag) fermoir m; (hook) agrafe f.

fat 1 n graisse f; (on meat) gras m. **2** adj gras (f grasse); (cheek, salary) gros (f grosse); **to get f.** grossir.

fa·tal adj mortel; (mistake etc) fatal (mpl fatals).

fate destin m, sort m.

fa·ther père m.

fa·ther-in-law, pl **fathers-in-law** beau-père m.

fa·tigue fatigue f.

fat·ten·ing adj (food) qui fait grossir.

fat·ty adj (food) gras (f grasse).

fau·cet (tap) robinet m.

fault faute f, (defect) défaut m; (mistake) erreur f, **it's your f.** c'est ta faute; **to find f.** (**with**) critiquer.

fault·y adj défectueux.

fa·vor 1 n (act of kindness) service m; **to do sb a f.** rendre service à qn; **to be in f. of** (support) être pour; (prefer) préférer. **2** vt (encourage) favoriser; (prefer) préférer.

fa·vor·a·ble adj favorable (**to** à).

fa·vor·ite adj & n favori, -ite mf, préféré, -ée mf.

fax 1 n (machine) télécopieur m, fax m; (message) télécopie f, fax m. **2** vt (message) faxer; **to f. sb** envoyer une télécopie or un fax à qn.

fear 1 n crainte f, peur f; **for f. of doing** de peur de faire. **2** vt craindre.

fear·ful adj (person) apeuré; (noise, pain) épouvantable.

fear·less adj intrépide.

feast festin m.

feat exploit m.

feath·er plume f.

fea·ture (of face, person) trait m; (of thing, place) caractéristique f.

Feb·ru·ar·y février m.

fed·er·al adj fédéral.

fed up adj **to be f. up** Fam en avoir marre (**with** de).

fee prix m; **fee(s)** (professional) honoraires mpl; (for registration) droits mpl; **school** or **tuition fees** frais mpl de scolarité.

fee·ble adj faible.

feed* vt donner à manger à; (breast-feed) allaiter; (bottle-feed) donner le biberon à (un bébé).

feed·back réaction(s) f(pl).

feel 1 n toucher m; (feeling) sensation f. **2** vt* (be aware of) sentir; (experience) éprouver; (touch) tâter; **to f. that** avoir l'impression que. **3** vi (tired, old etc) se sentir; **I f. hot/sleepy/**etc j'ai chaud/sommeil/etc; **she feels better** elle va mieux; **to f. like sth** (want) avoir envie de qch.

► **feel around** vi tâtonner; (in pocket etc) fouiller.

feel·ing sentiment m; (physical) sensation f.

► **feel up to** vt être en forme pour.

feet see **foot**.

fell pt of **fall**.

fel·low (man) type m.

fel·o·ny crime m.

felt[1] pt & pp of **feel**.

felt[2] feutre m.

felt-tip (pen) (crayon m) feutre m.

fe·male 1 adj (voice etc) féminin; (animal) femelle; **f. student** étudiante f. **2** n femme f, (animal) femelle f.

fem·i·nine adj féminin.

fence 1 n barrière f, (in race) obstacle m. **2** vi (with sword) faire de l'escrime.

fence (in) vt (land) clôturer.

fenc·ing (sport) escrime f.

fend vi **to f. for oneself** se débrouiller.

fend·er (on car) aile f.

fern fougère f.

fe·ro·cious adj féroce.

fer·ry ferry-boat m; (small, for river) bac m.

fer·tile adj (land) fertile.

fer·til·iz·er engrais m.

fes·ti·val festival m (pl -als).

fes·tiv·i·ties npl festivités fpl.

fetch[1] vt (bring) amener (qn); (object) apporter; **to (go and) f.** aller chercher.

fetch[2] vt (be sold for) rapporter.

fête fête f.

feud 1 n querelle f. **2** vi se quereller, se disputer.

fe·ver fièvre f; **to have a f.** avoir de la fièvre.

fe·ver·ish adj fiévreux.

few adj & pron peu (de); **f. towns/** etc peu de villes/etc; **a f. towns/**etc quelques villes/etc; **f. of them** peu d'entre eux; **a f.** quelques-un(e)s (of de); **a f. of us** quelques-uns d'entre nous; **quite a f., a good f.** bon nombre (de); **a f. more books/** etc encore quelques livres/etc; **every f. days** tous les trois ou quatre jours.

few·er adj & pron moins (de) (than que).

fi·an·cé(e) fiancé, -ée mf.

fi·ber fibre f.

fi·ber·board (bois) aggloméré m.

fic·tion (works of) f. romans mpl.

fid·dle (dishonest act) Fam combine f.

▶ **fiddle (around) with** vt (pen etc) tripoter; (cars etc) bricoler.

fidg·et vi gigoter.

field champ m; (for sports) terrain m.

fierce adj féroce; (attack) furieux.

fif·teen adj & n quinze (m).

fif·teenth adj & n quinzième (mf).

fifth adj & n cinquième (mf).

fif·ti·eth adj & n cinquantième (mf).

fif·ty adj & n cinquante (m).

fig figue f.

fight 1 n bagarre f, Boxing combat m; (struggle) lutte f, (quarrel) dispute f. **2** vi* se battre (**against** contre); (struggle) lutter (**for** pour); (quarrel) se disputer. **3** vt se battre avec (qn).

▶ **fight back** vi se défendre.

fight·er (determined person) battant, -ante mf.

▶ **fight off** vt (attacker) repousser; (disease) résister à.

▶ **fight over** vt se disputer.

fig·ure[1] (numeral) chiffre m; (price) prix m; (of woman) ligne f; (diagram, person) figure f.

fig·ure[2] vt **to f. that** (guess) penser que.

▶ **figure on doing** vt compter faire.

▶ **figure out** vt arriver à comprendre; (problem) résoudre.

file (tool) lime f, (folder, information) dossier m; (computer data) fichier m; **in single f.** en file.

file (a·way) vt (document) classer.

file (down) vt limer.

▶ **file in** vi entrer à la queue leu leu.

▶ **file out** vi sortir à la queue leu leu.

fil·ing cab·i·net classeur m.

fill 1 vt remplir (**with** de); (tooth) plomber. **2** vi se remplir.

fil·let filet m.

▶ **fill in** vt (form, hole) remplir.

fill·ing 1 adj (meal) nourrissant. **2** n (in tooth) plombage m; (in food) garniture f.

▶ **fill out** *vt (form)* remplir.

▶ **fill up 1** *vt (container, form)* remplir. **2** *vi* se remplir; *(with gas)* faire le plein.

film 1 *n* film *m*; *(for camera)* pellicule *f*. **2** *vt* filmer.

fil·ter filtre *m*; **f.-tipped cigarette** cigarette *f* (à bout) filtre.

filth saleté *f*.

filth·y *adj* sale.

fin *(of fish)* nageoire *f*.

fi·nal 1 *adj (last)* dernier. **2** *n (match)* finale *f*.

fi·nal·ize *vt* mettre au point; *(date)* fixer.

fi·nal·ly *adv* enfin.

fi·nance 1 *n* finance *f*. **2** *vt* financer.

fi·nan·cial *adj* financier.

find *n* trouvaille *f*. **2** *vt** trouver; *(sth or sb lost)* retrouver.

▶ **find out 1** *vt (secret etc)* découvrir; *(person)* démasquer. **2** *vi (inquire)* se renseigner (**about** sur); **to f. out about sth** *(discover)* découvrir qch.

fine¹ *n* amende *f*, *(for driving offense)* contravention *f*. **2** *vt* **to f. sb ($100/etc)** infliger une amende (de cent dollars/*etc*) à qn.

fine² *adj (thin, not coarse)* fin; *(very good)* excellent; **he's f.** *(healthy)* il va bien. **2** *adv (well)* très bien.

fin·ger doigt *m*; **little f.** petit doigt *m*.

fin·ger·nail ongle *m*.

fin·ger·print empreinte *f* (digitale); *(smudge)* trace *f* de doigt.

fin·ger·tip bout *m* du doigt.

fin·ish 1 *n* fin *f*; *(of race)* arrivée *f*. **2** *vt* finir; **to f. doing** finir de faire. **3** *vi* finir; **to have finished with** ne plus avoir besoin de; *(situation, person)* en avoir fini avec.

fin·ished *adj* fini.

fin·ish line ligne *f* d'arrivée.

▶ **finish off** *vti* finir.

▶ **finish up 1** *vt* finir. **2** *vi* **to f. up in** se retrouver à; **to f. up doing** finir par faire.

Finn Finlandais, -aise *mf*.

Finn·ish 1 *adj* finlandais. **2** *(language)* finnois *m*.

fir sapin *m*.

fire¹ feu *m*; *(accidental)* incendie *m*; **to set f. to** mettre le feu à; **on f.** en feu; **(there's a) f.!** au feu!

fire² **1** *vt* **to f. a gun** tirer un coup de fusil *or* de revolver; **to f. sb** *(dismiss)* renvoyer qn. **2** *vi* tirer (**at** sur).

fire a·larm alarme *f* d'incendie.

fire·crack·er pétard *m*.

fire de·part·ment pompiers *mpl*.

fire en·gine voiture *f* de pompiers.

fire es·cape escalier *m* de secours.

fire·man, *pl* **-men** pompier *m*.

fire·place cheminée *f*.

fire sta·tion caserne *f* de pompiers.

fire·wood bois *m* de chauffage.

fire·works **f. (display)** feu *m* d'artifice.

firm¹ *n* entreprise *f*. **2** *adj* ferme.

firm·ly *adv* fermement.

first 1 *adj* premier. **2** *adv (firstly)* premièrement; *(for the first time)* pour la première fois; **(at) f.** d'abord. **3** *n* premier, -ière *mf*; **(gear)** *(of vehicle)* première *f*.

first aid premiers secours *mpl*.

first-class 1 *adj* excellent; *(ticket, seat)* de première; *(mail)* ordinaire. **2** *adv (to travel)* en première.

first floor rez-de-chaussée *m inv*.

first grade cours *m* préparatoire.

first·ly *adv* premièrement.

first name prénom *m*.

fish 1 *n inv* poisson *m*. **2** *vi* pêcher.

fish·er·man, *pl* **-men** pêcheur *m*.

fish·ing pêche *f*; **to go f.** aller à la pêche.

fish·ing rod canne *f* à pêche.

fish·mar·ket poissonnerie *f*.

fish sticks bâtonnets *mpl* de poisson.

fist poing *m*.

fit¹ *adj* en bonne santé; (in good shape) en forme; (suitable) propre (**for** à; **to do** à faire); (worthy) digne (**for** de; **to do** de faire); (able) apte (**for** à; **to do** à faire); **f. to eat** bon à manger.

fit² 1 *vt* (of clothes) aller (bien) à (qn). 2 *vi* **this shirt fits** (fits me) cette chemise me va (bien).

fit³ (attack) accès *m*.

fit (in) 1 *vt* (object) faire entrer; **to f. sb in** (find time to see) prendre qn. 2 *vti* **to f. (in) sth** (go in) aller dans qch; **he doesn't f. in** il ne peut pas s'intégrer.

fit (on) 1 *vt* **to f. sth (on) to sb** (put) poser qch sur qn; (fix) fixer qch à qch. 2 *vti* **to f. (on) sth** (go on sth) aller sur qch.

fit·ness (health) santé *f*.

► **fit (out) with** *vt* (house etc) équiper de.

fit·ting 1 *adj* approprié (**to** à). 2 *n* (of dress) essayage *m*; **fittings** (in house) installations *fpl*; **f. room** cabine *f* d'essayage.

five *adj & n* cinq (*m*).

fix *vt* (make firm, decide) fixer; (mend) réparer; (deal with) arranger; (prepare, cook) préparer.

fix·ture Sports rencontre *f*; **fixtures** (in building) installations *fpl*.

► **fix up** *vt* (trip etc) arranger; **to f. sb up with a job**/etc procurer un travail/etc à qn.

fiz·zy *adj* pétillant.

flag drapeau *m*; (on ship) pavillon *m*.

flake (of snow) flocon *m*.

flake (off) *vi* (of paint) s'écailler.

flame flamme *f*; **to burst into f., to go up in flames** prendre feu.

flam·ma·ble *adj* inflammable.

flan tarte *f*.

flan·nel flanelle *f*.

flap 1 *vi* (of wings etc) battre. 2 *vt* **to f. its wings** battre des ailes. 3 *n* (of pocket, envelope) rabat *m*.

► **flare up** *vi* (of fire) prendre; (of violence) éclater.

flash 1 *n* (of light) éclat *m*; (for camera) flash *m*. 2 *vi* (shine) briller; (on and off) clignoter. 3 *vt* (a light) projeter; (aim) diriger (**on, at** sur); **to f. one's headlights** faire un appel de phares.

flash·ers (of vehicle) feux *mpl* de détresse.

flash·light lampe *f* électrique, lampe *f* de poche.

flask (bottle) bouteille *f*; (for pocket) flasque *f*.

flat¹ 1 *adj* plat; (punctured) crevé; (deflated) à plat; (beer) éventé; (rate, fare) fixe; **to put sth (down) f.** mettre qch à plat; **f. (on one's face)** à plat ventre. 2 *adv* **f. out** (to work) d'arrache-pied; (to run) à toute vitesse. 3 *n* crevaison *f*.

flat² (rooms) appartement *m*.

flat·ly *adv* (to deny, refuse) catégoriquement.

flat·ten (out) *vt* aplatir.

flat·ter *vt* flatter.

fla·vor goût *m*; (of ice cream etc) parfum *m*.

fla·vor·ing (in cake etc) parfum *m*.

flaw défaut *m*.

flea puce *f*.

flea mar·ket marché *m* aux puces.

flee* 1 *vi* s'enfuir. 2 *vt* (place) s'enfuir de.

fleet (of ships) flotte *f*.

Flem·ish 1 *adj* flamand. 2 *n* (language) flamand *m*.

flesh chair *f*.

flex 1 *vt* (limb) fléchir. 2 *n* (wire) fil *m* (souple); (for telephone) cordon *m*.

flex·i·ble *adj* souple.

flick (with finger) chiquenaude *f*.

flick·er 1 *n* (of eyes) tremblement *m*; (of flame, light) vacillement *m*; **a f. of hope** l'ombre d'un espoir. 2 *vi* (eyes) trembler; (flame, light) vaciller.

▶ **flick off** vt enlever (d'une chiquenaude).

flight (of bird, aircraft) vol m; (escape) fuite f; **f. of stairs** escalier m.

flight at·ten·dant (male) steward m; (female) hôtesse f de l'air.

flim·sy adj (light) (trop) léger; (thin) (trop) mince.

fling* vt lancer.

flint (for lighter) pierre f.

flip 1 n (flick) petit coup m; **f. chart** tableau m à feuilles. 2 vt (with finger) donner un petit coup à; (toss) envoyer; **to f. a coin** jouer à pile ou face.

flip-flops npl tongs fpl.

flip·per (of swimmer) palme f.

▶ **flip through** vt (book) feuilleter.

float 1 n Fishing flotteur m; (at carnival) char m. 2 vi flotter (**on** sur).

flock 1 n (of sheep) troupeau m; (of birds) volée f. 2 vi venir en foule.

flood 1 n inondation f; (of letters, tears) flot m. 2 vt (field, house etc) inonder. 3 vi (of river) déborder.

▶ **flood in** vt (of tourists etc) affluer.

▶ **flood into** vt (of tourists etc) envahir (un pays etc).

flood·light projecteur m.

floor (ground) sol m; (wooden etc in building) plancher m; (story) étage m; **on the f.** par terre; **on the first f.** au rez-de-chaussée.

floor·board planche f.

floor lamp lampadaire m.

flop 1 vi (of play etc) faire un four. 2 n four m.

flop·py adj (soft) mou (f molle).

flop·py disk disquette f.

flo·rist fleuriste mf.

floss (dental) **f.** fil m dentaire.

flour farine f.

flour·ish 1 n (gesture) grand geste m; (decoration) fioriture f. 2 vt brandir. 3 vi (business, economy, plant) prospérer; (person) être en pleine santé.

flow 1 vi couler; (of electric current, information) circuler; (of traffic)

s'écouler. 2 n (of river) courant m; (of current, information) circulation f.

flow chart tableau m.

flow·er 1 n fleur f; **in f.** en fleur(s). 2 vi fleurir.

flow·er bed parterre m de fleurs, plate-bande f.

flow·er shop (boutique f de) fleuriste mf.

flu grippe f.

flu·ent adj **he's f. in Russian, his Russian is f.** il parle couramment le russe.

flu·ent·ly adv (to speak a language) couramment.

fluff (of material) peluche(s) f(pl); (on floor) moutons mpl.

flu·id adj & n fluide (m).

flunk vt (exam) Fam être collé à.

flu·o·res·cent adj fluorescent.

flush vt **to f. the toilet** tirer la chasse d'eau.

flute flûte f.

flut·ter vi (of bird) voltiger; (of flag) flotter.

fly[1] (insect) mouche f.

fly[2] vi voler; (of passenger) aller en avion; (of flag) flotter. 2 vt (aircraft) piloter; (airline) voyager par.

fly[3] (on pants) braguette f.

▶ **fly across, fly over** vt (country etc) survoler.

▶ **fly away, fly off** vi s'envoler.

fly·ing vol m; (air travel) l'avion m; **f. saucer** soucoupe f volante.

foam écume f; (on beer) mousse f; **f. rubber** caoutchouc m mousse; **f. mattress**/etc matelas m/etc mousse.

fo·cus 1 n (of attention) centre m; **in f.** au point. 2 vt (image) mettre au point. 3 vti **to f. (one's attention) on** se tourner vers.

fog brouillard m.

fog·gy adj **it's f.** il y a du brouillard; **f. weather** brouillard m.

foil (for cooking) papier m alu(minium).

fold 1 n (in paper etc) pli m. 2 vt

plier; (*wrap*) envelopper (**in** dans);
to f. one's arms (se) croiser les
bras. **3** *vi* (*of chair etc*) se plier.
▶**fold back, fold over 1** *vt* (*blanket etc*) replier. **2** *vi* se replier.
fold·er (*file holder*) chemise *f*.
fold·ing *adj* (*chair etc*) pliant.
▶**fold up 1** *vt* (*chair etc*) plier. **2** *vi* se
plier.
folk 1 *adj* (*dance etc*) folklorique; **f.
music** (musique *f*) folk *m*. **2** *npl*
folks gens *mpl or fpl*.
fol·low *vt* suivre; (*career*) poursuivre; **followed by** suivi de. **2** *vi*
suivre.
▶**follow around** *vt* suivre partout.
fol·low·er partisan *m*.
fol·low·ing 1 *n* suivant. **2** *prep* à
la suite de.
▶**follow through** *vt* (*plan etc*)
poursuivre jusqu'au bout.
▶**follow up** *vt* (*idea, story*) creuser;
(*clue*) suivre.
fond *adj* **to be** (**very**) **f. of** aimer
(beaucoup).
food nourriture *f*; (*particular substance*) aliment *m*; (*for cats, dogs*)
pâtée *f*.
fool 1 *n* imbécile *mf*; **to play the
f.** faire l'imbécile. **2** *vt* (*trick*)
rouler.
▶**fool around** *vi* faire l'imbécile;
(*waste time*) perdre son temps.
fool·ish *adj* bête.
fool·ish·ly *adv* bêtement.
foot, *pl* **feet** pied *m*; (*of animal*)
patte *f*, (*measure*) pied *m* (=
30,48cm); **at the f. of** (*page, stairs*)
au bas de; **on f.** à pied.
foot·ball (*game*) football *m* américain; (*ball*) ballon *m* (de football
américain).
foot·ball play·er joueur, -euse
mf de football américain.
foot·bridge passerelle *f*.
foot·path sentier *m*.
foot·print empreinte *f* (de pied *or*
de pas).
foot·step pas *m*.

foot·stool repose-pieds *m inv*;
(*cushioned*) pouf *m*.
for *prep* pour; (*in exchange for*)
contre; (*for a distance of*) pendant;
what's it f.? ça sert à quoi?; **he was
away f. a month** il a été absent
pendant un mois; **he won't be back
f. a month** il ne sera pas de retour
avant un mois; **he's been here/I
haven't seen him f. a month** il est
ici/je ne l'ai pas vu depuis un mois;
I haven't seen him f. ten years
voilà dix ans que je ne l'ai pas vu; **it's
f. you to say** c'est à toi de dire; **f.
that to be done** pour que ça soit
fait.
for·bid* *vt* interdire (**sb to do** à qn
de faire); **she is forbidden to leave**
il lui est interdit de partir.
force 1 *n* force *f*; **the armed forces**
les forces armées. **2** *vt* forcer (*qn*)
(**to do** à faire); (*door*) forcer; **forced
to do** obligé *or* forcé de faire; **to f.
one's way into** entrer de force
dans.
fore·cast 1 *vt*** prévoir. **2** *n* prévision *f*, (*of weather*) météo *f*.
fore·head front *m*.
for·eign *adj* étranger; (*trade*) extérieur; (*travel*) à l'étranger.
for·eign·er étranger, -ère *mf*.
fore·man, *pl* -**men** (*worker*) contremaître *m*.
fore·most *adj* principal.
fore·run·ner précurseur *m*.
fore·see* *vt* prévoir.
for·est forêt *f*.
for·ev·er *adv* pour toujours; (*continually*) sans cesse.
forge *vt* (*signature, money*) contrefaire; (*document*) falsifier.
▶**forge ahead** *vi* (*progress*) aller de
l'avant.
for·ger·y faux *m*.
for·get* *vti* oublier (**to do** de
faire).
▶**forget about** *vt* oublier.
for·get·ful *adj* **he's f.** il n'a pas de
mémoire.

for·give* vt pardonner (**sb sth** qch à qn).

fork 1 n (for eating) fourchette f; (for gardening) fourche f; (in road) bifurcation f. 2 vi (of road) bifurquer.

fork out vt (money) Fam allonger.

form 1 n forme f; (document) formulaire m. 2 vt (group, basis etc) former; (habit) contracter; (an opinion) se former; **to f. part of** faire partie de. 3 vi (appear) se former.

for·mal adj (person, tone etc) cérémonieux; (stuffy) compassé; (official) officiel; **f. dress** tenue de cérémonie.

for·mal·i·ty formalité f.

for·mat 1 n format m. 2 vt Comput formater.

for·ma·tion formation f.

for·mer 1 adj (previous) ancien; (of two) premier. 2 pron the f. celui-là, celle-là.

for·mer·ly adv autrefois.

for·mu·la, pl -as or -ae formule f; (pl -as) (baby food) lait m maternisé.

fort fort m.

forth adv **and so f.** et ainsi de suite; **to walk back and f.** faire les cent pas.

forth·com·ing adj (event) à venir; (communicative) expansif (**about** sur); **no answer was f.** il n'y a eu aucune réponse.

for·ti·eth adj & n quarantième (mf).

for·tress forteresse f.

for·tu·nate adj (choice etc) heureux; **to be f.** (of person) avoir de la chance; **it's f. that** c'est heureux que (+ subjunctive).

for·tu·nate·ly adv heureusement.

for·tune n fortune f; **to make one's f.** faire fortune; **to have the good f. to do** avoir la chance de faire.

for·ty adj & n quarante (m).

fo·rum forum m.

for·ward 1 adv **forward(s)** en avant; **to go f.** avancer. 2 vt (letter) faire suivre; (goods) expédier.

fos·sil fossile m.

fos·ter 1 vt (child) accueillir; (hope, idea) nourrir, entretenir; (relations) favoriser. 2 adj **f. child** enfant mf placé(e) dans une famille d'accueil; **f. parents** parents mpl nourriciers.

foul 1 adj (smell, taste) infect; (language) grossier. 2 n Sports faute f.

found¹ pt & pp de **find**.

found² vt (town etc) fonder.

found·er¹ fondateur, -trice mf.

foun·der² vi (ship) sombrer; (plan, hopes) s'effondrer.

foun·tain fontaine f.

foun·tain pen stylo m à encre.

four adj & n quatre (m).

four·teen adj & n quatorze (m).

fourth adj & n quatrième (mf).

fowl volaille f.

fox renard m.

foy·er (in theater) foyer m.

frac·tion fraction f.

frac·ture 1 n fracture f. 2 vt **to f. one's leg/etc** se fracturer la jambe/etc.

frag·ile adj fragile.

frag·ment fragment m.

fra·grance parfum m.

frail adj fragile.

frame 1 n (of picture, bicycle) cadre m; (of window) châssis m; **f. of mind** humeur f. 2 vt (picture) encadrer.

frame·work structure f; **in the f. of** dans le cadre de.

franc franc m.

fran·chise n (right to vote) droit m de vote; (right to sell product) franchise f.

frank adj franc (f franche).

frank·ly adv franchement.

frank·ness franchise f.

fran·tic adj (activity) frénétique; (rush) effréné; (person) hors de soi.

fran·ti·cal·ly adv comme un fou.

fraud (crime) fraude f; (person) imposteur m.

fray vi (of garment) s'effilocher.

freck·le tache f de rousseur.

freck·led adj couvert de taches de rousseur.

free 1 adj libre; (lavish) généreux (with de); **f. (of charge)** gratuit; **to get f.** se libérer; **f. to do** libre de faire; **f. of** (pain etc) débarrassé de. **2** adv **f. (of charge)** gratuitement. **3** vt (pt & pp **freed**) (prisoner) libérer; (trapped person) dégager.

free·dom liberté f; **f. from** (worry) absence f de.

free·ly adv librement; (to give) libéralement.

free-range adj (chicken) fermier; **f. eggs** œufs mpl de poules élevées en plein air.

free·way autoroute f.

freeze* 1 vi geler. **2** vt (food) congeler; (prices) bloquer.

freez·er congélateur m; (in fridge) freezer m.

▸**freeze up, freeze over** vi geler; (of window) se givrer.

freez·ing adj (weather) glacial; (hands, person) gelé; **it's f.** on gèle.

freight (goods) fret m; **f. car** wagon m de marchandises; **f. train** train m de marchandises.

French 1 adj français; (teacher) de français; (embassy) de France. **2** n (language) français m; **the F.** les Français mpl.

French bread a loaf of F. une baguette.

French fries frites fpl.

French·man, pl -men Français m.

French-speak·ing adj francophone.

French·wom·an, pl -women Française f.

fre·quent adj fréquent; **f. visitor** habitué, -ée mf (**to** de).

fre·quent·ly adv fréquemment.

fresh adj frais (f fraîche); (new) nouveau (f nouvelle); **to get some f. air** prendre l'air.

fresh·en·er air f. désodorisant m.

▸**fresh·en up** vi faire un brin de toilette.

fret vi (worry) se faire du souci.

Fri·day vendredi m; **Good F.** Vendredi Saint.

fridge frigo m.

fried (pt & pp of **fry**) adj (fish) frit; **f. egg** œuf m sur le plat.

friend ami, -ie mf; (from school, work) camarade mf; **to be friends with sb** être ami avec qn.

friend·ly adj aimable (**to** avec); **to be f. with** être ami avec.

friend·ship amitié f.

fright peur f; **to get a f.** avoir peur; **to give sb a f.** faire peur à qn.

fright·en vt effrayer.

▸**frighten away, frighten off** vt (animal, person) faire fuir.

fright·ened adj effrayé; **to be f.** avoir peur (**of** de).

fright·en·ing adj effrayant.

frill (on dress etc) volant m.

fringe frange f; **on the f. of society** en marge de la société; **f. benefits** avantages mpl en nature.

fro adv **to go to and f.** aller et venir.

frog grenouille f.

from prep de; **where are you f.?** d'où êtes-vous?; **a train f.** un train en provenance de. ▪ (time onwards) à partir de, dès; **f. today (on), as f. today** à partir d'aujourd'hui, dès aujourd'hui. ▪ (numbers, prices onwards) à partir de. ▪ (away from); **to take/borrow f.** prendre/emprunter à. ▪ (out of) dans; sur; (box) prendre dans; (table) prendre sur; **to drink f. a cup/the bottle** boire dans une tasse/à la bouteille. ▪ (according to) d'après. ▪ (cause) par. ▪ (on behalf of) de la part de; **tell her f. me** dis-lui de ma part.

front 1 n (of garment, building) devant m; (of boat, car) avant m; (of *book*) début *m*; **in f. (of)** devant; **in f.** (*ahead*) en avant; (*in race*) en tête; **in the f.** (*in vehicle*) à l'avant. **2** *adj* (*tooth*) de devant; (*part, wheel, car seat*) avant *inv*; (*row, page*) premier; **f. door** porte *f* d'entrée.

fron·tier frontière *f*.

frost gel *m*; (*on window*) givre *m*.

frost·bite gelure *f*.

▶**frost up** *vi* (*of window etc*) se givrer.

frost·y *adj* (*window*) givré; **it's f.** il gèle.

froth mousse *f*.

frown *vi* froncer les sourcils.

fro·zen *adj* (*vegetables etc*) surgelé; **f. food** surgelés *mpl*.

fruit fruit *m*; **(some) f.** (*one piece*) un fruit; (*more than one*) des fruits; **f. drink** boisson *f* aux fruits; **f. salad** salade *f* de fruits; **f. tree** arbre *m* fruitier.

fruit·cake cake *m*.

frus·trate *vt* frustrer.

frus·trat·ed *adj* frustré.

frus·trat·ing *adj* irritant.

frus·tra·tion frustration *f*.

fry 1 *vt* faire frire. **2** *vi* frire.

fry·ing pan poêle *f* (à frire).

fudge caramel *m* mou.

fu·el combustible *m*; (*for vehicle*) carburant *m*.

fu·gi·tive fugitif, -ive *mf*.

ful·fill *vt* (*ambition*) réaliser; (*condition*) remplir; (*desire*) satisfaire.

ful·fill·ing *adj* satisfaisant.

full 1 *adj* plein (**of** de); (*bus, theater etc*) complet; (*life, day*) rempli; **the f. price** le prix fort; **to pay f. fare** payer plein tarif; **to be f.** (*of person*) n'avoir plus faim; (*of hotel*) être complet; **f. name** (*on form*) nom et prénom. **2** *n* **in f.** (*to read sth etc*) en entier.

full-scale, full-size *adj* (*model*) grandeur nature *inv*.

full-time *adj & adv* à plein temps.

ful·ly *adv* entièrement.

fumes *npl* vapeurs *fpl*; (*from car exhaust*) gaz *m inv*.

fun amusement *m*; **to be f.** être très amusant; **to have (some) f.** s'amuser; **to make f. of** se moquer de; **for f.** pour le plaisir.

func·tion fonction *f*; (*meeting*) réunion *f*.

func·tion·al *adj* fonctionnel.

fund 1 *n* (*for pension etc*) caisse *f*; **funds** (*money, resources*) fonds *mpl*. **2** *vt* fournir des fonds à.

fu·ner·al enterrement *m*; **f. home** entreprise *f* de pompes funèbres.

fun·nel (*of ship*) cheminée *f*; (*for pouring*) entonnoir *m*.

fun·ny *adj* drôle; (*strange*) bizarre; **a f. idea** une drôle d'idée; **to feel f.** ne pas se sentir très bien.

fur fourrure *f*.

fu·ri·ous *adj* furieux (**with, at** contre).

fur·nace fourneau *m*.

fur·nish *vt* (*room*) meubler.

fur·nished room pièce *f* meublée.

fur·ni·ture meubles *mpl*; **a piece of f.** un meuble.

fur·ther 1 *adv* = **farther**; (*more*) davantage. **2** *adj* supplémentaire; **f. details** de plus amples détails; **a f. case/etc** un autre cas/etc.

fur·ther·more *adv* en outre.

fur·thest *adj & adv* = **farthest**.

fu·ry fureur *f*.

fuss 1 *n* chichis *mpl*; **what a f.!** quelle histoire! **2** *vi* faire des chichis.

fuss (a·round) *vi* s'agiter.

▶**fuss over** *vt* être aux petits soins pour.

fuss·y *adj* tatillon; (*difficult*) difficile (**about** sur).

fu·ture 1 *n* avenir *m*; *Grammar* futur *m*; **in the f.** (*one day*) un jour (futur). **2** *adj* futur; (*date*) ultérieur.

fuze (*wire*) plomb *m*, fusible *m*; (*of bomb*) amorce *f*; **to blow a f.** faire sauter un plomb; **we've blown a f.** un plomb a sauté.

fuzz·y *adj* (*picture, idea*) flou.

G

gadg·et gadget m.

Gael·ic adj & n gaélique (m).

gag 1 n (over mouth) bâillon m; (joke) gag m. **2** vt (victim) bâillonner. **3** vi (choke) s'étouffer (**on** avec).

gai·e·ty gaieté f.

gai·ly adv gaiement.

gain 1 vt (obtain) gagner; (experience) acquérir; **to g. speed/weight** prendre de la vitesse/du poids. **2** n (increase) augmentation f (in de); (profit) bénéfice m.

▸ **gain on** vt (catch up with) rattraper.

ga·la gala m.

ga·lax·y galaxie f.

gale grand vent m.

gal·lant adj (chivalrous) galant.

gal·ler·y galerie f; (for public) tribune f; **art g.** (private) galerie f d'art; (public) musée m d'art.

gal·li·vant Fam vadrouiller.

gal·lon gallon m.

gal·lop 1 vi galoper. **2** n galop m.

gam·ble 1 vi jouer (**on** sur; **with** avec). **2** vt jouer. **3** n coup m risqué.

gam·ble (a·way) vt (lose) perdre (au jeu).

gam·bler joueur, -euse mf.

gam·bling jeu m.

game jeu m; (of football, etc) match m; (of tennis, chess, cards) partie f; **to play a g. of** (football etc) jouer un match de; (tennis, chess, cards) faire une partie de.

game ar·cade f galerie de jeux.

gang (of children, criminals) bande f, gang m; (of workers) équipe f.

gang·ster gangster m.

▸ **gang up on** vt se mettre à plusieurs contre.

gang·way (to ship, aircraft) passerelle f.

gap (empty space) trou m; (in time) intervalle m; (in knowledge) lacune f; **the g. between** (difference) l'écart m entre.

gape vi rester bouche bée.

▸ **gape at** vt regarder bouche bée.

ga·rage garage m.

gar·bage ordures fpl; (nonsense) idioties fpl; **g. bag** sac m poubelle; **g. man** éboueur m; **g. truck** camion-benne m.

gar·ban·zo (bean) pois m chiche.

gar·den 1 n jardin m. **2** vi jardiner.

gar·den·er jardinier, -ière mf.

gar·den hose tuyau m.

gar·den·ing jardinage m.

gar·gle vi se gargariser.

gar·land guirlande f.

gar·lic ail m.

gar·ment vêtement m.

gas 1 n gaz m inv; (gasoline) essence f; **g. mask/meter/etc** masque m/compteur m/etc à gaz; **g. heat** chauffage m au gaz; **g. heater** appareil m de chauffage à gaz; **g. station** station-service f; **g. stove** cuisinière f à gaz; (portable) réchaud m à gaz. **2** vt (poison) asphyxier (qn).

gash 1 n entaille f. **2** vt entailler.

gas·o·line essence f.

gasp 1 vi **to g. (for breath)** haleter. **2** n halètement m.

gas·sy adj (drink) gazeux.

gas·works usine f à gaz.

gate (at grade crossing, field etc) barrière f; (metal) grille f; (of castle, in airport) porte f; (at stadium) entrée f; (for tickets) portillon m.

gate-crash vi s'inviter (de force).

gath·er 1 vt (people, objects) rassembler; (pick up) ramasser; (information) recueillir; **I g. that...** je crois comprendre que...; **to g. speed** prendre de la vitesse. **2** vi (of people) se rassembler.

gath·er·ing (group) réunion f.

▸ **gather round** vi (come closer) s'approcher.

gaud·y adj voyant.

gauge 1 n (instrument) jauge f. **2** vt (estimate) évaluer.

gaunt adj décharné.

gauze gaze f.

gave pt de **give**.

gay 1 adj homo(sexuel). **2** n homo(sexuel) m.

gaze 1 n regard m (fixe). **2** vi regarder.

▸ **gaze at** vt regarder (longuement).

gear 1 n équipement m; (belongings) affaires fpl; (clothes) Fam vêtements mpl; (speed in vehicle) vitesse f, **in g.** en prise; **not in g.** au point mort. **2** vt adapter (**to** à).

▸ **gear up** vt to be geared up to do être prêt à faire; **to g. oneself up for** se préparer pour.

geek Fam ringard, -e mf.

geese see **goose**.

gel gel m.

gem pierre f précieuse.

gen·der Grammar genre m.

gen·er·al 1 adj général; **in g.** en général; **the g. public** le (grand) public; **for g. use** à l'usage du public. **2** n (in army) général m.

gen·er·al·ly adv généralement.

gen·er·a·tion génération f.

gen·er·a·tor groupe m électrogène.

gen·er·os·i·ty générosité f.

gen·er·ous adj généreux (**with** de); (helping) copieux.

gen·er·ous·ly adv généreusement.

gen·ius (ability, person) génie m.

gen·tle adj (person, slope etc) doux (f douce); (touch) léger; (exercise, speed) modéré.

gen·tle·man, pl -men monsieur m.

gen·tle·ness douceur f.

gent·ly adv doucement.

gen·u·ine adj véritable, authentique; (sincere) sincère.

gen·u·ine·ly adv véritablement, sincèrement.

ge·o·graph·i·cal adj géographique.

ge·og·ra·phy géographie f.

ge·o·met·ric, ge·o·met·ri·cal adj géométrique.

ge·om·e·try géométrie f.

germ (in body, food etc) microbe m.

Ger·man 1 adj allemand. **2** n (person) Allemand, -ande mf; (language) allemand m.

Ger·man mea·sles rubéole f.

Ger·man shep·herd (dog) berger m allemand.

ges·ture geste m.

get* 1 vt (obtain) obtenir; (find) trouver; (buy) acheter; (receive) recevoir; (catch) attraper; (bus, train) prendre; (seize) saisir; (fetch) aller chercher; (put) mettre; (derive) tirer (**from** de); (understand) comprendre; (prepare) préparer; (hit with fist, stick etc) atteindre; (reputation) se faire; **I have got** j'ai; **to g. sb to do sth** faire faire qch à qn; **to g. sth built/etc** faire construire/etc qch. **2** vi (go) aller; (arrive) arriver (**to** à); (become) devenir; **to g. caught/etc** se faire prendre/etc; **to g. cleaned up** se laver; **where have you gotten to?** où en es-tu?; **you've got to stay** (must) tu dois rester; **to g. working** se mettre à travailler.

▸ **get across 1** vt (road) traverser; (message) communiquer. **2** vi traverser.

▸ **get along** vi (manage) se débrouiller; (be on good terms) s'entendre (**with** avec).

▸ **get around** vi se déplacer; **to g. around to doing** en venir à faire.

▸ **get at** vt (reach) parvenir à.

▸ **get away** vi (leave) partir; (escape) s'échapper.

▸ **get back 1** vt (recover) récupérer; (replace) remettre. **2** vi (return) revenir; (move back) reculer.

▸ **get by** vi passer; (manage) se débrouiller.

▸ **get down** vti descendre.

▸ **get in 1** vt (laundry etc) rentrer;

(call for) faire venir *(qn)*. **2** *vi (enter)* entrer; *(come home)* rentrer; *(enter vehicle or train)* monter; *(of plane, train)* arriver.

▶ **get in (to)** *vt* entrer dans; *(vehicle, train)* monter dans; **to g. in (to) bed** se mettre au lit.

▶ **get off 1** *vi (leave)* partir; *(from vehicle or train)* descendre (**from** de); *(in court)* être acquitté. **2** *vt (remove)* enlever; *(send)* expédier; **to g. off a bus** descendre d'un bus.

▶ **get on 1** *vt (shoes, clothes)* mettre; *(bus, train)* monter dans. **2** *vi (progress)* marcher; *(manage)* se débrouiller; *(succeed)* réussir; *(enter bus or train)* monter; **to g. on with** *(task)* continuer.

▶ **get out 1** *vi* sortir; *(from vehicle or train)* descendre (**from** de); **to get out of** *(danger)* se tirer de; *(habit)* perdre. **2** *vt (remove)* enlever; *(bring out)* sortir *(qch)*.

▶ **get over 1** *vt (road)* traverser; *(obstacle)* surmonter; *(fence)* franchir; *(illness)* se remettre de. **2** *vi (cross)* traverser; *(visit)* passer.

▶ **get through 1** *vi* passer; *(finish)* finir; **to g. through to sb** *(on phone)* contacter qn. **2** *vt* passer par; *(meal)* venir à bout de.

▶ **get to** **to g. sth to sb** faire parvenir qch à qn; **to g. sb to the airport** amener qn à l'aéroport.

get-to·geth·er réunion *f*.

▶ **get up 1** *vi (rise)* se lever *(from* de*)*; **to g. up to something** *or* **mischief** faire des bêtises. **2** *vt (bring up)* monter *(qch)*; *(wake up)* réveiller.

ghast·ly *adj (horrible)* affreux.

ghet·to, *pl* -os ghetto *m*.

ghost fantôme *m*.

gi·ant 1 *n* géant *m*. **2** *adj (tree, packet)* géant.

gid·dy *adj* **to be** *or* **feel g.** avoir le vertige; **to make g.** donner le vertige à.

gift cadeau *m*; *(talent)* don *m*.

gift·ed *adj* doué.

gift vouch·er bon-cadeau *m*.

gig *Fam (pop or rock concert)* concert *m*.

gi·ga·byte gigaoctet *m*.

gi·gan·tic *adj* gigantesque.

gig·gle 1 *vi* pouffer (de rire). **2** *n* **to get/have the giggles** attraper/ avoir le fou rire.

gills *npl (of fish)* ouïes *fpl*.

gim·mick truc *m*.

gin *(drink)* gin *m*.

gin·ger gingembre *m*.

gi·raffe girafe *f*.

girl *(jeune)* fille *f*, *(daughter)* fille *f*, **American g.** jeune Américaine *f*.

girl·friend amie *f*, *(of boy)* petite amie *f*.

girl scout éclaireuse *f*.

give* *vt* donner (**to** à); *(support)* apporter; *(a smile)* faire; *(a sigh)* pousser; *(a look)* jeter.

▶ **give away** *vt (free of charge)* donner; *(prizes)* distribuer; *(betray)* trahir *(qn)*.

▶ **give back** *vt (return)* rendre.

▶ **give in 1** *vi (surrender)* céder (**to** à). **2** *vt (hand in)* remettre.

giv·en 1 *adj (specified)* donné; **at a g. moment** à un moment donné; **to be g. to sth** *(prone to)* avoir une tendance à qch. **2** *conj (considering)* étant donné.

▶ **give out** *vt (hand out)* distribuer.

▶ **give over** *vt (devote)* consacrer (**to** à).

▶ **give up 1** *vi* abandonner. **2** *vt* abandonner; *(seat)* céder (**to** à); *(prisoner)* livrer (**to** à); **to g. up smoking** cesser de fumer.

▶ **give way** *vi (of branch, person etc)* céder (**to** à); *(in vehicle)* céder la priorité (**to** à).

glad *adj* content (**of**, **about** de).

glad·ly *adv* volontiers.

glam·or *(charm)* enchantement *m*; *(splendor)* éclat *m*.

glam·or·ous *adj* séduisant.

glance 1 *n* coup d'œil *m*. **2** *vi* jeter un coup d'œil (**at** à, sur).

gland glande *f.*

glare 1 *n (light)* lumière *f* éblouissante; *(look)* regard *m* furieux. **2** *vi (dazzle)* briller d'un éclat éblouissant; **to g. at sb** regarder qn avec colère.

glar·ing *adj (light)* éblouissant; *(injustice)* flagrant.

glass verre *m; (mirror)* miroir *m;* **a pane of g.** une vitre.

glass·es *npl (for eyes)* lunettes *fpl.*

glee joie *f.*

glen vallon *m.*

glide *vi* glisser; *(of aircraft, bird)* planer.

glid·ing *(sport)* vol *m* à voile.

glim·mer *(of hope)* lueur *f.*

glimpse aperçu *m;* **to catch** *or* **get a g. of** entrevoir.

glit·ter·ing *adj* scintillant.

globe globe *m.*

gloom *(sadness)* tristesse *f.*

gloom·y *adj* triste; *(pessimistic)* pessimiste.

glo·ri·fied *adj* **it's a g. barn***/etc* ce n'est guère plus qu'une grange*/etc.*

glo·ri·ous *adj* glorieux; *(splendid)* magnifique.

glo·ry gloire *f.*

gloss *(shine)* brillant *m.*

gloss·y *adj (paint, finish)* brillant; *(magazine)* de luxe.

glove gant *m.*

glove box, glove com·part·ment *(in car)* boîte *f* à gants.

glow *vi (of sky, fire)* rougeoyer.

glue 1 *n* colle *f.* **2** *vt* coller **(to, on** à); **with eyes glued to** les yeux fixés sur.

glum *adj* triste.

glut *(of oil etc)* surplus *m.*

glut·ton glouton, -onne *mf.*

gnat *(insect)* moucheron *m.*

gnaw *vti* ronger.

go[1]* *vi* aller **(to** à; **from** de); *(depart)* partir, s'en aller; *(disappear)* disparaître, partir; *(function)* marcher; *(become)* devenir; *(of material)* s'user; **to go well/badly** *(of*

event) se passer bien/mal; **she's going to do** *(is about to, intends to)* elle va faire; **it's all gone** il n'y en a plus; **to go and get** aller chercher; **to go riding/on a trip***/etc* faire du cheval/un voyage*/etc;* **to let go of** lâcher; **to go to a doctor***/etc* aller voir un médecin*/etc;* **two hours***/etc* **to go** encore deux heures*/etc.*

go[2], *pl* **goes** *(attempt)* coup *m;* **to have a go at (doing) sth** essayer (de faire) qch; **on the go** actif.

▸**go about, go around 1** *vi* se déplacer; *(of news)* circuler. **2** *vt* **to know how to go about it** savoir s'y prendre.

▸**go across** *vti (cross)* traverser.

▸**go after** *vt (chase)* poursuivre; *(seek)* (re)chercher.

go-a·head to get the g. avoir le feu vert.

▸**go ahead** *vi* avancer; *(continue)* continuer; *(start)* commencer; **go ahead!** allez-y!; **to go ahead with** *(plan etc)* poursuivre.

goal but *m.*

goal·keep·er gardien *m* de but.

▸**go along** *vi* aller; **to go along with** *(agree)* être d'accord avec.

▸**go around 1** *vi (turn)* tourner; *(be sufficient)* suffire. **2** *vt (corner)* tourner; *(world)* faire le tour de.

goat chèvre *f.*

▸**go away** *vi* partir, s'en aller.

▸**go back** *vi* retourner; *(in time)* remonter; *(step back)* reculer; **to go back on** *(promise)* revenir sur.

go-be·tween intermédiaire *mf.*

god dieu *m;* **G.** Dieu *m.*

god·daugh·ter filleule *f.*

god·fa·ther parrain *m.*

god·moth·er marraine *f.*

▸**go down 1** *vi* descendre; *(fall down)* tomber; *(of ship)* couler; *(of sun)* se coucher; *(of price etc)* baisser. **2** *vt* **to go down the stairs/street** descendre l'escalier/la rue.

god·send to be a g. tomber à pic.

god·son filleul *m.*

goes *see* **go**¹.

gog·gles *npl* lunettes *fpl* (de protection, de plongée).

▸**go in 1** *vi* (r)entrer; *(of sun)* se cacher. **2** *vt* **to go into a room**/*etc* entrer dans une pièce/*etc*.

▸**go (in) for** *vt* s'intéresser à.

go·ing 1 *n (conditions)* conditions *fpl*; **it's slow** *or* **tough g.** c'est difficile. **2** *adj* **the g. price** le prix pratiqué (**for** pour).

go·ings-on *npl* activités *fpl*.

▸**go into** *vt (room etc)* entrer dans.

gold *or m*; **g. watch**/*etc* montre/*etc* en or.

gold·en *adj (in color)* doré; *(rule)* d'or.

gold·fish poisson *m* rouge.

gold mine mine *f* d'or.

gold-plat·ed *adj* plaqué or.

golf golf *m*.

golf·er golfeur, -euse *mf*.

gone *pp de* **go**¹.

good 1 *adj* bon (*f* bonne); *(kind)* gentil; *(weather)* beau (*f* belle); *(well-behaved)* sage; **very g.!** *(all right)* très bien!; **to feel g.** se sentir bien; **g. at French**/*etc* bon *or* fort en français/*etc*; **to be g. with** *(children)* savoir s'y prendre avec; **it's a g. thing (that)...** heureusement que...; **a g. many, a g. deal (of)** beaucoup (de); **g. morning** bonjour; *(on leaving)* au revoir; **g. evening** bonsoir; **g. night** bonsoir; *(going to bed)* bonne nuit. **2** *n (advantage, virtue)* bien *m*; **for her own g.** pour son bien; **it's no g. crying**/*etc* ça ne sert à rien de pleurer/*etc*; **that's no g.** *(worthless)* ça ne vaut rien; *(bad)* ça ne va pas; **what's the g.?** à quoi bon?; **for g.** pour de bon.

good·bye *int* au revoir.

good-look·ing *adj* beau (*f* belle).

good·ness bonté *f*; **my g.!** mon Dieu!; **thank g.!** Dieu merci!; **for g.' sake!** bon sang!

goods *npl* marchandises *fpl*; *(articles for sale)* articles *mpl*.

good·will bonne volonté *f*.

▸**go off** *vi (leave)* partir; *(of alarm)* se déclencher.

▸**go on** *vi* continuer (**doing** à faire); *(happen)* se passer; *(last)* durer.

goose, *pl* **geese** oie *f*.

goose·ber·ry groseille *f* à maquereau.

goose bumps *npl* chair *f* de poule.

▸**go out** *vi* sortir; *(of light, fire)* s'éteindre.

▸**go over 1** *vi* aller (**to** à); *(to enemy)* passer (**to** à); **to go over to sb's** faire un saut chez qn. **2** *vt* examiner; *(in one's mind)* repasser.

gorge *(ravine)* gorge *f*.

gor·geous *adj* magnifique.

go·ril·la gorille *m*.

Gos·pel Évangile *m*.

gos·sip 1 *n (talk)* bavardage(s) *m(pl)*; *(person)* commère *f*. **2** *vi (to talk)* bavarder; *(ill-naturedly)* se livrer à des commérages.

got *pt & pp de* **get**.

▸**go through 1** *vi* passer. **2** *vt (suffer)* subir; *(examine)* examiner; *(search)* fouiller; *(spend)* dépenser; *(wear out)* user.

got·ten *pp de* **get**.

▸**go under** *vi (of ship, company)* couler.

▸**go up 1** *vi* monter; *(of prices)* augmenter. **2** *vt* **to go up the stairs/ street** monter l'escalier/la rue.

gour·met gourmet *m*.

gov·ern 1 *vt (rule)* gouverner; *(city)* administrer; *(influence)* déterminer. **2** *vi* gouverner.

gov·ern·ment gouvernement *m*; *(local)* administration *f*.

gov·er·nor gouverneur *m*.

▸**go with** *vt (accompany)* accompagner, aller avec; *(colors)* aller avec.

▸**go without** *vt* se passer de.

gown *(of woman)* robe *f*.

grab *vt* **to g. (hold of)** saisir; **to g. sth from sb** arracher qch à qn.

grace *(charm)* grâce *f*.

grace·ful adj gracieux.

grade 1 n catégorie f; (in exam etc) note f; (class in school) classe f. **2** vt (classify) classer; (school paper) noter, corriger.

grade cross·ing passage m à niveau.

grade school école f primaire.

grad·u·al adj progressif.

gradu·al·ly adv progressivement.

grad·u·ate 1 vi obtenir son diplôme. **2** n diplômé, -ée mf.

grad·u·a·tion remise f des diplômes.

graf·fi·ti npl graffiti mpl.

graft 1 n greffe f. **2** vt greffer.

grain (seed) grain m; (cereal) céréales fpl.

gram gramme m.

gram·mar grammaire f.

gram·mar school = **grade school**.

gram·mat·i·cal adj grammatical.

grand adj (splendid) magnifique.

grand-dad(·dy) Fam papi m.

grand·child, pl -children petit(e)-enfant mf.

grand·daugh·ter petite-fille f.

grand·fa·ther grand-père m.

grand·ma Fam mamie f.

grand·moth·er grand-mère f.

grand·par·ents npl grands-parents mpl.

grand·son petit-fils m.

gran·ny Fam mamie f.

gra·no·la muesli m.

grant 1 vt accorder (to à); (request) accéder à; **to take sth for granted** considérer qch comme acquis; **I take it for granted that** je présume que. **2** n subvention f; (for study) bourse f.

grape grain m de raisin; **grapes** le raisin, les raisins mpl; **to eat (some) grapes** manger du raisin or des raisins.

grape·fruit pamplemousse m.

graph courbe f; **g. paper** papier m millimétré.

graph·ic adj graphique; **g. designer** graphiste mf.

graph·ics n (study) art m graphique. **2** npl graphiques mpl.

grasp 1 vt (seize, understand) saisir. **2** n (hold) prise f; (understanding) compréhension f.

grass herbe f; (lawn) gazon m.

grass·hop·per sauterelle f.

grate 1 n (for fireplace) grille f de foyer. **2** vt (cheese etc) râper.

grate·ful adj reconnaissant (to à; for de); **I'm g. (to you) for your help** je vous suis reconnaissant de votre aide.

grat·er râpe f.

grat·i·fy·ing adj très satisfaisant or agréable.

grat·i·tude reconnaissance f, gratitude f (for de).

grave^1 tombe f.

grave^2 adj (serious) grave.

grav·el gravier m.

grave·yard cimetière m.

grav·i·ty (force) pesanteur f.

gra·vy jus m de viande.

gray adj gris; **to be going g.** grisonner.

graze 1 vi (of cattle) paître. **2** vt (skin) écorcher. **3** n (wound) écorchure f.

grease 1 n graisse f. **2** vt graisser.

greas·y adj plein de graisse; (hair) gras.

great adj grand; (excellent) Fam magnifique; **a g. deal (of), a g. many** beaucoup (de); **the greatest team/etc** (best) la meilleure équipe/etc.

great-grand·fa·ther arrière-grand-père m.

great-grand·moth·er arrière-grand-mère f.

great·ly (much) beaucoup; (very) très.

greed avidité f; (for food) gourmandise f.

greed·y adj avide; (for food) gourmand.

Greek 1 adj grec (f grecque). **2** n Grec m, Greque f, (language) grec m.

green 1 adj vert; **to turn** or **go g.** verdir. **2** n (color) vert m; (lawn) pelouse f; **greens** légumes mpl verts.

green·house serre f; **g. effect** effet m de serre.

greet vt saluer.

greet·ing salutation f; **greetings** (for birthday, festival) vœux mpl.

gre·nade (bomb) grenade f.

grey·hound lévrier m.

grid (on map) quadrillage m; (bars) grille f.

grief chagrin m.

grieve vi **to g. for sb** pleurer qn.

grill 1 n (utensil) gril m; (dish) grillade f. **2** vti griller.

grim adj (face, future) sombre; (bad) Fam affreux.

grime crasse f.

grim·y adj crasseux.

grin 1 vi avoir un large sourire. **2** n large sourire m.

grind* vt moudre; **to g. one's teeth** grincer des dents.

grind·er coffee g. moulin m à café.

grip 1 vt saisir; (hold) tenir serré. **2** n (hold) prise f, (with hand) poigne f, **in the g. of** en proie à.

grip·ping adj (book etc) prenant.

groan 1 vi gémir. **2** n gémissement m.

gro·cer épicier, -ière mf.

gro·cer·y g. store magasin m d'alimentation; **groceries** (food) épicerie f.

groin aine f.

groom (bridegroom) marié m.

groove (slot) rainure f.

▸ **grope around** vi tâtonner.

▸ **grope for** vt chercher à tâtons.

gross adj (total) (income etc) brut.

gross·ly adv (very) extrêmement.

ground terre f, sol m; (for camping etc) terrain m; **grounds** (reasons) raisons fpl, (gardens) parc m; **on the g.** (lying, sitting) par terre.

ground meat hachis m (de viande).

ground·work préparation f.

group groupe m.

group (to·geth·er) vti (se) grouper.

grow* **1** vi (of person) grandir; (of plant, hair) pousser; (increase) augmenter, grandir; (of company, town) se développer. **2** vt (plant, crops) cultiver; (beard) laisser pousser.

▸ **grow into** vt devenir.

growl vi grogner (at contre).

grown adj (man, woman) adulte.

grown-up grande personne f.

▸ **grow out of** vt (clothes) devenir trop grand pour; (habit) perdre.

growth croissance f, (increase) augmentation f (in de); (lump) tumeur f (on à).

▸ **grow up** vi devenir adulte.

grub (food) Fam bouffe f.

grub·by adj sale.

grudge rancune f; **to have a g. against** garder rancune à.

gru·el·ing adj éprouvant.

grue·some adj horrible.

grum·ble vi râler, grogner (about, at contre).

grump·y adj grincheux.

grunt 1 vti grogner. **2** n grognement m.

guar·an·tee 1 n garantie f. **2** vt garantir (against contre; sb that à qn que).

guard 1 n (vigilance, soldiers) garde f, (individual person) garde m; **to keep a g. on** surveiller; **under g.** sous surveillance; **on one's g.** sur ses gardes; **on g. (duty)** de garde; **to stand g.** monter la garde. **2** vt protéger; (watch over) surveiller.

guard·i·an gardien, -enne mf; (of minor) tuteur, -trice mf; (of museum) conservateur, -trice mf; **g. angel** ange m gardien.

guess 1 n conjecture f, (intuition) intuition f; **to make a g.** (essayer de) deviner. **2** vt deviner (that que); (length, number) estimer; (suppose) supposer; (think) croire (that que).

guess·work hypothèse *f*; **by g.** au jugé.

guest invité, -ée *mf*; *(in hotel)* client, -ente *mf*; *(at meal)* convive *mf*.

guest room chambre *f* d'amis.

guid·ance conseils *mpl*.

guide 1 *n* guide *m*; **g. (book)** guide *m*. **2** *vt* guider; **guided tour** visite *f* guidée.

guide·lines *npl* indications *fpl* (à suivre).

guild association *f*.

guilt culpabilité *f*.

guilt·y *adj* coupable; **g. person** coupable *mf*.

gui·nea pig cobaye *m*.

gui·tar guitare *f*.

· **gui·tar·ist** guitariste *mf*.

gulf *(in sea)* golfe *m*; **a g. between** un abîme entre.

gull *(bird)* mouette *f*.

gulp *(of drink)* gorgée *f*.

▸ **gulp down** *vt* avaler (vite).

gum¹ *(around teeth)* gencive *f*.

gum² **1** *n* *(for chewing)* chewing-gum *m*; *(glue)* colle *f*. **2** *vt* coller.

gun pistolet *m*; *(rifle)* fusil *m*; *(firing shells)* canon *m*.

▸ **gun down** *vt* abattre.

gun·fire coups *mpl* de feu.

gun·man, *pl* **-men** bandit *m* armé.

gun·point at g. sous la menace d'une arme.

gun·pow·der poudre *f* à canon.

gun·shot coup *m* de feu.

gush (out) *vi* jaillir (*of* de).

gust **g. (of wind)** rafale *f* (de vent).

gut 1 *n* intestin *m*; **guts** *(insides)* entrailles *fpl*; *Fam (courage)* cran *m*. **2** *vt* *(poultry, fish)* étriper; *(house)* ravager.

gut·ter *(on roof)* gouttière *f*; *(in street)* caniveau *m*.

guy *Fam* type *m*.

gym gym *f*(nastique) *f*, *(gymnasium)* gymnase *m*.

gym·nas·tics gymnastique *f*.

gy·ne·col·o·gist gynécologue *mf*.

H

hab·it habitude *f*; **to be in/get into the h. of doing** avoir/prendre l'habitude de faire.

hab·i·tat habitat *m*.

hack *vt (cut)* tailler.

hack·er (computer) h. pirate *m* informatique.

had *pt & pp de* **have**.

had·dock aiglefin *m*; **smoked h.** haddock *m*.

hag (old) h. (vieille) sorcière *f*.

hag·gle *vi* marchander; **to h. over the price** discuter le prix.

hail 1 *n* grêle *f*. **2** *vi* grêler; **it's hailing** il grêle.

hail·stone grêlon *m*.

hair *(on head)* cheveux *mpl*; *(on body, of animal)* poils *mpl*; **a h.** *(on head)* un cheveu; *(on body, of animal)* un poil.

hair·brush brosse *f* à cheveux.

hair·cut coupe *f* de cheveux; **to get a h.** se faire couper les cheveux.

hair·do, *pl* **-dos** *Fam* coiffure *f*.

hair·dress·er coiffeur, -euse *mf*.

hair dry·er sèche-cheveux *m inv*.

-haired *suffix* **long-/red-h.** aux cheveux longs/roux.

hair·pin épingle *f* à cheveux.

hair-rais·ing *adj* effrayant.

hair spray (bombe *f* de) laque *f*.

hair·style coiffure *f*.

hair·y *adj (person, animal, body)* poilu.

half 1 *n* (*pl* **halves**) moitié *f*, demi, -ie *mf*; **h. (of) the apple/*etc*** la moitié de la pomme/*etc*; **ten and a h.** dix et demi; **ten and a h. weeks** dix semaines et demie; **to cut in h.** couper en deux. **2** *adj* demi; **h. a day, a h.-day** une demi-journée; **h. a dozen, a h.-dozen** une demi-douzaine; **at h. price** à moitié prix. **3** adv (full etc) à demi, à moitié; **h. past one** une heure et demie.

half·heart·ed adj peu enthousiaste.

half-hour demi-heure f.

half-time (in game) mi-temps f.

half·way adv à mi-chemin (**between** entre); **to fill/etc h.** remplir/etc à moitié.

hal·i·but (fish) flétan m.

hall salle f; **lecture h.** amphithéâtre m.

Hal·low·e'en Halloween m (la veille de la Toussaint).

hall·way entrée f.

halt halte f; **to call a h. to** mettre fin à.

halve vt (time, expense) réduire de moitié.

ham jambon m; **h. and eggs** œufs mpl au jambon.

ham·burg·er hamburger m; (raw meat) bœuf m haché.

ham·mer 1 n marteau m. **2** vt (nail) enfoncer (**into** dans).

ham·mer·ing (defeat) Fam raclée f.

ham·mock hamac m.

ham·per 1 vt gêner. **2** n panier m; (laundry basket) panier m à linge.

ham·ster hamster m.

hand[1] main f; (of clock) aiguille f; Cards jeu m; **to hold in one's h.** tenir à la main; **to give sb a (helping) h.** donner un coup de main à qn; **by h.** (to make, sew etc) à la main; **at** or **to h.** sous la main; **on h.** disponible; **out of h.** (situation) incontrôlable.

hand[2] vt (give) donner, passer (**to** à).

▸ **hand around** vt (cookies) passer.

hand·bag sac m à main.

hand·book manuel m; (guide) guide m.

hand·brake frein m à main.

hand·cuff vt passer les menottes à.

hand·cuffs npl menottes fpl.

hand·ful (group) poignée f.

hand·i·cap 1 n handicap m. **2** vt handicaper; **to be handicapped** (after an accident etc) rester handicapé.

hand·i·capped adj handicapé.

▸ **hand in** vt remettre.

hand·ker·chief, pl **-fs** mouchoir m.

han·dle 1 n (of door) poignée f; (of knife) manche m; (of bucket) anse f; (of saucepan) queue f. **2** vt (manipulate) manier; (touch) toucher à; (vehicle) manœuvrer; (deal with) s'occuper de.

han·dle·bars npl guidon m.

hand lug·gage bagages mpl à main.

hand·made adj fait à la main.

hand·out (leaflet) prospectus m; (money) aumône f; (papers for course, workshop) photocopies fpl.

▸ **hand out** vt distribuer.

▸ **hand over** vt remettre.

hand·rail rampe f.

hand·shake poignée f de main.

hand·some adj beau (f belle); (profit) considérable.

hand·writ·ing écriture f.

hand·y adj commode, pratique; (skillful) habile (**at doing** à faire); (within reach) sous la main; (place) accessible.

hand·y·man, pl **-men** bricoleur m.

hang[1]* **1** vt (pt & pp hung) suspendre (**on, from** à); (let dangle) laisser pendre (**from, out of** de). **2** vi pendre; (of fog) flotter. **3** n **to get the h. of sth** Fam arriver à comprendre qch.

hang[2] vt (pt & pp hanged) (criminal) pendre (**for** pour).

han·gar hangar m.

▸ **hang around** vi traîner; (wait) attendre.

▸ **hang down** vi pendre.

hang·er (coat) **h.** cintre m.

hang·glid·er deltaplane® *m*.

hang·ing *adj* suspendu (**from** à).

▸**hang on** *vi* résister; *(wait)* attendre; **h. on to** ne pas lâcher; *(keep)* garder.

▸**hang out 1** *vt (laundry)* étendre; *(flag)* arborer. **2** *vi (of tongue, shirt)* pendre.

hang·o·ver gueule *f* de bois.

▸**hang up 1** *vt (picture)* accrocher. **2** *vi (on phone)* raccrocher.

hang-up complexe *m*.

hap·pen *vi* arriver, se passer; **to h. to sb/sth** arriver à qn/qch; **I h. to know** il se trouve que je le sais; **do you h. to have…?** est-ce que par hasard vous avez…?

hap·pen·ing événement *m*.

hap·pi·ly *adv* joyeusement; *(contentedly)* tranquillement; *(fortunately)* heureusement.

hap·pi·ness bonheur *m*.

hap·py *adj* heureux (**to do** de faire; **about sth** de qch); **I'm not h. about it** ça ne me plaît pas beaucoup; **H. New Year!** bonne année!

ha·rass *vt* harceler.

ha·rass·ment harcèlement *m*.

har·bor port *m*.

hard 1 *adj (not soft, severe, difficult)* dur; **h. worker** gros travailleur *m*; **h. on sb** dur avec qn; **h. of hearing** malentendant. **2** *adv (to work, hit)* dur; *(to pull)* fort; *(to rain)* à verse; **to think h.** réfléchir bien.

hard·ball *(game)* base-ball *m*; *(ball)* balle *f* de base-ball.

hard-boiled *adj (egg)* dur.

hard cop·y *(document)* copie *f* (sur) papier.

hard-core *(group)* noyau *m*.

hard disk disque *m* dur.

hard·en *vti* durcir; **to become hardened to** s'endurcir à.

hard·ly *adv* à peine; **h. anyone** presque personne; **h. ever** presque jamais.

hard·ness dureté *f*.

hard·ship épreuve(s) *f(pl)*.

hard up *adj (broke) Fam* fauché.

hard·ware *n inv* quincaillerie *f*; *(of computer)* matériel *m*.

hard·ware store quincaillerie *f*.

hard-work·ing *adj* travailleur.

hare lièvre *m*.

harm 1 *n (hurt)* mal *m*; *(wrong)* tort *m*. **2** *vt (physically)* faire du mal à; *(health, interests etc)* nuire à.

harm·ful *adj* nuisible.

harm·less *adj* inoffensif.

har·mon·i·ca harmonica *m*.

har·mo·ni·ous *adj* harmonieux.

har·mo·ny harmonie *f*.

har·ness *(for horse)* harnais *m*; *(to carry baby)* porte-bébé *m* ventral.

harp harpe *f*.

▸**harp on** *vt Fam* ne pas s'arrêter de parler de.

harsh *adj* dur, sévère; *(sound, taste)* âpre.

harshly *adv* durement.

harshness dureté *f*.

har·vest 1 *n* moisson *f*, *(of fruit)* récolte *f*. **2** *vt* moissonner; récolter.

has *see* have.

has·sle *Fam (trouble)* histoires *fpl*; *(aggravation)* **it's a h.** c'est casse-pieds *inv*.

haste hâte *f*; **to make h.** se hâter.

has·ten 1 *vi* se hâter (**to do** de faire). **2** *vt* hâter.

has·ti·ly *adv* à la hâte.

hast·y *adj* précipité; *(visit)* rapide.

hat chapeau *m*; *(of child)* bonnet *m*; *(cap)* casquette *f*.

hatch *vi (of chick, egg)* éclore.

hatch·back *(three-door)* trois-portes *f inv*; *(five-door)* cinq-portes *f inv*.

hate *vt* détester, haïr; **to h. doing** *or* **to do** détester faire.

hate·ful *adj* haïssable.

ha·tred haine *f*.

haul *vt (pull)* tirer.

haunt 1 *n (place)* lieu *m* de prédilection; *(of criminal)* repaire *m*. **2** *vt* hanter.

haunt·ed *adj* hanté.

have* **1** *vt* avoir; *(meal, drink etc)* prendre; **to h. a party/dream** faire une fête/un rêve; **will you h...?** *(some cake, tea etc)* est-ce que tu veux...?; **to let sb h. sth** donner qch à qn; **you've had it!** *Fam* tu es fichu! **2** *v aux* avoir; *(with 'monter', 'sortir' etc and reflexive verbs)* être; **to h. decided/been** avoir décidé/été; **to h. gone** être allé; **to h. cut oneself** s'être coupé; **I've got to go, I h. to go** je dois partir; **to h. sth done** faire faire qch; **he's had his suitcase brought up** il a fait monter sa valise; **haven't I?, hasn't she?/etc** n'est-ce pas?; **no I haven't!** non!; **yes I h.!** oui!; *(after negative question)* si!

hav·oc ravages *mpl*.

hawk faucon *m*.

hay foin *m*.

hay fe·ver rhume *m* des foins.

hay·stack meule *f* de foin.

haz·ard **1** *n* risque *m*. **2** *vt* risquer; **to h. a guess** essayer de deviner.

haze brume *f*.

ha·zel·nut noisette *f*.

haz·y *adj (weather)* brumeux; *(photo, idea)* flou.

he *pron* il; *(stressed)* lui; **he's a happy man** c'est un homme heureux.

head **1** *n (of person, hammer etc)* tête *f*; *(leader)* chef *m*; **it didn't enter my h.** ça ne m'est pas venu à l'esprit; **heads or tails?** pile ou face?; **per h., a h.** *(each)* par personne. **2** *adj (salesperson etc)* principal. **3** *vt (group, company)* être à la tête de; *(list)* être en tête de.

head·ache mal *m* de tête; **to have a h.** avoir mal à la tête.

head·band bandeau *m*.

▸**head for, be head·ing or head·ed for** *vt (place)* se diriger vers; *(disaster)* aller à.

head·ing *(of chapter etc)* titre *m*; *(of subject)* rubrique *f*.

head·light *(of vehicle)* phare *m*.

head·line *(of newspaper)* manchette *f*; **the headlines** les titres *mpl*.

head·mas·ter *(of school)* directeur *m*.

head·mis·tress *(of school)* directrice *f*.

head·phones *npl* casque *m* (à écouteurs).

head·quar·ters *npl* siège *m* (central); *(military)* quartier *m* général.

head·wait·er maître *m* d'hôtel.

head·way progrès *mpl*.

heal *vi (of wound)* se cicatriser; *(of bruise)* disparaître; *(of bone)* se ressouder.

health santé *f*.

health care soins *mpl* médicaux.

health food aliment *m* naturel; **h. food store** magasin *m* diététique.

health in·sur·ance assurance *f* maladie.

health·y *adj (person)* en bonne santé; *(food, attitude etc)* sain.

heap **1** *n* tas *m*; **heaps of** *(money, people)* *Fam* des tas de. **2** *vt* entasser.

▸**heap on** *vt* **to h. sth on sb** *(praise)* couvrir qn de qch; *(insults)* accabler qn de qch.

hear* **1** *vt* entendre; *(listen to)* écouter; *(learn)* apprendre (**that** que). **2** *vi* entendre; *(get news)* recevoir des nouvelles (**from** de); **I've heard of** or **about him** j'ai entendu parler de lui.

hear·ing *(sense)* ouïe *f*.

hear·ing aid appareil *m* auditif.

hearse corbillard *m*.

heart cœur *m*; **heart(s)** *Cards* cœur *m*; **by h.** par cœur.

heart at·tack crise *f* cardiaque.

heart·beat battement *m* de cœur.

heart·break·ing *adj* navrant.

heart·en·ing *adj* encourageant.

heart·y *adj (appetite)* gros (*f* grosse).

heat chaleur *f; (heating)* chauffage *m.*

heat (up) *vti* chauffer.

heat·er radiateur *m.*

heath lande *f.*

heat·ing chauffage *m.*

heat wave vague *f* de chaleur.

heave 1 *vt (lift)* soulever; *(pull)* tirer; *(a sigh)* pousser. **2** *(feel sick)* avoir des haut-le-cœur.

heav·en ciel *m;* **h.** knows when Dieu sait quand.

heav·i·ly *adv* lourdement; *(to smoke, drink)* beaucoup; **to rain h.** pleuvoir à verse.

heav·y *adj* lourd; *(rain)* fort; *(traffic)* dense; *(smoker, drinker)* grand.

heav·y·weight *Boxing* poids *m* lourd; *(important person)* personnage *m* important.

He·brew *(language)* hébreu *m.*

hec·tic *adj* fiévreux; *(period)* très agité.

hedge haie *f.*

hedge·hog hérisson *m.*

heel talon *m.*

heft·y *adj* gros (*f* grosse).

height hauteur *f; (of person)* taille *f; (of success etc)* sommet *m;* **at the h. of** *(summer)* au cœur de.

heir héritier *m.*

heir·ess héritière *f.*

held *pt & pp de* **hold.**

hel·i·cop·ter hélicoptère *m.*

hell enfer *m;* **a h. of a lot (of)** *(very many, very much)* Fam énormément (de); **h.!** Fam zut!

hel·lo! *int* bonjour!; *(answering phone)* allô!; *(surprise)* tiens!

helm *(of boat)* barre *f.*

hel·met casque *m.*

help 1 *n* aide *f,* secours *m; (cleaning woman)* femme *f* de ménage; *(workers in office, store)* employés, -ées *mfpl;* **h.!** au secours! **2** *vt* aider *(do, to do* à faire); **to h. oneself (to)** se servir (de); **I can't h. laugh-**

ing/*etc* je ne peux pas m'empêcher de rire/*etc.*

help·er assistant, -ante *mf.*

help·ful *adj* utile; *(person)* serviable.

help·ing *(serving)* portion *f.*

help·less *adj (powerless)* impuissant; *(disabled)* impotent.

▶**help out** *vti* aider.

hem ourlet *m.*

hem·i·sphere hémisphère *m.*

hemmed in *adj* enfermé; *(surrounded)* cerné.

hem·or·rhage hémorragie *f.*

hep·a·ti·tis hépatite *f.*

her 1 *pron* la, l'; *(after prep, 'than', 'it is')* elle; **(to) h.** lui; **I see h.** je la vois; **I give it to h.** je le/la lui donne. **2** *poss adj* son, sa, *pl* ses.

herb herbe *f,* **herbs** *(in cooking)* fines herbes *fpl.*

herd troupeau *m.*

here *adv* ici; **h. is, h. are** voici; **h. she is** la voici; **summer is h.** l'été est là; **h.!** *(answering roll call)* présent!; **h. (you are)!** *(take this)* tenez!

he·red·i·ta·ry *adj* héréditaire.

her·mit solitaire *mf.*

he·ro, *pl* -oes héros *m.*

he·ro·ic *adj* héroïque.

her·o·in *(drug)* héroïne *f.*

her·o·ine héroïne *f.*

her·ring hareng *m.*

hers *poss pron* le sien, la sienne, *pl* les sien(ne)s; **this hat is h.** ce chapeau est à elle *or* est le sien.

her·self *pron* elle-même; *(reflexive)* se, s'; *(after prep)* elle.

hes·i·tant *adj* hésitant.

hes·i·tate *vi* hésiter (**about** sur; **to do** à faire).

hes·i·ta·tion hésitation *f.*

hey! *int* hé!; *(calling attention)* holà! le hoquet.

hi! *int* Fam salut!

hic·cups *npl* **to have (the) h.** avoir le hoquet.

hide¹ * **1** *vt* cacher (**from** à). **2** *vi* se cacher (**from** de).

hide² *(skin)* peau *f.*

hide-and-seek cache-cache *m inv.*

hid·e·ous *adj* horrible.

hid·e·ous·ly *adv* horriblement.

hide-out cachette *f.*

hid·ing a good h. *(beating)* une bonne raclée.

hid·ing place cachette *f.*

hi·er·ar·chy hiérarchie *f.*

hi-fi hi-fi *f inv.*

high 1 *adj* haut; *(speed)* grand; *(price, number)* élevé; *(on drugs) Fam* défoncé; **h. fever** forte fièvre *f*; **to be 16 feet h.** avoir 5 mètres de haut. **2** *adv* **h. (up)** *(to fly, throw etc)* haut. **3** *n* an all-time h. un nouveau record.

high·chair chaise *f* haute.

high-class *adj (service)* de premier ordre; *(building)* de luxe.

high·er *adj* supérieur (**than** à).

high·er ed·u·ca·tion enseignement *m* supérieur.

high·lands *npl* régions *fpl* montagneuses.

high·light 1 *n (of visit, day)* point *m* culminant; *(of show)* clou *m*. **2** *vt* souligner.

high·ly *adv (very)* très; *(to recommend)* chaudement; **h. paid** très bien payé.

high-pitched *adj (sound)* aigu (*f* -uë).

high-rise *adj* **h. apartment building** tour *f.*

high school *(ages 11–15)* = collège *m*; *(ages 15–18)* = lycée *m.*

high school di·plo·ma = baccalauréat *m.*

high-speed *adj* ultra-rapide; **h. train** rapide *m.*

high·way autoroute *f.*

hi·jack *vt (aircraft)* détourner.

hi·jack·er pirate *m* de l'air.

hi·jack·ing piraterie *f* aérienne; *(one incident)* détournement *m.*

hike 1 *n* excursion *f* à pied. **2** *vi* marcher à pied.

hik·er excursionniste *mf.*

hi·lar·i·ous *adj* hilarant.

hill colline *f.*

hill·side on the h. à flanc de colline.

hill·y *adj* accidenté.

him *pron* le, l'; *(after prep, 'than', 'it is')* lui; **(to) h.** lui; **I see h.** je le vois; **I give it to h.** je le/la lui donne.

him·self *pron* lui-même; *(reflexive)* se, s'; *(after prep)* lui.

hin·der *vt* gêner.

Hin·du 1 *n* Hindou, -oue *mf.* **2** *adj* hindou, -oue.

hinge charnière *f.*

hint 1 *n* allusion *f*, *(sign)* indication *f*, **hints** *(advice)* conseils *mpl.* **2** *vt* laisser entendre (**that** que).

▸ **hint at** *vt* faire allusion à.

hip hanche *f.*

hip·po·pot·a·mus hippopotame *m.*

hire *vt (worker)* engager, embaucher.

his 1 *poss adj* son, sa, *pl* ses. **2** *poss pron* le sien, la sienne, *pl* les sien(ne)s; **this hat is h.** ce chapeau est à lui *or* est le sien.

His·pan·ic 1 *n* Hispano-Américain, -aine *mf.* **2** *adj* hispano-américain, -aine.

hiss 1 *vti* siffler. **2** *n* sifflement *m.*

his·tor·i·c, his·tor·i·cal *adj* historique.

his·to·ry histoire *f.*

hit* 1 *vt (beat etc)* frapper; *(bump into)* heurter; *(reach)* atteindre; *(affect)* toucher. **2** *n (blow)* coup *m*; *(play, film)* succès *m*; **h. (song)** chanson *f* à succès.

hit-and-run driv·er chauffard *m.*

hitch 1 *n (snag)* problème *m*. **2** *vti* **to h. (a ride)** *Fam* faire du stop (**to** jusqu'à).

hitch·hike *vi* faire de l'auto-stop (**to** jusqu'à).

hitch·hik·er auto-stoppeur, -euse *mf.*

hitch·hik·ing auto-stop *m.*

▸ **hit (up)on** *vt (find)* tomber sur.

HIV *abbr (human immunodefi-*

ciency virus) VIH *m*, HIV *m*; **to be H. positive/negative** être séropositif/ séronégatif.

hive ruche *f*.

hoard *vt* amasser.

hoarse *adj* enroué.

hoax canular *m*.

hob·by passe-temps *m inv*.

ho·bo, *pl* **-os** vagabond, -onde *mf*.

hock·ey hockey *m*; **ice h.** hockey *m* sur glace.

hold 1 *n (grip)* prise *f*; *(of ship)* cale *f*; *(of aircraft)* soute *f*; **to get h. of** saisir; *(contact)* joindre; *(find)* trouver. **2** *vt** tenir; *(breath, interest, attention)* retenir; *(a post)* occuper; *(a record)* détenir; *(possess)* posséder; *(contain)* contenir; **to h. hands** se tenir par la main; **please h.** *(on phone)* ne quittez pas; **to be held** *(of event)* avoir lieu. **3** *vi (of nail, rope)* tenir; **if the rain holds off** s'il ne pleut pas.

▸**hold back** *vt (crowd)* contenir; *(hide)* cacher.

▸**hold down** *vt (price)* maintenir bas; *(job)* garder.

hold·er *(of passport)* titulaire *mf*; *(of record)* détenteur, -trice *mf*; *(container)* support *m*.

▸**hold on** *vi* attendre; *(stand firm)* tenir bon; **h. on!** *(on phone)* ne quittez pas!; **h. on (tight)** tenez bon!

▸**hold onto** *vt (cling to)* tenir bien; *(keep)* garder.

▸**hold out 1** *vt* offrir; *(arm)* étendre. **2** *vi* résister; *(last)* durer.

hold·up *(attack)* hold-up *m inv*; *(traffic jam)* bouchon *m*.

▸**hold up** *vt* lever; *(support)* soutenir; *(delay)* retarder; *(bank)* attaquer.

hole trou *m*.

hol·i·day *(legal)* jour *m* férié; **holidays** *(from school, work etc)* vacances *fpl*.

hol·low *adj & n* creux *(m)*.

hol·ly houx *m*.

ho·ly *adj* saint; *(water)* bénit.

home 1 *n* maison *f*, *(country)* pays *m* (natal); **at h.** à la maison, chez soi; **to make oneself at h.** se mettre à l'aise; **a good h.** une bonne famille; **(retirement) h.** maison *f* de retraite; **h. life/cooking/etc** la vie/ cuisine/etc familiale. **2** *adv* à la maison, chez soi; **to go** *or* **come (back) h.** rentrer; **to be h.** être rentré.

home·land patrie *f*.

home·less *adj* sans abri.

home·made *adj* (fait à la) maison *inv*.

home·sick *adj* **to be h.** *(when abroad)* avoir le mal du pays; *(in general)* être nostalgique.

home·town ville *f* natale.

home·work devoir(s) *m(pl)*.

ho·mo·sex·u·al *adj & n* homosexuel, -elle *(mf)*.

hon·est *adj* honnête; *(frank)* franc *(f* franche) *(with* avec).

hon·es·ty honnêteté *f*, *(frankness)* franchise *f*.

hon·ey miel *m*; *(person) Fam* chéri, -ie *mf*.

hon·ey·moon lune *f* de miel; *(trip)* voyage *m* de noces.

honk *vi (in vehicle)* klaxonner.

hon·or 1 *n* honneur *m*; **in h. of** en l'honneur de; **with honors** *(academic distinction)* avec mention. **2** *vt* honorer *(with* de).

hon·or·a·ble *adj* honorable.

hood capuchon *m*; *(mask of robber)* cagoule *f*, *(car or carriage roof)* capote *f*, *(of car engine)* capot *m*.

hoof, *pl* **-fs** *or* **-ves** sabot *m*.

hook crochet *m*; *(on clothes)* agrafe *f*; *Fishing* hameçon *m*; **off the h.** *(phone)* décroché.

hooked *adj (nose, object)* recourbé; **h. on** *(drugs, chess etc) Fam* accro de.

▸**hook on**, **hook up** *vt* accrocher *(to* à).

hook·y to play h. sécher (la classe).

hoo·li·gan vandale m.

hoop cerceau m.

hoot 1 vi (of owl) hululer. **2** n hululement m.

hop 1 vi sauter (à cloche-pied); (of bird) sautiller; **h. in!** (in car) montez! **2** n saut m.

hope 1 n espoir m. **2** vi espérer; **I h. so** j'espère que oui. **3** vt espérer (**to** do faire; **that** que).

▸**hope for** vt espérer.

hope·ful adj optimiste; (promising) prometteur; **to be h. that** avoir bon espoir que.

hope·ful·ly (one hopes) on espère (que).

hope·less adj désespéré; (useless) nul.

hope·less·ly (extremely) complètement.

hops npl houblon m.

hop·scotch marelle f.

ho·ri·zon horizon m; **on the h.** à l'horizon.

hor·i·zon·tal adj horizontal.

horn (of animal) corne f, (on vehicle) klaxon® m.

hor·ri·ble adj horrible.

hor·ri·bly adv horriblement.

hor·rif·ic adj horrible.

hor·ri·fy vt horrifier.

hor·ror horreur f.

horse cheval m.

horse·back on h. à cheval.

horse·pow·er cheval(-vapeur) m; **10 h.** 10 chevaux.

horse·rac·ing courses fpl.

horse·shoe fer m à cheval.

hose tuyau m; (pantyhose) collant m.

hos·pi·ta·ble adj accueillant.

hos·pi·tal hôpital m; **in the h.** à l'hôpital.

hos·pi·tal·i·ty hospitalité f.

hos·pi·tal·ize vt hospitaliser.

host hôte m; (of TV show) présentateur, -trice mf.

hos·tage otage m; **to take sb h.** prendre qn en otage.

hos·tel foyer m; **youth h.** auberge f de jeunesse.

host·ess hôtesse f.

hos·tile adj hostile (**to, towards** à).

hos·til·i·ty hostilité f (**to, towards** envers).

hot adj chaud; (spice) fort; **to be** or **feel h.** avoir chaud; **it's h.** (of weather) il fait chaud.

hot·cake crêpe f.

hot dog hot-dog m.

ho·tel hôtel m.

hot-wa·ter bottle bouillotte f.

hound vt (pursue) traquer.

hour heure f; **half an h.** une demi-heure; **a quarter of an h.** un quart d'heure.

hour·ly 1 adj (pay) horaire; **an h. bus/etc** un bus/etc toutes les heures. **2** adv toutes les heures.

house¹, pl **-ses** maison f, (audience in theatre) salle f.

house² vt loger; (of building) abriter.

house·hold famille f.

house·keep·er gouvernante.

house·keep·ing ménage m (entretien).

House of Rep·re·sen·ta·tives Chambre f des représentants.

house·warm·ing to have a h. (party) pendre la crémaillère.

house·wife, pl **-wives** ménagère f.

house·work (travaux mpl de) ménage m.

hous·ing logement m; (houses) logements mpl.

hov·el taudis m.

hov·er vi (of bird etc) planer.

hov·er·craft aéroglisseur m.

how adv comment; **h. kind!** comme c'est gentil!; **h. do you do?** enchanté; **h. long/high is?** quelle est la longueur/hauteur de?; **h. much?, h. many?** combien?; **h. much time/etc?** combien de temps/*etc*?; **h. many apples/***etc*? combien de pommes/*etc*?; **h. about some coffee?** du café?

how·e·ver 1 *adv* **h. big he may be** quelque grand qu'il soit; **h. she may do it** de quelque manière qu'elle le fasse. 2 *conj* cependant.

howl 1 *vi* hurler. 2 *n* hurlement *m*.

HQ *abbr* (*headquarters*) QG *m*.

hub·cap enjoliveur *m*.

hud·dle *vi* se blottir.

hug 1 *vt* serrer (dans ses bras). 2 *n* **to give sb a h.** serrer qn (dans ses bras).

huge *adj* énorme.

huh? *int Fam* hein?

hull (*of ship*) coque *f*.

hum 1 *vi* (*of insect*) bourdonner; (*of person*) fredonner. 2 *vt* (*tune*) fredonner.

hu·man *adj* humain; **h. being** être *m* humain.

hu·man·i·ty humanité *f*.

hum·ble *adj* humble.

hu·mid *adj* humide.

hu·mid·i·ty humidité *f*.

hu·mil·i·ate *vt* humilier.

hu·mil·i·a·tion humiliation *f*.

hu·mor·ous *adj* (*book etc*) humoristique; (*person*) plein d'humour.

hu·mor (*fun*) humour *m*.

hump (*lump*) bosse *f*.

hunch *Fam* intuition *f*.

hun·dred *adj & n* cent (*m*); **a h. pages** cent pages; **hundreds of** des centaines de.

hun·dredth *adj & n* centième (*mf*).

hun·ger faim *f*.

hun·gry *adj* **to be** or **feel h.** avoir faim; **to make h.** donner faim à.

hunt 1 *n* (*search*) recherche *f* (**for** de). 2 *vt* (*animals*) chasser; (*pursue*) poursuivre; (*seek*) chercher. 3 *vi* chasser.

▸ **hunt down** *vt* traquer.

hunt·er chasseur *m*.

▸ **hunt for** *vt* (re)chercher.

hunt·ing chasse *f*.

hur·dle (*fence*) haie *f*, (*problem*) obstacle *m*.

hurl *vt* lancer.

hur·ray! *int* hourra!

hur·ri·cane ouragan *m*.

hur·ry 1 *n* hâte *f*; **in a h.** à la hâte; **to be in a h.** être pressé. 2 *vi* se dépêcher (**to do** de faire); **to h. through a meal** manger à toute vitesse; **to h. towards** se précipiter vers. 3 *vt* (*person*) bousculer.

▸ **hurry up** *vi* se dépêcher.

hurt* 1 *vt* faire du mal à; (*emotionally*) faire de la peine à; (*reputation etc*) nuire à; **to h. sb's feelings** blesser qn. 2 *vi* faire mal. 3 *n* mal *m*.

hus·band mari *m*.

hush silence *m*.

hus·tle 1 *vt* (*shove*) bousculer (*qn*). 2 *n* **h. and bustle** tourbillon *m*.

hut cabane *f*.

hy·dro·gen hydrogène *m*.

hy·giene hygiène *f*.

hy·gi·en·ic *adj* hygiénique.

hymn cantique *m*.

hy·phen trait *m* d'union.

hy·phen·at·ed *adj* (*word*) à trait d'union.

hyp·no·tize *vt* hypnotiser.

hy·poc·ri·sy hypocrisie *f*.

hy·po·crite hypocrite *mf*.

hy·poth·e·sis, *pl* -ses hypothèse *f*.

hys·ter·i·cal *adj* (*upset*) qui a une crise de nerfs; (*funny*) *Fam* désopilant.

hys·ter·i·cal·ly *adv* (**to cry**) sans pouvoir s'arrêter.

I

I *pron* je, j'; (*stressed*) moi.

ice glace *f*, (*on road*) verglas *m*.

ice·berg iceberg *m*.

ice-cold *adj* glacial; (*drink*) glacé.

ice-cream glace *f*.

ice-cream bar esquimau® *m*.

ice cube glaçon *m*.
ice-skat·ing patinage *m* (sur glace).
▶ **ice up** *vi (of windshield)* givrer.
i·ci·cle glaçon *m*.
ic·ing *(on cake)* glaçage *m*.
ic·y *adj* glacé; *(weather)* glacial; *(road)* verglacé.
ID pièce *f* d'identité.
i·de·a idée *f*; **I have an i. that** j'ai l'impression que.
i·de·al 1 *adj* idéal (*mpl* -aux *or* -als). **2** *n* idéal *m* (*pl* -aux *or* -als).
i·de·al·ly *adv* idéalement; **i. we should stay** l'idéal, ce serait que nous restions.
i·den·ti·cal *adj* identique (**to,** **with** à).
i·den·ti·fi·ca·tion *(document)* pièce *f* d'identité.
i·den·ti·fy *vt* identifier; **to i.** (one-self) **with** s'identifier avec.
i·den·ti·ty identité *f*; **i. card** carte *f* d'identité; **i. theft** vol *m* d'identité.
id·i·om expression *f* idiomatique.
id·i·ot idiot, -ote *mf*.
id·i·ot·ic *adj* idiot.
i·dle *adj (unoccupied)* inactif; *(lazy)* paresseux.
i·dler paresseux, -euse *mf*.
i·dol idole *f*.
i·dol·ize *vt (adore)* traiter comme une idole.
i.e. *abbr* c'est-à-dire.
if *conj* si; **if he comes** s'il vient; **even if** même si; **if only I were rich** si seulement j'étais riche.
ig·loo igloo *m*.
ig·no·rance ignorance *f* (of de).
ig·no·rant *adj* ignorant (of de).
ig·nore *vt* ne prêter aucune attention à *(qch)*; *(pretend not to recognize)* faire semblant de ne pas reconnaître *(qn)*.
ill 1 *adj (sick)* malade; *(bad)* mauvais. **2** *n* **ills** maux *mpl*.
il·le·gal *adj* illégal.
il·leg·i·ble *adj* illisible.
il·lit·er·ate *adj* illettré.

ill·ness maladie *f*.
ill-treat *vt* maltraiter.
il·lu·sion illusion *f* (**about** sur).
il·lus·trate *vt* illustrer (**with** de).
il·lus·tra·tion illustration *f*.
im·age image *f*; **(public) i.** *(of firm)* image *f* de marque.
i·mag·i·na·ry *adj* imaginaire.
i·mag·i·na·tion imagination *f*.
i·mag·ine *vt* (s')imaginer (**that** que).
im·i·tate *vt* imiter.
im·i·ta·tion imitation *f*; **i. jewelry** bijoux *mpl* fantaisie.
im·mac·u·late *adj* impeccable.
im·ma·ture *adj (person)* qui manque de maturité.
im·me·di·ate *adj* immédiat.
im·me·di·ate·ly 1 *adv (at once)* tout de suite, immédiatement. **2** *conj (as soon as)* dès que.
im·mense *adj* immense.
im·mense·ly *adv* extraordinaire-ment.
im·mi·grant *n & adj* immigré, -ée *(mf)*.
im·mi·gra·tion immigration *f*.
im·mi·nent *adj* imminent.
im·mor·tal *adj* immortel.
im·mune *adj (naturally)* immunisé (**to** contre); *(vaccinated)* vacciné.
im·mu·nize *vt* vacciner (**against** contre).
im·pact effet *m* (**on** sur).
im·pa·tience impatience *f*.
im·pa·tient *adj* impatient (**to do** de faire).
im·pa·tient·ly *adv* avec impa-tience.
im·per·a·tive *Grammar* impératif *m*.
im·per·son·ate *vt* se faire passer pour; *(on TV etc)* imiter.
im·per·son·a·tor *(on TV etc)* imitateur, -trice *mf*.
im·per·ti·nent *adj* impertinent (**to** envers).
im·pe·tus impulsion *f*.

im·ple·ment¹ *(tool)* instrument *m*; *(utensil)* ustensile *m*.

im·ple·ment² *vt* mettre en œuvre.

im·pli·ca·tion conséquence *f*; *(impact)* portée *f*.

im·plic·it *adj (implied)* implicite; *(absolute)* absolu.

im·ply *vt* laisser entendre (**that** que); *(assume)* impliquer.

im·po·lite *adj* impoli.

im·port 1 *vt* importer (**from** de). **2** *n* importation *f*.

im·por·tance importance *f*; **of no i.** sans importance.

im·por·tant *adj* important.

im·port·er importateur, -trice *mf*.

im·pose 1 *vt* imposer (**on** à); *(fine)* infliger (**on** à). **2** *vi (cause trouble)* déranger; **to i. on sb** déranger qn.

im·pos·ing *adj (building)* impressionnant.

im·po·si·tion *(inconvenience)* dérangement *m*.

im·pos·si·bil·i·ty impossibilité *f*.

im·pos·si·ble *adj* impossible (**to do** à faire); **it is i. (for us) to do it** il (nous) est impossible de le faire.

im·pos·tor imposteur *m*.

im·prac·ti·cal *adj* peu réaliste.

im·press *vt* impressionner (qn).

im·pres·sion impression *f*.

im·pres·sive *adj* impressionnant.

im·pris·on *vt* emprisonner.

im·prob·a·ble *adj* peu probable.

im·prop·er *adj (obscene)* indécent; *(inappropriate)* inopportun, peu approprié.

▶ **im·prove 1** *vt* améliorer. **2** *vi* s'améliorer; *(of business)* reprendre.

im·prove·ment amélioration *f*.

▶ **improve on** *vt* faire mieux que.

im·pro·vise *vti* improviser.

im·pu·dent *adj* impudent.

im·pulse impulsion *f*; **on i.** sur un coup de tête.

im·pul·sive *adj* impulsif.

im·pul·sive·ly *adv* de manière impulsive.

im·pu·ri·ty impureté *f*.

in 1 *prep* dans; **in the box**/*etc* dans la boîte/*etc*; **in an hour('s) time** dans une heure. ▪ à; **in school** à l'école; **in Paris** à Paris; **in Portugal** au Portugal; **in ink** à l'encre. ▪ en; **in summer/May/French** en été/mai/français; **in Spain** en Espagne; **in an hour** *(within that period)* en une heure; **in doing** en faisant. ▪ de; **in a soft voice** d'une voix douce; **the best in** le meilleur de. ▪ **in the morning** le matin; **one in ten** un sur dix. **2** *adv* **to be in** *(home)* être là, être à la maison; *(of train)* être arrivé; *(in fashion)* être en vogue.

in- *prefix* in-.

in·a·bil·i·ty incapacité *f* (**to do** de faire).

in·ac·ces·si·ble *adj* inaccessible.

in·ac·cu·ra·cy *(error)* inexactitude *f*.

in·ac·cu·rate *adj* inexact.

in·ad·e·qua·cy insuffisance *f*.

in·ad·e·quate *adj* insuffisant; *(person)* pas à la hauteur.

in·ap·pro·pri·ate *adj* peu approprié.

in·au·gu·rate *vt (building)* inaugurer.

in·au·gu·ra·tion inauguration *f*.

in·box *(for e-mail)* boîte *f* de réception.

Inc *abbr (Incorporated)* = SARL.

in·ca·pa·ble *adj* incapable (**of doing** de faire).

in·cense *vt* mettre en colère.

in·cen·tive encouragement *m*, motivation *f*.

inch pouce *m* (= 2,54cm).

in·ci·dent incident *m*; *(in film etc)* épisode *m*.

in·ci·dent·al·ly *(by the way)* à propos.

in·cite *vt* inciter (**to do** à faire).

in·cite·ment incitation *f.*

in·cli·na·tion *(desire)* envie *f* (**to do** de faire).

in·cline *vt (bend)* incliner; **to be inclined to do** *(feel a wish to)* avoir bien envie de faire; *(tend to)* avoir tendance à faire.

in·clude *vt (contain)* comprendre; **to be included** être compris; *(on list)* être inclus.

in·clud·ing *prep* y compris; **i. service** service *m* compris; **up to and i. Monday** jusqu'à lundi inclus.

in·clu·sive *adj* inclus; **to be i. of** comprendre.

in·come revenu *m* (**from** de); **private i.** rentes *fpl.*

in·come tax impôt *m* sur le revenu.

in·com·pat·i·ble *adj* incompatible (**with** avec).

in·com·pe·tent *adj* incompétent.

in·com·plete *adj* incomplet.

in·con·ceiv·a·ble *adj* inconcevable.

in·con·sid·er·ate *adj (remark)* irréfléchi; *(person)* pas très gentil (**towards** avec).

in·con·sis·ten·cy incohérence *f.*

in·con·sis·tent *adj* en contradiction (**with** avec).

in·con·spic·u·ous *adj* peu en évidence.

in·con·ven·ience 1 *n (bother)* dérangement *m*; *(disadvantage)* inconvénient *m*. **2** *vt* déranger, gêner.

in·con·ven·ient *adj (moment, situation etc)* gênant; *(house)* mal situé; **it's i. (for me) to** ça me dérange de.

in·cor·po·rate *vt (contain)* contenir.

in·cor·rect *adj* inexact; **you're i.** vous avez tort.

in·crease 1 *vi* augmenter; *(of effort, noise)* s'intensifier. **2** *vt* augmenter; intensifier. **3** *n* augmenta-

tion *f* (**in, of** de); *(of effort, noise)* intensification *f*; **on the i.** en hausse.

in·creas·ing *adj (amount)* croissant.

in·creas·ing·ly *adv* de plus en plus.

in·cred·i·ble *adj* incroyable.

in·cred·i·bly *adv* incroyablement.

in·cu·ba·tor *(for baby, eggs)* couveuse *f.*

in·cur *vt (expenses)* faire; *(loss)* subir.

in·cur·a·ble *adj* incurable.

in·de·cent *adj (obscene)* indécent.

in·de·ci·sive *adj* indécis.

in·deed *adv* en effet; **very good/ etc i.** vraiment très bon/*etc*; **yes i.!** bien sûr!; **thank you very much i.!** merci infiniment!

in·def·i·nite *adj* indéfini.

in·def·i·nite·ly *adv* indéfiniment.

in·de·pend·ence indépendance *f.*

in·de·pend·ent *adj* indépendant (**of** de).

in·de·pend·ent·ly *adv* de façon indépendante; **i. of** indépendamment de.

in·dex 1 *n (in book)* index *m*. **2** *vt (classify)* classer.

in·dex card fiche *f.*

in·dex fin·ger index *m.*

in·dex-linked *adj* indexé (**to** sur).

In·di·an 1 *n* Indien, -ienne *mf*. **2** *adj* indien, -ienne.

in·di·cate *vt* indiquer (**that** que).

in·di·ca·tion *(sign)* indice *m*, indication *f.*

in·di·ca·tor *(instrument)* indicateur *m*; *(in vehicle)* clignotant *m.*

in·dif·fer·ence indifférence *f* (**to** à).

in·dif·fer·ent *adj* indifférent (**to** à).

in·di·ges·tion problèmes *mpl* de

digestion; **(an attack of) i.** une indigestion.

in·dig·nant *adj* indigné (**at** de).

in·dig·na·tion indignation *f.*

in·di·rect *adj* indirect.

in·di·rect·ly *adv* indirectement.

in·dis·creet *adj* indiscret.

in·dis·crim·i·nate *(random)* fait/donné/*etc* au hasard.

in·dis·crim·i·nate·ly *adv (at random)* au hasard.

in·dis·tin·guish·a·ble *adj* indifférenciable (**from** de).

in·di·vid·u·al 1 *adj* individuel; *(specific)* particulier. **2** *n (person)* individu *m.*

indi·vid·u·al·ly *adv (separately)* individuellement.

in·door *adj (games, shoes etc)* d'intérieur; *(swimming pool)* couvert.

in·doors *adv* à l'intérieur.

in·duce *vt* persuader (**to do** de faire); *(cause)* provoquer.

in·dulge 1 *vt (person)* gâter; *(whim)* satisfaire; **to i. oneself** se faire plaisir. **2** *vi* se faire plaisir.

▸**indulge in** *vt* se permettre.

in·dul·gent *adj* indulgent (**to** envers).

in·dus·tri·al *adj* industriel; *(conflict)* du travail; **i. park** zone *f* industrielle.

in·dus·try industrie *f.*

in·ed·i·ble *adj* immangeable.

in·ef·fec·tive *adj (measure)* inefficace.

in·ef·fi·cien·cy inefficacité *f.*

in·ef·fi·cient *adj (person, measure)* inefficace.

in·ept *adj (unskilled)* peu habile (**at** à); *(incompetent)* incapable.

in·e·qual·i·ty inégalité *f.*

in·ev·i·ta·ble *adj* inévitable.

in·ev·i·ta·bly *adv* inévitablement.

in·ex·cus·a·ble *adj* inexcusable.

in·ex·pen·sive *adj* bon marché *inv.*

in·ex·pe·ri·ence inexpérience *f.*

in·ex·pe·ri·enced *adj* inexpérimenté.

in·ex·pli·ca·ble *adj* inexplicable.

in·fal·li·ble *adj* infaillible.

in·fa·mous *adj (evil)* infâme.

in·fan·cy petite enfance *f.*

in·fant petit(e) enfant *mf*; *(baby)* nourrisson *m.*

in·fan·try infanterie *f.*

in·fat·u·at·ed *adj* amoureux (**with** de).

in·fat·u·a·tion engouement *m* (**for, with** pour).

in·fect *vt* infecter; **to get infected** s'infecter.

in·fec·tion infection *f.*

in·fec·tious *adj* contagieux.

in·fer *vt* déduire (**from** de).

in·fe·ri·or *adj* inférieur (**to** à); *(goods, work)* de qualité inférieure.

in·fe·ri·or·i·ty infériorité *f.*

in·fer·nal *adj* infernal.

in·fest *vt* infester (**with** de).

in·fi·nite *adj* infini.

in·fi·nite·ly *adv* infiniment.

in·fin·i·tive *Grammar* infinitif *m.*

in·fin·i·ty infini *m.*

in·firm *adj* infirme.

in·flamed *adj (throat etc)* enflammé.

in·flam·ma·tion inflammation *f.*

in·flate *vt* gonfler.

in·fla·tion inflation *f.*

in·flex·i·ble *adj* inflexible.

in·flict *vt (a wound)* occasionner (**on** à); **to i. pain on sb** faire souffrir qn.

in·flu·ence 1 *n* influence *f*; **under the i. (of drink)** en état d'ébriété. **2** *vt* influencer.

in·flu·en·tial *adj* **to be i.** avoir une grande influence.

in·flu·en·za grippe *f.*

in·flux flot *m.*

in·fo *Fam* renseignements *mpl* (**on** sur).

in·form *vt* informer (**of** de; **that** que).

in·for·mal *adj* simple, décontracté; *(expression)* familier; *(meeting)* non-officiel.

in·for·mal·ly *adv* sans cérémonie; *(to dress)* simplement; *(to discuss)* à titre non-officiel.

in·for·ma·tion renseignements *mpl* (**about, on** sur); **a piece of i.** un renseignement.

in·form·a·tive *adj* instructif.

▸ **inform on** *vt* dénoncer.

in·fu·ri·ate *vt* exaspérer.

in·gen·ious *adj* ingénieux.

in·grat·i·tude ingratitude *f*.

in·gre·di·ent ingrédient *m*.

in·hab·it *vt* habiter.

in·hab·i·tant habitant, -ante *mf*.

in·hale *vt* aspirer.

in·her·it *vt* hériter (de).

in·her·i·tance héritage *m*.

in·hib·it *vt (hinder)* gêner; **to be inhibited** avoir des inhibitions.

in·hi·bi·tion inhibition *f*.

in·hos·pi·ta·ble *adj* peu accueillant, inhospitalier.

in·hu·man *adj* inhumain.

in·i·tial 1 *adj* premier. **2** *n* initials initiales *fpl*; *(signature)* paraphe *m*. **3** *vt* parapher.

in·i·tial·ly *adv* au début.

in·i·ti·ate *vt (reform, negotiations)* amorcer; *(quarrel)* provoquer, déclencher; *(lawsuit)* entamer; *(into society)* initier (**into** à).

in·ject *vt* injecter (**into** à).

in·jec·tion injection *f*, piqûre *f*.

in·jure *vt (physically)* blesser, faire du mal à.

in·jured 1 *adj* blessé. **2** *n* **the i.** les blessés *mpl*.

in·ju·ry blessure *f*, *(fracture)* fracture *f*, *(sprain)* foulure *f*.

in·jus·tice injustice *f*.

ink encre *f*.

in·kling (petite) idée *f*.

in·land 1 *adj* intérieur. **2** *adv* à l'intérieur.

in·laws *npl* belle-famille *f*.

in·mate *(of prison)* détenu, -ue *mf*.

inn auberge *f*.

in·ner *adj* intérieur; **the i. city** les quartiers défavorisés du centre-ville.

in·ner tube *(of tire)* chambre *f* à air.

inn·keep·er aubergiste *mf*.

in·no·cence innocence *f*.

in·no·cent *adj* innocent.

in·oc·u·late *vt* vacciner (**against** contre).

in·oc·u·la·tion vaccination *f*.

in·put *(computer operation)* entrée *f*, *(data)* données *fpl*.

in·quire 1 *vi* se renseigner (**about** sur). **2** *vt* demander; **to i. how to get to** demander le chemin de.

▸ **inquire into** *vt* faire une enquête sur.

in·quir·y demande *f* de renseignements; *(investigation)* enquête *f*.

in·quis·i·tive *adj* curieux.

in·sane *adj* fou (*f* folle).

in·san·i·ty folie *f*.

in·scrip·tion inscription *f*, *(in book)* dédicace *f*.

in·sect insecte *m*.

in·sec·ti·cide insecticide *m*.

in·se·cure *adj (not securely fixed)* mal fixé; *(uncertain)* incertain; *(person)* qui manque d'assurance.

in·sen·si·tive *adj* insensible (**to** à).

in·sen·si·ti·vi·ty insensibilité *f*.

in·sert *vt* introduire, insérer (**in, into** dans).

in·side 1 *adv* dedans, à l'intérieur. **2** *prep* à l'intérieur de. **3** *n* dedans *m*, intérieur *m*; **on the i.** à l'intérieur (**of** de); **i. out** *(socks etc)* à l'envers. **4** *adj* intérieur.

in·sid·er initié, -ée *mf*.

in·sight *(into question)* aperçu *m* (**into** de).

in·sig·nif·i·cant *adj* insignifiant.

in·sin·cere *adj* peu sincère.

in·sist 1 *vi* insister (**on doing** pour faire). **2** *vt (order)* insister (**that** pour que + *subjunctive*); *(declare)* affirmer (**that** que).

in·sis·tence insistance *f*; **her i. on**

seeing me l'insistance qu'elle met à vouloir me voir.

in·sis·tent *adj* to be i. insister (**that** que + *subjunctive*).

▸**insist on** *vt (demand)* exiger; *(assert)* affirmer.

in·so·lence insolence *f.*

in·so·lent *adj* insolent.

in·som·ni·a insomnie *f.*

in·spect *vt* contrôler.

in·spec·tion inspection *f*, *(of tickets)* contrôle *m.*

in·spec·tor inspecteur, -trice *mf.*

in·spi·ra·tion inspiration *f.*

in·spire *vt* inspirer (**sb with sth** qch à qn).

in·stall *vt* installer.

in·stall·ment *(of money)* acompte *m*; *(of serial)* épisode *m.*

in·stance *(example)* cas *m*; **for i.** par exemple.

in·stant **1** *adj* immédiat; **i. coffee** café *m* soluble; **i. messaging** messagerie *f* instantanée. **2** *(moment)* instant *m.*

in·stant·ly *adv* immédiatement.

in·stead *adv* plutôt; **i. of (doing) sth** au lieu de (faire) qch; **i. of sb** à la place de qn; **i. (of him)** à sa place.

in·stinct instinct *m.*

in·stinc·tive *adj* instinctif.

in·stinc·tive·ly *adv* instinctivement.

in·sti·tu·tion institution *f.*

in·struct *vt (teach)* enseigner (**sb in sth** qch à qn); *(order)* charger qn de faire.

in·struc·tions *npl (for use)* mode *m* d'emploi; *(orders)* instructions *fpl.*

in·struc·tive *adj* instructif.

in·struc·tor *(for skiing etc)* moniteur, -trice *mf*, **driving i.** moniteur, -trice *mf* d'auto-école.

in·stru·ment instrument *m.*

in·stru·men·tal *adj Music* instrumental; **to be i. in sth** contribuer à qch.

in·suf·fi·cient *adj* insuffisant.

in·su·late *vt (against cold and electrically)* isoler.

in·su·la·tion *(material)* isolant *m.*

in·sult **1** *vt* insulter. **2** *n* insulte *f*(**to** à).

in·sur·ance assurance *f*; **i. company** compagnie *f* d'assurances.

in·sure *vt* assurer (**against** contre).

in·tact *adj* intact.

in·take *(of water)* prise *f*, arrivée *f*; *(of food, alcohol etc)* consommation *f*; *(of students, recruits)* admission *f.*

in·te·grate **1** *vt* intégrer. **2** *vi* s'intégrer.

in·teg·ri·ty intégrité *f.*

in·tel·lect intelligence *f.*

in·tel·lec·tu·al *adj & n* intellectuel, -elle *(mf).*

in·tel·li·gence intelligence *f.*

in·tel·li·gent *adj* intelligent.

in·tel·li·gi·ble *adj* compréhensible.

in·tend *vt (gift etc)* destiner (**for** à); **to be intended to do/for sb** être destiné à faire/à qn; **to i. to do** avoir l'intention de faire.

in·tense *adj* intense; *(interest)* vif.

in·ten·si·fy **1** *vt* intensifier. **2** *vi* s'intensifier.

in·ten·si·ty intensité *f.*

in·ten·sive *adj* intensif; **i. care** réanimation *f.*

in·tent *adj* **i. on doing** résolu à faire.

in·ten·tion intention *f* (**of doing** de faire).

in·ten·tion·al *adj* **it wasn't i.** ce n'était pas fait exprès.

in·ten·tion·al·ly *adv* exprès.

in·ter·act *vi (people)* communiquer.

in·ter·ac·tive *adj* interactif, -ive.

in·ter·cept *vt* intercepter.

in·ter·change *(on road)* échangeur *m.*

in·ter·change·a·ble *adj* interchangeable.

in·ter·com interphone *m.*

in·ter·con·nect·ed *adj (facts etc)* liés.

in·ter·course *(sexual)* rapports *mpl* sexuels.

in·ter·est 1 *n* intérêt *m; (money)* intérêts *mpl;* **to take an i.** s'intéresser à; **to be of i.** to sb intéresser qn. **2** *vt* intéresser.

in·ter·est·ed *adj* intéressé; **to be i. in sth/sb** s'intéresser à qch/qn; **I'm i. in doing** ça m'intéresse de faire.

in·ter·est·ing *adj* intéressant.

in·ter·fere *vi* se mêler des affaires d'autrui.

▸**interfere in** *vt* s'ingérer dans.

in·ter·fer·ence ingérence *f, (on radio)* parasites *mpl.*

▸**interfere with** *vt (upset)* déranger.

in·ter·im 1 *n* **in the i.** entretemps. **2** *adj* provisoire.

in·te·ri·or 1 *adj* intérieur. **2** *n* intérieur *m.*

in·ter·jec·tion *Grammar* interjection *f.*

in·ter·me·di·ar·y intermédiaire *mf.*

in·ter·me·di·ate *adj* intermédiaire; *(course)* de niveau moyen.

in·ter·mis·sion *(in theater)* entracte *m.*

in·tern *n (in office)* stagiaire *mf, (in hospital)* interne *mf.*

in·ter·nal *adj* interne; *(flight)* intérieur.

In·ter·nal Rev·e·nue Ser·vice service *m* des impôts.

in·ter·na·tion·al *adj* international.

In·ter·net the I. (l')Internet *m;* **on the I.** sur Internet; **I. surfer** internaute *mf.*

in·tern·ship *n (in office)* stage *m; (in hospital)* internat *m.*

in·ter·pret *vt* interpréter.

in·ter·pret·er interprète *mf.*

in·ter·ro·gate *vt* interroger.

in·ter·ro·ga·tion *(by police)* interrogatoire *m.*

in·ter·rog·a·tive *adj & n Grammar* interrogatif *(m).*

in·ter·rupt *vt* interrompre.

in·ter·rup·tion interruption *f.*

in·ter·sect 1 *vt* couper. **2** *vi* s'entrecouper.

in·ter·sec·tion *(of roads, lines)* intersection *f.*

in·ter·state autoroute *f.*

in·ter·val intervalle *m.*

in·ter·vene *vi (of person)* intervenir; *(of event)* survenir.

in·ter·ven·tion intervention *f.*

in·ter·view 1 *n* entrevue *f* (**with** avec); *(on TV etc)* interview *f.* **2** *vt* avoir une entrevue avec; *(on TV etc)* interviewer.

in·ter·view·er *(on TV etc)* interviewer *m.*

in·ti·mate *adj* intime.

in·tim·i·date *vt* intimider.

in·to *prep* dans; **to put i.** mettre dans. ▪ **en; to translate i.** traduire en; **i. pieces** en morceaux. ▪ **to be i. yoga** */etc Fam* être à fond dans le yoga */etc.*

in·tol·er·a·ble *adj* intolérable (**that** que + *subjunctive*).

in·tox·i·cate *vt* enivrer.

in·tox·i·cat·ed *adj* ivre.

in·tran·si·tive *adj Grammar* intransitif *f.*

in·tri·cate *adj* complexe.

in·tro·duce *vt (bring in)* introduire (**into** dans); *(program)* présenter; **to i. sb to sb** présenter qn à qn.

in·tro·duc·tion introduction *f, (of person to person)* présentation *f,* **i. to** *(initiation)* premier contact avec.

in·trude *vi* déranger (**on sb** qn).

in·trud·er intrus, -use *mf.*

in·tru·sion *(disturbance)* dérangement *m.*

in·tu·i·tion intuition *f.*

in·un·dat·ed *adj* submergé (**with work/letters**/*etc* de travail/lettres/*etc*).

in·vade vt envahir.

in·vad·er envahisseur, -euse mf.

in·val·id¹ malade mf; (through injury) infirme mf.

in·val·id² adj non valable.

in·val·u·a·ble adj inestimable.

in·var·i·a·bly adv (always) toujours.

in·va·sion invasion f.

in·vent vt inventer.

in·ven·tion invention f.

in·ven·tor inventeur, -trice mf.

in·ven·to·ry inventaire m.

in·vest vt (money) placer, investir (in dans).

in·ves·ti·gate vt examiner; (crime) enquêter sur.

in·ves·ti·ga·tion examen m; (inquiry by journalist, police etc) enquête f (of, into sur).

in·ves·ti·ga·tor enquêteur, -euse mf.

▶ **invest in** vt placer son argent dans; (firm) investir dans.

in·vest·ment investissement m, placement m.

in·ves·tor (in shares) actionnaire mf; (saver) épargnant, -ante mf.

in·vig·or·at·ing adj stimulant.

in·vis·i·ble adj invisible.

in·vi·ta·tion invitation f.

in·vite vt inviter (to do à faire); (ask for) demander; (give occasion for) provoquer.

in·vit·ing adj engageant.

in·voice 1 n facture f. **2** vt facturer.

in·voke vt invoquer.

in·volve vt (person) mêler (in à); (entail) entraîner; **the job involves** le poste nécessite.

in·volved adj (concerned) concerné; (committed) engagé (in dans); (complicated) compliqué; (at stake) en jeu; **the person i.** la personne en question; **to be i. with sb** avoir des liens intimes avec qn.

in·volve·ment participation f (in à); (commitment) engagement m; (emotional) liaison f.

in·ward(s) adv vers l'intérieur.

IOU abbr (I owe you) reconnaissance f de dette.

IQ abbr (intelligence quotient) QI m inv.

IRA abbr (individual retirement account) plan m d'épargne retraite personnel.

i·ris (plant, of eye) iris m.

I·rish 1 npl the I. les Irlandais mpl. **2** adj irlandais.

I·rish·man, pl -men Irlandais m.

I·rish·wom·an, pl -women Irlandaise f.

i·ron 1 n fer m; (for clothes) fer m (à repasser). **2** vt (clothes) repasser.

i·ron·ic, i·ron·i·cal adj ironique.

i·ron·ing repassage m.

i·ron·ing board planche f à repasser.

i·ro·ny ironie f.

ir·ra·tion·al adj (person) peu rationnel.

ir·reg·u·lar adj irrégulier.

ir·rel·e·vance manque m de rapport.

ir·rel·e·vant adj sans rapport (to avec); **that's i.** ça n'a rien à voir.

ir·re·sist·i·ble adj irrésistible.

ir·re·spec·tive of prep sans tenir compte de.

ir·ri·gate vt irriguer.

ir·ri·ta·ble adj irritable.

ir·ri·tate vt (annoy, inflame) irriter.

ir·ri·tat·ing adj irritant.

ir·ri·ta·tion irritation f.

is see **be**.

Is·lam·ic adj islamique.

is·land île f.

i·so·late vt isoler (from de).

i·so·lat·ed adj isolé.

i·so·la·tion isolement m; **in i.** isolément.

is·sue 1 vt publier; (tickets) distribuer; (passport) délivrer; (an order) donner; (warning) lancer; (supply) fournir (with de; to à). **2** n (matter) question f; (newspaper) numéro m.

IT *abbr (information technology)* l'informatique *f*.

it *pron (subject)* il, elle; *(object)* le, la, l'; **(to) it** *(indirect object)* lui; **it's ringing** il sonne; **I've done it** je l'ai fait. ■ *(impersonal)* il; **it's snowing** il neige. ■ *(non specific)* ce, cela, ça; **who is it?** qui est-ce?; **it was Paul who…** c'est Paul qui… ■ **of it, from it, about it** en; **in it, to it, at it** y; **on it** dessus; **under it** dessous.

I·tal·ian 1 *n* Italien, -ienne *mf*; *(language)* italien *m*. **2** *adj* italien, -ienne.

i·tal·ics *npl* italique *m*.

itch 1 *n* démangeaison(s) *f(pl)*. **2** *vi* démanger; **his arm itches** son bras le démange.

itch·ing démangeaison(s) *f(pl)*.

itch·y *adj* **I have an i. hand** j'ai une main qui me démange.

i·tem *(object)* article *m*; *(matter)* question *f*; **(news) i.** information *f*.

its *poss adj* son, sa, *pl* ses.

it·self *pron* lui-même, elle-même; *(reflexive)* se, s'.

i·vo·ry ivoire *m*.

i·vy lierre *m*.

J

jab 1 *vt* enfoncer *(into* dans); *(prick)* piquer *(qn)* **(with sth** du bout de qch). **2** *n (blow)* coup *m*.

jack *(for car)* cric *m*; *Cards* valet *m*; **j. of all trades** homme *m* à tout faire.

jack·et veste *f*; **j. potato** pomme *f* de terre en robe des champs.

jack·ham·mer marteau *m* piqueur.

Ja·cuz·zi® Jacuzzi® *m*.

jag·ged *adj* déchiqueté.

jag·uar jaguar *m*.

jail 1 *n* prison *f*. **2** *vt* emprisonner.

jam¹ confiture *f*.

jam² 1 *n (traffic)* **j.** embouteillage *m*. **2** *vt (squeeze, make stuck)* coincer; *(street etc)* encombrer. **3** *vi (get stuck)* se coincer.

▸ **jam into** *vt* to **j. sth into sth** *(cram)* (en)tasser qch dans qch.

jammed *adj (machine etc)* coincé, bloqué; *(street etc)* encombré.

jam-packed *adj* bourré de monde.

jan·i·tor concierge *m*.

Jan·u·ar·y janvier *m*.

Jap·a·nese 1 *n* Japonais, -aise *mf*; *(language)* japonais *m*. **2** *adj* japonais, -aise.

jar pot *m*; *(large, glass)* bocal *m*.

jaun·dice jaunisse *f*.

jave·lin javelot *m*.

jaw mâchoire *f*.

jay·walk·ing = délit *m* mineur qui consiste à traverser une rue en dehors des clous ou au feu vert.

jazz jazz *m*.

jea·lous *adj* jaloux (*f* -ouse) **(of** de).

jeal·ous·y jalousie *f*.

jeans *npl (pair of)* **j.** (blue-)jean *m*.

jeep® jeep® *f*.

jeer (at) *vti* railler; *(boo)* huer.

jeer·ing *(of crowd)* huées *fpl*.

jeers *npl* huées *fpl*.

Jell-O® *inv* gelée *f*.

jel·ly *(preserve, dessert)* gelée *f*.

jeop·ard·ize *vt* mettre en danger.

jeop·ard·y danger *m*.

jerk 1 *vt* donner une secousse à. **2** *n* secousse *f*; **(stupid) j.** *Fam* crétin, -ine *mf*.

jer·sey *(garment)* maillot *m*.

jet *(plane)* avion *m* à réaction.

jet lag fatigue *f* (due au décalage horaire).

jet-lagged *adj* qui souffre du décalage horaire.

jet·ty jetée *f*.

Jew Juif *m*, Juive *f*.

jew·el bijou m (pl -oux); (in watch) rubis m.

jew·el·er bijoutier, -ière mf.

jew·el·ry bijoux mpl.

Jew·ish adj juif.

jig·saw j. (puzzle) puzzle m.

jin·gle vi (of keys) tinter.

jit·ter·y adj to be j. Fam avoir la frousse.

job (task) travail m; (post) poste m.

job·less adj au chômage.

jock·ey jockey m.

jog 1 n (shake) secousse f. 2 vt secouer; (push) pousser; (memory) rafraîchir. 3 vi faire du jogging.

john Fam cabinets mpl.

join¹ 1 vt (put together) joindre; (wires, pipes) raccorder; (words, towns) relier; **to j. sb** (catch up with, meet) rejoindre qn; (go with) se joindre à qn (**in doing** pour faire). 2 vi (of roads etc) se rejoindre; (of objects) se joindre. 3 n raccord m.

join² 1 vt (become a member of) s'inscrire à (club, party); (firm, army) entrer dans. 2 vi devenir membre.

▶**join in** 1 vt to join in sth prendre part à qch. 2 vi prendre part.

joint 1 n (in body) articulation f. 2 adj (account) joint; (effort) conjugué.

joint·ly adv conjointement.

joke 1 n plaisanterie f; (trick) tour m. 2 vi plaisanter (**about** sur).

jok·er plaisantin m; Cards joker m.

jol·ly adj gai.

jolt vti secouer.

jos·tle 1 vti (push) bousculer. 2 vi (push each other) se bousculer.

▶**jot down** vt noter.

jour·nal·ist journaliste mf.

jour·ney voyage m; (distance) trajet m.

joy joie f.

joy·ful adj joyeux.

joy·stick manche m à balai.

judge 1 n juge m. 2 vti juger.

judg·ment jugement m.

ju·di·cial adj judiciaire.

ju·do judo m.

jug cruche f; (for milk) pot m.

jug·ger·naut force f irrésistible.

jug·gle vi jongler (**with** avec).

jug·gler jongleur, -euse mf.

juice jus m.

juic·y adj (fruit) juteux.

Ju·ly juillet m.

jum·ble (up) vt mélanger.

jum·bo adj géant.

jum·bo jet gros-porteur m.

jump 1 n saut m; (start) sursaut m; (increase) hausse f. 2 vi sauter; (start) sursauter; **to j. off sth** sauter de qch. 3 vt **to j. rope** sauter à la corde.

jump·er (garment) robe-chasuble f.

▶**jump in, jump on** 1 vt (train, vehicle) monter dans. 2 vi monter.

jump rope corde f à sauter.

jump·y adj nerveux.

junc·tion carrefour m.

June juin m.

jun·gle jungle f.

jun·ior 1 adj (younger) plus jeune; (in rank) subalterne; (doctor) jeune. 2 n cadet, -ette mf; (in school) petit(e) élève mf.

jun·ior high (school) = collège m d'enseignement secondaire.

junk bric-à-brac m inv; (metal) ferraille f; (goods) camelote f; (garbage) ordures fpl; **j. food** malbouffe f; **j. mail** prospectus mpl; (email) messages mpl publicitaires.

ju·ry jury m.

just adv (exactly, only) juste; **she has/had j. left** elle vient/venait de partir; **he'll (only) j. catch the bus** il aura son bus de justesse; **he j. missed it** il l'a manqué de peu; **j. as big/etc** tout aussi grand/etc (**as** que); **j. over ten** un peu plus de dix; **j. one** un(e) seul(e); **j. about** à peu près; (almost) presque; **j. about to do** sur le point de faire.

jus·tice justice *f.*
jus·ti·fi·ca·tion justification *f.*
jus·ti·fy *vt* justifier; **to be justified in doing** être fondé à faire.
▸ **jut out** *vi* faire saillie.

K

kan·ga·roo, *pl* -**oos** kangourou *m.*
ka·ra·oke karaoké *m.*
ka·ra·te karaté *m.*
ke·bab brochette *f.*
keen *adj (interest, emotion)* vif; **k. eyesight** vue *f* perçante; **he's a k. athlete** c'est un passionné de sport; **to be k. on doing** *(want)* tenir (beaucoup) à faire.
keep* 1 *vt* garder; *(shop, car)* avoir; *(diary, promise)* tenir; *(family)* entretenir; *(rule)* respecter; *(delay)* retenir; **to k. doing** continuer à faire; **to k. sb waiting/working** faire attendre/travailler qn; **to k. sb in/out** empêcher qn de sortir/d'entrer. **2** *vi (remain)* rester; *(of food)* se garder; **to k. going** continuer; **to k. (to the) right** tenir sa droite. **3** *n (food)* nourriture *f*, subsistance *f.*
▸ **keep away 1** *vt (person)* éloigner (**from** de). **2** *vi* ne pas s'approcher (**from** de).
▸ **keep back 1** *vt (crowd)* contenir; *(delay)* retenir; *(hide)* cacher (**from** à). **2** *vi* ne pas s'approcher (**from** de).
▸ **keep down** *vt (restrict)* limiter; *(price)* maintenir bas.
keep·er *(in park, zoo)* gardien, -ienne *mf.*
▸ **keep from** *vt (hide)* cacher à; **to k. sb from doing** *(prevent)* empêcher qn de faire.
▸ **keep off** *vi (not go near)* ne pas

s'approcher de; **the rain kept off** il n'a pas plu.
▸ **keep on** *vt (hat, employee)* garder; **to k. on doing** continuer à faire.
▸ **keep up** *vti* continuer (**doing sth** à faire qch); **to k. up (with sb)** *(follow)* suivre (qn).
ken·nel niche *f.*
kept *pt* & *pp* de **keep**.
ker·o·sene pétrole *m* (lampant).
ketch·up ketchup *m.*
ket·tle bouilloire *f*; **the k. is boiling** l'eau bout.
key 1 *n* clef *f*; *(of piano, typewriter, computer)* touche *f.* **2** *adj (industry, post etc)* clef *(f inv)*.
key·board clavier *m.*
key ring porte-clefs *m inv.*
kick 1 *n* coup *m* de pied. **2** *vt* donner un coup de pied à. **3** *vi* donner des coups de pied.
▸ **kick down, kick in** *vt (door etc)* démolir à coups de pied.
kick·off *Fam* coup *m* d'envoi.
▸ **kick off** *vi Sports* donner le coup d'envoi.
▸ **kick out** *vt (throw out) Fam* flanquer dehors.
kid 1 *n (child) Fam* gosse *mf.* **2** *vti (tease) Fam* blaguer.
kid·nap *vt* kidnapper.
kid·nap·per ravisseur, -euse *mf.*
kid·ney rein *m*; *(as food)* rognon *m.*
kill *vti* tuer.
kill·er tueur, -euse *mf.*
kill·ing *(of person)* meurtre *m; Fam* **to make a k.** se remplir les poches.
ki·lo, *pl* -os kilo *m.*
kil·o·gram kilogramme *m.*
kil·o·me·ter kilomètre *m.*
kin **my next of k.** mon plus proche parent.
kind¹ *(sort)* sorte *f*, genre *m*, espèce *f* (**of** de); **all kinds of** toutes sortes de; **what k. of drink/etc is it?** qu'est-ce que c'est comme boisson/*etc*?; **k. of worried/etc** plutôt inquiet/*etc.*

kind² adj (pleasant) gentil (**to** avec).

kin·der·gar·ten jardin m d'enfants.

kind·ly 1 adj bienveillant. **2** adv gentiment; **k. wait** ayez la bonté d'attendre.

kind·ness gentillesse f.

king roi m.

king·dom royaume m.

ki·osk kiosque m.

kiss 1 n baiser m. **2** vt (person) embrasser; **to k. sb's hand** baiser la main de qn. **3** vi s'embrasser.

kit équipement m; (set of articles) trousse f; (do-it-yourself) **k.** kit m; **tool k.** trousse f à outils.

kitch·en cuisine f.

kite (toy) cerf-volant m.

kit·ten chaton m.

klutz Fam balourd, -ourde mf.

knack to have a or the **k.** of doing avoir le don de faire.

knee genou m (pl genoux).

kneel* (**down**) vi s'agenouiller; **to be kneeling** (**down**) être à genoux.

knew pt of **know**.

knick·ers knickers mpl.

knife, pl knives couteau m; (penknife) canif m.

knight chevalier m; Chess cavalier m.

knit vti tricoter.

knit·ting (activity, material) tricot m; **k. needle** aiguille f à tricoter.

knob (on door etc) bouton m.

knock 1 vt (strike) frapper; (collide with) heurter; **to k. one's head on sth** se cogner la tête contre qch. **2** vi frapper. **3** n coup m; **there's a k. at the door** quelqu'un frappe; **I heard a k.** j'ai entendu frapper.

▶**knock against, knock into** vt (bump into) heurter.

▶**knock down** vt (vase, pedestrian etc) renverser; (house, wall etc) abattre.

knock·er (for door) marteau m.

▶**knock in** vt (nail) enfoncer.

▶**knock off** vt (person, object) faire tomber (**from** de).

▶**knock out** vt (make unconscious) assommer; Boxing mettre K.-O.; (beat in competition) éliminer.

▶**knock over** vt (pedestrian, vase etc) renverser.

knot 1 n nœud m. **2** vt nouer.

know* 1 vt (facts, language etc) savoir; (person, place etc) connaître; (recognize) reconnaître (**by** à); **to k. that** savoir que; **to k. how to do** savoir faire; **I'll let you k.** je te le ferai savoir; **to k. (a lot) about** (person, event) en savoir long sur; (cars, sewing etc) s'y connaître en; **to get to k. sb** apprendre à mieux connaître qn. **2** vi savoir; **I wouldn't k.** je n'en sais rien; **I k. about that** je suis au courant; **do you k. of a good dentist/etc?** connais-tu un bon dentiste/etc?

know-how savoir-faire m inv.

know-it-all Fam je-sais-tout mf.

knowl·edge connaissance f (**of** de); (learning) connaissances fpl.

known adj connu; **well k.** (bien) connu (**that** que); **she is k. to be** on sait qu'elle est.

knuck·le articulation f (du doigt).

Ko·ran the K. le Coran m.

L

lab Fam labo m.

la·bel 1 n étiquette f. **2** vt (goods) étiqueter.

la·bor 1 n (work) travail m; (workers) main-d'œuvre f; **in l.** en train d'accoucher. **2** adj (market, situation) du travail.

lab·o·ra·to·ry laboratoire m.

La·bor Day fête f du travail.

la·bor·er manœuvre *m*; *(on farm)* ouvrier *m* agricole.

la·bor pro·test mouvement *m* revendicatif.

la·bor un·ion syndicat *m*.

lace *(cloth)* dentelle *f*, *(of shoe)* lacet *m*.

lace (up) *vt (shoe)* lacer.

lack 1 *n* manque *m*. **2** *vt* manquer de. **3** *vi* to be lacking manquer (**in** de).

lad gamin *m*.

lad·der échelle *f*.

la·dle louche *f*.

la·dy dame *f*; **a young l.** une jeune fille; *(married)* une jeune femme; **the ladies' room** les toilettes *fpl* pour dames.

la·dy·bug coccinelle *f*.

la·ger bière *f* blonde.

lake lac *m*.

lamb agneau *m*.

lame *adj* to be l. boiter.

lamp lampe *f*.

lamp·post réverbère *m*.

lamp·shade abat-jour *m inv*.

land 1 *n* terre *f*, *(country)* pays *m*; **(plot of) l.** terrain *m*. **2** *vi (of aircraft)* atterrir; *(of passengers)* débarquer. **3** *vt (aircraft)* poser.

land·ing *(of aircraft)* atterrissage *m*; *(top of stairs)* palier *m*.

land·la·dy propriétaire *f*, *(of pub)* patronne *f*.

land·lord propriétaire *m*; *(of pub)* patron *m*.

land·own·er propriétaire *m* foncier.

land·scape paysage *m*.

land·slide éboulement *m*.

lane *(in country)* chemin *m*; *(in town)* ruelle *f*, *(division of road)* voie *f*.

lan·guage 1 *n (English etc)* langue *f*, *(means of expression, style)* langage *m*. **2** *adj (laboratory)* de langues; *(teacher, studies)* de langue(s).

lan·tern lanterne *f*.

lap *(of person)* genoux *mpl*; *(in race)* tour *m* (de piste).

la·pel *(of coat etc)* revers *m*.

lap·top portable *m*.

lar·ce·ny vol *m* simple.

lar·der *(storeroom)* garde-manger *m inv*.

large *adj* grand; *(in volume)* gros *(f* grosse).

large·ly *adv* en grande mesure.

large-scale *adj* de grande envergure.

lark *(bird)* alouette *f*, *(joke) Fam* rigolade *f*.

la·ser laser *m*.

last¹ 1 *adj* dernier; **next to l.** avant-dernier. **2** *adv (lastly)* en dernier lieu; *(on the last occasion)* (pour) la dernière fois; **to leave l.** sortir en dernier. **3** *n (person, object)* dernier, -ière *mf*; **the l. of the beer/etc** le reste de la bière/*etc*; **at (long) l.** enfin.

last² *vi* durer; *(endure)* tenir.

last·ly *adv* en dernier lieu, enfin.

latch loquet *m*.

late 1 *adj (not on time)* en retard (**for** à); *(meal, hour)* tardif; **he's an hour l.** il a une heure de retard; **it's l.** il est tard; **at a later date** à une date ultérieure; **at the latest** au plus tard; **of l.** dernièrement. **2** *adv (in the day, season etc)* tard; *(not on time)* en retard; **it's getting l.** il se fait tard; **later (on)** plus tard.

late·com·er retardataire *mf*.

late·ly *adv* dernièrement.

Lat·in 1 *adj* latin. **2** *n (language)* latin *m*.

La·tin A·mer·i·ca l'Amérique *f* latine.

lat·ter 1 *adj (last-named)* dernier; *(second)* deuxième. **2** *n (last)* dernier, -ière *mf*; *(second)* second, -onde *mf*.

laugh 1 *n* rire *m*. **2** *vi* rire (**at, about** de).

laugh·ter rire(s) *m(pl)*.

launch 1 *vt (rocket, fashion etc)* lancer. **2** *n* lancement *m*.

laun·dro·mat laverie *f* automatique.

laun·dry *(place)* blanchisserie *f*, *(clothes)* linge *m*.

laun·dry de·ter·gent lessive *f*.

lav·a·to·ry cabinets *mpl*.

law loi *f*; *(study, profession)* droit *m*; **court of l., l. court** cour *f* de justice.

lawn pelouse *f*, gazon *m*; **l. mower** tondeuse *f* (à gazon).

law·suit procès *m*.

law·yer avocat *m*; *(for wills, sales)* notaire *m*.

lay* *vt (put down)* poser; *(table)* mettre; *(blanket)* étendre (**over** sur); *(trap)* tendre; *(egg)* pondre.

▸ **lay down** *vt (put down)* poser.

lay·er couche *f*.

▸ **lay in** *vt (supplies)* faire provision de.

▸ **lay off** *vt (worker)* licencier.

lay·out disposition *f*.

▸ **lay out** *vt (garden)* dessiner; *(display)* disposer; *(money) Fam* mettre (**on** dans).

lay·per·son profane *mf*.

la·zy *adj* paresseux.

la·zy·bones *Fam* fainéant, -ante *mf*.

lead¹ *vt* (conduct)* mener, conduire (**to** à); *(team, government etc)* diriger; *(life)* mener; **to l. sb in/out/etc** être entrer/sortir/*etc* qn; **to l. sb to do** amener qn à faire. **2** *vi (of street, door etc)* mener (**to** à); *(in race)* être en tête; *(in match)* mener; *(go ahead)* aller devant. **3** *n (distance or time ahead)* avance *f* (**over** sur); *(example)* exemple *m*; *(leash)* laisse *f*, *(electric wire)* fil *m*; **to be in the l.** *(in race)* être en tête; *(in match)* mener.

lead² *(metal)* plomb *m*; *(of pencil)* mine *f*.

▸ **lead away, lead off** *vt* emmener.

lead·er chef *m*; *(of country, party)* dirigeant, -ante *mf*.

lead·ing *adj (main)* principal.

▸ **lead on 1** *vi (go ahead)* aller devant. **2** *vt (deceive)* tromper.

▸ **lead to** *vt (result in)* aboutir à; *(cause)* causer.

▸ **lead up to** *vt (of street etc)* conduire à; *(precede)* précéder.

leaf, *pl* **leaves** feuille *f*, *(of book)* feuillet *m*.

leaf·let prospectus *m*; *(containing instructions)* notice *f*.

▸ **leaf through** *vt (book)* feuilleter.

leak 1 *n (of gas etc)* fuite *f*. **2** *vi (of liquid, pipe etc)* fuir.

lean¹ 1 *vi (of object)* pencher; *(of person)* se pencher; **to l. against/on sth** *(of person)* s'appuyer contre/sur qch. **2** *vt* appuyer (**against** contre); **to l. one's head on/out of sth** pencher la tête sur/par qch.

▸ **lean forward** *vi (of person)* se pencher (en avant).

▸ **lean over** *vi (of person)* se pencher; *(of object)* pencher.

leap 1 *n* bond *m*. **2** *vi** bondir.

leap year année *f* bisextile.

learn* 1 *vt* apprendre (**that** que); **to l. (how) to do** apprendre à faire. **2** *vi* apprendre; **to l. about** *(study)* étudier; *(hear about)* apprendre.

learn·er débutant, -ante *mf*.

learn·ing *n (of language)* apprentissage *m* (**of** de).

lease 1 *n* bail *m*; **to give sb a new l. on life** redonner du tonus à qn. **2** *vt* louer à bail.

leash laisse *f*.

least 1 *adj* **the l.** *(smallest amount of)* le moins de; *(slightest)* le *or* la moindre. **2** *n* **the l.** le moins; **at l.** du moins; *(with quantity)* au moins. **3** *adv (to work etc)* le moins; *(with adjective)* le *or* la moins.

leath·er cuir *m*.

leave 1 *n (vacation)* congé *m*. **2** *vt** laisser; *(go away from)* quitter; **to be left (over)** rester; **there's no bread/*etc* left** il ne reste plus de pain/*etc*; **to l. go (of)** *(release)* lâcher. **3** *vi (go away)* partir (**from** de; **for** pour).

▸ **leave behind** *vt (not take)* laisser; *(in race, at school)* distancer.

▸ **leave on** *vt (hat, gloves)* garder.

▸ **leave out** *vt (forget to add)* oublier (de mettre); *(word, line)* sauter; *(exclude)* exclure.

lec·ture 1 *n (public speech)* conférence *f*; **to give a l.** faire une conférence. **2** *vt* **to l. sb** sermonner qn.

lec·tur·er conférencier, -ière *mf*.

leek poireau *m*.

left¹ *pt & pp de* **leave**.

left² **1** *adj (side, hand etc)* gauche. **2** *adv* à gauche. **3** *n* gauche *f*; **on** *or* **to the l.** à gauche (**of** de).

left-hand *adj* à *or* de gauche; **on the l. side** à gauche (**of** de).

left-hand·ed *adj (person)* gaucher.

left·o·vers *npl* restes *mpl*.

leg jambe *f*; *(of dog etc)* patte *f*; *(of table)* pied *m*; **l. (of chicken)** cuisse *f (de poulet)*; **l. of lamb** gigot *m (d'agneau)*.

le·gal *adj* légal.

le·gal·ly *adv* légalement.

leg·end légende *f*.

leg·i·ble *adj* lisible.

leg·is·la·tion législation *f*.

leg·is·la·tive *adj* législatif.

leg·is·la·ture *(corps m)* législatif *m*.

le·git·i·mate *adj* légitime.

lei·sure l. (time) loisirs *mpl*; **l. activities** loisirs *mpl*.

lem·on citron *m*; **tea with l.** thé *m* au citron.

lem·on·ade citronnade *f*.

lend* *vt* prêter (**to** à); *(color, charm etc)* donner (**to** à).

length longueur *f*; *(section of rope etc)* morceau *m*; *(duration)* durée *f*; **l. of time** temps *m*.

length·en *vt* allonger; *(in time)* prolonger.

length·y *adj* long (*f* longue).

le·nient *adj* indulgent (**to** envers).

lens lentille *f*; *(in spectacles)* verre *m*; *(of camera)* objectif *m*.

len·til lentille *f (graine)*.

leop·ard léopard *m*.

le·o·tard collant *m (de danse)*.

less 1 *adj & n* moins (de) (**than** que); **l. time/etc** moins de temps/etc; **l. than a quart/ten** *(with quantity, number)* moins d'un litre/de dix. **2** *adv* moins (**than** que); **l. (often)** moins souvent; **l. and l.** de moins en moins; **one l.** un(e) de moins. **3** *prep* moins.

les·son leçon *f*.

let* *vt (allow)* laisser (**sb do** qn faire); **to l. sb have sth** donner qch à qn; **l. us** *or* **l.'s eat/etc** mangeons/ etc; **l.'s go for a stroll** allons nous promener; **l. him come** qu'il vienne.

▸ **let down** *vt (lower)* baisser; **to l. sb down** *(disappoint)* décevoir qn.

▸ **let in** *vt (person)* faire entrer; *(noise, light)* laisser entrer.

▸ **let off** *vt (firework, gun)* faire partir; **to l. sb off** *(not punish)* ne pas punir qn; **to l. sb off doing** dispenser qn de faire.

▸ **let out** *vt (person)* laisser sortir; *(cry, secret)* laisser échapper.

let·ter lettre *f*.

let·ter·box boîte *f* aux *or* à lettres.

let·ter o·pen·er coupe-papier *m inv*.

let·tuce laitue *f*.

▸ **let up** *vi (of rain etc)* s'arrêter.

lev·el 1 *n* niveau *m*; *(rate)* taux *m*. **2** *adj (surface)* plat; *(object on surface)* d'aplomb; *(equal in score)* à égalité (**with** avec); *(in height)* au même niveau (**with** que).

lev·er levier *m*.

li·a·ble *adj* **to be l. to do** être capable *or* susceptible de faire.

li·ar menteur, -euse *mf*.

li·bel 1 *n* diffamation *f*. **2** *vt* diffamer.

lib·er·ty liberté *f*; **at l. to do** libre de faire.

li·brar·i·an bibliothécaire *mf*.

li·brar·y bibliothèque *f*.

lice *npl* poux *mpl*.

li·cense *(document)* permis *m*; **l.**

plate/number plaque f/numéro m d'immatriculation.

lick vt lécher.

lic·o·rice réglisse f.

lid (of box etc) couvercle m.

lie¹* vi (in flat position) s'allonger; (remain) rester; (be) être; **to be lying** (on the grass etc) être allongé.

lie² 1 vi* (tell lies) mentir. 2 n mensonge m.

▸ **lie around** vi (of objects, person) traîner.

▸ **lie down** vi s'allonger; **lying down** allongé.

life, pl **lives** vie f; **to come to l.** s'animer.

life·belt ceinture f de sauvetage.

life·boat canot m de sauvetage.

life·guard maître nageur m (sauveteur).

life in·sur·ance assurance-vie f.

life jack·et gilet m de sauvetage.

life pre·ser·ver ceinture f de sauvetage.

life·time in my l. de mon vivant.

lift 1 vt lever. 2 n (elevator) ascenseur m; **to give sb a l.** emmener qn (en voiture) (**to** à).

▸ **lift down, lift off** vt (take down) descendre (**from** de).

▸ **lift out** vt (take out) sortir (**of** de).

▸ **lift up** vt (arm, object) lever.

light¹ lumière f; (on vehicle) feu m; (vehicle headlight) phare m; **do you have a l.?** (for cigarette) est-ce que vous avez du feu?

light²*vt (match, fire, gas) allumer.

light³ adj (not dark) clair; **a l. green jacket** veste f vert clair.

light⁴ adj (in weight, quantity etc) léger; **to travel l.** voyager avec peu de bagages.

light (up) vt (room) éclairer; (cigarette) allumer.

light bulb ampoule f (électrique).

light·er (for cigarettes) briquet m; (for stove) allume-gaz m inv.

light·house phare m.

light·ing (lights) éclairage m.

light·ning (charge) foudre f; (flash of) l. éclair m.

like¹ 1 prep comme; **l. this** comme ça; **what's he l.?** comment est-il?; **to be** or **look l.** ressembler à; **what was the book l.?** comment as-tu trouvé le livre? 2 conj (as) Fam comme; **do l. I do** fais comme moi.

like² vt aimer (bien) (**to do, doing** faire); **she likes it here** elle se plaît ici; **to l. sth best** aimer mieux qch; **I'd l. to come** je voudrais (bien) or j'aimerais (bien) venir; **I'd l. some cake** je voudrais du gâteau; **would you l. an apple?** voulez-vous une pomme?; **if you l.** si vous voulez.

like·a·ble adj sympathique.

like·li·hood there's isn't much l. that il y a peu de chances que (+ subjunctive).

like·ly 1 adj probable; (excuse) vraisemblable; **it's l. (that) she'll come, she's l. to come** il est probable qu'elle viendra. 2 adv very l. très probablement.

like·wise adv de même.

lik·ing l. for (person) de la sympathie pour; (thing) du goût pour.

lil·y lis m.

limb membre m.

lime (fruit) citron m vert.

lim·it 1 n limite f (**to** à). 2 vt limiter (**to** à).

lim·ou·sine (airport shuttle) voiture-navette f.

limp 1 vi (of person) boiter. 2 n **to have a l.** boiter.

line¹ 1 n ligne f; (of poem) vers m; (wrinkle) ride f; (track) voie f; (rope) corde f; (row) rangée f; (of vehicles, people) file f; **on the l.** (phone) au bout du fil; **to stand in l.** faire la queue; **to drop a l.** (send a letter) envoyer un mot (**to** à). 2 vt **to l. the street** (of trees) border la rue; (of people) faire la haie le long de la rue.

line² vt (clothes) doubler.

lin·en (sheets etc) linge m.

lin·er (ocean) l. paquebot m.

▸**line up 1** vt (children, objects) aligner; (arrange) organiser. **2** vi s'aligner; (of people) faire la queue.

lin·ger vi (of person) s'attarder; (of smell, memory) persister; (of doubt) subsister.

lin·guis·tics linguistique f.

lin·ing (of clothes) doublure f.

link 1 vt (connect) relier; (relate) lier (to à). **2** n lien m; (of chain) maillon m; (by road, rail) liaison f.

▸**link up 1** vi (of people etc) s'associer; (of roads) se rejoindre.

li·on lion m.

lip lèvre f.

lip·stick bâton m de rouge; (substance) rouge m (à lèvres).

li·queur liqueur f.

liq·uid n & adj liquide (m).

liq·ui·date vt liquider.

liq·uor alcool m.

list 1 n liste f. **2** vt faire la liste de; (names) mettre sur la liste, inscrire; (name one by one) énumérer.

lis·ten (to) vt écouter.

lis·ten·er (to radio) auditeur, -trice mf.

▸**listen (out) for** vt guetter (un bruit ou les cris etc de).

li·ter litre m.

lit·er·al·ly adv litéralement.

lit·er·ar·y adj littéraire.

lit·er·a·ture littérature f; (pamphlets etc) documentation f.

lit·i·ga·tion litige m.

lit·ter (rubbish) détritus m; (papers) papiers mpl; (young animals) portée f.

lit·tle 1 adj (small) petit. **2** adj & n (not much) peu (de); l. time/etc peu de temps/etc; **she eats l.** elle mange peu; **as l. as possible** le moins possible; **a l. money/etc** (some) un peu d'argent/etc. **3** adv a l. heavy/etc un peu lourd/etc; **to work/etc a l.** travailler/etc un peu; **l. by l.** peu à peu.

live¹ vi vivre; (reside) habiter, vivre. **2** vt (life) mener.

live² 1 adj (electric wire) sous tension; (switch) mal isolé. **2** adj & adv (broadcast) en direct.

live·ly adj (person, style, interest, mind) vif; (discussion) animé.

▸**live off, live on** vt (eat) vivre de.

liv·er foie m.

▸**live through** vt (experience) vivre; (survive) survivre à.

liv·ing 1 adj (alive) vivant. **2** n vie f; **to make** or **earn a** or **one's l.** gagner sa vie; **the cost of l.** le coût de la vie.

liv·ing room salle f de séjour.

liz·ard lézard m.

load 1 n charge f; (weight) poids m; **a l. of, loads of** (people, money etc) Fam un tas de. **2** vt (truck, gun etc) charger (with de).

▸**load up 1** vt (car, ship etc) charger (with de). **2** vi charger la voiture, le navire etc.

loaf, pl **loaves** pain m.

loan 1 n (money lent) prêt m; (money borrowed) emprunt m. **2** vt (lend) prêter (to à).

lob·by (of hotel) hall m.

lob·ster homard m.

lo·cal adj local; (regional) régional; (of the neighborhood) du or de quartier; (of the region) de la région.

lo·cal·i·ty environs mpl.

lo·cal·ly adv dans le coin.

lo·cate vt (find) trouver, repérer; **to be located** être situé.

lo·ca·tion (site) emplacement m.

lock 1 vt (door etc) fermer à clef. **2** n (on door etc) serrure f; (on canal) écluse f; (of hair) mèche f.

▸**lock away** vt (prisoner, jewels etc) enfermer.

lock·er (for luggage) casier m de consigne automatique; (for clothes) vestiaire m (métallique).

lock·et médaillon m.

▸**lock in** vt enfermer; **to l. sb in sth** enfermer qn dans qch.

▸**lock out** vt (accidentally) enfermer dehors.

▸**lock up 1** vt (house etc) fermer à clef; (prisoner, jewels etc) enfermer. **2** vi fermer à clef.

lodge 1 n (porter's) loge f, (hunter's) pavillon m; (in park, resort) bâtiment m central.**2** vt (accommodate) héberger, loger; (claim) déposer; **to l. a complaint** porter plainte. **3** vi (live) loger, être logé; (get stuck) se loger.

lodg·er (room and meals) pensionnaire mf, (room only) locataire mf.

lodg·ing hébergement m; lodgings chambre(s) f(pl) meublée(s).

loft (attic) grenier m.

log (tree trunk) tronc m d'arbre; (for fire) bûche f.

log·ic logique f.

log·i·cal adj logique.

lol·li·pop sucette f.

lone adj solitaire.

lone·li·ness solitude f.

lone·ly adj solitaire.

long 1 adj long (f longue); **to be 33 feet l.** avoir dix mètres de long; **to be six weeks l.** durer six semaines; **a l. time** longtemps. **2** adv longtemps; **has he been here l.?** il y a longtemps qu'il est ici?; **how l. ago?** il y a combien de temps?; **before l.** sous peu; **she no longer swims** elle ne nage plus; **I won't be l.** je n'en ai pas pour longtemps; **all summer l.** tout l'été; **as l. as, so l. as** (provided that) pourvu que (+ subjunctive).

long-dis·tance (phone call) interurbain; (flight) long-courrier.

long johns caleçon m (long).

long-term adj à long terme.

look 1 n regard m; (appearance) air m; **to have a l. (at)** jeter un coup d'œil (à); **to have a l. (for)** chercher; **to have a l. around** regarder; (walk) faire un tour; **let me have a l.** fais voir. **2** vi regarder; **to l. tired/**
etc sembler or avoir l'air fatigué/etc; **you l. like** or **as if you're tired** on dirait que tu es fatigué; **to l. well** or **good** (of person) avoir bonne mine; **you l. good in that hat**/etc ce chapeau/etc te va très bien.

▸**look around 1** vt visiter. **2** vi regarder; (walk around) faire un tour; (look back) se retourner.

▸**look at** vt regarder.

▸**look back** vi regarder derrière soi; (remember) regarder en arrière.

▸**look down** vi baisser les yeux; (from a height) regarder en bas.

▸**look for** vt chercher.

▸**look forward to** vt (event) attendre avec impatience; **to l. forward to doing** avoir hâte de faire.

▸**look into** vt examiner; (find out about) se renseigner sur.

▸**look (out) on to** vt (of window etc) donner sur.

look·out (high place) observatoire m; **to be on the l.** faire le guet; **to be on the l. for** guetter.

▸**look out** vi (be careful) faire attention (for à).

▸**look over** or **through** vt examiner; (briefly) parcourir; (region, town) parcourir.

▸**look up 1** vi lever les yeux; (into the air) regarder en l'air; (improve) s'améliorer. **2** vt (word) chercher.

loom¹ métier m à tisser.

loom² vi (of mountain) apparaître indistinctement; (of event) paraître imminent.

loop boucle f.

loose 1 adj (screw, belt, knot) desserré; (tooth) branlant; (page) détaché; (clothes) flottant; (tea etc) au poids; (having escaped) (animal) échappé; (prisoner) évadé; **l. change** petite monnaie f; **to set** or **turn l.** (dog etc) lâcher. **2** n **on the l.** (prisoner) évadé; (animal) échappé.

loos·en vt (knot, belt, screw) desserrer.

lord seigneur *m*.

lose* **1** *vt* perdre; **to get lost** *(of person)* se perdre; **the ticket/etc got lost** on a perdu le billet/*etc*. **2** *vi* perdre.

los·er *(in contest etc)* perdant, -ante *mf*.

▸**lose to** *vt* être battu par.

loss perte *f*.

lost *adj* perdu.

lost and found objets *mpl* trouvés.

lot **a l. of, lots of** beaucoup de; **a l.** beaucoup; **quite a l.** pas mal *(of* de*)*; **such a l.** tellement *(of* de*)*; **what a l. of flowers/water/etc!** regarde toutes ces fleurs/toute cette eau/*etc*!

lo·tion lotion *f*.

lot·ter·y loterie *f*.

loud **1** *adj (voice, music)* fort; *(noise, cry)* grand; **the radio/TV is too l.** le son de la radio/télé est trop fort. **2** *adv (to shout etc)* fort; **out l.** tout haut.

loud·ly *adv (to speak etc)* fort.

loud·speak·er haut-parleur *m*; *(for speaking to crowd)* porte-voix *m inv*.

lounge salon *m*; **teachers' l.** salle *f* des professeurs.

lous·y *adj (food, weather etc) Fam* infect.

love **1** *n* amour *m*; **in l.** amoureux *(* **with** de*)*; **they're in l.** ils s'aiment. **2** *vt* aimer (beaucoup) *(* **to do, doing** faire*)*.

love·ly *adj* agréable; *(excellent)* excellent; *(pretty)* joli; *(charming)* charmant; *(kind)* gentil.

lov·er **a l. of music/etc** un amateur de musique/*etc*.

lov·ing *adj* affectueux.

low **1** *adj (voice)* bas; *(speed, income, intelligence)* faible; *(opinion, quality)* mauvais; **to feel l.** être déprimé; **in a l. voice** à voix basse; **lower** inférieur. **2** *adv* bas; **to turn down l.** baisser.

low beams *(of vehicle)* codes *mpl*.

low·er *vt* baisser; *(by rope)* descendre.

low-fat *adj (milk)* écrémé; *(cheese)* allégé.

loy·al *adj* fidèle *(* **to** à*)*, loyal *(* **to** envers*)*.

loy·al·ty loyauté *f*.

loz·enge *(tablet)* pastille *f*.

luck *(chance)* chance *f*; **bad l.** malchance *f*.

luck·i·ly *adv* heureusement.

luck·y *adj (person)* chanceux; *(guess, event)* heureux; **to be l.** avoir de la chance *(* **to do** de faire*)*; **it's l. that** c'est une chance que; **l. charm** porte-bonheur *m inv*; **l. number/etc** chiffre *m/etc* porte-bonheur.

lu·di·crous *adj* ridicule.

lug·gage bagages *mpl*.

luke·warm *adj* tiède.

lull·a·by berceuse *f*.

lum·ber bois *m* de charpente.

lum·ber·yard dépôt *m* de bois.

lu·mi·nous *adj* lumineux.

lump morceau *m*; *(bump)* bosse *f*; *(swelling)* grosseur *f*.

lump sum somme *f* forfaitaire.

lu·na·tic fou *m*, folle *f*.

lunch déjeuner *m*; **to have l.** déjeuner; **l. break, l. hour, l. time** heure *f* du déjeuner.

lung poumon *m*.

lux·u·ri·ous *adj* luxueux.

lux·u·ry **1** *n* luxe *m*. **2** *adj (goods etc)* de luxe.

M

MA *abbr* = **Master of Arts**.

mac·a·ro·ni macaroni(s) *m(pl)*.

ma·chine machine *f*.

ma·chine gun *(heavy)* mitrailleuse *f*; *(portable)* mitraillette *f*.

ma·chin·er·y machines *fpl*; *(works)* mécanisme *m*.

mack·er·el *n inv* maquereau *m*.

mad *adj* fou *(folle)*; **m. (at)** *(angry)* furieux (contre); **m. about** *(person)* fou de; *(films etc)* passionné de; **like m.** comme un fou *or* une folle.

Mad·am madame *f*; *(unmarried)* mademoiselle *f*.

made *pt & pp de* **make**.

mad·man, *pl* **-men** fou *m*.

mad·ness folie *f*.

mag·a·zine magazine *m*, revue *f*.

mag·got ver *m*.

mag·ic 1 *n* magie *f*. 2 *adj (wand etc)* magique.

mag·i·cal *adj* magique.

ma·gi·cian magicien, -ienne *mf*.

mag·is·trate magistrat *m*.

mag·net aimant *m*.

mag·nif·i·cent *adj* magnifique.

mag·ni·fy·ing glass loupe *f*.

ma·hog·a·ny acajou *m*.

maid *(servant)* bonne *f*.

mail 1 *n (system)* poste *f*, *(letters)* courrier *m*. 2 *adj (bag etc)* postal. 3 *vt (letter)* poster.

mail·box boîte *f* aux *or* à lettres.

mail·man, *pl* **-men** facteur *m*.

main¹ *adj* principal; **the m. thing is to** l'essentiel est de; **m. road** grand-route *f*.

main² **water/gas m.** conduite *f* d'eau/de gaz; **the mains** *(electricity)* le secteur.

main·land continent *m*.

main·ly *adv* surtout.

main street grand-rue *f*.

main·tain *vt (vehicle etc)* entretenir; *(law and order)* faire respecter; **to m. that** affirmer que.

main·te·nance *(of vehicle, road)* entretien *m*; *(alimony)* pension *f* alimentaire.

mai·son·ette duplex *m*.

mai·tre d' maître *m* d'hôtel.

maj·es·ty majesté *f*; **Your M.** Votre Majesté.

ma·jor 1 *adj* majeur; **a m. road** une

grande route. 2 *n (officer)* commandant *m*.

ma·jor·ette majorette *f*.

ma·jor·i·ty majorité *f (of* de); **the m. of people** la plupart des gens.

make* 1 *vt* faire; *(tool, vehicle etc)* fabriquer; *(decision)* prendre; *(friends, salary)* se faire; *(destination)* arriver à; **to m. happy/etc** rendre heureux/etc; **to m. sb do sth** faire faire qch à qn; **to m. do** *(manage)* se débrouiller (**with** avec); **to m. do with** *(be satisfied with)* se contenter de; **to m. it** arriver; *(succeed)* réussir; **what do you m. of it?** qu'en penses-tu? 2 *n (brand)* marque *f*.

▶ **make for** *vt* aller vers.

▶ **make good** *vt (loss)* compenser; *(damage)* réparer.

▶ **make off** *vi (run away)* se sauver.

▶ **make out 1** *vt (see)* distinguer; *(understand)* comprendre; *(write)* faire *(chèque, liste)*; *(claim)* prétendre *(that* que). 2 *vi Fam* se peloter.

mak·er *(of product)* fabricant, -ante *mf*.

make-up *(for face)* maquillage *m*.

▶ **make up 1** *vt (story)* inventer; *(put together)* faire *(collection, liste etc)*; *(form)* former; *(loss)* compenser; *(quantity)* compléter; *(quarrel)* régler; *(one's face)* maquiller. 2 *vti* **to m. (it) up** *(of friends)* se réconcilier.

▶ **make up for** *vt (loss, damage)* compenser; *(lost time, mistake)* rattraper.

ma·lar·i·a malaria *f*.

male 1 *adj* mâle; *(clothes, sex)* masculin. 2 *n* mâle *m*.

mal·ice méchanceté *f*.

ma·li·cious *adj* malveillant.

mall *(shopping)* **m.** galerie *f* marchande; *(large complex)* centre *m* commercial.

ma·ma, mam·ma *Fam* maman *f*.

mam·mal mammifère *m*.

man, *pl* **men** homme *m*.

man·age 1 vt (run) diriger; (handle) manier; **to m. to do** (succeed) réussir à faire; (by being smart) se débrouiller pour faire; **I'll m. it** j'y arriverai. **2** vi (succeed) y arriver; (make do) se débrouiller (**with** avec); **to m. without sth** se passer de qch.

man·age·ment (running, managers) direction f.

man·ag·er directeur, -trice mf; (of shop, café) gérant, -ante mf.

man·ag·ing di·rec·tor PDG m.

mane crinière f.

ma·neu·ver 1 n manœuvre f. **2** vti manœuvrer.

ma·ni·ac fou m, folle f.

man·kind l'humanité f.

man·made adj artificiel.

man·ner (way) manière f; (behavior) attitude f; **manners** (social habits) manières fpl; **to have no manners** être mal élevé.

man·pow·er main f d'œuvre.

man·tel·piece (shelf) cheminée f.

man·u·al 1 adj manuel. **2** n (book) manuel m.

man·u·fac·ture 1 vt fabriquer. **2** n fabrication f.

man·u·fac·tur·er fabricant, -ante mf.

ma·nure fumier m.

man·y adj & n beaucoup (de); **m. things** beaucoup de choses; **I don't have m.** j'en ai pas beaucoup; **m. came** beaucoup sont venus; **(a good** or **great) m. of** un (très) grand nombre de; **m. times** bien des fois; **as m. books/etc as** autant de livres/etc que.

map (of country, region) carte f; (of town etc) plan m.

mar·a·thon marathon m.

mar·ble marbre m; (toy) bille f.

March mars m.

march 1 n marche f (militaire). **2** vi (of soldiers) défiler.

mare jument f.

mar·ga·rine margarine f.

mar·gin (of page) marge f.

ma·rine 1 adj marin. **2** n marine m; **the M. Corps** les Marines mpl.

mark 1 n (symbol) marque f; (stain, trace) trace f; (token, sign) signe m; (for school exercise etc) note f; (target) but m. **2** vt marquer; (exam etc) corriger.

mark·er (pen) marqueur m.

mar·ket marché m.

mar·ket·ing marketing m.

▸ **mark off** vt (area) délimiter.

mar·ma·lade confiture f d'oranges.

mar·riage mariage m.

mar·ried adj marié; **to get m.** se marier.

mar·row (of bone) moelle f.

mar·ry 1 vt épouser, se marier avec; (of priest etc) marier. **2** vi se marier.

marsh marais m.

mar·shal 1 n (in army) maréchal m; (district police officer) commissaire m; (police chief) commissaire m de police; (fire chief) capitaine m des pompiers. **2** vt (troops) masser, rassembler; (facts, arguments etc) rassembler.

mar·vel·ous adj merveilleux.

mar·zi·pan pâte f d'amandes.

mas·car·a mascara m.

mas·cot mascotte f.

mas·cu·line adj masculin.

mash vt **to m. (up)** écraser, broyer; (food) faire une purée de; **mashed potatoes** purée f (de pommes de terre).

mask masque m.

mass¹ n (quantity) masse f; **a m. of** (many) une multitude de; (pile) un tas de; **masses of** des masses de. **2** adj (protests, departure) en masse.

mass² (church service) messe f.

mas·sa·cre 1 n massacre m. **2** vt massacrer.

mas·sage 1 n massage m. **2** vt masser.

mas·seur masseur m.

mas·seuse masseuse f.

mas·sive adj (huge) énorme.

mast (of ship) mât m.

mas·ter 1 n maître m; M. of Arts/ Science (person) Maître m ès lettres/sciences; **M. of Ceremonies** animateur, -trice mf. 2 vt (control) maîtriser; (subject, situation) dominer; **she has mastered Latin** elle possède le latin.

mas·ter·piece chef-d'œuvre m.

mat tapis m; (of straw) natte f; (at door) paillasson m; **(place) m.** set m (de table).

match¹ (stick) allumette f.

match² 1 n (game) match m; (equal) égal, -ale mf; **to be a good m.** (of colors, people etc) être bien assortis. 2 vt (of clothes, color etc) aller (bien) avec; **to be well-matched** être (bien) assortis. 3 vi être assortis.

match·box boîte f d'allumettes.

match·ing adj (dress etc) assorti.

match·stick allumette f.

▸ **match up** vt (plates etc) assortir.

▸ **match up to** vt égaler; (sb's hopes or expectations) répondre à.

mate (friend) camarade mf.

ma·ter·i·al matière f; (cloth) tissu m; **material(s)** (equipment) matériel m; **building materials** matériaux mpl de construction.

ma·ter·nal adj maternel.

math maths fpl.

math·e·mat·i·cal adj mathématique.

math·e·mat·ics mathématiques fpl.

mat·i·nee (in theater) matinée f.

matt adj (paint, paper) mat.

mat·ter¹ 1 n matière f; (subject, affair) affaire f; **what's the m. with you?** qu'est-ce que tu as?; **there's sth the m.** il y a qch qui ne va pas; **there's something the m. with my leg** j'ai quelque chose à la jambe. 2 vi importer (**to** à); **it doesn't m. if/ who/etc** peu importe si/qui/etc; **it**

doesn't m.! ça ne fait rien!

mat·tress matelas m.

ma·ture adj mûr; (cheese) fait.

max·i·mum adj & n maximum (m).

May mai m.

may v aux (pt might) (possibility) pouvoir; **he m. come** il peut arriver; **he might come** il pourrait arriver; **I m. or might have forgotten it** je l'ai peut-être oublié; **we m. or might as well go** nous ferions aussi bien de partir. ▪ (permission) pouvoir; **m. I stay?** puis-je rester?; **m. I?** vous permettez?; **you m. go** tu peux partir. ▪ (wish) **m. you be happy** (que) tu sois heureux.

may·be adv peut-être.

may·on·naise mayonnaise f.

may·or maire m.

maze labyrinthe m.

MBA abbr (Master of Business Administration) MBA m, maîtrise f de gestion.

me pron me, m'; (after prep, 'than', 'it is') moi; (to) **me** me, m'; **she knows me** elle me connaît; **he gives (to) me** il me donne.

mead·ow pré m.

meal repas m.

mean¹ vt (signify) vouloir dire; (intend) destiner (**for** à); (result in) entraîner; **to m. to do** avoir l'intention de faire; **I m. it** je suis sérieux; **to m. sth to sb** avoir de l'importance pour qn; **I didn't m. to!** je ne l'ai pas fait exprès!

mean² adj méchant.

mean·ing sens m.

mean·ing·ful adj significatif.

mean·ing·less adj qui n'a pas de sens.

mean·ness méchanceté f.

means n(pl) (method) moyen(s) m(pl) (**to do, of doing** de faire); (wealth) moyens mpl; **by m. of** (stick etc) au moyen de; (work etc) à force de; **by all m.!** très certainement!; **by no m.** nullement.

mean·time adv & n (in the) m. entre-temps.

mean·while adv entre-temps.

mea·sles rougeole f.

mea·sure 1 n (action, amount) mesure f. **2** vt mesurer.

meas·ure·ment (of chest etc) tour m; **measurements** mesures fpl.

▸**measure up** vt (plank etc) mesurer.

▸**measure up to** vt (task) être à la hauteur de.

meat viande f.

me·chan·ic mécanicien, -ienne mf.

me·chan·i·cal adj mécanique.

mech·a·nism mécanisme m.

med·al médaille f.

med·al·ist to be a gold m. être médaillé d'or.

me·di·a npl the (mass) m. les médias mpl.

me·di·an (in road) refuge m.

med·i·cal adj médical; (school, studies) de médecine; (student) en médecine.

med·i·ca·tion médicaments mpl.

med·i·cine médicament m; (science) médecine f.

med·i·cine cab·i·net, med·i·cine chest (armoire f à) pharmacie f.

me·di·e·val adj médiéval.

Med·i·ter·ra·ne·an 1 adj méditerranéen. **2** n the M. la Méditerranée.

me·di·um adj moyen.

me·di·um-sized adj moyen.

meet* 1 vt (person, team) rencontrer; (person by arrangement) retrouver; (pass in street etc) croiser; (fetch) (aller or venir) chercher; (wait for) attendre; (be introduced to) faire la connaissance de. **2** vi (of people, teams) se rencontrer; (of people by arrangement) se retrouver; (be introduced) se connaître; (of club etc) se réunir.

meet·ing réunion f, (large) assemblée f, (between two people) rencontre f, (arranged) rendez-vous m inv.

▸**meet up** vi (of people) se rencontrer; (by arrangement) se retrouver.

▸**meet up with** vt rencontrer; (by arrangement) retrouver.

▸**meet with** vt (accident) avoir; (difficulty) rencontrer; (person) rencontrer; (by arrangement) retrouver.

meg·a·byte mégaoctet m.

mel·o·dy mélodie f.

mel·on melon m.

melt 1 vi fondre. **2** vt (faire) fondre.

mem·ber membre m.

mem·o, pl -os note f.

mem·o·ra·ble adj mémorable.

me·mo·ri·al 1 adj (plaque etc) commémoratif. **2** n mémorial m.

mem·o·ry mémoire f, (recollection) souvenir m; **in m. of** à la mémoire de; **m. stick** clé f USB.

men see **man**.

mend vt réparer; (clothes) raccommoder.

men·tal adj mental.

men·tal·ly adv he's m. handicapped c'est un handicapé mental; she's m. ill c'est une malade mentale.

men·tion 1 vt mentionner; not to m... sans parler de...; **don't m. it!** il n'y a pas de quoi! **2** n mention f.

men·u menu m.

me·ow vi (of cat) miauler.

mer·cy pitié f, at the m. of à la merci de.

mere adj simple; (only) ne...que; she's a m. child ce n'est qu'une enfant.

mere·ly adv (tout) simplement.

merge vi (blend) se mêler (with à); (of roads) se (re)joindre; (of firms) fusionner.

merg·er fusion f.

mer·it 1 n mérite m. **2** vt mériter.

mer·ry adj gai.

mer·ry-go-round (at fair) manège m.

MEETING PEOPLE

Hello, how are you?
Bonjour, comment ça va ?

Hi, how's it going?
Salut, ça va ?

Fine thank you, how are you?
Bien, merci, et vous/toi ?

Good, and you?
Ça va, et toi/vous ?

Good morning/afternoon.
Bonjour.

Good evening.
Bonsoir.

What's your name?
Comment vous appelez-vous ?/
Comment t'appelles-tu ?

My name's Eve.
Je m'appelle Eve.

I'm Brian and this is my wife Kim.
Je suis Brian, et voici Kim, ma femme.

Nice to meet you.
Enchanté(e).

How old are you?
Quel âge avez-vous/as-tu ?

I'm 15/25 (years old).
J'ai quinze/vingt-cinq ans.

Where are you from?
D'où venez-vous/viens-tu ?

I'm from the United States./I'm American.
Je viens des États-Unis./Je suis
américain(e).

Where do you live?
Où habitez-vous/habites-tu ?

I live near San Francisco.
J'habite près de San Francisco.

What do you do?
Que faites-vous/fais-tu dans la vie ?

I'm a teacher/a student.
Je suis professeur/étudiant(e).

I'm in high school.
Je suis au lycée.

I'm a stay-at-home mom.
Je suis mère au foyer.

I work for an insurance company.
Je travaille dans les assurances.

I'm retired.
Je suis à la retraite.

Do you have any brothers and sisters?
Vous avez/Tu as des frères et des sœurs ?

I've got an older sister and two little brothers.
J'ai une sœur aînée et deux petits frères.

Do you have kids?
Vous avez/Tu as des enfants ?

We have a three-year-old son named Josh.
Nous avons un fils de trois ans qui
s'appelle Josh.

Are you married?
Est-ce que vous êtes/tu es marié(e) ?

I'm divorced/separated/widowed.
Je suis divorcé(e)/séparé(e)/veuf (veuve).

What do you do in your spare time?
Que faites-vous pendant votre temps
libre ?/
Qu'est ce que tu fais pendant ton temps libre ?

I like reading/going to the movies.
J'aime lire/aller au cinéma.

I play basketball/do yoga.
Je joue au basket/fais du yoga.

I'm taking French classes.
Je suis des cours de français.

See you soon/later!
À bientôt/plus tard !

Have a good weekend/trip!
Bon weekend/voyage !

We should keep in touch, here's my e-mail address.
Nous devrions garder le contact, voici mon adresse e-mail.

mesh (of net) maille f.

mess (confusion) désordre m; (dirt) saleté f; **in a m.** sens dessus dessous; (trouble) dans le pétrin.

mes·sage message m.

▸ **mess around** vi (have fun) s'amuser; (play the fool) faire l'idiot.

▸ **mess around with** vt (fiddle with) s'amuser avec.

mes·sen·ger messager m; (in office, hotel) coursier, -ière mf.

▸ **mess up** vt (ruin) gâcher; (dirty) salir; (room) mettre sens dessus dessous.

mess·y adj (untidy) en désordre; (dirty) sale.

met·al métal m; **m. ladder/etc** échelle f/etc métallique.

met·a·phor métaphore f.

me·ter¹ (device) compteur m; (parking) m. parcmètre m.

me·ter² mètre m.

meth·od méthode f.

me·thod·i·cal adj méthodique.

met·ric adj métrique.

mice see **mouse**.

mi·cro prefix micro-.

mi·cro·chip puce f.

mi·cro·phone micro m.

mi·cro·scope microscope m.

mi·cro·wave (ov·en) four m à micro-ondes.

mid adj (in) **m.-June** (à) la mi-juin; **in m. air** en plein ciel.

mid·day midi m.

mid·dle 1 n milieu m; (waist) taille f; (right) **in the m. of** au (beau) milieu de; **in the m. of saying/etc** en train de dire/etc. **2** adj du milieu; (class) moyen; (name) deuxième.

mid·dle-aged adj d'un certain âge.

mid·dle-class adj bourgeois.

mid·night minuit m.

mid·se·mes·ter break vacances fpl scolaires.

midst **in the m. of** au milieu de.

mid·way adv à mi-chemin.

mid·wife, pl -wives sage-femme f.

might see **may**.

might·y 1 adj (powerful) puissant; (great) énorme. **2** adv Fam rudement.

mild adj doux (f douce); (beer, punishment) léger; (medicine, illness) bénin (f bénigne).

mile mile m (= 1,6km).

mile·age ≃ kilométrage m.

mil·i·ta·ry adj militaire.

milk 1 n lait m. **2** adj (chocolate) au lait; (bottle) à lait. **3** vt (cow) traire.

milk·man, pl -men laitier m.

milk·shake milk-shake m.

mill moulin m; (factory) usine f.

mil·li·me·ter millimètre m.

mil·lion million m; **a m. men/etc** un million d'hommes/etc.

mil·lion·aire millionnaire mf.

mime vti mimer.

mim·ic 1 n imitateur, -trice mf. **2** vt (-ck-) imiter.

mince vt hacher; **she doesn't m. words** elle ne mâche pas ses mots.

mind 1 n esprit m; (sanity) raison f; (memory) mémoire f; **to change one's m.** changer d'avis; **to make up one's m.** se décider; **to be on sb's m.** préoccuper qn; **to have in m.** (person, plan) avoir en vue. **2** vti faire attention à; (look after) garder; (noise etc) être gêné par; **do you m. if?** (I smoke) ça vous gêne si?; (I leave) ça ne vous fait rien si?; **I don't m.** ça m'est égal; **I wouldn't m. a cup of tea** j'aimerais bien une tasse de thé; **never m.!** ça ne fait rien!; (don't worry) ne vous en faites pas!

mine¹ poss pron le mien, la mienne, pl les mien(ne)s; **this hat is m.** ce chapeau est à moi or est le mien.

mine² (for coal etc, explosive) mine f.

min·er mineur m.

min·er·al adj & n minéral (m).

min·i- prefix mini-.

min·i·a·ture adj (train etc) minia-

ture *inv;* **in m.** en miniature.

min·i·bus minibus *m.*

min·i·mum *adj & n* minimum (*m*).

min·ing 1 *n* exploitation *f* minière, extraction *f.* **2** *adj* minier.

min·is·ter *(clergyman)* pasteur *m.*

min·is·try **to enter the m.** devenir pasteur.

mi·nor *adj (detail, operation)* petit.

mi·nor·i·ty minorité *f.*

mint *(herb)* menthe *f; (candy)* bonbon *m* à la menthe; **m. tea/etc** thé *m/etc* à la menthe.

mi·nus *prep* moins; *(without)* sans.

min·ute[1] minute *f.*

mi·nute[2] *adj (tiny)* minuscule.

mir·a·cle miracle *m.*

mi·rac·u·lous *adj* miraculeux.

mir·ror miroir *m*, glace *f; (in vehicle)* rétroviseur *m.*

mis·be·have *vi* se conduire mal.

mis·cel·la·ne·ous *adj* divers.

mis·chief espièglerie *f; (malice)* méchanceté *f;* **to get into m.** faire des bêtises.

mis·chie·vous *adj* espiègle; *(harmful)* méchant, nuisible.

misdemeanor délit *m*

mi·ser avare *mf.*

mis·er·a·ble *adj (wretched)* misérable; *(unhappy)* malheureux.

mi·ser·ly *adj* avare.

mis·er·y souffrances *fpl; (sadness)* tristesse *f.*

mis·for·tune malheur *m.*

mis·hap contretemps *m.*

mis·lay* *vt* égarer.

mis·lead *vt* tromper.

mis·lead·ing *adj* trompeur.

miss[1] **1** *vt (train, opportunity etc)* manquer; *(not see)* ne pas voir; *(not understand)* ne pas comprendre; **he misses Paris/her** Paris/elle lui manque. **2** *vi* manquer.

miss[2] *(woman)* mademoiselle *f;* **Miss Brown** Mademoiselle *or* Mlle Brown.

mis·sile *(rocket)* missile *m; (object thrown)* projectile *m.*

mis·sing *adj* absent; *(after disaster)* disparu; *(object)* manquant; **there are two cups m.** il manque deux tasses.

mis·sion mission *f.*

▶ **miss out 1** *vt (leave out)* sauter. **2** *vi* rater l'occasion.

▶ **miss out on** *vt (opportunity etc)* rater.

mist *(fog)* brume *f; (on glass)* buée *f.*

mis·take 1 *n* erreur *f*, faute *f;* **to make a m.** se tromper; **by m.** par erreur. **2** *vt* (meaning etc)* se tromper sur; **to m. sb/sth for** prendre qn/qch pour; **you're mistaken** tu te trompes.

mis·ta·ken·ly *adv* par erreur.

mis·treat *vt* maltraiter.

mis·tress maîtresse *f.*

mis·trust 1 *n* méfiance *f.* **2** *vt* se méfier de.

mist·y *adj* brumeux.

mis·un·der·stand* *vt* mal comprendre.

mis·un·der·stand·ing malentendu *m.*

mit·ten *(glove)* moufle *f.*

mix 1 *vt* mélanger, mêler; *(cake)* préparer; *(salad)* remuer. **2** *vi* se mêler; **she doesn't m.** elle n'est pas sociable.

mixed *adj (school)* mixte; *(chocolates etc)* assortis.

mix·er *(electric, for cooking)* mixe(u)r *m.*

mix·ture mélange *m.*

mix-up confusion *f.*

▶ **mix up** *vt (drink, papers etc)* mélanger; *(make confused)* embrouiller *(qn); (mistake)* confondre (**with** avec).

▶ **mix with** *vt* fréquenter.

moan *vi (groan)* gémir; *(complain)* se plaindre (**to** à; **about** de; **that** que).

mob 1 *n* foule *f.* **2** *vt* assiéger.

mo·bile *adj* mobile.

mod·el 1 n (example etc) modèle m; (fashion) m. mannequin m; (scale) m. modèle m (réduit). 2 adj (car, plane etc) modèle réduit inv; m. train train m miniature.

mod·el·ing clay pâte f à modeler.

mo·dem modem m.

mod·er·ate adj modéré.

mod·er·a·tion modération f.

mod·ern adj moderne; **m. languages** langues fpl vivantes.

mod·ern·ize 1 vt moderniser. 2 vi se moderniser.

mod·est adj modeste.

mod·es·ty modestie f.

mod·i·fi·ca·tion modification f.

mod·i·fy vt modifier.

moist adj humide; (sticky) moite.

mois·ture humidité f, (on glass) buée f.

mold 1 n (shape) moule m; (growth) moisissure f. 2 vt (clay etc) mouler.

mold·y adj moisi; **to get m.** moisir.

mole (on skin) grain m de beauté; (animal) taupe f.

mom Fam maman f.

mo·ment moment m; **the m. she leaves** dès qu'elle partira.

mom·my Fam maman f.

Mon·day lundi m.

mon·ey argent m.

mon·ey or·der mandat m.

mon·i·tor (computer screen) moniteur m (d'ordinateur).

monk moine m.

mon·key singe m.

mo·nop·o·lize vt monopoliser.

mo·not·o·nous adj monotone.

mo·not·o·ny monotonie f.

mon·ster monstre m.

month mois m.

month·ly 1 adj mensuel. 2 adv mensuellement.

mon·u·ment monument m.

moo vi meugler.

mood (of person) humeur f, Grammar mode m; **in a good/bad m.** de bonne/mauvaise humeur; **to be in** the m. to do être d'humeur à faire.

mood·y adj (bad-tempered) de mauvaise humeur.

moon lune f.

moon·light clair m de lune.

moor lande f.

moose inv élan m.

mop 1 n balai m (à laver). 2 vt (floor etc) essuyer.

mo·ped mobylette® f.

▶ **mop up** vt (liquid) éponger.

mor·al (of story) morale f.

mo·rale moral m.

more 1 adj & n plus (de) (than que); (other) d'autres; **m. cars/etc** plus de voitures/etc; **he has m. (than you)** il en a plus (que toi); **a few m. months** encore quelques mois; **(some) m. tea/etc** encore du thé/etc; **m. than a quart/ten** (with quantity, number) plus d'un litre/de dix; **many m., much m.** beaucoup plus (de). 2 adv plus (than que); **m. and m.** de plus en plus; **m. or less** plus ou moins; **she doesn't have any m.** elle n'en a plus.

more·o·ver adv de plus.

morn·ing matin m; (duration of morning) matinée f, **in the m.** le matin; (tomorrow) demain matin; **at seven in the m.** à sept heures du matin; **every Tuesday m.** tous les mardis matin.

mor·tal adj & n mortel, -elle (mf).

mort·gage prêt-logement m.

Mos·lem adj & n musulman, -ane (mf).

mosque mosquée f.

mos·qui·to, pl -oes moustique m.

moss mousse f (plante).

most 1 adj & n **the m.** le plus (de); **I have the m. books** j'ai le plus de livres; **I have the m.** j'en ai le plus; **m. (of the) books/etc** la plupart des livres/etc; **m. of the cake/etc** la plus grande partie du gâteau/etc; **at (the very) m.** tout au plus. 2 adv (le) plus; (very) très; **the m. beautiful** le plus beau, la plus belle (in, of

de); **to talk (the) m.** parler le plus;
m. of all surtout.

most·ly adv surtout.

mo·tel motel m.

moth papillon m de nuit; (in
clothes) mite f.

moth·er mère f; **M.'s Day** la fête
des Mères.

moth·er-in-law, pl mothers-in-
law belle-mère f.

mo·tion 1 n (of arm etc) mouvement m. **2** vti **to m. (to) sb to do**
faire signe à qn de faire.

mo·ti·vat·ed adj motivé.

mo·tive motif m (**for** de).

mo·tor (engine) moteur m.

mo·tor·bike moto f.

mo·tor·boat canot m automobile.

mo·tor·cy·cle motocyclette f.

mo·tor·cy·clist motocycliste mf.

mo·tor·ist automobiliste mf.

mount 1 n (frame for photo) cadre
m. **2** vt (horse, photo) monter. **3** vi
(on horse) se mettre en selle.

moun·tain montagne f; **m. bike**
VTT m inv.

moun·tain·eer alpiniste mf.

moun·tain·eer·ing alpinisme m.

moun·tain·ous adj montagneux.

▸**mount up** vi (add up) chiffrer (**to**
à); (accumulate) s'accumuler.

mourn vt **to m. (for) sb,** **to m. the**
loss of sb pleurer (la perte de) qn;
she's mourning elle est en deuil.

mourn·ing deuil m; **in m.** en
deuil.

mouse, pl **mice** souris f.

mousse mousse f (dessert).

mouth, pl **-s** bouche f, (of dog, lion
etc) gueule f, (of river) embouchure
f.

mouth·wash bain m de bouche.

move 1 n mouvement m; (change
of house) déménagement m; (in
game) coup m; (one's turn) tour m;
(act) démarche f; **to make a m.**
(leave) se préparer à partir; **to get**

a m. on se remuer. **2** vt déplacer;
(arm, leg) remuer; (put) mettre;
(transport) transporter; (piece in
game) jouer; **to m. sb** (emotionally)
émouvoir qn; (transfer in job) muter
qn. **3** vi bouger; (go) aller (**to** à);
(out of house) déménager; (change
seats) changer de place; (play)
jouer; **to m. to a new house/etc** aller habiter une nouvelle maison/
etc; **to m. into a house** emménager
dans une maison.

▸**move along** vi avancer.

▸**move around** vi se déplacer; (fidget) remuer.

▸**move away** vi s'éloigner; (to new
house) déménager.

▸**move back 1** vt (chair etc) reculer;
(to its position) remettre. **2** vi reculer; (return) retourner.

▸**move down** vti descendre.

▸**move forward** vti avancer.

▸**move in** vi (into house) emménager.

move·ment (action, group etc)
mouvement m.

▸**move off** vi (go away) s'éloigner;
(of vehicle) démarrer.

▸**move on** vi avancer.

▸**move out** vi (out of house) déménager.

▸**move over 1** vt pousser. **2** vi se
pousser.

mov·er déménageur m.

▸**move up 1** vt (meeting) avancer. **2**
vi (on seats etc) se pousser.

mov·ie film m; **the movies** (art,
movie theater) le cinéma.

mov·ie cam·er·a caméra f.

mov·ie star vedette f de cinéma.

mov·ie the·a·ter cinéma m.

mov·ing adj en mouvement; (touching) émouvant.

mov·ing van camion m de déménagement.

mow vt (pp **mown** or **mowed**) **to**
m. the lawn tondre le gazon.

mow·er (lawn) m. tondeuse f (à
gazon).

MP3 *abbr (MPEG1 Audio Layer)* M. player lecteur *m* MP3.

Mr Mr Brown Monsieur *or* M. Brown.

Mrs Mrs Brown Madame *or* Mme Brown.

Ms Ms Brown Madame *or* Mme Brown.

MS, MSc *abbr* = Master of Science.

much 1 *adj & n* beaucoup (de); not m. time/etc pas beaucoup de temps/etc; I don't have m. je n'en ai pas beaucoup; as m. as autant que; as m. wine/etc as autant de vin/etc que; twice as m. deux fois plus (de). **2** *adv* very m. beaucoup; not (very) m. pas beaucoup.

mud boue *f*.

mud·dle *(mix-up)* confusion *f*; *(mess)* désordre *m*; in a m. *(person)* désorienté; *(mind, ideas)* embrouillé.

mud·dle (up) *vt (person, facts)* embrouiller; *(papers)* mélanger.

▸ **muddle through** *vi* se tirer d'affaire.

mud·dy *adj (water, road)* boueux; *(hands etc)* couvert de boue.

mues·li muesli *m*.

muf·fin muffin *m*.

mug¹ *(cup)* grande tasse *f*; *(beer)* m. chope *f*.

mug² *vt (in street)* agresser, attaquer.

mug·ger agresseur *m*.

mule *(male)* mulet *m*; *(female)* mule *f*.

mul·ti·cul·tur·al *adj* multiculturel.

mul·ti·ple *adj & n* multiple *(m)*.

mul·ti·plex multiplexe *m*.

mul·ti·pli·ca·tion multiplication *f*.

mul·ti·ply *vt* multiplier.

mum·ble *vti* marmotter.

mumps oreillons *mpl*.

mu·nic·i·pal *adj* municipal.

mur·der 1 *n* meurtre *m*, assassinat *m*. **2** *vt* tuer, assassiner.

mur·der·er meurtrier, -ière *mf*, assassin *m*.

mur·mur *vti* murmurer.

mus·cle muscle *m*.

mus·cu·lar *adj (arm etc)* musclé.

mu·se·um musée *m*.

mush·room champignon *m*.

mu·sic musique *f*.

mu·si·cal 1 *adj* musical; *(instrument)* de musique; to be m. être musicien. **2** *n* comédie *f* musicale.

mu·si·cian musicien, -ienne *mf*.

Mus·lim *adj & n* musulman, -ane *(mf)*.

mus·sel moule *f*.

must *v aux (necessity)* devoir; you m. obey tu dois obéir, il faut que tu obéisses. ▪ *(certainty)* devoir; she m. be smart elle doit être intelligente; I m. have seen it j'ai dû le voir.

mus·tache moustache *f*.

mus·tard moutarde *f*.

must·y to smell m. sentir le moisi.

mute **1** *adj* muet. **2** *n (person)* muet, -ette *mf*; *(on musical instrument)* sourdine *f*.

mut·ter *vti* marmonner.

mut·ton *(meat)* mouton *m*.

mu·tu·al *adj (help etc)* mutuel; *(friend)* commun.

muz·zle *(for animal)* muselière *f*.

my *poss adj* mon, ma, *pl* mes.

my·self *pron* moi-même; *(reflexive)* me, m'; *(after prep)* moi.

mys·te·ri·ous *adj* mystérieux.

mys·ter·y mystère *m*; *(novel)* roman *m* policier; *(movie)* film *m* policier.

myth mythe *m*.

N

nail *(of finger, toe)* ongle *m*; *(metal)* clou *m*; n. file/polish lime *f*/vernis *m* à ongles.

nail (down) *vt* clouer.

na·ïve *adj* naïf.

na·ked *adj* nu.

name 1 *n* nom *m*; *(reputation)* réputation *f*; **my n. is…** je m'appelle…; **first n.** prénom *m*; **last n.** nom *m* de famille. **2** *vt* nommer; *(date, price)* fixer; **he was named after** *or* **for** il a reçu le nom de.

name·ly *adv* à savoir.

nan·a *(grandmother) Fam* mamie *f*.

nan·ny nourrice *f*; *(grandmother) Fam* mamie *f*.

nap *(sleep)* petit somme *m*; **to have** *or* **take a n.** faire un petit somme.

nap·kin serviette *f*.

nar·ra·tive 1 *n* récit *m*. **2** *adj* narratif.

nar·row *adj* étroit.

nar·row (down) *vt (choice etc)* limiter.

nar·row·ly he n. escaped being killed/*etc* il a failli être tué/*etc*.

nast·i·ly *adv (to behave)* méchamment.

nas·ty *adj* mauvais; *(spiteful)* méchant (**to(wards)** avec).

na·tion nation *f*.

na·tion·al *adj* national.

na·tion·al·i·ty nationalité *f*.

na·tive 1 *adj (country)* natal *(mpl* -als); **to be an English n. speaker** avoir l'anglais comme langue maternelle. **2** *n* **to be a n. of** être originaire de.

nat·u·ral *adj* naturel; *(actor etc)* né.

nat·u·ral·ly *adv (as normal, of course)* naturellement; *(to behave etc)* avec naturel.

na·ture *(natural world, character)* nature *f*.

na·ture stud·y sciences *fpl* naturelles.

naught rien *m*.

naugh·ty *adj (child)* vilain.

nau·se·at·ing *adj* écœurant.

nau·seous *adj* **to feel n.** avoir envie de vomir.

na·val *adj* naval *(mpl* -als); *(officer)* de marine.

na·vel nombril *m*.

nav·i·gate 1 *vi* naviguer. **2** *vt (boat)* diriger.

nav·i·ga·tion navigation *f*.

na·vy 1 *n* marine *f*. **2** *adj* **n. (blue)** bleu marine *inv*.

near 1 *adv* près; **very n.** tout près; **n.** to près de; **to come n. to being killed/***etc* faillir être tué/*etc*; **n. enough** *(more or less)* plus ou moins. **2** *prep* **n. (to)** près de; **n. (to) the end** vers la fin; **to come n. sb** s'approcher de qn. **3** *adj* proche; **in the n. future** dans un avenir proche.

near·by 1 *adv* tout près. **2** *adj* proche.

near·ly *adv* presque; **she (very) n. fell** elle a failli tomber; **not n. as smart/***etc* **as** loin d'être aussi intelligent/*etc* que.

neat *adj (clothes, work)* soigné; *(room)* bien rangé.

neat·ly *adv* avec soin.

nec·es·sar·i·ly *adv* **not n.** pas forcément.

nec·es·sar·y *adj* nécessaire (**to do** de faire); **to do what's n.** faire le nécessaire.

ne·ces·si·ty nécessité *f*.

neck cou *m*; *(of dress, horse)* encolure *f*.

neck·lace collier *m*.

nec·tar·ine nectarine *f*.

need 1 *n* besoin *m*; **to be in n. of** avoir besoin de; **there's no n. (for you) to do** tu n'as pas besoin de faire; **if n. be** si besoin est. **2** *vt* avoir besoin de; **her hair needs cutting** il faut qu'elle se fasse couper les cheveux; **I needn't have rushed** ce n'était pas la peine de me presser.

nee·dle aiguille *f*.

need·less·ly *adv* inutilement.

nee·dle·work couture *f*; *(object)* ouvrage *m*.

neg·a·tive 1 *adj* négatif. **2** *n (of photo)* négatif *m*; *Grammar* forme *f* négative.

ne·glect vt (person, work, duty etc) négliger; (garden, car) ne pas s'occuper de.

ne·glect·ed adj (appearance) négligé; (garden, house) mal tenu; **to feel n.** se sentir délaissé.

neg·li·gence négligence f.

neg·li·gent adj négligent.

ne·go·ti·ate vti (discuss) négocier.

ne·go·ti·a·tion négociation f.

neigh vi (of horse) hennir.

neigh·bor voisin, -ine mf.

neigh·bor·hood quartier m; (neighbors) voisinage m.

neigh·bor·ing adj voisin.

nei·ther 1 adv n....nor ni...ni; **he n. sings nor dances** il ne chante ni ne danse. **2** conj (not either) **if you won't go, n. will I** si tu n'y vas pas, je n'irai pas non plus. **3** adj **n. boy (came)** aucun des deux garçons (n'est venu). **4** pron **n. (of them)** ni l'un(e) ni l'autre.

ne·on adj (lighting etc) au néon.

neph·ew neveu m.

nerve nerf m; (courage) courage m (**to do** de faire); (calm) sang-froid m; (cheek) culot m (**to do** de faire); **you get on my nerves** tu me tapes sur les nerfs.

nerv·ous adj (tense) nerveux; (worried) inquiet (**about** de); (uneasy) mal à l'aise; **to be** ou **feel n.** (before exam etc) avoir le trac.

nest nid m.

net 1 n filet m. **2** adj (profit, weight etc) net (f nette).

net·ting (wire) n. grillage m.

net·tle ortie f.

net·work réseau m.

neu·tral 1 adj neutre. **2** n **in n.** (gear) au point mort.

nev·er adv (ne...) jamais; **she n. lies** elle ne ment jamais; **n. again** plus jamais.

nev·er-end·ing adj interminable.

nev·er·the·less adv néanmoins.

new adj nouveau (f nouvelle); (brand-new) neuf (f neuve); **a n. glass/etc** (different) un autre verre/etc; **what's n.?** Fam quoi de neuf?

new-born adj **a n. baby** un nouveau-né, une nouveau-née.

new·ly adv (recently) nouvellement.

news nouvelle(s) f(pl); (in the media) informations fpl; **sports n.** (newspaper column) chronique f sportive; **a piece of n., some n.** une nouvelle; (in the media) une information.

news flash flash m.

news·let·ter bulletin m.

news·pa·per journal m.

news·stand kiosque m (à journaux).

next 1 adj prochain; (room, house) d'à côté; (following) suivant; **n. month** (in the future) le mois prochain; **the n. day** le lendemain; **the n. morning** le lendemain matin; (by) **this time n. week** d'ici (à) la semaine prochaine; **to live n. door** habiter à côté (**to** de); **n.-door neighbor** voisin m d'à côté. **2** n suivant, -ante mf. **3** adv (afterwards) ensuite; (now) maintenant; **when you come n.** la prochaine fois que tu viendras. **4** prep **n. to** (beside) à côté de.

nib (of pen) plume f.

nib·ble vti (eat) grignoter; (bite) mordiller.

nice adj (pleasant) agréable; (pretty) joli; (kind) gentil (**to** avec); **it's n. here** c'est bien ici; **n. and warm/etc** (very) bien chaud/etc.

nice·ly adv agréablement; (kindly) gentiment.

nick·el (coin) pièce f de cinq cents.

nick·el-and-dime-store = magasin m à prix unique.

nick·name surnom m.

niece nièce f.

night nuit f; (evening) soir m; **last n.** (evening) hier soir; (night) la nuit dernière; **to have an early/late n.** se coucher tôt/tard; **to have a good n.('s sleep)** bien dormir.

night·club boîte *f* de nuit.

night·gown, *Fam* **nightie** chemise *f* de nuit.

night·in·gale rossignol *m*.

night·mare cauchemar *m*.

night·stand table *f* de nuit.

night·time nuit *f*.

night watch·man veilleur *m* de nuit.

nil zéro *m*.

nine *adj & n* neuf (*m*).

nine·teen *adj & n* dix-neuf (*m*).

nine·ti·eth *adj & n* quatre-vingt-dixième (*mf*).

nine·ty *adj & n* quatre-vingt-dix (*m*).

ninth *adj & n* neuvième (*mf*).

nip 1 *n* (*bite*) morsure *f*; (*drink*) petit verre; (*coldness*) **there's a n. in the air** le fond de l'air est frais. **2** *vt* pincer.

nip·ple bout *m* de sein; (*of bottle*) tétine *f*.

ni·tro·gen azote *m*.

no 1 *adv & n* non (*m inv*); **no more than ten**/*etc* pas plus de dix/*etc*; **no more time**/*etc* plus de temps/*etc*. **2** *adj* aucun(e); pas de; **I have no idea** je n'ai aucune idée; **no child came** aucun enfant n'est venu; **I have no time**/*etc* je n'ai pas de temps/*etc*; **of no importance**/*etc* sans importance/*etc*; **'no smoking'** 'défense de fumer'; **no way!** *Fam* pas question!; **no one = nobody**.

no·ble *adj* noble.

no·bod·y *pron* (ne…) personne; **n. came** personne n'est venue; **n.!** personne!

nod 1 *vti* faire un signe de tête à (qn); (*one's head*) faire un signe de tête. **2** *n* signe *m* de tête.

▸ **nod off** *vi* s'assoupir.

noise bruit *m*; (*of bell, drum*) son *m*; **to make a n.** faire du bruit.

nois·i·ly *adv* bruyamment.

nois·y *adj* bruyant.

nom·i·nate *vt* (*appoint*) nommer.

nom·i·na·tion (*proposal*) proposition *f*; (*appointment*) nomination *f*.

non- *prefix* non-.

none *pron* aucun(e) *mf*; (*in filling out a form*) néant; **she has n. (at all)** elle n'en a pas (du tout); **n. (at all) came** pas un(e) seul(e) n'est venu(e); **n. of the cake**/*etc* pas une seule partie du gâteau/*etc*; **n. of the trees**/*etc* aucun des arbres/*etc*.

none·the·less *adv* néanmoins.

non·ex·ist·ent *adj* inexistant.

non·fic·tion (*in library*) ouvrages *mpl* généraux.

non·sense absurdités *fpl*; **that's n.** c'est absurde.

non-smok·er non-fumeur, -euse *mf*.

non-stick *adj* (*pan*) anti-adhésif.

non·stop 1 *adj* sans arrêt; (*train, flight*) direct. **2** *adv* sans arrêt; (*to fly*) sans escale.

noo·dles *npl* nouilles *fpl*; (*in soup*) vermicelle(s) *m(pl)*.

noon midi *m*; **at n.** à midi.

nor *conj* ni; **neither you n. me/I** ni toi ni moi; **she neither drinks n. smokes** elle ne fume ni ne boit; **I do not know, n. do I care** je ne sais pas et d'ailleurs je m'en moque.

norm norme *f*.

nor·mal 1 *adj* normal. **2** *n* **above/ below n.** au-dessus/au-dessous de la normale.

nor·mal·ly *adv* normalement.

north 1 *n* nord *m*; (**to the**) **n. of** au nord de. **2** *adj* (*coast*) nord *inv*. **3** *adv* au nord.

North A·mer·i·can 1 *n* Nord-Américain, -aine *mf*. **2** *adj* nord-américain, -aine.

north·bound *adj* en direction du nord.

north·east *n & adj* nord-est (*m & adj inv*).

north·ern *adj* (*coast*) nord *inv*; (*town*) du nord.

north·ern·er habitant, -ante *mf* du nord.

north·ward(s) *adj & adv* vers le nord.

north·west *n & adj* nord-ouest (*m & adj inv*).

Nor·we·gian 1 *n* Norvégien, -ienne *mf*. **2** *adj* norvégien, -ienne *mf*.

nose nez *m*; **her n. is bleeding** elle saigne du nez.

nose·bleed saignement *m* de nez.

nos·tril (*of person*) narine *f*; (*horse*) naseau *m*.

nos·(e)y *adj* indiscret.

not *adv* (ne…) pas; **he's n. there, he isn't there** il n'est pas là; **n. yet** pas encore; **why n.?** pourquoi pas?; **n. one reply**/*etc* pas une seule réponse/*etc*; (*after 'thank you'*) je vous en prie. ▪ non; **I think/hope n.** je pense/j'espère que non; **isn't she?, don't you?**/*etc* non?

no·ta·ble *adj* notable.

no·ta·bly *adv* (*noticeably*) notablement; (*particularly*) notamment.

note 1 *n* (*comment, musical etc*) note *f*, (*money*) billet *m*; (*message*) petit mot *m*; **to make a n. of** prendre note de. **2** *vt* noter.

note·book carnet *m*; (*for school*) cahier *m*; (*computer*) portable *m*.

▸ **note down** *vt* (*word etc*) noter.

note·pad bloc-notes *m*.

note·pa·per papier *m* à lettres.

noth·ing *pron* (ne…) rien; **he knows n.** il ne sait rien; **n. to eat**/*etc* rien à manger/*etc*; **n. big**/*etc* rien de grand/*etc*; **n. much** pas grand-chose; **I've got n. to do with it** je n'y suis pour rien; **to come to n.** (*of efforts etc*) ne rien donner; **for n.** (*in vain, free of charge*) pour rien; **to have n. on** être tout nu.

no·tice 1 *n* avis *m*; (*sign*) pancarte *f*; (*poster*) affiche *f*; **to give n.** don-

ner sa démission; **to give sb** (*advance*) **n.** avertir qn (**of** de); **to take n.** faire attention (**of** à); **until further n.** jusqu'à nouvel ordre. **2** *vt* remarquer (**that** que).

no·tice·a·ble *adj* visible.

no·ti·fi·ca·tion avis *m*.

no·ti·fy *vt* avertir (**sb of sth** qn de qch).

no·tion idée *f*.

no·to·ri·ous *adj* tristement célèbre; (*criminal*) notoire.

noun nom *m*.

nour·ish·ing *adj* nourrissant.

nov·el 1 *n* roman *m*. **2** *adj* nouveau (*f* nouvelle).

nov·el·ist romancier, -ière *mf*.

No·vem·ber novembre *m*.

now 1 *adv* maintenant; **just n., right n.** en ce moment; **I saw her just n.** je l'ai vue à l'instant; **for n.** pour le moment; **from n. on** désormais; **before n.** avant; **n. and then** de temps à autre. **2** *conj* **n. (that)** maintenant que.

now·a·days *adv* aujourd'hui.

no·where *adv* nulle part; **n. near the house** loin de la maison; **n. near enough** loin d'être assez.

noz·zle (*hose*) jet *m*.

nu·clear *adj* nucléaire.

nude **in the n.** (tout) nu.

nudge 1 *vt* pousser du coude. **2** *n* coup *m* de coude.

nui·sance embêtement *m*; (*person*) peste *f*; **that's a n.** c'est embêtant.

numb *adj* (*hand etc*) engourdi.

num·ber 1 *n* nombre *m*; (*of page, house, telephone etc*) numéro *m*; **a n. of** un certain nombre de. **2** *vt* (*page etc*) numéroter.

nu·mer·al chiffre *m*.

nu·mer·ous *adj* nombreux.

nun religieuse *f*.

nurse 1 *n* infirmière *f*; **(male) n.** infirmier *m*. **2** *vt* (*take care of*) soigner; (*baby*) allaiter. **3** *vi* (*of baby*) téter.

nurs·er·y (in house) chambre f d'enfants; (for plants) pépinière f.

nurs·er·y rhyme chanson f enfantine.

nurs·er·y school école f maternelle.

nurs·ing home (for elderly people) maison f de retraite; (for convalescents) maison f de repos; (for mentally ill) maison f de santé.

nut¹ (walnut) noix f; (hazelnut) noisette f; (peanut) cacah(o)uète f.

nut² (for bolt) écrou m.

nut·crack·er casse-noix m inv.

nut·shell in a n. en un mot.

ny·lon 1 n nylon m; **nylons** bas mpl nylon. **2** adj (shirt etc) en nylon.

O

oak chêne m.

oar aviron m.

oat·meal flocons mpl d'avoine.

oats npl avoine f.

o·be·di·ence obéissance f (to à).

o·be·di·ent adj obéissant.

o·bey 1 vt obéir à (qn); **to be obeyed** être obéi. **2** vi obéir.

ob·ject¹ (thing, aim) objet m; Grammar complément m (d'objet).

ob·ject² vi **to o. to sth/sb** désapprouver qch/qn; **it objects to my doing that** ça me gêne que tu fasses ça.

ob·jec·tion objection f.

ob·jec·tive (aim) objectif m.

ob·li·ga·tion obligation f.

o·blige vt (compel) contraindre (sb to do qn à faire); (help) rendre service à.

o·blig·ing adj serviable.

o·blique adj oblique.

ob·scene adj obscène.

ob·scure 1 adj obscur. **2** vt (hide)

cacher; (confuse) obscurcir.

ob·ser·vant adj observateur.

ob·ser·va·tion observation f.

ob·serve vt observer; (say) remarquer (**that** que).

ob·ses·sion obsession f.

ob·sta·cle obstacle m.

ob·sti·nate adj (person, resistance) obstiné.

ob·struct vt (block) boucher; (hinder) gêner.

ob·tain vt obtenir.

ob·tain·a·ble adj disponible.

ob·vi·ous adj évident (**that** que).

ob·vi·ous·ly adv évidemment.

oc·ca·sion (time, opportunity) occasion f; (event, ceremony) événement m.

oc·ca·sion·al adj (odd) qu'on fait/voit/etc de temps en temps; **she drinks the o. whisky** elle boit un whisky de temps en temps.

oc·ca·sion·al·ly adv de temps en temps.

oc·cu·pant occupant, -ante mf.

oc·cu·pa·tion (activity) occupation f; (job) emploi m; (trade) métier m; (profession) profession f.

oc·cu·py vt occuper; **to keep oneself occupied** s'occuper (**doing** à faire).

oc·cur vi (happen) avoir lieu; (be found) se rencontrer; **it occurs to me that...** il me vient à l'esprit que...

oc·cur·rence (event) événement m.

o·cean océan m.

o'clock adv (it's) **three o'c.**/etc (il est) trois heures/etc.

Oc·to·ber octobre m.

oc·to·pus pieuvre f.

odd adj (strange) bizarre. ▪ (number) (left over) **I have an o. penny** il me reste un penny; **a few o. stamps** quelques timbres (qui restent); **the o. man out** l'exception f; **sixty o.** soixante et quelques; **an o. glove**/etc un gant/etc dépareillé. ▪ qu'on fait/voit/*etc* de temps en temps; **I smoke the o. cigarette** je fume une cigarette de temps en temps; **o. jobs** menus travaux *mpl.*

odd·ly *adv* bizarrement.

odds *npl (in betting)* cote *f*; *(chances)* chances *fpl*; **at o.** en désaccord (**with** avec); **o. and ends** des petites choses.

o·dor odeur *f.*

of *prep* de, d' (de + le = du, de + les = des); **of the woman** de la femme; **of a book** d'un livre; **she has a lot of it** *or* **of them** elle en a beaucoup; **a friend of his** un ami à lui; **there are ten of us** nous sommes dix; **that's nice of you** c'est gentil de ta part.

off 1 *adv (gone away)* parti; *(light, radio etc)* éteint; *(faucet)* fermé; *(detached)* détaché; *(removed)* enlevé; *(canceled)* annulé; **6 miles o.** à 10km (d'ici *or* de là); **to be** *or* **go o.** *(leave)* partir; **a day o.** un jour de congé; **time o.** du temps libre; **5% o.** une réduction de 5%; **hands o.!** pas touche!; **to be better o.** être mieux. **2** *prep (from)* de; *(distant)* éloigné de; **to get o. the bus**/*etc* descendre du bus/*etc*; **to take sth o. the table**/*etc* prendre qch sur la table/*etc*; **o. New York** au large de New York.

off·col·or *adj* risqué.

of·fend *vt* froisser *(qn)*; **to be offended (at)** se froisser (de).

of·fend·er *(criminal)* délinquant, -ante *mf.*

of·fense *(crime)* délit *m*; **to take o.** s'offenser (**at** de).

of·fen·sive *adj (words etc)* insultant (**to sb** pour qn); *(person)* insultant (**to sb** avec qn).

of·fer 1 *n* offre *f*; **special o.** *(in store)* promotion *f.* **2** *vt* offrir (**to do** de faire).

of·fer·ing offre *f*; *(in church)* offrande *f.*

off·hand 1 *adj (abrupt)* brusque, impoli. **2** *adv (to say, know etc)* comme ça.

of·fice *(room)* bureau *m*; *(of doctor, lawyer)* cabinet *m*; *(post)* fonction *f*; **head o.** siège *m* central; **o. building** immeuble *m* de bureaux.

of·fi·cer *(in the army etc)* officier *m*; **(police) o.** agent *m* (de police).

of·fi·cial 1 *adj* officiel. **2** *n (civil servant)* fonctionnaire *mf.*

of·fi·cial·ly *adv* officiellement.

off·line *adj* *Comput* non connecté; *(printer)* déconnecté.

off·spring *inv (children)* progéniture *f.*

of·ten *adv* souvent; **how o.?** combien de fois?; **how o. do they run?** *(train etc)* il y en a tous les combien?; **every so o.** de temps en temps.

oh! *int* oh!, ah!; **oh yes!** mais oui!; **oh yes?** ah oui?

oil 1 *n* huile *f*; *(extracted from ground)* pétrole *m*; *(fuel)* mazout *m*; **o. spill** *(event)* marée *f* noire; *(result)* nappe *f* de pétrole. **2** *vt (machine)* graisser.

oil·can burette *f.*

oil change *(in vehicle)* vidange *f.*

oint·ment pommade *f.*

OK, o·kay 1 *adj (satisfactory)* bien *inv*, *(unharmed)* sain et sauf; *(un damaged)* intact; *(without worries)* tranquille; **it's o.** ça va; **I'm o.** *(healthy)* je vais bien. **2** *adv (well)* bien; **o.!** *(agreement)* d'accord!

old *adj* vieux *(f* vieille); *(former)* ancien; **how o. is he?** quel âge a-t-il?; **he's ten years o.** il a dix ans; **he's older than me** il est plus âgé que moi; **an older son** un fils aîné; **the oldest son** le fils aîné; **o. man** vieillard *m*; **o. woman** vieille femme *f*; **to get** *or* **grow old(er)** vieillir; **o. age** vieillesse *f.*

old-fash·ioned *adj* démodé; *(person)* rétro *inv.*

ol·ive olive f; **o. oil** huile f d'olive.

O·lym·pic adj olympique; **the O. games, the Olympics** les jeux mpl olympiques.

om·e·let(te) omelette f; **cheese/etc o.** omelette au fromage/etc.

o·mis·sion omission f.

o·mit vt omettre.

on 1 prep (position) sur; **to put on (to)** mettre sur. ▪ (about) sur; **to speak on** parler sur. ▪ (manner, means) **on foot** à pied; **on the train/etc** dans le train/etc; **to be on (salary)** toucher; (team) être membre de; **to keep or stay on** (path etc) suivre. ▪ (time) **on Monday** lundi; **on Mondays** le lundi; **on May 3rd** le 3 mai. ▪ (+ present participle) en; **on seeing this** en voyant ceci. **2** adv (ahead) en avant; (in progress) en cours; (lid, brake) mis; (light, radio) allumé; (gas, faucet) ouvert; **on (and on)** sans cesse; **to play/etc** continuer à jouer/etc; **what's on?** (television) qu'y a-t-il à la télé?; **from then on** à partir de là.

once 1 adv une fois; (formerly) autrefois; **o. a month** une fois par mois; **o. again, o. more** encore une fois; **at o.** tout de suite; **all at o.** tout à coup; (at the same time) à la fois. **2** conj une fois que.

one 1 adj un, une; **o. man** un homme; **o. woman** une femme; **page o.** la page un; **twenty-o.** vingt-et-un. ▪ (only) seul; **my o. (and only) aim** mon seul (et unique) but. ▪ (same) même; **on the o. bus** dans le même bus. **2** pron un, une; **do you want o.?** en veux-tu (un)?; **o. of them** l'un d'eux, l'une d'elles; **a big/etc o.** un grand/etc; **that o.** celui-là, celle-là; **the o. who or which** celui or celle qui; **another o.** un(e) autre. ▪ (impersonal) on; **o. knows** on sait; **it helps o.** ça nous or vous aide; **one's family** sa famille.

one·self pron soi-même; (reflexive) se, s'.

one-way adj (street) à sens unique; (ticket) simple.

on·ion oignon m.

on-line adj Comput en ligne.

on·look·er spectateur, -trice mf.

on·ly 1 adj seul; **the o. one** le seul, la seule; **an o. son** un fils unique. **2** adv seulement, ne… que; **I o. have ten** je n'en ai que dix, j'en ai dix seulement; **not o.** non seulement; **I have o. just seen it** je viens tout juste de le voir; **o. he knows** lui seul le sait. **3** conj (but) Fam seulement.

on·to prep = **on to**.

on·ward(s) adv en avant; **from that time o.** à partir de là.

o·paque adj opaque.

o·pen 1 adj ouvert; (ticket) open inv; **wide o.** grand ouvert. **2** n **(out) in the o.** en plein air. **3** vt ouvrir. **4** vi (of flower, door, eyes etc) s'ouvrir; (of shop, office, person) ouvrir.

o·pen-air adj (pool, market etc) en plein air.

o·pen·ing ouverture f; (career prospect) débouché m.

o·pen·ly adv ouvertement.

o·pen-mind·ed adj à l'esprit ouvert.

o·pen·ness franchise f.

▸ **open out 1** vt ouvrir. **2** vi s'ouvrir; (widen) s'élargir.

▸ **open up 1** vt ouvrir. **2** vi s'ouvrir; (open the door) ouvrir.

op·er·a opéra m.

op·er·ate 1 vi (of surgeon) opérer (**on sb** qn; **for** de); (of machine etc) fonctionner; (proceed) opérer. **2** vt faire fonctionner; (business) gérer.

op·er·a·tion opération f; (working) fonctionnement m.

op·er·a·tor (on phone) standardiste mf.

o·pin·ion opinion f, avis m; **in my o.** à mon avis.

op·po·nent adversaire mf.

op·por·tu·ni·ty occasion *f* (**to do** de faire).

op·pose *vt* s'opposer à.

op·posed *adj* opposé (**to** à).

op·pos·ing *adj (team)* opposé.

op·po·site 1 *adj (direction, opinion etc)* opposé; *(house)* d'en face. **2** *adv (to sit etc)* en face. **3** *prep* **o. (to)** en face de. **4** *n* **the o.** le contraire.

op·po·si·tion opposition *f* (**to** à).

opt *vi* **to o. for sth** décider pour qch.

op·ti·cal *adj* optique.

op·ti·cian opticien, -ienne *mf*.

op·ti·mist to be an o. être optimiste.

op·ti·mis·tic *adj* optimiste.

op·tion *(choice)* choix *m*.

op·tion·al *adj* facultatif.

or *conj* ou; **he doesn't drink or smoke** il ne boit ni ne fume.

o·ral 1 *adj* oral. **2** *n (exam)* oral *m*.

or·ange 1 *n (fruit)* orange *f*; **o. juice** jus *m* d'orange. **2** *adj & n (color)* orange (*m & adj inv*).

or·ange·ade orangeade *f*.

or·bit orbite *f*.

or·chard verger *m*.

or·ches·tra orchestre *m*.

or·deal épreuve *f*.

or·der 1 *n (command, arrangement)* ordre *m*; *(purchase)* commande *f*; **in o.** *(passport etc)* en règle; **in o. to do** pour faire; **in o. that** pour que (+ *subjunctive*); **out of o.** *(machine)* en panne; *(telephone)* en dérangement. **2** *vt* ordonner (**sb to do** à qn de faire); *(meal, goods etc)* commander; *(taxi)* appeler. **3** *vi (in café etc)* commander.

▸ **order around** *vt* commander.

or·di·nance ordonnance *f*.

or·di·na·ry *adj (usual, commonplace)* ordinaire; *(average)* moyen; **it's out of the o.** ça sort de l'ordinaire.

ore minerai *m*.

or·gan *(in body)* organe *m*; *(instrument)* orgue *m*, orgues *fpl*.

or·gan·ic *adj (vegetables etc)* biologique.

or·gan·i·za·tion organisation *f*.

or·gan·ize *vt* organiser.

or·gan·iz·er organisateur, -trice *mf*.

o·ri·en·tal *adj* oriental.

o·ri·gin origine *f*.

o·rig·i·nal 1 *adj (idea, artist etc)* original; *(first)* premier; *(copy, version)* original. **2** *n (document etc)* original *m*.

o·rig·i·nal·i·ty originalité *f*.

o·rig·i·nal·ly *adv (at first)* au départ.

o·rig·i·nate *vi (begin)* prendre naissance (**in** dans); **to o. from** émaner de.

or·na·ment *(on dress etc)* ornement *m*; *(vase etc)* bibelot *m*.

or·phan orphelin, -ine *mf*.

or·phan·age orphelinat *m*.

or·tho·dox *adj* orthodoxe.

os·trich autruche *f*.

oth·er 1 *adj* autre; **o. doctors** d'autres médecins; **the o. one** l'autre *mf*. **2** *pron* **the o.** l'autre *mf*; (some) **others** d'autres; **some do, others don't** les uns le font, les autres ne le font pas. **3** *adv* **o. than** autrement que.

oth·er·wise *adv* autrement.

ouch! *int* aïe!

ought *v aux (obligation, desirability)* devoir; **you o. to leave** tu devrais partir; **I o. to have done it** j'aurais dû le faire; **he said he o. to stay** il a dit qu'il devait rester. ▪ *(probability)* devoir; **it o. to be ready** ça devrait être prêt.

ounce once *f* (= 28,35g).

our *poss adj* notre, *pl* nos.

ours *pron* le nôtre, la nôtre, *pl* les nôtres; **this book is o.** ce livre est à nous *or* est le nôtre.

our·selves *pron* nous-mêmes; *(reflexive, after prep)* nous.

EXPRESSING YOUR OPINION

What do you think?
Qu'est-ce que tu en penses/vous en pensez ?

I really like it/liked it.
Ça me plaît beaucoup/Ça m'a beaucoup plu.

It was great/beautiful!
C'était génial/beau !

It was OK.
Ce n'était pas mal.

The tour of the castle was quite interesting.
La visite du château était assez intéressante.

I love croissants/hiking.
J'adore les croissants/faire de la randonné.

I hate snow/shopping.
Je déteste la neige/faire les magasins.

I'd rather have coffee.
Je préférerais du café.

Which do you prefer?
Tu préfères/Vous préférez lequel/ laquelle ?

I think she's very nice.
Je la trouve très sympa.

I agree (with you).
Je suis d'accord (avec toi/vous).

Absolutely!
Absolument !

I'm sure it'll be nice tomorrow.
Je suis sûr(e) qu'il fera beau demain.

That's true.
C'est vrai.

I've changed my mind.
J'ai changé d'avis.

I don't know.
Je ne sais pas.

Really?
Ah bon ?/C'est vrai ?

What a surprise!
Quelle surprise !

Did you like the art gallery?
Le musée d'art t'a/vous a plu ?

I don't like it/didn't like it at all.
Ça ne me plaît pas du tout/Ça ne m'a pas du tout plu.

It was a bit boring/too touristy.
C'était un peu ennuyeux/trop touristique.

The food's nothing special.
La nourriture n'a rien d'exceptionnel.

We had a great time!
On s'est éclatés !

I don't like jazz/cycling.
Je n'aime pas le jazz/faire du vélo.

This is delicious/disgusting!
C'est délicieux/dégoûtant !

I prefer small hotels to big ones.
Je préfère les petits hôtels aux grands.

I prefer the bigger/smaller one.
Je préfère le (la) plus grand(e)/le (la) plus petit(e).

I think/I don't think it's possible.
Je crois que c'est/Je ne crois pas que ce soit possible.

I disagree (with you).
Je ne suis pas d'accord (avec toi/vous).

Of course (not)!
Bien sûr (que non) !

Are you sure?
Tu en es/Vous en êtes sûr(e) ?

I don't believe you.
Je ne te/vous crois pas.

I'm not sure.
Je ne suis pas sûr(e).

It depends.
Ça dépend.

That's strange!
C'est étrange/bizarre !

What a pity!
Quel dommage !

out 1 adv (outside) dehors; (not at home etc) sorti; (light, fire) éteint; (news, secret) connu; (book) publié; (eliminated from game) éliminé; **to be** or **go o. a lot** sortir beaucoup; **to have a day o.** sortir pour la journée; **the tide's o.** la marée est basse; **o. there** là-bas. **2** prep **o. of** en dehors de; (danger, water) hors de; (because of) par; **o. of pity**/etc par pitié/etc; **o. of the window** par la fenêtre; **to drink/take/copy o. of sth** boire/prendre/copier dans qch; **made o. of** (wood etc) fait en; **to make sth o. of a box/**etc faire qch avec une boîte/etc; **she's o. of town** elle n'est pas en ville; **four o. of five** quatre sur cinq; **to feel o. of place** ne pas se sentir intégré.

out·bound adj **o. journey** or **trip** aller m.

out·break (of war) début m; (of violence) éruption f.

out·burst (of anger, joy) explosion f.

out·come résultat m.

out·dat·ed adj démodé.

out·do* vt surpasser (**in** en).

out·door adj (pool, market) en plein air; **o. clothes** tenue f pour sortir.

out·doors adv dehors.

out·er adj extérieur.

out·er space l'espace m (cosmique).

out·fit (clothes) costume m; (for woman) toilette f; (toy) panoplie f (de cow-boy etc); **ski/**etc **o.** tenue f de ski/etc.

out·grow vt (habit) passer l'âge de; (clothes) devenir trop grand pour.

out·ing sortie f, excursion f.

out·law 1 n hors-la-loi m inv. **2** vt proscrire.

out·let (market for goods) débouché m.

out·line (shape) contour m.

tive(s) f(pl); (point of view) perspective f (**on** sur).

out·num·ber vt être plus nombreux que.

out-of-date adj (expired) périmé; (old-fashioned) démodé.

out·put rendement m; (computer data) données fpl de sortie.

out·rage 1 n scandale m; (anger) indignation f. **2** vt **outraged by sth** indigné de qch.

out·ra·geous (shocking) scandaleux.

out·right adv (to say, tell) franchement.

out·set **at the o.** au debut; **from the o.** dès le début.

out·side 1 adv (au) dehors; **to go o.** sortir. **2** prep en dehors de. **3** n extérieur m. **4** adj extérieur.

out·sid·er (stranger) étranger, -ère mf; (athlete, horse etc) outsider m.

out·skirts npl banlieue f.

out·stand·ing adj remarquable; (problem) non réglé; (debt) impayé.

out·ward adj (sign, appearance) extérieur.

out·ward(s) adv vers l'extérieur.

o·val adj & n ovale (m).

ov·en four m.

ov·en mitt gant m isolant.

o·ver 1 prep (on) sur; (above) au-dessus de; (on the other side of) de l'autre côté de; **to jump/look/**etc **o. sth** sauter/regarder/etc par-dessus qch; **o. it** (on) dessus; (above) au-dessus; (to jump etc) par-dessus; **to be upset/**etc **o. sth** (about) avoir de la peine/etc à cause de qch; **o. the phone** au téléphone; **o. the holidays** pendant les vacances; **o. ten days** (more than) plus de dix jours; **men o. sixty** les hommes de plus de soixante ans; **all o. Spain** dans toute l'Espagne; **all o. the carpet** partout sur le tapis. **2** adv (above) (par-)dessus; **o. here** ici; **o. there** là-bas; **to come** or **go o.** (visit) passer; **to ask o.** inviter (à venir); **all o.**

(everywhere) partout; **it's (all) o.**
(finished) c'est fini; **a pound or o.**
une livre ou plus; **I have ten o.** il
m'en reste dix; **o. and o. (again)** à
plusieurs reprises; **o. pleased**/*etc*
trop content/*etc*.

o·ver·all *adj (length etc)* total.

o·ver·alls *npl (of workman)* bleu
m de travail; *(of child)* salopette *f*.

o·ver·board *adv* à la mer.

o·ver·charge to o. sb for sth
faire payer qch trop cher à qn.

o·ver·coat pardessus *m*.

o·ver·come *vt (problem)* surmonter.

o·ver·do* *vt* **to o. it** ne pas y aller
doucement; **don't o. it!** vas-y
doucement!

o·ver·draft découvert *m*.

o·ver·due *adj (train etc)* en retard.

o·ver·eat* *vi* manger trop.

o·ver·ex·cit·ed *adj* surexcité.

o·ver·flow *vi (of river, bath etc)*
déborder.

o·ver·head *adv* au-dessus.

o·ver·hear *vt (pt & pp overheard)*
surprendre.

o·ver·heat *vi (of engine)* chauffer.

o·ver·joyed *adj* fou *(f* folle*)* de
joie.

o·ver·lap 1 *vi* se chevaucher. **2** *vt*
chevaucher.

ov·er·leaf *adv* au verso.

o·ver·load *vt* surcharger.

o·ver·look *vt* ne pas remarquer;
(forget) oublier; *(ignore)* passer sur;
(of window etc) donner sur.

o·ver·night 1 *adv* (pendant) la
nuit; **to stay o.** passer la nuit. **2** *adj*
(train) de nuit.

o·ver·pass *(bridge)* toboggan *m*.

o·ver·rat·ed *adj* surfait.

o·ver·seas 1 *adv (abroad)* à
l'étranger. **2** *adj (visitor etc)* étranger; *(trade)* extérieur.

o·ver·sight oubli *m*.

o·ver·sleep* *vi (pt & pp over-
slept)* dormir trop longtemps.

o·ver·spend* *vi* dépenser trop.

o·ver·take* *vti (in vehicle)* dépasser.

o·ver·time 1 *n* heures *fpl* supplémentaires. **2** *adv* **to work o.** faire
des heures supplémentaires.

o·ver·turn *vi (of car, boat)* se retourner.

o·ver·weight *adj* **to be o.** *(of
person)* avoir des kilos en trop.

o·ver·whelm *vt* accabler; **overwhelmed with** *(work, offers)* submergé de.

o·ver·work 1 *n* surmenage *m*. **2** *vi*
se surmener.

owe *vt (money etc)* devoir (**to** à).

ow·ing *prep* **o. to** à cause de.

owl hibou *m (pl* hiboux*)*.

own 1 *adj* propre; **my o. house** ma
propre maison. **2** *pron* **it's my
(very) o.** c'est à moi (tout seul); **a
house of his o.** sa propre maison;
(all) on one's o. tout seul; **to get
one's o. back** se venger. **3** *vt* posséder; **who owns this ball**/*etc*? à qui
appartient cette balle/*etc*?

own·er propriétaire *mf*.

▶ **own up** *vi* avouer (**to sth** qch).

ox, *pl* **oxen** bœuf *m*.

ox·y·gen oxygène *m*.

oys·ter huître *f*.

o·zone ozone *m*; **o. layer** couche *f*
d'ozone.

P

pa *Fam* papa *m*.

pace pas *m*.

Pa·cif·ic 1 *adj* pacifique. **2** *n* **the P.**
le Pacifique.

pac·i·fi·er *(of baby)* sucette *f*.

pack 1 *n* paquet *m; (backpack)* sac
m à dos; *(of wolves)* meute *f*, *(of
cards)* jeu *m; (of lies)* tissu *m*. **2** *vt*
(fill) remplir (**with** de); *(suitcase)*

faire; *(object into box etc)* emballer; *(object into suitcase)* mettre dans sa valise.

pack·age paquet *m*; *Comput* progiciel *m*.

pack·age tour voyage *m* organisé.

pack·ag·ing emballage *m*.

▸**pack away** *vt (put away)* ranger.

▸**pack down** *vt (crush)* tasser.

packed *adj* (bus etc) bondé.

packed lunch panier-repas *m*.

pack·et paquet *m*.

▸**pack in** *vt (quit) Fam* laisser tomber.

pack·ing emballage *m*.

▸**pack into 1** *vt (cram)* entasser dans. **2** *vi (crowd into)* s'entasser dans.

▸**pack up 1** *vt (put into box)* emballer; *(give up) Fam* laisser tomber. **2** *vi Fam (stop)* s'arrêter; *(of machine)* tomber en panne.

pact pacte *m*.

pad *(of cloth etc)* tampon *m*; *(for writing etc)* bloc *m*.

pad·ded *adj (armchair etc)* rembourré.

pad·dle 1 *vi (dip one's feet)* se mouiller les pieds. **2** *n (for boat)* pagaie *f*, *(for ping-pong)* raquette *f*. **3** *vt* to p. a canoe pagayer.

pad·dle boat pédalo *m*.

pad·lock cadenas *m*; *(on bicycle)* antivol *m*.

page *(of book etc)* page *f*.

pain douleur *f*, *(grief)* peine *f*, **pains** *(efforts)* efforts *mpl*; **to be in p.** souffrir; **to take (great) pains to do** se donner du mal à faire.

pain·ful *adj* douloureux.

pain·kill·er calmant *m*; **on painkillers** sous calmants.

paint 1 *n* peinture *f*, **paints** *(in box, tube)* couleurs *fpl*. **2** *vti* peindre; **to p. sth blue/etc** peindre qch en bleu/ *etc*.

paint·brush pinceau *m*.

paint·er peintre *m*.

paint·ing *(activity, picture)* peinture *f*.

paint strip·per décapant *m*.

pair *(two)* paire *f*, *(of people)* couple *m*.

pa·ja·mas *npl* pyjama *m*; **a pair of p.** un pyjama.

Pa·ki·sta·ni 1 *n* Pakistanais, -aise *mf*. **2** *adj* pakistanais, -aise.

pal *Fam* copain *m*, copine *f*.

pal·ace palais *m*.

pal·ate *(in mouth)* palais *m*.

pale *adj* pâle.

pal·ette *(of artist)* palette *f*.

palm *(of hand)* paume *f*, **p. (tree)** palmier *m*; **p. (leaf)** palme *f*.

pam·phlet brochure *f*.

pan casserole *f*, *(for frying)* poêle *f*.

pan·cake crêpe *f*.

pane vitre *f*.

pan·el *(of door etc)* panneau *m*; *(of judges)* jury *m*; *(of experts)* groupe *m*; **(control) p.** console *f*.

pan·ic 1 *n* panique *f*. **2** *vi* s'affoler.

pant *vi* haleter.

pant·ies *npl (female)* slip *m*.

pan·to·mime spectacle *m* de mime.

pan·try *(larder)* garde-manger *m inv*.

pants *npl (trousers)* pantalon *m*.

pant·y·hose collant *m*.

pa·per 1 *n* papier *m*; *(newspaper)* journal *m*; *(wallpaper)* papier *m* peint; *(in high school, college)* dissertation *f*; **brown p.** papier *m* d'emballage; **to put down on p.** mettre par écrit. **2** *adj (bag, towel etc)* en papier; *(cup, plate)* en carton.

pa·per·back livre *m* de poche.

pa·per clip trombone *m*.

pa·per tow·el essuie-tout *m inv*.

pa·per·work écritures *fpl*.

par *(parity)* égalité *f*, *(in golf)* par *m*; **on a p.** au même niveau *(with de)*; **that's about p. for the course** c'est ce à quoi il faut s'attendre.

par·a·chute parachute *m*.

pa·rade *(procession)* défilé *m*; *(street)* avenue *f*.

par·a·dise paradis *m*.

par·a·graph paragraphe *m*; 'new p.' 'à la ligne'.

par·a·keet perruche *f*.

par·a·le·gal assistant, -ante *mf* *(d'un avocat)*.

par·al·lel *adj* parallèle (**with, to** à).

par·a·lyze *vt* paralyser.

par·a·site parasite *m*.

par·a·sol *(over table, on beach)* parasol *m*.

par·cel colis *m*, paquet *m*.

par·don 1 *n* I beg your p. je vous prie de m'excuser; *(not hearing)* vous dites?; **p.?** *(not hearing)* comment?; **p. (me)!** *(sorry)* pardon! **2** *vt* pardonner (**sb for sth** qch à qn).

par·ent père *m*, mère *f*; one's parents ses parents *mpl*.

par·ish paroisse *f*.

Pa·ris·ian 1 *n* Parisien, -ienne *mf*. **2** *n* parisien, -ienne.

park 1 *n* parc *m*. **2** *vt (vehicle)* garer. **3** *vi* se garer; *(remain parked)* stationner.

par·ka anorak *m*.

park·ing stationnement *m*; 'no p.' 'défense de stationner'.

park·ing en·force·ment of·fi·cer contractuel, -elle *mf*.

park·ing light *(of vehicle)* veilleuse *f*.

park·ing lot parking *m*.

park·ing me·ter parcmètre *m*.

park·ing place, parking space place *f* de parking.

park·ing tick·et contravention *f*.

par·lia·ment parlement *m*.

par·rot perroquet *m*.

pars·ley persil *m*.

pars·nip panais *m*.

part 1 *n* partie *f*; *(of machine)* pièce *f*; *(of serial)* épisode *m*; *(role)* rôle *m*; *(in hair)* raie *f*; **to take p.** participer (**in** à); **in p.** en partie; **for the most p.** dans l'ensemble; **to be a p. of sth** faire partie de qch; **in these parts** dans ces parages. **2** *adv (partly)* en partie. **3** *vi (of friends etc)* se quitter; *(of couple)* se séparer.

par·tial *adj* partiel; **to be p. to sth** *(fond of) Fam* avoir un faible pour qch.

par·tic·i·pant participant, -ante *mf*.

par·tic·i·pate *vi* participer (**in** à).

par·tic·i·pa·tion participation *f*.

par·ti·ci·ple *Grammar* participe *m*.

par·tic·u·lar 1 *adj* particulier; *(fussy)* difficile (**about** sur); *(showing care)* méticuleux; **in p.** en particulier. **2** *npl* particulars détails *mpl*; **sb's particulars** les coordonnées *fpl* de qn.

par·tic·u·lar·ly *adv* particulièrement.

par·ti·tion *(in room)* cloison *f*.

part·ly *adv* en partie.

part·ner partenaire *mf*; *(in business)* associé, -ée *mf*; **(dancing) p.** cavalier, -ière *mf*.

part·ner·ship association *f*.

part·ridge perdrix *f*.

part-time *adj & adv* à temps partiel.

par·ty *(formal)* réception *f*; *(with friends)* soirée *f*; *(for birthday)* fête *f*; *(group)* groupe *m*; *(political)* parti *m*.

pass 1 *n (entry permit)* laissez-passer *m inv*, *(over mountains)* col *m*; *Sports* passe *f*; *(for transportation)* carte *f* d'abonnement. **2** *vi* passer (**to** à; **through** par), *(overtake)* dépasser; *(in exam)* être reçu (**in French/etc** en français/etc). **3** *vt* passer (**to** à); *(go past)* passer devant *(immeuble etc)*; *(vehicle)* dépasser; *(exam)* être reçu à; **to p. sb** *(in street)* croiser qn.

pass·a·ble *adj (not bad)* passable; *(road)* praticable.

pas·sage *(of text etc)* passage *m*; *(corridor)* couloir *m*.

pas·sage·way (corridor) couloir m.

▸**pass around** vt (cake etc) faire passer.

▸**pass away** vi (die) mourir.

pass·book livret m de caisse d'épargne.

▸**pass by 1** vi passer (à côté). **2** vt (building etc) passer devant; **to p. by sb** (in street) croiser qn.

pas·sen·ger passager, -ère mf; (on train) voyageur, -euse mf.

pas·ser-by, pl **passers-by** passant, -ante mf.

pass·ing 1 n (of time) écoulement m; (of law) vote m; **in p.** en passant. **2** adj qui passe.

pass·ing grade (in school) moyenne f.

pas·sion passion f.

pas·sion·ate adj passionné.

pas·sive 1 adj passif. **2** n Grammar passif m.

▸**pass off** vt **to p. oneself off as** se faire passer pour.

▸**pass on** vt (message etc) transmettre (**to** à).

▸**pass out** vi (faint) s'évanouir.

▸**pass over** vt (ignore) passer sur.

pass·port passeport m.

▸**pass through** vi passer.

▸**pass up** vt (chance) laisser passer.

pass·word mot m de passe.

past 1 n passé m; **in the p.** (formerly) dans le temps. **2** adj (gone by) passé; (former) ancien; **these p. months** ces derniers mois; **in the p. tense** au passé. **3** prep (in front of) devant; (after) après; (further than) plus loin que; **p. four o'clock** quatre heures passées. **4** adv devant; **to go p.** passer.

pas·ta pâtes fpl.

paste 1 n (of meat) pâté m; (of fish) beurre m; (glue) colle f. **2** vt coller.

pas·teur·ized adj (milk) pasteurisé.

pas·tille pastille f.

pas·time passe-temps m inv.

pas·try pâte f, (cake) pâtisserie f.

pas·ture pâturage m.

pat vt (cheek etc) tapoter; (animal) caresser.

patch (for clothes) pièce f; (over eye) bandeau m; (of color) tache f; **cabbage p.** carré m de choux; **bad p.** mauvaise période f.

patch (up) vt (clothing) rapiécer.

pat·ent[1] n brevet m d'invention. **2** vt (faire) breveter.

pat·ent[2] **p.** (leather) cuir m verni.

path, pl **-s** sentier m; (in park) allée f.

pa·thet·ic adj (results etc) lamentable.

path·way sentier m.

pa·tience patience f; **to lose p.** perdre patience (**with sb** avec qn).

pa·tient 1 adj patient. **2** n malade mf; (on doctor's or dentist's list) patient, -ente mf.

pa·tient·ly adv patiemment.

pat·i·o, pl **-os** patio m.

pa·tri·ot·ic adj patriotique; (person) patriote.

pa·trol 1 n patrouille f. **2** vi patrouiller. **3** vt patrouiller dans.

pa·tron (of charity) patron, -onne mf; (of arts) mécène m; (customer) client, -e mf; **p. saint** (saint, -e mf) patron, -onne mf.

pat·tern dessin m; (paper model for garment) patron m.

pause 1 n pause f; (in conversation) silence m. **2** vi faire une pause; (hesitate) hésiter.

pave vt paver; **to p. the way for sth** ouvrir la voie à qch.

paved adj pavé.

pave·ment (roadway) chaussée f.

pa·vil·ion pavillon m.

pav·ing stone pavé m.

paw patte f.

pawn Chess pion m.

pay* 1 n salaire m; (of workman, soldier) paie f; **p. slip** bulletin m de paie. **2** vt (person, sum) payer; (deposit) verser; (of investment) rapporter; *(compliment, visit)* faire (**to** à); **to p. sb to do** *or* **for doing** payer qn pour faire; **to p. sb for sth** payer qch à qn; **to p. money into one's account** verser de l'argent sur son compte. **3** *vi* payer; **to p. a lot** payer cher.

pay·a·ble *adj* payable; **a check p. to** un chèque à l'ordre de.

▸ **pay back** *vt (person, loan)* rembourser.

pay·check chèque *m* de règlement de salaire.

▸ **pay for** *vt* payer.

pay·ment paiement *m*; *(of deposit)* versement *m*.

▸ **pay off** *vt (debt, person)* rembourser.

▸ **pay out** *vt (spend)* dépenser.

pay phone téléphone *m* public.

▸ **pay up** *vti* payer.

PC¹ *abbr (personal computer)* PC *m*.

PC² *adj abbr (politically correct)* politiquement correct.

PDA *abbr (personal digital assistant)* PDA *m*.

PE *abbr (physical education)* éducation *f* physique, EPS *f*.

pea pois *m*; **(green) peas** petits pois *mpl*; **p. soup** soupe *f* aux pois.

peace paix *f*; **p. of mind** tranquillité *f* d'esprit; **in p.** en paix; **to have (some) p. and quiet** avoir la paix.

peace·ful *adj* paisible; *(demonstration)* pacifique.

peach pêche *f*.

pea·cock paon *m*.

peak 1 *n (mountain top)* sommet *m*; *(mountain)* pic *m*; **to be at its p.** être à son maximum. **2** *adj (hours, period)* de pointe.

peaked *adj Fam (ill)* patraque.

pea·nut cacah(o)uète *f*; **p. butter** beurre *m* de cacah(o)uètes.

pear poire *f*; **p. tree** poirier *m*.

pearl perle *f*.

peb·ble caillou *m (pl* cailloux*)*; *(on beach)* galet *m*.

pe·can noix *f* de pécan.

peck *vti* **to p. (at)** *(of bird)* picorer *(du pain etc)*; donner un coup de bec à *(qn)*.

pe·cu·liar *adj* bizarre; *(special)* particulier (**to** à).

pe·cu·li·ar·i·ty *(feature)* particularité *f*.

ped·al 1 *n* pédale *f*. **2** *vi* pédaler. **3** *vt* **to p. a bicycle** faire marcher un vélo; *(ride)* rouler en vélo.

pe·des·tri·an piéton *m*; **p. crossing** passage *m* pour piétons; **p. street** rue *f* piétonne.

pe·dom·e·ter pédomètre *m*.

peek **to have a p.** jeter un petit coup d'œil (**at** à).

peel 1 *n* épluchure(s) *f(pl)*; **a piece of p., some p.** une épluchure. **2** *vt (apple, potato etc)* éplucher. **3** *vi (of sunburnt skin)* peler; *(of paint)* s'écailler.

▸ **peel off** *vt (label etc)* décoller.

peep 1 *n* coup *m* d'œil *(furtif)*. **2** *vi* **to p. (at)** regarder furtivement.

peer *vi* **to p. (at)** regarder attentivement.

peg *(for tent)* piquet *m*; *(for clothes)* pince *f* (à linge); *(for coat, hat)* patère *f*.

pen *(fountain, ballpoint)* stylo *m*; *(enclosure)* parc *m*.

pen·al·ty *(prison sentence)* peine *f*, *(fine)* amende *f*; *Sports* penalty *m*.

pen·cil crayon *m*; **in p.** au crayon.

pen·cil case trousse *f*.

▸ **pencil in** *vt (note down)* noter provisoirement.

pen·cil sharp·en·er taille-crayon(s) *m inv*.

pen·e·trate *vt (substance)* pénétrer; *(forest)* pénétrer dans.

pen·guin manchot *m*.

pen·i·cil·lin pénicilline *f*.

pen·in·su·la presqu'île *f*.

pen·knife *-knives* canif *m*.

pen·ni·less *adj* sans le sou.

pen·ny, *pl* **pennies** *(coin)* cent *m*; **not a p.!** pas un sou!

pen pal correspondant, -ante *mf*.
pen·sion pension *f*; **(retirement)** **p.** retraite *f*.
pen·sion·er (old age) **p.** retraité, -ée *mf*.
peo·ple 1 *npl* gens *mpl or fpl*; *(specific persons)* personnes *fpl*; **the p.** *(citizens)* le peuple; **old p.** les personnes *fpl* âgées; **old p.'s home** maison *f* de retraite; **English p.** les Anglais *mpl*. **2** *n (nation)* peuple *m*.
pep·per poivre *m*; *(vegetable)* poivron *m*.
pep·per·mint *(flavor)* menthe *f*; *(candy)* bonbon *m* à la menthe.
per *prep* par; **p. year** par an; **p. person** par personne; **p. cent** pour cent; **10 dollars p. pound** 10 dollars la livre.
per·ceive *vt* percevoir; *(notice)* remarquer.
per·cent·age pourcentage *m*.
perch 1 *n (for bird)* perchoir *m*. **2** *vi (of bird, person)* se percher.
per·co·la·tor cafetière *f*; *(in café etc)* percolateur *m*.
per·fect 1 *adj* parfait; *Grammar* **p. tense** parfait *m*. **2** *n Grammar* parfait *m*. **3** *vt (technique)* mettre au point; *(one's French etc)* parfaire ses connaissances en.
per·fec·tion perfection *f*.
per·fect·ly *adv* parfaitement.
per·form 1 *vt (task, miracle)* accomplir; *(one's duty)* remplir; *(surgical operation)* pratiquer (**on** sur); *(a play, piece of music)* jouer. **2** *vi (act, play)* jouer; *(sing)* chanter; *(dance)* danser; *(of machine)* fonctionner.
per·form·ance *(in theater)* représentation *f*, *(in movie theater, concert hall)* séance *f*, *(of actor, musician)* interprétation *f*, *(of athlete, machine)* performance *f*.
per·form·er *(entertainer)* artiste *mf*.
per·fume parfum *m*.

per·haps *adv* peut-être; **p. not** peut-être que non.
per·il péril *m*.
pe·ri·od période *f*; *(historical)* époque *f*, *(lesson)* leçon *f*; *(punctuation mark)* point *m*; **(monthly)** **period(s)** *(of woman)* règles *fpl*.
pe·ri·od·i·cal périodique *m*.
perk *(in job)* avantage *m* en nature.
▸ **perk up** *vi (become livelier)* reprendre du poil de la bête.
perm 1 *n* permanente *f*. **2** *vt* **to have one's hair permed** se faire faire une permanente.
per·ma·nent *adj* permanent; *(address)* fixe.
per·ma·nent·ly *adv* à titre permanent.
per·mis·sion permission *f* (**to do** de faire); **to ask p.** demander la permission.
per·mit 1 *vt* permettre (**sb to do à** qn de faire). **2** *n* permis *m*, *(entrance pass)* laissez-passer *m* inv.
per·pen·dic·u·lar *adj* perpendiculaire (**to** à).
per·se·cute *vt* persécuter.
per·se·cu·tion persécution *f*.
per·se·ver·ance persévérance *f*.
per·se·vere *vi* persévérer (**in** dans).
per·sist *vi* persister (**in doing à** faire; **in sth** dans qch).
per·sist·ent *adj (person)* obstiné; *(noise etc)* continuel.
per·son personne *f*, **in p.** en personne.
per·son·al *adj* personnel; *(application)* en personne; *(friend)* intime; *(life)* privé; *(indiscreet)* indiscret.
per·son·al·i·ty personnalité *f*.
per·son·al·ly *adv* personnellement; *(in person)* en personne.
per·son·nel personnel *m*.
per·suade *vt* persuader (**sb to do** qn de faire).
per·sua·sion persuasion *f*.
per·ti·nent *adj* pertinent.

pes·si·mist to be a p. être pessimiste.

pes·si·mis·tic *adj* pessimiste.

pest *n* animal *m* or insecte *m* nuisible; *(person)* casse-pieds *mf inv.*

pes·ter *vt* harceler (**with questions** de questions); **to p. sb to do sth/for sth** harceler qn pour qu'il fasse qch/jusqu'à ce qu'il donne qch.

pet 1 *n* animal *m* (domestique); *(favorite person)* chouchou, -oute *mf.* **2** *adj (dog, cat etc)* domestique; *(favorite)* favori (*f* -ite).

pet·al pétale *m.*

pe·ti·tion *(signatures)* pétition *f.*

pet·ti·coat jupon *m.*

pet·ty *adj (minor)* petit; *(mean)* mesquin; **p. cash** petite caisse *f.*

phar·ma·cist pharmacien, -ienne *mf.*

phar·ma·cy pharmacie *f.*

phase phase *f.*

▸ **phase in** *vt* introduire progressivement.

▸ **phase out** *vt* supprimer progressivement.

PhD *abbr (Doctor of Philosophy)* doctorat *m.*

pheas·ant faisan *m.*

phe·nom·e·nal *adj* phénoménal.

phe·nom·e·non, *pl* -ena phénomène *m.*

phi·los·o·pher philosophe *mf.*

phil·o·soph·i·cal *adj* philosophique; *(resigned)* philosophe.

phi·los·o·phy philosophie *f.*

phlegm *(in throat)* glaires *fpl.*

phone 1 *n* téléphone *m*; **on the p.** au téléphone; *(at other end)* au bout du fil. **2** *vt* téléphoner à. **3** *vi* téléphoner.

▸ **phone back** *vti* rappeler.

phone book annuaire *m.*

phone booth cabine *f* téléphonique.

phone call coup *m* de fil; **to make a p. call** téléphoner (**to** à).

phone numb·er numéro *m* de téléphone.

pho·net·ic *adj* phonétique.

pho·to, *pl* -os photo *f*; **to take a p.** of prendre une photo de; **to have one's p. taken** se faire prendre en photo.

pho·to·cop·i·er photocopieuse *f.*

pho·to·cop·y 1 *n* photocopie *f.* **2** *vt* photocopier.

pho·to·graph photographie *f.*

pho·tog·ra·pher photographe *mf.*

pho·to·graph·ic *adj* photographique.

pho·tog·ra·phy photographie *f.*

phrase expression *f*; *(idiom)* locution *f.*

phrase·book manuel *m* de conversation.

phys·i·cal *adj* physique; **p. examination** examen *m* médical; **p. education** éducation *f* physique.

phy·si·cian médecin *m.*

phys·ics physique *f.*

pi·an·ist pianiste *mf.*

pi·an·o, *pl* -os piano *m.*

pick 1 *n* to take one's p. faire son choix. **2** *vt* choisir; *(flower, fruit)* cueillir; *(hole)* faire (**in** dans); **to p. one's nose** se mettre les doigts dans le nez.

pick·ax pioche *f.*

pick·le cornichon *m.*

pick·led *adj (onion etc)* au vinaigre.

▸ **pick off** *vt* enlever.

▸ **pick on** *vt* s'en prendre à.

▸ **pick out** *vt* choisir; *(identify)* reconnaître.

pick·pock·et pickpocket *m.*

▸ **pick up 1** *vt (sth dropped)* ramasser; *(fallen person or chair)* relever; *(person into air, weight)* soulever; *(a cold)* attraper; *(habit, accent, speed)* prendre; *(fetch)* (passer) prendre; *(find)* trouver; *(learn)* apprendre. **2** *vi (improve)* s'améliorer;

(of business) reprendre; *(of patient)* aller mieux.

pic·nic pique-nique *m*.

pic·ture 1 *n* image *f*; *(painting)* tableau *m*; *(photo)* photo *f*; *(film)* film *m*. **2** *vt (imagine)* s'imaginer (**that** que).

pic·ture frame cadre *m*.

pic·tur·esque *adj* pittoresque.

pie *(open)* tarte *f*; *(with pastry on top)* tourte *f*.

piece morceau *m*; *(of fabric, machine, in game)* pièce *f*; *(coin)* pièce *f*; **in pieces** en morceaux; **to take to pieces** *(machine)* démonter; **a p. of news/etc** une nouvelle/etc; **in one p.** intact; *(person)* indemne.

pier jetée *f*.

pierce *vt* percer *(qch)*.

pierc·ing 1 *adj (cry, cold)* perçant; **2** *n (for body adornment)* piercing *m*.

pig cochon *m*.

pi·geon pigeon *m*.

pi·geon·hole casier *m*.

pig·gy·back to give sb a p. porter qn sur le dos.

pig·gy·bank tirelire *f*.

pig·tail *(hair)* natte *f*.

pile 1 *n* tas *m*; *(neatly arranged)* pile *f*; **piles of** *Fam* beaucoup de. **2** *vt* entasser; *(neatly)* empiler.

▸ **pile into** *vt (crowd into)* s'entasser dans.

piles *npl (illness)* hémorroïdes *fpl*.

pile·up 1 *(on road)* carambolage *m*.

▸ **pile up 1** *vt* entasser; *(neatly)* empiler. **2** *vi* s'accumuler.

pill pilule *f*; **to be on the P.** prendre la pilule.

pil·lar pilier *m*.

pil·low oreiller *m*.

pil·low·case taie *f* d'oreiller.

pi·lot pilote *m*.

pim·ple bouton *m*.

pin épingle *f*; *(drawing pin)* punaise *f*.

pin (on) *vt* épingler (**to** sur, à); *(to wall)* punaiser (**to, on** à).

pin·a·fore *(apron)* tablier *m*.

pin·ball flipper *m*; **p. machine** flipper *m*.

pin·cers *npl (tool)* tenailles *fpl*.

pinch 1 *n (of salt)* pincée *f*; **to give sb a p.** pincer qn. **2** *vt* pincer; *(steal)* *Fam* piquer (**from** à).

pin·cush·ion pelote *f* (à épingles).

pine pin *m*.

pine·ap·ple ananas *m*.

pink *adj & n (color)* rose *(m)*.

pink·ie petit doigt *m*.

pint pinte *f (= 0.47 litre)*.

▸ **pin up** *vt (on wall)* punaiser (**on** à); *(notice)* afficher.

pi·o·neer 1 *n (settler)* pionnier, -ère *mf*. **2** *vt* **to p. sth** être le premier/la première à mettre au point qch.

pipe tuyau *m*; *(of smoker)* pipe *f*; **to smoke a p.** fumer la pipe.

pi·rate pirate *m*.

pis·ta·chi·o pistache *f*.

pis·tol pistolet *m*.

pit *(hole)* trou *m*; *(coalmine)* mine *f*; *(quarry)* carrière *f*; *(stone of fruit)* noyau *m*; *(smaller)* pépin *m*.

pitch *vt (tent)* dresser; *(ball)* lancer.

pitch-black, pitch-dark *adj* noir comme dans un four.

pitch·er *(container)* cruche *f*.

pit·y 1 *n* pitié *f*; **(what) a p.!** (quel) dommage!; **it's a p.** c'est dommage (**that** que (+ *subjunctive*); **to do** de faire). **2** *vt* plaindre.

piz·za pizza *f*.

plac·ard *(notice)* affiche *f*.

place 1 *n* endroit *m*, lieu *m*; *(house)* maison *f*; *(seat, position, rank)* place *f*; **in the first p.** en premier lieu; **to take p.** avoir lieu; **p. of work** lieu *m* de travail; **market p.** place *f* du marché; **at my p., to my p.** *(house)* chez moi; **all over the p.** partout; **to change the p. of** remplacer; **in p. of** à la place de. **2** *vt* placer; *(an order)* passer (**with sb** qn); **to p. sb** *(identify)* remettre qn.

place mat set *m* (de table).
place set·ting couvert *m*.
plague 1 *n* peste *f*, *(nuisance)* plaie *f*. **2** *vt* harceler (**with** de).
plain¹ *adj (clear)* clair; *(simple)* simple; *(madness)* pur; *(without pattern)* uni; *(woman, man)* sans beauté; **to make it p. that** faire comprendre à qn que.
plain² plaine *f*.
plain·ly *adv* clairement; *(frankly)* franchement.
plait 1 *n* tresse *f*. **2** *vt* tresser.
plan 1 *n* projet *m*; *(economic, of house etc)* plan *m*; **according to p.** comme prévu. **2** *vt (foresee)* prévoir; *(organize)* organiser; *(design)* concevoir; **to p. to do** *or* **doing** avoir l'intention de faire; **as planned** comme prévu.
plane *(aircraft)* avion *m*; *(tool)* rabot *m*.
plan·et planète *f*.
plane tree platane *m*.
▶ **plan for** *vt (rain, disaster)* prévoir.
plank planche *f*.
plant 1 *n* plante *f*, *(factory)* usine *f*, **house p.** plante *f* verte. **2** *vt (flower etc)* planter.
plas·ter plâtre *m*, **in p.** dans le plâtre.
plas·tic 1 *adj (object)* en plastique. **2** *n* plastique *m*.
plas·tic bag sac *m* en plastique.
plas·tic sur·ge·ry chirurgie *f* esthétique.
plas·tic wrap film *m* alimentaire.
plate *(dish)* assiette *f*, *(metal sheet)* plaque *f*.
plat·form *(at train station)* quai *m*; *(on bus etc)* plate-forme *f*, *(for speaker etc)* estrade *f*.
plau·si·ble *adj* plausible.
play 1 *n (in theater)* pièce *f* (de théâtre). **2** *vt (part, tune etc)* jouer; *(game)* jouer à; *(instrument)* jouer de; *(team)* jouer contre; *(record, CD)* passer; **to p. a part in doing/ in sth** contribuer à faire/à qch. **3** *vi* jouer (**at** à); *(of tape recorder etc)* marcher; **what are you playing at?** qu'est-ce que tu fais?; **what's playing?** *(at movies etc)* qu'est-ce qu'on joue?
▶ **play around** *vi* jouer.
▶ **play back** *vt (tape)* réécouter.
▶ **play down** *vt* minimiser.
play·er *(in game, of instrument)* joueur, -euse *mf*, **CD/DVD p.** lecteur *m* de CD/DVD.
play·ground *(in school)* cour *f* de récréation; *(with swings etc)* terrain *m* de jeux.
play·ing card carte *f* à jouer.
play·ing field terrain *m* de jeux.
▶ **play on** *vt (feelings, fears etc)* jouer sur.
play·pen parc *m* (pour enfants).
play·school garderie *f* (d'enfants).
play·time récréation *f*.
plea *(request)* appel *m*; *Law (argument)* argument *m*; *(defense)* défense *f*.
plead 1 *vt (argue)* plaider; *(as excuse)* alléguer. **2** *vi (beg)* supplier; **to p. with sb to do sth** supplier qn de faire qch; *Law* **to p. guilty/not guilty** plaider coupable/non coupable.
pleas·ant *adj* agréable.
pleas·ant·ly *adv* agréablement.
please 1 *adv* s'il vous plaît, s'il te plaît. **2** *vt* **to p. sb** plaire à qn; *(satisfy)* contenter qn. **3** *vi* plaire; **do as you p.** fais comme tu veux.
pleased *adj* content (**with** de; **that** que (+ *subjunctive*); **to do** de faire); **p. to meet you!** enchanté!
pleas·ing *adj* agréable.
pleas·ure plaisir *m*.
pleat *(in skirt)* pli *m*.
pleat·ed *adj* plissé.
pledge 1 *n* promesse *f*. **2** *vt* promettre.
plen·ti·ful *adj* abondant.
plen·ty **p. of** beaucoup de; **that's p.** c'est assez.
pli·ers *npl* pince(s) *f(pl)*.
plot 1 *n* complot *m* (**against**

contre); **p. (of land)** terrain *m*. **2** *vti* comploter (**to do** de faire).

▸ **plot (out)** *vt (route)* déterminer.

plow 1 *n* charrue *f*. **2** *vt (field)* labourer.

pluck *vt (fowl)* plumer; *(flower)* cueillir.

plug *(of cotton wool)* tampon *m*; *(for sink, bath)* bonde *f*, *(electrical)* fiche *f*, prise *f (mâle)*; **(socket)** prise *f* de courant; **(wall) p.** *(for screw)* cheville *f*.

plug (up) *vt* boucher.

▸ **plug in** *vt (radio etc)* brancher.

plum prune *f*.

plumb·er plombier *m*.

plumb·ing plomberie *f*.

plump *adj* potelé.

plunge 1 *vt* plonger (**into** dans). **2** *vi (dive)* plonger (**into** dans); *(fall)* tomber (**from** de).

plu·ral 1 *adj (form)* pluriel; *(noun)* au pluriel. **2** *n* pluriel *m*; **in the p.** au pluriel.

plus 1 *prep* plus; **two p. two** deux plus deux. **2** *adj* **twenty p.** vingt et quelques.

p.m. *adv* de l'après-midi; *(evening)* du soir.

poach *vt (egg)* pocher.

PO Box boîte *f* postale.

pock·et poche *f*. **p. money**/*etc* argent *m*/*etc* de poche.

pock·et·book *(handbag)* sac *m* à main.

pock·et·ful **a p. of** une pleine poche de.

pock·et·knife, *pl* **-knives** canif *m*.

pod·cast podcast *m*.

po·em poème *m*.

po·et poète *m*.

po·et·ic *adj* poétique.

po·e·try poésie *f*.

point 1 *n (position, score etc)* point *m*; *(decimal)* virgule *f*, *(meaning)* sens *m*; *(of knife etc)* pointe *f*; **points** *(for train)* aiguillage *m*; **p. of view** point *m* de vue; **at this p. (in time)** en ce moment; **what's**

the **p.?** à quoi bon? (**of waiting**/ *etc* attendre/*etc*); **there's no p. (in) staying**/*etc* ça ne sert à rien de rester/*etc*. **2** *vt (aim)* pointer (**at** sur); **to p. one's finger (at)** montrer du doigt.

▸ **point at** *vt* montrer du doigt.

point·ed *adj* pointu.

point·less *adj* inutile.

▸ **point out** *vt (show)* indiquer; *(mention)* signaler (**that** que).

▸ **point to** *vt (indicate)* indiquer.

poi·son 1 *n* poison *m*; *(of snake)* venin *m*. **2** *vt* empoisonner.

poi·son·ous *adj* toxique; *(snake)* venimeux; *(plant)* vénéneux.

poke *vt* pousser *(de doigt etc)*; *(fire)* tisonner; **to p. sth into sth** fourrer qch dans qch; **to p. one's head out of the window** passer la tête par la fenêtre.

▸ **poke around in** *vt (drawer etc)* fouiner dans.

pok·er *(for fire)* tisonnier *m*.

po·lar bear ours *m* blanc.

Pole Polonais, -aise *mf*.

pole *(rod)* perche *f*; *(fixed)* poteau *m*; *(for flag)* mât *m*; **North/South P.** pôle *m* Nord/Sud.

po·lice police *f*.

po·lice car voiture *f* de police.

po·lice force police *f*.

po·lice·man, *pl* **-men** agent *m* de police.

po·lice·wom·an, *pl* **-women** femme-agent *f*.

pol·i·cy *(plan etc)* politique *f*, **(insurance) p.** police *f* (d'assurance).

po·li·o polio *f*.

Po·lish 1 *adj* polonais. **2** *n (language)* polonais *m*.

pol·ish 1 *vt* cirer; *(metal)* astiquer; *(rough surface)* polir. **2** *n (for shoes)* cirage *m*; *(for floor etc)* cire *f*; *(shine)* vernis *m*; **to give sth a p.** faire briller qch.

▸ **polish off** *vt (food etc)* Fam avaler.

▸ **polish up** *vt (one's French etc)* perfectionner.

po·lite *adj* poli (**to, with** avec).

po·lite·ly *adv* poliment.

po·lite·ness politesse *f.*

po·lit·i·cal *adj* politique.

pol·i·ti·cian homme *m*/femme *f* politique.

pol·i·tics politique *f.*

poll *(voting)* scrutin *m;* **to go to the polls** aller aux urnes; **(opinion) p.** sondage *m* (d'opinion).

pol·len pollen *m.*

poll·ing place bureau *m* de vote.

polls urnes *fpl;* **to go to the p.** aller aux urnes.

pol·lute *vt* polluer.

pol·lu·tion pollution *f.*

po·lo shirt polo *m.*

pol·y·es·ter 1 *n* polyester *m.* 2 *adj (shirt etc)* en polyester.

pome·gran·ate *(fruit)* grenade *f.*

pond étang *m; (artificial)* bassin *m.*

po·ny poney *m.*

po·ny·tail *(hair)* queue *f* de cheval.

poo·dle caniche *m.*

pool *(puddle)* flaque *f; (for swimming)* piscine *f; (billiards)* billard *m* américain.

pooped *adj (tired) Fam* vanné.

poor 1 *adj* pauvre; *(bad)* mauvais; *(weak)* faible. 2 *npl* **the p.** les pauvres *mpl.*

poor·ly *adv (badly)* mal.

pop¹ 1 *vti (burst)* crever. 2 *vt (put) Fam* mettre.

pop² 1 *n (music)* pop *m; (drink)* soda *m; (father) Fam* papa *m.* 2 *adj (concert etc)* pop *inv.*

pop·corn pop-corn *m.*

pope pape *m.*

▸ **pop in** *vi* entrer un instant.

▸ **pop out** *vi* sortir un instant.

▸ **pop over** *vi* faire un saut (**to** chez).

pop·py coquelicot *m.*

pop·si·cle® glace *f* à eau.

pop·u·lar *adj* populaire; *(fashionable)* à la mode; **to be p. with** plaire beaucoup à.

pop·u·lar·i·ty popularité *f.*

pop·u·lat·ed *adj* **highly/sparsely/etc p.** très/peu/etc peuplé; **p. by** peuplé de.

pop·u·la·tion population *f.*

porch porche *m; (veranda)* véranda *f.*

pork *(meat)* porc *m.*

por·ridge porridge *m (bouillie de flocons d'avoine).*

port *(harbor)* port *m.*

por·ta·ble *adj* portable, portatif.

por·ter *(for luggage)* porteur *m.*

port·fo·li·o *(for documents)* porte-documents *m inv; (of politician)* portefeuille *m; (of model, artist etc)* book *m.*

port·hole hublot *m.*

por·tion *(share)* portion *f; (of train, book etc)* partie *f.*

por·trait portrait *m.*

Por·tu·guese 1 *adj* portugais, -aise. 2 *n* Portugais, -aise *mf; (language)* portugais *m.*

pose 1 *n (of model)* pose *f.* 2 *vi* poser (**for** pour).

posh *adj Fam* chic *inv.*

po·si·tion position *f; (job, circumstances)* situation *f;* **in a p. to do** en mesure de faire.

pos·i·tive *adj* positif; *(progress, change)* réel; *(answer)* affirmatif; *(sure)* certain (**of** de; **that** que).

pos·sess *vt* posséder.

pos·ses·sions *npl* biens *mpl.*

pos·ses·sive *adj & n Grammar* possessif *(m).*

pos·si·bil·i·ty possibilité *f.*

pos·si·ble *adj* possible; **it is p. (for us) to do it** il (nous) est possible de le faire; **it is p. that** il est possible que *(+ subjunctive);* **as far as p.** autant que possible; **if p.** si possible; **as much** *or* **as many as p.** le plus possible.

pos·si·bly *adv (perhaps)* peut-être; **if you p. can** si cela t'est possible; **to do all one p. can** faire tout son possible.

post¹ *(job, place)* poste *m.*

post² (pole) poteau m; (of door) montant m.

post (up) vt (notice etc) afficher.

post·age tarif m (postal) (to pour).

post·age stamp timbre-poste m.

post·al adj (services etc) postal.

post·card carte f postale.

post·er affiche f; (for decoration) poster m.

post·grad·u·ate étudiant, -ante mf de troisième cycle.

post·man, pl -men facteur m.

post·mark cachet m de la poste.

post of·fice (bureau m de) poste f.

post·pone vt remettre (for de; until à).

post·pone·ment remise f.

pot pot m; (for cooking) marmite f; (drug) Fam hasch m; **pots and pans** casseroles fpl.

po·ta·to, pl -oes pomme f de terre.

po·tent adj puissant.

po·ten·tial 1 adj (client, sales) éventuel. **2** n to have p. (of firm etc) avoir de l'avenir.

pot·ter potier m.

pot·ter·y (art) poterie f; (objects) poteries fpl; **a piece of p.** une poterie.

pot·ty pot m (de bébé).

pouch petit sac m; (of kangaroo) poche f.

poul·try volaille f.

pounce vi sauter (on sur).

pound (weight) livre f (= 453,6g); (money) livre f (sterling); (for cars, dogs) fourrière f.

pour vt (liquid) verser; **to p. money into sth** investir beaucoup d'argent dans qch.

pour (down) vi **it's pouring (down)** il pleut à verse.

▸ **pour in 1** vt (liquid) verser. **2** vi (of water, rain) entrer à flots; (of people) affluer.

▸ **pour off** vt (liquid) vider.

▸ **pour out 1** vt (liquid) verser; (cup etc) vider. **2** vi (of liquid) couler à flots; (of people) sortir en masse.

pov·er·ty pauvreté f.

pow·der 1 n poudre f. **2** vt **to p. one's face** se poudrer.

pow·dered adj (milk, eggs) en poudre; **p. sugar** sucre m glace.

pow·er (ability, authority) pouvoir m; (strength, nation) puissance f; (energy) énergie f; (current) courant m; **in p.** au pouvoir; **p. outage** coupure f de courant.

pow·er·ful adj puissant.

pow·er plant centrale f (électrique).

prac·ti·cal adj pratique.

prac·ti·cal joke farce f.

prac·ti·cal·ly adv (almost) pratiquement.

prac·tice 1 n (exercise, way of proceeding) pratique f; (habit) habitude f; (sports training) entraînement m; (rehearsal) répétition f; **to be out of p.** avoir perdu la pratique. **2** vt (sports, art etc) pratiquer; (medicine, law) exercer; (flute, piano etc) s'exercer à; (language) (s'exercer à) parler (on avec). **3** vi s'exercer; (of doctor, lawyer) exercer.

praise 1 vt louer (for sth de qch); **to p. sb for doing** louer qn d'avoir fait. **2** n louange(s) f(pl).

prank (trick) farce f.

prawn crevette f (rose).

pray 1 vi prier; **to p. for good weather/a miracle** prier pour avoir du beau temps/pour un miracle. **2** vt **to p. that** prier pour que (+ subjunctive).

prayer prière f.

preach vi prêcher.

pre·cau·tion précaution f (of doing de faire); **as a p.** par précaution.

pre·cede vti précéder.

prec·e·dent précédent m.

pre·ced·ing adj précédent.

pre·cinct (electoral district) circonscription f; (police district) secteur m.

pre·cious adj précieux.

pre·cise adj précis; (person) minutieux.

pre·co·cious adj (child) précoce.

pred·a·tor prédateur m.

pred·e·ces·sor prédécesseur m.

pre·dic·a·ment situation f fâcheuse.

pre·dict vt prédire.

pre·dict·a·ble adj prévisible.

pre·dic·tion prédiction f.

pref·ace préface f.

pre·fer vt préférer (**to** à); **to p. to do** préférer faire.

pref·er·a·ble adj préférable (**to** à).

pref·er·a·bly adv de préférence.

pref·er·ence préférence f (**for** pour).

pre·fix préfixe m.

preg·nan·cy grossesse f.

preg·nant adj (woman) enceinte; **five months p.** enceinte de cinq mois.

pre·his·tor·ic adj préhistorique.

prej·u·dice préjugé m; **to be full of p.** être plein de préjugés.

pre·lim·i·nar·y adj préliminaire.

pre·ma·ture adj prématuré.

prem·is·es npl locaux mpl; **on the p.** sur les lieux.

pre·mi·um (insurance) p. prime f (d'assurance).

prep·a·ra·tion préparation f; **preparations** préparatifs mpl (**for** de).

pre·pare 1 vt préparer (**sth for** qch pour; **sb for** qn à); **to p. to do** se préparer à faire. **2** vi **to p. for** (journey, occasion) faire des préparatifs pour; (exam) préparer.

pre·pared adj (ready) prêt (**to do** à faire); **to be p. for sth** (expect) s'attendre à qch.

prep·o·si·tion Grammar préposition f.

prep school école f préparatoire.

pre·school adj préscolaire.

pre·scribe vt (of doctor) prescrire.

pre·scrip·tion (for medicine) ordonnance f.

pres·ence présence f; **in the p. of** en présence de.

pres·ent[1] **1** adj (not absent) présent (**at** à; **in** dans); (year, state, job, house etc) actuel; Grammar **p. tense** présent m. **2** n (gift) cadeau m; Grammar (tense) présent m; **at p.** à présent.

pre·sent[2] vt présenter (**to** à); **to p. sb with** (gift) offrir à qn; (prize) remettre à qn.

pres·en·ta·tion présentation f; (of prize) remise f.

pres·ent·ly adv (soon) tout à l'heure; (now) à présent.

pres·er·va·tion conservation f.

pre·ser·va·tive agent m de conservation.

pre·serve 1 vt (keep) conserver. **2** n (jam) confiture f.

pre·side vi présider; **to p. over** or **at sth** présider qch.

pres·i·den·cy présidence f.

pres·i·dent président, -ente mf.

pres·i·den·tial adj présidentiel.

press[1] **1** n (newspapers, machine) presse f. **2** adj (conference etc) de presse.

press[2] **1** vt (button etc) appuyer sur; (clothes) repasser; **to p. sb to do** (urge) presser qn de faire. **2** vi (with finger) appuyer (**on** sur); (of weight) faire pression (**on** sur).

▸ **press down** vt (button etc) appuyer sur.

pressed adj **to be p. (for time)** être très bousculé.

▸ **press on** vi (carry on) continuer (**with sth** qch).

pres·sure pression f; **the p. of work** le surmenage; **under p.** (worker, to work) sous pression.

pres·sure cook·er cocotte-minute® f.

pre·sume vt présumer (**that** que).

pre·tend vti (make believe) faire

semblant (**to do** de faire; **that** que).

pre·text prétexte m; **on the p. of/ that** sous prétexte de/que.

pret·ty 1 adj joli. **2** adv (rather, quite) assez; **p. well, p. much** (almost) pratiquement.

pre·vail vi prédominer; **to p. upon** or **on sb to do sth** (persuade) persuader qn de faire qch.

pre·vent vt empêcher (**from** doing de faire).

pre·ven·tion prévention f.

pre·vi·ous adj précédent; (experience) préalable; **p. to** avant.

pre·vi·ous·ly adv avant.

prey proie f; **bird of p.** rapace m.

price prix m.

price list tarif m.

prick vt piquer (**with** avec); (burst) crever.

prick·ly adj (plant, beard) piquant.

pride (satisfaction) fierté f, (exaggerated) orgueil m; (self-respect) amour-propre m; **to take p. in** être fier de; (take care of) prendre soin de.

▶ **pride on** vt **to p. oneself on sth/ on doing** s'enorgueillir de qch/de faire.

priest prêtre m.

pri·mar·i·ly adv essentiellement.

pri·mar·y 1 adj principal; **p. color** couleur f primaire (élection f) primaire. **2** n (election) primaire.

pri·mar·y school école f primaire.

prime min·is·ter premier ministre m.

prime numb·er nombre m premier.

prim·i·tive adj primitif.

prim·rose primevère f.

prince prince m.

prin·cess princesse f.

prin·ci·pal (of school) directeur, -trice mf.

print 1 n (of finger, foot etc) empreinte f, (letters) caractères mpl; (engraving) gravure f, (photo)

épreuve f; **out of p.** épuisé; **p. shop** imprimerie f. **2** vt (book etc) imprimer; (photo) tirer; (write) écrire en caractères d'imprimerie.

print·er (of computer) imprimante f.

print·ing (industry, process) imprimerie f, (print run) tirage m; **p. plant** imprimerie f; **p. press** presse f d'imprimerie.

print·out (of computer) sortie f sur imprimante.

▶ **print out** vti (of computer) imprimer.

pri·or adj précédent; (experience) préalable.

pri·or·i·ty priorité f (**over** sur).

pris·on prison f; **in p.** en prison.

pris·on·er prisonnier, -ière mf; **to take sb p.** faire qn prisonnier.

pri·va·cy intimité f.

pri·vate 1 adj privé; (lesson, car, secretary etc) particulier; (report) confidentiel; (dinner etc) intime. **2** n (soldier) (simple) soldat m; **in p.** en privé; (to have dinner etc) dans l'intimité.

pri·vate·ly adv en privé; (to have dinner etc) dans l'intimité.

prize prix m; (in lottery) lot m.

prize·win·ner lauréat, -ate mf; (in lottery) gagnant, -ante mf.

pro¹ pro m; **the pros and cons** le pour et le contre.

pro² abbr (professional) pro mf.

pro- prefix (in favour of) pro-.

prob·a·ble adj probable (**that** que); (convincing) vraisemblable.

prob·a·bly adv probablement.

probe 1 n (device) sonde f, (investigation) enquête f. **2** vt sonder; (investigate) enquêter sur.

▶ **probe into** vt enquêter sur.

prob·lem problème m; **no p.!** Fam pas de problème!; **to have a p. doing** avoir du mal à faire.

prob·lem·at·ic, prob·lem·at·i·cal adj problématique.

pro·ceed vi (go) avancer; (act)

procéder; *(continue)* continuer.

pro·ceeds *npl* recette *f.*

pro·cess *(method)* procédé *m* **(for doing** pour faire**)**; *(chemical, economic etc)* processus *m*; **in the p. of doing** en train de faire.

pro·cessed cheese fromage *m* en tranches.

pro·ces·sion cortège *m.*

pro·duce 1 *vt (manufacture, cause etc)* produire; *(bring out)* sortir *(pistolet, mouchoir etc)*; *(passport)* présenter. **2** *n* produits *mpl.*

pro·duc·er *(of goods, film)* producteur, -trice *mf.*

prod·uct produit *m.*

pro·duc·tion production *f*; *(of play)* mise *f* en scène.

pro·duc·tive *adj* productif.

pro·duc·tiv·i·ty productivité *f.*

pro·fes·sion profession *f.*

pro·fes·sion·al 1 *adj* professionnel; *(piece of work)* de professionnel. **2** *n* professionnel, -elle *mf.*

pro·fes·sor professeur *m* (d'université).

prof·it 1 *n* profit *m*, bénéfice *m*; **to sell at a p.** vendre à profit. **2** *vi* **to p. by** or **from sth** tirer profit de qch.

prof·it·a·ble *adj* rentable.

pro·found *adj* profond.

pro·gram 1 *n (schedule, of computer)* programme *m*; *(broadcast)* émission *f.* **2** *vt* programmer.

prog·ress 1 *n* progrès *m(pl)*; **to make p.** faire des progrès; *(when driving etc)* bien avancer; **in p.** en cours. **2** *vi* progresser; *(of story, meeting)* se dérouler.

pro·gres·sive *adj* progressif.

pro·hib·it *vt* interdire **(sb from doing** à qn de faire**).**

proj·ect projet *m* **(for sth** pour qch**)**; *(at school)* étude *f.*

pro·jec·tor *(for films etc)* projecteur *m.*

pro·long *vt* prolonger.

prom·i·nent *adj (person)* important.

prom·ise 1 *n* promesse *f*; **to show p.** être prometteur. **2** *vt* promettre **(sb sth, sth to sb** qch à qn; **to do** de faire; **that** que**).** **3** *vi* **I p.!** je te le promets!; **p.?** promis?

prom·is·ing *adj (situation)* prometteur (*f* -euse).

pro·mote *vt* **to p. sb** *(in job etc)* donner de l'avancement à qn.

pro·mo·tion *(of person)* avancement *m.*

prompt *adj (speedy)* rapide.

prone *adj* **p. to** *(illnesses, accidents)* prédisposé à.

pro·noun pronom *m.*

pro·nounce *vt* prononcer.

pro·nun·ci·a·tion prononciation *f.*

proof *(evidence)* preuve(s) *f(pl).*

prop 1 *n (physical support)* support *m*; *(psychological support)* soutien *m.* **2** *vt (lean)* appuyer.

prop·a·gan·da propagande *f.*

pro·pel·ler hélice *f.*

prop·er *adj (suitable, respectable)* convenable; *(downright)* véritable; *(noun, meaning)* propre; **the p. address/method/etc** *(correct)* la bonne adresse/méthode/*etc.*

prop·er·ly *adv* comme il faut, convenablement.

prop·er·ty *(building, possessions)* propriété *f.*

pro·por·tion *(ratio)* proportion *f*; *(portion)* partie *f*; **proportions** *(size)* dimensions *fpl.*

pro·por·tion·al *adj* proportionnel **(to** à**).**

pro·pos·al proposition *f*; *(of marriage)* demande *f* (en mariage).

pro·pose 1 *vt (suggest)* proposer **(to** à; **that** que **(+ subjunctive)).** **2** *vi* faire une demande (en mariage) **(to** à**).**

prop·o·si·tion proposition *f.*

props *npl (in theater)* accessoires *mpl.*

▶**prop up** *vt (ladder etc)* appuyer **(against** contre**)**; *(one's head)* caler; *(wall)* étayer.

prose prose f.

pros·e·cute vt poursuivre (en justice).

pros·e·cu·tion (action) poursuites fpl judiciaires; **the p.** = le ministère public.

pros·pect (outlook, possibility) perspective f (of de); (future) **prospects** perspectives fpl d'avenir.

pros·per·i·ty prospérité f.

pros·per·ous adj riche.

pro·tect vt protéger (**from** de; **against** contre).

pro·tec·tion protection f.

pro·tec·tive adj (clothes etc) de protection.

pro·test 1 n protestation f (**against** contre); (demonstration) manifestation f. **2** vi protester (**against** contre); (of students etc) contester.

Prot·es·tant adj & n protestant, -ante (mf).

pro·test·er (student etc) contestataire mf.

pro·trac·tor (for measuring) rapporteur m.

proud adj fier (**of** de; **to do** de faire); (conceited) orgueilleux.

proud·ly adv fièrement; (conceitedly) orgueilleusement.

prove 1 vt prouver (**that** que). **2** vi **to p. difficult/etc** s'avérer difficile/etc.

prov·erb proverbe m.

pro·vide vt (supply) fournir (**sb with sth** qch à qn); **to p. sb with sth** (equip) pourvoir qn de qch.

pro·vid·ed, pro·vid·ing conj **p.** (**that**) pourvu que (+ subjunctive).

▶ **provide for** vt pourvoir aux besoins de.

prov·ince province f; **the provinces** la province.

pro·vin·cial adj provincial.

pro·vi·sion·al adj provisoire.

pro·voke vt (annoy) agacer.

prowl (a·round) vi rôder.

prowl·er rôdeur, -euse mf.

prune 1 n pruneau m. **2** vt (tree, bush) tailler.

prun·ing shears sécateur m.

psy·chi·at·ric adj psychiatrique.

psy·chi·a·trist psychiatre mf.

psy·cho·log·i·cal adj psychologique.

psy·chol·o·gist psychologue mf.

psy·chol·o·gy psychologie f.

pub pub m.

pub·lic 1 adj public (f -ique); (library, swimming pool) municipal. **2** n public m; **in p.** en public.

pub·li·ca·tion publication f.

pub·lic·i·ty publicité f.

pub·lish vt publier; (book, author) éditer.

pub·lish·er éditeur, -trice mf.

pub·lish·ing (profession) édition f.

pud·ding pudding m; **rice p.** riz m au lait.

pud·dle flaque f (d'eau).

puff 1 n (of smoke, wind) bouffée f. **2** vi souffler.

▶ **puff at** vt (cigar etc) tirer sur.

pull 1 n **to give sth a p.** tirer qch. **2** vt tirer; (trigger) appuyer sur; (tooth) arracher; (muscle) se claquer; **to p. apart** or **to pieces** mettre en pièces. **3** vi tirer (**at, on** sur); (go, move) aller.

▶ **pull along** vt traîner (**to** jusqu'à).

▶ **pull away 1** vt (move) éloigner; (snatch) arracher (**from** à). **2** vi (in vehicle) démarrer; **to p. away from** s'éloigner de.

▶ **pull back 1** vi se retirer. **2** vt retirer; (curtains) ouvrir.

▶ **pull down** vt baisser; (knock down) faire tomber; (demolish) démolir.

▶ **pull in 1** vt (into room etc) faire entrer (de force); (crowd) attirer. **2** vi arriver; (stop in vehicle) se garer.

▶ **pull off** vt (remove) enlever.

▶ **pull on** vt (boots etc) mettre.

▶ **pull out 1** vt (tooth, hair) arracher; (cork, pin) enlever; (from pocket etc) tirer, sortir (**from** de). **2** vi (move out in vehicle) déboîter; (withdraw) se retirer (**from, of** de).

pull·o·ver pull(-over) m.

▸ **pull over 1** vt traîner (**to** jusqu'à); (knock down) faire tomber. **2** vi (in vehicle) se ranger (**to** sur le côté).

▸ **pull through** vi s'en tirer.

▸ **pull up 1** vt (socks, sleeve, collar, shade) remonter, relever; (plant, tree) arracher; (chair) approcher. **2** vi (in vehicle) s'arrêter.

pulse pouls m.

pump 1 n pompe f; (air) p. (in service station) gonfleur m. **2** vt pomper.

pump·kin potiron m, citrouille f.

▸ **pump up** vt (mattress etc) gonfler.

punch¹ 1 n (blow) coup m de poing. **2** vt donner un coup de poing à (qn).

punch² 1 n (for paper) perforeuse f. **2** vt (ticket) poinçonner; (with date) composter; **to p. a hole in sth** faire un trou dans qch.

punc·tu·al adj (on time) à l'heure; (regularly) ponctuel.

punc·tu·a·tion ponctuation f.

punc·ture 1 n crevaison f. **2** vti (burst) crever.

pun·ish vt punir (**for sth** de qch; **for doing** pour avoir fait).

pun·ish·ment punition f.

pup (dog) chiot m.

pu·pil élève mf; (of eye) pupille f.

pup·pet marionnette f.

pup·py chiot m.

pur·chase 1 n achat m. **2** vt acheter (**from sb** à qn; **for sb** à or pour qn).

pur·chas·er acheteur, -euse mf.

pure adj pur.

pure·ly adv (only) strictement.

pur·ple 1 adj violet (f -ette). **2** n violet m.

pur·pose (aim) but m; **for this p.** dans ce but; **on p.** exprès.

pur·pose·ly adv exprès.

purse (for coins) porte-monnaie m

inv; (handbag) sac m à main.

pur·sue vt (inquiry, aim etc) poursuivre.

pur·suit poursuite f; (of pleasure, glory) quête f; (pastime) occupation f.

push 1 n to give sb/sth a p. pousser qn/qch. **2** vt pousser (**to, as far as** jusqu'à); **to p. sth into/between** enfoncer qch dans/entre; **to p. sb into doing** pousser qn à faire. **3** vi pousser.

push (down) vt (button) appuyer sur; (lever) abaisser.

▸ **push around** vt (bully) marcher sur les pieds à.

▸ **push aside** vt écarter.

▸ **push away** or **back** vt repousser.

push-but·ton adj p. phone téléphone m à touches.

▸ **push on** vi continuer (**with sth** qch).

▸ **push over** renverser.

▸ **push through** vt to p. one's way through se frayer un chemin (**a crowd** à travers une foule).

▸ **push up** vt (lever, sleeve, collar) relever; (increase) augmenter.

push·y adj Fam batailleur, -euse.

puss* (cat) minou m.

put* vt mettre; (money) placer (**into** dans); (question) poser (**to** à); (say) dire.

▸ **put across** vt (message etc) communiquer (**to** à).

▸ **put aside** vt (money, object) mettre de côté.

▸ **put away** vt (book, car etc) ranger; (criminal) mettre en prison

▸ **put back** vt (replace, postpone) remettre; (telephone receiver) raccrocher.

▸ **put by** vt (money) mettre de côté.

▸ **put down** vt (on floor etc) poser; (passenger) déposer; (a deposit) verser; (write down) inscrire.

▸ **put forward** vt (candidate) proposer (**for** à).

▸ **put in** vt (sth into box etc) mettre dedans; (insert) introduire; (add)

ajouter; *(install)* installer; *(application)* faire.

▸ **put off** *vt* renvoyer (à plus tard); *(gas, radio)* fermer; **to p. sb off** dissuader qn *(doing* de faire); *(disgust)* dégoûter qn.

▸ **put on** *vt (clothes etc)* mettre; *(weight)* prendre; *(gas, radio)* mettre; *(record, cassette)* passer; *(clock)* avancer; *(lid)* mettre en place.

▸ **put out** *vt (take outside)* sortir; *(arm, leg)* étendre; *(hand)* tendre; *(gas, light)* éteindre; *(bother)* déranger.

▸ **put through** *vt (on phone)* passer qn *(to* à).

▸ **put together** *vt* mettre ensemble; *(assemble)* assembler; *(compose)* composer.

put·ty mastic *m*.

▸ **put up 1** *vi (stay)* descendre *(at a hotel* à un hôtel). **2** *vt (lift)* lever; *(window)* remonter; *(tent, statue, ladder)* dresser; *(building)* construire; *(umbrella)* ouvrir; *(picture)* mettre; *(price)* augmenter; *(candidate)* proposer *(for* à); *(guest)* loger.

▸ **put up with** *vt* supporter.

puz·zle 1 *n* mystère *m*; *(jigsaw)* puzzle *m*. **2** *vt* laisser perplexe.

puz·zled *adj* perplexe.

puz·zling *adj* curieux.

py·lon pylône *m*.

pyr·a·mid pyramide *f*.

Q

qual·i·fi·ca·tion diplôme *m*; **qualifications** *(skills)* qualités *fpl* nécessaires *(for* pour; **to do** pour faire).

qual·i·fied *adj (able)* qualifié *(to do* pour faire); *(teacher etc)* diplômé.

qual·i·fy *vt* obtenir son diplôme *(as a doctor/etc* de médecin/*etc*); *(in sports)* se qualifier *(for* pour).

qual·i·ty qualité *f*.

quan·ti·ty quantité *f*.

quar·rel 1 *n* dispute *f*; **to pick a q.** chercher des histoires *(with sb* à qn). **2** *vi* se disputer *(with sb* avec qn).

quar·rel·ing disputes *fpl*.

quar·ry *(to extract stone etc)* carrière *f*.

quart litre *m (mesure approximative = 0.95 litre)*.

quar·ter¹ quart *m*; *(money)* quart *m* de dollar; *(of fruit)* quartier *m*; *(of school/fiscal year)* trimestre *m*; **to divide sth into quarters** diviser qch en quatre; **q. (of a) pound** quart *m* de livre; **a q. past** *or* **after nine** neuf heures et quart *or* un quart; **a q. to nine** neuf heures moins le quart.

quar·ter² *(district)* quartier *m*.

quar·ter·back quarterback *m*.

quartz *adj (watch etc)* à quartz.

quay quai *m*, débarcadère *m*.

queen reine *f*, *Chess, Cards* dame *f*.

quench *vt* **to q. one's thirst** se désaltérer.

que·ry *(question)* question *f*.

ques·tion 1 *n* question *f*; **it's out of the q.** il n'en est pas question. **2** *vt* interroger *(qn) (about* sur); *(doubt)* mettre *(qch)* en question.

ques·tion·a·ble *adj* discutable.

ques·tion mark point *m* d'interrogation.

ques·tion·naire questionnaire *m*.

quib·ble *vi* ergoter *(over* sur).

quiche quiche *f*.

quick 1 *adj* rapide; **be q.!** fais vite!; **to have a q. meal**/*etc* manger/*etc* en vitesse. **2** *adv* vite.

quick·ly *adv* vite.

qui·et *adj (silent, peaceful)* tranquille; *(machine, vehicle)* silencieux; *(voice, sound)* doux *(f* douce); **to be** or **keep q.** (shut up) se taire; (make no noise) ne pas faire de bruit; **q.!** silence!; **to keep q. about sth** ne pas parler de qch.

qui·et·ly adv tranquillement; (not loudly) doucement; (silently) silencieusement.

quilt édredon m.

quit* 1 to q. doing arrêter de faire. **2** vi abandonner; (resign) démissionner.

quite adv (entirely) tout à fait; (really) vraiment; (rather) assez; **q. a lot** pas mal (**of** de).

quiz, pl **quizzes** (in school) contrôle m; **q. show** jeu(-concours) m.

quo·ta quota m.

quo·ta·tion citation f; (estimate) devis m.

quo·ta·tion marks guillemets mpl; **in q.** entre guillemets.

quote 1 vt citer; (reference) rappeler; (price) indiquer. **2** vi **to q. from** citer. **3** n = **quotation**.

R

rab·bi rabbin m.
rab·bit lapin m.
ra·bies rage f.
race[1] n (contest) course f. **2** vt (horse) faire courir; **to r. (against** or **with) sb** faire une course avec qn. **3** vi (run) courir.
race[2] n (group) race f.
race·car voiture f de course.
race·car driv·er coureur m automobile.
race·horse cheval m de course.
race·track champ m de courses.
ra·cial adj racial.
ra·cial·ism, rac·ism racisme m.
rac·ing courses fpl.
ra·cist adj & n raciste (mf).

rack (for bottles, letters etc) casier m; (for drying dishes) égouttoir m; **(luggage) r.** (on bus, train) filet m à bagages.

rack·et (for tennis) raquette f; (din) vacarme m.

ra·dar radar m.

ra·di·a·tion radiation f.

ra·di·a·tor radiateur m.

rad·i·cal adj radical.

ra·di·o, pl -os radio f; (set) poste m de radio; **on** or **over the r.** à la radio.

ra·di·o·ac·tive adj radioactif.

rad·ish radis m.

ra·di·us, pl -dii (of circle) rayon m.

raf·fle tombola f.

raft (boat) radeau m.

rag (old clothing) haillon m; (for dusting etc) chiffon m; **in rags** (clothes) en loques; (person) en haillons.

rage rage f; **to fly into a r.** se mettre en rage.

rag·ged adj (clothes) en loques; (person) en haillons.

raid 1 n (military) raid m; (by police) descente f; (by thieves) hold-up m inv; **air r.** raid m aérien. **2** vt faire un raid dans; (of police) faire une descente dans; (of thieves) faire un hold-up dans.

rail (for train) rail m; (rod on balcony) balustrade f; (on stairs) rampe f; **by r.** (to travel) par le train; (to send) par chemin de fer.

rail·ing (of balcony) balustrade f; **railings** (fence) grille f.

rail·road 1 n chemin m de fer; **r. (track)** voie f ferrée. **2** adj (ticket) de chemin de fer; **r. line** ligne f de chemin de fer.

rain 1 n pluie f; **in the r.** sous la pluie. **2** vi pleuvoir; **it's raining** il pleut.

rain·bow arc-en-ciel m.

rain·coat imper(méable) m.

rain·y adj pluvieux.

raise 1 vt (lift) lever; (child, family, voice) élever; (salary, price) augmenter; *(question)* soulever; **to r. money** réunir des fonds. **2** *n* augmentation *f* (de salaire).

rai·sin raisin *m* sec.

rake 1 *n* râteau *m*. **2** *vt (garden)* ratisser.

rake (up) *vt (leaves)* ratisser.

ral·ly *(political)* rassemblement *m*.

▶ **rally (a)round 1** *vt* venir en aide à. **2** *vi* venir en aide.

ram 1 *n (animal)* bélier *m*. **2** *vt (vehicle)* emboutir; **to r. sth into sth** enfoncer qch dans qch.

ram·ble randonnée *f*.

ramp *(slope for wheelchair etc)* rampe *f* (d'accès).

ran *pt de* **run**.

ranch ranch *m*.

ran·dom 1 *n* **at r.** au hasard. **2** *adj (choice)* (fait) au hasard; *(sample)* prélevé au hasard; **r. check** *(by police)* contrôle-surprise *m*.

range 1 *n (of gun, voice etc)* portée *f*; *(of singer's voice)* étendue *f*; *(of colors, prices, products)* gamme *f*; *(of sizes)* choix *m*; *(of mountains)* chaîne *f*; *(stove)* cuisinière *f*. **2** *vi (vary)* varier (**from** de; **to** à).

rank rang *m*.

ran·som *(money)* rançon *f*.

rape 1 *vt* violer. **2** *n* viol *m*.

rap·id *adj* rapide.

rap·id·ly *adv* rapidement.

rap·ist violeur *m*.

rare *adj* rare; *(meat)* saignant.

rare·ly *adv* rarement.

ras·cal coquin, -ine *mf*.

rash 1 *n* éruption *f*. **2** *adj* irréfléchi.

rash·ly *adv* sans réfléchir.

rasp·ber·ry framboise *f*; **r. jam** confiture *f* de framboises.

rat rat *m*.

rate 1 *n (level)* taux *m*; *(speed)* vitesse *f*; *(price)* tarif *m*; **at the r. of** à une vitesse de; *(amount)* à raison de; **at this r.** *(slow speed)* à ce train-là; **at any r.** en tout cas. **2** *vt* évaluer (**at** à); *(regard)* considérer (**as** comme); *(deserve)* mériter.

rath·er *adv (preferably, quite)* plutôt; **I'd r. stay** j'aimerais mieux rester (**than** que); **r. than leave**/*etc* plutôt que de partir/*etc*.

rat·ing *(ranking)* classement *m*; *(appraisal)* évaluation *f*; **ratings** *(for TV, radio program)* indice *m* d'écoute.

ra·tio, *pl* -os proportion *f*.

ra·tion 1 *n* ration *f*; **rations** *(food)* vivres *mpl*. **2** *vt* rationner.

ra·tion·al *adj (person)* raisonnable.

ra·tion·ing rationnement *m*.

rat·tle 1 *n (baby's toy)* hochet *m*. **2** *vi* faire du bruit; *(of window)* trembler. **3** *vt (shake)* secouer.

rav·en·ous *adj* **I'm r.** j'ai une faim de loup.

raw *adj (vegetable etc)* cru; *(skin)* écorché; **r. material** matière *f* première.

ray *(of light, sun)* rayon *m*.

ra·zor rasoir *m*.

re- *prefix* ré-, re-, r-.

reach 1 *vt (place, distant object, aim)* atteindre; *(gain access to)* accéder à; *(of letter)* parvenir à *(qn)*; *(contact)* joindre *(qn)*; *(conclusion)* arriver à; **to r. sb sth** passer qch à qn. **2** *vi* s'étendre (**to** à); *(with arm)* (é)tendre le bras (**for** pour prendre). **3** *n* portée *f*; **within r. of** à portée de; *(near)* à proximité de; **within (easy) r.** *(object)* à portée de main.

▶ **reach out** *vi* (é)tendre le bras (**for** pour prendre).

re·act *vi* réagir (**against** contre; **to** à).

re·ac·tion réaction *f*.

re·ac·tor réacteur *m (nucléaire)*.

read* 1 *vt* lire; *(meter)* relever; *(of instrument)* indiquer. **2** *vi* lire; **to r. to sb** faire la lecture à qn.

▶ **read aloud** *vt* lire (à haute voix).

▶ **read back, read over** *vt* relire.

read·er lecteur, -trice *mf*; *(book)* livre *m* de lecture.

read·i·ly adv *(willingly)* volontiers; *(easily)* facilement.

read·ing lecture f, *(of meter)* relevé m; *(by instrument)* indication f.

▶**read through** vt parcourir.

▶**read up (on)** vt étudier.

read·y adj prêt (**to do** à faire; **for sth** à or pour qch); **to get sth/sb r.** préparer qch/qn; **to get r.** se préparer (**for sth** à or pour qch; **to do** à faire); **r. cash** argent m liquide.

read·y-made adj tout fait.

read·y-to-wear adj **r. clothes** prêt-à-porter m inv.

real adj vrai; *(life, world)* réel.

real es·tate biens mpl immobiliers; **r. estate agent** agent m immobilier.

re·al·is·tic adj réaliste.

re·al·i·ty réalité f.

re·al·ize vt *(know)* se rendre compte de; *(understand)* comprendre (**that** que).

real·ly adv vraiment.

Real·tor® agent m immobilier.

rear 1 n *(back part)* arrière m; **in** or **at the r.** à l'arrière. 2 adj arrière inv, de derrière. 3 vt *(family, animals)* élever.

rear (up) vi *(of horse)* se cabrer.

re·ar·range vt *(hair, room)* réarranger; *(plans)* changer.

rea·son 1 n raison f; **the r. for/ why...** la raison de/pour laquelle...; **for no r.** sans raison. 2 vi raisonner.

rea·son·a·ble adj raisonnable.

rea·son·a·bly adv *(fairly, rather)* assez.

rea·son·ing raisonnement m.

▶**reason with** vt raisonner.

re·as·sure vt rassurer.

re·as·sur·ing adj rassurant.

re·bel 1 n rebelle mf; *(against parents etc)* révolté, -ée mf. 2 vi se révolter (**against** contre).

re·bel·lion révolte f.

re·bound 1 vi *(of ball)* rebondir;

(of stone) ricocher. 2 n rebond m; ricochet m.

re·build vt reconstruire.

re·call vt *(remember)* se rappeler (**that** que; **doing** avoir fait); **to r. sth to sb** rappeler qch à qn.

re·ceipt *(for payment, object left etc)* reçu m (**for** de); **on r. of** dès réception de.

re·ceive vt recevoir.

re·ceiv·er *(of phone)* combiné m; **to pick up the r.** *(of phone)* décrocher.

re·cent adj récent; **in r. months** ces mois-ci.

re·cent·ly adv récemment.

re·cep·tion *(party, of radio etc)* réception f; **r. (desk)** réception f, accueil m.

re·cep·tion·ist secrétaire mf, réceptionniste mf.

re·charge vt *(battery)* recharger.

rec·i·pe recette f (**for** de).

re·cip·i·ent *(of gift, letter)* destinataire mf, *(of award)* lauréat, -ate mf.

re·cite vt *(poem)* réciter; *(list)* énumérer.

reck·less adj *(rash)* imprudent.

reck·on vt *(calculate)* calculer; *(think)* Fam penser (**that** que).

▶**reckon on** vt *(rely on)* compter sur; **to r. on doing** compter faire.

▶**reckon with** vt *(take into account)* compter avec.

re·claim vt *(baggage at airport)* récupérer.

rec·og·nize vt reconnaître (**by** à).

rec·ol·lect vt se souvenir de; **to r. that** se souvenir que.

rec·ol·lec·tion souvenir m.

rec·om·mend vt recommander (**to** à; **for** pour); **to r. sb to do** recommander à qn de faire.

rec·om·men·da·tion recommandation f.

re·cord 1 n *(best performance)* record m; *(register)* registre m; *(mention)* mention f; *(background)*

antécédents *mpl*; **(public) records**
archives *fpl*; **to keep a r. of** noter.
2 *adj (time, number etc)* record *inv*.
3 *vt (on tape, in register)* enregistrer; *(in diary)* noter. **4** *vi* enregistrer.

re·cord·ed *adj (music, message,
tape)* enregistré; *(TV broadcast)* en
différé.

re·cord·er flûte *f* à bec; **(tape) r.**
magnétophone *m*; **(video) r.** magnétoscope *m*.

re·cord·ing enregistrement *m*.

re·cov·er 1 *vt (get back)* retrouver.
2 *vi (from illness etc)* se remettre
(**from** de); *(of economy)* se redresser.

rec·re·a·tion récréation *f*.

re·cruit recrue *f*.

rec·tan·gle rectangle *m*.

rec·tan·gu·lar *adj* rectangulaire.

re·cy·cle *vt* recycler.

red 1 *adj* rouge; *(hair)* roux (*f*
rousse); **to turn r.** rougir; **r. light**
(traffic light) feu *m* rouge. **2** *n (color)* rouge *m*; **in the r.** *(company, account)* dans le rouge, en déficit.

red-hand·ed *adj* **caught r.** pris
en flagrant délit.

red·head roux *m*, rousse *f*.

red-hot *adj* brûlant.

re·di·rect *vt (mail)* faire suivre.

re·do* *vt (exercise, house etc)*
refaire.

re·duce *vt* réduire (**to** à; **by** de); **at
a reduced price** *(ticket, goods)* à
prix réduit.

re·duc·tion réduction *f* (**in** de).

re·dun·dan·cy superfluité *f*.

re·dun·dant *adj* superflu.

reed *(plant)* roseau *m*.

reef récif *m*.

reel *(of thread, film)* bobine *f*; *(film
itself)* bande *f*.

re·fec·to·ry réfectoire *m*.

re·fer 1 *vi* **to r.** *(mention)* faire
allusion à; *(speak of)* parler de; *(apply to)* s'appliquer à. **2** *vt* **to r. sth to
sb** soumettre qch à qn.

ref·er·ee 1 *n Sports* arbitre *m*. **2** *vt*
arbitrer.

ref·er·ence *(in book, for job)* référence *f*; *(mention)* mention *f* (**to**
de); **with r. to** concernant; **r. book**
ouvrage *m* de référence.

ref·er·en·dum référendum *m*.

re·fill 1 *vt* remplir (à nouveau);
(lighter, pen) recharger. **2** *n* recharge *f*; **a r.** *(drink)* un autre
verre.

re·flect *vt (light etc)* refléter; **to be
reflected** se refléter.

re·flec·tion *(image)* reflet *m*.

re·flex réflexe *m*.

re·form réforme *f*.

re·frain *vi* s'abstenir (**from doing**
de faire).

re·fresh *vt (of bath, drink)* rafraîchir; *(of sleep, rest)* délasser.

re·fresh·er course cours *m* de
recyclage.

re·fresh·ing *adj (drink)* rafraîchissant.

re·fresh·ments *npl (drinks)* rafraîchissements *mpl*; *(snacks)* petites choses *fpl* à grignoter.

re·frig·er·ate *vt (food)* conserver
au frais.

re·frig·er·a·tor réfrigérateur *m*.

ref·uge refuge *m*; **to take r.** se
réfugier.

ref·u·gee réfugié, -ée *mf*.

re·fund 1 *vt* rembourser. **2** *n* remboursement *m*.

re·fus·al refus *m*.

re·fuse 1 *vt* refuser (**sb sth** qch à
qn; **to do** de faire). **2** *vi* refuser.

re·gain *vt (lost ground)* regagner;
(health, strength) retrouver.

re·gard 1 *vt* considérer; **as regards**
en ce qui concerne. **2** *n* considération *f* (**for** pour); **to have (a) high r.
for sb** estimer qn; **to give one's regards to sb** transmettre son meilleur souvenir à qn.

re·gard·ing *prep* en ce qui concerne.

re·gard·less 1 *adj* **r. of** sans tenir

compte de. **2** *adv (all the same)* quand même.

reg·i·ment régiment *m*.

re·gion région *f*; **in the r. of $50/ etc** *(about)* dans les 50 dollars/ *etc*.

re·gion·al *adj* régional.

reg·is·ter *n* registre *m*. **2** *vt(birth etc)* déclarer; **registered letter** lettre recommandée; **to send by registered mail** envoyer en recommandé. **3** *vi (enroll)* s'inscrire (**for a course** à un cours); *(in hotel)* signer le registre.

reg·is·tra·tion *(enrollment)* inscription *f*; **r. (number)** *(of vehicle)* numéro *m* d'immatriculation.

re·gret 1 *vt* regretter (**doing, to do** de faire; **that** que (+ *subjunctive*)). **2** *n* regret *m*.

reg·u·lar *adj (steady)* régulier; *(surface)* uni; *(usual)* habituel; *(price, size)* normal; *(listener)* fidèle.

reg·u·lar·ly *adv* régulièrement.

reg·u·late *vt (adjust)* régler; *(control)* réglementer.

reg·u·la·tions *npl (rules)* règlement *m*.

re·hears·al répétition *f*.

re·hearse 1 *vt (a play etc)* répéter. **2** *vi* répéter.

reign 1 *n* règne *m*; **in the r. of** sous le règne de. **2** *vi* régner (**over** sur).

rein·deer *inv* renne *m*.

re·in·force *vt* renforcer (**with** de).

re·in·force·ments *npl (troops)* renforts *mpl*.

reins *npl (for horse)* rênes *fpl*; *(for baby)* bretelles *fpl* de sécurité (avec laisse).

re·ject *vt* rejeter.

re·jec·tion rejet *m*; *(of candidate)* refus *m*.

re·joice *vi (celebrate)* faire la fête; *(be delighted)* se réjouir (**over** or **at sth** de qch).

re·lat·ed *adj (linked)* lié (**to** à); **to be r. to sb** *(by family)* être parent de qn.

▶ **relate to** *vt (apply to)* se rapporter à.

re·la·tion *(relative)* parent, -ente *mf*; *(relationship)* rapport *m*; **international relations** relations *fpl* internationales.

re·la·tion·ship *(in family)* lien(s) *m(pl)* de parenté; *(relations)* relations *fpl*; *(connection)* rapport *m*.

rel·a·tive 1 *n (person)* parent, -ente *mf*. **2** *adj* relatif; **r. to** en rapport avec.

rel·a·tive·ly *adv* relativement.

re·lax 1 *vt (person)* détendre; *(grip, pressure)* relâcher. **2** *vi* se détendre; **r.!** *(calm down)* du calme!

re·lax·a·tion *(rest)* détente *f*.

re·laxed *adj* décontracté.

re·lease 1 *vt (free)* libérer (**from** de); *(bomb)* lâcher; *(brake)* desserrer; *(film, record)* sortir; *(trapped person)* dégager. **2** *n (of prisoner)* libération *f*; *(of film etc)* sortie *f*; **press r.** communiqué *m* de presse.

rel·e·vant *adj* pertinent (**to** à); *(useful)* utile; **that's not r.** ça n'a rien à voir.

re·li·a·bil·i·ty fiabilité *f*; *(of person)* sérieux *m*.

re·li·a·ble *adj* fiable; *(person)* sérieux.

re·lief *(from pain etc)* soulagement *m* (**from** à); *(help)* secours *m*; *(in geography etc)* relief *m*.

re·lieve *vt (pain, person etc)* soulager; *(take over from)* relayer *(qn)*.

re·li·gion religion *f*.

re·li·gious *adj* religieux.

rel·ish 1 *n* condiment *m*. **2** *vt (food, wine)* savourer.

re·load *vt (gun, camera)* recharger.

re·luc·tance manque *m* d'enthousiasme (**to do** de faire).

re·luc·tant *adj* peu enthousiaste (**to do** pour faire).

re·luc·tant·ly *adv* sans enthousiasme.

▸ **re·ly on** vt (count on) compter sur; (be dependent on) dépendre de.

re·main vi rester.

re·main·ing adj qui reste(nt).

re·mark 1 n remarque f. **2** vt (faire) remarquer (**that** que). **3** vi **to r. on sth** faire des remarques sur qch.

re·mark·a·ble adj remarquable (**for** par).

re·mark·a·bly adv remarquablement.

re·match Sports revanche f.

re·me·di·al adj **r. class** cours m de rattrapage.

rem·e·dy 1 n remède m. **2** vt remédier à.

re·mem·ber 1 vt se souvenir de, se rappeler; **to r. that/doing** se rappeler que/d'avoir fait; **to r. to do** penser à faire. **2** vi se souvenir, se rappeler.

re·mind vt rappeler (**sb of sth** qch à qn; **sb that** qch que); **to r. sb to do** faire penser à qn à faire.

re·mind·er rappel m; **to give sb a r. to do** faire penser à qn à faire.

re·morse remords m(pl).

re·mote adj (far-off) lointain; (isolated) isolé; (slight) petit.

re·mote con·trol télécommande f.

re·mov·al (of clothes, stain etc) enlèvement m; (of obstacle, word) suppression f.

re·move vt (clothes, stain etc) enlever (**from sb** à qn; **from sth** de qch); (obstacle, word) supprimer.

re·new vt renouveler; (resume) reprendre; (library book) renouveler le prêt de.

rent 1 n (for house etc) loyer m. **2** vt louer.

rent·al (of house, car) location f.

▸ **rent out** vt louer.

re·or·gan·ize vt (firm etc) réorganiser.

re·pair 1 vt réparer. **2** n réparation f; **in bad r.** en mauvais état.

re·pair·man, pl **-men** réparateur m, dépanneur m.

re·pay vt (pt & pp repaid) (pay back) rembourser; (reward) récompenser (**for** de).

re·pay·ment (paying back) remboursement m; (rewarding) récompense f.

re·peat 1 vt répéter (**that** que); (promise, threat) réitérer; (class) redoubler; **to r. oneself** se répéter. **2** n (on TV, radio) rediffusion f.

re·peat·ed adj (attempts etc) répétés.

re·peat·ed·ly adv à maintes reprises, de nombreuses fois.

re·pel vt repousser.

rep·e·ti·tion répétition f.

re·pet·i·tive adj répétitif.

re·place vt (take the place of) remplacer (**by, with** par); (put back) remettre; (telephone receiver) raccrocher.

re·place·ment (person) remplaçant, -ante mf; (machine part) pièce f de rechange.

re·play 1 n match m rejoué; (instant or action) **r.** répétition f d'une séquence précédente. **2** vt (match) rejouer.

rep·li·ca copie f exacte.

re·ply 1 vti répondre (**to** à; **that** que). **2** n réponse f.

re·port 1 n (account) rapport m; (of meeting) compte rendu m; (in media) reportage m; (of pupil) bulletin m; (rumor) rumeur f. **2** vt rapporter; (announce) annoncer (**that** que); (notify) signaler (**to** à); (inform on) dénoncer (**to** à). **3** vi faire un rapport; (of journalist) faire un reportage (**on** sur); (go) se présenter (**to** à; **to sb** chez qn).

re·port card bulletin m (scolaire).

re·port·ed adj (speech) indirect.

re·port·er reporter m.

rep·re·sent vt représenter.

rep·re·sen·ta·tive représentant, -ante mf.

re·pro·duce 1 *vt* reproduire. **2** *vi* se reproduire.

re·pro·duc·tion reproduction *f.*

rep·tile reptile *m.*

re·pub·lic république *f.*

rep·u·ta·ble *adj* de bonne réputation.

rep·u·ta·tion réputation *f*; **to have a r. for being** avoir la réputation d'être.

re·quest 1 *n* demande *f* (**for** de). **2** *vt* demander (**sth from sb** qch à qn; **sb to do** à qn de faire).

re·quire *vt* (*of thing*) demander; (*of person*) avoir besoin de; **if required** s'il le faut.

re·quired *adj* the r. qualities/*etc* les qualités/*etc* qu'il faut.

re·run (*on TV, radio*) rediffusion *f.*

res·cue *vt* (*save*) sauver; (*set free*) délivrer (**from** de). **2** *n* sauvetage *m* (**of** de); (*help*) secours *m*; **to go to sb's r.** aller au secours de qn.

re·search 1 *n* recherches *fpl* (**on**, **into** sur). **2** *vi* faire des recherches.

re·search·er chercheur, -euse *mf.*

re·sem·blance ressemblance *f* (**to** avec).

re·sem·ble *vt* ressembler à.

re·sent *vt* (*person*) en vouloir à; (*remark, criticism*) ne pas apprécier.

re·sent·ment ressentiment *m.*

res·er·va·tion (*of hotel room etc*) réservation *f*; (*doubt*) réserve *f.*

re·serve 1 *vt* réserver; (*right*) se réserver. **2** *n* nature r. réserve *f* naturelle; **in r.** en réserve.

re·served *adj* (*person, place*) réservé.

re·serve tank réservoir *m* de secours.

res·er·voir réservoir *m.*

re·side *vi* to r. in New York résider à New York.

res·i·dence (*home*) résidence *f*; (*of students*) foyer *m.*

res·i·dent habitant, -ante *mf*; (*of hotel*) pensionnaire *mf.*

res·i·den·tial *adj* (*district*) résidentiel.

re·sign 1 *vt* to r. oneself to sth/to doing se résigner à qch/à faire. **2** *vi* démissionner; **to r. from one's job** démissionner.

res·ig·na·tion (*from job*) démission *f.*

re·sist 1 *vt* (*attack etc*) résister à; **to r. doing sth** se retenir de faire qch; **she can't r. cakes** elle ne peut pas résister devant des gâteaux. **2** *vi* résister.

re·sis·tance résistance *f* (**to** à).

re·sort[1] **1** *vi* to r. to doing en venir à faire; **to r. to sth** avoir recours à qch. **2** *n* as a last r. en dernier ressort.

re·sort[2] (*vacation*) r. station *f* de vacances; **beach r.** station *f* balnéaire; **ski r.** station *f* de ski.

re·sour·ces *npl* (*wealth, means*) ressources *fpl.*

re·spect 1 *n* respect *m* (**for** pour, de); **with r. to** en ce qui concerne. **2** *vt* respecter.

re·spect·a·ble *adj* (*honorable, quite good*) respectable; (*clothes, behavior*) convenable.

re·spec·tive *adj* respectif.

re·spond *vi* répondre (**to** à); **to r. to treatment** bien réagir au traitement.

re·sponse réponse *f.*

re·spon·si·bil·i·ty responsabilité *f.*

re·spon·si·ble *adj* responsable (**for** de; **to sb** devant qn); (*job*) à responsabilités.

rest[1] **1** *n* repos *m*; (*support*) support *m*; **to have** *or* **take a r.** se reposer. **2** *vi* (*relax*) se reposer; **to be resting on sth** (*of hand etc*) être posé sur qch. **3** *vt* (*lean*) appuyer (**on** sur; **against** contre).

rest[2] (*remaining part*) reste *m* (**of** de); **the r.** (*others*) les autres *mfpl*; **the r. of the men**/*etc* les autres hommes/*etc.*

res·tau·rant restaurant *m.*

rest·ful *adj* reposant.

rest·less *adj* agité.

re·store *vt (give back)* rendre (**to** à); *(building etc)* restaurer.

re·strain *vt (person, dog)* maîtriser; *(crowd, anger)* contenir; **to r. oneself from doing sth** s'empêcher de faire qch.

re·straint *(restriction)* restriction *f*; *(moderation)* mesure *f*.

re·strict *vt* restreindre (**to** à).

re·strict·ed *adj* restreint.

re·stric·tion restriction *f.*

rest·room toilettes *fpl.*

re·sult résultat *m*; **as a r. of** par suite de.

re·sume *vti* reprendre.

ré·su·mé CV *m inv.*

re·tail 1 *adj (price, shop)* de détail. **2** *adv (to sell)* au détail.

re·tail·er détaillant, -ante *mf.*

re·tain *vt (freshness etc)* conserver.

re·take *vt (exam)* repasser.

re·tire *vi (from work)* prendre sa retraite; *(withdraw)* se retirer (**from** de; **to** à); *(go to bed)* aller se coucher.

re·tired *adj (no longer working)* retraité.

re·tir·ee retraité, -ée *mf.*

re·tire·ment retraite *f.*

re·treat 1 *n (withdrawal)* retraite *f*; *(shelter)* refuge *m.* **2** *vi* se retirer; *(of army)* battre en retraite.

re·trieve *vt (recover)* récupérer; *(of dog)* rapporter.

re·turn 1 *vi (come back)* revenir; *(go back)* retourner; *(go back home)* rentrer. **2** *vt (give back)* rendre; *(put back)* remettre; *(send back)* renvoyer. **3** *n* retour *m*; *(on investment)* rendement *m*; **tax r.** déclaration *f* de revenus; **in r.** en échange (**for** de). **4** *adj (flight etc)* (de) retour.

re·turn·a·ble *adj (bottle)* consigné.

re·veal *vt (make known)* révéler (**that** que).

rev·e·la·tion révélation *f.*

re·venge vengeance *f*; **to get one's r.** se venger (**on sb** de qn; **for sth** de qch); **in r.** pour se venger.

re·verse 1 *adj (order)* inverse. **2** *n* contraire *m*; **in r.** (gear) en marche arrière. **3** *vti* **to r.** (the car) faire marche arrière; **to r. in/out** rentrer/sortir en marche arrière.

re·vert *vi* **to r.** to revenir à.

re·view 1 *vt (book)* faire la critique de. **2** *n* critique *f.*

re·vise 1 *vt (opinion, notes, text)* réviser. **2** *vi (for exam)* réviser (**for** pour).

re·vi·sion révision *f.*

re·viv·al *(of custom, business, play)* reprise *f*; *(of fashion)* renouveau *m.*

re·vive *vt (unconscious person)* ranimer.

re·volt révolte *f.*

re·volt·ing *adj* dégoûtant.

rev·o·lu·tion révolution *f.*

rev·o·lu·tion·ar·y *adj & n* révolutionnaire (*mf*).

re·volve *vi* tourner (**around** autour de).

re·volv·er revolver *m.*

re·volv·ing door(s) (porte *f* à) tambour *m.*

re·ward 1 *n* récompense *f* (**for** de, pour). **2** *vt* récompenser (**sb for sth** qn de *or* pour qch).

re·wind* 1 *vt (tape)* rembobiner. **2** *vi* se rembobiner.

rhet·o·ric rhétorique *f.*

rheu·ma·tism rhumatisme *m*; **to have r.** avoir des rhumatismes.

rhi·noc·er·os rhinocéros *m.*

rhu·barb rhubarbe *f.*

rhyme 1 *n* rime *f*; *(poem)* vers *mpl.* **2** *vi* rimer (**with** avec).

rhythm rythme *m.*

rhyth·mi·cal *adj* rythmé.

rib *(in body)* côte *f.*

rib·bon ruban *m.*

rice riz *m.*

rich 1 *adj* riche. **2** *npl* **the r.** les riches *mpl*.

rich·es *npl* richesses *fpl*.

rid *adj* **to get r. of** se débarrasser de.

rid·dle *(puzzle)* énigme *f*.

ride 1 *n (on bicycle, by car, on horse etc)* promenade *f; (distance)* trajet *m*; **to go for a r. (in car)** faire une promenade (en voiture); **to give sb a r. (in car)** emmener qn en voiture. **2** *vi** aller (à bicyclette/à moto/à cheval/*etc*) (**to** à); **to r., to go riding** *(on horse)* monter (à cheval). **3** *vt (a particular horse)* monter; *(distance)* faire (à cheval *etc*); **to r. a horse or horses** monter à cheval; **I was riding a bicycle** j'étais à bicyclette; **to r. a bicycle to** aller à bicyclette à.

rid·er *(on horse)* cavalier, -ière *mf*.

ridge crête *f; (of roof)* faîte *m*.

ri·dic·u·lous *adj* ridicule.

rid·ing *(horseback)* r. équitation *f*.

ri·fle fusil *m*.

rig (oil) r. derrick *m; (at sea)* plateforme *f* pétrolière.

right¹ 1 *adj (correct)* bon (*f* bonne); *(fair)* juste; *(angle)* droit; **to be r. (of person)** avoir raison (**to do** de faire); **she did r.** elle a bien fait; **the r. choice/time** le bon choix/moment; **it's the r. time** *(accurate)* c'est l'heure exacte; **the clock's r.** la pendule est à l'heure; **it's not r. to steal** ce n'est pas bien de voler; **to put r.** *(error)* corriger; **r.!** bien!; **that's r.** c'est ça. **2** *adv (straight)* (tout) droit; *(completely)* tout à fait; *(correctly)* juste; *(well)* bien; **she did r.** elle a bien fait; **r. here** ici même; **r. away, r. now** tout de suite. **3** *n* **r. and wrong** le bien et le mal.

right² 1 *adj (hand, side etc)* droit. **2** *adv* à droite. **3** *n* droite *f*; **on** *or* **to the r.** à droite (**of** de).

right³ *(claim)* droit *m* (**to do** de faire); **to have a r. to sth** avoir droit à qch.

right-hand *adj* à *or* de droite; **on the r. side** à droite (**of** de).

right-hand·ed *adj (person)* droitier.

right·ly *adv* à juste titre.

rig·id *adj* rigide.

rim *(of cup etc)* bord *m*.

rind *(of cheese)* croûte *f*.

ring¹ *(on finger, curtain etc)* anneau *m; (with jewel)* bague *f; (of people, chairs)* cercle *m; Boxing* ring *m*; **diamond r.** bague *f* de diamants; **to make a r. around** entourer (**with** de).

ring² 1 *n (sound)* sonnerie *f*; **to give sb a r.** *(phone call)* passer un coup de fil à qn. **2** *vi* (of bell, phone, person)* sonner. **3** *vt* sonner; **to r. the (door)bell** sonner à la porte).

ring·lead·er meneur, -euse *mf*.

▶ **ring out** *vi (of bell)* sonner; *(of sound)* retentir.

rinse 1 *vt* rincer; **to r. one's hands** se rincer les mains. **2** *n* **to give sb a r.** rincer qch.

▶ **rinse out** *vt* rincer.

ri·ot 1 *n (uprising)* émeute *f; (fight)* bagarre *f*. **2** *vi* faire une émeute; *(fight)* se bagarrer.

rip 1 *vt* déchirer. **2** *vi (of fabric)* se déchirer. **3** *n* déchirure *f*.

ripe *adj* mûr; *(cheese)* fait.

rip·en *vti* mûrir.

rip-off *Fam* **it's a r.** c'est du vol organisé.

▶ **rip off** *vt (button etc)* arracher (**from** de); **to r. sb off** *Fam* rouler qn.

▶ **rip out** *vt* arracher (**from** de).

▶ **rip up** *vt* déchirer.

rise *vi* (of temperature, balloon, price)* monter; *(of sun, curtain, person)* se lever; **to r. in price** augmenter de prix. **2** *n (in price etc)* hausse *f* (**in** de); *(slope in ground)* montée *f*; **to give r. to sth** donner lieu à qch.

ris·ing 1 *adj (sun)* levant; *(prices)* en hausse. **2** *n (of sun)* lever *m; (of prices)* hausse *f*.

risk 1 *n* risque *m* (**of doing** de faire; **in doing** à faire); **at r.** *(person)* en danger; *(job)* menacé. **2** *vt* risquer; **she won't r.** **leaving** elle ne se risquera pas à partir.

risk·y *adj* risqué.

rit·u·al *adj & n* rituel *(m)*.

ri·val 1 *adj (company etc)* rival. **2** *n* rival, -ale *mf*. **3** *vt (compete with)* rivaliser avec (**in** de); *(equal)* égaler (**in** en).

riv·er rivière *f*; *(flowing into sea)* fleuve *m*.

Riv·i·er·a the (French) R. la Côte d'Azur.

roach *(cockroach)* cafard *m*.

road 1 *n* route *f* (**to** qui va à); *(small)* chemin *m*; *(in town)* rue *f*; *(roadway)* chaussée *f*; **across the r.** *(building etc)* en face; **by r.** par la route. **2** *adj (map, safety)* routier; *(accident)* de la route; **r. sign** panneau *m* (routier).

road·side bord *m* de la route; **r. bar/hotel/etc** bar *m*/ hôtel *m*/etc situé au bord de la route.

road·way chaussée *f*.

road·work travaux *mpl*.

roam *vt* parcourir; **to r. the streets** *(of child, dog etc)* traîner dans les rues.

roar 1 *vi (of lion)* rugir; *(of person)* hurler. **2** *n (of lion)* rugissement *m*.

roast 1 *vt* rôtir; *(coffee)* griller. **2** *vi (of meat)* rôtir. **3** *n (meat)* rôti *m*. **4** *adj (chicken etc)* rôti; **r. beef** rosbif *m*.

rob *vt (person)* voler; *(bank)* attaquer; *(by breaking in)* cambrioler; **to r. sb of sth** voler qch à qn.

rob·ber voleur, -euse *mf*.

rob·ber·y vol *m*.

robe *(bathrobe)* robe *f* de chambre.

rob·in rouge-gorge *m*.

ro·bot robot *m*.

rock¹ 1 *vt (baby, boat)* bercer. **2** *vi (sway)* se balancer; *(of building)* trembler. **3** *n (music)* rock *m*.

rock² *(substance)* roche *f*, *(boulder, rock face)* rocher *m*; *(stone)* pierre *f*; **r. face** paroi *f* rocheuse.

rock·et fusée *f*.

rock·ing chair fauteuil *m* à bascule.

rod *(wooden)* baguette *f*; *(metal)* tige *f*, *(of curtain)* tringle *f*; *(for fishing)* canne *f* (à pêche).

rogue *(dishonest)* crapule *f*, *(mischievous)* coquin, -ine *mf*.

role rôle *m*.

roll 1 *n (of paper etc)* rouleau *m*; *(small bread loaf)* petit pain *m*; *(of drum)* roulement *m*; *(attendance list)* cahier *m* d'appel; **to call** *or* **take the r.** faire l'appel. **2** *vi (of ball etc)* rouler; *(of person, animal)* se rouler. **3** *vt* rouler.

▶**roll down** *vt (car window etc)* baisser; *(slope)* descendre (en roulant).

roll·er *(for hair, painting etc)* rouleau *m*.

roll·er·blade 1 *n* roller *m*. **2** *vi* faire du roller.

roll·er·skate 1 *n* patin *m* à roulettes. **2** *vi* faire du patin à roulettes.

roll·ing pin rouleau *m* à pâtisserie.

▶**roll over 1** *vi (many times)* se rouler; *(once)* se retourner. **2** *vt* retourner.

▶**roll up** *vt (map, cloth)* rouler; *(sleeve, pants)* retrousser.

Ro·man 1 *n* Romain, -aine *mf*. **2** *adj* romain, -aine.

Ro·man Cath·o·lic *adj & n* catholique *(mf)*.

ro·mance *(love)* amour *m*; *(affair)* aventure *f* amoureuse.

ro·man·tic *adj* romantique.

roof toit *m*; *(of tunnel, cave)* plafond *m*.

roof rack *(of car)* galerie *f*.

room *(in house etc)* pièce *f*; *(bedroom)* chambre *f*; *(large, public)* salle *f*; *(space)* place *f* (**for** pour); **men's r., ladies' r.** toilettes *fpl*.

room·mate colocataire *mf.*

room·y *adj* spacieux; *(clothes)* ample.

root racine *f*, *(origin)* origine *f*; **to take r.** *(of plant)* prendre racine.

▸**root for** *vt Fam* encourager.

rope corde *f.*

▸**rope off** *vt (of police etc)* interdire l'accès de.

rose *(flower)* rose *f*; **r. bush** rosier *m.*

ro·ta·tion rotation *f.*

rot (a·way) *vti* pourrir.

rot·ten *adj (fruit, weather etc)* pourri; *(bad) Fam* moche; **to feel r.** *(ill)* être mal fichu.

rough¹ *adj (surface, plank)* rugueux; *(ground)* inégal; *(brutal)* brutal; *(sea)* agité.

rough² *adj (calculation etc)* approximatif; **r. guess** approximation *f*, **r. draft** brouillon *m.*

rough·ly¹ *adv (not gently)* rudement; *(brutally)* brutalement.

rough·ly² *adv (more or less)* à peu (de choses) près.

round 1 *adj* rond. **2** *n Boxing* round *m*; *(of drinks, visits)* tournée *f*; *(of policeman)* ronde *f.*

round·a·bout *adj* indirect.

▸**round off** *vt (meal etc)* terminer (**with** par); *(figure)* arrondir.

round trip aller (et) retour *m.*

▸**round up** *vt (people, animals)* rassembler.

route itinéraire *m*; *(of ship, aircraft)* route *f*; **bus r.** ligne *f* d'autobus.

rou·tine routine *f.*

row¹ 1 *n (line)* rang *m*, rangée *f*, *(one behind another)* file *f*; **two days in a r.** deux jours de suite. **2** *vi (in boat)* ramer. **3** *vt (boat)* faire aller à la rame.

row² 1 *n Fam (noise)* vacarme *m*; *(quarrel)* dispute *f.* **2** *vi Fam* se disputer (**with** avec).

row·boat bateau *m* à rames.

row house maison *f* attenante aux maisons voisines.

roy·al *adj* royal.

roy·al·ty personnages *mpl* royaux.

rub *vti* frotter; *(person)* frictionner.

rub·ber caoutchouc *m*; *(eraser)* gomme *f.*

rub·ber band élastique *m.*

rub·ber boots bottes *fpl* de caoutchouc.

rub·ber stamp tampon *m.*

rub·ble décombres *mpl.*

▸**rub down** *vt (person)* frictionner; *(wall, door)* poncer.

▸**rub in** *vt (cream)* faire pénétrer (en massant).

▸**rub off** *or* **out** *vt (mark)* effacer.

ru·by rubis *m.*

ruck·sack sac *m* à dos.

rud·der gouvernail *m.*

rude *adj* impoli (**to** envers); *(coarse, insolent)* grossier (**to** envers).

rude·ness impolitesse *f*, *(coarseness, insolence)* grossièreté *f.*

rug carpette *f.*

rug·by rugby *m.*

ru·in 1 *n* ruine *f*; **in ruins** *(building)* en ruine. **2** *vt (health, person etc)* ruiner; *(clothes)* abîmer.

rule 1 *n* règle *f*; **against the rule(s)** contraire au règlement; **as a r.** en règle générale. **2** *vt (country)* gouverner. **3** *vi (of king etc)* régner (**over** sur).

▸**rule out** *vt* exclure.

rul·er *(for measuring)* règle *f*, *(king, queen etc)* souverain, -aine *mf.*

rul·ing 1 *adj (party)* au pouvoir; *(monarch)* régnant; *(class)* dirigeant. **2** *n* décision *f.*

rum rhum *m.*

rum·mage sale vente *f* de charité.

ru·mor bruit *m*, rumeur *f.*

run 1 *n (period)* période *f*; *(for skiing)* piste *f*; **to go for a r.** (aller) faire une course à pied; **on the r.** *(prisoner)* en fuite; **in the long r.** à la longue. **2** *vi** courir; *(of river, nose,* *faucet)* couler; *(of color in laundry)* déteindre; *(of play, movie)* se jouer; *(function)* marcher; *(of car engine)* tourner; **to r. down/in/etc** descendre/entrer/etc en courant; **to go running** faire du jogging. **3** *vt (race, risk)* courir; *(temperature, errand)* faire; *(business, country etc)* diriger; *(bath)* faire couler.

▸ **run across** *vt (meet)* tomber sur.

▸ **run along** *vi* filer.

▸ **run away** *vi* s'enfuir (**from** de).

▸ **run down** *vt (pedestrian)* renverser.

rung *(of ladder)* barreau *m*.

▸ **run into** *vt (meet)* tomber sur; *(crash into)* percuter.

run·ner *(athlete)* coureur *m*.

run·ner-up second, -onde *mf*.

run·ning 1 *n (on foot)* course *f*. **2** *adj* **r. water** eau *f* courante; *(place, investment, method)* sûr; **six days/etc r.** six jours/etc de suite.

run·ny *adj (nose)* qui coule.

▸ **run off** *vi (flee)* s'enfuir.

▸ **run out** *vi (of inventory)* s'épuiser; *(of lease)* expirer; **to r. out of** *(time, money)* manquer de; **we've r. out of coffee** on n'a plus de café.

▸ **run over** *vt (kill)* écraser; *(knock down)* renverser.

run·way *f* (d'envol).

rush 1 *vi* se précipiter (**at** sur; **towards** vers); *(hurry)* se dépêcher (**to do** de faire). **2** *vt (hurry)* bousculer *(qn)*; **to r. sb to the hospital** transporter qn d'urgence à l'hôpital; **to r. (through) sth** *(job, meal etc)* faire/manger/etc qch en vitesse. **3** *n* ruée *f* (**for** vers); *(confusion)* bousculade *f*; *(hurry)* hâte *f*; **in a r.** pressé (**to do** de faire).

rush hour heure *f* de pointe.

▸ **rush out** *vi* partir en vitesse.

Russian 1 *adj* russe. **2** *n* Russe *mf*; *(language)* russe *m*.

rust 1 *n* rouille *f*. **2** *vi (se)* rouiller.

rust·y *adj (metal, memory etc)* rouillé.

RV *abbr (recreational vehicle)* camping-car *m*.

rye bread pain *m* de seigle.

S

sack 1 *n (bag)* sac *m*; **to get the s.** *(from one's job)* se faire virer; **to give sb the s.** virer qn. **2** *vt (dismiss)* virer.

sa·cred *adj* sacré.

sac·ri·fice 1 *n* sacrifice *m*. **2** *vt* sacrifier (**to** à; **for** pour).

sad *adj* triste.

sad·den *vt* attrister.

sad·dle selle *f*.

sad·ly *adv* tristement; *(unfortunately)* malheureusement.

sad·ness tristesse *f*.

safe¹ *adj (person)* en sécurité; *(equipment, toy, animal)* sans danger; *(place, investment, method)* sûr; *(bridge, ladder)* solide; **s. (and sound)** sain et sauf; **it's s. to go out** on peut sortir sans danger; **s. from** à l'abri de.

safe² *(for money etc)* coffre-fort *m*.

safe·guard 1 *n* sauvegarde *f*. **2** *vt* sauvegarder.

safe·ly *adv (without accident)* sans accident; *(without risk)* sans risque; *(in a safe place)* en lieu sûr.

safe·ty sécurité *f*.

safe·ty pin épingle *f* de sûreté.

sag *vi (of roof, ground)* s'affaisser.

said *pt & pp de* **say**.

sail 1 *vi* naviguer; *(leave)* partir; *(as sport)* faire de la voile; **to s. around the world/an island** faire le tour du monde/d'une île en bateau. **2** *vt (boat)* piloter. **3** *n* voile *f*.

sail·board planche *f* (à voile).

sail·boat voilier *m*.

sail·ing navigation *f*; *(sport)* voile *f*; *(departure)* départ *m*.

sail·or marin *m*.

saint saint *m*, sainte *f*.

sake for my/your/his/etc s. pour moi/ toi/lui/etc; **(just) for the s. of eating/**

etc simplement pour manger/*etc*.

sal·ad salade f.

sal·ad bowl saladier m.

sal·ad dress·ing sauce f pour salade.

sal·a·ry *(professional)* salaire m, traitement m; *(wage)* salaire m.

sale vente f; **sale(s)** *(at reduced prices)* soldes mpl; **on s.** *(cheaply)* en solde; *(available)* en vente; **(up) for s.** à vendre.

sales·clerk vendeur, -euse mf.

sales·man pl -men *(in store)* vendeur m; **(traveling) s.** représentant m (de commerce).

sales tax = TVA f.

sales·wom·an pl -women vendeuse f; *(who travels)* représentante f (de commerce).

sa·li·va salive f.

salm·on saumon m.

sa·lon salon m.

salt 1 n sel m; **bath salts** sels mpl de bain. **2** vt saler.

salt·cel·lar, salt·sha·ker salière f.

salt·y adj salé.

sal·va·tion salut m; **S. Army** Armée f du salut.

same 1 adj même; **the (very) s. house as** (exactement) la même maison que. **2** pron **the s.** le or la même, pl les mêmes; **it's all the s. to me** ça m'est égal; **all** or **just the s.** tout de même; **to do the s.** en faire autant.

sam·ple 1 n échantillon m; *(of blood)* prélèvement m. **2** vt *(wine etc)* goûter.

sand 1 n sable m. **2** vt *(road)* sabler.

san·dal sandale f.

sand·cas·tle château m de sable.

sand·pa·per papier m de verre.

sand·wich sandwich m; **cheese/** *etc* **s.** sandwich au fromage/*etc*; **s. shop** sandwicherie f.

sand·y adj *(beach)* de sable; *(road)* sablonneux.

san·i·tar·y nap·kin serviette f hygiénique.

San·ta Claus le père Noël.

sar·dine sardine f.

sat pt & pp de **sit**.

satch·el cartable m.

sat·el·lite satellite m.

sat·in satin m.

sat·is·fac·tion satisfaction f.

sat·is·fac·to·ry adj satisfaisant.

sat·is·fy vt satisfaire *(qn)*; **to s. oneself that** s'assurer que; **satisfied (with)** satisfait (de).

sat·is·fy·ing adj satisfaisant.

sat·su·ma *(fruit)* mandarine f, satsuma f.

sat·u·rate vt *(soak)* tremper; **saturated fats** graisses fpl saturées.

Sat·ur·day samedi m.

sauce sauce f; *(stewed fruit)* compote f; **tomato s.** sauce f tomate.

sauce·pan casserole f.

sau·cer soucoupe f.

sau·na sauna m.

sau·sage saucisse f; *(dried, for slicing)* saucisson m.

save 1 vt *(rescue)* sauver *(from de)*; *(keep)* garder; *(money, time)* économiser; *(stamps)* collectionner; **to s. sb from doing** empêcher qn de faire; **that will s. him the trouble of going** ça lui évitera d'y aller. **2** n Sports arrêt m.

► **save up 1** vt *(money)* économiser. **2** vi faire des économies **(for sth, to buy sth** pour acheter qch).

sav·ings npl *(money)* économies fpl.

sav·ings and loan = société f de crédit immobilier.

sav·ings bank caisse f d'épargne.

saw¹ 1 n scie f. **2** vt* scier.

saw² pt de **see**.

saw·dust sciure f.

► **saw off** vt scier.

sax·o·phone saxophone m.

say* vt dire **(to** à; **that** que); *(of dial etc)* marquer; **to s. again** répéter; **(let's) s. tomorrow** disons demain; **that is to s.** c'est-à-dire.

say·ing proverbe m.

scab *(of wound)* croûte *f.*

scaf·fold·ing échafaudage *m.*

scald *vt* ébouillanter.

scale *(of map, wages etc)* échelle *f*; *(on fish)* écaille *f*; *(in music)* gamme *f.*

scales *npl (for weighing)* balance *f*; **(bathroom) s.** pèse-personne *m.*

scal·lion oignon *m* vert.

scan 1 *vt (text, graphics)* passer au scanner; *(scrutinize)* scruter; *(glance at)* parcourir. **2** *n* échographie *f*; **to have a s.** passer une échographie.

scan·dal scandale *m*; *(gossip)* médisances *fpl.*

Scan·di·na·vi·an 1 *n* Scandinave *mf.* **2** *adj* scandinave.

scan·ner scanner *m.*

scar cicatrice *f.*

scarce *adj* rare.

scarce·ly *adv* à peine.

scare *vt* faire peur à.

scare·crow épouvantail *m.*

scared *adj* effrayé; **to be s. (stiff)** avoir (très) peur.

scarf, *pl* **scarves** *(long)* écharpe *f*; *(square, for women)* foulard *m.*

scar·let fe·ver scarlatine *f.*

scar·y *adj* **it's s.** ça fait peur.

scat·ter 1 *vt (crowd, clouds etc)* disperser; *(throw around)* éparpiller *(papiers etc).* **2** *vi (of crowd)* se disperser.

sce·nar·i·o scénario *m.*

scene *(setting, fuss, part of play or movie)* scène *f*; *(of crime, accident)* lieu *m*; *(view)* vue *f.*

scen·er·y paysage *m*; *(for play or movie)* décor(s) *m(pl).*

scent *(fragrance, perfume)* parfum *m.*

sched·ule 1 *n (of work etc)* programme *m*; *(timetable)* horaire *m*; **on s.** *(on time)* à l'heure; **according to s.** comme prévu. **2** *vt (to plan)* prévoir; *(event)* fixer le programme de.

sched·uled *adj (planned)* prévu; *(service, flight)* régulier.

scheme plan *m* (**to do** pour faire); *(dishonest trick)* combine *f.*

schmuck *Fam* andouille *f.*

schol·ar *(learned person)* érudit, -ite *mf.*

schol·ar·ship *(grant)* bourse *f* (d'études).

school 1 *n* école *f*; *(teaching, lessons)* classe *f*; **in** *or* **at s.** à l'école; **public s.** école *f* publique; **summer s.** cours *mpl* d'été. **2** *adj (year etc)* scolaire.

school·boy écolier *m.*

school·girl écolière *f.*

school·teach·er *(primary)* instituteur, -trice *mf*; *(secondary)* professeur *m.*

sci·ence science *f*; **to study s.** étudier les sciences.

sci·ence fic·tion science-fiction *f.*

sci·en·tif·ic *adj* scientifique.

sci·en·tist scientifique *mf*, savant *m.*

scis·sors *npl* ciseaux *mpl.*

scold *vt* gronder (**for doing** pour avoir fait).

scone petit pain *m* au lait.

scoot·er *(child's)* trottinette *f*; *(motorcycle)* scooter *m.*

scope *(range)* étendue *f*; *(limits)* limites *fpl*; **s. for sth/for doing** *(opportunity)* des possibilités *fpl* de qch/de faire.

scorch *vt* roussir.

score¹ **1** *n (in sports)* score *m*; *(at cards)* marque *f*; *(music)* partition *f.* **2** *vt (point, goal)* marquer. **3** *vi (point)* marquer un point; *(goal)* marquer un but; *(count points)* marquer les points.

score² **a s. (of)** une vingtaine (de).

scorn mépris *m.*

Scot Écossais, -aise *mf.*

Scotch *(whisky)* scotch *m.*

scotch (tape)® scotch® *m.*

Scots·man, *pl* **-men** Écossais *m.*

Scots·wom·an, pl -women Écossaise f.

Scot·tish adj écossais.

scoun·drel vaurien m.

scout (boy) s. scout m; girl s. éclaireuse f.

scram·ble 1 vi to s. up a hill gravir une colline en s'aidant des mains. **2** vt (message) brouiller; **scrambled eggs** œufs mpl brouillés. **3** n (rush) bousculade f.

scrap 1 n petit morceau m (of de); (of information) fragment m; (metal) ferraille f; **scraps** (food) restes mpl. **2** vt se débarrasser de; (vehicle) mettre à la ferraille; (plan) abandonner.

scrap·book album m (pour collages etc).

scrape 1 vt racler; (skin, knee etc) érafler. **2** vi to s. against sth frotter contre qch. **3** n (on skin) éraflure f.

▸ **scrape away, scrape off** vt (mud etc) racler.

▸ **scrape through** vi (in exam) réussir de justesse.

▸ **scrape together** vt (money, people) réunir (difficilement).

scrap met·al ferraille f.

scrap pa·per (papier m) brouillon m.

scratch 1 n (mark, injury) éraflure f; **to start from s.** (re)partir de zéro; **it isn't up to s.** ce n'est pas au niveau. **2** vt (arm etc that itches) gratter; (skin, furniture etc) érafler; (one's name) graver (**on** sur). **3** vi (relieve an itch) se gratter.

scratch·card carte f à gratter.

scratch pa·per (for draft) (papier m) brouillon m.

scream 1 vti crier; **to s. at sb** crier après qn. **2** n cri m (perçant).

screen écran m; (folding) s. paravent m.

screw 1 n vis f. **2** vt visser (**to** à).

screw an·chor cheville f.

▸ **screw down** vt visser.

screw·driv·er tournevis m.

▸ **screw on** vt visser.

scrib·ble vti griffonner.

script (of movie) scénario m; (of play) texte m.

scrub vt nettoyer (à la brosse); (pan) récurer.

scrub brush brosse f dure.

scu·ba div·ing plongée f sous-marine.

sculp·tor sculpteur m.

sculp·ture (art, object) sculpture f.

scum (on liquid) écume f; Fam (people) racaille f.

sea mer f; (out) **at s.** en mer; **by s.** par mer; **by** or **beside the sea** au bord de la mer.

sea·food fruits mpl de mer.

sea·front bord m or front m de mer.

sea·gull mouette f.

seal 1 n (animal) phoque m; (mark, design) sceau m; (of wax) cachet m (de cire). **2** vt (document, container) sceller; (envelope) cacheter; (with putty) boucher.

sea li·on otarie f.

▸ **seal off** vt (of police etc) interdire l'accès de.

seam (in cloth) couture f.

search 1 n recherche f (**for** de); (of person, place) fouille f; **in s. of** à la recherche de. **2** vt (person, place) fouiller (**for** pour trouver); **to s. (through) one's papers/etc for sth** chercher qch dans ses papiers/etc. **3** vi chercher; **to s. for sth** chercher qch.

sea·shell coquillage m.

sea·shore bord m de la mer.

sea·sick adj **to be s.** avoir le mal de mer.

sea·sick·ness mal m de mer.

sea·side bord m de la mer.

sea·son 1 n saison f. **2** vt (food) assaisonner.

sea·son·al adj saisonnier.

sea·son·ing assaisonnement m.

sea·son tick·et abonnement m.

seat 1 n siège m; (on train, bus) banquette f; (in theater) fauteuil m; (place) place f; **to take** or **have a s.** s'asseoir. **2** vt (at table) placer (qn); **the room seats 50** la salle a 50 places (assises); **be seated!** asseyez-vous!

seat belt ceinture f de sécurité.

seat·ed adj (sitting) assis.

seat·ing (seats) places fpl assises.

sea·weed algue(s) f(pl).

sec·ond¹ **1** adj deuxième, second; **every s. week** une semaine sur deux; **in s. (gear)** en seconde. **2** adv **to come s.** se classer deuxième. **3** n (person, object) deuxième mf, second, -onde mf.

sec·ond² (part of minute) seconde f.

sec·ond·ar·y adj secondaire.

sec·ond-class adj (ticket) de seconde (classe); (mail) non urgent.

sec·ond-hand adj & adv (not new) d'occasion.

sec·ond·ly adv deuxièmement.

se·cret adj & n secret (m); **in s.** en secret.

se·cre·tar·y secrétaire mf; (cabinet official) ministre m; **S. of State** Ministre des Affaires étrangères.

se·cret·ly adv en secret, secrètement.

sec·tion (of town, book etc) partie f; (of machine, furniture) élément m; (in store) rayon m; **the sports/etc s.** (of newspaper) la page des sports/etc.

sec·u·lar adj (music, art) profane; (education, school) laïque.

se·cure 1 adj (person, valuables) en sûreté; (place) sûr; (solid) solide; (door, window) bien fermé. **2** vt (fasten) attacher; (window etc) bien fermer.

se·cure·ly adv (firmly) solidement; (safely) en sûreté.

se·cu·ri·ty sécurité f, (for loan) caution f.

se·dan berline f.

se·da·tion **under s.** sous calmants.

sed·a·tive calmant m.

see* vti voir; **we'll s.** on verra (bien); **I saw him run(ning)** je l'ai vu courir; **s. you (later)!** à tout à l'heure!; **s. you (soon)!** à bientôt!; **to s. that** (take care that) veiller à ce que (+ subjunctive); (check) s'assurer que.

▸ **see about** vt s'occuper de; (consider) songer à.

seed graine f, (in grape) pépin m.

see·ing conj **s. (that)** vu que.

seek* vt chercher (to do à faire); (ask for) demander (from à).

seem vi sembler (to do faire); **it seems that** (impression) il semble que (+ subjunctive or indicative); (rumor) il paraît que (+ indicative); **it seems to me that** il me semble que (+ indicative).

seem·ing·ly adv apparemment.

▸ **see off** vt accompagner (qn).

▸ **see out** vt raccompagner (qn).

see·saw (jeu m de) bascule f.

▸ **see through** vt **to s. sth through** (carry out) mener qch à bien; **to s. through sb** voir dans le jeu de qn; **$20 should s. me through** 20 dollars devraient me suffire.

▸ **see to** vt (deal with) s'occuper de; (mend) réparer; **to see to it that** veiller à ce que (+ subjunctive); (check) s'assurer que.

seg·ment segment m; (of orange) quartier m.

seize vt saisir; (power, land) s'emparer de.

sel·dom adv rarement.

se·lect vt choisir (from parmi); (candidates, players etc) sélectionner.

se·lec·tion sélection f.

se·lec·tive adj sélectif.

self-as·sur·ance assurance f.

self-as·sured adj sûr de soi.

self-con·fi·dence assurance f.

self-con·fi·dent adj sûr de soi.

self-con·scious adj gêné.

self-con·trol maîtrise f de soi.

self·de·fense légitime défense f.

self·em·ployed adj qui travaille à son compte.

self·ev·i·dent adj évident.

self·ish adj égoïste.

self·re·spect amour-propre m.

self·righ·teous adj suffisant.

self·serv·ice n & adj libre-service (m inv).

sell* 1 vt vendre; **to have** or **be sold out of** sth n'avoir plus de qch. 2 vi (of product) se vendre.

sell·er vendeur, -euse mf.

se·mes·ter semestre m.

sem·i- prefix demi-, semi-.

sem·i·cir·cle demi-cercle m.

sem·i·co·lon point-virgule m.

sem·i·de·tached house maison f jumelle.

sem·i·fi·nal demi-finale f.

sem·i·nar séminaire m.

sem·i·trail·er semi-remorque m.

sem·o·li·na semoule f.

sen·a·tor sénateur m.

send* vt envoyer (to à); **to s. sb for** sth/sb envoyer qn chercher qch/qn.

▸**send away**, **send off** 1 vt envoyer (**to** à); (dismiss) renvoyer. 2 vi **to s. away** or **off for** sth commander qch (par courrier).

▸**send back** vt renvoyer.

send·er expéditeur, -trice mf.

▸**send for** vt (doctor etc) faire venir; (by mail) commander (par courrier).

▸**send in** vt (form etc) envoyer; (person) faire entrer.

▸**send on** vt (letter, luggage) faire suivre.

▸**send out** vt (invitation etc) envoyer; (from room etc) faire sortir (qn); **to s. out for** (meal) envoyer chercher.

▸**send up** vt (luggage) faire monter.

sen·ior 1 adj (older) plus âgé; (position, rank) supérieur. 2 n aîné, -ée mf; (in school) grand m, grande f,

étudiant, -ante mf de dernière année.

sen·ior high (school) = lycée m.

sen·sa·tion sensation f.

sen·sa·tion·al adj (terrific) Fam sensationnel.

sense 1 n (meaning) sens m; **s. of smell** odorat m; **a s. of** (shame etc) un sentiment de; **to have a s. of humor** avoir de l'humour; **to have (good) s.** avoir du bon sens; **to have the s. to do** avoir l'intelligence de faire; **to make s.** (of story) avoir un sens, tenir debout. 2 vt sentir (intuitivement) (**that** que).

sense·less adj (stupid) insensé.

sen·si·ble adj (wise) raisonnable.

sen·si·tive adj sensible (**to** à); (skin) délicat; (touchy) susceptible (**about** à propos de).

sen·tence 1 n Grammar phrase f; (punishment, prison) peine f. 2 vt **to s. sb to 3 years (in prison)** condamner qn à 3 ans de prison.

sen·ti·ment sentiment m.

sen·ti·men·tal adj sentimental.

sep·a·rate 1 adj (distinct) séparé; (independent) indépendant; (different) différent. 2 vt séparer (**from** de). 3 vi se séparer (**from** de).

sep·a·rate·ly adv séparément.

sep·a·ra·tion séparation f.

Sep·tem·ber septembre m.

se·quence (order) ordre m; (series) succession f.

se·quin paillette f.

ser·geant sergent m; (in police force) brigadier m.

se·ri·al (story, film) feuilleton m.

se·ries inv série f.

se·ri·ous adj sérieux; (illness, mistake) grave.

se·ri·ous·ly adv sérieusement; (ill) gravement; **to take s.** prendre au sérieux.

ser·vant (in house etc) domestique mf.

serve vt servir (**to sb** à qn; **sb with**

sth qch à qn); *(of train, bus etc)* desservir *(un village etc);* **(it) serves you right!** ça t'apprendra!

▸ **serve up** *vt (meal etc)* servir.

serv·ice 1 *n* service *m; (machine or vehicle repair)* révision *f;* **s. charge** *(in restaurant)* service *m.* **2** *vt (machine, vehicle)* réviser.

ser·vice ar·e·a *(on highway)* aire *f* de service.

ser·vice sta·tion station-service *f.*

ses·sion séance *f.*

set 1 *n (of keys, tools etc)* jeu *m; (of stamps, numbers)* série *f; (of people)* groupe *m; (in mathematics)* ensemble *m; (of books)* collection *f; (scenery)* décor *m; (hairstyle)* mise *f* en plis; *Tennis* set *m;* **chess s.** jeu *m* d'échecs. **2** *adj (time, price etc)* fixe; **the s. menu** le plat du jour; **s. on doing** résolu à faire; **to be s. on sth** vouloir qch à tout prix; **all s.** *(ready)* prêt **(to do** pour faire). **3** *vt* (put)* mettre; *(date, limit etc)* fixer; *(record)* établir; *(mechanism, clock)* régler; *(alarm clock)* mettre **(for** pour); *(arm etc in plaster)* plâtrer; *(task)* donner **(for sb** à qn); *(trap)* tendre; **to have one's hair s.** se faire faire une mise en plis. **4** *vi (of sun)* se coucher; *(of jelly)* prendre.

▸ **set about** *vt* **to s. about sth/ about doing** *(begin)* se mettre à qch/à faire.

set·back revers *m.*

▸ **set back** *vt (clock)* retarder.

▸ **set down** *vt (object)* déposer.

▸ **set forward** *vt (clock)* avancer.

▸ **set off 1** *vt (bomb)* faire exploser; *(mechanism)* déclencher. **2** *vi (leave)* partir.

▸ **set out 1** *vt (display, explain)* exposer **(to** à); *(arrange)* disposer. **2** *vi (leave)* partir; **to s. out to do** entreprendre de faire.

set·tee canapé *m.*

set·ting *(surroundings)* cadre *m.*

set·tle **1** *vt (decide, arrange, pay)* régler; *(date)* fixer; **that's (all) settled** c'est décidé. **2** *vi (live)* s'installer.

▸ **settle down** *vi (in chair or house)* s'installer; *(calm down)* se calmer; *(in one's lifestyle)* se ranger.

set·tle·ment *(agreement)* accord *m.*

set·tler colon *m.*

▸ **settle (up) with** *vt (pay)* régler.

▸ **set up 1** *vt (tent)* dresser; *(business)* créer. **2** *vi* **to s. up shop** monter une affaire.

sev·en *adj & n* sept *(m).*

sev·en·teen *adj & n* dix-sept *(m).*

sev·enth *adj & n* septième *(mf).*

sev·en·ti·eth *adj & n* soixante-dixième *(mf).*

sev·en·ty *adj & n* soixante-dix *(m);* **s.-one** soixante et onze.

sev·er·al *adj & pron* plusieurs **(of** d'entre).

se·vere *adj (tone etc)* sévère; *(winter)* rigoureux; *(test)* dur.

sew* *vti* coudre.

sew·er égout *m.*

sew·ing couture *f.*

sew·ing ma·chine machine *f* à coudre.

▸ **sew on** *vt (button)* (re)coudre.

▸ **sew up** *vt (tear)* (re)coudre.

sex 1 *n* sexe *m; (activity)* relations *fpl* sexuelles; **to have s. with sb** coucher avec qn. **2** *adj (education, life etc)* sexuel.

sex·u·al *adj* sexuel.

sex·y *adj* sexy *inv.*

sh! *int* chut!

shab·by *adj (room etc)* minable.

shade ombre *f; (of colour)* ton *m; (of lamp)* abat-jour *m inv; (window)* store *m;* **in the s.** à l'ombre.

shad·ow ombre *f.*

shad·y *adj (place)* ombragé.

shaft *(of tool)* manche *m; (in mine)* puits *m; (of elevator)* cage *f; (of light)* rayon *m.*

shake 1 vt secouer; (bottle) agiter; (upset) bouleverser; **to s. one's head** (say no) secouer la tête; **to s. hands with sb** serrer la main à qn; **we shook hands** nous nous sommes serré la main. **2** vi trembler (with de).

shall v aux (future) **I s. come, I'll come** je viendrai; **we s. not come, we shan't come** nous ne viendrons pas. ▪ (question) **s. I leave?** veux-tu que je parte?; **s. we leave?** on part?

shal·low adj (water, river etc) peu profond.

shame (feeling, disgrace) honte f; **it's a s.** c'est dommage (**to do** de faire); **it's a s. (that)** c'est dommage que (+ subjunctive); **what a s.!** (quel) dommage!

shame·ful adj honteux.

sham·poo 1 n shampooing m. **2** vt **to s. sb's hair** faire un shampooing à qn.

shan't = shall not.

shape forme f; **in (good) s.** (fit) en (pleine) forme; **to stay in s.** se maintenir en forme; **to be in good/bad s.** (of vehicle etc) être en bon/mauvais état; (of business) marcher bien/mal; **to take s.** (of plan, book etc) prendre forme; (progress well) avancer.

-shaped suffix **pear-s./etc** en forme de poire/etc.

share 1 n part f (**of, in** de); (of stock) action f. **2** vt (meal, opinion etc) partager (**with** avec); (characteristic) avoir en commun.

share·hold·er actionnaire mf.

▸ **share in** vt avoir sa part de.

▸ **share out** vt partager, répartir (**among** entre).

shark requin m.

sharp 1 adj (knife etc) tranchant; (pointed) pointu; (point, pain) aigu (f -uë); (bend) brusque. **2** adv **five o'clock/etc s.** cinq heures/etc pile.

sharp·en vt (knife) aiguiser; (pencil) tailler.

sharp·ly adv (suddenly) brusquement.

shat·ter 1 vt (door, arm etc) fracasser; (glass) faire voler en éclats. **2** vi fracasser; (of glass) voler en éclats.

shave 1 vt (person, head) raser; **to s. off one's beard** se raser la barbe. **2** vi se raser. **3** n **to have a s.** se raser.

shav·er rasoir m électrique.

shav·ing cream crème f à raser.

shav·ing kit trousse f de toilette (d'homme).

shawl châle m.

she pron elle; **she's a happy woman** c'est une femme heureuse.

shed¹ (in garden) abri m (de jardin); (for goods or machines) hangar m.

shed² vt (lose) perdre; (tears) répandre.

sheep inv mouton m.

sheep·skin peau f de mouton.

sheer adj (utter) pur; (cliff) à pic; (stockings, fabric) extra fin.

sheet (on bed) drap m; (of paper) feuille f; (of glass, ice) plaque f.

shelf, pl **shelves** étagère f, (in shop) rayon m.

shell 1 n (of egg etc) coquille f, (of tortoise) carapace f, (seashell) coquillage m; (explosive) obus m. **2** vt (peas) écosser.

shell·fish (oysters etc) fruits mpl de mer.

shel·ter 1 n abri m; **to take s.** se mettre à l'abri (**from** de). **2** vt abriter (**from** de). **3** vi s'abriter.

shelv·ing rayonnage(s) m(pl).

shep·herd berger m.

sher·iff shérif m.

sher·ry sherry m.

shield 1 n bouclier m; (screen) écran m. **2** vt protéger (**from** de).

shift 1 n (change) changement m (**of, in** de); (period of work) poste m; (workers) équipe f; **gear s.** levier m de vitesse. **2** vt (move) bouger; **to s. gear(s)** changer de vitesse. **3** vi bouger.

shin tibia *m*.

shine 1 *vi** briller. **2** *vt (polish)* faire briller; **to s. a light on sth** éclairer qch. **3** *n (on shoes, cloth)* brillant *m*.

shin·y *adj* brillant.

ship navire *m*, bateau *m*; **by s.** en bateau.

ship·ping *(traffic)* navigation *f*.

ship·wreck naufrage *m*.

ship·wrecked *adj* naufragé; **to be s.** faire naufrage.

ship·yard chantier *m* naval.

shirt chemise *f*, *(of woman)* chemisier *m*; *(of sportsman)* maillot *m*.

shiv·er 1 *vi* frissonner (**with** de). **2** *n* frisson *m*.

shock 1 *n (emotional, physical)* choc *m*; **(electric) s.** décharge *f* (électrique); **suffering from s., in s.** en état de choc. **2** *vt (offend)* choquer; *(surprise)* stupéfier.

shock ab·sorb·er amortisseur *m*.

shock·ing *adj* affreux; *(outrageous)* scandaleux.

shoe chaussure *f*, soulier *m*.

shoe·lace lacet *m*.

shoe pol·ish cirage *m*.

shoe re·pair shop cordonnerie *f*.

shoe store magasin *m* de chaussures.

shoot* 1 *vt (kill)* tuer (d'un coup de feu); *(wound)* blesser (d'un coup de feu); *(execute)* fusiller; *(gun)* tirer un coup de; *(film)* tourner. **2** *vi (with gun)* tirer (**at** sur).

▶**shoot ahead** *vi (rush)* avancer à toute vitesse.

shoot·ing *(shots)* coups *mpl* de feu; *(murder)* meurtre *m*.

▶**shoot off** *vi (rush)* partir à toute vitesse.

▶**shoot up** *vi (of price)* monter en flèche.

shop 1 *n* magasin *m*; *(small)* boutique *f*; **at the flower s.** chez le fleuriste. **2** *vi* faire ses courses (**at** chez).

shop·keep·er commerçant, -ante *mf*.

shop·ping to go s. faire des courses.

shop·ping bag sac *m* à provisions.

shop·ping dis·trict quartier *m* commerçant.

shop·ping mall centre *m* commercial.

shore *(of sea, lake)* rivage *m*; *(coast)* côte *f*.

short 1 *adj* court; *(person, distance)* petit; **a s. time** *or* **while (ago)** (il y a) peu de temps; **to be s. of money/time** être à court d'argent/de temps; **we're s. ten men** il nous manque dix hommes; **to be s. for sth** *(of name)* être l'abréviation de qch. **2** *adv* **to cut s.** *(hair)* couper court; *(visit etc)* raccourcir; *(person)* couper la parole à; **to get** *or* **run s.** manquer (**of** de).

short·age manque *m*.

short·cut raccourci *m*.

short·en *vt (dress, text etc)* raccourcir.

short·ly *adv (soon)* bientôt; **s. after** peu après.

shorts *npl* **(a pair of) s.** un short.

short·sight·ed *adj* myope.

short-term *adj* à court terme.

shot *(from gun)* coup *m*; *(with camera)* prise *f* de vues.

shot·gun fusil *m* (de chasse).

should *v aux (ought to)* **you s. do it** vous devriez le faire; **I s. have stayed** j'aurais dû rester; **that s. be Paul** ça doit être Paul. ▪ *(would)* **it's strange she s. say no** il est étrange qu'elle dise non. ▪ *(possibility)* **if he s. come** s'il vient.

shoul·der épaule *f*, **(hard) s.** *(of highway)* bas-côté *m*.

shoul·der bag sac *m* à bandoulière.

shout 1 *n* cri *m*. **2** *vti* crier; **to s. to sb to do** crier à qn de faire.

▶**shout at** *vt (scold)* crier après.

shout·ing *(shouts)* cris *mpl*.
▸ **shout out** *vti* crier.
shove 1 *n* poussée *f*; **to give a s.
(to)** pousser. **2** *vt* pousser; *(put)
Fam* fourrer. **3** *vi* pousser.
shov·el 1 *n* pelle *f*. **2** *vt* *(snow etc)*
enlever à la pelle.
show 1 *n* *(in theater)* spectacle *m*;
(at movies) séance *f*; **the Auto S.** le
Salon de l'Automobile; **on s.** *(painting etc)* exposé. **2** *vt** montrer *(to à;
that* que); *(in exhibition)* exposer;
(movie) passer; *(indicate)* indiquer;
to s. sb to the door reconduire qn.
3 *vi* *(be visible)* se voir; *(of movie)*
passer.
▸ **show around** *vt* faire visiter; **to s.
sb around the house** faire visiter la
maison à qn.
show·er *(bath)* douche *f*; *(of rain)*
averse *f*.
▸ **show in** *vt* *(visitor)* faire entrer.
show·ing *(of movie)* séance *f*.
show·off crâneur, -euse *mf*.
▸ **show off** *vi* crâner.
▸ **show out** *vt* *(visitor)* reconduire.
▸ **show up 1** *vi* *(of person)* arriver. **2**
vt *(embarrass)* mettre *(qn)* dans
l'embarras.
shrimp crevette *f* (grise).
shrink* *vi* *(of clothes)* rétrécir.
shrub arbuste *m*.
shrug *vt* **to s. one's shoulders**
hausser les épaules.
shud·der *vi* frémir (**with** de).
shuf·fle *(cards)* battre.
shush! *int* chut!
shut* 1 *vt* fermer. **2** *vi* *(of door
etc)* se fermer, *(of shop etc)*
fermer.
▸ **shut down** *vti* fermer.
▸ **shut in** *vt* enfermer.
▸ **shut off** *vt* *(gas etc)* fermer; *(engine)* arrêter; *(isolate)* isoler.
▸ **shut out** *vt* *(light)* empêcher d'entrer; **to s. sb out** *(accidentally)* enfermer qn dehors.
shut·ter *(on window)* volet *m*; *(of
store)* rideau *m* (métallique).

shut·tle **s.** *(service)* navette *f*;
space s. navette spatiale.
▸ **shut up 1** *vt* *(house etc)* fermer;
(lock up) enfermer *(personne, objet
précieux)*. **2** *vi* *(be quiet)* se taire.
shy *adj* timide.
shy·ness timidité *f*.
sick 1 *adj* malade; **to be s.** *(vomit)*
vomir; **off s.** en congé de maladie;
to feel s. avoir mal au cœur; **to be
s. (and tired) of** sth/sb *Fam* en
avoir marre de qch/qn. **2** *npl* **the s.**
les malades *mpl*.
sick·ness maladie *f*.
side côté *m*; *(of hill, animal)* flanc
m; *(of road, river)* bord *m*; *(team)*
équipe *f*; **at** or **by the s. of** à côté
de; **at** or **by my s.** à côté de moi, à
mes côtés; **s. by s.** l'un à côté de l'autre; **to move to one s.** s'écarter; **to
take sides with sb** se ranger du côté de qn; **on our s.**
de notre côté.
side·board buffet *m*.
side·burns *npl* pattes *fpl*.
side·walk trottoir *m*.
side·ways *adv & adj* de côté.
sid·ing *(for train)* voie *f* d'évite-
ment; *(of wall)* parement *m* (extérieur).
siege siège *m*; **under s.** assiégé.
sieve tamis *m*; *(for liquids)* passoire
f.
sift *vt* *(flour etc)* tamiser.
sigh 1 *n* soupir *m*. **2** *vi* soupirer.
sight vue *f*; *(thing seen)* spectacle
m; **to lose s. of** perdre de vue; **to
catch s. of** apercevoir; **by s.** de
vue; **in s.** *(target etc)* en vue; **out of
s.** caché; **the (tourist) sights** les at-
tractions *fpl* touristiques.
sight·see·ing **to go s.** faire du
tourisme.
sign 1 *n* signe *m*; *(notice)* panneau
m; *(over shop, inn)* enseigne *f*; **no
s. of** aucune trace de. **2** *vti* *(with
signature)* signer.
sig·nal 1 *n* signal *m*; *(of vehicle)* cli-

gnotant *m*; **traffic signals** feux *mpl* de signalisation. **2** *vi* faire signe (**to** à); **to s. (left/right)** (*in car*) mettre son clignotant (à gauche/à droite).

sig·na·ture signature *f*.

sig·nif·i·cant *adj* (*important, large*) important.

sig·nif·i·cant·ly *adv* sensiblement.

sig·ni·fy *vt* signifier.

▸**sign in** *vi* (*in hotel etc*) signer le registre.

▸**sign on, sign up** *vi* (*of soldier, worker*) s'engager; (*for course*) s'inscrire (**for** à).

sign·post poteau *m* indicateur.

si·lence 1 *n* silence *m*; **in s.** en silence. **2** *vt* faire taire.

si·lent *adj* silencieux; (*movie*) muet (*f* muette); **to keep s.** garder le silence (**about** sur).

si·lent·ly *adv* silencieusement.

silk soie *f*.

sill (*of window*) rebord *m*.

sil·ly *adj* bête; **to do something s.** faire une bêtise.

sil·ver 1 *n* argent *m*; (*plates etc*) argenterie *f*. **2** *adj* (*spoon etc*) en argent; **s. paper** papier *m* d'argent.

sil·ver·plat·ed *adj* plaqué argent.

sil·ver·ware *inv* argenterie *f*.

sim·i·lar *adj* semblable (**to** à).

sim·i·lar·i·ty ressemblance *f* (**to** avec).

sim·ple *adj* simple.

sim·pli·fy *vt* simplifier.

sim·ply *adv* (*plainly, merely*) simplement; (*absolutely*) absolument.

si·mul·ta·ne·ous *adj* simultané.

si·mul·ta·ne·ous·ly *adv* simultanément.

sin péché *m*.

since 1 *prep* depuis. **2** *conj* depuis que; (*because*) puisque; **s. she's been here** depuis qu'elle est ici; **it's a year s. I saw him** ça fait un an que je ne l'ai pas vu. **3** *adv* (*ever*) **s.** depuis.

sin·cere *adj* sincère.

sin·cere·ly *adv* sincèrement; **yours s.** (*in letter*) veuillez croire à mes sentiments dévoués.

sin·cer·i·ty sincérité *f*.

sing* *vti* chanter.

sing·er chanteur, -euse *mf*.

sin·gle *adj* seul; (*room, bed*) pour une personne; (*unmarried*) célibataire; **not a s. book/etc** pas un seul livre/*etc*; **every s. day** tous les jours sans exception.

Sin·gle Mar·ket Marché *m* unique.

sin·gle·mind·ed *adj* résolu.

▸**single out** *vt* choisir.

sin·gu·lar 1 *adj* (*form*) singulier; (*noun*) au singulier. **2** *n* singulier *m*; **in the s.** au singulier.

sin·is·ter *adj* sinistre.

sink¹ (*in kitchen*) évier *m*; (*washbasin*) lavabo *m*.

sink*² *vi* (*of ship, person etc*) couler.

▸**sink (down) into** *vt* (*mud*) s'enfoncer dans; (*armchair*) s'affaler dans.

sip *vi* boire à petites gorgées.

sir monsieur *m*; **S.** (*title*) sir.

si·ren (*of factory etc*) sirène *f*.

sis·ter sœur *f*.

sit* 1 *vi* s'asseoir; **to be sitting** être assis; **she was sitting reading** elle était assise à lire. **2** *vt* (*child on chair etc*) asseoir.

sit (for) *vt* (*exam*) se présenter à.

▸**sit around** *vi* traîner; (*do nothing*) ne rien faire.

▸**sit down 1** *vi* s'asseoir; **to be sitting down** être assis. **2** *vt* asseoir (*qn*).

site (*position*) emplacement *m*; (*building*) **s.** chantier *m*.

sit·ting room salon *m*.

sit·u·ate *vt* situer; **to be situated** être situé, se situer.

sit·u·a·tion situation *f*.

▸**sit up (straight)** *vi* s'asseoir (bien droit).

six *adj & n* six (m).

six·teen *adj & n* seize (m).

sixth *adj & n* sixième (mf).

six·ti·eth *adj & n* soixantième (mf).

six·ty *adj & n* soixante (m).

size *(of person, clothes, packet etc)* taille f; *(measurements)* dimensions fpl; *(of town, sum)* importance f; *(of shoes, gloves)* pointure f; *(of shirt)* encolure f; **hip/chest s.** tour m de hanches/de poitrine.

skate 1 *n* patin m. 2 *vi* patiner.

skate·board planche f (à roulettes).

skat·er patineur, -euse mf.

skat·ing patinage m; **to go s.** faire du patinage.

skat·ing rink *(ice-skating)* patinoire f.

skel·e·ton squelette m.

sketch 1 *n (drawing)* croquis m; *(comic play)* sketch m. 2 *vi* faire un *or* des croquis.

skew·er *(for meat etc)* broche f; *(for kebab)* brochette f.

ski 1 *n* ski m. 2 *vi* faire du ski.

skid 1 *vi* déraper; **to s. into sth** déraper et heurter qch. 2 *n* dérapage m.

ski·er skieur, -euse mf.

ski·ing 1 *n* ski m. 2 *adj (school, clothes, etc)* de ski.

ski lift remonte-pente m.

skill habileté f (**at** à); *(technique)* technique f.

skilled *adj* habile.

skilled work·er ouvrier, -ière mf qualifié(e).

skill·ful *adj* habile (**at doing** à faire; **at sth** à qch).

skim milk lait m écrémé.

skin peau f.

skin div·ing plongée f sous-marine.

skin·ny *adj* maigre.

skip 1 *vi (hop)* sautiller; *(with rope)* sauter à la corde. 2 *vt (miss)* sauter *(repas, classe etc)*.

skirt jupe f.

skull crâne m.

sky ciel m.

sky·scrap·er gratte-ciel m inv.

slack *adj (rope)* lâche; **to be s.** *(of rope)* avoir du mou; *(in office etc)* être calme.

slack·en *vt (rope)* relâcher.

slacks *npl* pantalon m.

slam 1 *vt (door, lid)* claquer. 2 *vi (of door)* claquer. 3 *n* claquement m.

slang argot m.

slant 1 *n* inclinaison f. 2 *vi (of roof)* être en pente.

slap 1 *n* tape f; *(on face)* gifle f. 2 *vt (person)* donner une tape à; **to s. sb's face** gifler qn; **to s. sb's bottom** donner une fessée à qn.

slate ardoise f.

slaugh·ter 1 *vt* massacrer; *(animal)* abattre. 2 *n* massacre m; *(of animal)* abattage m.

slave esclave mf.

▸ **slave away** *vi* se crever (au travail).

slav·er·y esclavage m.

sled luge f; *(horse-drawn)* traîneau m.

sleep 1 *n* sommeil m; **to get some s.** dormir. 2 *vi* dormir; *(spend the night)* coucher; **to go** *or* **get to s.** s'endormir.

sleep·er *(bed in train)* couchette f; *(train)* train m couchettes.

sleep·ing *adj (asleep)* endormi.

sleep·ing bag sac m de couchage.

sleep·ing car wagon-lit m.

sleep·ing pill somnifère m.

sleep·y *adj* **to be s.** *(of person)* avoir sommeil.

sleet 1 *n* neige f fondue. 2 *vi* **it's sleeting** il tombe de la neige fondue.

sleeve *(of shirt etc)* manche f; *(of record)* pochette f; **long-/short-sleeved** à manches longues/courtes.

sleigh traîneau m.

slen·der *adj (person)* svelte;

(wrist, neck etc) fin; *(hope, chance)* maigre, faible.

slept *pt & pp de* **sleep**.

slice tranche *f.*

slice (up) *vt* couper (en tranches).

slide 1 *n (in playground)* toboggan *m; (film)* diapositive *f.* **2** *vi** glisser. **3** *vt (letter etc)* glisser *(into* dans); *(table, chair etc)* faire glisser.

slid·ing door porte *f* à glissière or coulissante.

slight *adj (noise, mistake etc)* léger, petit; *(chance)* faible; **the slightest thing** la moindre chose; **not in the slightest** pas le moins du monde.

slight·ly *adv* légèrement.

slim 1 *adj* mince. **2** *vi* maigrir.

sling *(for arm)* écharpe *f,* **in a s.** en écharpe.

slip 1 *n (mistake)* erreur *f, (woman's undergarment)* combinaison *f,* **a s. of paper** un bout de papier. **2** *vi* glisser. **3** *vt (slide)* glisser *(qch)* (*to* à; *into* dans).

▸**slip away** *vi* s'esquiver.

slip·cov·er *(on furniture)* housse *f.*

▸**slip in** *vi* entrer furtivement.

▸**slip into** *vt (room etc)* se glisser dans; *(bathrobe etc)* mettre, passer.

▸**slip off** *vt (garment)* enlever.

▸**slip on** *vt (garment)* mettre.

▸**slip out** *vi* sortir furtivement; *(for a moment)* sortir (un instant).

slip·per pantoufle *f.*

slip·per·y *adj* glissant.

▸**slip up** *vi (make a mistake)* gaffer.

slit *(opening)* fente *f, (cut)* coupure *f.*

slo·gan slogan *m.*

slope 1 *n* pente *f, (of mountain)* versant *m; (of skiing)* piste *f.* **2** *vi (of ground, roof etc)* être en pente.

slop·ing *adj* en pente.

slot *(slit)* fente *f, (groove)* rainure *f.*

slot ma·chine distributeur *m* automatique; *(for gambling)* machine *f* à sous.

slow 1 *adj* lent; **to be s.** *(of clock,*

watch) retarder; **to be five minutes s.** retarder de cinq minutes; **in s. motion** au ralenti. **2** *adv* lentement.

▸**slow down, slow up** *vti* ralentir.

slow·ly *adv* lentement; *(bit by bit)* peu à peu.

slow·poke *Fam* tortue *f.*

slug limace *f.*

slum *(house)* taudis *m;* **the slums** les quartiers *mpl* pauvres.

slump 1 *n (in sales, prices etc)* baisse *f* soudaine; *(economic depression)* crise *f.* **2** *vi (sales, prices, person)* s'effondrer; *(morale)* baisser soudainement.

sly *adj (cunning)* rusé.

smack 1 *n* claque *f,* gifle *f, (on bottom)* fessée *f.* **2** *vt (person)* donner une claque à; **to s. sb's face** gifler qn; **to s. sb's bottom** donner une fessée à qn.

small 1 *adj* petit. **2** *adv (to cut, chop)* menu.

small·pox petite vérole *f.*

smart *adj (fashionable, elegant)* élégant; *(clever)* intelligent.

smash 1 *vt (break)* briser; *(shatter)* fracasser. **2** *vi* se briser.

smash·ing *adj Fam* formidable.

▸**smash into** *vt (of vehicle)* (r)entrer dans.

smash-up collision *f.*

smell 1 *n* odeur *f,* (sense of) s. odorat *m.* **2** *vt** sentir. **3** *vi (stink)* sentir (mauvais); *(have a smell)* avoir une odeur; **to s. of smoke/etc** sentir la fumée/etc.

smell·y *adj* qui sent mauvais, qui pue; **to be s.** sentir mauvais, puer.

smile 1 *n* sourire *m.* **2** *vi* sourire (**at sb** à qn).

smock blouse *f.*

smoke 1 *n* fumée *f;* **to have a s.** fumer une cigarette/etc. **2** *vti* fumer; **'no smoking'** 'défense de fumer'; **smoking compartment** compartiment *m* fumeurs.

smok·er fumeur, -euse *mf, (train*

compartment) compartiment *m* fumeurs.

smooth *adj (surface, skin etc)* lisse; *(flight)* agréable.

▶**smooth down, smooth out** *vt (dress, hair etc)* lisser.

smug‧gle *vt* passer (en fraude).

smug‧gler contrebandier, -ière *mf.*

smug‧gling contrebande *f.*

snack *(meal)* casse-croûte *m inv;* **snacks** *(things to eat)* petites choses *fpl* à grignoter; *(candies)* friandises *fpl;* **to eat a s. or snacks** grignoter.

snack bar snack(-bar) *m.*

snail escargot *m.*

snake serpent *m.*

snap 1 *vt (break)* casser (avec un bruit sec). **2** *vi* se casser net. **3** *n (fastener)* bouton-pression *m.*

snap(‧shot) photo *f.*

snatch *vt* saisir *(d'un geste vif);* **to s. sth from sb** arracher qch à qn.

sneak‧er basket *m.*

sneer *vi* ricaner.

sneeze 1 *vi* éternuer. **2** *n* éternuement *m.*

sniff *vti* **to s. (at)** renifler.

snip (off) *vt* couper.

snook‧er snooker *m (sorte de jeu de billard).*

snore *vi* ronfler.

snor‧ing ronflements *mpl.*

snout museau *m.*

snow 1 *n* neige *f.* **2** *vi* neiger; **it's snowing** il neige.

snow‧ball boule *f* de neige.

snow‧drift congère *f.*

snow‧flake flocon *m* de neige.

snow‧man bonhomme *m* de neige.

snow‧plow chasse-neige *m inv.*

snow‧storm tempête *f* de neige.

so 1 *adv (to such a degree)* si, tellement *(that* que); *(thus)* ainsi; **so that** *(purpose)* pour que *(+ subjunctive); (result)* si bien que *(+ indicative);* **so as to do** pour faire; **I**

think so je le pense; **if so** si oui; **is that so?** c'est vrai?; **so am I, so do I/etc** moi aussi; **so much** *(to work etc)* tant *(that* que); **so much courage/etc** tant de courage/etc; **so many** tant; **so many books/etc** tant de livres/etc; **ten or so** environ dix; **and so on** et ainsi de suite. **2** *conj (therefore)* donc; **so what?** et alors?

soak 1 *vt (drench)* tremper *(qn); (laundry, food)* faire tremper. **2** *vi (of laundry etc)* tremper.

soaked (through) *adj (person)* trempé jusqu'aux os.

soak‧ing *adj & adv* **s. (wet)** trempé.

▶**soak up** *vt* absorber.

soap savon *m.*

soap pow‧der lessive *f.*

soap‧y *adj* savonneux.

sob 1 *n* sanglot *m.* **2** *vi* sangloter.

so‧ber *adj* **he's s.** *(not drunk)* il n'est pas ivre.

soc‧cer football *m.*

so‧cial *adj* social; **s. club** club *m;* **s. evening** soirée *f;* **to have a good s. life** sortir beaucoup; **s. security** *(pension)* pension *f* de retraite; **s. services, S. Security** = Sécurité *f* sociale; **s. worker** assistant, -ante *mf* social(e).

so‧cial‧ist *adj & n* socialiste *(mf).*

so‧ci‧e‧ty société *f.*

sock chaussette *f.*

sock‧et *(for electric plug)* prise *f* de courant.

so‧da (pop) soda *m.*

so‧da (wa‧ter) eau *f* gazeuse.

so‧fa canapé *m;* **s. bed** canapé-lit *m.*

soft *adj (gentle, not stiff)* doux *(f* douce); *(butter, ground)* mou *(f* molle); **s. drink** boisson *f* non alcoolisée.

soft‧ball = sorte de base-ball.

soft‧en **1** *vt (object)* ramollir; *(skin)* adoucir. **2** *vi (object)* ramollir; *(skin)* s'adoucir.

soft‧ly *adv* doucement.

soft·ware *inv* logiciel *m*.

soil sol *m*, terre *f*.

so·lar *adj* solaire.

sol·dier soldat *m*.

sole *(of shoe)* semelle *f*; *(of foot)* plante *f*; *(fish)* sole *f*; **lemon s.** limande *f*.

sol·emn *adj (formal)* solennel; *(serious)* grave.

sol·id 1 *adj (car, meal etc)* solide; *(wall, line)* plein; *(gold)* massif; **s. line** ligne *f* continue. **2** *n* solide *m*.

sol·i·dar·i·ty solidarité *f*.

so·lo *adj & n* solo *(m)*.

so·lu·tion solution *f* (to de).

solve *vt (problem)* résoudre.

sol·vent 1 *n* solvant *m*. **2** *adj (financially)* solvable.

some 1 *adj (amount, number)* du, de la, des; **s. wine** du vin; **s. water** de l'eau; **s. dogs** des chiens; **s. pretty flowers** de jolies fleurs. ▪ *(unspecified)* un, une; **s. man** *(or other)* un homme (quelconque). ▪ *(a few)* quelques; *(a little)* un peu de. **2** *pron (number)* quelques-un(e)s en; *(a certain quantity)* en; **I want s.** j'en veux.

some·bod·y *pron* = **someone**.

some·day *adv* un jour.

some·how *adv* d'une manière ou d'une autre; *(for some reason)* on ne sait pourquoi.

some·one *pron* quelqu'un; **s. small**/*etc* quelqu'un de petit/*etc*.

some·place *adv* quelque part.

som·er·sault culbute *f*.

some·thing *pron* quelque chose; **s.** **awful**/*etc* quelque chose d'affreux/*etc*; **s. of a liar**/*etc* un peu menteur/*etc*.

some·time *adv* un jour.

some·times *adv* quelquefois.

some·what *adv* quelque peu.

some·where *adv* quelque part.

son fils *m*.

song chanson *f*.

son-in-law, *pl* sons-in-law gendre *m*.

soon *adv* bientôt; *(quickly)* vite; *(early)* tôt; **s. after** peu après; **as s. as she leaves** aussitôt qu'elle partira; **no sooner had he spoken than** à peine avait-il parlé que; **I'd sooner leave** je préférerais partir; **I'd just as s. leave** j'aimerais autant partir; **sooner or later** tôt ou tard.

soot suie *f*.

soothe *vt (pain, nerves)* calmer.

sore 1 *adj (painful)* douloureux; *(angry) Fam* fâché (**at** contre); **she has a s. throat** elle a mal à la gorge. **2** *n* plaie *f*.

sor·row chagrin *m*.

sor·ry *adj* **to be s.** *(regret)* être désolé (**to do de faire**); **I'm s. she can't come** je regrette qu'elle ne puisse pas venir; **I'm s. about the delay** je m'excuse pour ce retard; **s.!** pardon!; **to feel** *or* **be s. for sb** plaindre qn.

sort¹ sorte *f*, espèce *f* (**of** de); **all sorts of** toutes sortes de; **what s. of drink**/*etc* **is it?** qu'est-ce que c'est comme boisson/*etc*?

sort² *vt (papers etc)* trier.

▶ **sort out** *vt (classify, select)* trier; *(separate)* séparer (**from** de); *(tidy)* ranger; *(problem)* régler.

soul âme *f*.

sound¹ 1 *n* son *m*; *(noise)* bruit *m*; **I don't like the s. of it** ça ne me plaît pas du tout. **2** *vt (bell, alarm etc)* sonner; **to s. one's horn** klaxonner. **3** *vi (of bell etc)* sonner; *(seem)* sembler; **to s. like** sembler être; *(resemble)* ressembler à.

sound² 1 *adj (healthy)* sain; *(good, reliable)* solide. **2** *adv* **s. asleep** profondément endormi.

sound·proof *vt* insonoriser.

soup soupe *f*, potage *m*.

sour *adj* aigre.

source source *f*.

south 1 *n* sud *m*; **(to the) s. of** au sud de. **2** *adj (coast)* sud *inv.* **3** *adv* au sud.

south·bound *adj* en direction du sud.

south·east n & adj sud-est (m & adj inv).

south·ern adj (town) du sud; (coast) sud inv.

south·ern·er habitant, -ante mf du sud.

south·ward(s) adj & adv vers le sud.

south·west n & adj sud-ouest (m & adj inv).

sou·ve·nir (object) souvenir m.

sow* vt (seeds) semer.

space (gap, emptiness, atmosphere) espace m; (period) période f; (for parking) place f; **to take up s.** (room) prendre de la place.

space heat·er radiateur m d'appoint.

▸ **space out** vt espacer.

space·ship engin m spatial.

space·suit combinaison f spatiale.

spa·cious adj spacieux.

spade bêche f; (of child) pelle f; **spade(s)** Cards pique m.

spa·ghet·ti spaghetti(s) mpl.

spam (e-mail) messages mpl publicitaires, pourriels mpl; **a s. e-mail** un message publicitaire, un pourriel.

span 1 n (of hand, wing) envergure f; (of arch) portée f; (of bridge) travée f; (duration) durée m. 2 vt (river etc) enjamber; (period of time etc) couvrir.

Span·iard Espagnol, -ole m.

Span·ish 1 adj espagnol. 2 n (language) espagnol m.

spank vt donner une fessée à.

spank·ing fessée f.

spare 1 adj (extra) de trop; (clothes) de rechange; (wheel) de secours; (bed, room) d'ami; **s. time** loisirs mpl. 2 n s. (part) pièce f détachée. 3 vt (do without) se passer de (qn, qch); **to s. sb** (details etc) épargner à qn; (time) accorder à qn; (money) donner à qn.

spark étincelle f.

spar·kle vi (of diamond, star) étinceler.

spar·kling adj (wine, water) pétillant.

spark·plug bougie f.

spar·row moineau m.

speak* 1 vi parler (**about, of** de); **English-/French-speaking** qui parle anglais/français. 2 vt (language) parler; (say) dire.

speak·er (public) orateur m; (loudspeaker) haut-parleur m; (of stereo system) enceinte f.

▸ **speak up** vi parler plus fort.

spear lance f.

spe·cial 1 adj spécial; (care, attention) (tout) particulier. 2 n **today's s.** (in restaurant) le plat du jour.

spe·cial·ist spécialiste mf (in de).

spe·cial·ize vi se spécialiser (in dans).

spe·cial·ly adv spécialement.

spe·cial·ty spécialité f.

spe·cies inv espèce f.

spe·cif·ic adj précis.

spec·i·fi·ca·tion spécification f.

spec·i·men (example, person) spécimen m.

spec·ta·cle spectacle m; **spectacles** (glasses) lunettes fpl.

spec·tac·u·lar adj spectaculaire.

spec·ta·tor spectateur, -trice mf.

spec·trum spectre m; (range) gamme f.

spec·u·late vi s'interroger; (financially) spéculer; **to s. that** conjecturer que.

speech (talk, lecture) discours m (on, about sur); (power of language) parole f; (spoken language) langage m.

speed 1 n (rate) vitesse f; (quickness) rapidité f; **s. limit** limitation f de vitesse. 2 vi* (drive too fast) aller trop vite.

speed·boat vedette f.

speed·om·e·ter compteur m (de vitesse).

▸ **speed* up 1** vt accélérer. **2** vi (of person) aller plus vite.

spell¹ (period) (courte) période f; (magic) charme m; **cold s.** vague f de froid.

spell*² vt (write) écrire; (say aloud) épeler; (of letters) former (mot); **how is it spelled?** comment cela s'écrit-il?

spell·ing orthographe f.

spend* 1 vt (money) dépenser (**on** pour); (time etc) passer (**on sth** sur qch; **doing** à faire). **2** vi dépenser.

sphere sphère f.

spice n épice f. **2** vt épicer.

spic·y adj (food) épicé.

spi·der araignée f; **s.'s web** toile f d'araignée.

spike pointe f.

spill* 1 vt répandre, renverser. **2** vi se répandre, se renverser (**on, over** sur).

▸ **spill out 1** vt (empty) vider (café, verre etc). **2** vi (of coffee etc) se renverser.

▸ **spill over** vi déborder.

spin* vt (wheel etc) faire tourner; (washing) essorer.

spin·ach (food) épinards mpl.

spin (a·round) vi (of dancer, wheel etc) tourner.

spine (of back) colonne f vertébrale.

spi·ral spirale f.

spire flèche f.

spir·its npl (drinks) alcool m.

spir·i·tu·al adj spirituel.

spit 1 vti* cracher. **2** n (for meat) broche f.

spite in s. of malgré.

spite·ful adj malveillant.

splash 1 vt éclabousser (**with** de; **over** sur). **2** n (mark) éclaboussure f.

splash (a·round) vi (in river, mud) patauger; (in bath) barboter.

splen·did adj splendide.

splin·ter (in finger) écharde f.

split 1 n fente f; (tear) déchirure f. **2** vt* (break apart) fendre; (tear) déchirer.

split (up) 1 vt (group) diviser; (money, work) partager (**between** entre). **2** vi (of group) se diviser (**in-to** en); (because of disagreement) se séparer.

spoil* vt gâter; (damage, ruin) abîmer; (child, dog etc) gâter.

spoke (of wheel) rayon m.

spoke, spo·ken pt & pp de **speak**.

spokes·man, pl -men porteparole m inv (**for, of** de).

sponge éponge f.

sponge cake gâteau m de Savoie.

▸ **sponge down** vt to s. oneself down se laver à l'éponge.

spon·sor 1 vt sponsoriser. **2** n sponsor mf.

spon·ta·ne·ous adj spontané.

spool bobine f.

spoon cuillère f.

spoon·ful cuillerée f.

sport sport m; **sports** (in general) sport m; **my favorite s.** mon sport préféré; **to play sports** faire du sport; **sports club** club m sportif; **sports car/jacket/ground** voiture f/veste f/terrain m de sport.

sports·man, pl -men sportif m.

sports·wom·an, pl -women sportive f.

spot¹ (stain, mark) tache f; (dot) point m; (place) endroit m; **on the s.** sur place.

spot² vt (notice) apercevoir.

spot·less adj (clean) impeccable.

spot·light (in theater etc) projecteur m; (for photography) spot m.

spot·ted adj (animal) tacheté.

spouse époux, -ouse mf.

spout (of teapot etc) bec m.

sprain 1 n foulure f. **2** vt to s. one's ankle/wrist se fouler la cheville/le poignet.

spray 1 n (can) bombe f; **hair s.** laque f à cheveux. **2** vt (liquid, surface) vaporiser; (plant) arroser;

(car) peindre à la bombe.

spread 1 *vt* (stretch, open out)* étendre; *(legs, fingers)* écarter; *(distribute)* répandre (**over** sur); *(paint, payment, visits)* étaler; *(news, germs)* propager. **2** *vi (of fire)* s'étendre; *(of news, epidemic)* se propager. **3** *n (paste)* pâte *f* (à tartiner); **cheese s.** fromage *m* à tartiner.

▶**spread out 1** *vt (stretch, open out)* étendre; *(legs, fingers)* écarter; *(distribute)* répandre; *(paint, payment, visits)* étaler. **2** *vi (of people)* se disperser.

spring¹ 1 *n (metal device)* ressort *m*. **2** *vi* (leap)* bondir.

spring² *(season)* printemps *m*; **in (the) s.** au printemps.

spring³ *(of water)* source *f*.

spring·board tremplin *m*.

spring on·ion oignon *m* vert.

spring·time printemps *m*.

sprin·kle *vt (sand etc)* répandre (**on, over** sur); **to s. with water, to s. water on** asperger d'eau; **to s. with** *(sugar, salt, flour)* saupoudrer de.

sprin·kler *(in garden)* arroseur *m*.

sprout (**Brussels**) **s.** chou *m* (*pl* choux) de Bruxelles.

spur *(of horse rider)* éperon *m*.

spurt (**out**) *vi (of liquid)* jaillir.

spy espion, -onne *mf*.

spy·ing espionnage *m*.

▶**spy on** *vt* espionner.

square 1 *n* carré *m*; *(in town)* place *f*; *(for drawing right angles)* équerre *f*. **2** *adj* carré; *(meal)* solide.

squash 1 *vt (crush)* écraser; *(squeeze)* serrer. **2** *n (game)* squash *m*; *(vegetable)* courge *f*.

squat (**down**) *vi* s'accroupir.

squeak *vi (of door)* grincer; *(of shoe)* craquer.

squeal 1 *vi* pousser des cris aigus. **2** *n* cri *m* aigu.

squeeze 1 *vt* presser; **to s. sb's hand** serrer la main à qn. **2** *vi (force oneself)* se glisser (**through/into/**

etc par/dans/etc). **3** *n (pressure)* pression *f*; *(hug)* étreinte; **to give sth a s.** presser qch; **a s. of lemon** quelques gouttes de citron.

▶**squeeze in** *vi (of person)* trouver un peu de place.

▶**squeeze into** *vt* **to s. sth into sth** faire rentrer qch dans qch.

▶**squeeze out** *vt (juice etc)* faire sortir (**from** de).

▶**squeeze up** *vi* se serrer (**against** contre).

squint 1 *n* **to have a s.** loucher. **2** *vi* loucher; *(in the sunlight etc)* plisser les yeux.

squir·rel écureuil *m*.

squirt 1 *vt (liquid)* faire gicler. **2** *vi* gicler.

stab *vt (with knife)* poignarder.

sta·bil·i·ty stabilité *f*.

sta·ble¹ *adj* stable.

sta·ble² écurie *f*.

stack *(heap)* tas *m*; **stacks of** *Fam* un *or* des tas de.

stack (**up**) *vt* entasser.

sta·di·um stade *m*.

staff personnel *m*; *(of school)* professeurs *mpl*; *(of army)* état-major *m*.

stag cerf *m*.

stage¹ 1 *n (platform)* scène *f*. **2** *vt (play)* monter.

stage² *(phase, of journey)* étape *f*.

stage·coach diligence *f*.

stag·ger *vi* chanceler.

stain 1 *vt (to mark)* tacher (**with** de). **2** *n* tache *f*.

stained glass win·dow vitrail *m* (*pl* vitraux).

stain·less steel *adj (knife etc)* en inox.

stain re·mov·er détachant *m*.

stair·case escalier *m*.

stairs *npl* escalier *m*.

stake *(post)* pieu *m*.

stale *adj (bread etc)* rassis (*f* rassie)

stalk¹ *(of plant)* tige *f*.

stalk² *vt (animal)* traquer; *(celebrity)* harceler.

stalk·er = admirateur obsessionnel.

stall 1 n (in market) étal m (pl étals); (for newspapers, flowers) kiosque m. **2** vti (of car engine) caler.

stam·mer vti bégayer.

stamp 1 n (for postage, instrument) timbre m; (mark) cachet m. **2** vt (document) tamponner; (letter) timbrer; **self-addressed stamped envelope** enveloppe f timbrée à votre adresse. **3** vti **to s. (one's feet)** taper des pieds.

stance position f.

stand 1 n (support) support m; (at exhibition) stand m; (for spectators) tribune f; **news/flower s.** kiosque m à journaux/à fleurs. **2** vt* (pain, person etc) supporter; (put) mettre (debout); **to s. a chance** avoir une chance. **3** vi être or se tenir (debout); (get up) se lever; (remain) rester (debout); (be situated) se trouver.

stan·dard 1 n norme f; (level) niveau m; **standards (of behavior)** principes mpl; **s. of living** niveau m de vie; **up to s.** (of work etc) au niveau. **2** adj (model, size) standard inv.

▸**stand around** vi traîner.

▸**stand aside** vi s'écarter.

▸**stand back** vi reculer.

stand·by adj (ticket) sans garantie.

▸**stand by 1** vi rester là (sans rien faire); (be ready) être prêt. **2** vt (friend) rester fidèle à.

▸**stand for** vt (mean) signifier, représenter; (put up with) supporter.

▸**stand in for** vt remplacer.

stand·ing adj debout inv.

▸**stand out** vi ressortir (**against** sur).

stand·point point m de vue.

stand·still to bring to a s. immobiliser; **to come to a s.** s'immobiliser.

▸**stand up 1** vt mettre debout. **2** vi se lever.

▸**stand up for** vt défendre.

▸**stand up to** vt résister à (qch); (defend oneself) tenir tête à (qn).

sta·ple 1 n (for paper etc) agrafe f. **2** vt agrafer.

sta·pler agrafeuse f.

star 1 n étoile f; (person) vedette f. **2** vi (of actor) être la vedette (**in** de). **3** vt (of movie) avoir pour vedette.

stare 1 n regard m (fixe). **2** vi **to s. at** fixer (du regard).

Star-Span·gled Ban·ner (flag) drapeau m américain; (hymn) hymne m national américain.

start¹ 1 n commencement m, début m; (of race) départ m; (lead) avance f (**on** sur); **to make a s.** commencer. **2** vt commencer; **to s. doing** or **to do** commencer à faire. **3** vi commencer (**with sth** par qch; **by doing** par faire); **starting from** (price etc) à partir de.

start² vi (jump) sursauter.

start (off or **out)** vi partir (**for** pour).

start (up) 1 vt (engine, vehicle) mettre en marche; (business) fonder. **2** vi (of engine, vehicle) démarrer.

start·er (in vehicle) démarreur m.

star·tle vt (make jump) faire sursauter.

▸**start on** vt commencer.

star·va·tion faim f.

starve vi souffrir de la faim; (die) mourir de faim; **I'm starving!** (hungry) je meurs de faim!

state¹ (condition) état m; **S.** (nation etc) État m; **the States** Fam les États-Unis mpl.

state² vt déclarer (**that** que); (time, date) fixer.

state·ment déclaration f; (bank) s. relevé m de compte.

states·man, pl **-men** homme m d'État.

stat·ic 1 adj statique. **2** n (on radio)

parasites *mpl*; *(electricity)* électricité *f* statique.

sta·tion *n (for trains)* gare *f*; *(underground)* station *f*; **(police) s.** commissariat *m* (de police); **bus s.** gare *f* routière; **radio s.** station *f* de radio; **service** *or* **gas s.** station-service *f*.

sta·tion·ar·y *adj (vehicle)* à l'arrêt.

sta·tion·er·y articles *mpl* de bureau.

sta·tion·er·y store papeterie *f*.

sta·tion·mas·ter chef *m* de gare.

sta·tion wag·on break *m*, commerciale *f*.

sta·tis·tic *(fact)* statistique *f*.

stat·ue statue *f*.

stay **1** *n (visit)* séjour *m*. **2** *vi* rester; *(reside)* loger; *(visit)* séjourner; **to s. put** ne pas bouger.

▸ **stay away** *vi* ne pas s'approcher (**from** de); **to s. away from** *(school etc)* ne pas aller à.

▸ **stay in** *vi* rester à la maison; *(of nail, screw)* tenir.

▸ **stay out** *vi* rester dehors; *(not come home)* ne pas rentrer.

▸ **stay out of** *vt (not interfere in)* ne pas se mêler de.

▸ **stay up** *vi* ne pas se coucher; *(of fence etc)* tenir; **to s. up late** se coucher tard.

stead·i·ly *adv (gradually)* progressivement; *(regularly)* régulièrement; *(without stopping)* sans arrêt.

stead·y *adj* stable; *(hand)* sûr; *(progress, speed)* régulier; **s. (on one's feet)** solide sur ses jambes.

steak steak *m*, bifteck *m*.

steal* *vti* voler (**from sb** à qn).

steam **1** *n* vapeur *f*; *(on glass)* buée *f*. **2** *vt (food)* cuire à la vapeur.

steam·roll·er rouleau *m* compresseur.

steel acier *m*.

steep *adj (stairs, slope etc)* raide; *(hill, path)* escarpé; *(price)* excessif.

stee·ple clocher *m*.

steer *vt (vehicle, ship, person)* diriger (**towards** vers).

steer·ing wheel volant *m*.

stem *(of plant)* tige *f*.

step **1** *n* pas *m*; *(of stairs)* marche *f*; *(on train, bus)* marchepied *m*; *(doorstep)* pas *m* de la porte; *(action)* mesure *f*; **(flight of) steps** escalier *m*; *(outdoors)* perron *m*; **(pair of) steps** *(ladder)* escabeau *m*. **2** *vi (walk)* marcher (**on** sur).

▸ **step aside** *vi* s'écarter.

▸ **step back** *vi* reculer.

step·broth·er demi-frère *m*.

step·daugh·ter belle-fille *f*.

step·fa·ther beau-père *m*.

▸ **step forward** *vi* faire un pas en avant.

▸ **step into** *vt (car etc)* monter dans.

▸ **step out of** *vt (car etc)* descendre de.

step·lad·der escabeau *m*.

step·mo·ther belle-mère *f*.

▸ **step over** *vt (obstacle)* enjamber.

step·sis·ter demi-sœur *f*.

step·son beau-fils *m*.

▸ **step up** *vt (increase)* augmenter; *(quicken)* accélérer.

ster·e·o **1** *n (pl -os) (equipment)* chaîne (stéréo *inv*). **2** *adj* stéréo *inv*.

ster·il·ize *vt* stériliser.

ster·ling *(currency)* sterling *m inv*; **s. silver** argent *m* fin; **the pound s.** la livre sterling.

stew ragoût *m*.

stew·ard *(on plane, ship)* steward *m*.

stew·ard·ess hôtesse *f*.

stewed fruit compote *f*.

stick¹ *n* bâton *m*; *(for walking)* canne *f*.

stick*² **1** *vt (glue)* coller; *(put) Fam* mettre, fourrer; **to s. sth into sth** fourrer qch dans qch. **2** *vi* coller (**to** à); *(of food in pan)* attacher (**to** dans); *(of drawer etc)* se coincer, être coincé.

stick·er autocollant *m*.

▸**stick on** vt (stamp) coller.

▸**stick out 1** vt (tongue) tirer. **2** vi (of petticoat etc) dépasser.

▸**stick up** vt (notice) afficher.

▸**stick up for** vt défendre.

stick·y adj collant; (label) adhésif.

stiff adj raide; (leg etc) ankylosé; (brush) dur; **to have a s. neck** avoir le torticolis; **to feel s.** être courbaturé.

sti·fle vi it's stifling on étouffe.

still¹ adv encore, toujours; (even) encore; (nevertheless) tout de même.

still² adj (not moving) immobile; (calm) calme; **to keep** or **stand s.** rester tranquille.

stim·u·late vt stimuler.

sting 1 vti* (of insect, ointment etc) piquer. **2** n piqûre f.

stin·gy adj avare.

stink* vi puer; **to s. of smoke/etc** empester la fumée/etc.

▸**stink up** vt (room) empester.

stir vt (coffee, leaves etc) remuer.

stir·rup étrier m.

stitch point m; (in knitting) maille f; (in wound) point m de suture.

stitch (up) vt (sew) coudre; (repair) recoudre.

stock 1 n (supply) provision f; (soup) bouillon m; **stock(s)** (securities) valeurs fpl (boursières); **in s.** en magasin, en stock; **out of s.** épuisé; **the S. Market** la Bourse. **2** vt (sell) vendre.

stock·ing bas m.

stock·pile 1 n réserve f. **2** vt faire des réserves de.

▸**stock up** vi s'approvisionner (**with** de, en).

stock·y adj trapu.

sto·len pp of **steal**.

stom·ach (for digestion) estomac m; (front of body) ventre m.

stom·ach·ache mal m de ventre; **to have a s.** avoir mal au ventre.

stone pierre f; (pebble) caillou m (pl cailloux); (in fruit) noyau m.

stood pt & pp de **stand**.

stool tabouret m.

stop 1 n (place, halt) arrêt m; (for plane, ship) escale f; **bus s.** arrêt m d'autobus; **to put a s. to sth** mettre fin à qch; **s. sign** (on road) stop m. **2** vt arrêter; (end) mettre fin à; (prevent) empêcher (**from doing** de faire). **3** vi s'arrêter; (of pain, conversation etc) cesser; (stay) rester; **to s. eating/etc** s'arrêter de manger/etc; **to s. snowing/etc** cesser de neiger/etc; 'no stopping (no standing)' (street sign) 'arrêt interdit'.

▸**stop by** vi passer (**sb's** chez qn).

stop·light (on vehicle) stop m.

stop·off, stop·o·ver halte f.

▸**stop off, stop over** vi (on trip) s'arrêter.

stop·per bouchon m.

▸**stop up** vt (sink, pipe etc) boucher.

stop·watch chronomètre m.

store (supply) provision f; (warehouse) entrepôt m; (shop) magasin m.

store (a·way) vt (furniture) entreposer.

store (up) vt (in warehouse etc) stocker; (for future use) mettre en réserve.

store·keep·er commerçant, -ante mf.

store·room (in house) débarras m; (in office, store) réserve f.

stork cigogne f.

storm tempête f; (thunderstorm) orage m.

storm·y adj orageux.

sto·ry¹ histoire f; (newspaper article) article m; (plot) intrigue f; **short s.** nouvelle f.

sto·ry² (of building) étage m.

stove (for cooking) cuisinière f; (portable) réchaud m; (for heating) poêle m.

straight 1 adj droit; (hair) raide; (route) direct; (tidy) en ordre; (frank) franc (f franche). **2** adv (to *walk etc)* droit; *(directly)* tout droit; *(to drink whisky etc)* sec; **s. away** tout de suite; **s. ahead** *or* **on** tout droit.

straight·en *vt (wire, tie, picture)* redresser; *(hair)* défriser; *(room, papers)* ranger.

▶**straighten out** *vt (problem)* résoudre.

straight·for·ward *adj (easy, clear)* simple.

strain 1 *n (tiredness)* fatigue *f; (mental)* tension *f* nerveuse. 2 *vt (eyes)* fatiguer; *(voice)* forcer; **to s. one's back** se faire mal au dos.

strain·er passoire *f.*

strand *(of wool)* brin *m; (of hair)* mèche *f.*

strand·ed *adj* en rade.

strange *adj (odd)* étrange; *(unknown)* inconnu.

strang·er *(unknown)* inconnu, -ue *mf; (person from outside)* étranger, -ère *mf.*

stran·gle *vt* étrangler.

strap sangle *f,* courroie *f, (on dress)* bretelle *f; (on watch)* bracelet *m; (on sandal)* lanière *f.*

strap (down *or* **in)** *vt* attacher *(avec une courroie).*

straw paille *f;* **a (drinking) s.** une paille.

straw·ber·ry 1 *n* fraise *f.* 2 *adj (ice-cream)* à la fraise; *(jam)* de fraises; *(tart)* aux fraises.

streak *(line)* raie *f; (of color)* strie *f; (of paint)* traînée *f.*

stream *(brook)* ruisseau *m; (flow)* flot *m.*

street rue *f;* **s. door** porte *f* d'entrée.

street·car *(tram)* tramway *m.*

street lamp, street light réverbère *m.*

street map plan *m* des rues.

strength force *f, (health, energy)* forces *fpl; (of wood etc)* solidité *f.*

strength·en *vt* renforcer.

stress 1 *n (mental)* stress *m; (emphasis)* & *Grammar* accent *m;* **under s.** stressé. 2 *vt* insister sur;

(word) accentuer; **to s. that** souligner que.

stressed *adj (person)* stressé.

stretch 1 *vt (rope, neck)* tendre; *(shoe, rubber)* étirer; **to s. one's legs** se dégourdir les jambes. 2 *vi (of person, elastic)* s'étirer. 3 *n (area)* étendue *f.*

stretch (out) 1 *vt (arm, leg)* étendre; **to s. (out) one's arm** *(reach out)* tendre le bras (**to take** pour prendre). 2 *vi (of plain etc)* s'étendre.

stretch·er brancard *m.*

strict *adj* strict.

strict·ly *adv* strictement; **s. forbidden** formellement interdit.

strict·ness sévérité *f.*

stride *(grand)* pas *m,* enjambée *f.*

▶**stride* along/out/***etc vi* avancer/sortir/*etc* à grands pas.

strike*[1] *vt (hit, impress)* frapper; *(collide with)* heurter; *(a match)* frotter; *(of clock)* sonner *(l'heure);* **it strikes me that** il me semble que *(+ indicative).*

strike[2] *(of workers)* grève *f;* **to go on s.** se mettre en grève (**for** pour obtenir).

▶**strike out** 1 *vt (cross out)* rayer, barrer. 2 *vi* **to s. out at sb** essayer de frapper qn.

strik·er *(worker)* gréviste *mf.*

strik·ing *adj (impressive)* frappant.

string ficelle *f, (of parka, apron)* cordon *m; (of violin, racket etc)* corde *f, (of pearls)* collier *m.*

strip *(piece)* bande *f,* **(thin) s.** *(of metal etc)* lamelle *t.*

strip (off) *vi* se déshabiller.

stripe rayure *f.*

striped *adj* rayé.

strip mall = centre *m* commercial qui longe une route.

strive *vi* **to s. to do sth** s'efforcer de faire qch.

stroke 1 *n (movement)* coup *m; (illness)* hémorragie *f* cérébrale; **(swimming) s.** nage *f;* **a s. of luck** un coup de chance. **2** vt (beard, cat etc) caresser.

stroll 1 n promenade f. **2** vi se promener.

stroll·er (for baby) poussette f.

strong adj fort; (shoes, chair etc) solide.

struc·ture structure f; (building) construction f.

strug·gle 1 n (fight) lutte f (**to do** pour faire). **2** vi (fight) lutter, se battre (**with** avec); (thrash around) se débattre; **to s. to do** (try hard) s'efforcer de faire; (have difficulty) avoir du mal à faire.

stub (of cigarette etc) bout m; (of ticket, check) talon m, souche f.

stub·born adj (person) entêté.

stub·born·ness entêtement m.

▸**stub out** vt (cigarette) écraser.

stuck (pt & pp of stick) adj (caught, jammed) coincé.

stud (for collar) bouton m de col.

stu·dent n étudiant, -ante mf; (at school) élève mf; **music/etc s.** étudiant, -ante en musique/etc. **2** adj (life, protest) étudiant; (restaurant, housing) universitaire.

stu·di·o, pl -os (of artist etc) studio m; **s. apartment** studio m.

stud·y 1 n étude f; (office) bureau m. **2** vt (learn, observe) étudier. **3** vi étudier; **to s. to be a doctor/etc** faire des études de médecine/etc; **to s. for an exam** préparer un examen.

stuff 1 n (things) trucs mpl; (possessions) affaires fpl; **it's good s.** c'est bon. **2** vt (fill) bourrer (**with** de); (cushion etc) rembourrer (**with** avec); (put) fourrer (**into** dans); (chicken etc) farcir.

stuffed (up) adj (nose) bouché.

stuff·ing (for chicken etc) farce f.

stuff·y adj (room etc) mal aéré; **it smells s.** ça sent le renfermé.

stum·ble vi trébucher (**over** sur).

stump (of tree) souche f.

stun vt (with punch etc) étourdir.

stunned adj (amazed) stupéfait (**by** par).

stun·ning adj (astounding) stupéfiant; (beautiful) superbe.

stu·pid adj stupide; **a s. thing** une stupidité; **s. fool** idiot, -ote mf.

stu·pid·i·ty stupidité f.

stur·dy adj robuste.

stut·ter 1 vi bégayer. **2** n to have a **s.** être bègue.

sty (for pigs) porcherie f.

style style m; (fashion) mode f; (design of dress etc) modèle m; (of hair) coiffure f.

styl·ish adj chic inv.

sub·ject (matter) & Grammar sujet m; (at school, university) matière f; (citizen) ressortissant, -ante mf.

sub·junc·tive Grammar subjonctif m.

sub·ma·rine sous-marin m.

sub·scrib·er abonné, -ée mf.

▸**sub·scribe to** vt (take out subscription) s'abonner à (journal etc); (be a subscriber) être abonné à (journal etc).

sub·scrip·tion (to newspaper etc) abonnement m.

sub·side vi (of ground) s'affaisser.

sub·si·dy subvention f.

sub·stance substance f.

sub·stan·tial adj important; (meal) copieux.

sub·sti·tute produit m de remplacement; (person) remplaçant, -ante mf (**for** de).

sub·ti·tle sous-titre m.

sub·tle adj subtil.

sub·tract vt soustraire (**from** de).

sub·trac·tion soustraction f.

sub·urb banlieue f; **the suburbs** la banlieue.

sub·ur·ban adj (train etc) de banlieue.

sub·way métro m.

suc·ceed vi réussir (**in doing** à faire; **in sth** dans qch).

suc·cess succès m, réussite f; **he**

was a s. il a eu du succès; **it was a s.** c'était réussi.

suc·cess·ful *adj* (effort etc) couronné de succès; (firm) prospère; (candidate in exam) admis; (writer, film etc) à succès; **to be s.** réussir (in dans; **in an exam** à un examen; **in doing** à faire).

suc·cess·ful·ly *adv* avec succès.

suc·ces·sion succession *f*, série *f*; **ten days in s.** dix jours consécutifs.

suc·ces·sive *adj* successif.

suc·ces·sor successeur *m* (**to** de).

such 1 *adj* tel, telle; **s. a car/etc** une telle voiture/etc; **s. happiness/etc** tant de bonheur/etc, tel que. **2** *adv* (so very) si; (in comparisons) aussi; **s. a large helping** une si grosse portion; **s. a kind woman as you** une femme aussi gentille que vous.

suck *vt* sucer.

suck (up) *vi* (with straw) aspirer.

sud·den *adj* soudain; **all of a s.** tout à coup.

sud·den·ly *adv* subitement.

suds *npl* (soap) **s.** mousse *f* de savon.

sue 1 *vt* poursuivre (en justice). **2** *vi* engager des poursuites judiciaires.

suede 1 *n* daim *m*. **2** *adj* de daim.

suf·fer 1 *vi* souffrir (**from** de). **2** *vt* (loss) subir; (pain) ressentir.

suf·fer·er victime *f*; **AIDS s.** malade *mf* du SIDA.

suf·fer·ing souffrance(s) *f(pl)*.

suf·fi·cient *adj* (quantity) suffisant, **s. money/etc** suffisamment d'argent/etc.

suf·fi·cient·ly *adv* suffisamment.

suf·fix suffixe *m*.

suf·fo·cate *vti* étouffer.

sug·ar 1 *n* sucre *m*; **granulated/lump s.** sucre cristallisé/en morceaux. **2** *vt* sucrer.

sug·ar bowl sucrier *m*.

sug·gest *vt* (propose) suggérer, proposer (**to** à; **doing** de faire; **that**

que (+ *subjunctive*)); (imply) suggérer.

sug·ges·tion suggestion *f*.

su·i·cide suicide *m*; **to commit s.** se suicider; **s. bombing** attentat-suicide *m*.

suit¹ (man's) costume *m*; (woman's) tailleur *m*; Cards couleur *f*; **flying/diving/ski s.** combinaison *f* de vol/plongée/ski.

suit² *vt* (please, be acceptable to) convenir à; (of dress, color etc) aller (bien) à; **it suits me to stay** ça m'arrange de rester; **suited to** (job, activity) fait pour.

suit·a·ble *adj* qui convient (**for** à), convenable (**for** pour); (dress, color) qui va (bien).

suit·case valise *f*.

suite (rooms) suite *f*, (furniture) mobilier *m*.

sulk *vi* bouder.

sul·len *adj* maussade.

sum (amount of money, total) somme *f*; (calculation) calcul *m*.

sum·ma·rize *vt* résumer.

sum·ma·ry résumé *m*.

sum·mer 1 *n* été *m*; **in (the) s.** en été. **2** *adj* d'été; **s. vacation** grandes vacances *fpl*.

sum·mer·time été *m*.

sum·mon *vt* (meeting, person) convoquer; (aid) appeler à; (to court etc) citer.

sum·mons 1 *n* (to court etc) assignation *f* à comparaître. **2** *vt* (to court etc) assigner à comparaître.

▶ **summon up** *vt* **to s. up one's courage/strength** rassembler son courage/ses forces.

▶ **sum up** *vti* (facts etc) résumer.

sun soleil *m*; **in the s.** au soleil; **the sun is shining** il fait (du) soleil.

sun·bathe *vi* prendre un bain de soleil, se faire bronzer.

sun·burn coup *m* de soleil.

sun·burned, **sun·burnt** *adj* brûlé par le soleil.

sun·dae glace *f* aux fruits.

SUGGESTIONS, INVITATIONS AND DESIRES

What do you want to do?
Qu'est-ce que tu veux/vous voulez faire ?

Do you want to go to a restaurant?
Tu veux/Vous voulez allez au restaurant ?

How about going for a walk?
Et si on allait faire une promenade ?

Let's meet at noon/outside the movie theater.
On se retrouve à midi/devant le cinéma ?

I don't want to go to the art gallery.
Je ne veux pas aller au musée d'art.

I feel like an ice-cream.
J'ai envie d'une glace.

What would you rather do?
Qu'est-ce que tu préfères/vous préférez faire ?

I'd like to learn French.
J'aimerais apprendre le français.

I don't mind.
Ça m'est égal.

I'd love to!
Avec plaisir !

I don't feel like it.
Je n'en ai pas envie.

Are you free tomorrow night?
Est-ce que tu es/vous êtes libre demain soir ?

That's very kind of you.
C'est très gentil.

Shall we go for a coffee?
On va prendre un café ?

Would you like to go for a drink?
Ça te/vous dit d'aller boire un verre ?

Let's go for a swim!
Allons nous baigner !

I'd like to go to the beach.
J'aimerais aller à la plage.

I'd rather go shopping.
Je préférerais faire les magasins.

I don't feel like going to the market.
Je n'ai pas envie d'aller au marché.

I think we should leave around 6.30.
Je propose qu'on parte vers six heures et demie.

I wouldn't mind living here.
J'aimerais bien habiter ici.

It's up to you.
C'est comme tu veux/vous voulez.

That's a good idea.
C'est une bonne idée.

I'm sorry, I can't.
Je suis désolé(e), je ne peux pas.

I'm afraid I already have plans.
Je regrette, j'ai déjà quelque chose de prévu.

Thank you for inviting me.
Merci de m'avoir invité.

Sun·day dimanche m.

sun·glass·es npl lunettes fpl de soleil.

sun·lamp lampe f à bronzer.

sun·light (lumière f du) soleil m.

sun·ny adj (day etc) ensoleillé; **it's s.** il fait (du) soleil; **s. periods** or **intervals** éclaircies fpl.

sun·rise lever m du soleil.

sun·roof toit m ouvrant.

sun·set coucher m du soleil.

sun·shine soleil m.

sun·stroke insolation f.

sun·tan bronzage m; **s. lotion/oil** crème f/huile f solaire.

sun·tanned adj bronzé.

su·per adj Fam sensationnel.

su·perb adj superbe.

su·per·fi·cial adj superficiel.

su·per·glue colle f extra-forte.

su·per·in·ten·dent (of apartment building) gardien, -enne mf; **(police) s.** = commissaire mf (de police).

su·pe·ri·or adj supérieur (**to** à).

su·pe·ri·or·i·ty supériorité f.

su·per·mar·ket supermarché m.

su·per·mo·del top model m.

su·per·sti·tion superstition f.

su·per·sti·tious adj superstitieux.

su·per·vise vt (person, work) surveiller; (office, research) diriger.

su·per·vi·sor surveillant, -ante mf; (in office) chef m de service; (in store) chef m de rayon.

sup·per dîner m; (late-night) souper m; **to have s.** dîner; (late at night) souper.

sup·ple adj souple.

sup·ple·ment 1 n supplément m. **2** vt compléter.

sup·ply 1 vt fournir; (with electricity, gas, water) alimenter (**with** en); (equip) équiper (**with** de); **to s. sb with sth, to s. sth to sb** fournir qch à qn. **2** n (stock) provision f; **(food) supplies** vivres mpl.

sup·port 1 vt (bear weight of, help, encourage) soutenir; (be in favor of) être en faveur de; (family etc) subvenir aux besoins de. **2** n (help) soutien m; (object) support m.

sup·port·er partisan m; (in sport) supporter m.

sup·pose vti supposer (**that** que); **I'm supposed to work** or **be working** je suis censé travailler; **he's supposed to be rich** on le dit riche; **I s. (so)** je pense; **you're tired, I s.** vous êtes fatigué, je suppose; **s. we go** (suggestion) si nous partions; **s. or supposing you're right** supposons que tu aies raison.

sup·press vt (feelings, smile, revolution) supprimer; (news, truth, evidence) faire disparaître.

sure adj sûr (**of** de; **that** que); **she's s. to accept** il est sûr qu'elle acceptera; **to make s. of sth** s'assurer de qch; **be s. to do it!** ne manquez pas de le faire!

sure·ly adv sûrement; **s. he didn't refuse?** (I hope) il n'a tout de même pas refusé?

surf 1 vt **to s. the Net** naviguer sur Internet. **2** vi (as sport) faire du surf.

sur·face surface f; **s. area** superficie f; **s. mail** courrier m par voie normale.

surf·board planche f (de surf).

surf·ing surf m; **to go s.** faire du surf.

surge 1 n (increase) augmentation f; (of anger, pity) accès m. **2** vi **to s. forward** (people) se ruer en avant.

sur·geon chirurgien, -enne mf.

sur·ge·ry **to have s.** avoir une opération (**for** pour).

sur·gi·cal adj chirurgical.

sur·name nom m de famille.

sur·plus 1 n surplus m. **2** adj en surplus.

sur·prise 1 n surprise f; **to take sb by s.** prendre qn au dépourvu. **2** adj (visit etc) inattendu. **3** vt (astonish) étonner, surprendre.

sur·prised adj surpris (**that** que (+ subjunctive); **at sth** de qch); **I'm s. to see you** je suis surpris de te voir.

sur·pris·ing adj surprenant.

sur·ren·der vi se rendre (**to** à).

sur·round vt entourer (**with** de); (of army, police) encercler; **surrounded by** entouré de.

sur·round·ing adj environnant.

sur·round·ings npl environs mpl; (setting) cadre m.

sur·veil·lance surveillance f.

sur·vey enquête f, (of opinion) sondage m.

sur·vey·or (of land) géomètre m.

sur·vive 1 vi survivre. 2 vt survivre à.

sur·vi·vor survivant, -ante mf.

sus·pect 1 n suspect, -ecte mf. 2 vt soupçonner (**that** que; **of sth** de qch; **of doing** d'avoir fait).

sus·pend vt (postpone, dismiss) suspendre; (student) renvoyer; (driver's license) retirer.

sus·pend·ers npl bretelles fpl.

sus·pense (in book etc) suspense m.

sus·pen·sion (of vehicle) suspension f.

sus·pi·cion soupçon m.

sus·pi·cious adj (person) méfiant; (behavior) suspect; **s.(-looking)** suspect; **to be s. of** se méfier de.

SUV abbr (sport-utility vehicle) quatre-quatre m ou f.

swal·low 1 vti avaler. 2 n (bird) hirondelle f.

▸ **swallow down** vt avaler.

swamp marécage m.

swan cygne m.

swap 1 n échange m. 2 vt échanger (**for** contre); **to s. seats** changer de place. 3 vi échanger.

swarm (of bees etc) essaim m.

sway vi se balancer.

swear* 1 vt (promise) jurer (**to do** de faire; **that** que). 2 vi (curse) jurer (**at** contre).

swear·word gros mot m.

sweat 1 n sueur f. 2 vi transpirer, suer; **I'm sweating** je suis en sueur.

sweat·er pull m.

sweat·shirt sweat-shirt m.

Swede Suédois, -oise mf.

Swed·ish 1 adj suédois. 2 n (language) suédois m.

sweep* 1 vt (with broom) balayer; (chimney) ramoner. 2 vi balayer.

▸ **sweep aside** vt écarter.

▸ **sweep away** vt (leaves etc) balayer; (carry off) emporter.

▸ **sweep out** vt (room etc) balayer.

▸ **sweep up** vt balayer.

sweet adj (not sour) doux (f douce); (tea, coffee etc) sucré; (child, house, cat) mignon (f mignonne); (kind) aimable.

sweet·corn maïs m.

sweet·en vt (tea etc) sucrer.

sweet·ly adv (kindly) aimablement; (agreeably) agréablement.

swell* (up) vi (of hand, leg etc) enfler; (of wood, dough) gonfler.

swell·ing enflure f.

swerve vi (of vehicle) faire une embardée.

swift 1 adj rapide. 2 n (bird) martinet m.

swim 1 n **to go for a s.** se baigner. 2 vi* nager; (as sport) faire de la natation; **to go swimming** aller nager. 3 vt (crawl etc) nager.

swim meet (competition) concours m de natation.

swim·mer nageur, -euse mf.

swim·ming natation f.

swim·ming pool piscine f.

swim·ming trunks slip m de bain.

swim·suit maillot m de bain.

swing 1 n (in playground etc) balançoire f. 2 vi* (sway) se balancer. 3 vt (arms etc) balancer.

▸ **swing around** vi (turn) virer; (of person) se retourner (vivement).

Swiss 1 adj suisse. **2** n inv Suisse m, Suissesse f; **the S.** les Suisses mpl.

switch 1 n (electric) bouton m (électrique). **2** vt (money, employee) transférer (**to** à); (exchange) échanger (**for** contre); **to s. places** or **seats** changer de place.

▸**switch off** vt (lamp, gas etc) éteindre; (engine) arrêter.

▸**switch on** vt (lamp, gas etc) mettre, allumer; (engine) mettre en marche.

swol·len (pp of swell) adj (leg etc) enflé; (stomach) gonflé.

sword épée f.

syl·la·ble syllabe f.

syl·la·bus programme m (scolaire).

sym·bol symbole m.

sym·bol·ic adj symbolique.

sym·pa·thet·ic adj (showing pity) compatissant; (understanding) compréhensif.

sym·pa·thize vi **l s. (with you)** (pity) je suis désolé (pour vous); (understanding) je vous comprends.

sym·pa·thy (pity) compassion f; (understanding) compréhension f; (when sb dies) condoléances fpl.

sym·pho·ny symphonie f.

symp·tom symptôme m.

syn·a·gogue synagogue f.

syn·o·nym synonyme m.

sy·ringe seringue f.

syr·up sirop m.

sys·tem système m; (human body) organisme m; (order) méthode f.

T

tab (cloth etc flap) patte f.

ta·ble (furniture, list) table f; **bedside t.** table f de chevet; **to lay** or **set/clear the t.** mettre/débarrasser la table.

ta·ble·cloth nappe f.

ta·ble·mat (of cloth) napperon m; (hard) dessous-de-plat m inv.

ta·ble·spoon = cuillère f à soupe.

ta·ble·spoon·ful = cuillerée f à soupe.

tab·let (pill) comprimé m.

tack (nail) petit clou m; (thumbtack) punaise f.

tack·le vt (problem etc) s'attaquer à; Rugby, Football plaquer; Soccer tacler.

tack·y adj (remark etc) de mauvais goût.

tact tact m.

tact·ful adj **to be t.** (of person) avoir du tact.

tac·tic a t. une tactique; **tactics** la tactique.

taf·fy caramel n (dur).

tag (label) étiquette f.

tail (of animal etc) queue f.

tai·lor tailleur m.

take* vt prendre; (prize) remporter; (exam) passer; (subtract) soustraire (**from** de); (tolerate) supporter; (bring) amener (qn) (**to** à); (by car) conduire (qn) (**to** à); **to t. sth to sb** (ap)porter qch à qn; **to t. sb (out) to the theater/** etc emmener qn au théâtre/etc; **to t. sth with one** emporter qch; **to t. sb home** ramener qn; **it takes courage/**etc il faut du courage/etc (**to do** pour faire); **it took me an hour to do it** j'ai mis une heure à le faire.

▸**take after** vt ressembler à.

▸**take along** vt (object) emporter; (person) emmener.

▸**take apart** vt (machine) démonter.

▸**take away** vt (thing) emporter; (person) emmener; (remove) enlever; (subtract) soustraire (**from** de).

▸**take back** vt reprendre; (return) rapporter; (accompany) ramener (qn) (**to** à).

▸**take down** vt (object) descendre; (notes) prendre.

▸**take in** vt (chair, car etc) rentrer; (include) inclure; (understand) comprendre; (deceive) Fam rouler.

tak·en adj (seat) pris.

take·off (of aircraft) décollage m.

▸**take off 1** vt (remove) enlever; (lead away) emmener; (subtract) déduire (**from** de). **2** vi (of aircraft) décoller.

▸**take on** vt (work, staff, passenger) prendre.

take·out 1 adj (meal) à emporter; (restaurant) qui fait des plats à emporter. **2** n (food) plat m à emporter.

▸**take out** vt (from pocket etc) sortir; (stain) enlever; (tooth) arracher; (insurance) prendre.

take·o·ver (of company etc) rachat m; **t. bid** OPA f.

▸**take over 1** vt (company etc) racheter; **to t. over sb's job** remplacer qn. **2** vi prendre la relève (**from** de); (permanently) prendre la succession (**from** de).

▸**take up** vt (carry up) monter; (space, time) prendre; (hobby) se mettre à.

tak·ings npl recette f.

tale (story) conte m.

tal·ent talent m; **to have a t. for** avoir du talent pour.

tal·ent·ed adj doué.

talk 1 n propos mpl; (gossip) bavardage(s) m(pl); (conversation) conversation f, (lecture) exposé m (**on** sur); **talks** pourparlers mpl; **to have a t. with sb** parler avec qn; **there's t. of** on parle de. **2** vi parler (**to** à; **with** avec; **about, of** de). **3** vt (nonsense) dire; **to t. sb into do-ing/out of doing** persuader qn de faire/de ne pas faire.

talk·a·tive adj bavard.

▸**talk over** vt discuter (de).

tall adj (person) grand; (tree, house) haut; **how t. are you?** combien mesures-tu?

tam·bou·rine tambourin m.

tame 1 adj (animal) apprivoisé. **2** vt apprivoiser.

tam·pon tampon m hygiénique.

tan 1 n (suntan) bronzage m. **2** vti bronzer.

tan·ger·ine mandarine f.

tan·gled adj enchevêtré.

tank (storing liquid or gas) réservoir m; (vehicle) char m; (fish) **t.** aquarium m.

tank·er (oil) **t.** (ship) pétrolier m.

tap 1 n (for water) robinet m; (blow) petit coup m. **2** vti (hit) frapper légèrement.

tape¹ n (of cloth, paper) ruban m; (adhesive) **t.** ruban m adhésif. **2** vt (stick) coller (avec du ruban adhésif).

tape² **1** n (for sound or video recording) bande f (magnétique/vidéo). **2** vt (a movie etc) enregistrer, magnétoscoper; (music, voice) enregistrer; (event) faire une cassette de. **3** vi enregistrer.

tape meas·ure mètre m (à) ruban.

tape re·cord·er magnétophone m.

tar goudron m.

tar·get cible f, (objective) objectif m.

tar·iff (list of prices) tarif m; (at customs) tarif m douanier.

tar·pau·lin bâche f.

tart (pie) (open) tarte f, (with pastry on top) tourte f.

tar·tan adj (skirt etc) écossais.

task travail m.

taste 1 n goût m. **2** vt (eat, drink) goûter à; (make out the taste of) sentir le goût de). **3** vi **to t. of** or **like sth** avoir un goût de qch; **to t. delicious/etc** avoir un goût délicieux/etc.

tast·y adj savoureux.

tat·tered adj (clothes) en lambeaux.

tat·tle vi rapporter (**on** sur).

tat·tle·tale *Fam* rapporteur, -euse *mf*.

tat·too 1 *n* (*pl* -oos) (*on body*) tatouage *m*. **2** *vt* tatouer.

tax 1 *n* (*on goods*) taxe *f*, (*on income*) impôt *m*, contributions *fpl*; **t. free** (*goods*) non taxé; **t. collector** percepteur *m* d'impôt. **2** *vt* (*goods*) taxer; (*person, company*) imposer.

tax·a·ble *adj* imposable.

tax·i taxi *m*; **t. stand** station *f* de taxis.

tax·pay·er contribuable *mf*.

TB tuberculose *f*.

tea thé *m*; **to have t.** prendre le thé; **t. party** thé *m*; **t. set** service *m* à thé.

tea·bag sachet *m* de thé.

teach*1 *vt* apprendre (**sb sth** qch à qn); (*that* que); (*in school etc*) enseigner (**sb sth** qch à qn); **to t. sb (how) to do** apprendre à qn à faire. **2** *vi* enseigner.

teach·er professeur *m*; (*in primary school*) instituteur, -trice *mf*.

teach·ing enseignement *m*; **t. staff** personnel *m* enseignant.

tea·cup tasse *f* à thé.

team équipe *f*.

▸ **team up** *vi* faire équipe (**with** avec).

tea·pot théière *f*.

tear¹ 1 *n* (*rip*) déchirure. **2** *vt** déchirer.

tear² (*in eye*) larme *f*; **in tears** en larmes.

▸ **tear off, tear out** *vt* (*with force*) arracher; (*receipt, stamp etc*) détacher.

▸ **tear up** *vt* (*letter etc*) déchirer.

tease *vt* taquiner.

tea·spoon petite cuillère *f*, cuillère *f* à café.

tea·spoon·ful cuillerée *f* à café.

tech·ni·cal *adj* technique.

tech·ni·cian technicien, -ienne *mf*.

tech·nique technique *f*.

tech·no·log·i·cal *adj* technologique.

tech·nol·o·gy technologie *f*.

ted·dy bear ours *m* (en peluche).

teen·age *adj* (*boy, girl, behavior*) adolescent; (*magazine, fashion*) pour adolescents.

teen·ag·er adolescent, -ente *mf*.

tee-shirt tee-shirt *m*.

teeth *see* **tooth**.

tee·tot·al·er = personne *f* qui ne boit jamais d'alcool.

tele- *prefix* télé-.

tel·e·com·mu·ni·ca·tions *npl* télécommunications *fpl*.

tel·e·gram télégramme *m*.

tel·e·graph pole poteau *m* télégraphique.

tel·e·phone 1 *n* téléphone *m*; **on the t.** (*speaking*) au téléphone. **2** *adj* (*call, line etc*) téléphonique; (*number*) de téléphone; **t. booth** cabine *f* téléphonique; **t. directory** annuaire *m* du téléphone. **3** *vi* téléphoner. **4** *vt* **to t. sb** téléphoner à qn.

tel·e·scope télescope *m*.

tel·e·vise *vt* retransmettre à la télévision.

tel·e·vi·sion télévision *f*; **on t.** à la télévision; **t. set** téléviseur *m*.

tell*1 *vt* dire (**sb sth** qch à qn; *that* que); (*story*) raconter; (*distinguish*) distinguer (**from** de); (*know*) savoir; **to t. sb to do** dire à qn de faire; **to t. the difference** voir la différence. **2** *vi* **to t. of** *or* **about sth/sb** parler de qch/qn; **to t. on sb** rapporter sur qn.

tell·er (*bank*) **t.** guichetier, -ière *mf* (*de banque*).

▸ **tell off** *vt* disputer.

tem·per **to lose one's t.** se mettre en colère; **in a bad t.** de mauvaise humeur.

tem·per·a·ture température *f*; **to have a t.** avoir de la température.

tem·ple (*building*) temple *m*.

tem·po·rar·i·ly *adj* temporairement.

tem·po·rar·y *adj* provisoire;

USING THE TELEPHONE

Hello?
Allô ?

Hi Claire, it's Alex.
Salut Claire, c'est Alex (à l'appareil).

Hello, Alan Wright speaking?
Allô, Alan Wright à l'appareil ?

Good morning/afternoon, Staff Solutions!
Staff Solutions, bonjour !

Hello, could you put me through to Customer Services, please?
Bonjour, pouvez-vous me passer le service clientèle, s'il vous plaît ?

Can I speak to Julie Rey, please? This is Steve Brown from CPS.
Est-ce que je peux parler à Julie Rey, s'il vous plaît ? C'est Steve Brown de la part de CPS.

Speaking!
C'est moi!

Who's calling, please?
C'est de la part de qui ?

Could you repeat that/spell it?
Pourriez-vous répéter/l'épeler ?

Just a moment, I'll get him/her.
Un instant, je vais le/la chercher.

Hold the line please, I'll put you through.
Ne quittez pas, je vous le/la passe.

I'm afraid she's in a meeting/she's not in.
Je regrette, elle est en réunion/elle n'est pas là.

The line's busy, would you like to hold?
Ça sonne occupé, voulez-vous patienter ?

There's no reply.
Ça ne répond pas.

Would you like to leave a message?
Voulez-vous laisser un message ?

Please leave a message after the tone.
Veuillez laisser un message après le bip.

No thanks, I'll call back later.
Non merci, je rappellerai plus tard.

Can you tell him/her I called?
Vous pouvez lui dire que j'ai appelé ?

Can you ask him/her to call me back as soon as possible?
Pouvez-vous lui demander de me rappeler dès que possible ?

My number is 42-35-59-01.
Mon numéro est le quarante-deux, trente-cinq, cinquante-neuf, zéro-un.

The French read out phone numbers in pairs of digits.

Thank you for calling.
Merci d'avoir appelé.

Talk to you later!
On s'appelle !

Can I take your number?
Je peux avoir votre/ton numéro ?

You can reach me on my cell.
Vous pouvez/Tu peux me joindre sur mon portable.

I'll text you later.
Je vous/t'envoie un SMS plus tard.

I can't get a signal in here.
Je ne capte pas ici.

I don't have many minutes left.
Il ne me reste plus beaucoup de crédit.

I need to charge my cellphone.
J'ai besoin de recharger mon portable.

You've got the wrong number.
Vous vous êtes trompé(e) de numéro.

Sorry, I must have the wrong number.
Désolé(e), j'ai dû me tromper de numéro.

I can barely hear you.
Je vous/t'entends très mal.

We got cut off.
On a été coupés.

Is there a payphone around here?
Est-ce qu'il y a une cabine téléphonique par ici ?

I'd like to call collect.
Je voudrais appeler en PCV.

(job) temporaire; *(secretary)* intérimaire.

tempt *vt* tenter; **tempted to do** tenté de faire.

temp·ta·tion tentation *f.*

tempt·ing *adj* tentant.

ten *adj & n* dix *(m).*

ten·an·cy location *f; (period)* occupation *f.*

ten·ant locataire *mf.*

tend *vi* to t. to do avoir tendance à faire.

ten·den·cy tendance *f* (**to do** à faire).

ten·der *adj (soft, loving)* tendre; *(painful)* sensible.

ten·nis tennis *m*; **table t.** tennis *m* de table; **t. court** court *m* (de tennis); **t. shoes** (chaussures *fpl* de) tennis *fpl.*

tense 1 *adj (person, muscle, situation)* tendu. **2** *n (of verb)* temps *m.*

ten·sion tension *f.*

tent tente *f.*

tenth *adj & n* dixième *(mf).*

term *(word)* terme *m*; *(period)* période *f*; *(semester)* semestre *m*; **terms** *(conditions)* conditions *fpl*; *(prices)* prix *mpl*; **on good/bad terms** en bons/mauvais termes (**with** avec).

ter·mi·nal (air) t. aérogare *f*; **(computer) t.** terminal *m* (d'ordinateur).

ter·mi·nate 1 *vt (work, project)* terminer; *(contract)* résilier; *(pregnancy)* interrompre. **2** *vi* se terminer.

ter·race *(next to house etc)* terrasse *f.*

ter·ri·ble *adj* affreux.

ter·ri·bly *adv (badly, very)* affreusement.

ter·ri·fic *adj Fam (excellent, very great)* formidable.

ter·ri·fy *vt* terrifier; **to be terrified of** avoir très peur de.

ter·ri·fy·ing *adj* terrifiant.

ter·ri·to·ry territoire *m.*

ter·ror terreur *f.*

ter·ror·ist *n & adj* terroriste *(mf).*

test 1 *vt (try)* essayer; *(product, machine)* tester; *(pupil)* interroger; *(of doctor)* examiner *(les yeux etc)*; *(analyze)* analyser *(le sang etc).* **2** *n* essai *m*; *(of product)* test *m*; *(in school)* interrogation *f*, test *m*; *(by doctor)* examen *m*; *(of blood etc)* analyse *f*; **eye t.** examen *m* de la vue.

tes·ta·ment testament *m*; *(tribute)* preuve *f*; **Old/New T.** Ancien/Nouveau Testament *m.*

tes·ti·mo·ny témoignage *m.*

test tube éprouvette *f.*

test-tube ba·by bébé-éprouvette *m.*

text 1 *n* texte *m*; **t. (message)** SMS *m*, texto *m.* **2** *vt (send text message to)* envoyer un SMS *or* un texto à.

text·book manuel *m* (scolaire).

tex·tile *adj & n* textile *(m).*

tex·ture texture *f.*

than *conj* que; **happier t.** plus heureux que. ■ *(with numbers)* de; **more t. six** plus de six.

thank 1 *vt* remercier (**for sth** pour qch; **for doing** d'avoir fait); **t. you!** merci!; **no t. you!** (non) merci! **2** *n* **thanks** remerciements *mpl*; **(many) thanks!** merci (beaucoup)!; **thanks to** *(because of)* grâce à.

thank·ful *adj* reconnaissant (**for** de).

Thanks·giv·ing (day) = 4ème jeudi de novembre, fête commémorant la première action de grâce des colons anglais.

that 1 *conj* que; **to say t.** dire que. **2** *rel pron (subject)* qui; *(object)* que; *(after prep)* lequel, laquelle, *pl* lesquel(le)s; **the boy t. left** le garçon qui est parti; **the book t. I read** le livre que j'ai lu; **the carpet t. I put it on** le tapis sur lequel je l'ai mis; **the house t. she told me about** la maison dont elle m'a parlé; **the**

day/moment t. le jour/moment où.
3 *dem adj* (*pl see* **those**) ce, cet (*before vowel or mute h*); cette; (*opposed to 'this'*) ce… + -là; **t. day** ce jour; ce jour-là; **t. girl** cette fille; cette fille-là. **4** *dem pron* (*pl see* **those**) ça, cela; **t. (one)** celui-ci *m*, celle-la *f*; **give me t.** donne-moi ça or cela; **t.'s right** c'est juste; **who's t.?** qui est-ce?; **t.'s the house** c'est la maison; (*pointing*) voilà la maison; **t. is (to say)** c'est-à-dire. **5** *adv* (*so*) si; **not t. good** pas si bon; **t. much** (*to cost etc*) (au)tant que ça.

thaw 1 *n* dégel *m*. **2** *vi* dégeler; (*of snow*) fondre; (*of food*) décongeler; **it's thawing** ça dégèle. **3** *vt* (*food*) (faire) décongeler.

the le, l', la, *pl* les; **t. roof** le toit; **t. man** l'homme; **t. moon** la lune; **t. boxes** les boîtes; **of t., from t.** du, de l', de la, *pl* des; **to t., at t.** au, à l', à la, *pl* aux.

the·a·ter théâtre *m*.

theft vol *m*.

their *poss adj* leur, *pl* leurs.

theirs *poss pron* le leur, la leur, *pl* les leurs; **this book is t.** ce livre est à eux or est le leur.

them *pron les*; (*after prep, 'than', 'it is'*) eux *mpl*, elles *fpl*; (*to*) **t.** leur; **I see t.** je les vois; **I give (to) t.** je leur donne; **ten of t.** dix d'entre eux/elles; **all of t. came** tous sont venus, toutes sont venues; **I like all of t.** je les aime tous/toutes.

them·selves *pron* eux-mêmes *mpl*, elles-mêmes *fpl*; (*reflexive*) se, s'; (*after prep*) eux *mpl*, elles *fpl*.

then 1 *adv* (*at that time*) à cette époque-là; (*just a moment ago*) à ce moment-là; (*next*) ensuite; **from t. on** dès lors; **before t.** avant cela; **until t.** jusque-là. **2** *conj* (*therefore*) donc.

the·o·ry théorie *f*.

the·ra·py thérapie *f*.

there *adv* là; (*down or over*) **t.** là-bas; **on t.** là-dessus; **t. is, t. are** il y

a; (*pointing*) voilà; **t. he is** le voilà; **that man t.** cet homme-là.

there·fore *adv* donc.

ther·mom·e·ter thermomètre *m*.

Ther·mos® thermos® *m or f*.

ther·mo·stat thermostat *m*.

these 1 *dem adj* (*sing see* **this**) ces; (*opposed to 'those'*) ces… + ci; **t. men** ces hommes; ces hommes-ci. **2** *dem pron* (*sing see* **this**) **t. (ones)** ceux-ci *mpl*, celles-ci *fpl*; **t. are my friends** ce sont mes amis.

the·sis, *pl* -ses thèse *f*.

they *pron* ils *mpl*, elles *fpl*; (*stressed*) eux *mpl*, elles *fpl*; **t. are doctors** ce sont des médecins. ■ (*people in general*) on; **t. say** on dit.

thick 1 *adj* épais (*f* épaisse). **2** *adv* (*to spread*) en couche épaisse.

thick·en 1 *vt* épaissir. **2** *vi* (*of fog etc*) s'épaissir; (*of cream etc*) épaissir.

thick·ly *adv* (*to spread*) en couche épaisse.

thick·ness épaisseur *f*.

thief, *pl* **thieves** voleur, -euse *mf*.

thigh cuisse *f*.

thim·ble dé *m* (à coudre).

thin 1 *adj* (*slice, paper etc*) mince; (*person, leg*) maigre; (*soup*) peu épais (*f* épaisse). **2** *adv* (*to spread*) en couche mince.

thin (down) *vt* (*paint etc*) diluer.

thing chose *f*; **one's things** (*belongings*) ses affaires *fpl*; **it's a good t.** (that) heureusement que.

think*1 *vi* penser (**about, of** à); **to t. (carefully)** réfléchir (**about, of** à); **to t. of doing** penser à faire; **she doesn't t. much of it** ça ne lui dit pas grand-chose. **2** *vt* penser (that que); **I t. so** je pense que oui; **what do you t. of him?** que penses-tu de lui?

▸ **think over** *vt* réfléchir à.

▸ **think up** *vt* inventer.

thin·ly *adv* (*to spread*) en couche mince.

third 1 *adj* troisième. **2** *n* troisième

mf; **a t.** *(fraction)* un tiers. **3** *adv* **to come t.** se classer troisième.

third·ly *adv* troisièmement.

thirst *n* soif *f*.

thirst·y *adj* to be *or* feel t. avoir soif; **to make sb t.** donner soif à qn.

thir·teen *adj & n* treize *(m)*.

thir·teenth *adj & n* treizième *(mf)*.

thir·ti·eth *adj & n* trentième *(mf)*.

thir·ty *adj & n* trente *(m)*.

this **1** *dem adj (pl see these)* ce, cet *(before vowel or mute h)*, cette; *(opposed to 'that')* ce… + ci; **t. book** ce livre; ce livre-ci; **t. photo** cette photo; cette photo-ci. **2** *dem pron (pl see these)* ceci; **t. (one)** celui-ci *m*, celle-ci *f*; **give me t.** donne-moi ceci; **t. is Paul** c'est Paul; *(pointing)* voici Paul. **3** *adv* **t. high** *(pointing)* haut comme ceci; **t. far** jusqu'ici.

thong *(underwear)* string *m*; *(sandal)* tong *f*.

thorn épine *f*.

thor·ough *adj (careful)* minutieux; *(knowledge, examination)* approfondi; **to give sth a t. clean/** *etc* nettoyer/*etc* qch à fond.

thor·ough·ly *adv (completely)* tout à fait; *(carefully)* avec minutie; *(to know, clean etc)* à fond.

those **1** *dem adj (sing see that)* ces; *(opposed to 'these')* ces… + -là; **t. men** ces hommes; ces hommes-là. **2** *dem pron (sing see that)* **t. (ones)** ceux-là *mpl*, celles-là *fpl*; **t. are my friends** ce sont mes amis.

though **1** *conj (even)* **t.** bien que *(+ subjunctive)*; **as t.** comme si. **2** *adv (however)* cependant.

thought *(pt & pp of* think*)* pensée *f*, *(careful)* réflexion *f*.

thought·ful *adj (considerate)* gentil, attentionné.

thought·less *adj (towards others)* pas très gentil; *(absent-minded)* étourdi.

thou·sand *adj & n* mille *(m & adj inv)*; **a t. pages** mille pages; **two t.**

pages deux mille pages; **thousands of** des milliers de.

thread **1** *n (yarn)* fil *m*. **2** *vt (needle, beads)* enfiler.

threat menace *f*.

threat·en *vt* menacer *(to do de faire;* **with sth** de qch*)*.

threat·en·ing *adj* menaçant.

three *adj & n* trois *(m)*.

thresh·old seuil *m*.

threw *pt de* throw.

thrill frisson *m*.

thrilled *adj* ravi *(with sth de qch;* **to do** de faire*)*.

thrill·er film *m*/roman *m* à suspense.

thrill·ing *adj* passionnant.

thrive *vi (person, business, plant)* prospérer; **to t. on sth** avoir besoin de qch pour s'épanouir.

thriv·ing *adj* prospère.

throat gorge *f*.

throne trône *m*.

through **1** *prep (place)* à travers; *(window, door)* par; *(time)* pendant; *(means)* par; **to go** *or* **get t.** *(forest etc)* traverser; *(hole etc)* passer par; *(wall etc)* passer à travers. **2** *adv* à travers; **to let t.** laisser passer; **to be t.** *(finished)* avoir fini; **t. to** *or* **till** jusqu'à; **I'll put you t. (to him)** *(on phone)* je vous le passe.

▸ **through·out** **1** *prep* **t. the neighborhood/***etc* dans tout le quartier/ *etc*; **t. the day/***etc* pendant toute la journée/*etc*. **2** *adv (everywhere)* partout; *(all the time)* tout le temps.

throw* *vt* jeter *(to, at* à*)*; *(party)* donner.

▸ **throw away** *vt (unwanted object)* jeter.

▸ **throw out** *vt (unwanted object)* jeter; *(expel)* mettre à la porte.

▸ **throw up** *vti (vomit)* Fam rendre.

thrust **1** *vt* **t. sth into sth** enfoncer qch dans qch. **2** *n (movement)* mouvement *m* en avant; *(of argument etc)* idée *f* principale.

thud bruit *m* sourd.

thug voyou *m*.

thumb pouce *m*.

thumb·tack punaise *f*.

thun·der 1 *n* tonnerre *m*. 2 *vi* tonner; **it's thundering** il tonne.

thun·der·storm orage *m*.

Thurs·day jeudi *m*.

thus *adv* ainsi.

tick (off) *vt (on list etc)* cocher.

tick·et billet *m*; *(for bus, subway, cloakroom)* ticket *m*; **(price) t.** étiquette *f*.

tick·et col·lec·tor contrôleur, -euse *mf*.

tick·et of·fice guichet *m*.

tick·le *vt* chatouiller.

tick·lish *adj* chatouilleux.

tic-tac-toe morpion *m (jeu)*.

tide marée *f*.

ti·di·ly *adv (to put away)* soigneusement.

ti·dy *adj (place, toys etc)* bien rangé; *(clothes, hair)* soigné; *(person)* ordonné; *(in appearance)* soigné.

tidy (up or away) *vt* ranger.

tie 1 *n (around neck)* cravate *f*; *(game)* match *m* nul. 2 *vt (fasten)* attacher (**to** à); *(a knot)* faire (**in** à); *(shoe)* lacer.

▶ **tie down** *vt* attacher.

▶ **tie up** *vt* attacher (**to** à); *(person)* ligoter.

ti·ger tigre *m*.

tight 1 *adj (clothes fitting too closely)* (trop) étroit; *(drawer, lid)* dur; *(knot, screw)* serré; *(rope, wire)* raide. 2 *adv (to hold, shut)* bien; *(to squeeze)* fort.

tight·en (up) *vt (bolt, screw)* (res)serrer; *(security)* renforcer.

tight·ly *adv (to hold)* bien; *(to squeeze)* fort.

tights *npl* collant(s) *m(pl)*.

tile 1 *n (on roof)* tuile *f*; *(on wall or floor)* carreau *m*. 2 *vt (wall, floor)* carreler.

till 1 *prep & conj* = **until**. 2 *n (for money)* caisse *f* (enregistreuse).

tilt *vti* pencher.

tim·ber bois *m* (de construction).

time 1 *n* temps *m*; *(point in time)* moment *m*; *(period in history)* époque *f*; *(on clock)* heure *f*; *(occasion)* fois *f*; **some/most of the t.** une partie/la plupart du temps; **all of the t.** tout le temps; **in a year's t.** dans un an; **it's t. (to do)** il est temps (de faire); **to have a good t.** s'amuser; **to have a hard t. doing** avoir du mal à faire; **in t.** *(to arrive)* à temps; **from t. to t.** de temps en temps; **what t. is it?** quelle heure est-il?; **on t.** à l'heure; **at the same t.** en même temps (**as** que); *(simultaneously)* à la fois; **for the t. being** pour le moment; **one at a t.** un à un. 2 *vt (athlete etc)* chronométrer; *(activity)* minuter; *(choose the time of)* choisir le moment de.

tim·er *(device)* minuteur *m*; *(built into appliance)* programmateur *m*; *(plugged into socket)* prise *f* programmable.

time·ta·ble horaire *m*; *(of activities)* emploi *m* du temps.

tim·id *adj (afraid)* craintif; *(shy)* timide.

tim·ing **what good t.!** ça tombe bien!

tin *(metal)* étain *m*; *(coated steel or iron)* fer-blanc *m*; *(can)* boîte *f*.

tin·foil papier *m* (d')alu.

ti·ny *adj* tout petit.

tip 1 *n (end)* bout *m*; *(pointed)* pointe *f*; *(money)* pourboire *m*; *(advice)* conseil *m*. 2 *vt (waiter etc)* donner un pourboire à.

tip (out) *vt (liquid, load)* déverser (**into** dans).

tip·toe on t. sur la pointe des pieds.

▶ **tip up, tip over** 1 *vt (tilt)* pencher; *(overturn)* faire basculer. 2 *vi (tilt)* pencher; *(overturn)* basculer.

tire¹ 1 *vt* fatiguer. 2 *vi* se fatiguer.

tire² pneu *m (pl* pneus).

tired vt fatigué; **to be t.** of sth/sb/
doing en avoir assez de qch/de qn/
de faire.

tired·ness fatigue f.

▸**tire out** vt épuiser.

tir·ing adj fatigant.

tis·sue (handkerchief etc) mouchoir m en papier.

ti·tle titre m.

to prep à; (towards) vers; (of attitude) envers; (right up to) jusqu'à;
give it to him donne-le-lui; **to**
France en France; **to Portugal** au
Portugal; **to the butcher(s)/etc**
chez le boucher/etc; **the road to Pa-**
ris la route de Paris; **the train to Pa-**
ris le train pour Paris; **kind/cruel to**
sb gentil/cruel envers qn; **it's ten**
(minutes) to one il est une heure
moins dix. ▪ (with infinitive) **to**
say/do/etc dire/faire/etc, (in order)
to pour. ▪ (with adjective) de; à;
happy/etc to do heureux/etc de
faire; **it's easy/difficult to do** c'est
facile/difficile à faire.

toad crapaud m.

toad·stool champignon m (vénéneux).

toast 1 n pain m grillé; **piece or**
slice of t. tranche f de pain grillé,
toast m. 2 vt (faire) griller.

toast·er grille-pain m inv.

to·bac·co tabac m.

to·bac·co store (bureau m de)
tabac m.

to·bog·gan luge f.

to·day adv aujourd'hui.

tod·dler enfant mf (en bas âge).

toe orteil m.

toe·nail ongle m du pied.

tof·fee caramel m (dur).

to·geth·er adv ensemble; (at the
same time) en même temps; **t. with**
avec.

toi·let (room) toilettes fpl; (bowl,
seat) cuvette f or siège m des cabinets; **to go to the t.** aller aux
toilettes.

toi·let pa·per papier m hygiénique.

toi·let·ries npl articles mpl de toilette.

toi·let wa·ter (perfume) eau f de
toilette.

to·ken (for subway etc) jeton m.

told pt & pp de **tell**.

tol·er·ance tolérance f.

tol·er·ant adj tolérant (**of** à
l'égard de).

tol·er·ate vt tolérer.

toll (fee) péage m; **t. road/bridge**
route f/pont m à péage.

toll-free num·ber = numéro m
vert.

to·ma·to, pl -oes tomate f.

tomb tombeau m.

to·mor·row adv demain; **t.**
morning demain matin; **the day af-**
ter t. après-demain.

ton tonne f (= 907kg); **tons of** (lots
of) Fam des tonnes de.

tone ton m; (dial) **t.** tonalité f.

tongs npl pince f.

tongue langue f.

ton·ic t. (water) Schweppes® m;
gin and t. gin-tonic m.

to·night adv (this evening) ce
soir; (during the night) cette nuit.

tonne = **ton**.

ton·sil amygdale f.

ton·sil·li·tis to have t. avoir une
angine.

too adv trop; (also) aussi; (moreover) en plus; **t. tired to play** trop
fatigué pour jouer; **t. hard to solve**
trop difficile à résoudre; **t. much, t.**
many trop; **t. much salt/t. many**
people/etc trop de sel/gens/etc;
one t. many un de trop.

took pt de **take**.

tool outil m.

tooth, pl **teeth** dent f.

tooth·ache mal m de dents; **to**
have a t. avoir mal aux dents.

tooth·brush brosse f à dents.

tooth·paste dentifrice m.

tooth·pick cure-dent m.

top¹ 1 n (of mountain, tower, tree)
sommet m; (of wall, ladder, page,

garment) haut *m*; *(of table)* dessus *m*; *(of list)* tête *f*; *(of bottle, tube)* bouchon *m*; *(bottle cap)* capsule *f*; *(of saucepan)* couvercle *m*; *(of pen)* capuchon *m*; **at the t. of the class** le premier de la classe; **on t. of** sur. **2** *adj (drawer, shelf)* du haut; *(step, layer)* dernier; *(in competition)* premier; *(maximum)* maximum; **on the t. floor** au dernier étage; **at t. speed** à toute vitesse.

top² *(spinning)* **t.** toupie *f*.

top·ic sujet *m*.

▸ **top up** *vt (glass)* remplir; *(coffee, tea)* remettre.

torch torche *f*.

tor·ment *vt (annoy)* agacer.

tor·na·do, *pl* **-oes** tornade *f*.

tor·toise tortue *f*.

tor·toise·shell écaille *f*.

tor·ture 1 *n* torture *f*. **2** *vt* torturer.

toss 1 *vt (throw)* jeter (**to** à); **to t. a coin** jouer à pile ou face. **2** *vi* **let's t.** jouons à pile ou face.

to·tal *adj & n* total (*m*).

to·tal·ly *adv* totalement.

touch 1 *n (contact)* contact *m*; *(sense)* toucher *m*; **in t. with sb** en contact avec qn; **to get in t.** se mettre en contact. **2** *vt* toucher. **3** *vi (of lines, hands etc)* se toucher; **don't t.!** n'y *or* ne touche pas!

touch·down *(of plane)* atterrissage *m*; *(in football)* essai *m*.

▸ **touch down** *vi (of aircraft)* atterrir.

touch·y *adj* susceptible.

tough *adj (meat)* dur; *(sturdy)* solide; *(strong)* fort; *(difficult, harsh)* dur.

tour 1 *n (journey)* voyage *m*; *(visit)* visite *f*; *(by artist etc)* tournée *f*. **2** *vt* visiter.

tour·ism tourisme *m*.

tour·ist 1 *n* touriste *mf*. **2** *adj* touristique.

tour·ist (in·for·ma·tion) of·fice syndicat *m* d'initiative.

tour·na·ment tournoi *m*.

tow *vt (car, boat)* remorquer; *(trailer)* tracter.

to·ward(s) *prep* vers; *(of feelings)* envers; **cruel/etc t. sb** cruel/etc envers qn.

tow·el serviette *f* (de toilette); *(for dishes)* torchon *m*.

tow·er tour *f*.

town ville *f*; **in t.**, **(in)to t.** en ville.

town coun·cil conseil *m* municipal.

town hall mairie *f*.

town·house maison *f* mitoyenne (en ville).

town·ship canton *m*.

tow truck dépanneuse *f*.

tox·ic *adj* toxique.

toy 1 *n* jouet *m*. **2** *adj (gun)* d'enfant; *(house, car)* miniature.

toy·shop magasin *m* de jouets.

trace 1 *n* trace *f* (**of** de). **2** *vt (with tracing paper)* (dé)calquer; *(find)* retrouver.

trac·ing pa·per papier-calque *m inv*.

track *(of animal, sports stadium etc)* piste *f*; *(of record)* plage *f*; *(for train)* voie *f*; *(path)* chemin *m*; *(racetrack)* champ *m* de courses; **tracks** *(of wheels)* traces *fpl*; **on the right t.** sur la bonne voie.

track shoe *(running shoe)* jogging *m*.

track·suit survêtement *m*.

trac·tor tracteur *m*.

trac·tor-trail·er semi-remorque *m*.

trade 1 *n* commerce *m*; *(job)* métier *m*. **2** *vi* faire du commerce (**with** avec); *(swap)* échanger; **to t. places** changer de place. **3** *vt* échanger (**for** contre).

trade-in *(car etc)* reprise *f*.

trade·mark marque *f* de fabrique; *(registered)* **t.** marque déposée.

trad·er commerçant, -ante *mf*, marchand, -ande *mf*.

trade un·ion syndicat *m*.

trad·ing commerce *m*.

tra·di·tion tradition *f*.

tra·di·tion·al *adj* traditionnel.

traf·fic circulation f, *(air, sea, rail)* trafic m.

traf·fic jam embouteillage m.

traf·fic laws Code m de la route.

traf·fic lights npl feux mpl (de signalisation); *(when red)* feu m rouge.

traf·fic sign panneau m de signalisation.

trag·e·dy tragédie f.

trag·ic adj tragique.

trail 1 n *(of smoke, blood etc)* traînée f. 2 vti *(on the ground etc)* traîner.

trail·er *(for car)* remorque f; *(caravan)* camping-car m; **t. park** = terrain aménagé pour les campingcars.

train¹ train m; *(underground)* rame f; **to go** or **come by t.** prendre le train; **t. set** petit train m; **t. ticket** billet m de train; **t. station** gare f, **t. tracks** voie f ferrée.

train² vt *(teach)* former **(to do** à faire); *(in sport)* entraîner; *(animal, child)* dresser **(to do** à faire). 2 vi recevoir une formation **(as a doctor/etc** de médecin/etc); *(of athlete)* s'entraîner.

trained adj *(skilled)* qualifié; *(nurse, engineer)* diplômé.

train·ee stagiaire mf.

train·er *(of athlete, sportsperson, racehorse)* entraîneur, -euse mf; *(of animal)* dresseur, -euse mf.

train·ing formation f; *(in sports)* entraînement m.

trai·tor traître m.

tramp clochard, -arde mf.

tran·quil·iz·er tranquillisant m.

trans·fer 1 vt *(person, goods etc)* transférer **(to** à). 2 n transfert m **(to** à); *(image)* décalcomanie f.

trans·fu·sion (blood) **t.** transfusion f (sanguine).

tran·sis·tor **t.** (radio) transistor m.

tran·sit transit m; **in t.** en transit.

tran·si·tive adj Grammar transitif.

trans·late vt traduire **(from** de; **into** en).

trans·la·tion traduction f.

trans·la·tor traducteur, -trice mf.

trans·mis·sion transmission f.

trans·mit vt transmettre.

trans·par·ent adj transparent.

trans·plant greffe f.

trans·port 1 vt transporter. 2 n transport m **(of** de); **means of t.** moyen m de transport; **public t.** les transports en commun.

trap 1 n piège m. 2 vt *(animal)* prendre (au piège); *(jam)* coincer; *(cut off by snow etc)* bloquer **(by** par).

trap door trappe f.

trash *(nonsense)* sottises fpl; *(junk)* bric-à-brac m inv; *(waste)* ordures fpl.

trash·can poubelle f.

trash·y adj *(book, movie)* nul; *(goods)* de mauvaise qualité.

trav·el 1 vi voyager. 2 vt *(country, distance)* parcourir. 3 n travel(s) voyages mpl; **t. agent** agent m de voyages; **t. guide** guide m.

trav·el·er voyageur, -euse mf.

trav·el·er's check chèque m de voyage.

trav·el·ing voyages mpl.

trav·el sick·ness *(in car)* mal m de la route; *(in aircraft)* mal m de l'air.

tray plateau m.

treach·er·ous adj *(road, conditions)* très dangereux.

tread* vi marcher **(on** sur).

treas·ure trésor m.

treas·ur·er trésorier, -ère mf.

treat 1 vt traiter; *(consider)* considérer **(as** comme); **to t. sb to sth** offrir qch à qn. 2 n *(special)* **t.** petit extra m; **to give sb a (special) t.** donner une surprise à qn.

treat·ment traitement m.

tre·ble vti tripler.

tree arbre m.

trem·ble vi trembler (**with** de).

tre·men·dous adj (huge) énorme; (dreadful) affreux; Fam (marvellous) formidable.

trench tranchée f.

trend·y adj Fam branché.

tri·al (in court) procès m; **to go** or **be on t.** être jugé, passer en jugement.

tri·an·gle triangle m.

tri·an·gu·lar adj triangulaire.

tribe tribu f.

trib·ute (mark of respect) hommage m; **to pay t.** rendre hommage à.

trick 1 n (joke, of magician etc) tour m; (clever method) astuce f; **to play a t. on sb** jouer un tour à qn. **2** vt tromper.

trick·le 1 n (of liquid) filet m. **2** vi dégouliner.

trick·y adj (problem etc) difficile.

tri·cy·cle tricycle m.

trig·ger (of gun) gâchette f.

trim vt couper (un peu).

trip (journey) voyage m; (outing) excursion f.

trip (over or **up)** vi trébucher; **to t. over sth** trébucher contre qch.

tri·ple vti tripler.

▸**trip up** vi faire trébucher.

tri·umph 1 n triomphe m (**over** sur). **2** vi triompher (**over** de).

triv·i·al adj (unimportant) insignifiant.

trol·ley (streetcar) tramway m.

trom·bone trombone m.

troop·er (soldier) soldat m de cavalerie; (policeman) gendarme m.

troops npl troupes fpl.

tro·phy coupe f, trophée m.

trop·i·cal adj tropical.

trot 1 n trot m. **2** vi trotter.

trou·ble 1 n (difficulty) ennui(s) m(pl); (effort) peine f; (disorder, illness) troubles mpl; **to be in t.** avoir des ennuis; **to get into t.** s'attirer des ennuis (**with** avec); **to go to the t. of doing, take the t. to do**

se donner la peine de faire. **2** vt (inconvenience) déranger; (worry, annoy) ennuyer.

trou·sers npl pantalon m; **a pair of t., some t.** un pantalon.

trout truite f.

tru·ant **to play t.** sécher (la classe).

truck camion m.

truck driv·er, truck·er camionneur m; (over long distances) routier m.

true adj vrai; (accurate) exact; **t. to** (one's promise etc) fidèle à; **to come t.** se réaliser.

trump (card) atout m.

trum·pet trompette f.

trunk (of tree, body) tronc m; (of elephant) trompe f; (case) malle f; (of vehicle) coffre m; **trunks** (for swimming) slip m de bain.

trust 1 n (faith) confiance f (**in** en). **2** vt (person, judgment) avoir confiance en; **to t. sb with sth, to t. sth to sb** confier qch à qn.

truth vérité f.

try 1 vt essayer (**to do, doing** de faire); **to t. one's luck** tenter sa chance. **2** vi essayer; **to t. hard** faire un gros effort. **3** n (attempt) essai m; **to give sth/a t.** essayer qch.

try (out) vt (car, method etc) essayer; (person) mettre à l'essai.

try·ing adj (person) difficile.

▸**try on** vt (clothes, shoes) essayer.

T-shirt tee-shirt m.

tub (basin) baquet m; (bath) baignoire f.

tube tube m.

▸**tuck in** vt (shirt, blanket) rentrer; (person in bed) border.

Tues·day mardi m.

tuft touffe f.

tug vti tirer (**at** sur).

tug(·boat) remorqueur m.

tu·i·tion enseignement m; (lessons) leçons fpl.

tu·lip tulipe f.

tum·ble dégringolade f.

tum·ble (down) vi dégringoler.
tum·ble dry·er sèche-linge m inv.
tum·bler (glass) gobelet m.
tum·my Fam ventre m.
tu·mor tumeur f.
tu·na (fish) thon m.
tune 1 n air m; **in t./out of t.** (instrument) accordé/désaccordé; **to sing in t./out of t.** chanter juste/faux. 2 vt (instrument) accorder; (engine) régler.
tun·ing (of engine) réglage m.
tun·nel tunnel m.
tur·ban turban m.
tur·key dindon m, dinde f; (as food) dinde f.
turn 1 n (movement, in game) tour m; (in road) tournant m; **to take turns** se relayer; **it's your t. (to play)** c'est à toi or (à) ton tour (de jouer). 2 vt tourner; (mattress, pancake) retourner; **to t. sth red/etc** rendre qch rouge/etc; **she's turned twenty** elle a vingt ans passés. 3 vi (of wheel etc) tourner; (turn head or body) se tourner; (become) devenir; **to t. red/etc** devenir rouge/etc.
▸ **turn around** 1 vt (head, object) tourner; (vehicle) faire faire demi-tour à. 2 vi (of person) se retourner.
▸ **turn away** 1 vt (eyes) détourner; (person) renvoyer. 2 vi se détourner.
▸ **turn back** vi retourner.
▸ **turn down** vt (gas, radio etc) baisser; (offer, person) refuser.
▸ **turn into** vt **to t. sb into sth** (change) changer qn en qch; **to t. into sb/sth** se changer en qn/qch.
tur·nip navet m (plante).
▸ **turn off** vt (light, radio etc) éteindre; (faucet) fermer; (machine) arrêter.
▸ **turn on** vt (light, radio etc) mettre; (faucet) ouvrir; (machine) mettre en marche.
▸ **turn out** 1 vt (light) éteindre. 2 vi (happen) se passer.
▸ **turn over** 1 vt (page) tourner. 2 vi (of vehicle, person) se retourner.
turn·pike autoroute f à péage.
▸ **turn up** 1 vt (radio, light etc) mettre plus fort; (collar) remonter. 2 vi (arrive) arriver.
tur·tle tortue f; **sea t.** tortue f de mer.
tur·tle·neck (sweater) col m roulé.
tusk défense f.
tu·tor 1 n précepteur, -trice mf. 2 vt donner des cours particuliers à.
TV télé f.
tweez·ers npl pince f à épiler.
twelfth adj & n douzième (mf).
twelve adj & n douze (m).
twen·ti·eth adj & n vingtième (mf).
twen·ty adj & n vingt (m).
twice adv deux fois; **t. as heavy/etc** deux fois plus lourd/etc.
twig brindille f.
twi·light crépuscule m.
twin jumeau m, jumelle f; **t. brother** frère m jumeau; **t. sister** sœur f jumelle; **t. beds** lits mpl jumeaux.
twine (grosse) ficelle f.
twin·kle vi (of star) scintiller.
twirl 1 vt faire tournoyer. 2 vi tournoyer.
twist 1 vt (wire, arm etc) tordre; (roll) enrouler (**around** autour de); (knob) tourner; **to t. one's ankle** se tordre la cheville. 2 n (turn) tour m; (in road) zigzag m.
▸ **twist off** vt (lid) dévisser.
two adj & n deux (m); **t.-way traffic** circulation f dans les deux sens.
type¹ (sort) genre m, type m.
type² 1 n (print) caractères mpl. 2 vti (write) taper (à la machine).
typed adj tapé à la machine.
type·writ·er machine f à écrire.
typ·i·cal adj typique (**of** de); **that's t. (of him)!** c'est bien lui!
typ·ist dactylo f.

U

UFO abbr (unidentified flying object) OVNI m.

ug·li·ness laideur f.

ug·ly adj laid.

ul·cer ulcère m.

ul·ti·mate adj (last) final; (supreme, best) absolu.

um·brel·la parapluie m; (over table, on beach) parasol m.

um·pire arbitre m.

ump·teen adj Fam je ne sais combien de, des tas de.

un- prefix in-, peu, non, sans.

un·a·ble adj to be u. to do être incapable de faire; **he's u. to swim** il ne sait pas nager.

un·ac·cept·a·ble adj inacceptable.

un·ac·cus·tomed to be u. to sth/to doing ne pas être habitué à qch/à faire.

u·nan·i·mous adj unanime.

u·nan·i·mous·ly adv à l'unanimité.

un·at·trac·tive adj (idea, appearance) peu attrayant; (ugly) laid.

un·a·vail·a·ble adj (person) qui n'est pas disponible; (product) épuisé.

un·a·void·a·ble adj inévitable.

un·a·void·a·bly adv inévitablement; (delayed) pour une raison indépendante de sa volonté.

un·a·ware adj to be u. of sth ignorer qch; to be u. that ignorer que.

un·a·wares adv to catch sb u. prendre qn au dépourvu.

un·bear·a·ble adj insupportable.

un·be·liev·a·ble adj incroyable.

un·break·a·ble adj incassable.

un·but·ton vt déboutonner.

un·cer·tain adj incertain (about,

of de); **it's u. whether** il n'est pas certain que (+ subjunctive); **I'm u. whether to stay** je ne sais pas très bien si je dois rester.

un·cer·tain·ty incertitude f.

un·changed adj inchangé.

un·cle oncle m.

un·clear adj (meaning) qui n'est pas clair; (result) incertain; **it's u. whether** on ne sait pas très bien si.

un·com·fort·a·ble adj (chair etc) inconfortable; (uneasy) mal à l'aise.

un·com·mon adj rare.

un·con·nect·ed adj (facts etc) sans rapport (with avec).

un·con·scious adj (person) sans connaissance.

un·con·sti·tu·tion·al adj inconstitutionnel.

un·con·vinc·ing adj peu convaincant.

un·co·op·er·a·tive adj peu coopératif.

un·cork vt (bottle) déboucher.

un·cov·er vt découvrir.

un·dam·aged adj (goods) en bon état.

un·de·cid·ed adj (person) indécis (about sur).

un·de·ni·a·ble adj incontestable.

un·der 1 prep sous; (less than) moins de; (according to) selon; **children u. nine** les enfants de moins de neuf ans; **u. the circumstances** dans les circonstances; **u. there** là-dessous; **u. it** dessous. **2** adv au-dessous.

un·der- prefix sous-.

un·der·charge vt **I** undercharged him (for it) je ne (le) lui ai pas fait payer assez.

un·der·clothes npl sous-vêtements mpl.

un·der·done adj pas assez cuit.

un·der·es·ti·mate vt sous-estimer.

un·der·go* vt subir.

un·der·grad·u·ate étudiant, -ante *mf* (qui prépare la licence).

un·der·ground *adj* souterrain; **u. passage** passage souterrain.

un·der·line *vt (word etc)* souligner.

un·der·mine *vt* saper.

un·der·neath 1 *prep* sous. **2** *adv* (en) dessous; **the book u.** le livre d'en dessous. **3** *n* dessous *m*.

un·der·pants *npl* slip *m*.

un·der·pass *(on highway)* passage *m* inférieur.

un·der·shirt tricot *m* de corps; *(woman's)* chemise *f* (américaine).

un·der·stand* *vti* comprendre.

un·der·stand·a·ble *adj* compréhensible.

un·der·stand·ing 1 *n* compréhension *f*; *(agreement)* accord *m*; *(sympathy)* entente *f*. **2** *adj (person)* compréhensif.

un·der·stood *adj (agreed)* entendu.

un·der·take* *vt* entreprendre (**to do** de faire).

un·der·tak·er entrepreneur *m* de pompes funèbres.

un·der·tak·ing *(task)* entreprise *f*.

un·der·wa·ter 1 *adj* sous-marin. **2** *adv* sous l'eau.

un·der·wear sous-vêtements *mpl*; *(underpants)* slip *m*.

un·do* *vt* défaire.

un·done *adj* **to come u.** *(of knot etc)* se défaire.

un·doubt·ed·ly *adv* sans aucun doute.

un·dress 1 *vi* se déshabiller. **2** *vt* déshabiller; **to get undressed** se déshabiller.

un·eas·y *adj (ill at ease)* mal à l'aise.

un·em·ployed 1 *adj* au chômage. **2** *n* **the u.** les chômeurs *mpl*.

un·em·ploy·ment chômage *m*; *(payment)* allocation *f* de chômage; **to go on u.** s'inscrire au chômage.

un·em·ploy·ment of·fice = agence *f* nationale pour l'emploi, ANPE *f*.

un·e·ven *adj* inégal.

un·e·vent·ful *adj (trip etc)* sans histoires.

un·ex·pect·ed *adj* inattendu.

un·ex·pect·ed·ly *adv* à l'improviste; *(suddenly)* subitement.

un·fair *adj* injuste (**to sb** envers qn).

un·fair·ly *adv* injustement.

un·fair·ness injustice *f*.

un·faith·ful *adj* infidèle (**to** à).

un·fa·mil·iar *adj* inconnu; **to be u. with sth** ne pas connaître qch.

un·fash·ion·a·ble *adj (subject etc)* démodé; *(restaurant etc)* peu chic *inv*.

un·fas·ten *vt* défaire.

un·fa·vor·a·ble *adj* défavorable.

un·fin·ished *adj* inachevé.

un·fit *adj* en mauvaise santé; *(in bad shape)* pas en forme; *(unsuitable)* impropre (**for** à; **to do** à faire); *(unworthy)* indigne (**for** de; **to do** de faire); *(unable)* inapte (**for** à; **to do** à faire).

un·fold *vt* déplier.

un·for·get·ta·ble *adj* inoubliable.

un·for·giv·a·ble *adj* impardonnable.

un·for·tu·nate *adj* malheureux; **you were u.** tu n'as pas eu de chance.

un·for·tu·nate·ly *adv* malheureusement.

un·friend·ly *adj* froid, peu aimable (**to** avec).

un·fur·nished *adj* non meublé.

un·grate·ful *adj* ingrat.

un·hap·pi·ness tristesse *f*.

un·hap·py *adj (sad)* malheureux; **u. with** *or* **about sth** mécontent de qch.

un·harmed *adj (person)* indemne.

un·health·y *adj (climate etc)* malsain; *(person)* en mauvaise santé.

un·help·ful *adj (person)* peu serviable.

un·hook *vt (picture, curtain)* décrocher; *(dress)* dégrafer.

un·hurt *adj* indemne.

un·hy·gi·en·ic *adj* pas très hygiénique.

u·ni·form uniforme *m.*

un·im·por·tant *adj* peu important.

un·in·hab·it·ed *adj* inhabité.

un·in·jured *adj* indemne.

un·in·ten·tion·al *adj* involontaire.

un·in·ter·est·ing *adj (book etc)* peu intéressant.

un·ion **1** *n* union *f; (labor union)* syndicat *m.* **2** *adj* syndical; **u. member** syndiqué, -ée *mf.*

u·nique *adj* unique.

u·nit unité *f; (of furniture etc)* élément *m; (team)* groupe *m.*

u·nite 1 *vt* unir; *(country, party)* unifier. **2** *vi (of students etc)* s'unir.

u·ni·ver·sal *adj* universel.

u·ni·verse univers *m.*

u·ni·ver·si·ty 1 *n* université *f;* **at u.** à l'université. **2** *adj* universitaire; *(student)* d'université.

un·just *adj* injuste.

un·kind *adj* peu gentil (**to sb** avec qn).

un·know·ing·ly *adj* inconsciemment.

un·known *adj* inconnu.

un·lead·ed *adj (gasoline)* sans plomb.

un·less *conj* à moins que *(+ subjunctive);* **u. she comes** à moins qu'elle ne vienne.

un·like *prep* **u. me, she…** à la différence de moi, elle…; **that's u. him** ça ne lui ressemble pas.

un·like·ly *adj* peu probable; *(unbelievable)* incroyable; **she's u. to win** il est peu probable qu'elle gagne.

un·lim·it·ed *adj* illimité.

un·list·ed *adj (phone number)* sur la liste rouge.

un·load *vt* décharger.

un·lock *vt* ouvrir *(avec une clef).*

un·luck·i·ly *adv* malheureusement.

un·luck·y *adj (person)* malchanceux; *(number etc)* qui porte malheur; **you're u.** tu n'as pas de chance.

un·made *adj (bed)* défait.

un·mar·ried *adj* célibataire.

un·nec·es·sar·y *adj* inutile.

un·no·ticed *adj* **to go u.** passer inaperçu.

un·oc·cu·pied *adj (house)* inoccupé; *(seat)* libre.

un·pack 1 *vt (suitcase)* défaire; *(goods, belongings)* déballer. **2** *vi* défaire sa valise.

un·paid *adj (bill, sum)* impayé; *(work, worker)* bénévole.

un·pleas·ant *adj* désagréable (**to sb** avec qn).

un·plug *vt (appliance)* débrancher.

un·pop·u·lar *adj* peu populaire; **to be u. with sb** ne pas plaire à qn.

un·pre·dict·a·ble *adj* imprévisible; *(weather)* indécis.

un·pre·pared *adj* **to be u. for sth** *(not expect)* ne pas s'attendre à qch.

un·rea·son·a·ble *adj* qui n'est pas raisonnable.

un·rec·og·niz·a·ble *adj* méconnaissable.

un·re·lat·ed *adj (facts etc)* sans rapport (**to** avec).

un·re·li·a·ble *adj (person)* peu sûr; *(machine)* peu fiable.

un·rest agitation *f.*

un·roll 1 *vt* dérouler. **2** *vi* se dérouler.

un·safe *adj (place, machine etc)* dangereux; *(person)* en danger.

un·sat·is·fac·to·ry *adj* peu satisfaisant.

un·screw *vt* dévisser.

un·skilled work·er ouvrier, -ière *mf* non qualifié(e).

un·sta·ble *adj* instable.

un·stead·i·ly *adv (to walk)* d'un pas mal assuré.

un·stead·y *adj (hand, step)* mal assuré; *(table, ladder etc)* instable.

un·suc·cess·ful *adj (attempt etc)* vain; *(candidate)* malheureux; **to be u.** ne pas réussir *(in doing* à faire).

un·suc·cess·ful·ly *adv* en vain.

un·suit·a·ble *adj* qui ne convient pas *(for* à).

un·suit·ed *adj* u. to *(job, activity)* peu fait pour.

un·sure *adj* incertain *(of, about* de).

un·tan·gle *vt* démêler.

un·ti·dy *adj (clothes, hair)* peu soigné; *(room)* en désordre; *(person)* désordonné; *(in appearance)* peu soigné.

un·tie *vt (person, hands)* détacher; *(knot, parcel)* défaire.

un·til 1 *prep* jusqu'à; **u. then** jusque-là; **I didn't come u. yesterday** je ne suis venu qu'hier; **not u. tomorrow** pas avant demain. **2** *conj* jusqu'à ce que *(+ subjunctive)*; **do nothing u. I come** ne fais rien avant que j'arrive.

un·true *adj* faux *(f* fausse).

un·used *adj (new)* neuf *(f* neuve).

un·u·su·al *adj* exceptionnel; *(strange)* étrange.

un·u·su·al·ly *adv* exceptionnellement.

un·veil *vt* dévoiler.

un·want·ed *adj* non désiré.

un·well *adj* indisposé.

un·will·ing *adj* he's u. to do il ne veut pas faire.

un·will·ing·ly *adv* à contrecœur.

un·wor·thy *adj* indigne *(of* de).

un·wrap *vt* ouvrir.

un·zip *vt* ouvrir (la fermeture éclair® de).

up 1 *adv* en haut; *(in the air)* en l'air; *(out of bed)* levé, debout; **to come or go up** monter; **prices are up** les prix ont augmenté; **up there** là-haut; **further or higher up** plus

haut; **up to** *(as far as)* jusqu'à; **it's up to you to do it** c'est à toi de le faire; **that's up to you** ça dépend de toi; **what are you up to?** que fais-tu?; **to walk up and down** marcher de long en large. **2** *prep (a hill)* en haut de; *(a tree)* dans; *(a ladder)* sur; **to go up** *(hill, stairs)* monter.

up·date *vt* mettre à jour.

up·grade 1 *vt (improve)* améliorer; *(promote)* promouvoir; *(software)* mettre à jour. **2** *n (of software)* mise *f* à jour.

up·hill *adv* to go u. monter.

up·hold *vt* maintenir.

up·on *prep* sur.

up·per *adj* supérieur.

up·right *adj & adv (straight)* droit.

up·roar vacarme *m*, tapage *m*.

up·scale *adj* haut de gamme.

up·set *vt* (stomach, routine etc)* déranger; **to u. sb** *(make sad)* peiner qn; *(offend)* vexer qn. **2** *adj (sad)* peiné; *(offended)* vexé; *(stomach)* dérangé; **to have an u. stomach** avoir l'estomac dérangé.

up·side down *adv* à l'envers.

up·stairs 1 *adv* en haut; **to go u.** monter (l'escalier). **2** *adj (people, room)* du dessus.

up-to-date *adj* moderne; *(information)* à jour; *(well-informed)* au courant *(on* de).

up·town les quartiers *mpl* résidentiels.

up·ward(s) *adv* vers le haut; **upwards of five euros** cinq euros et plus.

urge *vt* to u. sb to do conseiller vivement à qn de faire.

ur·gen·cy urgence *f*.

ur·gent *adj* urgent.

ur·gent·ly *adv* d'urgence.

u·rine urine *f*.

us *pron* nous; **(to) us** nous; **she sees us** elle nous voit; **he gives (to) us** il nous donne; **all of us** nous tous; **let's or let us eat!** mangeons!

us·age usage *m*.

use 1 *n* usage *m*, emploi *m*; **to make u. of sth** se servir de qch; **not in u.** hors d'usage; **to be of u.** être utile; **it's no u. crying**/*etc* ça ne sert à rien de pleurer/*etc*; **what's the u. of worrying**/*etc*? à quoi bon s'inquiéter/*etc*? **2** *vt* se servir de, utiliser (**as** comme; **to do, for doing** pour faire); **it's used to do** *or* **for doing** ça sert à faire; **it's used as** ça sert de.

use (up) *vt (fuel)* consommer; *(supplies)* épuiser; *(money)* dépenser.

used 1 *adj (secondhand)* d'occasion. **2** *v aux* **I u. to sing**/*etc* avant, je chantais/*etc*. **3** *adj* **u. to sth/to doing** habitué à qch/à faire; **to get u. to** s'habituer à.

use·ful *adj* utile (**to** à); **to come in u.** être utile.

use·ful·ness utilité *f*.

use·less *adj* inutile; *(person)* nul.

us·er *(of road)* usager *m*; *(of machine, dictionary)* utilisateur, -trice *mf*.

us·er-friend·ly *adj* convivial.

u·su·al *adj* habituel; **as u.** comme d'habitude.

u·su·al·ly *adv* d'habitude.

u·ten·sil ustensile *m*.

u·til·i·ty *(public)* **u.** service *m* public.

ut·ter 1 *adj* complet; *(idiot)* parfait. **2** *vt (a cry)* pousser; *(a word)* dire.

ut·ter·ly *adv* complètement.

U-turn *(in vehicle)* demi-tour *m*.

V

va·can·cy *(post)* poste *m* vacant; *(room)* chambre *f* libre.

va·cant *adj (room, seat)* libre; **v. lot** terrain *m* vague.

va·ca·tion vacances *fpl*; **on v.** en vacances.

va·ca·tion·er vacancier, -ière *mf*.

vac·ci·nate *vt* vacciner.

vac·ci·na·tion vaccination *f*.

vac·cine vaccin *m*.

vac·u·um *vt (carpet etc)* passer à l'aspirateur.

vac·u·um clean·er aspirateur *m*.

vague *adj* vague; *(outline)* flou.

vague·ly *adv* vaguement.

vain *adj* **in v.** en vain.

val·id *adj (ticket etc)* valable.

val·ley vallée *f*.

val·u·a·ble 1 *adj (object)* de (grande) valeur. **2** *npl* **valuables** objets *mpl* de valeur.

val·ue valeur *f*; **it's good v. (for money)** ça a un bon rapport qualité/prix.

valve *(of machine)* soupape *f*; *(in pipe, tube, heart)* valve *f*.

van camionnette *f*, fourgonnette *f*; *(large)* camion *m*.

van·dal vandale *mf*.

van·dal·ize *vt* saccager.

va·nil·la 1 *n* vanille *f*. **2** *adj (ice cream)* à la vanille.

van·ish *vi* disparaître.

var·i·a·ble *adj & n* variable (*f*).

var·i·ant variante *f*.

var·ied *adj* varié.

va·ri·e·ty variété *f*; **a v. of reasons**/*etc* diverses raisons/*etc*; **v. show** spectacle *m* de variétés.

var·i·ous *adj* divers.

var·nish 1 *vt* vernir. **2** *n* vernis *m*.

var·y *vti* varier.

vase vase *m*.

Vas·e·line® vaseline *f*.

vast *adj* vaste.

VCR *abbr (video cassette recorder)* magnétoscope *m*.

veal *(meat)* veau *m*.

veg·e·ta·ble légume *m*.

veg·e·tar·i·an *adj & n* végétarien, -ienne (*mf*).

veg·e·ta·tion végétation *f*.

ve·hi·cle véhicule *m*.

veil voile *m*.

vein *(in body)* veine *f*.

vel·vet 1 *n* velours *m.* **2** *adj* de velours.

vend·ing ma·chine distributeur *m* automatique.

ven·dor vendeur, -euse *mf.*

ve·ne·tian blind store *m* vénitien.

ven·ti·la·tion *(in room)* aération *f.*

ven·ture 1 *vt* hasarder; **to v. to do sth** se hasarder à faire qch. **2** *vi* **to v. out of doors** se risquer à sortir. **3** *n* entreprise *f* (hasardeuse).

ven·ue *(meeting place)* lieu *m* (de rendez-vous); *(for concert etc)* salle *f.*

verb verbe *m.*

ver·bal *adj* verbal.

ver·dict verdict *m.*

verse *(part of song)* couplet *m*; *(poetry)* poésie *f*; **in v.** en vers.

ver·sion version *f.*

ver·sus *prep* contre.

ver·ti·cal *adj* vertical.

ver·y 1 *adv* très; **v. much** beaucoup; **at the v. latest** au plus tard. **2** *adj* *(actual)* même; **his** *or* **her v. brother** son frère même.

vest *(waistcoat)* gilet *m.*

vet vétérinaire *mf.*

vet·er·an *(of war)* ancien combattant *m*; *(experienced person)* vétéran *m.*

vet·er·i·nar·i·an vétérinaire *mf.*

vi·a *prep* par.

vi·brate *vi* vibrer.

vi·bra·tion vibration *f.*

vic·ar pasteur *m.*

vice vice *m*; *(tool)* étau *m.*

vi·cious *adj (spiteful)* méchant; *(violent)* brutal.

vic·tim victime *f*; **to be the v. of** être victime de.

vic·to·ry victoire *f.*

vid·e·o 1 *n (cassette)* cassette *f*; **on v.** sur cassette. **2** *adj (game, camera etc)* vidéo *inv.* **3** *vt (event)* faire une (vidéo)cassette de.

vid·e·o·cas·sette vidéocassette *f*; **v. recorder** magnétoscope *m.*

vid·e·o game jeu *m* vidéo.

vid·e·o·tape cassette *f* vidéo.

view vue *f*; **to come into v.** apparaître; **in my v.** à mon avis; **in v. of** compte tenu de.

view·er *(person)* téléspectateur, -trice *mf.*

view·find·er viseur *m.*

view·point point *m* de vue.

vil·la villa *f.*

vil·lage village *m.*

vil·lag·er villageois, -oise *mf.*

vil·lain scélérat *m*; *(in movie, play)* méchant, -ante *mf.*

vin·e·gar vinaigre *m.*

vine·yard vignoble *m.*

vi·o·lence violence *f.*

vi·o·lent *adj* violent.

vi·o·lent·ly *adv* violemment.

vi·o·lin violon *m.*

VIP *abbr (very important person)* VIP *mf.*

vir·gin vierge *f.*

vir·tu·al *adj* quasi; **v. reality** réalité *f* virtuelle.

vir·tue *(goodness)* vertu *f*; *(advantage)* mérite *m*; **by v. of** en vertu de.

vi·rus virus *m.*

vi·sa visa *m.*

vise étau *m.*

vis·i·ble *adj* visible.

vis·it 1 *n* visite *f*, *(stay)* séjour *m.* **2** *vt (place)* visiter; **to v. sb** rendre visite à qn; *(stay with)* faire un séjour chez qn. **3** *vi* être en visite.

vis·it·ing hours heures *fpl* de visite.

vis·i·tor visiteur, -euse *mf*, *(guest)* invité, -ée *mf.*

vi·tal *adj* essentiel; **it's v. that** il est essentiel que (+ *subjunctive*).

vi·ta·min vitamine *f.*

viv·id *adj* vif; *(description)* vivant.

vo·cab·u·lar·y vocabulaire *m.*

vo·ca·tion·al *adj* profesionnel, -elle.

vod·ka vodka *f.*

voice voix *f*; **at the top of one's v.** à tue-tête.

voice·mail (service) messagerie f vocale; (message) message m vocal.

vol·ca·no, pl -oes volcan m.

volt·age voltage m.

vol·ume (book, capacity, loudness) volume m.

vol·un·tar·y adj volontaire; (unpaid) bénévole.

vol·un·teer 1 n volontaire mf. **2** vi se proposer (**for sth** pour qch; **to do** pour faire).

vom·it vti vomir.

vote 1 n vote m. **2** vi voter; **to v. Republican** voter républicain.

vot·er électeur, -trice mf.

vouch·er (for meal, gift etc) chèque m.

vow·el voyelle f.

voy·age voyage m (par mer).

vul·gar adj vulgaire.

W

wad (of money etc) liasse f; (of cotton wool) tampon m.

wad·dle vi se dandiner.

▸ **wade through** vt (mud, water etc) patauger dans.

wad·ing pool (small, inflatable) piscine f gonflable.

▸ **wad up** vt (paper) chiffonner.

wa·fer gaufrette f.

waf·fle gaufre f.

wag vti (tail) remuer.

wage(·s) n(pl) salaire m.

wage earn·er salarié, -ée mf.

wag·on (horse-drawn) charrette f, chariot m.

waist taille f; **stripped to the w.** torse nu.

waist·coat gilet m.

wait 1 n attente f. **2** vi attendre; **to w. for sb/sth** attendre qn/qch; **w.**

until I've gone, w. for me to go attends que je sois parti; **to keep sb waiting** faire attendre qn.

▸ **wait behind** vi rester.

wait·er garçon m (de café).

wait·ing attente f.

wait·ing room salle f d'attente.

wait·ress serveuse f.

wait·staff serveurs mpl.

▸ **wait up** vi veiller; **to w. up for sb** attendre le retour de qn avant de se coucher.

wake* (up) 1 vi se réveiller. **2** vt réveiller.

walk 1 n promenade f; (shorter) (petit) tour m; (path) allée f; **to go for a w.** faire une promenade; (shorter) faire un (petit) tour; **to take for a w.** (child) emmener se promener; (baby, dog) promener; **five minutes' w. (away)** à cinq minutes à pied. **2** vi marcher; (stroll) se promener; (go on foot) aller à pied. **3** vt (distance) faire à pied; (take for a walk) promener (chien).

▸ **walk away** vi s'éloigner (**from** de).

walk·er (for pleasure) promeneur, -euse mf.

▸ **walk in** vi entrer.

walk·ing stick canne f.

Walk·man®, pl **Walkmans** baladeur m.

▸ **walk off** vi s'en aller; **to walk off with sth** (steal) partir avec qch.

▸ **walk out** vi (leave) partir.

wall mur m; (of cabin, tunnel) paroi f.

wal·let portefeuille m.

wall·pa·per 1 n papier m peint. **2** vt tapisser.

wall-to-wall car·pet(·ing) moquette f.

wal·nut (nut) noix f.

wal·rus (animal) morse m.

wan·der (a·round) vi errer; (stroll) flâner.

want vt vouloir (**to do** faire); (ask for) demander (qn); (need) avoir besoin de; **I w. him to go** je veux qu'il parte; **you're wanted** on vous demande.

WAP *abbr (Wireless Application Protocol)* WAP *m*.

war guerre *f*; **at w.** en guerre (**with** avec).

ward *(in hospital)* salle *f*.

war·den directeur, -trice *mf*.

ward·robe *(built-in)* penderie *f*; *(free-standing)* armoire *f*.

ware·house, *pl* -ses entrepôt *m*.

warm 1 *adj* chaud; **to be** or **feel w.** avoir chaud; **it's (nice and) w.** *(of weather)* il fait *(agréablement)* chaud. **2** *vt (person, food etc)* réchauffer.

warmth chaleur *f*.

▶ **warm up 1** *vt (person, food etc)* réchauffer. **2** *vi (of person, room, engine)* se réchauffer; *(of food, water)* chauffer.

warn *vt* avertir (**that** que); **to w. sb against sth** mettre qn en garde contre qch; **to w. sb against doing** conseiller à qn de ne pas faire.

warn·ing avertissement *m*; *(advance notice)* (pré)avis *m*; **(hazard) w. flashers** *(of vehicle)* feux *mpl* de détresse.

war·rant 1 *n (legal order)* mandat *m*. **2** *vt (justify)* justifier.

war·ran·ty *(for goods)* garantie *f*.

war·ri·or guerrier, -ère *mf*.

war·ship navire *m* de guerre.

wart verrue *f*.

war·time in w. en temps de guerre.

was *pt de* **be**.

wash 1 *n* **to give sth a w.** laver qch; **in the w.** *(of dirty clothes)* au sale. **2** *vt* laver; **to w. one's hands** se laver les mains.

wash·a·ble *adj* lavable.

▶ **wash away, wash off, wash out 1** *vt (stain)* faire partir (en lavant). **2** *vt (floor etc)* partir (au lavage).

wash·ba·sin lavabo *m*.

wash·cloth gant *m* de toilette.

wash·ing *(act)* lavage *m*.

wash·ing ma·chine machine *f* à laver.

▶ **wash out** *(bowl etc)* laver.

wash·room toilettes *fpl*.

▶ **wash up** *vi (wash hands and face)* se laver.

wasp guêpe *f*.

waste 1 *n* gaspillage *m*; *(of time)* perte *f*. **2** *vt (money, food etc)* gaspiller; *(time, opportunity)* perdre.

waste·pa·per vieux papiers *mpl*.

waste·pa·per bas·ket corbeille *f* (à papier).

watch 1 *n (small clock)* montre *f*. **2** *vt* regarder; *(be careful of)* faire attention à. **3** *vi* regarder.

watch·band bracelet *m* de montre.

watch (o·ver) *vt (suspect, baby etc)* surveiller.

watch (out) for *vt (wait for)* guetter.

▶ **watch out** *vi (take care)* faire attention (**for** à); **w. out!** attention!

wa·ter 1 *n* eau *f*; **w. pistol** pistolet *m* à eau. **2** *vt (plant etc)* arroser.

wa·ter·col·or *(picture)* aquarelle *f*; *(paint)* couleur *f* pour aquarelle.

wa·ter·cress cresson *m* (de fontaine).

▶ **water down** *vt (wine etc)* couper (d'eau).

wa·ter·fall chute *f* d'eau.

wa·ter·front bord *m* or front *m* de mer.

wa·ter·ing can arrosoir *m*.

wa·ter·mel·on pastèque *f*.

wa·ter·proof *adj (material)* imperméable.

wa·ter·ski·ing ski *m* nautique.

wa·ter·tight *adj* étanche.

wave 1 *n (of sea)* vague *f*; *(in hair)* ondulation *f*; **medium/short w.** *(on radio)* ondes *fpl* moyennes/ courtes; **long w.** grandes ondes *fpl*, ondes *fpl* longues. **2** *vi (with hand)* faire signe (de la main); **to w. to sb** *(greet)* saluer qn de la main. **3** *vt (arm, flag etc)* agiter.

wave·length longueur *f* d'ondes.
wav·y *adj (hair)* ondulé.
wax 1 *n* cire *f*. **2** *vt* cirer; **to have one's legs waxed** se faire épiler les jambes (à la cire).
wax pa·per papier *m* sulfurisé.
way¹ 1 *n (path)* chemin *m* (**to** de); *(direction)* sens *m*; *(distance)* distance *f*; **all the w., the whole w.** *(to talk etc)* pendant tout le chemin; **this w.** par ici; **that w.** par là; **which w.?** par où?; **to lose one's w.** se perdre; **the w. there** l'aller *m*; **the w. back** le retour; **the w. in** l'entrée *f*; **the w. out** la sortie; **on the w.** en route (**to** pour); **to be** *or* **stand in sb's w.** être sur le chemin de qn; **to get out of the w.** s'écarter; **a long w. (away** *or* **off)** très loin. **2** *adv (behind etc)* très loin; **w. ahead** très en avance (**of** sur).
way² *(manner)* façon *f*; *(means)* moyen *m*; **(in) this w.** de cette façon; **no w.!** *Fam* pas question!
we *pron* nous; **we teachers** nous autres professeurs.
weak *adj* faible; *(tea, coffee)* léger.
weak·en 1 *vt* affaiblir. **2** *vi* faiblir.
weak·ness faiblesse *f*; *(fault)* point *m* faible.
wealth richesse(s) *f(pl)*.
wealth·y *adj* riche.
weap·on arme *f*.
wear* 1 *vt (have on body)* porter; *(put on)* mettre. **2** *n* **w. (and tear)** usure *f*.
▶ **wear off** *vi (of color, effect etc)* disparaître.
▶ **wear out 1** *vt (clothes etc)* user; *(person)* épuiser. **2** *vi* s'user.
wea·ry *adj* fatigué.
wea·sel belette *f*.
weath·er temps *m*; **what's the w. like?** quel temps fait-il?; **it's nice w.** il fait beau; **under the w.** *(ill)* patraque.
weath·er fore·cast, weather report météo *f*.
weave* *vt (cloth)* tisser.

web *(of spider)* toile *f*; **the W.** le Web; **w. page** page *f* web; **w. site** site *m* web.
web·cam webcam *m*.
wed·ding mariage *m*.
wed·ding ring alliance *f*.
wedge 1 *n (under wheel etc)* cale *f*. **2** *vt (table etc)* caler.
Wednes·day mercredi *m*.
weed mauvaise herbe *f*.
week semaine *f*; **a w. from tomorrow** demain en huit.
week·day jour *m* de semaine.
week·end week-end *m*; **over the w.** ce week-end.
week·ly 1 *adj* hebdomadaire. **2** *adv* toutes les semaines. **3** *n (magazine)* hebdomadaire *m*.
weep* *vi* pleurer.
weigh *vti* peser.
weight poids *m*; **by w.** au poids; **to put on w.** grossir; **to lose w.** maigrir.
weird *adj (odd)* bizarre.
wel·come 1 *adj* **to be w.** *(warmly received, of person)* être bien reçu; **w.!** bienvenue!; **to make sb (feel) w.** faire bon accueil à qn; **you're w.!** *(after 'thank you')* il n'y a pas de quoi!; **some coffee/a break would be w.** un café/une pause ne ferait pas de mal. **2** *n* accueil *m*. **3** *vt* accueillir; *(warmly)* faire bon accueil à.
weld *vt* souder.
wel·fare to be on w. vivre d'allocations.
well¹ *(for water)* puits *m*; *(oil)* **w.** puits *m* de pétrole.
well² 1 *adv* bien; **w. done!** bravo!; **as w.** *(also)* aussi; **as w. as** aussi bien que; **as w. as two cats, he has a dog** en plus de deux chats, il a un chien. **2** *adj* bien *inv*; **she's w.** *(healthy)* elle va bien; **to get w.** se remettre. **3** *int* eh bien!; **huge, w., very big** énorme, enfin, très grand.
well-be·haved *adj* sage.
well-be·ing bien-être *m*.

well-in·formed *adj* bien informé.

well-known *adj* (bien) connu.

well-man·nered *adj* bien élevé.

well-off *adj* riche.

well-to-do *adj* aisé.

Welsh 1 *adj* gallois. **2** *n (language)* gallois *m*; **the W.** les Gallois *mpl.*

Welsh·man, *pl* **-men** Gallois *m.*

Welsh·wom·an, *pl* **-women** Galloise *f.*

went *pt de* **go**[1].

were *pt de* **be.**

west 1 *n* ouest *m*; **(to the) w. of** à l'ouest de. **2** *adj (coast)* ouest *inv.* **3** *adv* à l'ouest.

west·bound *adj* en direction de l'ouest.

west·ern 1 *adj (coast)* ouest *inv*; *(culture etc)* occidental. **2** *n (film)* western *m.*

west·ward(s) *adj & adv* vers l'ouest.

wet 1 *adj* mouillé; *(damp, rainy)* humide; *(day, month)* de pluie; '**w. paint**' 'peinture fraîche'; **to get w.** se mouiller; **to make w.** mouiller; **it's w.** *(raining)* il pleut. **2** *vt* mouiller.

whale baleine *f.*

wharf quai *m*, débarcadère *m.*

what 1 *adj* quel, quelle, *pl* quel(le)s; **w. book?** quel livre?; **w. a fool!** quel idiot! **2** *pron (in questions)* qu'est-ce qui; *(object)* (qu'est-ce) que; *(after prep)* quoi; **w.'s happening?** qu'est-ce qui se passe?; **w. does he do?** qu'est-ce qu'il fait?, que fait-il?; **w. is it?** qu'est-ce que c'est?; **w.'s that book?** c'est quoi, ce livre?; **w.!** *(surprise)* quoi!; **w.'s it called?** comment ça s'appelle?; **w. for?** pourquoi?; **w. about me?** et moi?; **w. about leaving?** si on partait? **3** *pron (indirect, relative)* ce qui; *(object)* ce que; **I know w. will happen/w. she'll do** je sais ce qui arrivera/ce qu'elle fera; **w. I need** ce dont j'ai besoin.

what·ev·er 1 *adj* **w. (the) mistake/etc** quelle que soit l'erreur/*etc*; **no chance w.** pas la moindre chance; **nothing w.** rien du tout. **2** *pron (no matter what)* quoi que (+ *subjunctive*); **w. you do** quoi que tu fasses; **w. is important** tout ce qui est important; **do w. you want** fais tout ce que tu veux.

wheat blé *m.*

wheel 1 *n* roue *f*; **at the w.** *(driving)* au volant. **2** *vt* pousser.

wheel·bar·row brouette *f.*

wheel·chair fauteuil *m* roulant.

when 1 *adv* quand. **2** *conj* quand; **w. I finish, w. I've finished** quand j'aurai fini; **w. I saw him** *or* **w. I'd seen him, I left** après l'avoir vu, je suis parti; **the day/moment w.** le jour/moment où.

when·ev·er *conj* quand; *(each time that)* chaque fois que.

where 1 *adv* où; **w. are you from?** d'où êtes-vous? **2** *conj* (là) où; **I found it w. she'd left it** je l'ai trouvé là où elle l'avait laissé; **the place/house w.** l'endroit/la maison où.

where·a·bouts 1 *adv* où (donc). **2** *n* **his w.** l'endroit *m* où il est.

where·as *conj* alors que.

where·by *adv* par quoi.

wher·ev·er *conj* **w. you go** partout où tu iras; **I'll go w. you like** j'irai (là) où vous voudrez.

wheth·er *conj* si; **I don't know w. to leave** je ne sais pas si je dois partir; **w. she does it or not** qu'elle le fasse ou non.

which 1 *adj (in questions etc)* quel, quelle, *pl* quel(le)s; **w. hat?** quel chapeau?; **in w. case** auquel cas. **2** *rel pron (subject)* qui; *(object)* que; *(after prep)* lequel, laquelle, *pl* lesquel(le)s; *(after clause)* ce qui, ce que; **the house w. is old** la maison qui est vieille; **the book w. I like** le livre que j'aime; **the table w. I put it on** la table sur laquelle je l'ai mis; **the film of w.** le film dont; **she's**

sick, w. is sad elle est malade, ce qui est triste; **he lies, w. I don't like** il ment, ce que je n'aime pas. **3** *pron* **w. (one)** *(in questions)* lequel, laquelle, *pl* lesquel(le)s; **w. (one) of us?** lequel *or* laquelle d'entre nous *or* de nous? ■ **w. (one)** *(the one that)* celui qui, celle qui, *pl* ceux qui, celles qui; *(object)* celui *etc* que; **show me w. (one) is red** montrez-moi celui *or* celle qui est rouge; **I know w. (ones) you want** je sais ceux *or* celles que vous désirez.

which·ev·er *adj & pron* **w. book/** *etc or* **w. of the books/***etc* **you buy** quel que soit le livre/*etc* que tu achètes; **take w. books interest you** prenez les livres qui vous intéressent; **take w. (one) you like** prends celui *or* celle que tu veux; **w. (ones) remain** ceux *or* celles qui restent.

while 1 *conj (when)* pendant que; *(although)* bien que *(+ subjunctive)*; *(as long as)* tant que; *(whereas)* tandis que; **while eating/***etc* en mangeant/*etc*. **2** *n* **a w.** un moment; **all the w.** tout le temps.

whim caprice *m*.

whine *vi* gémir.

whip 1 *n* fouet *m*. **2** *vt* fouetter.

▶**whip out** *vt* sortir brusquement.

whirl (a·round) *vi* tourbillonner.

whisk 1 *n (for eggs etc)* fouet *m*. **2** *vt* fouetter.

whisk·ers *npl (of cat)* moustaches *fpl*.

whis·key whisky *m*.

whis·per 1 *vti* chuchoter. **2** *n* chuchotement *m*.

whis·tle 1 *n* sifflement *m*; *(object)* sifflet *m*; **to blow the** *or* **one's w.** siffler. **2** *vti* siffler.

white 1 *adj* blanc *(f* blanche); **to turn w.** blanchir; **w. man** blanc *m*; **w. woman** blanche *f*. **2** *n (color, of egg)* blanc *m*.

white·wash *vt (wall)* badigeonner.

▶**whizz past** *vi* passer à toute vitesse.

who *pron* qui; **w. did it?** qui (est-ce qui) a fait ça?

who·ev·er *pron* qui que ce soit qui; *(object)* qui que ce soit que; **this man, w. he is** cet homme, quel qu'il soit.

whole 1 *adj* entier; *(intact)* intact; **the w. time/village/***etc* tout le temps/village/*etc*; **the w. thing** le tout. **2** *n* **on the w.** dans l'ensemble.

whole·sale 1 *adj (price)* de gros. **2** *adv (to sell)* au prix de gros; *(in bulk)* en gros.

whole·sal·er grossiste *mf*.

whole-wheat *adj (bread)* complet.

whol·ly *adv* entièrement.

whom *pron (object)* que; *(in questions and after prep)* qui; **of w.** dont.

whoop·ing cough coqueluche *f*.

whose *poss pron & adj* à qui, de qui; **w. book is this?** à qui est ce livre?; **w. daughter are you?** de qui es-tu la fille?; **the woman w. book I have** la femme de qui j'ai le livre.

why 1 *adv* pourquoi; **w. not?** pourquoi pas? **2** *conj* **the reason w. they…** la raison pour laquelle ils….

wick mèche *f (de bougie)*.

wick·ed *adj (evil)* méchant; *(mischievous)* malicieux.

wick·er 1 *n* osier *m*. **2** *adj (basket etc)* en osier.

wide 1 *adj* large; *(choice, variety)* grand; **to be three yards w.** avoir trois mètres de large. **2** *adv (to open)* tout grand.

wide-a·wake *adj* éveillé.

wide·ly *adv (to travel)* beaucoup.

wid·en 1 *vt* élargir. **2** *vi* s'élargir.

wide·spread *adj (très)* répandu.

wid·ow veuve *f*.

wid·ow·er veuf *m*.

width largeur *f*.

wife, *pl* **wives** femme *f*.

wig perruque f.
wild adj (animal, flower etc) sauvage.
wil·der·ness désert m.
wild·life nature f.
wild·ly adv (cheer) frénétiquement; (guess) au hasard.
will¹ v aux he will come, he'll come (future tense) il viendra; you will not come, you won't come tu ne viendras pas; you'll come, won't you? tu viendras, n'est-ce pas?; w. you have a cup of tea? veux-tu prendre un thé?; w. you be quiet! veux-tu te taire!; I w.! (yes) oui!
will² volonté f, (legal document) testament m; ill w. mauvaise volonté f, against one's w. à contrecœur.
will·ing adj (helper, worker) de bonne volonté; to be w. to do vouloir bien faire.
will·ing·ly adv (with pleasure) volontiers; (voluntarily) volontairement.
will·ing·ness bonne volonté f, his or her w. to do son empressement m à faire.
wil·low saule m.
win 1 n victoire f. **2** vi* gagner. **3** vt (money, prize, race) gagner.
wind¹ vent m.
wind² * **1** vt (roll) enrouler (around autour de); (clock) remonter. **2** vi (of river, road) serpenter.
wind·break·er blouson m.
wind·mill moulin m à vent.
win·dow fenêtre f, (pane, in vehicle or train) vitre f, (in store) vitrine f, (counter) guichet m; to go w. shopping faire du lèche-vitrines.
win·dow box jardinière f.
win·dow·pane vitre f.
win·dow screen grillage m.
win·dow·sill (inside) appui m de (la) fenêtre; (outside) rebord m de (la) fenêtre.
wind·shield pare-brise m inv; w. wiper essuie-glace m.

wind·surf·ing to go w. faire de la planche (à voile).
wind·y adj it's w. (of weather) il y a du vent.
wine vin m; w. bottle bouteille f à vin; w. list carte f des vins.
wine·glass verre m à vin.
wing aile f.
wink 1 vi faire un clin d'œil (at, to à). **2** n clin m d'œil.
win·ner gagnant, -ante mf, (of argument, fight) vainqueur m.
win·ning 1 adj (number, horse etc) gagnant; (team) victorieux. **2** n winnings gains mpl.
win·ter 1 n hiver m; in (the) w. en hiver. **2** adj d'hiver.
win·ter·time hiver m.
wipe vt essuyer; to w. one's feet/hands s'essuyer les pieds/les mains.
▸ **wipe off, wipe up** vt (liquid) essuyer.
wip·er (in vehicle) essuie-glace m.
wire·less adj sans fil.
wire fil m.
wir·ing (electrical) installation f électrique.
wis·dom sagesse f.
wise adj (in knowledge) sage; (advisable) prudent.
wish 1 vt souhaiter, vouloir (to do faire); I w. (that) you could help me/could have helped me je voudrais que/j'aurais voulu que vous m'aidiez; I w. I hadn't done that je regrette d'avoir fait ça; if you w. si tu veux; I w. you a happy birthday je vous souhaite un bon anniversaire; I w. I could si seulement je pouvais. **2** vi to w. for sth souhaiter qch. **3** n (specific) souhait m; (general) désir m; best wishes (on greeting card) meilleurs vœux mpl; (in letter) amitiés fpl; send him or her my best wishes fais-lui mes amitiés.
wit (humor) esprit m; (person) homme m/femme f d'esprit; wits

(intelligence) intelligence *f*; **to be at one's wits' end** ne plus savoir que faire.

witch sorcière *f*.

with *prep* avec; **come w. me** viens avec moi; **w. no hat**/*etc* sans chapeau/*etc*. ▪ *(at the house of)* chez; **she's staying w. me** elle loge chez moi. ▪ *(cause)* de; **to jump w. joy** sauter de joie. ▪ *(instrument, means)* avec, de; **to write w. a pen** écrire avec un stylo; **to fill w.** remplir de. ▪ *(description)* à; **w. blue eyes** aux yeux bleus.

with·draw *1 vt* retirer. *2 vi* se retirer (**from** de).

with·draw·al retrait *m*.

with·er *vi (of plant etc)* se flétrir.

with·hold* *vt (permission, help)* refuser (**from** à); *(decision)* différer; *(money)* retenir (**from** de); *(information)* cacher (**from** à).

with·in *prep (place, box etc)* à l'intérieur de; **w. 6 miles (of)** *(less than)* à moins de 10 km (de); *(inside an area of)* dans un rayon de 10 km (de); **w. a month** *(to return etc)* avant un mois; *(to finish sth)* en moins d'un mois.

with·out *prep* sans; **w. a tie**/*etc* sans cravate/*etc*; **w. doing** sans faire.

wit·ness *1 n (person)* témoin *m*. *2 vt (accident etc)* être (le) témoin de.

wob·bly *adj (table, tooth)* branlant.

wolf, *pl* **wolves** loup *m*.

wom·an, *pl* **women** femme *f*; **women's** *(clothes etc)* féminin.

won·der *1 n (it's) no w.* ce n'est pas étonnant **(that** que (+ *subjunctive*)**). 2** *vt* se demander **(if** si; **why** pourquoi**). 3** *vi (think)* réfléchir; **I was just wondering** je réfléchissais.

won·der·ful *adj* merveilleux.

won't = will not.

wood *(material, forest)* bois *m*.

wood·en *adj* de *or* en bois.

wood·work *(school subject)* menuiserie *f*.

wool laine *f*.

wool·en 1 *adj* en laine. **2** *n* **woolens** lainages *mpl*.

word *mot m*; *(spoken, promise)* parole *f*; **words** *(of song etc)* paroles *fpl*; **to have a w. with sb** parler à qn; *(advise, criticize)* avoir un mot avec qn; **in other words** autrement dit.

word·ing termes *mpl*.

word pro·cess·ing traitement *m* de texte.

wore *pt* de **wear**.

work 1 *n* travail *m*; *(product, book etc)* œuvre *f*; *(building or repair work)* travaux *mpl*; **out of w.** au chômage; **a day off w.** un jour de congé; **he's off w.** il n'est pas allé travailler; **the works** *(of clock etc)* le mécanisme. **2** *vi* travailler; *(of machine etc)* marcher; *(of drug)* agir. **3** *vt (machine)* faire marcher; **to get worked up** s'exciter.

▸ **work at, work on** *vt (improve)* travailler.

work·bench établi *m*.

work·er travailleur, -euse *mf*; *(manual)* ouvrier, -ière *mf*; **(office) w.** employé, -ée *mf* (de bureau).

work·force main-d'œuvre *f*.

work·ing *adj* **w. class** classe *f* ouvrière; **in w. order** en état de marche.

work·man, *pl* **-men** ouvrier *m*.

▸ **work on** *vt (book, problem etc)* travailler à.

work·out séance *f* d'entraînement.

▸ **work out** *vi (succeed)* marcher; *(do exercises)* s'entraîner; **it works out at 50 euros** ça fait 50 euros. **2** *vt* calculer; *(problem)* résoudre; *(scheme)* préparer; *(understand)* comprendre.

work·shop atelier *m*.

world 1 *n* monde *m*; **all over the w.** dans le monde entier. **2** *adj (war etc)* mondial; *(champion, cup, record)* du monde.

world·wide *adj* mondial.

worm *ver m.*

worn *(pp of* wear*) adj (clothes etc)* usé.

worn-out *adj (object)* complètement usé; *(person)* épuisé.

wor·ri·some *adj* inquiétant.

wor·ry **1** *n* souci *m.* **2** *vi* s'inquiéter (**about sth** de qch; **about sb** pour qn). **3** *vt* inquiéter; **to be worried** être inquiet.

worse **1** *adj* pire, plus mauvais (**than** que); **to get w.** se détériorer; **he's getting w.** *(in health)* il va de plus en plus mal. **2** *adv* plus mal (**than** que); **to be w. off** aller moins bien financièrement.

wors·en *vti* empirer.

wor·ship *vt (person, god)* adorer.

worst **1** *adj* pire, plus mauvais. **2** *adv* (**the) w.** le plus mal. **3** *n* **the w. (one)** le *or* la pire, le *or* la plus mauvais(e); **at w.** au pire.

worth **1** *n* valeur *f;* **to buy 50 dollars w. of gas** acheter pour 50 dollars d'essence. **2** *adj* **to be w. sth** valoir *m;* **how much** *or* **what is it w.?** ça vaut combien?; **the movie's w. seeing** le film vaut la peine d'être vu; **it's w. (one's) while** ça (en) vaut la peine; **it's w. (while) waiting** ça vaut la peine d'attendre.

worth·while *adj (activity)* qui vaut la peine; *(book, movie)* qui vaut la peine d'être lu/vu; *(plan, contribution)* valable; *(cause)* louable.

wor·thy *adj* **w. of sth/sb** digne de qch/qn.

would *v aux* **I w. stay, I'd stay** *(conditional tense)* je resterais; **he w. have done it** il l'aurait fait; **w. you help me, please?** voulez-vous m'aider, s'il vous plaît?; **w. you like some tea?** voudriez-vous (prendre) du thé?; **I w. see her every day** *(in the past)* je la voyais chaque jour.

wound **1** *vt* blesser; **the wounded** les blessés *mpl.* **2** *n* blessure *f.*

wrap (up) **1** *vt* envelopper; *(par-cel)* emballer. **2** *vti* **to w. (oneself) up** *(dress warmly)* se couvrir. **3** *n* plastic w. film *m* plastique.

wrap·per *(of candy)* papier *m.*

wrap·ping *(action, material)* emballage *m;* **w. paper** papier *m* d'emballage.

wreath, *pl* **-s** couronne *f.*

wreck **1** *n (ship)* épave *f; (sinking)* naufrage *m; (train etc)* train *m etc* accidenté; *(accident)* accident *m.* **2** *vt* détruire.

wrench *(tool)* clef *f* (à écrous), clef *f* à molette.

wres·tle *vi* lutter (**with sb** avec qn).

wres·tler lutteur, -euse *mf; (no holds barred)* catcheur, -euse *mf.*

wres·tling *(sport)* lutte *f; (no holds barred)* catch *m.*

wring* (**out**) *vt (clothes by hand)* tordre.

wrin·kle *(on skin)* ride *f.*

wrist poignet *m.*

wrist·watch montre *f.*

write* *vti* écrire.

► **write away for, write off for** *vt (details etc)* écrire pour.

► **write back** *vi* répondre.

► **write down** *vt* noter.

► **write off** *vt (debt)* annuler.

► **write out** *vt* écrire; *(copy)* recopier.

writ·er auteur *m (* **of** de*); (literary)* écrivain *m.*

writ·ing *(handwriting)* écriture *f;* **to put sth (down) in w.** mettre qch par écrit; **some w.** *(on page)* quelque chose d'écrit.

writ·ing desk secrétaire *m.*

writ·ing pad bloc *m* de papier à lettres; *(for notes)* bloc-notes *m.*

writ·ing pa·per papier *m* à lettres.

wrong **1** *adj (sum, idea etc)* faux *(f* fausse*); (direction, time etc)* mauvais; *(unfair)* injuste; **to be w.** *(of person)* avoir tort *(to do* de faire*); (mistaken)* se tromper; **it's w. to swear/etc** c'est mal de jurer/etc; **the clock's w.** la pendule n'est pas à l'heure; **something's w.** quelque chose ne va pas; **something's w. with the phone** le téléphone ne marche pas bien; **something's w. with her arm** elle a quelque chose au bras; **what's w. with you?** qu'est-ce que tu as?; **the w. way around** *or* **up** à l'envers. **2** *adv* mal; **to go w.** *(of plan)* mal tourner. **3** *n* to be in the w. être dans son tort. **wrong·ly** *adv (incorrectly)* mal.

X

X·mas *Fam* Noël *m*.
X-ray 1 *n (photo)* radio(graphie) *f*, *(beam)* rayon *m* X; **to have an X-ray** passer une radio. **2** *vt* radiographier.

Y

yacht yacht *m*.
yard *(of farm, school etc)* cour *f*, *(for storage)* dépôt *m*; *(measure)* yard *m* (= 91,44cm).
yarn *(thread)* fil *m*.
yawn 1 *vi* bâiller. **2** *n* bâillement *m*.
year an *m*, année *f*; **school/fiscal y.** année *f* scolaire/fiscale; **this y.** cette année; **in the y. 1992** en (l'an) 1992; **he's ten years old** il a dix ans; **New Y.** Nouvel An; **New Year's Day** le jour de l'An; **New Year's Eve** la Saint-Sylvestre.
year·ly *adj* annuel.
yeast levure *f*.
yell hurlement *m*.
yell (out) *vti* hurler.

▸**yell at** *vt (scold)* crier après.
yel·low *adj* & *n (color)* jaune *(m)*.
yes *adv* oui; *(contradicting negative question)* si.
yes·ter·day *adv* hier; **y. morning** hier matin; **the day before y.** avant-hier.
yet 1 *adv* encore; *(already)* déjà; **she hasn't come (as) y.** elle n'est pas encore venue; **has he come y.?** est-il déjà arrivé? **2** *conj (nevertheless)* pourtant.
yield *vi* **'y.'** *(road sign)* 'cédez la priorité'.
yo·gurt yaourt *m*.
yolk jaune *m (of egg)*.
you *pron (polite form singular)* vous; *(familiar form singular)* tu; *(polite and familiar form plural)* vous; *(object)* vous; te, t'; *pl* vous; *(after prep, 'than', 'it is')* vous; toi; *pl* vous; **(to) y.** vous; te, t'; *pl* vous; **y. are** vous êtes; tu es; **I see y.** je vous vois; je te vois; **y. teachers** vous autres professeurs; **y. idiot!** espèce d'imbécile! ▪ *(indefinite)* on; *(object)* vous; te, t'; *pl* vous; **y. never know** on ne sait jamais.
young 1 *adj* jeune; **my young(er) brother** mon (frère) cadet; **his** *or* **her youngest brother** le cadet de ses frères; **the youngest son** le cadet. **2** *n (of animals)* petits *mpl*; **the y.** *(people)* les jeunes *mpl*.
young·ster jeune *mf*.
your *poss adj (polite form singular, polite and familiar form plural)* votre, *pl* vos; *(familiar form singular)* ton, ta, *pl* tes; *(one's)* son, sa, *pl* ses.
yours *poss pron* le vôtre, la vôtre, *pl* les vôtres; *(familiar form singular)* le tien, la tienne, *pl* les tien(ne)s; **this book is y.** ce livre est à vous *or* est le vôtre; ce livre est à toi *or* est le tien.
your·self *pron (polite form)* vous-même; *(familiar form)* toi-même; *(reflexive)* vous; te, t'; *(after prep)* vous; toi.

your·selves *pron pl* vous-mêmes;
(reflexive, after prep) vous.

youth jeunesse *f, (young man)* jeune
m, **y. center** maison *f* des jeunes.

Z

ze·bra zèbre *m*.

ze·ro, *pl* -os zéro *m*.

zig·zag 1 *n* zigzag *m*. **2** *adj* en zigzag. **3** *vi* zigzaguer.

zip (up) *vt* fermer (avec une fermeture éclair®).

zip code code *m* postal; *(geo-
graphic area)* division *f* postale.

Zip® drive Comput lecteur *m*
Zip®.

zip·per fermeture *f* éclair®.

zit *(pimple)* Fam bouton *m*.

zone zone *f*.

zoo, *pl* zoos zoo *m*.

zuc·chi·ni, *pl* -ni *or* -nis courgette
f.

French verb conjugations

Regular verbs

	-ER Verbs	**-IR Verbs**	**-RE Verbs**
Infinitive	*donn / er*	*fin / ir*	*vend / re*
1 Present	je donne	je finis	je vends
	tu donnes	tu finis	tu vends
	il donne	il finit	il vend
	nous donnons	nous finissons	nous vendons
	vous donnez	vous finissez	vous vendez
	ils donnent	ils finissent	ils vendent
2 Imperfect	je donnais	je finissais	je vendais
	tu donnais	tu finissais	tu vendais
	il donnait	il finissait	il vendait
	nous donnions	nous finissions	nous vendions
	vous donniez	vous finissiez	vous vendiez
	ils donnaient	ils finissaient	ils vendaient
3 Past historic	je donnai	je finis	je vendis
	tu donnas	tu finis	tu vendis
	il donna	il finit	il vendit
	nous donnâmes	nous finîmes	nous vendîmes
	vous donnâtes	vous finîtes	vous vendîtes
	ils donnèrent	ils finirent	ils vendirent
4 Future	je donnerai	je finirai	je vendrai
	tu donneras	tu finiras	tu vendras
	il donnera	il finira	il vendra
	nous donnerons	nous finirons	nous vendrons
	vous donnerez	vous finirez	vous vendrez
	ils donneront	ils finiront	ils vendront
5 Subjunctive	je donne	je finisse	je vende
	tu donnes	tu finisses	tu vendes
	il donne	il finisse	il vende
	nous donnions	nous finissions	nous vendions
	vous donniez	vous finissiez	vous vendiez
	ils donnent	ils finissent	ils vendent
7 Present participle	donnant	finissant	vendant
8 Past participle	donné	fini	vendu

Note The conditional is formed by adding the following endings to the infinitive: -ais, -ais, -ait, -ions, -iez, -aient. Final 'e' is dropped in infinitives ending '-re'.

(1)

Spelling anomalies of -er verbs

Verbs in **-ger** (eg **manger**) take an extra **e** before endings beginning with **o** or **a**: *Present* je mange, nous mangeons; *Imperfect* je mangeais, nous mangions; *Past historic* je mangeai, nous mangeâmes; *Present participle* mangeant. Verbs in **-cer** (eg **commencer**) change **c** to **ç** before endings beginning with **o** or **a**: *Present* je commence, nous commençons; *Imperfect* je commençais, nous commencions; *Past historic* je commençai, nous commençâmes; *Present participle* commençant. Verbs containing mute **e** in their penultimate syllable fall into two groups. In the first (eg **mener, peser, lever**), **e** becomes **è** before an unpronounced syllable in the present and subjunctive, and in the future and conditional tenses (eg je mène, ils mèneront). The second group contains most verbs ending in **-eler** and **-eter** (eg **appeler, jeter**). These verbs change **l** to **ll** and **t** to **tt** before an unpronounced syllable (eg j'appelle, ils appelleront; je jette, ils jetteront). However, the following four verbs in **-eler** and **-eter** fall into the first group in which **e** changes to mute **e** (eg je pèle, ils pèleront; j'achète, ils achèteront): **geler, peler; acheter, haleter**. Derived verbs (eg **dégeler, racheter**) are conjugated in the same way. Verbs containing **é** in their penultimate syllable change **é** to **è** before the unpronounced endings of the present and subjunctive only (eg je cède but je céderai). Verbs in **-yer** (eg **essuyer**) change **y** to **i** before an unpronounced syllable in the present and subjunctive, and in the future and conditional tenses (eg j'essuie, ils essuieront). In verbs in **-ayer** (eg **balayer**), **y** may be retained before mute **e** (eg je balaie or balaye, ils balaieront or balayeront).

Irregular verbs

Listed below are those verbs considered to be the most useful. Forms and tenses not given are fully derivable, such as the third person singular of the present tense which is normally formed by substituting 't' for the final 's' of the first person singular, eg 'crois' becomes 'croit', 'dis' becomes 'dit'. Note that the endings of the past historic fall into three categories, the 'a' and 'i' categories shown at *donner*, and at *finir* and *vendre*, and the 'u' category which has the following endings: -us, -ut, -ûmes, -ûtes, -urent. Most of the verbs listed below form their past historic with 'u'. The imperfect may usually be formed by adding -ais, -ait, -ions, -iez, -aient to the stem of the first person plural of the present tense, eg 'je buvais' etc may be derived from 'nous buvons' (stem 'buv-' and ending '-ons'); similarly, the present participle may generally be formed by substituting -ant for -ons (eg buvant). The future may usually be formed by adding -ai, -as, -a, -ons, -ez, -ont to the infinitive or to an infinitive without final 'e' where the ending is -re (eg conduire). The imperative usually has the same forms as the second persons singular and plural and first person plural of the present tense.

1 = Present   2 = Imperfect   3 = Past historic   4 = Future
5 = Subjunctive   6 = Imperative   7 = Present participle
8 = Past participle   n = nous   v = vous   † verbs conjugated with **être** only.

Irregular French verbs

abattre	*like* **battre**
† **s'abstenir**	like **tenir**
accourir	*like* **courir**
accueillir	*like* **cueillir**
acquérir	1 j'acquiers, n acquérons 2 j'acquérais 3 j'acquis 4 j'acquerrai 5 j'acquière 7 acquérant 8 acquis
admettre	*like* **mettre**
† **aller**	1 je vais, tu vas, il va, n allons, v allez, ils vont 4 j'irai 5 j'aille, nous allions, ils aillent 6 va, allons, allez (*but note* vas-y)
apercevoir	*like* **recevoir**
apparaître	*like* **connaître**
appartenir	*like* **tenir**
apprendre	*like* **prendre**
asseoir	1 j'assieds, il assied, n asseyons, ils asseyent 2 j'asseyais 3 j'assis 4 j'assiérai 5 j'asseye 7 asseyant 8 assis
atteindre	1 j'atteins, n atteignons, ils atteignent 2 j'atteignais 3 j'atteignis 4 j'atteindrai 5 j'atteigne 7 atteignant 8 atteint
avoir	1 j'ai, tu as, il a, n avons, v avez, ils ont 2 j'avais 3 j'eus 4 j'aurai 5 j'aie, il ait, n ayons, ils aient 6 aie, ayons, ayez 7 ayant 8 eu
battre	1 je bats, il bat, n battons 5 je batte
boire	1 je bois, n buvons, ils boivent 2 je buvais 3 je bus 5 je boive, n buvions 7 buvant 8 bu
bouillir	1 je bous, n bouillons, ils bouillent 2 je bouillais 3 *not used* 5 je bouille 7 bouillant
combattre	*like* **battre**
commettre	*like* **mettre**
comprendre	*like* **prendre**
conclure	1 je conclus, n concluons, ils concluent 5 je conclue
conduire	1 je conduis, n conduisons 3 je conduisis 5 je conduise 8 conduit
connaître	1 je connais, il connaît, n connaissons 3 je connus 5 je connaisse 7 connaissant 8 connu
conquérir	*like* **acquérir**
consentir	*like* **conduire**
contenir	*like* **tenir**
contraindre	*like* **atteindre**
contredire	*like* **dire** *except* 1 v contredisez
convaincre	*like* **vaincre**
convenir	*like* **tenir**
coudre	1 je couds, il coud, n cousons, ils cousent 3 je cousis 5 je couse 7 cousant 8 cousu

courir	1 je cours, n courons 3 je courus 4 je courrai 5 je coure 8 couru
couvrir	1 je couvre, n couvrons 2 je couvrais 5 je couvre 8 couvert
craindre	*like* **atteindre**
croire	1 je crois, n croyons, ils croient 2 je croyais 3 je crus 5 je croie, n croyions 7 croyant 8 cru
cueillir	1 je cueille, n cueillons 2 je cueillais 4 je cueillerai 5 je cueille 7 cueillant
cuire	1 je cuis, n cuisons 2 je cuisais 3 je cuisis 5 je cuise 7 cuisant 8 cuit
débattre	*like* **battre**
décevoir	*like* **recevoir**
découvrir	*like* **couvrir**
décrire	*like* **écrire**
déduire	*like* **conduire**
défaire	*like* **faire**
déplaire	*like* **plaire**
déteindre	*like* **atteindre**
détruire	*like* **conduire**
† **devenir**	*like* **tenir**
devoir	1 je dois, n devons, ils doivent 2 je devais 3 je dus 4 je devrai 5 je doive, n devions 6 *not used* 7 devant 8 dû, due, *pl* dus, dues
dire	1 je dis, n disons, v dites 2 je disais 3 je dis 5 je dise 7 disant 8 dit
disparaître	*like* **connaître**
dissoudre	1 je dissous, n dissolvons 2 je dissolvais 5 je dissolve 7 dissolvant 8 dissous, dissoute
distraire	1 je distrais, n distrayons 2 je distrayais 3 *none* 5 je distraie 7 distrayant 8 distrait
dormir	*like* **mentir**
éclore	1 il éclôt, ils éclosent 8 éclos
écrire	1 j'écris, n écrivons 2 j'écrivais 3 j'écrivis 5 j'écrive 7 écrivant 8 écrit
élire	*like* **lire**
émettre	*like* **mettre**
émouvoir	1 j'émeus, n émouvons, ils émeuvent 2 j'émouvais 3 j'émus (*rare*) 4 j'émouvrai 5 j'émeuve, n émouvions 8 ému
endormir	*like* **mentir**
enfreindre	*like* **atteindre**
† **s'enfuir**	*like* **fuir**
entretenir	*like* **tenir**
envoyer	4 j'enverrai
éteindre	*like* **atteindre**
être	1 je suis, tu es, il est, n sommes, v êtes, ils sont 2 j'étais 3 je fus 4 je serai 5 je sois, n soyons, ils soient 6 sois, soyons, soyez 7 étant 8 été

French verb conjugations

exclure	*like* **conclure**
extraire	*like* **distraire**
faillir	*(defective)* 3 je faillis 4 je faillirai 8 failli
faire	1 je fais, n faisons, v faites, ils font 2 je faisais 3 je fis 4 je ferai 5 je fasse 7 faisant 8 fait
falloir	*(impersonal)* 1 il faut 2 il fallait 3 il fallut 4 il faudra 5 il faille 6 *none* 7 *none* 8 fallu
frire	*(defective)* 1 je fris, tu fris, il frit 4 je frirai *(rare)* 6 fris *(rare)* 8 frit *(for other persons and tenses use* faire frire*)*
fuir	1 je fuis, n fuyons, ils fuient 2 je fuyais 3 je fuis 5 je fuie 7 fuyant 8 fui
haïr	1 je hais, il hait, n haïssons
inscrire	*like* **écrire**
instruire	*like* **conduire**
interdire	*like* **dire** *except* 1 v interdisez
interrompre	*like* **rompre**
intervenir	*like* **tenir**
introduire	*like* **conduire**
joindre	*like* **atteindre**
lire	1 je lis, n lisons 2 je lisais 3 je lus 5 je lise 7 lisant 8 lu
maintenir	*like* **tenir**
mentir	1 je mens, n mentons 2 je mentais 5 je mente 7 mentant
mettre	1 je mets, n mettons 2 je mettais 3 je mis 5 je mette 7 mettant 8 mis
moudre	je mouds, il moud, n moulons 2 je moulais 3 je moulus 5 je moule 7 moulant 8 moulu
† mourir	1 je meurs, n mourons, ils meurent 2 je mourais 3 je mourus 4 je mourrai 5 je meure, n mourions
† naître	1 je nais, il naît, n naissons 2 je naissais 3 je naquis 4 je naîtrai 5 je naisse 7 naissant 8 né
nuire	1 je nuis, n nuisons 2 je nuisais 3 je nuisis 5 je nuise 7 nuisant 8 nui
obtenir	*like* **tenir**
offrir	*like* **couvrir**
ouvrir	*like* **couvrir**
paître	*(defective)* 1 il paît 2 il paissait 3 *none* 4 il paîtra 5 il paisse 7 paissant 8 *none*
paraître	*like* **connaître**
parcourir	*like* **courir**
† partir	*like* **mentir**
† parvenir	*like* **tenir**
peindre	*like* **atteindre**
permettre	*like* **mettre**
plaindre	*like* **atteindre**
plaire	1 je plais, il plaît, n plaisons 2 je plaisais 3 je plus 5 je plaise 7 plaisant 8 plu
pleuvoir	*(impersonal)* 1 il pleut 2 il pleuvait 3 il plut 4 il pleuvra 5 il pleuve 6 *none* 7 pleuvant 8 plu
poursuivre	*like* **suivre**

(5)

pouvoir	1 je peux *or* je puis, tu peux, il peut, n pouvons, ils peuvent 2 je pouvais 3 je pus 4 je pourrai 5 je puisse 6 *not used* 7 pouvant 8 pu
prédire	*like* **dire** *except* 1 v prédisez
prendre	1 je prends, il prend, n pronons, ils prennent 2 je prenais 3 je pris 5 je prenne 7 prenant 8 pris
prescrire	*like* **écrire**
pressentir	*like* **mentir**
prévenir	*like* **tenir**
prévoir	*like* **voire** *except* 4 je prévoirai
produire	*like* **conduire**
promettre	*like* **mettre**
† **provenir**	*like* **tenir**
rabattre	*like* **battre**
recevoir	1 je reçois, n recevons, ils reçoivent 2 je recevais 3 je reçus 4 je recevrai 5 je reçoive, n recevions, ils reçoivent 7 recevant 8 reçu
reconduire	*like* **conduire**
reconnaître	*like* **connaître**
reconstruire	*like* **conduire**
recoudre	*like* **coudre**
recouvrir	*like* **couvrir**
recueillir	*like* **cueillir**
redire	*like* **dire**
réduire	*like* **conduire**
refaire	*like* **faire**
rejoindre	*like* **atteindre**
relire	*like* **lire**
reluire	*like* **nuire**
rendormir	*like* **mentir**
renvoyer	*like* **envoyer**
† **repartir**	*like* **mentir**
repentir	*like* **mentir**
reprendre	*like* **prendre**
reproduire	*like* **conduire**
résoudre	1 je résous, n résolvons 2 je résolvais 3 je résolus 5 je résolve 7 résolvant 8 résolu
ressentir	*like* **mentir**
resservir	*like* **mentir**
ressortir	*like* **mentir**
restreindre	*like* **atteindre**
retenir	*like* **tenir**
† **revenir**	*like* **tenir**
revivre	*like* **vivre**
revoir	*like* **voir**
rire	1 je ris, n rions 2 je riais 3 je ris 5 je rie, n riions 7 riant 8 ri
rompre	*regular except* 1 il rompt
satisfaire	*like* **faire**

French verb conjugations

savoir	1 je sais, n savons, il savent 2 je savais 3 je sus 4 je saurai 5 je sache 6 sache, sachons, sachez 7 sachant 8 su
sentir	*like* **mentir**
servir	*like* **mentir**
sortir	*like* **mentir**
souffrir	*like* **couvrir**
sourire	*like* **rire**
soustraire	*like* **distraire**
soutenir	*like* **tenir**
† **se souvenir**	*like* **tenir**
suffire	1 je suffis, n suffisons 2 je suffisais 3 je suffis 5 je suffise 7 suffisant 8 suffi
suivre	1 je suis, n suivons 2 je suivais 3 je suivis 5 je suive 7 suivant 8 suivi
surprendre	*like* **prendre**
survivre	*like* **vivre**
taire	1 je tais, n taisons 2 je taisais 3 je tus 5 je taise 7 taisant 8 tu
teindre	*like* **atteindre**
tenir	1 je tiens, n tenons, ils tiennent 2 je tenais 3 je tins, tu tins, il tint, n tînmes, v tîntes, ils tinrent 4 je tiendrai 5 je tienne 7 tenant 8 tenu
traduire	*like* **conduire**
traire	*like* **distraire**
transmettre	*like* **mettre**
vaincre	1 je vaincs, il vainc, n vainquons 2 je vainquais 3 je vainquis 5 je vainque 7 vainquant 8 vaincu
valoir	1 je vaux, il vaut, n valons 2 je valais 3 je valus 4 je vaudrai 5 je vaille 6 *not* used 7 valant 8 valu
† **venir**	*like* **tenir**
vivre	1 je vis, n vivons 2 je vivais 3 je vécus 5 je vive 7 vivant 8 vécu
voir	1 je vois, n voyons 2 je voyais 3 je vis 4 je verrai 5 je voie, n voyions 7 voyant 8 vu
vouloir	1 je veux, il veut, n voulons, ils veulent 2 je voulais 3 je voulus 4 je voudrai 5 je veuille 6 veuille, veuillons, veuillez 7 voulant 8 voulu

Countries and regions

Africa *(African)* — Afrique f *(africain)*
South/North Africa *(South/North African)* — Afrique du Sud/Nord *(sud-/nord-africain)*
Algeria *(Algerian)* — Algérie f *(algérien)*
America *(American)* — Amérique f *(américain)*
South/North America *(South/North American)* — Amérique du Sud/Nord *(sud-/nord-américain)*
Argentina *(Argentinian)* — Argentine f *(argentin)*
Asia *(Asian)* — Asie f *(asiatique)*
Australia *(Australian)* — Australie f *(australien)*
Austria *(Austrian)* — Autriche f *(autrichien)*
Belgium *(Belgian)* — Belgique f *(belge)*
Brazil *(Brazilian)* — Brésil m *(brésilien)*
Canada *(Canadian)* — Canada m *(canadien)*
Caribbean (the) *(Caribbean)* — Antilles fpl (les) *(antillais)*
China *(Chinese)* — Chine f *(chinois)*
CIS *(abbr* Commonwealth of Independent States) — CEI f *(abrév* Communauté des États Indépendants)
Cuba *(Cuban)* — Cuba m *(cubain)*
Cyprus *(Cypriot)* — Chypre f *(c(h)ypriote)*
Czech Republic *(Czech)* — République f tchèque *(tchèque)*
Denmark *(Danish)* — Danemark m *(danois)*
Egypt *(Egyptian)* — Égypte f *(égyptien)*
England *(English)* — Angleterre f *(anglais)*
Europe *(European)* — Europe f *(européen)*
Finland *(Finnish)* — Finlande f *(finlandais)*
France *(French)* — France f *(français)*
Germany *(German)* — Allemagne f *(allemand)*
Great Britain *(British)* — Grande-Bretagne f *(britannique)*
Greece *(Greek)* — Grèce f *(grec)*
Holland *(Dutch)* — Pays-Bas mpl *(néerlandais)*
Hungary *(Hungarian)* — Hongrie f *(hongrois)*
India *(Indian)* — Inde f *(indien)*
Indonesia *(Indonesian)* — Indonésie f *(indonésien)*
Iran *(Iranian)* — Iran m *(iranien)*
Iraq *(Iraqi)* — Irak m *(irakien)*
Ireland *(Irish)* — Irlande f *(irlandais)*
Israel *(Israeli)* — Israël m *(israélien)*

Countries and regions

Italy *(Italian)*	Italie f *(italien)*
Jamaica *(Jamaican)*	Jamaïque f *(jamaïcain)*
Japan *(Japanese)*	Japon m *(japonais)*
Kenya *(Kenyan)*	Kenya m *(kényan)*
Korea *(Korean)*	Corée f *(coréen)*
South/North Korea	Corée du Sud/Nord
(South/North Korean)	*(sud-nord-coréen)*
Lebanon *(Lebanese)*	Liban m *(libanais)*
Libya *(Libyan)*	Libye f *(libyen)*
Luxembourg *(Luxembourgish)*	Luxembourg m *(luxembourgeois)*
Malaysia *(Malaysian)*	Malaisie *(malais)*
Mexico *(Mexican)*	Mexique m *(mexicain)*
Morocco *(Moroccan)*	Maroc m *(marocain)*
New Zealand	Nouvelle-Zélande f *(néo-zélandais)*
Nigeria *(Nigerian)*	Nigéria m *(nigérian)*
Norway *(Norwegian)*	Norvège f *(norvégien)*
Pakistan *(Pakistani)*	Pakistan m *(pakistanais)*
Philippines *(Filipino)*	Philippines fpl *(philippin)*
Poland *(Polish)*	Pologne f *(polonais)*
Portugal *(Portuguese)*	Portugal m *(portugais)*
Romania *(Romanian)*	Roumanie f *(roumain)*
Russia *(Russian)*	Russie f *(russe)*
Saudi Arabia *(Saudi)*	Arabie f Saoudite *(saoudien)*
Scotland *(Scottish)*	Écosse f *(écossais)*
Slovakia *(Slovak)*	Slovaquie *(slovaque)*
Spain *(Spanish)*	Espagne f *(espagnol)*
Sweden *(Swedish)*	Suède f *(suédois)*
Switzerland *(Swiss)*	Suisse f *(suisse)*
Syria *(Syrian)*	Syrie f *(syrien)*
Thailand *(Thai)*	Thaïlande f *(thaïlandais)*
Tunisia *(Tunisian)*	Tunisie f *(tunisien)*
Turkey *(Turkish)*	Turquie f *(turc)*
United Kingdom *(British)*	Royaume-Uni m *(britannique)*
United States *(American)*	États-Unis mpl *(américain)*
Vietnam *(Vietnamese)*	Viêt-nam m *(vietnamien)*
Wales *(Welsh)*	Pays m de Galles *(gallois)*
West Indies *(West Indian)*	Antilles fpl *(antillais)*

Français – Anglais
French – English

A

a *voir* **avoir**.

à *prép* (à + le = **au** [o], à + les = **aux** [o]) *(direction: lieu)* to; *(temps)* till, to; **aller à Paris** to go to Paris; **de 3 à 4 h** from 3 till *ou* to 4 (o'clock). ▪ *(position: lieu)* at, in; *(surface)* on; *(temps)* at; **être au bureau/à la ferme/au jardin/à Paris** to be at *ou* in the office/on *ou* at the farm/in the garden/in Paris; **à 8 h** at 8 (o'clock); **à mon arrivée** on (my) arrival; **à lundi!** see you (on) Monday! ▪ *(description)* **l'homme à la barbe** the man with the beard; **verre à liqueur** liqueur glass. ▪ *(attribution)* **donner qch à qn** to give sth to sb, to give sb sth. ▪ *(devant infinitif)* **apprendre à lire** to learn to read; **travail à faire** work to do; **maison à vendre** house for sale. ▪ *(appartenance)* **c'est (son livre) à lui** it's his (book); **c'est à vous de** *(décider, protester etc)* it's up to you to; *(lire, jouer etc)* it's your turn to. ▪ *(prix)* for; **pain à un euro** loaf for one euro. ▪ *(poids)* by; **vendre au poids** to sell by weight. ▪ *(moyen, manière)* **à bicyclette** by bicycle; **à la main** by hand; **à pied** on foot; **au crayon** in pencil; **au galop** at a gallop; **deux à deux** two by two. ▪ *(appel)* **au voleur!** (stop) thief!

abaisser *vt* to lower.

abaisser (s') *vpr (barrière)* to lower; *(température)* to drop.

abandon *m (de sportif)* withdrawal; **à l'a.** in a neglected state.

abandonner 1 *vt (travail)* to give up; *(endroit)* to desert. **2** *vi* to give up; *(sportif)* to withdraw.

abasourdi, -ie *adj* stunned.

abat-jour *m inv* lampshade.

abattoir *m* slaughterhouse.

abattre* *vt (mur)* to knock down; *(arbre)* to cut down; *(animal)* to slaughter; *(avion)* to shoot down; *(personne)* to shoot.

abattre (s') *vpr* **s'a. sur** *(pluie)* to come down on; *(tempête)* to hit.

abattu, -ue *adj (mentalement)* dejected; *(physiquement)* exhausted.

abbaye *f* abbey.

abbé *m (prêtre)* priest.

abcès *m* abscess.

abdomen *m* stomach, abdomen.

abeille *f* bee.

aberrant, -ante *adj* absurd.

abîmer *vt* to ruin.

abîmer (s') *vpr* to get ruined.

aboiement *m* bark; **aboiements** barking.

abolir *vt* to abolish.

abominable *adj* terrible.

abondance *f* **une a. de** plenty of.

abondant, -ante *adj* plentiful.

abonné, -ée *mf (à un journal, au téléphone)* subscriber.

abonnement *m* subscription; **(carte d')a.** *(de train)* season pass.

abonner (s') *vpr* to subscribe, to take out a subscription (**à** to).

abord (d') *adv* first.

abordable *adj (prix, marchandises)* affordable.

abordage *m (assaut)* boarding.

aborder 1 *vi* to land. **2** *vt (personne)* to approach; *(problème)* to tackle; *(navire)* to board.

aboutir *vi* to succeed; **a. à** to lead to; **n'a. à rien** to come to nothing.

aboyer *vi* to bark.

abréger *vt (récit)* to shorten.

abreuvoir *m (récipient)* drinking trough.

abréviation *f* abbreviation.

abri *m* shelter; **a. (de jardin)** (garden) shed; **à l'a. de** *(vent)* sheltered from; *(besoin)* safe from; **sans a.** homeless.

abricot *m* apricot.

abricotier *m* apricot tree.

abriter *vt* to shelter.

abriter (s') *vpr* to (take) shelter.

abrupt, -e *adj (pente etc)* steep.

abrutir *vt (télévision)* to stupefy, to numb; *(travail)* to exhaust.

absence *f* absence.

absent, -ente 1 *adj* absent, away. **2** *mf* absentee.

absenter (s') *vpr* to go away (**de** from).

absolu, -ue *adj* absolute.

absolument *adv* absolutely.

absorbant, -ante *adj (papier)* absorbent; *(travail, lecture)* absorbing.

absorber *vt* to absorb.

abstenir* (s') *vpr* to refrain (**de faire** from doing).

absurde *adj* absurd.

absurdité *f* absurdity. **dire des absurdités** to talk nonsense.

abus *m* abuse; *(de nourriture)* overindulgence (**de** in).

abuser *vi* to go too far; **a. de** *(situation, personne)* to take unfair advantage of; *(friandises)* to overindulge in.

acajou *m* mahogany.

accabler *vt* to overwhelm (**de** with).

accalmie *f* lull.

accéder *vi* **a. à** *(lieu)* to reach.

accélérateur *m* accelerator.

accélérer *vi* to accelerate.

accélérer (s') *vpr* to speed up.

accent *m* accent; *(sur une syllabe)* stress.

accepter *vt* to accept; **a. de faire** to agree to do.

accès *m* access (**à** to); *(de folie, colère, toux)* fit; *(de fièvre)* bout; **'a. Interdit'** 'no entry'.

accessoires *mpl (de voiture etc)* accessories; *(de théâtre)* props.

accident *m* accident; **a. d'avion/ de train** plane/train crash.

accidentel, -elle *adj* accidental.

acclamations *fpl* cheers.

acclamer *vt* to cheer.

accolade *f (embrassade)* embrace; *(signe)* curly bracket.

accommoder *vt (assaisonner)* to prepare.

accompagnateur, -trice *mf (musical)* accompanist; *(d'un groupe)* guide.

accompagnement *m (musical)* accompaniment.

accompagner *vt (personne)* to go *ou* come with; *(chose, musique)* to accompany.

accomplir *vt* to carry out.

accord *m* agreement; *(musical)* chord; **tomber d'a.** to reach an agreement; **être d'a.** to agree (**avec** with); **d'a.!** all right!

accordéon *m* accordion.

accorder *vt (donner)* to grant; *(instrument)* to tune; *(verbe)* to make agree.

accorder (s') *vpr (s'entendre)* to get along.

accotement *m (of road)* shoulder.

accouchement *m* delivery.

accoucher *vi* to give birth (**de** to).

accouder (s') *vpr* **s'a. à** *ou* **sur** to lean on *(with one's elbows)*.

accoudoir *m* armrest.

accourir* *vi* to come running.

accoutumer (s') *vpr* to get accustomed (**à** to).

accroc *m* tear (**à** in).

accrochage *m (de voitures)* minor collision.

accrocher *vt (déchirer)* to catch; *(fixer)* to hook; *(suspendre)* to hang up *(on a hook)*; *(heurter)* to hit.

accrocher (s') *vpr (se cramponner)* to cling (**à** to); *(ne pas céder)* to persevere.

accroissement *m* increase (**de** in).

accroître *vt*, **s'accroître** *vpr* to increase.

accroupi, -ie *adj* squatting.

accroupir (s') *vpr* to squat (down).

accueil *m* welcome.

accueillant, -ante *adj* welcoming.

accueillir* *vt* to welcome.

accumuler *vt*, **s'accumuler** *vpr* to pile up.

accusation *f* accusation; *(au tribunal)* charge.

accusé, -ée *mf* accused; *(à la cour d'assises)* defendant.

accuser *vt* to accuse (**de** of); *(rendre responsable)* to blame (**de** for).

acharnement *m* (stubborn) determination.

acharner (s') *vpr* **s'a. sur** *(attaquer)* to lay into; **s'a. à faire** to struggle to do.

achat *m* purchase; **faire des achats** to go shopping.

acheter *vti* to buy; **a. à qn** to buy from sb; *(pour qn)* to buy for sb.

acheteur, -euse *mf* buyer; *(dans un magasin)* shopper.

achever *vt* to finish (off); **a. de faire qch** *(personne)* to finish doing sth; **a. qn** *(tuer)* to finish sb off.

acide 1 *adj* sour. **2** *m* acid.

acier *m* steel.

acné *f* acne.

acompte *m* deposit.

acquéreur *m* purchaser.

acquérir* *vt (acheter)* to purchase; *(obtenir)* to acquire.

acquisition *f (achat)* purchase.

acquittement *m (d'un accusé)* acquittal.

acquitter *vt (dette)* to pay; *(accusé)* to acquit.

acquitter (s') *vpr* **s'a. envers qn** to repay sb.

acrobate *mf* acrobat.

acrobatie(s) *f(pl)* acrobatics.

acrobatique *adj* acrobatic.

acte *m (action, de pièce de théâtre)* act.

acteur, -trice *mf* actor, actress.

actif, -ive 1 *adj* active. **2** *m Grammaire* active.

action *f* action; *(en Bourse)* share, stock.

actionnaire *mf* shareholder.

activer *vt (feu)* to boost.

activer (s') *vpr (se dépêcher) Fam* to get a move on.

activité *f* activity.

actualité *f (événements)* current affairs; **actualités** *(à la télévision etc)* news.

actuel, -elle *adj (présent)* present; *(contemporain)* topical.

actuellement *adv* at the present time.

adaptateur *m* adapter.

adaptation *f* adjustment; *(de roman)* adaptation.

adapter *vt* to adapt; *(ajuster)* to fit (**à** to).

adapter (s') *vpr* **s'a. à** *(s'habituer)* to adapt to, to adjust to; *(tuyau etc)* to fit.

additif *m* additive.

addition *f* addition; *(au restaurant)* check.

additionner *vt* to add (**à** to); *(nombres)* to add up.

adepte *mf* follower.

adéquat, -ate *adj* appropriate; *(quantité)* adequate.

adhérent, -ente *mf* member.

adhérer *vi* **a. à** *(coller)* to stick to; *(s'inscrire)* to join.

adhésif, -ive *adj & m* adhesive.

adieu, -x *int & m* farewell.

adjectif *m* adjective.

adjoint, -ointe *mf* assistant; **a. au maire** deputy mayor.

adjuger *vt* **a. qch à qn** *(prix, contrat)* to award sth to sb; *(aux enchères)* to knock sth down to sb.

admettre* *vt (laisser entrer, accueillir, reconnaître)* to admit; *(autoriser, tolérer)* to allow; *(candidat)* to pass; **être admis à** *(examen)* to have passed.

administratif, -ive *adj* administrative.

administration *f* administration; **l'A.** *(service public)* the Civil Service.

administrer *vt (gérer, donner)* to administer.

admirable *adj* admirable.
admirateur, -trice *mf* admirer.
admiratif, -ive *adj* admiring.
admiration *f* admiration.
admirer *vt* to admire.
admissible *adj (tolérable)* acceptable, admissible; **candidat a.** = candidate who has qualified for the oral examination.
admission *f* admission (**à, dans** to).
adolescent, -ente *mf* adolescent, teenager.
adopter *vt* to adopt.
adoptif, -ive *adj (fils, patrie)* adopted.
adoption *f* adoption.
adorable *adj* adorable.
adoration *f* worship.
adorer *vt* to love, to adore (**faire** doing); *(dieu)* to worship.
adosser (s') *vpr* to lean back (**à** against).
adoucir *vt (voix, traits)* to tone down.
adoucir (s') *vpr (temps)* to turn milder.
adresse *f (domicile)* address; *(habileté)* skill.
adresser *vt (lettre)* to send; *(compliment, remarque)* to address; **a. la parole à** to speak to.
adresser (s') *vpr* s'a. à to speak to; *(aller trouver)* to go and see; *(bureau)* to (go and) ask at; *(être destiné à)* to be aimed at.
adroit, -oite *adj* skillful.
ADSL *m abrév (asymmetric digital subscriber line)* broadband.
adulte *mf adj* adult, grown-up.
adverbe *m* adverb.
adversaire *mf* opponent.
aération *f* ventilation.
aérer *vt* to air (out).
aérien, -ienne *adj (photo)* aerial; **attaque/transport aérien(ne)** air attack/transport.
aérobic *m* aerobics.
aérogare *f* air terminal.

aéroglisseur *m* hovercraft.
aéroport *m* airport.
aérosol *m* aerosol.
affaiblir *vt,* s'affaiblir *vpr* to weaken.
affaire *f (question)* matter; **affaires** business; *(effets)* things; **avoir a. à** to have to deal with; **c'est mon a.** that's my business; **faire une bonne a.** to get a bargain.
affamé, -ée *adj* starving.
affection *f (attachement)* affection.
affectueux, -euse *adj* affectionate, loving.
affichage *m* **panneau d'a.** billboard.
affiche *f* poster.
afficher *vt (affiche)* to stick up.
affirmatif, -ive *adj (ton, réponse)* positive, affirmative.
affirmation *f* assertion.
affirmer *vt* to assert.
affliger *vt* to distress.
affluence *f* crowd; **heure(s) d'a.** rush hour(s).
affluent *m* tributary.
affolant, -ante *adj* terrifying.
affolement *m* panic.
affoler *vt* to drive crazy.
affoler (s') *vpr* to panic.
affranchir *vt (lettre)* to stamp.
affranchissement *m (tarif)* postage.
affreux, -euse *adj* horrible.
affront *m* insult; **faire un a. à** to insult.
affrontement *m* confrontation.
affronter *vt* to confront; *(mauvais temps, difficultés etc)* to brave.
affûter *vt* to sharpen.
afin 1 *prép* **a. de** *(+ infinitif)* in order to. 2 *conj* **a. que** *(+ subjonctif)* so that.
africain, -aine 1 *adj* African. 2 *mf* **A.** African.
agaçant, -ante *adj* irritating.
agacer *vt* to irritate.
âge *m* age; **quel â. as-tu?** how old

are you?; **d'un certain â.** middle-aged; **le moyen â.** the Middle Ages.
âgé, -ée *adj* elderly; **â. de six ans** six years old; **enfant â. de six ans** six-year-old child.
agence *f* agency; *(succursale)* branch office; **a. immobilière** real estate office.
agenda *m* appointment book.
agenouiller (s') *vpr* to kneel (down); **être agenouillé** to be kneeling (down).
agent *m* agent; **a. (de police)** police officer; **a. immobilier** real estate agent.
agglomération *f* built-up area; *(ville)* town.
aggloméré *n* fiberboard.
aggravation *f (de maladie)* aggravation; *(de situation)* worsening.
aggraver *vt*, **s'aggraver** *vpr (situation, maladie)* to get worse; *(état de santé)* to deteriorate; *(difficultés)* to increase.
agile *adj* agile.
agilité *f* agility.
agir *vpr* to act.
agir (s') *vpr* **il s'agit d'argent/***etc* it's a question *ou* matter of money/*etc*; **de quoi s'agit-il?** what is it?, what's it about?
agitation *f (de la mer)* roughness; *(d'une personne)* restlessness.
agité, -ée *adj (mer)* rough; *(personne)* restless.
agiter *vt (remuer)* to stir; *(secouer)* to shake; *(brandir)* to wave.
agiter (s') *vpr (enfant)* to fidget.
agneau, -x *m* lamb.
agrafe *f* hook; *(pour papiers)* staple.
agrafer *vt (robe)* to do up; *(papiers)* to staple.
agrafeuse *f* stapler.
agrandir *vt* to enlarge.
agrandir (s') *vpr* to expand.
agrandissement *m (de ville)* expansion; *(de maison)* extension; *(de photo)* enlargement.

agréable *adj* pleasant.
agréer *vt* **veuillez a. (l'expression de) mes salutations distinguées** *(dans une lettre)* sincerely yours.
agresser *vt* to attack.
agresseur *m* attacker; *(dans la rue)* mugger.
agressif, -ive *adj* aggressive.
agression *f (dans la rue)* mugging.
agressivité *f* aggressiveness.
agricole *adj* **ouvrier/machine a.** farm worker/machine; **travaux agricoles** farm work.
agriculteur *m* farmer.
agriculture *f* farming.
aguets (aux) *adv* on the look-out.
ah! *int* ah!, oh!
ai *voir* **avoir**.
aide 1 *f* help; **à l'a. de** with the aid of. **2** *mf (personne)* assistant.
aider *vt* to help (**à faire** to do).
aider (s') *vpr* **s'a. de** to make use of.
aïe! *int* ouch!
aie(s), aient *voir* **avoir**.
aigle *m* eagle.
aigre *adj* sour.
aigu, -uë *adj (douleur)* acute; *(dents)* sharp; *(voix)* shrill.
aiguillage *m (pour train)* switches.
aiguille *f (à coudre, de pin)* needle; *(de montre)* hand.
aiguiller *vt (train)* to switch.
aiguilleur *m* signalman; **a. du ciel** air-traffic controller.
aiguiser *vt* to sharpen.
ail *m* garlic.
aile *f* wing; *(de moulin à vent)* sail; *(d'automobile)* fender.
ailier *m Sport* wing.
aille(s), aillent *voir* **aller**[1].
ailleurs *adv* somewhere else; **d'a.** *(du reste)* anyway.
aimable *adj (gentil)* kind; *(sympathique)* likeable.
aimant *m* magnet.
aimanter *vt* to magnetize.
aimer *vt* to love; **a. (bien)** *(apprécier)* to like, to be fond of; **a. faire**

to like doing *ou* to do; **a. mieux** to prefer.

aimer (s') *vpr* ils s'aiment they're in love.

aîné, -ée 1 *adj (de deux frères etc)* elder, older; *(de plus de deux)* eldest, oldest. **2** *mf (de deux)* elder *ou* older (child); *(de plus de deux)* eldest *ou* oldest (child).

ainsi *adv (comme ça)* (in) this *ou* that way; **a. que** as well as; **et a. de suite** and so on.

air¹ *m* air; *(mélodie)* tune; **en plein a.** in the open (air), outdoors; **ficher en l'a.** *Fam (jeter)* to chuck, to pitch; *(gâcher)* to mess up; **en l'a.** *(jeter)* (up) in the air; *(paroles)* empty.

air² *m (expression)* look; **avoir l'a.** to look, to seem; **avoir l'a. de** to look like.

aire *f* area; **a. de stationnement** parking area.

aisance *f (facilité)* ease; *(prospérité)* affluence.

aise *f* à l'a. *(dans un vêtement etc)* comfortable; *(dans une situation)* at ease; **mal à l'a.** uncomfortable.

aisé, -ée *adj (facile)* easy; *(riche)* comfortably off.

aisselle *f* armpit.

ait *voir* **avoir**.

ajourner *vt* to postpone; *(après le début de la séance)* to adjourn.

ajout *m* addition (à to).

ajouter *vti* to add (à to).

ajuster *vt (pièce, salaires)* to adjust; **a. à** *(adapter)* to fit to.

alaise *f* (waterproof) undersheet.

alarme *f (signal)* alarm, **a. antivol/ d'incendie** burglar/fire alarm.

alarmer *vt* to alarm.

album *m (de timbres etc)* album.

alcool *m* alcohol; *(spiritueux)* spirits; **a. à 90°** rubbing alcohol.

alcoolique *adj & mf* alcoholic.

alcoolisé, -ée *adj* alcoholic.

alcootest® *m* breath test; *(appareil)* Breathalyzer®.

alentours *mpl* surroundings.

alerte *f* alarm; **en état d'a.** on the alert.

alerter *vt* to warn.

algèbre *f* algebra.

algérien, -ienne 1 *adj* Algerian. **2** *mf* A. Algerian.

algue(s) *f(pl)* seaweed.

alibi *m* alibi.

aliéné, -ée *mf* insane person.

alignement *m* alignment.

aligner *vt*, **s'aligner** *vpr* to line up.

aliment *m* food.

alimentaire *adj* ration/*etc* **a.** food rations/*etc*; **produits alimentaires** foods.

alimentation *f (action)* feeding; *(régime)* diet; *(nourriture)* food; **magasin d'a.** grocery store.

alimenter *vt (nourrir)* to feed.

allaiter *vti* to breastfeed.

allécher *vt* to tempt.

allée *f (de parc etc)* path; *(de cinéma, supermarché etc)* aisle.

allégé, -ée *adj (fromage etc)* low-fat.

alléger *vt* to make lighter.

allemand, -ande 1 *adj* German. **2** *mf* A. German. **3** *m (langue)* German.

aller¹* *vi (aux être)* to go; **a. à** *(convenir à)* to suit; **a. avec** *(vêtement)* to go with; **a. bien/mieux** *(personne)* to be well/better; **il va savoir/***etc* he'll know/*etc*, he's going to know/*etc*; **il va partir** he's about to leave, he's going to leave; **va voir!** go and see!; **comment vas-tu?**, **(comment) ça va?** how are you?; **ça va!** all right!, fine!; **allez-y!** go on!, go ahead!; **allez! au lit!** come on *ou* go on to bed!

aller² *m* outward journey; **a. (simple)** one-way (ticket); **a. (et) retour** round-trip (ticket).

aller (s'en) *vpr* to go away; *(tache)* to come out.

allergie *f* allergy.

allergique *adj* allergic (à to).

alliance *f (anneau)* wedding ring; *(de pays)* alliance.

allié, -ée *mf* ally.

allier *vt* to combine (**à** with); *(pays)* to ally (**à** with).

allier (s') *vpr (pays)* to become allied (**à** with, to).

allô! *int* hello!

allocation *f* allowance, benefit; **a. (de) chômage** unemployment benefit; **allocations familiales** child benefit.

allongé, -ée *adj (étiré)* elongated.

allonger 1 *vt (bras)* to stretch out; *(jupe)* to lengthen. **2** *vi (jours)* to get longer.

allonger (s') *vpr* to stretch out.

allouer *vt* **a. qch à qn** *(ration)* to allocate sb sth; *(indemnité)* to grant sb sth.

allumage *m (de voiture)* ignition.

allumer *vt (feu, cigarette, gaz)* to light; *(électricité)* to turn *ou* switch on.

allumer (s') *vpr (lumière)* to come on.

allumette *f* match.

allure *f (vitesse)* pace; *(de véhicule)* speed; *(air)* look.

allusion *f* allusion; **faire a. à** to refer to.

alors *adv (en ce cas-là)* so; **a. que** *(tandis que)* whereas.

alouette *f* (sky)lark.

alourdir *vt* to weigh down.

alourdir (s') *vpr* to become heavy *ou* heavier.

Alpes (les) *fpl* the Alps.

alphabet *m* alphabet.

alphabétique *adj* alphabetical.

alpinisme *m* mountain climbing.

alpiniste *mf* mountain climber.

alterner *vti* to alternate.

altitude *f* height.

alu *m* **papier (d')a.** tinfoil.

aluminium *m* aluminum; **papier a.** tinfoil.

amabilité *f* kindness.

amaigri, -ie *adj* thin(ner).

amaigrissant *adj* **régime a.** (weight-loss) diet.

amande *f* almond.

amant *m* lover.

amarrer *vt* to moor.

amarres *fpl* moorings.

amas *m* heap, pile.

amasser *vt*, **s'amasser** *vpr* to pile up.

amateur *m (d'art etc)* lover; *(sportif)* amateur; **une équipe a.** an amateur team.

ambassade *f* embassy.

ambassadeur, -drice *mf* ambassador.

ambiance *f* atmosphere.

ambigu, -uë *adj* ambiguous.

ambitieux, -euse *adj* ambitious.

ambition *f* ambition.

ambulance *f* ambulance.

ambulant, -ante *adj* traveling.

âme *f* soul.

amélioration *f* improvement.

améliorer *vt*, **s'améliorer** *vpr* to improve.

aménagement *m (disposition)* fitting out; *(transformation)* conversion.

aménager *vt (arranger)* to fit out (**en** as); *(transformer)* to convert (**en** into).

amende *f* fine.

amener *vt* to bring.

amer, -ère *adj* bitter.

américain, -aine 1 *adj* American. **2** *mf* **A.** American.

amertume *f* bitterness.

ameublement *m* furniture.

ami, -ie *mf* friend; *(de la nature etc)* lover (**de** of); **petit a.** boyfriend; **petite amie** girlfriend.

amical, -e, -aux *adj* friendly.

amincir *vt* to make thin *or* thinner; **cette robe t'amincit** that dress makes you look thinner.

amiral, -aux *m* admiral.

amitié *f* friendship.

amonceler (s') *vpr* to pile up.

amont (en) *adv* upstream.

amorce *f (de pêcheur)* bait; *(de pistolet d'enfant)* cap.

amortir *vt (coup)* to cushion; *(bruit)* to deaden.

amortisseur *m* shock absorber.

amour *m* love; **pour l'a. de** for the sake of.

amoureux, -euse 1 *mf* lover. **2** *adj* **a. de qn** in love with sb.

amour-propre *m* self-respect.

amovible *adj* removable.

amphithéâtre *m* *(romain)* amphitheater; *(à l'université)* lecture hall.

ample *adj* *(vêtement)* full, ample.

amplement *adv* fully, amply; **c'est a. suffisant** it's more than enough.

ampleur *f* *(de robe)* fullness.

amplificateur *m* amplifier.

amplifier *vt* *(son, courant)* to amplify.

ampoule *f* *(électrique)* (light) bulb; *(aux pieds etc)* blister; *(de médicament)* phial.

amputer *vt* to amputate.

amusant, -ante *adj* amusing.

amusement *m* amusement.

amuser *vt* to entertain.

amuser (s') *vpr* to enjoy oneself, to have fun; **s'a. avec** to play with; **s'a. à faire** to amuse oneself doing.

amygdales *fpl* tonsils.

an *m* year; **il a dix ans** he's ten (years old); **Nouvel A.** New Year.

analogue *adj* similar.

analphabète *adj & mf* illiterate.

analyse *f* analysis.

analyser *vt* to analyze.

ananas *m* pineapple.

anarchie *f* anarchy.

anatomie *f* anatomy.

ancêtre *m* ancestor.

anchois *m* anchovy.

ancien, -ienne *adj* old, *(meuble)* antique; *(qui n'est plus)* former; *(antique)* ancient; *(dans une fonction)* senior.

anciennement *adv* formerly.

ancienneté *f* *(âge)* age; *(expérience)* seniority.

ancre *f* anchor.

ancrer *vt* to anchor.

andouille *f* *Fam* fool; **espèce d'a.!** (you) fool!

âne *m* *(animal)* donkey; *(personne)* ass.

anéantir *vt* to wipe out.

anecdote *f* anecdote.

ânesse *f* female donkey.

anesthésie *f* anesthesia; **a. générale** general anesthetic.

anesthésier *vt* to anesthetize.

ange *m* angel.

angine *f* throat infection.

anglais, -aise 1 *adj* English. **2** *mf* **A.** Englishman, Englishwoman; **les A.** the English. **3** *m* *(langue)* English.

angle *m* angle; *(de rue)* corner.

anglophone 1 *adj* English-speaking. **2** *mf* English speaker.

angoissant, -ante *adj* distressing.

angoisse *f* (great) anxiety, anguish.

angoisser (s') *vpr* to get anxious.

anguille *f* eel.

animal, -e, -aux *m & adj* animal.

animateur, -trice *mf* *(de télévision)* emcee; *(de club)* leader, organizer.

animation *f* *(des rues)* activity; *(de réunion)* liveliness.

animé, -ée *adj* lively.

animer *vt* *(débat)* to lead; *(soirée)* to liven up; *(mécanisme)* to drive.

animer (s') *vpr* *(rue etc)* to come to life.

anis *m* aniseed.

ankylosé, -ée *adj* stiff.

anneau, -x *m* ring.

année *f* year; **bonne a.!** Happy New Year!

annexe *f* *(bâtiment)* annex(e).

anniversaire *m* *(d'événement)* anniversary; *(de naissance)* birthday.

annonce *f* *(publicitaire)* advertisement; **petites annonces** classified advertisements.

annoncer *vt* to announce; *(vente)* to advertise.

annoncer (s') *vpr* **s'a. pluvieux/difficile/etc** to look rainy/difficult/etc.

annuaire *m* (*téléphonique*) directory, phone book.

annuel, -elle *adj* yearly.

annulaire *m* ring finger.

annulation *f* cancelation.

annuler *vt* to cancel.

ânonner *vt* to stumble through.

anonymat *m* anonymity; **garder l'a.** to remain anonymous.

anonyme 1 *adj* anonymous. **2** *mf* anonymous person.

anorak *m* parka.

anorexie *f* anorexia.

anormal, -e, -aux *adj* abnormal.

anse *f* (*de tasse etc*) handle.

Antarctique (l') *m* the Antarctic.

antécédent *m* Grammaire antecedent; **antécédents** (*de personne*) past record; **antécédents médicaux** medical history.

antenne *f* (*de radio, d'insecte*) antenna.

antérieur, -eure *adj* (*précédent*) former; (*placé devant*) front.

antibiotique *m* antibiotic.

antibrouillard *adj & m* (**phare**) **a.** fog light.

antichoc *adj inv* shockproof.

anticipé, -ée *adj* (*retraite, retour*) early; (*paiement*) advance.

anticorps *m* antibody.

antilope *f* antelope.

antipathique *adj* disagreeable.

antiquaire *mf* antique dealer.

antique *adj* ancient.

antiquité *f* (*temps, ancienneté*) antiquity; (*objet ancien*) antique.

antivol *m* anti-theft device.

anxiété *f* anxiety.

anxieux, -euse *adj* anxious.

août *m* August.

apaisant, -ante *adj* soothing.

apaiser *vt* (*personne*) to calm; (*douleur*) to soothe.

apercevoir* *vt* to see; (*brièvement*) to catch a glimpse of.

apercevoir (s') *vpr* **s'a. de** to realize.

aperçu *m* (*idée*) general idea.

apéritif *m* aperitif.

aphte *m* mouth ulcer.

apitoyer (s') *vpr* **s'a. sur son sort** to feel sorry for oneself.

aplanir *vt* (*terrain*) to level; (*difficulté*) to iron out, to smooth out.

aplati, -ie *adj* flat.

aplatir *vt* to flatten (out).

aplomb (d') *adv* (*meuble etc*) level, straight.

apostrophe *f* (*signe*) apostrophe.

apparaître* *vi* to appear.

appareil *m* (*électrique*) appliance; (*téléphonique*) telephone; (*avion*) aircraft; (*dentaire*) braces; (*digestif*) system; **a. (photo)** camera.

apparemment *adv* apparently.

apparence *f* appearance.

apparent, -ente *adj* apparent; (*visible*) conspicuous, noticeable.

apparition *f* appearance; (*spectre*) apparition.

appartement *m* apartment.

appartenance *f* (*de groupe*) belonging (**à** to); (*de parti*) membership (**à** of).

appartenir* *vi* to belong (**à** to).

appât *m* bait.

appâter *vt* to lure.

appauvrir (s') *vpr* to become impoverished.

appauvrissement *m* impoverishment.

appel *m* (*cri*) call; (*en justice*) appeal; **faire l'a.** to call the roll; **faire a. à** to call upon.

appeler *vt* (*personne, nom etc*) to call; (*en criant*) to call out to (*sb*); **a. à l'aide** to call for help.

appeler (s') *vpr* to be called; **il s'appelle Paul** his name is Paul.

appellation *f* (*nom*) term; **a. contrôlée** (*de vin*) guaranteed vintage.

appendicite *f* appendicitis.

appétissant, -ante *adj* appetizing.

appétit *m* appetite (**de** for); **bon a.!** enjoy your meal!

applaudir *vti* to applaud.
applaudissements *mpl* applause.
application *f* application.
applique *f* wall lamp.
appliqué, -ée *adj* painstaking.
appliquer (s') *vpr* s'a. à *(un travail)* to apply oneself to; *(concerner)* to apply to; **s'a. à faire** to take pains to do.
appoint *m* **faire l'a.** to give the exact money.
apporter *vt* to bring.
appréciation *f (de professeur)* comment (**sur** on).
apprécier *vt (aimer, percevoir)* to appreciate.
appréhender *vt (craindre)* to dread (**de faire** doing).
apprendre* *vti (étudier)* to learn; *(événement, fait)* to hear of; *(nouvelle)* to hear; **a. à faire** to learn to do; **a. qch à qn** to teach sb sth; *(informer)* to tell sb sth; **a. à qn à faire** to teach sb to do; **a. que** to learn that; *(être informé)* to hear that.
apprenti, -ie *mf* apprentice.
apprentissage *m* apprenticeship; *(d'une langue)* learning (**de** of).
apprêter (s') *vpr* to get ready (**à faire** to do).
apprivoisé, -ée *adj* tame.
apprivoiser *vt* to tame.
approcher 1 *vt (chaise etc)* to draw up (**de** to); *(personne)* to come *ou* get close to, to approach. **2** *vi* to draw near(er), to get close(r) (**de** to).
approcher (s') *vpr* to come *ou* get near(er) (**de** to); **il s'est approché de moi** he came up to me.
approfondir *vt (trou)* to dig deeper; *(question)* to go into thoroughly.
approprier (s') *vpr* to take, to help oneself to.
approuver *vt* to approve.
approvisionner (s') *vpr* to get one's supplies (**de** of).

approximatif, -ive *adj* approximate.
appui *m* support; *(pour coude etc)* rest.
appuyer 1 *vt (soutenir)* to support; **a. qch sur** *(poser)* to rest sth on. **2** *vi* **a. sur** to rest on; *(bouton)* to press.
appuyer (s') *vpr* **s'a. sur** to lean on, to rest on.
après 1 *prép (temps)* after; *(espace)* beyond; **a. un an** after a year; **a. le pont** beyond the bridge; **a. avoir mangé** after eating. **2** *adv* after(-wards); **l'année d'a.** the following year.
après (d') *prép* according to.
après-demain *adv* the day after tomorrow.
après-midi *m ou f inv* afternoon.
après-rasage, *pl* **après-rasages** *m* aftershave.
après-shampooing *m inv* conditioner.
après-ski, *pl* **après-skis** *m* snowboot.
apte *adj* capable (**à** of).
aptitudes *fpl* aptitude (**pour** for).
aquarelle *f* watercolor.
aquarium *m* aquarium.
aquatique *adj* aquatic.
arabe 1 *adj* Arab. **2** *mf* A. Arab. **3** *adj & m (langue)* Arabic; **chiffres arabes** Arabic numerals.
arachide *f* peanut.
araignée *f* spider.
arbitre *m* Football, Boxe referee; *Tennis* umpire.
arbitrer *vt* Football, Boxe to referee; *Tennis* to umpire.
arbre *m* tree.
arbuste *m (small)* shrub.
arc *m (arme)* bow; *(voûte)* arch; *(de cercle)* arc.
arcades *fpl* arcade, arches.
arc-en-ciel, *pl* **arcs-en-ciel** *m* rainbow.
arche *f (voûte)* arch.
archer *m* archer.

archiplein, -pleine *adj* jam-packed.

architecte *m* architect.

architecture *f* architecture.

archives *fpl* records.

Arctique (l') *m* the Arctic.

ardent, -ente *adj (passionné)* ardent.

ardeur *f (énergie)* enthusiasm.

ardoise *f* slate.

are *m* = 100 square meters.

arène *f (pour taureaux)* bullring; **arènes** *(romaines)* amphitheater.

arête *f (de poisson)* bone; *(de cube)* edge, ridge.

argent *m (métal)* silver; *(monnaie)* money; **a. comptant** cash.

argenterie *f* silverware.

argile *f* clay.

argot *m* slang.

argument *m* argument.

argumenter *vi* to argue.

arithmétique *f* arithmetic.

armature *f (de lunettes, tente)* frame.

arme *f* arm, weapon; **a. à feu** firearm.

armée *f* army; **a. de l'air** air force.

armement(s) *m(pl)* arms.

armer *vt (personne)* to arm (**de** with); *(fusil)* to cock.

armer (s') *vpr* to arm oneself (**de** with).

armoire *f (penderie)* wardrobe, closet; **a. à pharmacie** medicine chest *ou* cabinet.

armure *f* armor.

arobase *f* = **arrobas**.

aromate *m (herbe)* herb; *(épice)* spice.

arôme *m (goût)* flavor; *(odeur)* (pleasant) smell.

arracher *vt (clou, dent, cheveux, page)* to pull out; *(plante)* to pull up; **a. qch à qn** to snatch sth from sb.

arranger *vt (chambre, visite etc)* to fix up; *(voiture, texte)* to put right; **ça m'arrange** that suits me.

arranger (s') *vpr* to come to an agreement; *(finir bien)* to turn out fine; **s'a. pour faire** to manage to do.

arrestation *f* arrest.

arrêt *m (halte, endroit)* stop; *(action)* stopping; **temps d'a.** pause; **sans a.** constantly; **'a. interdit'** *(panneau de signalisation)* 'no stopping (no standing)'.

arrêté *m* order.

arrêter 1 *vt* to stop; *(voleur etc)* to arrest. **2** *vi* to stop; **il n'arrête pas de critiquer/etc** he's always criticizing/etc.

arrêter (s') *vpr* to stop (**de faire** doing).

arrière 1 *adv* **en a.** *(marcher)* backwards; *(rester)* behind. **2** *m & adj inv* rear, back; **faire marche a.** to reverse, to back. **3** *m Sport* (full)back.

arrière-boutique, *pl* **arrière-boutiques** *f* back (room) *(of a shop)*.

arrière-goût, *pl* **arrière-goûts** *m* aftertaste.

arrière-grand-mère, *pl* **arrière-grands-mères** *f* great-grandmother.

arrière-grand-père, *pl* **arrière-grands-pères** *m* great-grandfather.

arrière-pays *m inv* hinterland.

arrière-pensée, *pl* **arrière-pensées** *f* ulterior motive.

arrière-plan, *pl* **arrière-plans** *m* background; **à l'a.** in the background.

arrivage *m* shipment.

arrivée *f* arrival; **ligne d'a.** finish line.

arriver *vi (aux être)* to arrive; *(survenir)* to happen; **a. à** to reach; **a. à qn** to happen to sb; **a. à faire** to manage to do; **il m'arrive d'oublier/etc** I (sometimes) forget/etc.

arrobas *m* at sign.

arrogant, -ante *adj* arrogant.

arrondir *vt (chiffre, angle)* to round off.

arrondissement *m (d'une ville)* district.

arrosage *m* watering.

arroser *vt (terre)* to water.

arrosoir *m* watering can.

art *m* art.

artère *f* artery; *(rue)* main road.

artichaut *m* artichoke.

article *m (de presse, de commerce, en grammaire)* article; **articles de toilette** toiletries.

articulation *f (de membre)* joint; **a. (du doigt)** knuckle.

articuler *vt (mot etc)* to articulate.

artifice *m* **feu d'a.** firework display.

artificiel, -elle *adj* artificial.

artisan *m* craftsman.

artisanal, -e, -aux *adj* **objet a.** object made by craftsmen.

artisanat *m* craft industry.

artiste *mf* artist.

artistique *adj* artistic.

as¹ *voir* **avoir**.

as² *m (carte, champion)* ace.

ascenseur *m* elevator.

ascension *f* ascent; **l'A.** Ascension Day.

asiatique **1** *adj* Asian. **2** *mf* **A.** Asian.

asile *m (abri)* shelter.

aspect *m (air)* appearance.

asperge *f* asparagus.

asperger *vt* to spray (**de** with).

asphyxie *f* suffocation.

asphyxier *vt* to suffocate.

aspirateur *m* vacuum cleaner; **passer (à) l'a.** to vacuum.

aspirer *vt (liquide)* to suck up.

aspirine *f* aspirin.

assaisonnement *m* seasoning.

assaisonner *vt* to season.

assassin *m* murderer.

assassinat *m* murder.

assassiner *vt* to murder.

assaut *m* onslaught; **prendre d'a.** to (take by) storm.

assemblée *f (personnes réunies)* gathering; *(parlement)* assembly.

assembler *vt* to put together.

assembler (s') *vpr* to gather.

asseoir* (s') *vpr* to sit (down).

assez *adv* enough; **a. de pain/gens** enough bread/people; **j'en ai a.** I've had enough; **a. grand/etc** *(suffisamment)* big/etc enough (**pour faire** to do); **a. fatigué/etc** *(plutôt)* fairly *ou* quite tired/etc.

assiéger *vt (magasin, vedette)* to mob.

assiette *f* plate; **a. anglaise** (assorted) cold cuts.

assis, -ise *(pp de* **asseoir**) *adj* sitting (down).

assises *fpl* **cour d')a.** court of assizes.

assistance *f (assemblée)* audience; *(aide)* assistance.

assistant, -ante *mf* assistant; **assistant(e) social(e)** social worker; **assistante maternelle** *(dans une garderie)* daycare worker; *(à domicile)* babysitter.

assister **1** *vt (aider)* to help. **2** *vi* **a. à** *(réunion, cours etc)* to attend; *(accident)* to witness.

association *f* association.

associé, -ée *mf* partner.

associer (s') *vpr* to associate (**à** with).

assoiffé, -ée *adj* thirsty.

assombrir (s') *vpr (ciel)* to cloud over.

assommer *vt (personne)* to knock unconscious.

assorti, -ie *adj (objet semblable)* matching; *(bonbons)* assorted; **a. de** accompanied by.

assortiment *m* assortment.

assortir *vt, s'assortir* *vpr* to match.

assoupir (s') *vpr* to doze off.

assouplir *vt (corps)* to limber up, to stretch.

assouplissement *m* **exercices d'a.** stretching exercises.

assourdir *vt* to deafen.

assourdissant, -ante *adj* deafening.

assumer vt (tâche, rôle) to assume, to take on; (risque) to take.

assurance f (aplomb) self-assurance; (contrat) insurance.

assuré, -ée 1 adj (succès) guaranteed; (air, personne) confident. **2** mf policyholder.

assurer vt (par un contrat) to insure; (travail) to carry out; **a. à qn que** to assure sb that; **a. qn de qch** to assure sb of sth.

assurer (s') vpr s'a. to insure oneself (contre against); **s'a. que/de** to make sure that/of.

astérisque m asterisk.

asthmatique adj & mf asthmatic.

asthme m asthma.

asticot m maggot.

astiquer vt to polish.

astre m star.

astrologie f astrology.

astronaute mf astronaut.

astronomie f astronomy.

astuce f (pour faire qch) knack, trick.

astucieux, -euse adj clever.

atelier m (d'ouvrier etc) workshop; (de peintre) studio.

athée 1 adj atheistic. **2** mf atheist.

athlète mf athlete.

athlétique adj athletic.

athlétisme m athletics.

atlantique 1 adj Atlantic. **2** m l'A. the Atlantic.

atlas m atlas.

atmosphère f atmosphere.

atome m atom.

atomique adj (bombe etc) atomic.

atout m trump (card).

atroce adj atrocious.

atrocités fpl atrocities.

attabler (s') vpr to sit down at the table.

attachant, -ante adj (enfant etc) likeable.

attaché-case, pl attachés-cases m attaché case, briefcase.

attacher vt (lier) to tie (up) (à to); (boucler, fixer) to fasten.

attacher (s') vpr s'a. à qn to become attached to sb.

attaquant, -ante mf attacker.

attaque f attack.

attaquer vti to attack.

attaquer (s') vpr s'a. à to attack.

attarder (s') vpr (en chemin) to dawdle.

atteindre* vt to reach; **être atteint de** (maladie) to be suffering from.

attelage m (crochet) hook (for towing).

atteler vt (bêtes) to harness; (remorque) to hook up.

attendre 1 vt to wait for; **elle attend un bébé** she's expecting a baby. **2** vi to wait; **a. que qn vienne** to wait for sb to come; **faire a. qn** to keep sb waiting; **en attendant** meanwhile; **en attendant que** (+ subjonctif) until.

attendre (s') vpr s'a. à to expect.

attendrir (s') vpr to be moved (sur by).

attendrissant, -ante adj moving.

attentat m attempt on sb's life; **a. (à la bombe)** (bomb) attack.

attentat-suicide m suicide bombing.

attente f wait(ing); **salle d'a.** waiting room.

attentif, -ive adj (personne) attentive; (travail, examen) careful.

attention f attention; **faire a. à** to pay attention to; **a.!** watch out!, be careful!; **a. à la voiture!** watch out for the car!

attentionné, -ée adj considerate.

attentivement adv attentively.

atténuer vt (effet) to reduce; (douleur) to ease.

atténuer (s') vpr (douleur) to ease.

atterrir vi to land.

atterrissage m landing.

attestation f (document) certificate.

attester *vt* to testify to; **a. que...** to testify that...

attirant, -ante *adj* attractive.

attirer *vt* to attract; *(attention)* to draw *(sur* to).

attitude *f* attitude.

attraction *f* attraction.

attraper *vt (ballon, maladie, voleur, train etc)* to catch; *(accent, contravention etc)* to pick up; **se laisser a.** *(duper)* to get taken in.

attrayant, -ante *adj* attractive.

attribuer *vt (donner)* to assign *(à* to); *(décerner)* to award *(à* to).

attribut *m* attribute.

attrister *vt* to sadden.

attroupement *m* (disorderly) crowd.

attrouper *vt*, **s'attrouper** *vpr* to gather.

au *voir* **à, le**.

aube *f* dawn.

auberge *f* inn; **a. de jeunesse** youth hostel.

aubergine *f* eggplant.

aucun, -une 1 *adj* no, not any; **il n'a a. talent** he has no talent, he doesn't have any talent; **a. professeur n'est venu** no teacher has come. **2** *pron* none, not any; **il n'en a a.** he has none (at all), he doesn't have any (at all).

audace *f (courage)* daring.

audacieux, -euse *adj* daring.

au-delà 1 *adv* beyond; **100 euros mais pas a.** 100 euros but no more. **2** *prép* **a. de** beyond.

au-dessous 1 *adv* below, under; *(à l'étage inférieur)* downstairs. **2** *prép* **a. de** under, below.

au-dessus 1 *adv* above, over; *(à l'étage supérieur)* upstairs. **2** *prép* **a. de** above; *(âge, température, prix)* over.

audience *f (entretien)* audience; *(de tribunal)* hearing; **l'a. est suspendue** the case is adjourned.

audio *adj inv* audio.

auditeur, -trice *mf* listener; **les auditeurs** the audience.

auditoire *m* audience.

auge *f* (feeding) trough.

augmentation *f* increase (**de** in, of); **a. de salaire** (pay) raise.

augmenter *vti* to increase (**de** by).

aujourd'hui *adv* today.

auparavant *adv (avant)* before(-hand); *(d'abord)* first.

auprès de *prép* by, close to.

auquel *voir* **lequel**.

aura, aurai(t) *etc voir* **avoir**.

auriculaire *m* pinkie, little finger.

aurore *f* dawn.

ausculter *vt* to examine *(with a stethoscope)*.

aussi *adv (comparaison)* as; **a. sage que** as wise as. ■ *(également)* too, also, as well; **moi a.** so do/can/am/ etc I. ■ *(tellement)* so; **un repas a. délicieux** so delicious a meal, such a delicious meal.

aussitôt *adv* immediately; **a. que** as soon as; **a. levé, il partit** as soon as he was up, he left.

australien, -ienne 1 *adj* Australian. **2** *mf* **A.** Australian.

autant *adv* **a. de...que** *(quantité)* as much...as; *(nombre)* as many... as. ■ **a. de** *(tant de)* so much; *(nombre)* so many. ■ **a. (que)** *(souffrir, lire etc)* as much (as); **en faire a.** to do the same; **j'aimerais a. aller au cinéma** I'd just as soon go to the movies.

autel *m* altar.

auteur *m (de livre)* author; *(de chanson)* composer.

authentique *adj* genuine.

auto *f* car; **autos tamponneuses** bumper cars.

autobus *m* bus.

autocar *m* bus, coach.

autocollant *m* sticker.

auto-école *f* driving school.

autographe *m* autograph.

automatique *adj* automatic.

automatiquement *adv* automatically.

automne *m* autumn, fall.

automobile *f* & *adj* car, automobile.

automobiliste *mf* motorist, driver.

autonome *adj* (*région*) autonomous, self-governing; (*personne*) self-sufficient.

autoradio *m* car radio.

autorisation *f* permission.

autoriser *vt* to permit (**à faire** to do).

autoritaire *adj* authoritarian.

autorité *f* authority.

autoroute *f* highway.

auto-stop *m* hitchhiking; **faire de l'a.** to hitchhike.

auto-stoppeur, -euse *mf* hitchhiker.

autour 1 *adv* around. **2** *prép* **a. de** around.

autre *adj* & *pron* other; **un a. livre** another book; **un a.** another (one); **d'autres** others; **d'autres médecins** other doctors; **d'autres questions?** any other questions?; **quelqu'un/personne/rien d'a.** someone/no one/nothing else; **a. chose/part** something/somewhere else; **qui/quoi d'a.?** who/what else?; **l'un l'a., les uns les autres** each other; **l'un et l'a.** both (of them); **l'un ou l'a.** either (of them); **ni l'un ni l'a.** neither (of them); **les uns...les autres** some...others; **d'un moment à l'a.** any moment.

autrefois *adv* in the past.

autrement *adv* differently; (*sinon*) otherwise.

autrichien, -ienne 1 *adj* Austrian. **2** *mf* **A.** Austrian.

autruche *f* ostrich.

aux *voir* **à, le.**

auxiliaire *adj* & *m* (*verbe*) **a.** auxiliary (verb).

auxquel(le)s *voir* **lequel.**

aval (en) *adv* downstream.

avalanche *f* avalanche.

avaler *vti* to swallow.

avance *f* **à l'a., d'a.** in advance; **en a.** (*arriver, partir*) early; (*avant l'horaire prévu*) ahead (of time); **en a. sur** ahead of; **avoir une heure d'a.** (*train etc*) to be an hour early.

avancement *m* (*de personne*) promotion.

avancer 1 *vt* (*date*) to move up; (*main, chaise*) to move forward; (*travail*) to speed up. **2** *vi* to advance, to move forward; (*montre*) to be fast.

avancer (s') *vpr* to move forward.

avant 1 *prép* before; **a. de voir** before seeing; **a. qu'il (ne) parte** before he leaves; **a. tout** above all. **2** *adv* before; **en a.** (*mouvement*) forward; (*en tête*) ahead; **la nuit d'a.** the night before. **3** *m* & *adj inv* front. **4** *m* (*joueur*) forward.

avantage *m* advantage.

avantager *vt* to favor.

avantageux, -euse *adj* (*offre*) attractive; (*prix*) reasonable.

avant-bras *m inv* forearm.

avant-dernier, -ière *adj* & *mf* last but one.

avant-hier *adv* the day before yesterday.

avant-première, *pl* avant-premières *f* preview.

avant-veille *f* **l'a. (de)** two days before.

avare 1 *adj* miserly, stingy. **2** *mf* miser.

avarice *f* miserliness, avarice.

avarie *f* damage; **subir une a.** to be damaged.

avarié, -ée *adj* (*aliment*) rotting, rotten.

avec *prép* with; (*envers*) to(wards); **et a. ça?** (*dans un magasin*) anything else?

avenir *m* future; **à l'a.** in future.

aventure *f* adventure.

aventurer (s') *vpr* to venture.

aventurier, -ière *mf* adventurer.

avenue *f* avenue.

avérer (s') *vpr* (*se révéler*) to prove

to be; **il s'avère que...** it turns out that...

averse *f* shower.

avertir *vt* (*mettre en garde*) to warn; (*informer*) to notify.

avertissement *m* warning; notification.

avertisseur *m* (*klaxon®*) horn; **a. d'incendie** fire alarm.

aveu, -x *m* confession.

aveugle 1 *adj* blind. **2** *mf* blind man, blind woman; **les aveugles** the blind.

aveugler *vt* to blind.

aveuglette (à l') *adv* **chercher qch à l'a.** to grope for sth.

aviateur, -trice *mf* airman, airwoman.

aviation *f* (*armée de l'air*) air force; (*avions*) aircraft *inv*; **l'a.** (*activité*) flying; **base d'a.** air base.

avide *adj* (*cupide*) greedy; (*passionné*) eager (**de** for).

avion *m* aircraft *inv*, (air)plane; **a. à réaction** jet; **a. de ligne** airliner; **par a.** (*lettre*) airmail; **en a., par a.** (*voyager*) by plane, by air.

aviron *m* oar; **l'a.** (*sport*) rowing.

avis *m* opinion; (*communiqué*) notice; **à mon a.** in my opinion; **changer d'a.** to change one's mind.

avocat, -ate 1 *mf* attorney. **2** *m* (*fruit*) avocado.

avoine *f* oats.

avoir* 1 *v aux* to have; **je l'ai vu** I've seen him. **2** *vt* (*posséder*) to have; (*obtenir*) to get; **qu'est-ce que tu as?** what's the matter with you?; **il n'a qu'à essayer** all he has to do is try; **a. faim/chaud/etc** to be *ou* feel hungry/hot/etc; **a. cinq ans** to be five (years old); **j'en ai pour dix minutes** this will take me ten minutes. **3** (*locution*) **il y a** there is, *pl* there are; **il y a six ans** six years ago; (*voir* **il**).

avortement *m* abortion.

avouer *vti* to confess (**que** that).

avril *m* April.

axe *m* (*ligne*) axis; (*essieu*) axle; **grands axes** (*routes*) main roads.

ayant, ayez, ayons *voir* **avoir**.

azote *m* nitrogen.

azur *m* (*sky*) blue; **la Côte d'A.** the (French) Riviera.

B

baby-foot *m inv* foosball.

bac 1 *m* (*bateau*) ferry(boat); (*cuve*) tank. **2** *abrév* = **baccalauréat**.

baccalauréat *m* = high school diploma.

bâche *f* tarpaulin.

bachelier, -ière *mf* holder of the *baccalauréat*.

bâcher *vt* to cover over (with a tarpaulin).

bâcler *vt Fam* to botch (up).

badaud, -aude *mf* onlooker.

badigeonner *vt* (*mur*) to whitewash; (*écorchure*) to coat, to paint.

bafouiller *vti* to stammer.

bagage *m* piece of baggage; **bagages** baggage.

bagarre *f* fight(ing).

bagarrer (se) *vpr* to fight.

bagnole *f Fam* car.

bague *f* (*anneau*) ring.

baguette *f* stick; (*de chef d'orchestre*) baton; (*pain*) (long thin) loaf; **baguettes** (*de tambour*) drumsticks; (*pour manger*) chopsticks; **b. (magique)** (*magic*) wand.

baie¹ *f* (*de côte*) bay.

baie² *f* (*fruit*) berry.

baignade *f* (*bain*) bath, swim; (*endroit*) swimming place.

baigner 1 *vt* to bathe. **2** *vi* **b. dans** (*aliment*) to be steeped in.

baigner (se) *vpr* to go swimming.

baigneur, -euse 1 *mf* bather, swimmer. **2** *m* (*poupée*) baby doll.

baignoire f bath (tub).

bail, pl **baux** m lease; **ça fait un b. que je ne l'ai pas vu** Fam I haven't seen him for ages.

bâillement m yawn.

bâiller vi to yawn.

bâillon m gag.

bâillonner vt to gag.

bain m bath; **prendre un b. de soleil** to sunbathe; **salle de bain(s)** bathroom; **être dans le b.** Fam to have gotten into the swing of things; **b. de bouche** mouthwash.

baiser m kiss.

baisse f fall, drop (**de** in); **en b.** falling.

baisser 1 vt to lower, to drop; (tête) to bend; (radio, chauffage) to turn down. **2** vi to go down, to drop.

baisser (se) vpr to bend down.

bal, pl **bals** m ball; (populaire) dance.

balade f Fam walk; (en auto) drive.

balader (se) vpr Fam (à pied) to (go for a) walk; **se b. (en voiture)** to go for a drive.

baladeur m Walkman®.

balai m broom; **manche à b.** broomstick.

balance f (pair of) scales.

balancer vt to sway; (lancer) Fam to pitch; (se débarrasser de) Fam to chuck, to pitch.

balancer (se) vpr to swing (from side to side).

balançoire f (suspendue) swing.

balayer vt to sweep (up); (enlever) to sweep away.

balayette f (hand)brush.

balayeur, -euse 1 mf (personne) roadsweeper. **2** f (véhicule) road-sweeper.

balbutier vti to stammer.

balcon m balcony.

baleine f whale.

balisage m beacons.

balise f (pour naviguer) beacon.

baliser vt to mark with beacons.

ballast m ballast.

balle f (de tennis, golf etc) ball; (projectile) bullet.

ballerine f ballerina.

ballet m ballet.

ballon m (jouet d'enfant, appareil) balloon; (sports) ball; **b. de football** soccer ball.

ballot m bundle.

ballottage m (scrutin) second ballot.

balnéaire adj **station b.** beach resort.

balustrade f (hand)rail.

bambin m tiny tot.

bambou m bamboo.

ban m (applaudissements) round of applause; **un (triple) b. pour...** three cheers for...

banal, -e, -als adj (objet, gens) ordinary; (idée) trite, banal; **pas b.** unusual.

banane f banana.

banc m (siège) bench; **b. de sable** sandbank.

bancaire adj **compte b.** bank account.

bancal, -e, -als adj (meuble) wobbly.

bandage m bandage.

bande[1] f (de terrain, papier etc) strip; (de film) reel; (rayure) stripe; (pansement) bandage; (sur la chaussée) line; **b. d'arrêt d'urgence** shoulder; **b. (magnétique)** tape; **b. vidéo** videotape; **b. dessinée** comic strip.

bande[2] f (groupe) gang.

bande-annonce, pl **bandes-annonces** f preview.

bandeau, -x m (sur les yeux) blindfold; (pour la tête) headband.

bander vt (blessure) to bandage; (yeux) to blindfold.

banderole f (sur montants) banner.

bandit m robber.

bandoulière f (de sac) shoulder strap; **en b.** slung across the shoulder.

banlieue f la b. the outskirts (of town).

banque f bank; (activité) banking; b. électronique e-banking.

banquette f (de véhicule, train) seat.

banquier m banker.

banquise f ice floe.

baptême m christening, baptism.

baptiser vt (enfant) to christen, to baptize.

baquet m tub, basin.

bar m (lieu, comptoir) bar.

baraque f hut, shack.

baraquement m (makeshift) huts.

baratin m Fam (verbiage) waffle; (de séducteur) sweet talk; (de vendeur) sales patter.

barbare adj (cruel) barbaric.

barbe f beard; **se faire la b.** to shave; **quelle b.!** Fam what a bore!

barbecue m barbecue.

barbelé adj fil de fer b. barbed wire.

barbiche f goatee.

barboter vi to splash around.

barbouillage m smear(ing); (gribouillage) scribble, scribbling.

barbouiller vt (salir) to smear; (gribouiller) to scribble.

barbu, -ue adj bearded.

barème m (de notes, de salaires, de prix) scale; (pour calculer) ready reckoner.

baril m barrel; **b. de poudre** powder keg.

barman, pl -men ou -mans m bartender.

baromètre m barometer.

baron m baron.

baronne f baroness.

barque f (small) boat.

barquette f (de fruit) punnet; (de plat cuisiné) container.

barrage m (sur une route) roadblock; (sur un fleuve) dam.

barre f bar; (de bateau) helm; (trait) stroke.

barreau, -x m (de fenêtre) bar; (d'échelle) rung.

barrer vt (route etc) to block; (mot, phrase) to cross out.

barrette f barrette.

barricade f barricade.

barricader vt to barricade.

barricader (se) vpr to barricade oneself (in).

barrière f (porte) gate; (clôture) fence; (obstacle) barrier.

barrique f (large) barrel.

bas, basse 1 adj low. **2** adv low; (parler) in a whisper; **plus b.** further ou lower down. **3** m (de côte, page, mur etc) bottom; **tiroir/etc du b.** bottom drawer/etc; **en b.** down (below); (par l'escalier) downstairs; **en ou au b. de** at the bottom of.

bas m (chaussette) stocking.

bas-côté m roadside, verge, shoulder.

bascule f weighing machine; (jeu d'enfant) seesaw.

basculer vti to topple over.

base f base; bases (d'un argument, accord etc) basis; **salaire de b.** base pay; **à b. de lait/citron** milk-/lemon-based.

baser vt to base (sur on).

basket(-ball) m basketball.

baskets fpl (chaussures) sneakers.

basque 1 adj Basque. **2** mf B. Basque.

basse voir **bas**.

basse-cour, pl basses-cours f farmyard.

bassin m pond; (rade) dock; (du corps) pelvis; **b. houiller** coalfield.

bassine f bowl.

bataille f battle.

batailleur, -euse 1 mf fighter. **2** adj fond of fighting, belligerent.

bateau, -x m boat; (grand) ship.

bateau-mouche, pl bateaux-mouches m river boat (on the Seine).

bâtiment m building; (navire) vessel; **le b.** (industrie) the construction industry.

bâtir *vt* to build; **bien bâti** well-built.
bâton *m* stick; *(d'agent)* baton; **b. de rouge** lipstick; **donner des coups de b. à qn** to beat sb (with a stick).
battante *adj f* **pluie b.** driving rain.
battement *m* beat(ing); *(de paupières)* blink(ing); *(délai)* interval; **b. de cœur** heartbeat.
batterie *f* battery; **la b.** *(d'un orchestre)* the drums.
batteur *m (d'orchestre)* drummer.
battre* 1 *vt* to beat. **2** *vi* to beat; **b. des mains** to clap (one's hands); **b. des paupières** to blink; **b. des ailes** *(oiseau)* to flap its wings.
battre (se) *vpr* to fight.
baume *m* balm.
bavard, -arde *adj* talkative.
bavardage *m* chatting.
bavarder *vi* to chat.
bave *f* drool.
baver *vi* to drool; **en b.** *Fam* to have a rough time of it.
bavoir *m* bib.
bavure *f (tache)* smudge.
bazar *m (magasin)* bazaar; *(désordre)* mess.
BD *f abrév (bande dessinée)* comic strip.
beau *(or* **bel** *before vowel or mute* h*),* **belle,** *pl* **beaux, belles** *adj* beautiful, attractive; *(voyage, temps etc)* fine, lovely; **au b. milieu** right in the middle; **j'ai b. crier/***etc* it's no use (my) shouting/*etc.*
beaucoup *adv (lire etc)* a lot; **aimer b.** to like very much *ou* a lot; **b. de** *(livres etc)* many, a lot of; *(courage etc)* a lot of; **pas b. d'argent/***etc* not much money/*etc*; **j'en ai b.** *(quantité)* I have a lot; *(nombre)* I have lots; **b. plus** much more; many more (**que** than).
beau-fils, *pl* **beaux-fils** *m (gendre)* son-in-law; *(après remariage)* stepson.
beau-frère, *pl* **beaux-frères** *m* brother-in-law.

beau-père, *pl* **beaux-pères** *m (père du conjoint)* father-in-law; *(après remariage)* stepfather.
beauté *f* beauty.
beaux-arts *mpl* fine arts; **école des b., les B.** art school.
beaux-parents *mpl* parents-in-law.
bébé *m* baby.
bec *m (d'oiseau)* beak; *(de cruche)* spout; **coup de b.** peck.
bécane *f Fam* bike.
bêche *f* spade.
bêcher *vt (cultiver)* to dig.
becquée *f* **donner la b. à** *(oiseau)* to feed.
bedonnant, -ante *adj* potbellied.
bégayer *vi* to stutter.
bègue 1 *mf* stutterer. **2** *adj* **être b.** to stutter.
beige *adj & m* beige.
beignet *m (pâtisserie)* fritter; *(rond)* donut.
bel *voir* **beau.**
bêler *vi* to bleat.
belette *f* weasel.
belge 1 *adj* Belgian. **2** *mf* **B.** Belgian.
bélier *m* ram.
belle *voir* **beau.**
belle-famille, *pl* **belles-familles** *f* in-laws.
belle-fille, *pl* **belles-filles** *f (épouse du fils)* daughter-in-law; *(après remariage)* stepdaughter.
belle-mère, *pl* **belles-mères** *f (mère du conjoint)* mother-in-law; *(après remariage)* stepmother.
belle-sœur, *pl* **belles-sœurs** *f* sister-in-law.
belliqueux, -euse *adj (agressif)* aggressive.
bénédiction *f* blessing.
bénéfice *m (gain)* profit; *(avantage)* benefit.
bénéficiaire 1 *mf (de chèque)* payee. **2** *adj (entreprise)* profit-making; *(compte)* in credit.

bénéficier *vi* to benefit (**de** from).

bénéfique *adj* beneficial.

bénévolat *m* voluntary work.

bénévole 1 *adj* voluntary. **2** *mf* volunteer.

bénin, -igne *adj (accident, opération)* minor; *(tumeur)* benign.

bénir *vt* to bless; *(remercier)* to give thanks to.

bénit, -ite *adj (pain)* consecrated; **eau bénite** holy water.

benjamin, -ine *mf* youngest child.

benne *f (de camion)* (movable) container; **camion à b. basculante** dump truck.

BEP *m abrév (brevet d'études professionnelles)* = vocational diploma taken at 18.

béquille *f (canne)* crutch; *(de moto)* stand.

berceau, -x *m* cradle.

bercer *vt (balancer)* to rock; *(apaiser)* to soothe, to lull.

berceuse *f* lullaby.

béret *m* beret.

berge *m (rive)* (raised) bank.

berger *m* shepherd; **b. allemand** German shepherd.

bergère *f* shepherdess.

bergerie *f* sheepfold.

berline *f (voiture)* sedan.

berner *vt* to fool.

besogne *f* job, task.

besoin *m* need; **avoir b. de** to need.

bestiole *f (insecte)* bug.

bétail *m* livestock.

bête¹ *f* animal; *(insecte)* bug; **b. noire** pet peeve.

bête² *adj* stupid.

bêtement *adv* stupidly; **tout b.** quite simply.

bêtise *f* stupidity; *(action, parole)* stupid thing.

béton *m* concrete; **mur/etc en b.** concrete wall/etc.

betterave *f* beet.

beurre *m* butter.

beurrer *vt* to butter.

beurrier *m* butter dish.

biais *m* **regarder qn de b.** to look sideways at sb; **par le b. de** through.

bibelot *m* (small) ornament, trinket.

biberon *m* (feeding) bottle.

bible *f* bible; **la B.** the Bible.

bibliothécaire *mf* librarian.

bibliothèque *f* library; *(meuble)* bookcase.

bic® *m* ballpoint.

biceps *m (muscle)* biceps.

biche *f* doe.

bicyclette *f* bicycle.

bidon 1 *m* (jerry) can. **2** *adj inv* *Fam* phoney.

bidonville *m* shantytown.

bidule *m (chose) Fam* whatchamacallit.

bien 1 *adv* well; **b. fatigué/souvent/etc (très)** very tired/often/etc; **merci b.!** thanks very much!; **b.!** fine!, right!; **b. des fois/des gens/** *etc* lots of *ou* many times/people/ *etc*; **je l'ai b. dit** *(intensif)* I *did* say so; **tu as b. fait** you did right; **c'est b. fait (pour lui)** it serves him right. **2** *adj inv (convenable, compétent etc)* fine. **3** *m (avantage)* good; *(chose)* possession; **ça te fera du b.** it will do you good; **pour ton b.** for your own good; **le b. et le mal** good and evil.

bien-être *m* wellbeing.

bienfaisant, -ante *adj* beneficial.

bien que *conj (+ subjonctif)* although.

bientôt *adv* soon; **à b.!** see you soon!; **il est b. midi/etc** it's nearly twelve/etc.

bienveillant, -ante *adj* kind.

bienvenu, -ue 1 *adj* welcome. **2** *f* welcome; **souhaiter la bienvenue à** to welcome.

bière *f* beer; **b. pression** draft beer.

bifteck *m* steak.

bifurcation *f (route etc)* fork.

bifurquer *vi* to fork.

bigoudi *m* (hair) roller.

bijou, -x *m* jewel.

bijouterie *f* (commerce) jewelry store, jeweler's.

bijoutier, -ière *mf* jeweler.

bilan *m* (financier) balance sheet; (résultat) outcome; (d'un accident) (casualty) toll; **b. de santé** check-up; **déposer le b.** to file for bankruptcy.

bile *f* bile; **se faire de la b.** *Fam* to worry.

bilingue *adj* bilingual.

billard *m* (jeu) billiards; (table) billiard table.

bille *f* (d'enfant) marble; **stylo à b.** ballpoint (pen).

billet *m* ticket; **b. (de banque)** bill; **b. aller, b. simple** one-way ticket; **b. aller-retour** round trip ticket; **b. électronique** e-ticket.

billeterie *f* (lieu) ticket office; **b. automatique** (de billet de transport) ticket machine.

biologie *f* biology.

biologique *adj* biological; (légumes etc) organic.

biotechnologie *f* biotechnology.

bip *m* beeper.

biscotte *f* Melba toast.

biscuit *m* cookie.

bise¹ *f* (vent) north wind.

bise² *f* (baiser) Fam kiss; **faire la b. à qn** to kiss sb on both cheeks.

bison *m* (American) buffalo.

bisou *m* Fam kiss.

bissextile *adj* f année b. leap year.

bistouri *m* scalpel.

bistro(t) *m* Fam bar.

bitume *m* (revêtement) asphalt.

bizarre *adj* peculiar, odd.

blague *f* (plaisanterie, farce) joke; **b. à part** seriously.

blaguer *vi* to be joking.

blaireau, -x *m* (animal) badger; (brosse) shaving brush.

blâmer *vt* to criticize, to blame.

blanc, blanche 1 *adj* white;

(page) blank. **2** *mf* (personne) white person. **3** *m* (couleur) white; (de poulet) breast; (espace) blank; **b. (d'œuf)** (egg) white; **laisser en b.** to leave blank; **chèque en b.** blank check; **donner carte blanche à qn** to give sb free rein.

blancheur *f* whiteness.

blanchir *vi* to turn white.

blanchisserie *f* (lieu) laundry.

blatte *f* (cock)roach.

blé *m* wheat.

blême *adj* sickly pale; **b. de colère** livid.

blêmir *vi* to turn pale.

blessant, -ante *adj* hurtful.

blessé, -ée *mf* casualty.

blesser *vt* to injure, to hurt; (avec un couteau, une balle etc) to wound; (offenser) to hurt.

blesser (se) *vpr* se b. le *ou* au bras/etc to hurt one's arm/etc.

blessure *f* injury; wound.

bleu, -e 1 *adj* (mpl bleus) blue. **2** *m* (pl bleus) (couleur) blue; (contusion) bruise; (vêtement) overalls.

blindé, -ée *adj* (voiture etc) armored; **porte blindée** reinforced steel door; **une vitre blindée** bullet-proof glass.

bloc *m* block; (de papier) pad; **à b.** (visser etc) tight.

bloc-notes, *pl* **blocs-notes** *m* writing pad.

blog *m* blog.

blogueur, -euse *mf* blogger.

blond, -onde 1 *adj* fair(-haired), blond. **2** *mf* fair-haired *ou* blond person; **(bière) blonde** beer.

bloquer *vt* (obstruer) to block; (coincer) to jam; (roue) to lock; (prix) to freeze.

bloquer (se) *vpr* to jam; (roue) to lock.

blottir (se) *vpr* to crouch; (dans son lit) to snuggle in; **se b. contre** to snuggle up to.

blouse *f* (tablier) smock.

blouson *m* windbreaker.

bobine f reel, spool.

bocal, -aux m glass jar; (à poissons) bowl.

bœuf, pl -fs m ox (pl oxen); (viande) beef.

boire* vti to drink; **offrir à b. à qn** to offer sb a drink.

bois m wood; (de construction) timber; **en** ou **de b.** wooden; **b. de chauffage** firewood.

boisé, -ée adj wooded.

boisson f drink.

boîte f box; (de conserve) can; **b. aux** ou **à lettres** mailbox. ▪ (entreprise) Fam firm; **b. de nuit** nightclub; **b. de réception** (pour e-mails) in-box.

boiter vi to limp.

boîtier m (de montre) case.

bol m bowl; **un b. d'air** a breath of fresh air.

bombardement m bombing; shelling.

bombarder vt to bomb; (avec des obus) to shell.

bombe f bomb; (de laque etc) spray.

bon¹, bonne adj good; (qui convient) right; (apte) fit; **b. anniversaire!** happy birthday!; **le b. choix/ moment** the right choice/time; **b. à manger** fit to eat; **c'est b. à savoir** it's worth knowing; **croire b. de** to think it wise to; **b. en français/etc** good at French/etc; **un b. moment** (intensif) a good while; **pour de b.** really (and truly); **ah b.?** is that so?

bon² m (billet) coupon, voucher.

bonbon m candy.

bond m leap.

bondé, -ée adj packed.

bondir vi to leap.

bonheur m happiness; (chance) good luck; **par b.** luckily.

bonhomme, pl **bonshommes** m fellow; **b. de neige** snowman.

bonjour m & int good morning; (après-midi) good afternoon; **donner le b. à, dire b. à** to say hello to.

bonne¹ voir bon.

bonne² f maid.

bonnet m (de ski etc) cap; (de femme, d'enfant) bonnet, hat.

bonsoir m & int (en rencontrant qn) good evening; (en quittant qn) goodbye; (au coucher) good night.

bonté f kindness.

bord m (rebord) edge; (rive) bank; **au b. de la mer** at the beach; **au b. de la route** by the roadside; **b. du trottoir** curb; **à bord (de)** (avion, bateau) on board.

border vt (vêtement) to edge; (lit, personne) to tuck in; **b. la rue/etc** (maisons, arbres) to line the street/ etc.

bordereau, -x m (de livraison etc) note.

bordure f border.

borne f boundary mark; **b. kilométrique** = milestone.

borné, -ée adj (personne) narrow-minded; (esprit) narrow.

bosse f (dans le dos) hump; (enflure, de terrain) bump.

bosser vi Fam to work (hard).

bossu, -ue 1 adj hunchbacked. **2** m f hunchback.

botte f (chaussure) boot; (de fleurs etc) bunch.

bottine f (ankle) boot.

bouc m billy goat; (barbe) goatee.

boucan m Fam din, row; **faire du b.** to kick up a row.

bouche f mouth; **b. de métro** métro entrance; **b. d'égout** drain opening.

bouché, -ée adj **j'ai le nez b.** my nose is stuffed up.

bouchée f mouthful.

boucher¹ vt (évier etc) to stop up; (bouteille) to cork; (vue, rue etc) to block.

boucher², -ère m butcher.

boucher (se) vpr **se b. le nez** to hold one's nose.

boucherie f butcher's (shop).

bouchon m stopper; (de liège)

cork; *(de tube, bidon)* cap; *(embouteillage)* traffic jam.

boucle f *(de ceinture)* buckle; **b. d'oreille** earring; **b. (de cheveux)** curl.

bouclé, -ée *adj (cheveux)* curly.

boucler 1 *vt (attacher)* to fasten; *(cheveux)* to curl. **2** *vi* to be curly.

bouclier m shield.

bouder *vi* to sulk.

boudin m blood sausage.

boue f mud.

bouée f buoy; **b. de sauvetage** lifebuoy.

boueux, -euse *adj* muddy.

bouffe f *(nourriture) Fam* grub.

bouffée f *(de fumée)* puff.

bouffer *vti (manger) Fam* to eat.

bougeoir m candlestick.

bouger *vti* to move.

bougie f candle; *(d'automobile)* spark plug.

bouillie f porridge.

bouillir* *vi* to boil.

bouilloire f kettle.

bouillon m *(aliment)* broth; *(bulles)* bubbles.

bouillonner *vi* to bubble.

boulanger, -ère mf baker.

boulangerie f baker's (shop).

boule f ball; **boules** (French) bowling game; **b. de neige** snowball.

bouleau, -x m (silver) birch.

bouledogue m bulldog.

boulet m **b. de canon** cannonball.

boulette f *(de papier)* ball; *(de viande)* meatball.

boulevard m boulevard.

bouleversant, -ante *adj (perturbant)* distressing; *(émouvant)* deeply moving.

bouleversement m upheaval.

bouleverser *vt (déranger)* to turn upside down; *(perturber)* to distress; *(émouvoir)* to move deeply.

boulimie f bulimia.

boulon m bolt.

boulot m *Fam (emploi)* job; *(travail)* work.

bouquet m *(de fleurs)* bunch.

bouquin m *Fam* book.

bourdon m *(insecte)* bumblebee.

bourdonnement m buzzing.

bourdonner *vi* to buzz.

bourg m (small) market town.

bourgeois, -oise *adj & mf* middle-class (person).

bourgeon m bud.

bourgeonner *vi* to bud.

bourrasque f squall, gust of wind.

bourré, -ée *adj (ivre) Fam* wasted.

bourrer *vt* to stuff, to cram (**de** with); *(pipe)* to fill.

bourse f *(sac)* purse; *(d'études)* grant, scholarship; **la B.** the Stock Exchange.

bousculade f jostling.

bousculer *vt (heurter, pousser)* to jostle.

boussole f compass.

bout m end; *(de langue, canne, doigt)* tip; *(de papier, pain, ficelle)* piece; **un b. de temps** a little while; **au b. d'un moment** after a moment; **à b.** exhausted; **à b. de souffle** out of breath.

bouteille f bottle; *(de gaz)* cylinder.

boutique f shop.

bouton m *(bourgeon)* bud; *(au visage etc)* pimple; *(de vêtement, de machine)* button; *(de porte, télévision)* knob.

bouton-d'or, pl **boutons-d'or** m buttercup.

boutonner *vt,* **se boutonner** *vpr* to button (up).

boutonnière f buttonhole.

bouton-pression, pl **boutons-pression** m snap (fastener).

box, pl **boxes** m *(garage)* garage facility; *(de cheval)* stall; *(au bureau)* cubicle.

boxe f boxing.

boxer *vi* to box.

boxeur m boxer.

boycotter *vt* to boycott.

BP f *abrév (boîte postale)* PO Box.

bracelet *m* bracelet; *(de montre)* strap, band.

braconner *vi* to poach.

braconnier *m* poacher.

braguette *f (de pantalon)* fly.

brailler *vti* to bawl.

braise(s) *f(pl)* embers.

brancard *m (civière)* stretcher.

branchages *mpl* (cut) branches.

branche *f (d'arbre)* branch; *(de compas)* arm, leg.

branchement *m* connection.

brancher *vt* to plug in.

brandir *vt* to flourish.

branlant, -ante *adj (table etc)* wobbly, shaky.

braquer 1 *vt (arme etc)* to point (**sur** at). **2** *vi* to turn the steering wheel, to steer.

bras *m* arm; **b. dessus b. dessous** arm in arm; **à b. ouverts** with open arms.

brasier *m* blaze.

brassard *m* armband.

brasse *f (nage)* breaststroke.

brasserie *f (usine)* brewery; *(café)* brasserie.

brassière *f (de bébé)* undershirt.

brave *adj & m* brave (man).

bravement *adv* bravely.

bravo 1 *int* bravo. **2** *m* cheer.

bravoure *f* bravery.

break *m (voiture)* station wagon.

brebis *f* ewe.

brèche *f* gap.

bredouille *adj* rentrer b. to come back empty-handed.

bredouiller *vti* to mumble.

bref, brève 1 *adj* brief, short. **2** *adv* **(enfin) b.** in a word.

bretelle *f* strap; *(d'accès)* access road; **bretelles** *(pour pantalon)* suspenders.

breton, -onne 1 *adj* Breton. **2** *mf* **B.** Breton.

brevet *m* diploma; **b. (des collèges)** = exam at end of junior high school; **b. (d'invention)** patent.

bricolage *m (passe-temps)* do-it-yourself.

bricoler 1 *vi* to do odd jobs. **2** *vt (fabriquer)* to put together.

bricoleur, -euse *mf* handyman, handywoman.

bride *f* bridle.

brider *vt* to hold in *ou* back.

bridés *adj* avoir les yeux bridés to have slanting eyes.

brièvement *adv* briefly.

brièveté *f* shortness, brevity.

brigand *m* robber; *(enfant)* rascal.

brillamment *adv* brilliantly.

brillant, -ante 1 *adj (luisant)* shining; *(astiqué)* shiny; *(couleur)* bright; *(doué)* brilliant. **2** *m* shine; *(couleur)* brightness.

briller *vi* to shine; **faire b.** *(meuble)* to polish (up).

brin *m (d'herbe)* blade; *(de corde, fil)* strand; *(de muguet)* spray.

brindille *f* twig.

brioche *f* brioche *(light sweet bun)*.

brique *f* brick; *(de lait, jus de fruit)* carton.

briquet *m* (cigarette) lighter.

brise *f* breeze.

briser *vt*, **se briser** *vpr* to break.

britannique 1 *adj* British. **2** *mf* **B.** Briton; **les Britanniques** the British.

broc *m* pitcher, jug.

brocante *f (commerce)* second-hand trade *(in furniture etc)*.

brocanteur, -euse *mf* second-hand dealer *(in furniture etc)*.

broche *f (pour rôtir)* spit; *(bijou)* brooch.

brochet *m* pike.

brochette *f (tige)* skewer; *(plat)* kebab.

brochure *f* brochure, booklet.

brocolis *mpl* broccoli.

broder *vt* to embroider (**de** with).

broderie *f* embroidery.

bronches *fpl* bronchial tubes.

bronchite *f* bronchitis.

bronzage *m* (sun)tan.

bronze *m* bronze.

bronzer 1 *vt* to tan. **2** *vi* to get (sun)tanned.

bronzer (se) *vpr* se (faire) b. to sunbathe, to get a (sun)tan.

brosse *f* brush; **b. à dents** toothbrush.

brosser *vt* to brush.

brosser (se) *vpr* se b. les dents/cheveux to brush one's teeth/hair.

brouette *f* wheelbarrow.

brouhaha *m* hubbub.

brouillard *m* fog; **il y a du b.** it's foggy.

brouiller *vt* (œufs) to scramble; **b. la vue à qn** to blur sb's vision.

brouiller (se) *vpr* (temps) to cloud over; (vue) to get blurred; (amis) to fall out (**avec** with).

brouillon *m* rough draft.

broussailles *fpl* bushes.

brousse *f* **la b.** the bush.

brouter *vti* to graze.

broyer *vt* to grind.

brugnon *m* nectarine.

bruine *f* drizzle.

bruit *m* noise, sound; (nouvelle) rumor; **faire du b.** to make noise.

brûlant, -ante *adj* (objet, soleil) burning (hot).

brûlé *m* **odeur de b.** smell of burning.

brûler *vti* to burn; **b. un feu (rouge)** to go through the lights.

brûler (se) *vpr* to burn oneself.

brûlure *f* burn.

brume *f* mist, haze.

brumeux, -euse *adj* misty, hazy.

brun, brune 1 *adj* brown; (cheveux) dark, brown; (personne) dark-haired. **2** *m* (couleur) brown. **3** *mf* dark-haired person.

brunir *vi* to turn brown; (cheveux) to get darker.

brushing *m* blow-dry.

brusque *adj* (manière, personne) abrupt; (subit) sudden.

brusquement *adv* suddenly.

brusquerie *f* abruptness.

brut *adj* (pétrole) crude; (poids, salaire) gross.

brutal, -e, -aux *adj* (violent) brutal; (enfant) rough.

brutaliser *vt* to ill-treat.

brutalité *f* brutality.

brute *f* brute.

bruyamment *adv* noisily.

bruyant, -ante *adj* noisy.

BTS *m abrév* (brevet de technicien supérieur) = advanced vocational training certificate.

bu, bue *pp of* **boire**.

bûche *f* log.

bûcheron *m* lumberjack.

bûcheur, -euse *mf Fam* grind.

budget *m* budget.

buée *f* mist.

buffet *m* (armoire) sideboard; (table, repas) buffet.

buisson *m* bush.

bulldozer *m* bulldozer.

bulle *f* bubble; (de BD) balloon.

bulletin *m* (météo) report; (scolaire) report card; **b. de paie** pay slip; **b. de vote** ballot paper.

bureau, -x *m* (table) desk; (lieu) office; **b. de change** foreign exchange office, bureau de change; **b. de tabac** tobacco store.

burette *f* oilcan.

bus *m* bus.

buste *m* (torse) chest; (sculpture) bust.

but *m* (objectif) aim, goal; *Sport* goal.

buté, -ée *adj* obstinate.

buter *vi* b. contre to stumble over.

butoir *m* (de porte) stop(per).

butte *f* mound.

buvard *m* blotting paper.

buvette *f* refreshment bar.

buveur, -euse *mf* drinker.

C

ça *pron dém* (abrév de cela) (pour désigner) that; (plus près) this; (sujet indéfini) it, that; **ça m'amuse que...** it amuses me that...; **où/quand/comment/etc ça?** where?/

when?/how?/*etc*; **ça va (bien)?** how's it going?; **ça va!** fine!, OK!; **ça alors!** *(surprise, indignation)* I'll be!, how about that!; **c'est ça** that's right.
cabane *f* hut, cabin; *(à outils)* shed; *(à lapins)* hutch.
cabine *f (de bateau)* cabin; *(téléphonique)* phone booth *ou* box; *(à la piscine)* cubicle; **c. (de pilotage)** cockpit; *(d'un grand avion)* flight deck; **c. d'essayage** fitting room.
cabinet *m (de médecin)* office; *(de ministre)* department; **cabinets** *(toilettes)* bathroom, men's/ladies' room; **c. de toilette** (small) bathroom; **c. de travail** study.
câble *m* cable; *(cordage)* rope; **la télévision par c.** cable television.
cabosser *vt* to dent.
cabrer (se) *vpr (cheval)* to rear (up).
cacah(o)uète *f* peanut.
cacao *m* cocoa.
cachalot *m* sperm whale.
cache-cache *m inv* hide-and-seek.
cache-nez *m inv* scarf, muffler.
cacher *vt* to hide (à from); **je ne cache pas que...** I don't hide the fact that...
cacher (se) *vpr* to hide.
cachet *m (de la poste)* postmark; *(comprimé)* tablet.
cacheter *vt* to seal.
cachette *f* hiding place; **en c.** in secret.
cachot *m* dungeon.
cactus *m* cactus.
cadavre *m* corpse.
caddie® *m* (supermarket) cart.
cadeau, -x *m* present, gift.
cadenas *m* padlock.
cadence *f (vitesse)* rate; **en c.** in time.
cadet, -ette 1 *adj (de deux frères etc)* younger; *(de plus de deux)* youngest. **2** *mf (de deux)* younger (child); *(de plus de deux)* youngest (child); *(sportif)* junior.

cadran *m (de téléphone)* dial; *(de montre)* face.
cadre *m (de photo, vélo etc)* frame; *(décor)* setting; *(sur un imprimé)* box; *(chef)* executive, manager.
cadrer 1 *vt (photo)* to center. **2** *vi (correspondre)* to tally (**avec** with).
cafard *m (insecte)* (cock)roach; **avoir le c.** to feel blue; **ça me donne le c.** it depresses me.
café *m* coffee; *(bar)* café; **c. au lait, c. crème** coffee with milk; **c. noir, c. nature** black coffee; **c. soluble** *ou* **instantané** instant coffee; **tasse de c.** cup of black coffee.
cafétéria *f* cafeteria.
cafetière *f* coffeepot; *(électrique)* percolator.
cage *f* cage; *(d'escalier)* well; *Sport* goal (area).
cageot *m* crate, box.
cagnotte *f (caisse commune)* kitty; *(de jeux)* pool.
cagoule *f* ski mask; *(de bandit, moine)* hood.
cahier *m* exercise book; **c. de brouillon** scratch pad; **c. d'appel** roll *(in school)*.
cahot *m* jolt, bump.
cailler *vti (sang)* to clot; *(lait)* to curdle; **faire c.** *(lait)* to curdle.
caillot *m* (blood) clot.
caillou, -x *m* stone.
caisse *f* case, box; *(guichet)* cash desk; *(de supermarché)* checkout; *(tambour)* drum; **c. (enregistreuse)** till, cash register; **c. d'épargne** savings bank.
caissier, -ière *mf* cashier; *(de supermarché)* checkout assistant.
cake *m* fruit cake.
calcaire *adj (eau)* hard.
calciné, -ée *adj* charred.
calcul *m* calculation; *(discipline)* arithmetic.
calculatrice *f* calculator.
calculer *vt* to calculate.
cale *f (pour maintenir)* wedge; *(de bateau)* hold.

caleçon m underpants; **c. de bain** bathing trunks.

calendrier m calendar.

calepin m notebook.

caler 1 vt (meuble etc) to wedge; (appuyer) to prop (up). **2** vti (moteur) to stall.

calfeutrer vt to draftproof.

calfeutrer (se) vpr **se c. (chez soi)** to shut oneself away.

calibre m (diamètre) caliber; (d'œuf) grade.

califourchon (à) adv astride; **se mettre à c. sur** to straddle.

câlin, -ine 1 adj affectionate. **2** m cuddle.

calmant m (pour la nervosité) sedative; (pour la douleur) painkiller; **sous calmants** (pour la nervosité) under sedation; (pour la douleur) on painkillers.

calme 1 adj calm. **2** m calm(ness); **du c.!** keep quiet!; (pas de panique) keep calm!; **dans le c.** (travailler, étudier) in peace and quiet.

calmer vt (douleur) to soothe; (inquiétude) to calm; **c. qn** to calm sb (down).

calmer (se) vpr to calm down.

calomnie f (en paroles) slander; (par écrit) libel.

calorie f calorie.

calque m (dessin) tracing; (papier-)c. tracing paper.

camarade mf friend; **c. de jeu** playmate.

camaraderie f friendship.

cambouis m (dirty) oil.

cambrer (se) vpr to arch one's back.

cambriolage m burglary.

cambrioler vt to burglarize.

cambrioleur, -euse mf burglar.

camelote f junk.

camembert m Camembert (cheese).

caméra f (TV ou film) camera.

caméscope® m camcorder.

camion m truck.

camion-benne, pl **camions-bennes** m garbage truck.

camionnette f van.

camp m camp; **feu de c.** campfire; **lit de d.** camp bed; **dans mon c.** (jeu) on my side.

campagnard, -arde mf countryman, countrywoman.

campagne f country(side); (électorale, militaire etc) campaign; **à la c.** in the country.

camper vi to camp.

campeur, -euse mf camper.

camping m camping; (terrain) camp(ing) site.

camping-car m camper.

canadien, -ienne 1 adj Canadian. **2** mf C. Canadian.

canal, -aux m (pour bateaux) canal.

canalisation f (de gaz etc) mains.

canaliser vt (foule) to channel.

canapé m (siège) sofa, couch, settee.

canapé-lit, pl **canapés-lits** m sofa bed.

canard m duck.

canari m canary.

cancer m cancer.

cancéreux, -euse mf cancer sufferer.

candidat, -ate mf candidate; **être** ou **se porter c. à** to apply for.

candidature f application; (aux élections) candidacy; **poser sa c.** to apply (à for).

cane f (female) duck.

caneton m duckling.

canette f (de bière) (small) bottle.

caniche m poodle.

canicule f heatwave.

canif m penknife.

canine f canine (tooth).

caniveau, -x m gutter (in street).

canne f (walking) stick; **c. à pêche** fishing rod.

cannelle f cinnamon.

cannibale mf cannibal.

canoë m canoe; (sport) canoeing.

canon m (big) gun; *(de fusil etc)* barrel.

canot m boat; **c. de sauvetage** lifeboat; **c. pneumatique** rubber dinghy.

canoter vi to go boating.

cantine f canteen; *(à l'école)* cafeteria.

cantique m hymn.

cantonnier m road mender.

caoutchouc m rubber; **balle/etc en c.** rubber ball/etc.

CAP m abrév *(certificat d'aptitude professionnelle)* technical and vocational diploma.

cap m *(pointe de terre)* cape; *(direction)* course; **mettre le c. sur** to steer a course for.

capable adj capable, able; **c. de faire** able to do, capable of doing.

capacité f ability; *(contenance)* capacity.

cape f cape; *(grande)* cloak.

capitaine m captain.

capitale f *(lettre, ville)* capital.

capitulation f surrender.

capituler vi to surrender.

capot m *(de véhicule)* hood.

capote f *(de véhicule)* (convertible) top.

caprice m *(passing)* whim.

capricieux, -euse adj temperamental.

capsule f *(spatiale)* capsule; *(de bouteille)* cap.

capter vt *(signal, radio)* to pick up.

captiver vt to fascinate.

capture f capture.

capturer vt to capture.

capuche f hood.

capuchon m hood; *(de stylo)* cap.

car 1 conj because, for. **2** m bus, coach; **c. de police** police van.

carabine f rifle; **c. à air comprimé** airgun.

caractère[1] m *(lettre)* character; **petits caractères** small letters; **caractères d'imprimerie** capitals.

caractère[2] m *(tempérament, na-ture)* character; **avoir bon c.** to be good-natured.

caractéristique adj & f characteristic.

carafe f decanter.

carambolage m pileup *(of vehicles)*.

caramel m caramel; *(bonbon dur)* taffy.

carapace f shell.

caravane f *(pour camper)* trailer.

carbone m **(papier) c.** carbon (paper).

carbonisé, -ée adj *(nourriture)* burnt to a cinder.

carburant m fuel.

carburateur m carburetor.

carcasse f carcass; *(d'immeuble etc)* frame, shell.

cardiaque adj **être c.** to have a weak heart; **crise/problème c.** heart attack/trouble.

cardinal, -aux 1 adj *(nombre, point)* cardinal. **2** m cardinal.

caressant, -ante adj loving.

caresse f caress.

caresser vt to stroke.

cargaison f cargo.

cargo m cargo boat.

carie f **la c. (dentaire)** tooth decay; **une c.** a cavity.

cariée adj **dent c.** decayed ou bad tooth.

carillon m *(cloches)* chimes; *(horloge)* chiming clock.

caritatif, -ive adj charitable.

carlingue f *(d'avion)* cabin.

carnaval, pl -als m carnival.

carnet m notebook; *(de timbres, chèques, adresses)* book; **c. de notes** report card.

carotte f carrot.

carpe f carp.

carpette f rug.

carré, -ée adj & m square.

carreau, -x m *(vitre)* (window) pane; *(pavé)* tile; *Cartes (couleur)* diamonds; **à carreaux** *(nappe etc)* check.

carrefour m crossroads.

carrelage *m (sol)* tiled floor.

carrément *adv (dire etc)* bluntly; *(complètement)* downright.

carrière *f (terrain)* quarry; *(métier)* career.

carrosse *m* (horse-drawn) carriage.

carrosserie *f* body(work).

carrure *f* build.

cartable *m* satchel.

carte *f* card; *(routière)* map; *(menu)* menu; **c. (postale)** (post)card; **c. à jouer** playing card; **c. à gratter** scratchcard; **jouer aux cartes** to play cards; **c. de visite** business card; **c. de crédit** credit card; **c. des vins** wine list; **c. grise** vehicle registration document.

carton *m* cardboard; *(boîte)* cardboard box.

cartonné *adj* livre c. hardback.

cartouche *f* cartridge; *(de cigarettes)* carton.

cas *m* case; **en tout c.** in any case; **en aucun c.** on no account; **en c. de besoin** if need be; **en c. d'accident** in the event of an accident; **en c. d'urgence** in an emergency; **au c. où elle tomberait** if she should fall; **pour le c. où il pleuvrait** in case it rains.

casanier, -ière *adj* stay-at-home.

cascade *f* waterfall; *(de cinéma)* stunt.

cascadeur, -euse *mf* stunt man, stunt woman.

case *f* pigeonhole; *(de tiroir)* compartment; *(d'échiquier etc)* square; *(de formulaire)* box; *(hutte)* hut, cabin.

caserne *f* barracks; **c. de pompiers** fire station.

casier *m* pigeonhole; *(fermant à clef)* locker; **c. à bouteilles/à disques** bottle/record rack; **c. judiciaire** criminal record.

casino *m* casino.

casque *m* helmet; *(de coiffeur)* (hair)-dryer; **c. (à écouteurs)** headphones.

casqué, -ée *adj* helmeted.

casquette *f (coiffure)* cap.

casse-cou *mf inv (personne)* daredevil.

casse-croûte *m inv* snack.

casse-noisettes *m inv*, **casse-noix** *m inv* nutcracker(s).

casse-pieds *mf inv (personne) Fam* pain.

casser 1 *vt* to break; *(noix)* to crack; **elle me casse les pieds** *Fam* she's getting on my nerves. **2** *vi*, **se casser** *vpr* to break; **se c. la figure** *(tomber) Fam* to take a spill.

casserole *f (sauce)* pan.

casse-tête *m inv (problème)* headache; *(jeu)* puzzle.

cassette *f (audio)* cassette; *(vidéo)* video (cassette); **sur c.** *(film)* on video.

cassis *m (fruit)* blackcurrant; *(obstacle)* dip *(across road)*.

castor *m* beaver.

catalogue *m* catalog.

catastrophe *f* disaster; **atterrir en c.** to make an emergency landing.

catastrophique *adj* disastrous.

catch *m* (all-in) wrestling.

catcheur, -euse *mf* wrestler.

catéchisme *m* catechism.

catégorie *f* category.

cathédrale *f* cathedral.

catholique *adj & mf* Catholic.

cauchemar *m* nightmare.

cause *f* cause; **à c. de** because of, on account of.

causer 1 *vt (provoquer)* to cause. **2** *vi (bavarder)* to chat *(de* about).

caution *f (d'appartement)* deposit; *(d'un détenu)* bail; *(personne)* guarantor; *(appui)* backing.

cavalier, -ière *mf* rider; *(pour danser)* partner.

cave *f* cellar.

caveau, -x *m* (burial) vault.

caverne *f* cave.

cavité *f* hollow.

CCP *m abrév (compte chèque post-*

al) Post Office checking account.

ce¹ (**c'** *before e and é*) *pron dém* it, that; **c'est toi/bon/***etc* it's *ou* that's you/good/*etc*; **c'est mon médecin** he's my doctor; **ce sont eux qui…** they are the ones who…; **c'est elle de jouer** it's her turn to play; **est-ce que tu viens?** are you coming? **ce que, ce qui** what; **je sais ce qui est bon/ce que tu veux** I know what is good/what you want; **ce que c'est beau!** it's so beautiful!

ce², **cette**, *pl* **ces** (**ce** *becomes* **cet** *before a vowel or mute h*) *adj dém* this, that, *pl* these, those; **(+ ci)** this, *pl* these; **(+ là)** that, *pl* those; **cet homme** this/that man; **cet homme-ci** this man; **cet homme-là** that man.

ceci *pron dém* this.

céder **1** *vt* to give up (**à** to). **2** *vi (personne)* to give in (**à** to); *(branche, chaise etc)* to give way.

cédille *f Grammaire* cedilla.

CEI *f abrév (Communauté d'États Indépendants)* CIS.

ceinture *f* belt; *(taille)* waist; **c. de sécurité** seatbelt; **c. de sauvetage** life preserver.

cela *pron dém (pour désigner)* that; *(sujet indéfini)* it, that; **c. m'attriste que…** it saddens me that…; **quand/comment/***etc* **c.?** when?/how?/*etc*.

célèbre *adj* famous.

célébrer *vt* to celebrate.

célébrité *f* fame.

céleri *m (en branches)* celery.

célibataire **1** *adj* single, unmarried. **2** *m* bachelor. **3** *f* unmarried woman.

cellophane® *f* cellophane®.

cellule *f* cell.

celui, **celle**, *pl* **ceux**, **celles** *pron dém* the one, *pl* those, the ones; **c. de Jean** Jean's (one); **ceux de Jean** Jean's (ones). ■ **(+ ci)** this one, *pl* these (ones) *(dont on vient de parler)* the latter; **(+ là)** that one, *pl*

those (ones); the former; **ceux-ci sont gros** these (ones) are big.

cendre *f* ash.

cendrier *m* ashtray.

censé, -ée *adj* être c. faire qch to be supposed to do sth.

censure *f (activité)* censorship; *(comité)* board of censors.

censurer *vt (film)* to censor.

cent *adj & m* hundred; **c. pages** a *ou* one hundred pages; **cinq pour c.** five percent.

centaine *f* une c. a hundred (or so); **des centaines de** hundreds of.

centenaire **1** *adj* hundred-year-old; **être c.** to be a hundred. **2** *mf* centenarian. **3** *m (anniversaire)* centenary.

centième *adj & mf* hundredth.

centigrade *adj* centigrade.

centime *m* centime.

centimètre *m* centimeter; *(ruban)* tape measure.

central, -e, -aux **1** *adj* central. **2** *m* **c. (téléphonique)** (telephone) exchange.

centrale *f (usine)* power plant.

centre *m* center; **c. commercial** shopping mall.

centre-ville *m inv* downtown area.

cependant *conj* however, yet.

céramique *f (matière)* ceramic; **de c.** ceramic.

cerceau, -x *m* hoop.

cercle *m* circle.

cercueil *m* coffin.

céréale *f* cereal.

cérémonie *f* ceremony.

cerf *m* deer.

cerf-volant, *pl* **cerfs-volants** *m* kite.

cerise *f* cherry.

cerisier *m* cherry tree.

cerne *m* ring.

cerner *vt* to surround; **avoir les yeux cernés** to have rings under one's eyes.

certain¹, **-aine** *adj (sûr)* certain,

sure; **c'est c. que tu réussiras** you're certain *ou* sure to succeed; **je suis c. de réussir** I'm certain *ou* sure I'll succeed; **être c. de qch** to be certain *ou* sure of sth.

certain², -aine *adj (difficile à fixer)* certain; **un c. temps** a certain (amount of) time.

certainement *adv* certainly.

certains *pron pl* some (people).

certificat *m* certificate.

certifier *vt* to certify.

certitude *f* certainty; **avoir la c. que** to be certain that.

cerveau, -x *m* brain; **rhume de c.** head cold.

cervelle *f* brain; *(plat)* brains.

ces *voir* **ce²**.

CES *m abrév (collège d'enseignement secondaire)* = (junior) high school.

cesse *f* **sans c.** constantly.

cesser *vti* to stop; **faire c.** to put a stop to; **il ne cesse (pas) de parler** he doesn't stop talking.

cessez-le-feu *m inv* ceasefire.

c'est-à-dire *conj* that is (to say).

cet, cette *voir* **ce²**.

ceux *voir* **celui**.

chacun, -une *pron* each (one), every one; *(tout le monde)* everyone.

chagrin *m* grief; **avoir du c.** to be very upset.

chahut *m* racket.

chahuter *vi* to create a racket.

chahuteur, -euse *mf* rowdy.

chaîne *f* chain; *(de télévision)* channel; *(de montagnes)* chain, range; **travail à la c.** assembly-line work; **c. hi-fi** hi-fi system.

chaînette *f* (small) chain.

chair *f* flesh; *(couleur)* **c.** flesh-colored; **en c. et on os** in the flesh; **la c. de poule** goose pimples *ou* bumps; **c. à saucisses** sausage meat.

chaise *f* chair; **c. longue** deckchair; **c. haute** high-chair.

châle *m* shawl.

chalet *m* chalet.

chaleur *f* heat; *(douce)* warmth.

chaleureux, -euse *adj* warm.

chaloupe *f (bateau)* launch.

chalumeau, -x *m* blowtorch.

chalutier *m* trawler.

chamailler (se) *vpr* to squabble.

chambouler *vt Fam* to make topsy-turvy.

chambre *f* (bed)room; **c. à coucher** bedroom; *(mobilier)* bedroom suite *ou* set; **c. à air** *(de pneu)* inner tube; **c. de commerce** chamber of commerce; **c. d'amis** guest room; **garder la c.** to stay indoors.

chameau, -x *m* camel.

chamois *m* **peau de c.** chamois.

champ *m* field; **c. de bataille** battlefield; **c. de courses** racetrack.

champagne *m* champagne.

champignon *m* mushroom.

champion, -onne *mf* champion.

championnat *m* championship.

chance *f* luck; *(probabilité, occasion)* chance; **avoir de la c.** to be lucky; **c'est une c. que** it's lucky that.

chanceler *vi* to stagger.

chanceux, -euse *adj* lucky.

chandail *m* (thick) sweater.

chandelier *m* candlestick.

chandelle *f* candle; **en c.** *(tir)* straight into the air.

change *m (de devises)* exchange.

changement *m* change.

changer *vti* to change; **c. qn en** to change sb into; **ça la changera de ne pas travailler** it'll be a change for her not to be working; **c. de train/voiture/etc** to change trains/one's car/etc; **c. de vitesse/sujet** to change gear/the subject.

changer (se) *vpr* to change (one's clothes).

chanson *f* song.

chant *m* singing; *(chanson)* song; **c. de Noël** Christmas carol.

chantage *m* blackmail.

chanter 1 *vi* to sing; *(coq)* to crow;

si ça te chante *Fam* if you feel like it. **2** *vt* to sing.

chanteur, -euse *mf* singer.

chantier *m* (building) site; **c. naval** shipyard, dockyard.

chantilly *f* whipped cream.

chantonner *vti* to hum.

chaos *m* chaos.

chapeau, -x *m* hat.

chapelet *m* rosary; **un c. de** *(saucisses etc)* a string of.

chapelle *f* chapel.

chapelure *f* breadcrumbs.

chapiteau, -x *m* (de cirque) big top; *(pour expositions etc)* marquee, tent.

chapitre *m* chapter.

chaque *adj* each, every.

char *m* (romain) chariot; (de carnaval) float; **c. (d'assaut)** tank.

charade *f* (énigme) riddle.

charbon *m* coal; **c. de bois** charcoal.

charcuterie *f* pork butcher's shop; *(aliments)* cooked pork meats.

charcutier, -ière *mf* pork butcher.

chardon *m* thistle.

charge *f* (poids) load; (fardeau) burden; **à la c. de qn** (personne) dependent on sb; (frais) payable by sb; **prendre en c.** to take charge of.

chargé, -ée *adj* (véhicule, arme etc) loaded; (journée) busy.

chargement *m* loading; (objet) load.

charger *vt* to load; (soldats, batterie) to charge; **c. qn de** (travail etc) to entrust sb with; **c. qn de faire** to instruct sb to do.

charger (se) *vpr* **se c. de** (enfant, travail etc) to take charge of.

chargeur *m* (pour batterie, portable) charger.

chariot *m* (à bagages etc) cart.

charité *f* (secours) charity.

charmant, -ante *adj* charming.

charme *m* charm; (magie) spell.

charmer *vt* to charm.

charnière *f* hinge.

charpente *f* frame(work).

charpentier *m* carpenter.

charrette *f* cart.

charrier *vt* (transporter) to cart; *(rivière)* to carry along (sand etc).

charrue *f* plow.

charter *m* charter (flight).

chasse[1] *f* hunting, hunt; **c. à courre** hunting; **avion de c.** fighter plane; **faire la c. à** to hunt for.

chasse[2] *f* **c. d'eau** toilet flush; **tirer la c.** to flush the toilet.

chasse-neige *m inv* snowplow.

chasser **1** *vt* (animal) to hunt; (personne, odeur) to chase away; *(mouche)* to brush away. **2** *vi* to hunt.

chasseur, -euse *mf* hunter.

châssis *m* frame; (d'automobile) chassis.

chat *m* cat; **pas un c.** not a soul; **c. perché** (jeu) tag.

châtaigne *f* chestnut.

châtaignier *m* chestnut tree.

châtain *adj inv* (chestnut) brown.

château, -x *m* castle; (palais) palace; **c. fort** fortified castle; **c. d'eau** water tower.

châtiment *m* punishment.

chaton *m* kitten.

chatouiller *vt* to tickle.

chatouilleux, -euse *adj* ticklish.

chatte *f* (she-)cat.

chatterton *m* electrician's tape.

chaud, chaude **1** *adj* hot; (doux) warm. **2** *m* **avoir c.** to be hot; (doux) to be warm; **il fait c.** it's hot; **être au c.** to be in the warm.

chaudement *adv* warmly.

chaudière *f* boiler.

chauffage *m* heating.

chauffant, -ante *adj* (couverture) electric; **plaque chauffante** hot plate.

chauffard *m* reckless driver.

chauffé, -ée *adj* (piscine etc) heated.

chauffe-eau *m inv* water heater.

chauffer 1 *vt* to heat (up). **2** *vi* to heat (up); *(moteur)* to overheat.

chauffeur *m* driver; *(employé)* chauffeur.

chaume *m (pour toiture)* thatch; **toit de c.** thatched roof.

chaumière *f* thatched cottage.

chaussée *f* road(way).

chausse-pied, *pl* **chausse-pieds** *m* shoehorn.

chausser *vt* **c. qn** to put shoes on (to) sb; **c. du 40** to take a size 40 shoe.

chausser (se) *vpr* to put on one's shoes.

chaussette *f* sock.

chausson *m* slipper; *(de danse)* shoe.

chaussure *f* shoe.

chauve 1 *adj* bald. **2** *mf* bald person.

chauve-souris, *pl* **chauves-souris** *f (animal)* bat.

chauvin, -ine 1 *adj* chauvinistic. **2** *mf* chauvinist.

chaux *f* lime.

chavirer *vti* to capsize.

chef *m* leader, head; **c. d'entreprise** head of (a) company; **c. de gare** stationmaster; **c. d'orchestre** conductor; **en c.** *(commandant, rédacteur)* in chief.

chef-d'œuvre, *pl* **chefs-d'œuvre** *m* masterpiece.

chef-lieu, *pl* **chefs-lieux** *m* chief town *(of a département)*.

chemin *m* road, path; *(trajet, direction)* way; **beaucoup de c. à faire** a long way to go; **se mettre en c.** to set out.

chemin de fer *m* railroad.

cheminée *f* fireplace; *(encadrement)* mantelpiece; *(sur le toit)* chimney; *(de navire)* funnel.

cheminot *m* railroad employee.

chemise *f* shirt; *(cartonnée)* folder; **c. de nuit** *(de femme)* nightgown; *(d'homme)* nightshirt.

chemisette *f* short-sleeved shirt.

chemisier *m* blouse.

chêne *m* oak.

chenil *m* kennel.

chenille *f* caterpillar.

chèque *m* check; **c. de voyage** traveler's check.

chèque-repas, *pl* **chèques-repas** *m* meal voucher.

chéquier *m* checkbook.

cher, chère *adj (aimé)* dear (**à** to); *(coûteux)* expensive; **payer c.** *(objet)* to pay a lot for; *(erreur etc)* to pay dearly for.

chercher *vt* to look for; *(dans un dictionnaire)* to look up; **aller c.** to (go and) fetch *ou* get; **c. à faire** to attempt to do.

chercheur, -euse *mf* research worker.

chéri, -ie 1 *adj* dearly loved. **2** *mf* darling.

cherté *f* high cost.

chétif, -ive *adj* puny.

cheval, -aux *m* horse; **à c.** on horseback; **faire du c.** to go horseback riding; **chevaux de bois** merry-go-round.

chevalier *m* knight.

chevaline *adj f* **boucherie c.** horse butcher's (shop).

chevelure *f* (head of) hair.

chevet *m* **table/livre de c.** bedside table/book; **au c. de** at the bedside of.

cheveu, -x *m* **un c.** a hair; **cheveux** hair; **tiré par les cheveux** far-fetched.

cheville *f* ankle; *(pour vis)* (wall) plug.

chèvre *f* goat.

chevreau, -x *m (petit de la chèvre)* kid.

chez *prép* **c. qn** at sb's house/apartment/*etc*; **il est c. Jean/c. le médecin** he's at Jean's (place)/at the doctor's; **il va c. Jean/c. le médecin** he's going to Jean's (place)/to the doctor's; **c. moi, c. nous** at home; **je vais c. moi** I'm going home; **une habitude c. elle** a habit with her; **c.**

Mme Dupont *(adresse)* care of Mme Dupont.

chic 1 *adj inv* smart; *(gentil) Fam* nice. **2** *int* **c. (alors)!** great! **3** *m* style.

chicorée *f (à café)* chicory; *(pour salade)* endive.

chien *m* dog; **un mal de c.** an awful lot of trouble; **temps de c.** rotten weather.

chien-loup, *pl* **chiens-loups** *m* wolfhound.

chienne *f* dog, bitch.

chiffon *m* rag; **c. (à poussière)** dust cloth.

chiffonner *vt* to crumple.

chiffre *m* figure, number; *(romain, arabe)* numeral; **c. d'affaires** sales.

chimie *f* chemistry.

chimique *adj* chemical.

chimpanzé *m* chimpanzee.

chinois, -oise 1 *adj* Chinese. **2** *mf* **C.** Chinese man, Chinese woman, Chinese *inv*; **les C.** the Chinese. **3** *m (langue)* Chinese.

chiot *m* puppy.

chipoter *vi (contester)* to quibble *(sur* about).

chips *mpl* (potato) chips.

chirurgical, -e, -aux *adj* surgical.

chirurgie *f* surgery.

chirurgien *m* surgeon.

choc *m (d'objets, émotion)* shock.

chocolat *m* chocolate; **c. à croquer** bittersweet chocolate; **c. au lait** milk chocolate.

chocolaté, -ée *adj* chocolate-flavored.

chœur *m (chanteurs, nef)* choir; **en c.** (all) together.

choisir *vt* to choose, to pick.

choix *m* choice; *(assortiment)* selection.

cholestérol *m* cholesterol.

chômage *m* unemployment; **au c.** unemployed.

chômer *vi* to be unemployed.

chômeur, -euse *mf* unemployed

person; **les chômeurs** the unemployed.

choquant, -ante *adj* shocking.

choquer *vt* to shock.

chorale *f* choral society.

chose *f* thing; **monsieur C.** Mr What's-his-name.

chou, -x *m* cabbage; **choux de Bruxelles** Brussels sprouts.

choucroute *f* sauerkraut.

chouette 1 *f* owl. **2** *adj Fam* super, great.

chou-fleur, *pl* **choux-fleurs** *m* cauliflower.

choyer *vt* to pamper.

chrétien, -ienne *adj & mf* Christian.

chrome *m* chrome.

chromé, -ée *adj* chrome-plated.

chronique *f (à la radio)* report; *(dans le journal)* column.

chronomètre *m* stopwatch.

chronométrer *vt* to time.

chrysanthème *m* chrysanthemum.

chuchotement *m* whisper(ing).

chuchoter *vti* to whisper.

chut! *int* sh!, shush!

chute *f* fall; **c. d'eau** waterfall; **c. de neige** snowfall; **c. de pluie** rainfall.

chuter *vi (diminuer)* to fall, to drop; *(tomber) Fam* to fall.

ci 1 *adv* **par-ci par-là** here and there. **2** *pron dém* **comme ci comme ça** so so.

cible *f* target.

cicatrice *f* scar.

cicatrisation *f* healing (up).

cicatriser *vt*, **se cicatriser** *vpr* to heal up *(leaving a scar)*.

cidre *m* cider.

Cie *abrév (compagnie)* Co.

ciel *m (pl* **ciels)** sky; *(pl* **cieux)** *(paradis)* heaven.

cierge *m* candle.

cigale *f (insecte)* cicada.

cigare *m* cigar.

cigarette *f* cigarette.

cigogne *f* stork.

ci-joint, -jointe 1 *adj* le document c. the enclosed document. **2** *adv* vous trouverez c. copie de… please find enclosed a copy of…

cil *m* (eye)lash.

cime *f* (*d'un arbre*) top; (*d'une montagne*) peak.

ciment *m* cement.

cimenter *vt* to cement.

cimetière *m* cemetery.

ciné *m Fam* movies.

cinéaste *m* movie maker.

ciné-club *m* film club.

cinéma *m* (*art, industrie*) movies; (*bâtiment*) movie theater; **faire du c.** to make movies.

cinéphile *mf* movie enthusiast.

cinglé, -ée *adj Fam* crazy.

cinq *adj & m* five.

cinquantaine *f* about fifty.

cinquante *adj & m* fifty.

cinquantième *adj & mf* fiftieth.

cinquième *adj & mf* fifth.

cintre *m* coathanger.

cirage *m* (shoe) polish.

circonférence *f* circumference.

circonflexe *adj Grammaire* circumflex.

circonstance *f* circumstance; **pour la c.** for this occasion.

circonstanciel, -ielle *adj Grammaire* adverbial.

circuit *m* (*électrique, sportif etc*) circuit; (*voyage*) tour.

circulaire 1 *adj* circular. **2** *f* (*lettre*) circular.

circulation *f* circulation; (*automobile*) traffic.

circuler *vi* to circulate; (*véhicule, train*) to travel; (*passant*) to walk around; (*rumeur*) to go around; **faire c.** (*piétons etc*) to move on.

cire *f* wax.

ciré *m* (*vêtement*) oilskins.

cirer *vt* to polish.

cirque *m* circus.

ciseau, -x *m* chisel; (une paire de) **ciseaux** (a pair of) scissors.

citadin, -ine *mf* city dweller.

citation *f* quotation.

cité *f* city; **c. universitaire** (university) dormitory complex.

citer *vt* to quote.

citerne *f* (*réservoir*) tank.

citoyen, -enne *mf* citizen.

citoyenneté *f* citizenship.

citron *m* lemon; **c. pressé** (fresh) lemon juice.

citronnade *f* lemonade.

citrouille *f* pumpkin.

civière *f* stretcher.

civil, -e 1 *adj* civil; (*non militaire*) civilian; **année civile** calendar year. **2** *m* civilian; **en c.** (*policier*) in plain clothes.

civilisation *f* civilization.

civilisé, -ée *adj* civilized.

civique *adj* civic; **instruction c.** civics.

clair, -e 1 *adj* (*distinct, limpide, évident*) clear; (*éclairé*) light; (*pâle*) light(-colored); **bleu/vert c.** light blue/green. **2** *adv* (*voir*) clearly. **3** *m* **c. de lune** moonlight.

clairement *adv* clearly.

clairière *f* clearing.

clairon *m* bugle.

clairsemé, -ée *adj* sparse.

clairvoyant, -ante *adj* perceptive.

clandestin, -ine *adj* (*journal, mouvement*) underground; **passager c.** stowaway.

claque *f* smack, slap.

claquement *m* (*de porte*) slam(ming).

claquer 1 *vt* (*porte*) to slam, to bang. **2** *vi* (*porte*) to slam, to bang; (*coup de feu*) to ring out; **c. des mains** to clap one's hands; **elle claque des dents** her teeth are chattering.

claquer (se) *vpr* se c. un muscle to tear a muscle.

claquettes *fpl* tap dancing; **faire des c.** to do tap dancing.

clarinette *f* clarinet.

clarté *f* light; (*précision*) clarity.

classe f class; **aller en c.** to go to school.

classement m classification; filing; grading; (rang) place; (en sport) placing.

classer vt to classify; (papiers) to file; (candidats) to grade.

classer (se) vpr **se c. premier** to come first.

classeur m (meuble) filing cabinet; (portefeuille) (loose leaf) binder.

classique adj classical.

clavicule f collarbone.

clavier m keyboard.

clé, clef f key; (outil) wrench; **fermer à c.** to lock; **sous c.** under lock and key; **c. de contact** ignition key; **c. USB** memory stick.

clémentine f tangerine.

clergé m clergy.

clic m (avec une souris) click.

cliché m (de photo) negative.

client, -ente mf customer; (d'un avocat) client; (d'un médecin) patient; (d'hôtel) guest.

clientèle f customers; (d'un avocat, d'un médecin) practice.

cligner vi **c. des yeux** to blink; (fermer à demi) to squint; **c. de l'œil** to wink.

clignotant m (de voiture) turn signal.

clignoter vi to blink; (lumière) to flicker.

climat m climate.

climatisation f air conditioning.

climatisé, -ée adj air-conditioned.

clin d'œil m wink; **en un c.** in no time (at all).

clinique f (private) clinic.

cliquer vi to click (sur on); **c. deux fois** to double-click.

clochard, -arde mf down-and-out, tramp.

cloche f bell.

cloche-pied (à) adv **sauter à c.** to hop on one foot.

clocher m bell tower; (en pointe) steeple.

clochette f (small) bell.

cloison f partition.

clone m clone.

cloner vt to clone.

clope m ou f Fam smoke, cigarette.

clopin-clopant adv **aller c.** to hobble.

cloque f blister.

clos, close adj closed.

clôture f (barrière) fence.

clôturer vt to enclose.

clou m nail; **les clous** (passage) crosswalk.

clouer vt to nail; **cloué au lit** confined to bed.

clouté, -ée adj (pneus) studded; **passage c.** crosswalk.

clown m clown.

club m (association) club.

cm abrév (centimètre) cm.

coaguler vti, **se coaguler** vpr to clot.

coalition f coalition.

cobaye m guinea pig.

coca mf (Coca-Cola®) Coke®.

cocaïne f cocaine.

coccinelle f ladybug.

cocher[1] vt to tick (off), to check (off).

cocher[2] m coachman.

cochon, -onne 1 m pig; **c. d'Inde** guinea pig. **2** mf (personne sale) (dirty) pig.

cochonnerie f (chose sans valeur) trash; (obscénité) smutty remark; **manger des cochonneries** to eat junk food.

cocorico int & m cock-a-doodle-doo.

cocotier m coconut palm.

cocotte f casserole; **c. minute®** pressure cooker.

code m code; **codes, phares c.** low beams; **C. de la route** traffic laws.

cœur m heart; (couleur), Cartes hearts; **au c. de** (ville, hiver etc) in the middle ou heart of; **par c.**

by heart; **avoir mal au c.** to feel sick; **avoir le c. gros** to have a heavy heart; **avoir bon c.** to be kind-hearted; **de bon c.** *(offrir)* willingly; *(rire)* heartily.

coffre *m* chest; *(de banque)* safe; *(de voiture)* trunk.

coffre-fort, *pl* coffres-forts *m* safe.

coffret *m (à bijoux etc)* box.

cogner *vti* to knock, to bang.

cogner (se) *vpr* **se c. la tête/etc** to knock *ou* bang one's head/*etc;* **se c. à qch** to knock *ou* bang into sth.

cohabiter *vi* to live together; **c. avec qn** to live with sb.

cohérent, -ente *adj (discours)* coherent; *(attitude)* consistent.

cohue *f* crowd.

coiffer *vt* **c. qn** to do sb's hair.

coiffer (se) *vpr* to do one's hair.

coiffeur, -euse *mf* hairdresser.

coiffure *f* hat; *(arrangement)* hairstyle.

coin *m (angle)* corner; *(endroit)* spot; **du c.** *(magasin etc)* local; **dans le c.** in the (local) area.

coincé, -ée *adj* stuck.

coincer *vt (mécanisme etc)* to jam.

coincer (se) *vpr* to get stuck *ou* jammed; **se c. le doigt** to get one's finger stuck.

coïncidence *f* coincidence.

coing *m* quince.

col *m* collar; *(de montagne)* pass; **c. roulé** turtleneck.

colère *f* anger; **une c.** a fit of anger; **en c.** angry (**contre** with); **se mettre en c.** to lose one's temper.

coléreux, -euse *adj* quick-tempered.

colique *f* diarrhea.

colis *m* parcel.

collaboration *f* collaboration.

collaborer *vi* collaborate (**à** on).

collant, -ante 1 *adj (papier)* sticky; *(vêtement)* skin-tight. **2** *m (de danse)* leotard.

colle *f* glue; *(blanche)* paste.

collecte *f (quête)* collection.

collectif, -ive *adj* collective; **billet c.** group ticket.

collection *f* collection.

collectionner *vt* to collect.

collectionneur, -euse *mf* collector.

collectivité *f (groupe)* community.

collège *m* = (junior) high school.

collégien, -enne *mf* = (junior) high school student.

collègue *mf* colleague.

coller *vt* to stick; *(à la colle transparente)* to glue; *(à la colle blanche)* to paste; *(affiche)* to stick up; *(papier peint)* to hang; *(mettre) Fam* to stick; **c. contre** *(nez, oreille etc)* to press against.

collier *m (bijou)* necklace; *(de chien)* collar.

colline *f* hill.

collision *f* collision; **entrer en c. avec** to collide with.

colocataire *mf* roommate.

colombe *f* dove.

colonel *m* colonel.

colonie *f* colony; **c. de vacances** summer camp.

colonne *f* column; **c. vertébrale** spine.

coloré, -ée *adj* colorful; *(verre, liquide)* colored.

colorer *vt* to color.

coloriage *m* album de coloriages coloring book.

colorier *vt (dessin)* to color (in).

coloris *m (nuance)* shade.

colosse *m* giant.

colza *m (plante)* rape.

coma *m* coma; **dans le c.** in a coma.

combat *m* fight.

combatif, -ive *adj* eager to fight; *(instinct, esprit)* fighting.

combattant *m* fighter, brawler.

combattre* *vti* to fight.

combien *adv (quantité)* how much; *(nombre)* how many; **c. de** *(temps, argent etc)* how much;

(gens, livres etc) how many. ■ *(à quel point)* how; **c. y a-t-il d'ici à…?** how far is it to…? **2** m inv **le c. sommes-nous?** Fam what is the date?; **tous les c.?** Fam how often?

combinaison f combination; *(vêtement de femme)* slip; *(de mécanicien)* overalls; **c. de vol/plongée/ski** flying/diving/ski suit; **c. spatiale** spacesuit.

combiné m *(de téléphone)* receiver.

combiner vt *(assembler)* to combine.

comble 1 m **le c. de** *(la joie etc)* the height of; **c'est un** ou **le c.!** that's the limit! **2** adj *(bondé)* packed.

combler vt *(trou etc)* to fill; **c. son retard** to make up lost time.

combustible m fuel.

comédie f comedy; **c. musicale** musical; **jouer la c.** to put on an act, to pretend.

comédien m actor.

comédienne f actress.

comestible adj edible.

comique adj *(amusant)* funny; *(acteur etc)* comic.

comité m committee.

commandant m *(d'un navire)* captain; **c. de bord** *(d'un avion)* captain.

commande f *(achat)* order; **sur c.** to order; **les commandes** *(d'un avion etc)* the controls.

commandement m *(autorité)* command.

commander 1 vt to command; *(acheter)* to order. **2** vi **c. à qn de faire** to command sb to do.

comme 1 adv & conj like; **c. moi** like me; **c. cela** like that; **qu'as-tu c. vins?** what kind of wines do you have? ■ as; **blanc c. neige** (as) white as snow; **c. si** as if; **c. pour faire** as if to do; **c. par hasard** as if by chance. **2** adv *(exclamatif)* **regarde c. il pleut!** look how (hard) it's raining!; **c. c'est petit!** how

small it is! **3** conj *(temps, cause)* as; **c. elle entrait** as she was coming in.

commencement m beginning, start.

commencer vti to begin, to start *(à faire* to do, doing; **par** with; **par faire** by doing); **pour c.** to begin with.

comment adv how; **c. le sais-tu?** how do you know?; **c.?** *(répétition, surprise)* what?; **c. est-il?** what is he like?; **c. faire?** what's to be done?; **c. t'appelles-tu?** what's your name?; **c. allez-vous?** how are you?

commentaire m *(remarque)* comment; *(de radio, de télévision)* commentary.

commerçant, -ante mf merchant; **rue commerçante** shopping street.

commerce m trade, commerce; *(magasin)* store, business; **dans le c.** *(objet)* (on sale) in stores.

commercial, -e, -aux adj commercial.

commère f gossip.

commettre* vt *(délit etc)* to commit; *(erreur)* to make.

commissaire m **c. (de police)** police chief.

commissariat m **c. (de police)** (central) police station.

commission f *(course)* errand; *(pourcentage)* commission *(sur* on); **faire les commissions** to go shopping, to run (the) errands.

commode 1 adj *(pratique)* handy. **2** f chest of drawers, dresser.

commun, -une adj *(collectif, habituel etc)* common; *(frais, cuisine)* shared; **ami c.** mutual friend; **en c.** in common; **avoir** ou **mettre en c.** to share.

communautaire adj *(de la CE)* Community; **vie c.** community life.

communauté f *(collectivité)* community; **la C.** *(économique)* **européenne** the European (Economic) Community; **la C. des États in-**

dépendants the Commonwealth of Independent States.

commune f commune.

communication f communication; **c. (téléphonique)** (telephone) call.

communier vi to receive (Holy) Communion.

communion f (Holy) Communion.

communiqué m (official) statement; (publicitaire) message; **c. de presse** press release.

communiquer vti to communicate.

communiste adj & mf communist.

compact, -e adj dense.

compagne f friend; (épouse) companion.

compagnie f (présence, société) company; **tenir c. à qn** to keep sb company.

compagnon m companion; **c. de jeu** playmate; **c. de travail** coworker.

comparable adj comparable.

comparaison f comparison (avec with).

comparaître* vi (devant tribunal) to appear (**devant** before).

comparer vt to compare (**à** to, with).

compartiment m compartment.

compas m compass.

compatir vi to sympathize.

compatriote mf compatriot.

compenser 1 vt to compensate for. **2** vi to compensate.

compétence f competence.

compétent, -ente adj competent.

compétition f competition; (épreuve sportive) event; **de c.** (esprit, sport) competitive.

complaisance f kindness.

complaisant, -ante adj kind.

complément m Grammaire complement.

complet, -ète 1 adj complete;

(train, hôtel etc) full; (aliment) whole. **2** m suit.

complètement adv completely.

compléter vt to complete; (somme) to make up.

complexe 1 adj complex. **2** m (sentiment, construction) complex.

complication f complication.

complice m accomplice.

compliment m compliment; **mes compliments!** congratulations!

complimenter vt to compliment (**sur, pour** on).

compliqué, -ée adj complicated.

compliquer vt to complicate.

compliquer (se) vpr to get complicated.

complot m plot.

comploter vti to plot (**de faire** to do).

comportement m behavior.

comporter (se) vpr to behave; (joueur, voiture) to perform.

composé, -ée adj & m (mot, en chimie etc) compound; **temps c.** compound tense; Grammaire **passé c.** perfect (tense).

composer vt to make up, to compose; (numéro) to dial; **être composé de** to be made up ou composed of.

composer (se) vpr se c. de to be made up ou composed of.

compositeur, -trice mf composer.

composter vt (billet) to cancel.

compote f sauce; **c. de pommes** applesauce.

compréhensible adj understandable.

compréhensif, -ive adj (personne) understanding.

comprendre* vt to understand; (comporter) to include; **je n'y comprends rien** I don't understand anything about it.

comprendre (se) vpr ça se comprend that's understandable.

comprimé m tablet.

comprimer *vt* to compress.

compris, -ise *adj (inclus)* included (**dans** in); **tout c.** (all) inclusive; **y c.** including.

compromettre* *vt (personne)* to compromise; *(sécurité)* to jeopardize.

comptabilité *f (comptes)* accounts; *(science)* bookkeeping, accounting; *(service)* accounts department.

comptable *mf* bookkeeper; *(expert)* accountant.

comptant 1 *adj* **argent c.** (hard) cash. **2** *adv* **payer c.** to pay (in) cash.

compte *m* account; *(calcul)* count; *(nombre)* (right) number; **avoir un c. en banque** to have a bank(ing) account; **c. courant** checking account; **c. à rebours** countdown; **tenir c. de** to take into account; **c. tenu de** considering; **se rendre c. de** to realize; **à son c.** *(travailler)* for oneself; *(s'installer)* on one's own; **en fin de c.** all things considered.

compte-gouttes *m inv* dropper; *Fig* **au c.** a little at a time.

compter 1 *vt (calculer)* to count; **c. faire** to expect to do; *(avoir l'intention de)* to intend to do; **c. qch à qn** *(facturer)* to charge sb for sth. **2** *vi (calculer, avoir de l'importance)* to count; **c. sur** to rely on.

compte rendu *m* report; *(de livre, film)* review.

compteur *m* meter; **c. (de vitesse)** speedometer; **c. (kilométrique)** odometer.

comptoir *m (de magasin)* counter; *(de café)* bar; *(de bureau)* (reception) desk.

comte *m* count.

comtesse *f* countess.

concentré, -ée 1 *adj (lait)* condensed; *(attentif)* concentrating (hard). **2** *m* **c. de tomates** tomato purée.

concentrer *vt*, **se concentrer** *vpr* to concentrate.

concerner *vt* to concern.

concert *m* concert.

concerter (se) *vpr* to consult each other.

concessionnaire *mf (authorized)* dealer.

concevoir *vt* to conceive.

concierge *mf* caretaker, janitor.

concitoyen, -enne *mf* fellow citizen.

conclure* *vti* to conclude (**que** that).

conclusion *f* conclusion.

concombre *m* cucumber.

concordant, -ante *adj* in agreement.

concorder *vi* to agree; **c. avec** to match.

concours *m (examen)* competitive examination; *(jeu)* competition; **c. hippique** horse show.

concret, -ète *adj* concrete.

concrétiser *vt (rêve)* to realize; *(projet)* to carry out.

conçu, -ue *adj* **c. pour faire/pour qn** designed to do/for sb; **bien c.** *(maison etc)* well designed.

concubinage *m* cohabitation; **vivre en c.** to cohabit.

concurrence *f* competition; **faire c. à** to compete with.

concurrencer *vt* to compete with.

concurrent, -ente *mf* competitor.

condamnation *f* sentence; *(censure)* condemnation.

condamné, -ée *mf* condemned man/woman.

condamner *vt* to condemn; *(accusé)* to sentence (**à** to); *(porte)* to block up; **c. à une amende** to fine.

condition *f* condition; **conditions** *(clauses, tarifs)* terms; **à c. de faire, à c. que l'on fasse** providing *ou* provided (that) one does.

conditionné *adj* à air c. *(pièce etc)* air-conditioned.

conditionnel *m* *Grammaire* conditional.

condoléances *fpl* sympathy.

conducteur, -trice *mf* driver.

conduire* *vt* to lead; *(voiture)* to drive; *(eau)* to carry; **c. qn à** *(accompagner)* to take sb to.

conduire (se) *vpr* to behave.

conduite *f* behavior; *(de voiture)* driving **(de** of); *(d'eau, de gaz)* main.

cône *m* cone.

confection *f* making **(de** of); **vêtements de c.** ready-to-wear clothes.

confectionner *vt* to make.

conférence *f* conference.

confesser *vt,* **se confesser** *vpr* to confess.

confession *f* confession.

confettis *mpl* confetti.

confiance *f* trust; **faire c. à qn, avoir c. en qn** to trust sb; **c. en soi** (self-)confidence.

confiant, -ante *adj* trusting; *(sûr de soi)* confident.

confidence *f (secret)* confidence; **faire une c. à qn** to confide in sb.

confidentiel, -ielle *adj* confidential.

confier *vt* **c. qch à qn** *(enfant, objet)* to give sb sth to take care of; **c. un secret/etc à qn** to confide a secret/etc to sb.

confier (se) *vpr* **se c. à qn** to confide in sb.

confirmation *f* confirmation.

confirmer *vt* to confirm **(que** that).

confiserie *f* candy store; **confiseries** *(produits)* candy.

confiseur, -euse *mf* confectioner.

confisquer *vt* to confiscate **(à qn** from sb).

confit *adj* **fruits confits** candied fruit.

confiture *f* jelly.

conflit *m* conflict.

confondre *vt (choses, personnes)* to mix up, to confuse; **c. avec** to mistake for.

conformément *adv* **c. à** in accordance with.

confort *m* comfort.

confortable *adj* comfortable.

confrère *m* colleague.

confus, -use *adj* confused; *(gêné)* embarrassed; **je suis c.!** *(désolé)* I'm terribly sorry!

confusion *f* confusion; *(gêne, honte)* embarrassment.

congé *m (vacances)* vacation; **c. de maladie** sick leave; **congés payés** paid vacation.

congélateur *m* freezer, deep-freeze.

congeler *vt* to freeze.

congère *f* snowdrift.

congrès *m* congress.

conjoint *m* spouse.

conjonction *f* *Grammaire* conjunction.

conjoncture *f* circumstances.

conjugaison *f* conjugation.

conjugal, -e, -aux *adj (bonheur)* marital; *(vie)* married; *(devoir)* conjugal.

conjuguer *vt (verbe)* to conjugate.

connaissance *f* knowledge; *(personne)* acquaintance; **connaissances** knowledge (of); **faire la c. de qn, faire c. avec qn** to meet sb; **perdre c.** to lose consciousness; **sans c.** unconscious.

connaître *vt* to know; *(rencontrer)* to meet; **nous nous connaissons déjà** we've met before; **s'y c. à ou en qch** to know (all) about sth.

connu, -ue *(pp* of **connaître)** *adj (célèbre)* well-known.

conquérant, -ante *mf* conqueror.

conquérir* *vt* to conquer.

conquête *f* conquest; **faire la c. de** to conquer.

consacrer *vt (temps, vie etc)* to devote **(à** to).

FAIRE CONNAISSANCE

Bonjour, comment ça va?
Hello, how are you?

Salut, ça va ?
Hi, how's it going?

Bien, merci, et vous ?
Fine thank you, how are you?

Ça va, et toi ?
Good, and you?

Bonjour.
Good morning/afternoon.

Bonsoir.
Good evening.

**Comment vous appelez-vous ?/
Comment t'appelles-tu ?**
What's your name?

Je m'appelle Marie.
My name's Marie.

**Je m'appelle Paul, et voici Nicole,
ma femme.**
I'm Paul and this is my wife Nicole.

Enchanté(e).
Pleased to meet you.

Quel âge avez-vous/as-tu ?
How old are you?

J'ai quinze/vingt-cinq ans.
I'm 15/25 (years old).

D'où venez-vous/viens-tu?
Where are you from?

Je viens de France./Je suis français(e).
I'm from France./I'm French.

Où habitez-vous/habites-tu ?
Where do you live?

J'habite près de Bordeaux.
I live near Bordeaux.

Que faites-vous/fais-tu dans la vie ?
What do you do?

Je suis professeur/étudiant(e).
I'm a teacher/a student.

Je suis au lycée.
I'm in high school.

Je suis mère au foyer.
I'm a stay-at-home mom.

Je travaille dans les assurances.
I work for an insurance company.

Je suis à la retraite.
I'm retired.

Vous avez/Tu as des frères et des sœurs ?
Do you have any brothers and sisters?

J'ai une sœur aînée et deux petits frères.
I've got an older sister and two little brothers.

Vous avez/Tu as des enfants ?
Do you have kids?

**Nous avons un fils de trois ans qui
s'appelle Luc.**
We have a three-year-old son named Luc.

Est-ce que vous êtes/tu es marié(e) ?
Are you married?

Je suis divorcé(e)/séparé(e)/veuf (veuve).
I'm divorced/separated/widowed.

**Que faites-vous pendant votre temps
libre ?/
Qu'est-ce que tu fais pendant ton temps
libre ?**
What do you do in your spare time?

J'aime lire/aller au cinéma.
I like reading/going to the movies.

Je joue au basket/fais du yoga.
I play basketball/do yoga.

Je suis des cours de français.
I'm taking French classes.

À bientôt/plus tard !
See you soon/later!

Bon weekend/voyage !
Have a good weekend/trip!

Nous devrions garder le contact, voici mon adresse e-mail.
We should keep in touch, here's my e-mail address.

consacrer (se) *vpr* se c. à to devote oneself to.

conscience *f (psychologique)* consciousness; *(morale)* conscience; **avoir/prendre c. de** to be/become conscious *ou* aware of; **c. professionnelle** conscientiousness.

consciencieux, -euse *adj* conscientious.

conscient, -ente *adj* c. de aware of.

conseil[1] *m* un c. a piece of advice; **des conseils** advice.

conseil[2] *m (assemblée)* council; **c. d'administration** board of directors; **c. des ministres** *(réunion)* cabinet meeting.

conseiller *vt* to advise; **c. qch à qn** to recommend sth to sb; **c. à qn de faire** to advise sb to do.

conseiller, -ère *mf (expert)* consultant, adviser; *(d'un conseil)* councilor; **c. municipal** city councilman/councilwoman.

consentement *m* consent.

consentir* *vi* c. à to consent to.

conséquence *f* consequence.

conservation *f* preservation.

conservatoire *m* school *(of music, drama)*.

conserve *f* conserves canned food; **de** *ou* **en c.** canned; **mettre en c.** to can.

conserver *vt* to keep; *(fruits, vie, tradition etc)* to preserve.

conserver (se) *vpr (aliment)* to keep.

considérable *adj* considerable.

considération *f (respect)* regard, esteem; **prendre qch en c.** to take sth into consideration.

considérer *vt* to consider (**que** that; **comme** to be).

consigne *f (instruction)* orders; *(de gare)* baggage check; *(somme)* deposit; **c. automatique** baggage lockers.

consigner *vt (bouteille etc)* to charge a deposit on.

consistant, -ante *adj (sauce etc)* thick; *(repas)* solid.

consister *vi* c. en/dans to consist of/in; **c. à faire** to consist in doing.

consolation *f* comfort.

console *f* console.

consoler *vt* to comfort, to console (**de** for).

consoler (se) *vpr* se c. de *(la mort de qn etc)* to get over.

consolider *vt* to strengthen.

consommateur, -trice *mf* consumer; *(au café)* customer.

consommation *f* consumption; *(boisson)* drink.

consommer 1 *vt (aliment etc)* to consume. **2** *vi (au café)* to drink; **c. beaucoup/peu** *(véhicule)* to get good/bad mileage.

consonne *f* consonant.

conspirateur, -trice *mf* conspirator.

conspiration *f* plot.

conspirer *vi* to plot (**contre** against).

constamment *adv* constantly.

constat *m* (official) report.

constatation *f* observation.

constater *vt* to note, to observe (**que** that); *(enregistrer)* to record.

consternation *f* distress.

consterner *vt* to distress.

constipé, -ée *adj* constipated.

constituer *vt (composer)* to make up; *(représenter)* to represent; **constitué de** made up of.

constituer (se) *vpr* se c. prisonnier to give oneself up.

constitution *f* constitution; *(composition)* composition.

constructeur *m (bâtisseur)* builder; *(fabricant)* maker (**de** of); **c. automobile** car manufacturer.

construction *f* construction; **matériaux/jeu de c.** construction materials/set.

construire* *vt* to build.

consul *m* consul.

consulat *m* consulate.

consultation f consultation; **cabinet de c.** (doctor's) office.

consulter vt, **se consulter** vpr to consult.

contact m contact; (toucher) touch; (de voiture) ignition; **être en c. avec** to be in touch ou contact with; **entrer en c. avec** to come into contact with; **mettre/couper le c.** (dans une voiture) to turn on/off the ignition; **lentilles** ou **verres de c.** contact lenses.

contacter vt to contact.

contagieux, -euse adj contagious, infectious.

contagion f infection.

conte m tale; **c. de fée** fairy tale.

contempler vt to gaze at.

contemporain, -aine adj & mf contemporary.

contenance f (d'un récipient) capacity.

contenir* vt to contain; (avoir comme capacité) to hold.

content, -ente adj pleased, happy (**de faire** to do; **de qn/qch** with sb/sth); **c. de soi** self-satisfied.

contenter vt to satisfy, to please.

contenter (se) vpr **se c. de** to be content ou happy with.

contenu m (de récipient) contents.

conter vt (histoire etc) to tell.

contestable adj debatable.

contestataire mf protester.

contestation f protest.

contesté, -ée adj (théorie, dirigeant) controversial.

contester 1 vi (étudiants etc) to protest. **2** vt to protest against.

conteur, -euse mf storyteller.

contexte m context.

continent m continent; (opposé à une île) mainland.

continu, -ue adj continuous.

continuel, -elle adj continual.

continuellement adv continually.

continuer 1 vt to continue, to carry on (**à** ou **de faire** doing). **2** vi to continue, to go on.

contour m outline.

contourner vt (colline etc) to go around.

contraceptif, -ive adj & m contraceptive.

contracter vt, **se contracter** vpr to contract.

contractuel, -elle mf parking enforcement officer.

contradiction f contradiction.

contradictoire adj contradictory; (théories) conflicting.

contraindre* vt to compel (**à faire** to do).

contrainte f compulsion.

contraire 1 adj opposite; **c. à** contrary to. **2** m opposite; **au c.** on the contrary.

contrairement adv **c. à** contrary to.

contrariant, -ante adj (action etc) annoying; (personne) difficult.

contrarier vt (projet etc) to spoil; (personne) to annoy.

contrariété f annoyance.

contraste m contrast.

contrat m contract.

contravention f (pour stationnement interdit) (parking) ticket.

contre prép & adv against; (en échange de) (in exchange) for; **échanger c.** to exchange for; **fâché c.** angry with; **six voix c. deux** six votes to two; **Nîmes c. Arras** (match) Nîmes versus Arras; **un médicament c.** (toux etc) medicine for; **par c.** on the other hand; **tout c. qch/qn** close to sth/sb

contre- préfixe counter-.

contre-attaque f counterattack.

contrebande f (fraude) smuggling; **de c.** (tabac etc) smuggled; **passer qch en c.** to smuggle sth.

contrebandier, -ière mf smuggler.

contrebas (en) adv & prép (down) below; **en c. de** below.

contrebasse f (instrument) double bass.

contrecarrer vt to thwart.

contrecœur (à) *adv* reluctantly.
contrecoup *m* repercussions.
contredire* *vt* to contradict.
contredire (se) *vpr* **se c.** to contradict oneself.
contrefaçon *f (pratique)* counterfeiting; *(produit)* fake.
contre-jour (à) *adv* against the (sun)light.
contremaître *m* foreman.
contre-plaqué *m* plywood.
contretemps *m* hitch.
contribuable *mf* taxpayer.
contribuer *vi* to contribute (**à** to).
contribution *f* contribution; *(impôt)* tax.
contrôle *m* inspection, check(ing) (**de** of); *(des prix, de la qualité)* control; *(maîtrise)* control.
contrôleur, -euse *mf (de train)* conductor; *(au quai)* ticket collector; *(de bus)* conductor.
contrordre *m* change of orders.
contusion *f* bruise.
convaincant, -ante *adj* convincing.
convaincre* *vt* to convince (**de** of); **c. qn de faire** to persuade sb to do.
convaincu, -ue *adj (certain)* convinced (**de** of).
convalescence *f* convalescence; **être en c.** to convalesce.
convalescent, -ente 1 *mf* convalescent. **2** *adj* **être c.** to convalesce.
convenable *adj* suitable; *(correct)* decent.
convenablement *adv* suitably; decently.
convenir* *vi* **c. à** *(être fait pour)* to be suitable for; *(plaire à, aller à)* to suit; **ça convient** *(date etc)* that's suitable, that suits me/us/*etc*.
convention *f (accord)* agreement; *(règle)* convention.
convenu, -ue *adj (prix etc)* agreed.
conversation *f* conversation.

convertir *vt* to convert (**à** to; **en** into).
conviction *f (certitude)* conviction.
convive *mf* guest *(at table)*.
convivial, -e, -aux *adj* convivial; *(système informatique)* user-friendly.
convocation *f (lettre)* (written) notice to attend.
convoi *m (véhicules)* convoy.
convoquer *vt* to summon (**à** to).
coopération *f* cooperation.
coopérer *vi* to cooperate (**à** in; **avec** with).
coordonnées *fpl (adresse, téléphone)* contact details.
copain *m* Fam *(camarade)* pal; *(petit ami)* boyfriend; **être c. avec** to be pals with.
copeau, -x *m (de bois)* shaving.
copie *f* copy; *(devoir, examen)* paper.
copier *vti* to copy (**sur** from).
copieux, -euse *adj* plentiful.
copine *f* Fam *(camarade)* pal; *(petite amie)* girlfriend; **être c. avec** to be pals with.
copropriété *f (immeuble en)* **c.** condominium.
coq *m* rooster.
coque *f (de navire)* hull; *(de noix)* shell; *(fruit de mer)* cockle; **œuf à la c.** soft-boiled egg.
coquelicot *m* poppy.
coqueluche *f* whooping cough.
coquet, -ette *adj (chic)* stylish, chic.
coquetier *m* egg cup.
coquetterie *f (élégance)* style, elegance.
coquillage *m (mollusque)* shellfish; *(coquille)* shell.
coquille *f* shell; **c. Saint-Jacques** scallop.
coquin, -ine *adj* mischievous.
cor *m (instrument)* horn; *(au pied)* corn.
corail, -aux *m* coral.

Coran *m* le C. the Koran.

corbeau, -x *m* crow.

corbeille *f* basket; **c. à papier** waste paper basket.

corbillard *m* hearse.

corde *f* rope; (*plus mince*) cord; (*de raquette, violon etc*) string; **c. à linge** clothesline; **c. à sauter** jump rope.

cordial, -e, -aux *adj* warm.

cordon *m* (*de tablier, sac etc*) string; (*de rideau*) cord.

cordon-bleu, *pl* **cordons-bleus** *m* cordon-bleu cook.

cordonnerie *f* shoe repair shop.

cordonnier *m* shoe repairman.

coriace *adj* tough.

corne *f* (*de chèvre etc*) horn; (*de cerf*) antler; (*matière, instrument*) horn.

corneille *f* crow.

cornet *m* (*de glace*) cornet, cone; **c. (de papier)** (paper) cone.

cornichon *m* (*concombre*) pickle.

corps *m* body; **lutter c. à c.** to fight hand-to-hand; **prendre c.** (*projet*) to take shape.

correct, -e *adj* (*exact, décent*) correct.

correctement *adv* correctly.

correcteur, -trice 1 *adj* **verres correcteurs** corrective lenses. **2** *mf* (*d'examen*) examiner; (*en typographie*) proofreader. **3** *m* **c. d'orthographe** spellchecker.

correction *f* correction; (*punition*) beating; (*exactitude, décence*) correctness; **la c. de** (*devoirs, examen*) the marking of.

correspondance *f* correspondence; (*de train, d'autocar*) connection, transfer.

correspondant, -ante *adj* corresponding. **2** *mf* (*d'un adolescent etc*) pen pal; (*au téléphone*) caller.

correspondre *vi* to correspond (**à** to, with); (*écrire*) to correspond (**avec** with).

corrida *f* bullfight.

corriger *vt* to correct; (*devoir*) to mark; **c. qn de** (*défaut*) to cure sb of.

corrompu, -ue *adj* corrupt.

corsage *m* (*chemisier*) blouse.

cortège *m* procession; **c. officiel** (*automobiles*) motorcade.

corvée *f* chore.

cosmonaute *mf* cosmonaut.

cosmos *m* (*univers*) cosmos; (*espace*) outer space.

cosse *f* (*de pois etc*) pod.

costaud, -aude *adj Fam* brawny.

costume *m* (*déguisement*) costume; (*complet*) suit.

costumé *adj* **bal c.** costume ball.

côte *f* rib; (*de mouton*) chop; (*de veau*) cutlet; (*montée*) hill; (*littoral*) coast; **c. à c.** side by side.

côté *m* side; (*direction*) way; **de l'autre c.** on the other side (**de** of); (*direction*) the other way; **du c. de** (*vers, près de*) towards; **de c.** (*mettre de l'argent etc*) to one side; (*regarder*) sideways; **à c.** nearby; (*pièce*) in the other room; (*maison*) next door; **à c. de** next to, beside; (*comparaison*) compared to; **à mes côtés** by my side.

coteau, -x *m* (*small*) hill.

côtelette *f* (*d'agneau, de porc*) chop; (*de veau*) cutlet.

côtier, -ière *adj* coastal.

cotisation *f* (*de club*) dues.

cotiser *vi* (*à un cadeau, pour la retraite*) to contribute (**à** to; **pour** towards).

cotiser (se) *vpr* to club together (**pour acheter** to buy).

coton *m* cotton; **c. (hydrophile)** absorbent cotton.

cou *m* neck.

couchage *m* **sac de c.** sleeping bag.

couchant *adj* (*soleil*) setting.

couche *f* (*épaisseur*) layer; (*de peinture*) coat; (*linge de bébé*) diaper.

couché, -ée *adj* **être c.** to be in

bed; (*étendu*) to be lying (down).
couche-culotte, *pl* **couches-culottes** *f* disposable diaper.
coucher 1 *vt* to put to bed; (*héberger*) to put up; (*allonger*) to lay (down *ou* out). **2** *vi* to sleep (**avec** with).
coucher (se) *vpr* to go to bed; (*s'allonger*) to lie flat *ou* down; (*soleil*) to set.
couchette *f* (*de train*) sleeper, sleeping berth; (*de bateau*) bunk.
coucou *m* (*oiseau*) cuckoo; (*fleur*) cowslip.
coude *m* elbow; **se serrer les coudes** to help one another; **c. à c.** side by side; **coup de c.** nudge; **pousser du c.** to nudge.
coudre* *vti* to sew.
couette *f* duvet, down comforter.
couler[1] *vi* (*eau etc*) to flow; (*robinet, nez, sueur*) to run; (*fuir*) to leak.
couler[2] *vti* (*bateau, nageur*) to sink.
couleur *f* color; *Cartes* suit; (*couleurs*) (*teint*) color; **de c.** colored; **photo/etc en couleurs** color photo/etc; **téléviseur c.** *ou* **en couleurs** color TV set.
couleuvre *f* (grass) snake.
coulisses *fpl* **dans les c.** in the wings, backstage.
couloir *m* corridor; (*de circulation, d'une piste*) lane.
coup *m* blow, knock; (*léger*) tap; (*choc moral*) blow; (*de fusil etc*) shot; (*de crayon, d'horloge*) stroke; (*aux échecs etc*) move; (*fois*) *Fam* time; **donner des coups à** to hit; **c. de brosse** brush(-up); **c. de chiffon** wipe (with a rag); **c. de sonnette** ring (on a bell); **c. de dents** bite; **c. de chance** stroke of luck; **tenter le c.** *Fam* to give it a try; **tenir le c.** to hold out; **sous le c. de** (*émotion*) under the influence of; **après c.** afterwards; **tué sur le c.** killed outright; **à c. sûr** for sure; **tout à c., tout d'un c.** suddenly; **d'un seul c.** all at once; **du c.** (*de ce fait*) as a result.

coupable 1 *adj* guilty (**de** of). **2** *mf* guilty person, culprit.
coupant, -ante *adj* sharp.
coupe *f* (*trophée*) cup; (*à boire*) goblet; (*de vêtement etc*) cut; **c. de cheveux** haircut.
coupe-ongles *m inv* (fingernail) clippers.
coupe-papier *m inv* letter opener.
couper 1 *vt* to cut; (*arbre*) to cut down; (*téléphone*) to cut off; (*courant etc*) to switch off; (*morceler*) to cut up; (*croiser*) to cut across; **c. la parole à qn** to cut sb short. **2** *vi* to cut; **ne coupez pas!** (*au téléphone*) hold on!
couper (se) *vpr* (*routes*) to intersect; **se c. au doigt** to cut one's finger.
couple *m* pair, couple.
couplet *m* verse.
coupure *f* cut; (*de journal*) clipping; **c. d'électricité** blackout, power outage.
cour *f* court(yard); (*de roi*) court; **c. (de récréation)** playground.
courage *m* courage; **bon c.!** good luck!
courageux, -euse *adj* courageous.
couramment *adv* (*parler*) fluently; (*souvent*) frequently.
courant, -ante 1 *adj* (*fréquent*) common; (*eau*) running; (*modèle, taille*) standard. **2** *m* (*de l'eau, électrique*) current; **c. d'air** draft; **coupure de c.** blackout, power outage; **être/mettre au c.** to know/tell (**de** about).
courbature *f* ache; **avoir des courbatures** to be aching (all over).
courbaturé, -ée *adj* aching (all over).
courbe 1 *adj* curved. **2** *f* curve.
courber *vti* to bend.
coureur *m* runner; (*cycliste*) cyclist; (*automobile*) racecar driver.
courgette *f* zucchini.

courir* 1 *vi* to run; *(se hâter)* to rush; *(à bicyclette, en auto)* to race; **le bruit court que…** there's a rumor going around that… **2** *vt (risque)* to run; *(épreuve sportive)* to run (in); *(danger)* to face.

couronne *f* crown; *(de fleurs)* wreath.

couronnement *m (de roi etc)* coronation.

couronner *vt* to crown.

courriel *m Can* e-mail.

courrier *m* mail; **c. électronique** e-mail.

courroie *f* strap; *(de transmission)* belt.

cours *m* course; *(d'une monnaie etc)* rate; *(leçon)* class; *(série de leçons)* course; **c. d'eau** river, stream; **en c.** *(travail)* in progress; *(année)* current; **en c. de route** on the way; **au c. de** during.

course¹ *f (action)* run(ning); *(épreuve de vitesse)* race; **courses** *(de chevaux)* races; **cheval de c.** racehorse; **voiture de c.** racecar.

course² *f (commission)* errand; **courses** *(achats)* shopping; **faire une c.** to run an errand; **faire les courses** to go shopping.

coursier, -ière *mf* messenger.

court, courte 1 *adj* short. **2** *adv (couper, s'arrêter)* short; **à c.** **de** *(argent etc)* short of. **3** *m Tennis* court.

court-circuit, *pl* **courts-circuits** *m* short-circuit.

couscous *m* couscous.

cousin, -ine *mf* cousin.

coussin *m* cushion.

coût *m* cost; **le c. de la vie** the cost of living.

couteau, -x *m* knife.

coûter *vti* to cost; **ça coûte combien?** how much does it cost?; **coûte que coûte** at all costs.

coûteux, -euse *adj* costly, expensive.

coutume *f* custom; **avoir c. de**

faire to be accustomed to doing.

couture *f* sewing; *(métier)* dressmaking; *(raccord)* seam.

couturier *m* fashion designer.

couturière *f* dressmaker.

couvée *f (oiseaux)* brood.

couvent *m* convent.

couver 1 *vt (œufs)* to sit on. **2** *vi (poule)* to brood.

couvercle *m* lid, cover.

couvert *m (set of)* cutlery; **mettre le c.** to set *ou* lay the table.

couvert, -erte *adj* covered (**de** with, in); *(de ciel)* overcast.

couverture *f (de lit)* blanket; *(de livre etc)* cover.

couveuse *f* incubator.

couvrir* *vt* to cover (**de** with).

couvrir (se) *vpr (s'habiller)* to wrap up; *(ciel)* to cloud over.

cow-boy *m* cowboy.

crabe *m* crab.

crachat *m* spit, spittle.

cracher 1 *vi* to spit. **2** *vt* to spit (out).

crachin *m (fine)* drizzle.

craie *f* chalk.

craindre* *vt* to be afraid of, to fear; *(chaleur, froid)* to be sensitive to; **c.** **de faire** to be afraid of doing; **ne craignez rien** don't be afraid.

crainte *f* fear.

craintif, -ive *adj* timid.

crampe *f* cramp.

cramponner (se) *vpr* **se c. à** to hold on to, to cling to.

crampons *mpl (de chaussures)* cleats.

cran *m (entaille)* notch, *(de ceinture)* hole; **couteau à c. d'arrêt** switchblade; **c. de sûreté** safety catch.

crâne *m* skull.

crapaud *m* toad.

craquement *m* snapping *ou* cracking (sound).

craquer *vi (branche)* to snap; *(bois sec)* to crack; *(sous la dent)* to crunch; *(se déchirer)* to split, to rip;

(personne) to break down.

crasse *f* filth.

crasseux, -euse *adj* filthy.

cratère *m* crater.

cravate *f* tie.

crawl *m (nage)* crawl.

crayon *m* pencil; **c. de couleur** colored pencil; *(en cire)* crayon; **c. à bille** ballpoint (pen).

crayonner *vt* to pencil.

créancier, -ière *mf* debtor.

création *f* creation; **1000 créations d'emplois** 1000 new jobs.

créature *f* creature.

crèche *f (de Noël)* crib; *(pour bébé)* daycare (center).

crédit *m* credit; **à c.** on credit; **faire c.** *(prêter)* to give credit (**à** to).

créditeur *adj* **compte c.** account in credit.

créer *vt* to create.

crémaillère *f* **pendre la c.** to have a house-warming (party).

crématorium *m* crematorium.

crème *f* cream; *(dessert)* cream dessert; **c. Chantilly** whipped cream; **c. glacée** ice cream; **c. à raser** shaving cream; **c. anglaise** custard sauce.

créneau, -x *m* **faire un c.** to parallel park.

crêpe *f* pancake, crepe.

crépiter *vi* to crackle.

crépu, -ue *adj* frizzy.

crépuscule *m* twilight, dusk.

cresson *m* (water)cress.

crête *f (de montagne etc)* crest.

creuser *vt* to dig.

creuser (se) *vpr* **se c. la tête** to rack one's brains.

creux, -euse **1** *adj* hollow; *(estomac)* empty; **assiette creuse** soup plate. **2** *m* hollow; *(de l'estomac)* pit.

crevaison *f (de pneu)* flat.

crevasse *f (trou)* crevice.

crevé, -ée *adj (fatigué) Fam* worn out; *(mort) Fam* dead.

crever 1 *vi (bulle etc)* to burst; *(pneu)* to go flat; *(mourir) Fam* to

die. **2** *vt* to burst; *(œil)* to put out.

crevette *f (grise)* shrimp; *(rose)* prawn.

cri *m (de joie, surprise)* cry, shout; *(de peur)* scream; *(de douleur)* cry; *(appel)* call, cry.

cric *m (de voiture)* jack.

crier 1 *vi* to shout (out), to cry (out); *(de peur)* to scream; **c. après qn** *Fam* to shout at sb. **2** *vt (injure, ordre)* to shout (out).

crime *m* crime; *(assassinat)* murder.

criminel, -elle 1 *adj* criminal. **2** *mf* criminal; *(assassin)* murderer.

crinière *f* mane.

crise *f* crisis; *(accès)* attack; *(de colère etc)* fit; **c. cardiaque** heart attack.

crisper *vt (visage)* to make tense; *(poing)* to clench.

cristal, -aux *m* crystal.

critique 1 *adj* critical. **2** *f (reproche)* criticism.

critiquer *vt* to criticize.

croc *m (dent)* fang.

croche-pied *m* **faire un c. à qn** to trip sb up.

crochet *m* hook; *(aiguille)* crochet hook; *(travail)* crochet; **faire qch au c.** to crochet sth; **faire un c.** *(personne)* to make a detour.

crochu, -ue *adj (nez)* hooked.

crocodile *m* crocodile.

croire* 1 *vt* to believe; *(estimer)* to think, to believe (**que** that); **j'ai cru la voir** I thought I saw her. **2** *vi* to believe (**à, en** in).

croisement *m (de routes)* crossroads.

croiser *vt (jambes, ligne etc)* to cross; **c. qn** to pass *ou* meet sb.

croiser (se) *vpr (voitures etc)* to pass (each other); *(routes)* to cross.

croisière *f* cruise.

croissance *f* growth.

croissant, -ante 1 *adj (nombre)* growing. **2** *m* crescent; *(pâtisserie)* croissant.

croix f cross.

croque-monsieur m inv = toasted cheese and ham sandwich.

croquer vti to crunch.

croquis m sketch.

crosse f (de fusil) butt.

crotte f (de lapin etc) droppings, dung.

crottin m (horse) dung.

crouler vi (édifice) to crumble; **c. sous le travail** to be snowed under with work.

croustillant, -ante adj (pain) crusty.

croustiller vi to be crusty.

croûte f (de pain etc) crust; (de fromage) rind; (de plaie) scab.

croûton m crust (at end of loaf).

croyant, -ante 1 adj être c. to be a believer. **2** mf believer.

CRS abrév mpl (Compagnies républicaines de sécurité) riot police.

cru¹, crue pp of **croire**.

cru², crue adj (aliment etc) raw.

cruauté f cruelty (**envers** to).

cruche f pitcher, jug.

crudités fpl assorted raw vegetables.

cruel, -elle adj cruel (**envers, avec** to).

crustacés mpl shellfish.

cube 1 m cube; **cubes** (jeu) building blocks. **2** adj (mètre etc) cubic.

cueillette f picking; (fruits cueillis) harvest.

cueillir* vt to pick.

cuiller, cuillère f spoon; **petite c., c. à café** teaspoon; **c. à soupe** soup spoon, tablespoon.

cuillerée f spoonful; **c. à café** teaspoonful; **c. à soupe** tablespoonful.

cuir m leather.

cuire* **1** vt to cook; (à l'eau) to boil; **c. (au four)** to bake; (viande) to roast. **2** vi to cook; (à l'eau) to boil; (au four) to bake; (viande) to roast; **faire c.** to cook.

cuisine f (pièce) kitchen; (art, aliments) cooking; **faire la c.** to cook,

to do the cooking; **livre de c.** cook book.

cuisiner vti to cook.

cuisinier, -ière 1 mf cook. **2** f (appareil) stove, range.

cuisse f thigh; (de poulet) leg.

cuisson m cooking.

cuit, cuite (pp of **cuire**) adj cooked; **bien c.** well done.

cuivre m (rouge) copper; (jaune) brass.

culbute f (saut) somersault; (chute) (backward) tumble.

culbuter vi to tumble over (backwards).

cul-de-sac, pl culs-de-sac m dead end.

culot m (d'ampoule, de lampe) base; (audace) Fam nerve.

culotte f (de femme) (pair of) panties; **culottes (courtes)** knickers.

culpabiliser vt c. qn to make sb feel guilty.

culte m (de dieu) worship; (religion) form of worship.

cultivateur, -trice mf farmer.

cultivé, -ée adj (personne) cultivated.

cultiver vt (terre) to farm; (plantes) to grow.

cultiver (se) vpr to improve one's mind.

culture f culture; (agriculture) farming; (de légumes) growing.

culturel, -elle adj cultural.

cupide adj avaricious.

cure f (course of) treatment, cure.

curé m (parish) priest.

cure-dent m toothpick.

curer vt (fossé etc) to clean out.

curieux, -euse 1 adj (bizarre) curious; (indiscret) inquisitive, curious (**de** about). **2** mf inquisitive person; (badaud) onlooker.

curiosité f curiosity.

curriculum (vitae) m inv résumé.

curseur m (d'ordinateur) cursor.

cuve f (réservoir) tank.

cuvette f (récipient) basin, bowl; (des toilettes) bowl.

CV m abrév (curriculum vitae) résumé.

cycle m (série) cycle.

cyclisme m cycling.

cycliste mf cyclist; **course c.** cycling ou bicycle race; **champion c.** cycling champion.

cyclomoteur m moped.

cyclone m cyclone.

cygne m swan.

cylindre m cylinder.

cylindrée f (engine) capacity.

cylindrique adj cylindrical.

cymbale f cymbal.

cyprès m (arbre) cypress.

D

dactylo f (personne) typist; (action) typing.

daim m fallow deer; (cuir) suede.

dallage m paving.

dalle f paving stone.

dallé, -ée adj paved.

dame f lady; (mariée) married lady; Échecs, Cartes queen; (au jeu de dames) king; **(jeu de) dames** checkers.

damier m checkerboard.

dandiner (se) vpr to waddle.

danger m danger; **en d.** in danger; **mettre en d.** to endanger; **en cas de d.** in an emergency; **en d. de mort** in peril of death; **'d. de mort'** (panneau) 'danger'; **être sans d.** to be safe.

dangereusement adv dangerously.

dangereux, -euse adj dangerous (**pour** to).

danois, -oise 1 adj Danish. **2** mf D. Dane. **3** m (langue) Danish.

dans prép in; (changement de lieu) into; (à l'intérieur de) inside; **entrer d.** to go in(to); **boire/prendre/etc d.** to drink/take/etc from ou out of; **d. deux jours/etc** (temps futur) in two days/etc; **d. les dix euros/etc** about ten euros/etc.

danse f dance; (art) dancing.

danser vti to dance.

danseur, -euse mf dancer.

date f date; **en d. du...** dated the...; **d. d'expiration** expiry date; **d. limite** deadline.

dater 1 vt (lettre etc) to date. **2** vi d. de to date from; **à d. de** as from.

datte f (fruit) date.

dauphin m dolphin.

davantage adv (quantité) more; (temps) longer; **d. de temps/etc** more time/etc; **d. que** more than; longer than.

de¹ (d' before a vowel or mute h, **de + le = du**, **de + les = des**) prép (complément d'un nom) of; **les rayons du soleil** the rays of the sun; **le livre de Paul** Paul's book; **un pont de fer** an iron bridge; **une augmentation d'impôts/etc** an increase in taxes/etc. ▪ (complément d'un adjectif) digne de worthy of; **heureux de** happy to; **content de qch/qn** pleased with sth/sb. ▪ (complément d'un verbe) parler de to speak of ou about; **décider de faire** to decide to do. ▪ (provenance: lieu & temps) from; **mes amis du village** my friends from the village. ▪ (agent) accompagné de accompanied by. ▪ (moyen) armé de armed with; **se nourrir de** to live on. ▪ (manière) d'une voix douce in ou with a gentle voice. ▪ (cause) **mourir de faim** to die of hunger. ▪ (temps) **travailler de nuit** to work by night; **six heures du matin** six o'clock in the morning. ▪ (mesure) **avoir** ou **faire six mètres de haut** to be 20 feet high; **homme de trente ans** thirty-year-old man; **ga-**

LA DATE ET L'HEURE

On est quel jour aujourd'hui ?
What day is it today?

On est le combien aujourd'hui ?
What's today's date?

On est le mercredi douze avril.
It's Wednesday April 12th.

Je suis né(e) en mille neuf cent quatre-vingt.
I was born in 1980.

Vous restez jusqu'à quand ?
How long are you staying?

Nous sommes arrivés le weekend dernier.
We got here last weekend.

À samedi !
See you on Saturday!

Prenez-le trois fois par jour.
Take it three times a day.

Quelle heure est-il ?
What's the time?

Il est presque midi/minuit.
It's nearly midday/midnight.

Il est sept heures moins le quart.
It's a quarter to seven.

Je me lève à 6h.
I get up at 6 a.m.

Je serai là vers huit heures.
I'll be there about eight.

Mon avion a eu deux heures de retard.
My plane was two hours late.

Je n'ai pas le temps (de...).
I don't have time (to...).

On est vendredi.
It's Friday.

On est le quinze avril deux mille huit.
It's April 15th, 2008.

Demain c'est jeudi.
It's Thursday tomorrow.

Je suis venu(e) à Paris il y a quelques années.
I came to Paris a few years ago.

Nous partons dimanche/le huit.
We leave on Sunday/the 8th.

J'ai attendu toute la journée.
I waited all day.

À la semaine prochaine !
See you next week!

Je les vois toutes les deux semaines.
I see them every two weeks.

Il est deux heures.
It's 2 o'clock.

Il est quatre heures et demie/quatre heures trente.
It's half past four/four-thirty.

Il est sept heures vingt.
It's twenty after seven.

Je me couche à 22h.
I go to bed at 10 p.m.

On se retrouve dans une demi-heure.
I'll meet you in half an hour.

Je suis en avance/en retard/à l'heure.
I'm early/late/on time.

C'est l'heure de partir.
It's time to go.

gner quinze euros de l'heure to earn fifteen euros an hour.

de² *art partitif* some; **elle boit du vin** she drinks (some) wine; **il ne boit pas de vin** *(négation)* he doesn't drink (any) wine; **des fleurs** (some) flowers; **de jolies fleurs** (some) pretty flowers; **il y en a six de tués** *(avec un nombre)* there are six dead.

dé *m (à jouer)* dice; *(à coudre)* thimble; **jouer aux dés** to play dice.

déballer *vt* to unpack.

débarbouiller (se) *vpr* to wash one's face.

débarquement *m (de passagers)* landing; *(de marchandises)* unloading.

débarquer 1 *vt (passagers)* to land; *(marchandises)* to unload. **2** *vi (passagers)* to land.

débarras *m* storeroom; **bon d.!** *Fam* good riddance!

débarrasser *vt (table etc)* to clear (**de** of); **d. qn de** *(ennemi, soucis etc)* to rid sb of; *(manteau etc)* to relieve sb of.

débarrasser (se) *vpr* **se d. de** to get rid of.

débat *m* discussion, debate.

débattre* *vt* to discuss, to debate.

débattre (se) *vpr* to struggle (to get free).

débile 1 *adj (esprit, enfant etc)* weak; *Fam* idiotic. **2** *mf Fam* idiot.

débit *m (vente)* sales; *(compte)* debit; *(de fleuve)* flow; **d. de boissons** bar, café.

débiter *vt (découper)* to cut up (**en** into); *(vendre)* to sell; *(compte)* to debit.

débiteur, -trice 1 *mf* debtor. **2** *adj* **compte d.** debit account.

déblayer *vt (terrain, décombres)* to clear.

débloquer *vt (mécanisme)* to unjam; *(crédits)* to release.

déboîter 1 *vt (tuyau)* to disconnect; *(os)* to dislocate. **2** *vi (véhi-*

cule) to pull out, to change lanes.

déborder 1 *vi (fleuve, liquide)* to overflow; **l'eau déborde du vase** the water is overflowing the vase. **2** *vt (dépasser)* to go beyond; **débordé de travail** snowed under with work.

débouché *m (carrière)* opening; *(marché pour produit)* outlet.

déboucher *vt (bouteille)* to open, to uncork; *(lavabo, tuyau)* to unclog.

débourser *vti* to pay out.

debout *adv* standing (up); **mettre d.** *(planche etc)* to stand up, to put upright; **se mettre d.** to stand *ou* get up; **rester d.** to remain standing; **être d.** *(levé)* to be up; **d.!** get up!

déboutonner *vt* to unbutton, to undo.

débraillé, -ée *adj (tenue etc)* slovenly, sloppy.

débrancher *vt* to unplug, to disconnect.

débrayer *vi (conducteur)* to depress the clutch.

débris *mpl* fragments; *(restes)* remains; *(détritus)* garbage.

débrouillard, -arde *adj* smart, resourceful.

débrouiller (se) *vpr* to manage (**pour faire** to do).

début *m* start, beginning; **au d.** at the beginning.

débutant, -ante *mf* beginner.

débuter *vi* to start, to begin.

décaféiné, -ée *adj* decaffeinated.

décalage *m (écart)* gap; **d. horaire** time difference.

décalcomanie *f (image)* decal.

décaler *vt* to shift.

décalquer *vt (dessin)* to trace.

décapant *m* cleaning agent; *(pour enlever la peinture)* paint stripper.

décaper *vt (métal)* to clean; *(surface peinte)* to strip.

décapiter *vt* to behead.

décapotable adj (voiture) convertible.

décapsuler vt d. une bouteille to take the top off a bottle.

décapsuleur m bottle-opener.

décéder vi to die.

déceler vt (trouver) to detect.

décembre m December.

décemment adv decently.

décennie f decade.

décent, -ente adj (convenable) decent.

déception f disappointment.

décerner vt (prix) to award.

décès m death.

décevant, -ante adj disappointing.

décevoir* vt to disappoint.

déchaîné, -ée adj (foule) wild.

déchaîner vt d. les rires to cause an outburst of laughter; d. la colère to arouse anger.

déchaîner (se) vpr (tempête, rires) to break out; (foule) to run riot; (personne) to fly into a rage.

décharge f d. (publique) (garbage) dump; d. (électrique) (electric) shock.

déchargement m unloading.

décharger vt to unload; (batterie) to discharge.

décharger (se) vpr (batterie) to go dead.

déchausser (se) vpr to take one's shoes off.

déchet m déchets (restes) waste; il y a du d. there's some waste.

déchiffrer vt to decipher.

déchiqueter vt to tear to shreds.

déchirer vt (page etc) to tear (up); (vêtement) to tear; (ouvrir) to tear open.

déchirer (se) vpr (robe etc) to tear.

déchirure f tear.

décidé, -ée adj (air, ton) determined; d. à faire determined to do.

décidément adv undoubtedly.

décider 1 vt (opération) to decide

on; d. que to decide that. **2** vi d. de faire to decide to do.

décider (se) vpr se d. à faire to make up one's mind to do.

décimal, -e, -aux adj decimal.

décimètre m decimeter; double d. ruler.

décisif, -ive adj decisive.

décision f decision; (fermeté) determination.

déclaration f declaration; (de vol etc) notification; (commentaire) statement; d. de revenus tax return.

déclarer vt to declare (que that); (vol etc) to notify.

déclarer (se) vpr (incendie) to break out.

déclencher vt (mécanisme, réaction) to trigger, to start (off); (attaque) to launch.

déclencher (se) vpr (alarme etc) to go off.

déclic m (bruit) click.

déclin m decline; être en d. to be in decline.

décoiffer vt d. qn to mess up sb's hair.

décollage m (d'avion) takeoff.

décoller 1 vi (avion) to take off. **2** vt (timbre) to unstick.

décoller (se) vpr to come unstuck.

décolleté, -ée 1 adj (robe) low-cut. **2** m (de robe) low neckline.

décolorer (se) vpr to fade.

décombres mpl rubble.

décongeler 1 vt (faire) d. (aliment) to thaw. **2** vi to thaw.

déconseiller vt d. qch à qn to advise sb against sth; d. à qn de faire to advise sb against doing.

décontracté, -ée adj (ambiance, personne) relaxed; (vêtement) casual.

décontracter (se) vpr to relax.

décor m (théâtre, paysage) scenery; (d'intérieur) decoration.

décorateur, -trice mf (interior) decorator.

décoratif, -ive *adj* decorative.

décoration *f* decoration.

décorer *vt (maison, soldat)* to decorate (**de** with).

découdre *vt* to unstitch.

découdre (se) *upr* to come unstitched.

découpage *m (image)* cutout.

découper *vt (viande)* to carve; *(article)* to cut out.

découragement *m* discouragement.

décourager *vt* to discourage.

décourager (se) *upr* to get discouraged.

découvert *m (d'un compte)* overdraft.

découverte *f* discovery.

découvrir (se) *upr (dans son lit)* to push the bedcovers off; *(ciel)* to clear (up); *(enlever son chapeau)* to remove one's hat.

décrasser *vt (nettoyer)* to clean.

décrire* *vt* to describe.

décroché *adj (téléphone)* off the hook.

décrocher *vt (détacher)* to unhook; *(tableau)* to take down; **d. (le téléphone)** to pick up the phone.

décrocher (se) *upr (tableau)* to fall down.

décrotter *vt* to clean (the mud off).

déçu, -ue *(pp of décevoir) adj* disappointed.

déculotter (se) *upr* to take off one's pants.

dédaigner *vt* to scorn, to despise.

dédaigneux, -euse *adj* scornful.

dédain *m* scorn.

dedans 1 *adv* inside; **en d.** on the inside; **tomber d.** *(trou)* to fall in (it); **je me suis fait rentrer d.** *(accident de voiture)* someone crashed into me. **2** *m* **le d.** the inside.

dédommagement *m* compensation.

dédommager *vt* to compensate (**de** for).

déduction *f* deduction.

déduire* *vt (soustraire)* to deduct (**de** from).

déesse *f* goddess.

défaillance *f (évanouissement)* fainting fit; *(faiblesse)* weakness; *(panne)* failure; **avoir une d.** *(s'évanouir)* to faint; *(faiblir)* to feel weak.

défaire* *vt (nœud etc)* to undo.

défaire (se) *upr* to come undone.

défait *adj (lit)* unmade.

défaite *f* defeat.

défaut *m (faiblesse)* fault; *(de fabrication)* defect.

défavorable *adj* unfavorable (**à** to).

défavorisé, -ée *adj (milieu)* underprivileged.

défavoriser *vt* to put at a disadvantage.

défectueux, -euse *adj* faulty, defective.

défendre¹ *vt (protéger)* to defend.

défendre² *vt (interdire)* **d. à qn de faire** to forbid sb to do; **d. qch à qn** to forbid sb sth.

défendre (se) *upr* to defend oneself.

défense¹ *f (protection)* defense; *(d'éléphant)* tusk.

défense² *f (interdiction)* **'d. de fumer'** 'no smoking'; **'d. (absolue) d'entrer'** '(strictly) no entry'.

défenseur *m* defender.

défi *m* challenge; **lancer un d. à qn** to challenge sb.

déficitaire *adj (budget)* in deficit; *(entreprise)* loss-making; *(compte)* in debit.

défier *vt* to challenge (**à** to); **d. qn de faire** to challenge sb to do.

défiguré, -ée *adj* disfigured.

défilé *m (militaire)* parade; *(gorge)* pass.

défiler *vi (soldats)* to march.

définir *vt* to define; **article défini** *Grammaire* definite article.

définitif, -ive *adj* final, definitive.

définition *f* definition; *(de mots croisés)* clue.

définitivement *adv (partir, exclure)* for good.

défoncé, -ée *adj (route)* bumpy; *(drogué)* Fam high.

défoncer *vt (porte, mur)* to smash in, to knock down; *(trottoir, route)* to dig up.

déformé, -ée *adj* misshapen; **chaussée déformée** uneven road surface, bumpy road.

déformer *vt* to put out of shape.

déformer (se) *vpr* to lose its shape.

défouler (se) *vpr* to let off steam.

défricher *vt (terrain)* to clear.

défroisser *vt* to smooth out.

défunt, -unte 1 *adj (mort)* departed; **mon d. mari** my late husband. **2** *mf* **le d., la défunte** the deceased.

dégagé, -ée *adj (ciel)* clear.

dégagement *m (action)* clearing; *Football* kick (down the field); **itinéraire de d.** alternative route *(to ease traffic congestion)*.

dégager 1 *vt (table etc)* to clear (**de** *of)*; *(odeur)* to give off; **d. qn de** *(décombres etc)* to pull sb out of. **2** *vi Football* to clear the ball (down the field); **dégagez!** get lost!

dégager (se) *vpr (ciel)* to clear; **se d. de** *(personne)* to pull oneself free from *(rubble)*; *(odeur)* to come out of *(room)*.

dégainer *vti (arme)* to draw.

dégarni, -ie *adj* bare; **front d.** receding hairline.

dégarnir *vt (arbre de Noël)* to take down the decorations from.

dégarnir (se) *vpr (crâne)* to go bald.

dégâts *mpl* damage.

dégel *m* thaw.

dégeler *vti* to thaw (out).

dégivrer *vt (réfrigérateur)* to defrost.

déglingué, -ée *adj* falling to pieces.

dégonfler *vt (pneu)* to deflate.

dégonfler (se) *vpr (pneu)* to deflate; *(se montrer lâche)* Fam to chicken out.

dégouliner *vt* to trickle.

dégourdi, -ie *adj (malin)* smart. **2** *mf* smart boy/girl.

dégourdir *vt* se d. les jambes to stretch one's legs.

dégoût *m* disgust; **avoir du d. pour qch** to have a (strong) dislike for sth.

dégoûtant, -ante *adj* disgusting.

dégoûté, -ée *adj* disgusted (**de** with, by); **il n'est pas d.** *(difficile)* he's not fussy.

dégoûter *vt* to disgust; **d. qn de qch** to (be enough to) make sb sick of sth.

dégrader (se) *vpr (situation)* to deteriorate.

degré *m (angle, température)* degree.

dégringolade *f* tumble.

dégringoler *vi* to tumble (down).

déguerpir *vi* to clear out, to make tracks.

dégueulasse *adj* Fam disgusting.

déguisement *m* disguise; *(de bal costumé)* costume.

déguiser *vt* to disguise; **d. qn (en)** *(costumer)* to dress sb up (as).

déguiser (se) *vpr* to dress oneself up (**en** as).

déguster *vt (goûter)* to taste.

dehors 1 *adv* out(side); **en d.** on the outside; **en d. de la maison** outside the house; **en d. de la ville** out of town; **au-d. (de), au d. (de)** outside. **2** *m (extérieur)* outside.

déjà *adv* already; **elle l'a d. vu** she's seen it before, she's already seen it; **quand partez-vous, d.?** when did you say you were leaving?

déjeuner 1 *vi (à midi)* to have lunch; *(le matin)* to have breakfast. **2** *m* lunch; **petit d.** breakfast.

delà *adv* **au-d. (de), au d. (de)** beyond.

délabré, -ée *adj* dilapidated.

délacer vt (chaussures) to undo, to untie.

délai m time limit; **sans d.** without delay; **dernier d.** final date.

délasser (se) vpr to relax.

délayer vt (mélanger) to mix (with liquid).

délégation f delegation.

délégué, -ée mf delegate.

délibérer vi (se consulter) to deliberate (**de** about).

délicat, -ate adj (santé, travail) delicate; (geste) tactful; (exigeant) particular.

délicatement adv (doucement) delicately.

délicatesse f (tact) tact.

délice m delight.

délicieux, -euse adj (plat) delicious.

délier vt to undo.

délier (se) vpr (paquet) to come undone.

délimiter vt (terrain) to mark off.

délinquant, -ante mf delinquent.

délirer vi (dire n'importe quoi) to rave.

délit m offense.

délivrer vt (prisonnier) to release, to (set) free; (billet) to issue.

déloger vt to drive out.

deltaplane® m hang glider.

déluge m flood; (de pluie) downpour.

demain adv tomorrow; **à d.!** see you tomorrow!

demande f request (**de qch** for sth); **demandes d'emploi** positions wanted.

demander vt to ask for; (nécessiter) to require; **d. le chemin/l'heure** to ask the way/the time; **d. qch à qn** to ask sb for sth; **d. à qn de faire** to ask sb to do; **ça demande du temps** it takes time; **être très demandé** to be in great demand.

demander (se) vpr to wonder (**pourquoi** why; **si** if).

demandeur, -euse mf **d. d'emploi** job seeker.

démangeaison f itch; **avoir des démangeaisons** to be itching.

démanger vti to itch; **son bras le démange** his arm itches.

démaquillant m cleanser.

démaquiller (se) vpr to take off one's make-up.

démarche f walk; **faire des démarches** to go through the process (**pour faire** of doing).

démarrage m start.

démarrer vi (moteur) to start (up); (voiture) to move off.

démarreur m starter.

démasquer vt to expose.

démêler vt (cheveux) to untangle.

déménagement m move, moving; **camion de d.** moving van.

déménager vi to move.

déménageur m mover.

démesuré, -ée adj excessive.

démettre (se) vpr **se d. le pied/etc** to dislocate one's foot/etc.

demeure f (belle maison) mansion.

demeurer vi (aux être) (rester) to remain; (aux avoir) (habiter) to live.

demi, -ie 1 adj half; **une heure et demie** an hour and a half; (horloge) half past one. **2** adv (**à**) **d. plein/etc** half-full/etc. **3** m (verre) (half-pint) glass of beer.

demi-cercle m semicircle.

demi-douzaine f une d. (de) half a dozen.

demi-finale f semifinal.

demi-frère m stepbrother.

demi-heure f une d. a half-hour, half an hour.

demi-journée f half-day.

demi-pension f breakfast and one meal.

demi-pensionnaire mf day student.

démission f resignation.

démissionner vt to resign.

demi-sœur f stepsister.

demi-tarif *adj inv (billet)* half-price.

demi-tour *m (en voiture)* U-turn; **faire d.** *(à pied)* to turn back; *(en voiture)* to make a U-turn.

démocratie *f* democracy.

démocratique *adj* democratic.

démodé, -ée *adj* old-fashioned.

demoiselle *f (célibataire)* single woman; **d. d'honneur** *(à un mariage)* bridesmaid.

démolir *vt (maison)* to demolish, to knock down.

démolition *f* demolition.

démonstratif, -ive *adj & m Grammaire* demonstrative.

démonstration *f* demonstration, proof.

démonter *vt (mécanisme)* to take apart; *(tente)* to take down.

démonter (se) *vpr* to come apart, to come down.

démontrer *vt* to show.

démoraliser *vt* to demoralize.

démoraliser (se) *vpr* to become demoralized.

déneiger *vt* to clear of snow.

dénicher *vt (trouver)* to dig up.

dénombrer *vt* to count.

dénoncer *vt* **d. qn** *(au professeur)* to tell on sb *(à to).*

dénoncer (se) *vpr* to own up *(à to).*

dénouement *m (de livre)* ending; *(de pièce de théâtre)* dénouement; *(d'affaire)* outcome.

dénouer *vt (corde)* to undo, to untie.

dénouer (se) *vpr (nœud)* to come undone *ou* untied.

denrées *fpl* **d. alimentaires** foods.

dense *adj* dense.

dent *f* tooth *(pl* teeth); *(de fourchette)* prong; **faire ses dents** *(enfant)* to be teething; **coup de d.** bite.

dentaire *adj* dental.

dentelle *f* lace.

dentier *m (set of)* false teeth.

dentifrice *m* toothpaste.

dentiste *mf* dentist.

déodorant *m* deodorant.

dépannage *m (emergency)* repair.

dépanner *vt (voiture)* to repair.

dépanneur *m (de télévision)* repairman; *(de voiture)* roadside mechanic.

dépanneuse *f (voiture)* tow truck.

départ *m* departure; *(d'une course)* start; **ligne de d.** starting post; **au d.** at the start.

départager *vt* to decide between.

département *m* department.

départementale *adj f* **route d.** secondary road.

dépassé, -ée *adj (démodé)* outdated; *(incapable)* unable to cope.

dépasser 1 *vt (véhicule)* to overtake; **d. qn** *(en hauteur)* to be taller than sb; *(surclasser)* to be ahead of sb. **2** *vi (clou etc)* to stick out.

dépêcher (se) *vpr* to hurry (up).

dépeigné, -ée *adj* **être d.** to have untidy hair.

dépendre *vi* to depend (**de** on, upon).

dépense *f (frais)* expense.

dépenser *vt (argent)* to spend.

dépenser (se) *vpr* to exert oneself.

dépensier, -ière *adj* wasteful.

dépilatoire *adj* **crème d.** hair-removing cream.

dépister *vt (criminel)* to track down; *(maladie)* to detect.

dépit *m* **en d. de** in spite of; **en d. du bon sens** *(mal)* atrociously.

déplacé, -ée *adj (mal à propos)* out of place.

déplacement *m (voyage)* (business) trip.

déplacer *vt* to shift, to move.

déplacer (se) *vpr (voyager)* to travel (around).

déplaire* *vi* **ça me déplaît** I don't like it.

dépliant *m (prospectus)* leaflet.

déplier *vt*, **se déplier** *vpr* to unfold.

déplorable adj regrettable, deplorable.

déplorer vt (regretter) to deplore; **d. que** (+ subjonctif) to regret that.

déployer vt (ailes) to spread.

déporter vt (dévier) to carry (off course).

déposer vt (poser) to put down; (laisser) to leave; (plainte) to lodge; (ordures) to dump; **d. qn** (en voiture) to drop sb (off).

déposer (se) vpr (poussière) to settle.

dépôt m (d'ordures) dump; (dans une bouteille) deposit.

dépotoir m garbage dump.

dépouillé, -ée adj (arbre) bare.

dépression f depression; **d. nerveuse** nervous breakdown.

déprimé, -ée adj depressed.

déprimer vt to depress.

depuis 1 prép since; **d. lundi** since Monday; **d. qu'elle est partie** since she left; **j'habite ici d. un mois** I've been living here for a month; **d. quand êtes-vous là?** how long have you been here?; **d. Paris** from Paris. 2 adv since (then).

député m (à l'Assemblée Nationale) = Congressman, Congresswoman.

déraciner vt (arbre) to uproot.

déraillement m derailment.

dérailler vi (train) to jump the rails.

dérangement m en d. (téléphone) out of order.

déranger vt (affaires) to disturb, to upset; **d. qn** to disturb ou bother sb; **ça vous dérange si je fume?** do you mind if I smoke?

déranger (se) vpr (se déplacer) to bother to come ou go; **ne te dérange pas!** don't bother!

dérapage m skid.

déraper vi to skid.

déréglé, -ée adj out of order.

dérégler vt (télévision etc) to put out of order.

dérégler (se) vpr (montre etc) to go wrong.

dériver vi (bateau) to drift.

dernier, -ière 1 adj last; (mode) latest; (étage) top; **en d.** last. 2 mf last (person ou one); **ce d.** the latter; **être le d. de la classe** to be (at the) bottom of the class.

dernièrement adv recently.

dérober vt (voler) to steal (à from).

dérouiller (se) vpr se d. les jambes to stretch one's legs.

dérouler vt (tapis) to unroll; (fil) to unwind.

dérouler (se) vpr (événement) to take place.

derrick m oil rig.

derrière 1 prép & adv behind; **assis d.** (dans une voiture) sitting in the back; **par d.** (attaquer) from behind. 2 m back; (fesses) behind; **pattes de d.** hind legs.

des voir **de**[1,2], **le**.

dès prép from; **d. le début** (right) from the start; **d. qu'elle viendra** as soon as she comes.

désabusé, -ée adj disillusioned.

désaccord m disagreement.

désaccordé, -ée adj (violon etc) out of tune.

désaffecté, -ée adj (gare etc) disused.

désagréable adj unpleasant.

désaltérer vt d. qn to quench sb's thirst.

désaltérer (se) vpr to quench one's thirst.

désapprobation f disapproval.

désapprouver vt to disapprove of.

désarmement m (de nation) disarmament.

désarmer vt to disarm.

désastre m disaster.

désastreux, -euse adj disastrous.

désavantage m disadvantage.

désavantager vt to handicap.

desceller (se) vpr to come loose.

descendre 1 vi (aux être) to come ou go down; (d'un train) to get off; (d'un arbre) to climb down (de from); (thermomètre) to fall; (marée) to go out; **d. de cheval** to dismount; **d. en courant** to run down. **2** vt (aux avoir) (escalier) to come ou go down; (objet) to bring ou take down.

descente f (d'avion etc) descent; (pente) slope; **d. de lit** (tapis) bedside rug.

description f description.

désemparé, -ée adj (personne) at a loss.

désenchanté, -ée adj disillusioned.

désenfler vi to go down.

déséquilibre (en) adv (meuble) unsteady.

déséquilibrer vt to throw off balance.

désert, -erte adj deserted; **île déserte** desert island.

désert m desert.

désespérant, -ante adj (enfant) hopeless.

désespéré, -ée adj (personne) in despair; (situation) hopeless; (efforts) desperate.

désespérer vt to drive to despair.

désespoir m despair.

déshabiller vt, **se déshabiller** vpr to undress.

désherbant m weed killer.

désherber vti to weed.

désigner vt (montrer) to point to; (élire) to appoint; (signifier) to indicate.

désinfectant m disinfectant.

désinfecter vt to disinfect.

désintéresser (se) vpr **se d. de qch** to lose interest in sth.

désinvolte adj (dégagé) casual; (insolent) offhand.

désir m desire.

désirer vt to want; **je désire que tu viennes** I want you to come.

désister (se) vpr to withdraw.

désobéir vi to disobey; **d. à qn** to disobey sb.

désobéissant, -ante adj disobedient.

désobligeant, -ante adj disagreeable.

désodorisant m air freshener.

désolé, -ée adj **être d.** (navré) to be sorry (**que** (+ subjonctif) that; **de faire** to do).

désoler vt to upset (very much).

désordonné, -ée adj (personne) messy, untidy.

désordre m (dans une chambre) mess; (dans une classe) disturbance; **en d.** messy, untidy.

désorganisé, -ée adj disorganized.

désormais adv from now on.

desquel(le)s voir **lequel**.

dessécher (se) vpr (plante) to wither; (peau) to get dry.

desserrer vt (ceinture) to loosen; (poing) to open; (frein) to release.

desserrer (se) vpr to come loose.

dessert m dessert.

desservir vt (table) to clear; **le car dessert ce village** the bus stops at this village.

dessin m drawing; **d. (humoristique)** cartoon; **d. animé** (film) cartoon; **école de d.** art school.

dessinateur, -trice mf drawer; **d. humoristique** cartoonist.

dessiner vt to draw.

dessous 1 adv under(neath), below; **en d.** under(neath); **par-d.** (passer) under(neath). **2** m underside, underneath; **drap de d.** bottom sheet; **les gens du d.** the people downstairs.

dessous-de-plat m inv tablemat.

dessus 1 adv (marcher, monter) on it; (passer) over it; **par-d.** (sauter) over (it). **2** m top; **drap de d.** top sheet; **les gens du d.** the people upstairs.

dessus-de-lit m inv bedspread.

destin m fate.

destinataire *mf* addressee.
destination *f (lieu)* destination; **à d. de** *(train)* to, for.
destiner *vt* **d. qch à qn** to intend sth for sb.
destruction *f* destruction.
désuet, -ète *adj* obsolete.
détachant *m* stain remover.
détacher¹ *vt (ceinture)* to undo; *(personne)* to untie; *(ôter)* to take off.
détacher² *vt (linge)* to remove the stains from.
détacher (se) *upr (chien)* to break loose; *(se dénouer)* to come un-done; **se d. (de qch)** *(fragment)* to come off (sth).
détail¹ *m* detail; **en d.** in detail.
détail² *m* de d. *(magasin, prix)* re-tail; **vendre au d.** to sell retail.
détaillant, -ante *mf* retailer.
détaillé, -ée *adj (récit etc)* de-tailed.
détaler *vi* to run off.
détecteur *m* detector.
détective *m* **d. (privé)** (private) detective.
déteindre* *vi (couleur)* to run; **ton tablier bleu a déteint sur ma che-mise** the blue of your apron has come off on my shirt.
détendre *vt* **d. qn** to relax sb.
détendre (se) *upr (se reposer)* to relax; *(corde etc)* to slacken.
détendu, -ue *adj* relaxed; *(res-sort etc)* slack.
détenir* *vt (record, pouvoir, titre, prisonnier)* to hold; *(secret, objet volé)* to be in possession of.
détente *f (repos)* relaxation.
détenu, -ue *m* prisoner.
détergent *m* detergent.
détérioration *f* deterioration (**de** in).
détériorer (se) *upr* to deterior-ate.
déterminant, -ante *adj* deci-sive.
déterminer *vt (préciser)* to deter-mine.

déterrer *vt* to dig up.
détester *vt* to hate (**faire** doing, to do).
détonation *f* explosion.
détour *m (crochet)* detour.
détourné, -ée *adj (chemin)* round-about, indirect.
détournement *m (d'avion)* hi-jacking.
détourner *vt (dévier)* to divert; *(tête)* to turn (away); *(avion)* to hi-jack; **d. les yeux** to look away.
détourner (se) *upr* to turn away; **se d. de** *(chemin)* to stray from.
détraqué, -ée *adj* out of order.
détraquer *vt (mécanisme)* to put out of order.
détraquer (se) *upr (machine)* to break down.
détresse *f* distress; **en d.** *(navire)* in distress.
détritus *mpl* garbage.
détroit *m* strait(s).
détruire* *vt* to destroy.
dette *f* debt; **avoir des dettes** to be in debt.
deuil *m (vêtements)* mourning; **en d.** in mourning.
deux *adj & m* two; **d. fois** twice; **tous (les) d.** both.
deuxième *adj & mf* second.
deuxièmement *adv* secondly.
deux-pièces *m inv (maillot de bain)* bikini.
deux-points *m inv* Grammaire colon.
deux-roues *m inv* two-wheeled vehicle.
dévaler **1** *vt (escalier)* to race down. **2** *vi (tomber)* to tumble down.
dévaliser *vt* to rob.
devancer *vt* to get *ou* be ahead of.
devant 1 *prép & adv* in front (of); **d. (l'hôtel/etc)** in front (of the hotel/etc); **passer d. (l'église/etc)** to go past (the church/etc); **assis d.** *(dans une voiture)* sitting in the front. **2** *m*

front; **roue de d.** front wheel; **patte de d.** foreleg.

devanture f (vitrine) shop ou store window.

dévaster vt to ruin, to devastate.

développement m development; (de photos) developing; **en plein d.** (entreprise, pays) growing fast.

développer vt, **se développer** to develop.

devenir* vi (aux être) to become; **qu'est-il devenu?** what's become of him?

déverser vt, **se déverser** vpr (liquide) to pour out (**dans** into).

déviation f (itinéraire provisoire) detour.

dévier 1 vt (circulation) to divert. **2** vi (de sa route) to veer (off course).

deviner vt to guess.

devinette f riddle.

devis m estimate (of cost of work to be done).

devise f (légende) motto; **devises** (argent) (foreign) currency.

dévisser vt to unscrew.

dévisser (se) vpr (bouchon) to unscrew; (se desserrer) to come loose.

dévoiler vt (secret) to disclose.

devoir*[1] **1** v aux (nécessité) **je dois refuser** I must refuse, I have (got) to refuse; **j'ai dû refuser** I had to refuse. ▪ (probabilité) **il doit être tard** it must be late; **elle a dû oublier** she must have forgotten; **il ne doit pas être bête** he can't be stupid. ▪ (obligation) **tu dois apprendre tes leçons** you must study your lessons; **il aurait dû venir** he should have come; **vous devriez rester** you should stay. ▪ (événement prévu) **elle doit venir** she's supposed to be coming, she's due to come.

devoir*[2] **1** vt (argent etc) to owe (**à** to). **2** m (obligation) duty; (exercice) exercise; **devoirs** (à faire à la mai-

son) homework; **d. sur table** exam(ination) in class.

dévorer vt (manger) to eat up.

dévoué, -ée adj (soldat etc) dedicated.

dévouement m dedication.

dévouer (se) vpr **se d. (pour qn)** to sacrifice oneself (for sb).

diabète m diabetes.

diabétique mf diabetic.

diable m devil; **habiter au d.** to live miles from anywhere.

diagnostic m diagnosis.

diagonale f diagonal (line); **en d.** diagonally.

dialecte m dialect.

dialogue m conversation; (de film) dialogue.

diamant m diamond.

diamètre m diameter.

diapositive, Fam **diapo** f (color) slide.

diarrhée f diarrhea.

dictature f dictatorship.

dictée f dictation.

dicter vt to dictate (**à** to).

dictionnaire m dictionary.

dicton m saying.

diesel adj & m (moteur) **d.** diesel (engine).

diète f (jeûne) **à la d.** on a diet.

diététique adj **produit d.** health food.

dieu, -x m god; **D.** God.

différence f difference (**de** in).

différent, -ente adj different (**de** than, from, to).

difficile adj difficult; (exigeant) fussy; **d. à faire** difficult to do; **il nous est d. de** it's difficult for us to.

difficulté f difficulty; **en d.** in a difficult situation.

diffuser vt (émission) to broadcast.

digérer vti to digest.

digestif, -ive 1 adj digestive. **2** m after-dinner liqueur.

digestion f digestion.

digne adj **d. de** worthy of.

digue f dike; (en bord de mer) sea wall.

dilater vt, **se dilater** vpr to expand.

diligence f (véhicule) stagecoach.

dimanche m Sunday.

dimension f dimension.

diminuer 1 vt to reduce. **2** vi (réserves) to decrease; (jours) to get shorter; (prix) to drop.

diminutif m (prénom) nickname.

diminution f reduction, decrease (de in).

dinde f turkey.

dindon m turkey (cock).

dîner 1 vi to have dinner; (au Canada, en Belgique) to have lunch. **2** m dinner.

dînette f (jouet) doll's dinner service ou set.

dinosaure m dinosaur.

diphtongue f diphthong.

diplôme m certificate, diploma.

diplômé, -ée 1 adj qualified; (de l'université) être d. (de) to be a graduate (of). **2** mf holder of a diploma; (de l'université) graduate.

dire* vt (mot) to say; (vérité, secret, heure) to tell; **d. des bêtises** to talk nonsense; **d. qch à qn** to tell sb sth, to say sth to sb; **d. à qn que** to tell sb that, to say to sb that; **d. à qn de faire** to tell sb to do; **on dirait un château/du Mozart** it looks like a castle/sounds like Mozart; **ça ne me dit rien** (envie) I don't feel like it; (souvenir) it doesn't ring a bell.

dire (se) vpr **ça ne se dit pas** you don't say that.

direct, -e 1 adj direct; **train d.** fast train. **2** m (émission) live.

directement adv directly.

directeur, -trice mf director; (d'école) principal.

direction f (sens) direction; **en d. de** (train) to, for; **sous la d. de** (orchestre) conducted by; **la d.** (équipe dirigeante) the management.

dirigeable adj & m (ballon) **d.** airship, dirigible.

dirigeant m (de parti etc) leader; (d'entreprise, club) manager.

diriger vt (société) to run; (parti, groupe) to lead; (véhicule) to steer; (orchestre) to conduct; (arme etc) to point (**vers** towards).

diriger (se) vpr **se d. vers** (lieu) to make one's way towards.

dis, disant voir **dire**.

discipline f (règle) discipline.

discipliné, -ée adj well-disciplined.

discipliner (se) vpr to discipline oneself.

disco f disco.

discontinu, -ue adj (ligne) broken; (bruit) intermittent.

discothèque f (club) disco/theque.

discours m speech.

discret, -ète adj (personne) discreet.

discrètement adv discreetly.

discrétion f discretion.

discrimination f discrimination.

discussion f discussion; (conversation) talk; **pas de d.!** no argument!

discuter vi (parler) to talk (**de** about); (répliquer) to argue; **d. sur qch** to discuss sth.

dise(nt) etc voir **dire**.

disjoncter vi (circuit électrique) to fuse.

disloquer (se) vpr (meuble) to fall apart.

disparaître* vi to disappear; (être porté manquant) to be reported missing.

disparition f disappearance.

disparu, -ue adj (soldat) missing.

dispense f exemption.

dispenser vt **d. qn de** (obligation) to exempt sb from.

disperser vt (objets) to scatter.

disperser (se) vpr (foule) to disperse.

disponible adj (article, place etc) available.

disposé, -ée *adj* **bien d.** in a good mood; **d. à faire** prepared to do.

disposer 1 *vt (objets)* to arrange. **2** *vi* **d. de qch** to make use of sth.

disposer (se) *vpr* **se d. à faire** to prepare to do.

dispositif *m (mécanisme)* device.

disposition *f* arrangement; **à la d. de qn** at sb's disposal; **prendre ses dispositions** to make arrangements.

disproportionné, -ée *adj* disproportionate.

dispute *f* quarrel.

disputer *vt (match)* to play; *(rallye)* to compete in; **d. qn** *(gronder) Fam* to tell sb off.

disputer (se) *vpr* to quarrel (**avec** with).

disqualifier *vt (équipe)* to disqualify.

disque *m* disk; **d. compact** compact disk.

disquette *f (d'ordinateur)* floppy (disk), diskette.

dissertation *f (au lycée etc)* essay.

dissimuler *vt*, **se dissimuler** *(cacher)* to hide (**à** from).

dissipé, -ée *adj (élève)* unruly.

dissiper *vt (brouillard)* to dispel; **d. qn** to distract sb.

dissiper (se) *vpr (brume)* to lift; *(élève)* to misbehave.

dissolvant *m* solvent; *(pour vernis à ongles)* nail polish remover.

dissoudre* *vt*, **se dissoudre** *vpr* to dissolve.

dissuader *vt* to dissuade (**de qch** from sth; **de faire** from doing).

distance *f* distance; **à deux mètres de d.** seven feet apart.

distancer *vt* to leave behind.

distinct, -incte *adj* distinct.

distinctement *adv* clearly.

distinguer *vt* to distinguish; *(voir)* to make out; **d. le blé de l'orge** to tell wheat from barley.

distinguer (se) *vpr* **se d. de** to be distinguishable from.

distraction *f* amusement; *(étourderie)* absent-mindedness.

distraire* *vt (divertir)* to entertain.

distraire (se) *vpr* to amuse oneself.

distrait, -aite *adj* absent-minded.

distribuer *vt (donner)* to hand out; *(courrier)* to deliver; *(cartes)* to deal.

distributeur *m* **d. (automatique)** vending machine; **d. de billets** ticket machine; *(de banque)* automatic teller machine, ATM.

distribution *f* distribution; *(du courrier)* delivery.

dit, dite, dites *voir* **dire**.

divan *m* couch.

divergent, -ente *adj (lignes)* divergent; *(opinions)* differing.

divers, -erses *adj pl (distincts)* varied; *(plusieurs)* various.

diversifier *vt*, **se diversifier** *vpr* to diversify.

divertir *vt* to entertain.

divertir (se) *vpr* to enjoy oneself.

divertissement *m* entertainment.

diviser *vt*, **se diviser** *vpr* to divide (**en** into).

division *f* division.

divorce *m* divorce.

divorcé, -ée 1 *adj* divorced. **2** *mf* divorcee.

divorcer *vi* to get divorced.

dix *adj & m* ten.

dix-huit *adj & m* eighteen.

dixième *adj & mf* tenth.

dix-neuf *adj & m* nineteen.

dix-sept *adj & m* seventeen.

dizaine *f* **une d. (de)** about ten.

docile *adj* docile.

docker *m* docker.

docteur *m* doctor.

doctorat *m* doctorate, = PhD.

document *m* document.

documentaire *m (film)* documentary.

documentaliste *mf (à l'école)* (school) librarian.

documentation *f (documents)* documentation.

documenter (se) *vpr* to collect information.

dodo *m (langage enfantin)* **faire d.** to sleep.

doigt *m* finger; **d. de pied** toe; **petit d.** little finger, pinkie.

dois, doit, doivent(nt) *voir* **devoir**[1,2].

dollar *m* dollar.

domaine *m (terres)* estate.

dôme *m* dome.

domestique 1 *adj (animal)* domestic; **travaux domestiques** housework. **2** *mf* servant.

domicile *m* home; **livrer à d.** to deliver (to the house).

domination *f* domination.

dominer 1 *vt* to dominate. **2** *vi (être le plus fort)* to dominate.

domino *m* domino; **dominos** *(jeu)* dominoes.

dommage *m* **c'est d.!** it's a pity *ou* a shame! **(que** + *subjonctif* that); **dommages** *(dégâts)* damage.

dompter *vt (animal)* to tame.

dompteur, -euse *mf (de lions)* lion tamer.

DOM-TOM *mpl abrév (départements et territoires d'outre-mer)* = French overseas departments and territories.

don *m (cadeau, aptitude)* gift; *(charité)* donation.

donc *conj (par conséquent)* so; **asseyez-vous d.!** won't you sit down!

donjon *m* keep.

données *fpl (information)* data.

donner 1 *vt* to give; *(récolte)* to produce; *(sa place)* to give up; *(cartes)* to deal; **d. un coup à** to hit; **d. à réparer** to take (in) to be repaired; **ça donne soif/faim** it makes you thirsty/hungry. **2** *vi* **d. sur** *(fenêtre)* to overlook; *(porte)* to open onto.

donner (se) *vpr* **se d. du mal** to go to a lot of trouble **(pour faire** to).

dont *pron rel* (= *de qui, duquel, de quoi etc)* *(personne)* of whom; *(chose)* of which; *(appartenance: personne, chose)* whose; **une mère d. le fils est malade** a mother whose son is ill; **la fille d. il est fier** the daughter he is proud of *ou* of whom he is proud; **la façon d.** the way in which.

doper (se) *vpr* to take drugs.

doré, -ée *adj (objet)* gilt, gold; *(couleur)* golden.

dorénavant *adv* from now on.

dorer *vt (objet)* to gild.

dorer (se) *vpr* **se d. au soleil** to sunbathe.

dormir* *vi* to sleep.

dortoir *m* dormitory.

dos *m (de personne, d'animal)* back; **à d. d'âne** *(riding)* on a donkey; **'voir au d.'** *(verso)* 'see over'.

dose *f* dose.

dossier *m (de siège)* back; *(papiers)* file.

doter *vt (équiper)* to equip **(de** with); **doté d'une grande intelligence** endowed with great intelligence.

douane *f* customs.

douanier *m* customs officer.

doublage *m (de film)* dubbing.

double 1 *adj & adv* double. **2** *m* **le d. (de)** *(quantité)* twice as much (as), double; **je l'ai en d.** I have two of them.

doubler 1 *vt (vêtement)* to line; *(film)* to dub. **2** *vti (augmenter)* to double; *(en voiture)* to overtake.

doublure *f (étoffe)* lining.

douce *voir* **doux**.

doucement *adv (délicatement)* gently; *(à voix basse)* softly; *(lentement)* slowly.

douceur *f (de miel)* sweetness; *(de peau)* softness; *(de temps)* mildness.

douche *f* shower.

doucher *vt* **d. qn** to give sb a shower.

doucher (se) *vpr* to take a shower.

doué, -ée *adj* gifted **(en** at); *(intelligent)* clever.

douillet, -ette *adj (lit)* soft, cozy; **tu es d.** *(délicat)* you're such a baby.
douleur *f (mal)* pain; *(chagrin)* sorrow.
douloureux, -euse *adj* painful.
doute *m* doubt; **sans d.** probably, no doubt.
douter *vi* to doubt.
douter (se) *vpr* **se d. de qch** to suspect sth; **je m'en doute** I would think so.
douteux, -euse *adj (peu certain)* doubtful; *(louche, médiocre)* dubious.
doux, douce *adj (miel etc)* sweet; *(peau)* soft; *(temps)* mild.
douzaine *f* dozen; *(environ)* about twelve; **une d. d'œufs/etc** a dozen eggs/etc.
douze *adj & m* twelve.
douzième *adj & mf* twelfth.
dragée *f* sugared almond.
dragon *m (animal)* dragon.
draguer *vt (rivière)* to dredge; *(personne) Fam* to come on to.
dramatique *adj* dramatic; **film d.** drama.
drame *m* drama; *(catastrophe)* tragedy.
drap *m (de lit)* sheet; **d. housse** fitted sheet; **d. de bain** bath towel.
drapeau, -x *m* flag.
dressage *m* training.
dresser *vt (échelle)* to put up; *(animal)* to train.
dresser (se) *vpr (personne)* to stand up; *(montagne)* to stand.
dribbler *vti Sport* to dribble.
drogue *f* **une d.** *(stupéfiant)* a drug; **la d.** drugs.
drogué, -ée *mf* drug addict.
droguer (se) *vpr* to take drugs.
droguerie *f* hardware store.
droit[1] *m (privilège)* right (**de faire** to do); *(d'inscription etc)* fee(s); **le d.** *(science)* law; **avoir d. à** to be entitled to.

droit[2], droite 1 *adj (route etc)* straight; *(vertical)* upright; *(angle)* right. **2** *adv* straight; **tout d.** straight ahead.
droit[3], droite *adj (côté etc)* right.
droite *f* **la d.** *(côté)* the right (side); **à d.** *(tourner)* (to the) right; *(rouler etc)* on the right; **de d.** *(fenêtre etc)* right-hand; **à d. de** on *ou* to the right of.
droitier, -ière *adj & mf* right-handed (person).
drôle *adj* odd, strange; **d. d'air/de type** strange look/guy.
drôlement *adv (extrêmement)* terribly.
du *voir* **de[1,2], le.**
dû, due *(pp of devoir[1,2])* *adj* **d. à** due to.
duc *m* duke.
duchesse *f* duchess.
duel *m* duel.
dune *f* (sand) dune.
duplex *m* duplex.
duquel *voir* **lequel.**
dur, -e 1 *adj (substance)* hard; *(difficile)* hard, tough; *(hiver, personne, ton)* harsh; *(œuf)* hard-boiled. **2** *adv (travailler)* hard.
durable *adj* lasting.
durant *prép* during.
durcir *vti,* **se durcir** *vpr* to harden.
durée *f (de film etc)* length.
durer *vi* to last; **ça dure depuis** it's been going on for *ou* since.
dureté *f* hardness; *(de ton etc)* harshness.
duvet *m (d'oiseau)* down; *(sac)* sleeping bag.
DVD *m abrév (digital video disk, digital versatile disk)* DVD.
dynamique *adj* dynamic.
dynamite *f* dynamite.
dynamo *f* dynamo.
dyslexique *adj & mf* dyslexic.

E

eau, -x *f* water; **e. douce/salée** fresh/salt water; **e. de Cologne** cologne; **tomber à l'e.** *(projet)* to fall through.

eau-de-vie, *pl* **eaux-de-vie** *f* brandy.

ébahi, -ie *adj* astounded.

ébaucher *vt (tableau, roman)* to rough out.

ébéniste *m* cabinet-maker.

éblouir *vt* to dazzle.

éboueur *m* garbage collector.

ébouillanter (s') *vpr* to scald oneself.

éboulement *m* landslide.

ébouler (s') *vpr (falaise)* to crumble; *(roches)* to fall.

ébouriffé, -ée *adj (cheveux)* disheveled.

ébranler *vt* to shake; *(santé)* to weaken.

ébranler (s') *vpr (train etc)* to move off.

ébrécher *vt (assiette)* to chip.

ébruiter *vt*, **s'ébruiter** *vpr (nouvelle)* to spread.

ébullition *f* **être en é.** *(eau)* to be boiling.

écaille *f (de poisson)* scale; *(de tortue)* shell; *(pour lunettes)* tortoiseshell; *(de peinture)* flake.

écailler *vt (poisson)* to scale; *(huître)* to shell.

écailler (s') *vpr (peinture)* to flake (off), to peel.

écarlate *adj* scarlet.

écarquiller *vt* **é. les yeux** to open one's eyes wide.

écart *m (intervalle)* gap; *(embardée)* swerve; *(différence)* difference *(de* in; *entre* between); **à l'é.** out of the way; **à l'é. de** away from.

écarté, -ée *adj (endroit)* remote;

les jambes écartées with legs apart.

écarter *vt (objets)* to move apart; *(jambes, rideaux)* to open; **é. qch de qch** to move sth away from sth; **é. qn de** *(exclure)* to keep sb out of.

écarter (s') *vpr (s'éloigner)* to move away *(de* from).

échafaud *m* scaffold.

échafaudage *m (de peintre etc)* scaffold(ing).

échalote *f* shallot.

échancré, -ée *adj* low-cut.

échange *m* exchange; **en é.** in exchange *(de* for).

échanger *vt* to exchange *(contre* for).

échangeur *m (autoroute)* interchange.

échantillon *m* sample.

échapper *vi* **é. à qn** to escape from sb; **é. à la mort** to escape death; **son nom m'échappe** her name escapes me.

échapper (s') *vpr (s'enfuir)* to escape *(de* from); *(gaz, eau)* to escape.

écharde *f* splinter.

écharpe *f* scarf; *(de maire)* sash; **en é.** *(bras)* in a sling.

échauffer (s') *vpr (sportif)* to warm up.

échec *m* failure; **les échecs** *(jeu)* chess; **é.!** check!; **é. et mat!** checkmate!

échelle *f (marches)* ladder; *(dimension)* scale; **faire la courte é. à qn** to give sb a leg up *ou* a boost.

échelon *m (d'échelle)* rung; *(de fonctionnaire)* grade.

échiquier *m* chessboard.

écho *m (d'un son)* echo.

échographie *f* (ultrasound) scan; **passer une é.** to have a scan.

échouer *vi* to fail; **é. à** *(examen)* to fail.

échouer (s') *vpr (navire)* to run aground.

éclabousser *vt* to splash (**de** with).

éclaboussure *f* splash.

éclair *m* (*lumière*) flash; (*d'orage*) flash of lightning.

éclairage *m* (*de pièce etc*) lighting.

éclaircie *f* (*durée*) sunny interval.

éclaircir *vt* (*couleur etc*) to make lighter; (*mystère*) to clear up.

éclaircir (s') *vpr* (*ciel*) to clear (up); (*situation*) to become clear.

éclaircissement *m* explanation.

éclairé, -ée *adj* **bien/mal é.** well/badly lit.

éclairer *vt* (*pièce etc*) to light (up); **é. qn** (*avec une lampe*) to give sb some light.

éclairer (s') *vpr* (*visage*) to brighten up; (*situation*) to become clear; **s'é. à la bougie** to use candlelight.

éclaireur, -euse *mf* boy/girl scout.

éclat[1] *m* (*de la lumière*) brightness; (*de phare*) glare.

éclat[2] *m* (*de verre ou de bois*) splinter; (*de rire*) (out)burst.

éclatant, -ante *adj* (*lumière, succès*) brilliant.

éclatement *m* (*de ballon etc*) bursting; (*de bombe*) explosion.

éclater *vi* (*ballon etc*) to burst; (*bombe*) to go off; (*verre*) to shatter; (*guerre, incendie*) to break out; (*orage*) to break; **é. de rire** to burst out laughing; **é. en sanglots** to burst into tears.

éclore* *vi* (*œuf*) to hatch.

éclosion *f* hatching.

écluse *f* (*de canal*) lock.

écœurant, -ante *adj* disgusting, sickening.

écœurer *vt* **é. qn** to make sb feel sick.

école *f* school; **à l'é.** in *ou* at school; **aller à l'é.** to go to school.

écolier, -ière *mf* schoolboy, schoolgirl.

écologiste *mf* environmentalist.

économe *adj* thrifty.

économie *f* economy; **économies** (*argent*) savings; **une é. de temps** time saved; **faire des économies** to save (up).

économique *adj* (*bon marché*) economical.

économiser *vti* to economize (**sur** on).

écorce *f* (*d'arbre*) bark; (*de fruit*) peel, skin.

écorcher *vt* (*érafler*) to scrape; **é. les oreilles** to grate on one's ears.

écorcher (s') *vpr* to scrape oneself.

écorchure *f* scrape.

écossais, -aise 1 *adj* Scottish; (*tissu*) tartan; (*whisky*) Scotch. **2** *mf* **E.** Scot.

écosser *vt* (*pois*) to shell.

écoulement *m* (*de liquide*) flow; (*de temps*) passage.

écouler (s') *vpr* (*eau*) to flow out; (*temps*) to pass.

écourter *vt* (*séjour*) to cut short; (*texte, tige*) to shorten.

écouter 1 *vt* to listen to. **2** *vi* to listen.

écouteur *m* (*de téléphone*) earpiece; **écouteurs** (*casque*) earphones.

écran *m* screen; **le petit é.** television.

écrasant, -ante *adj* overwhelming.

écraser *vt* to crush; (*cigarette*) to put *ou* stub out; (*piéton*) to run over; **se faire é.** to get run over.

écraser (s') *vpr* to crash (**contre** into).

écrémé *adj* (*lait*) skim.

écrevisse *f* crayfish.

écrier (s') *vpr* to exclaim (**que** that).

écrire* **1** *vt* to write; (*en toutes lettres*) to spell; **é. à la machine** to type. **2** *vi* to write.

écrire (s') *vpr* (*mot*) to be spelled *ou* spelt.

écrit *m* **par é.** in writing.

écriteau, -x m notice, sign.

écriture f writing.

écrivain m author, writer.

écrou m (de boulon) nut.

écrouler (s') vpr to collapse.

écueil m reef; (obstacle) pitfall.

écuelle f bowl.

écume f (de mer etc) foam.

écureuil m squirrel.

écurie f stable.

écusson m (en étoffe) badge.

édifice m building.

édifier vt to erect.

éditer vt to publish.

éditeur, -trice mf publisher.

édition f (livre, journal) edition; (métier) publishing.

édredon m eiderdown.

éducateur, -trice mf educator.

éducatif, -ive adj educational.

éducation f education; **avoir de l'é.** to have good manners.

éduquer vt to educate.

effacer vt to rub out, to erase; (en lavant) to wash out; (avec un chiffon) to wipe away.

effarant, -ante adj astounding.

effaroucher vt to scare away.

effectif m (de classe etc) total number.

effectivement adv actually.

effectuer vt (expérience etc) to carry out; (trajet etc) to make.

effet m effect (sur on); **faire de l'e.** (remède) to be effective; **en e.** indeed, in fact; **sous l'e. de la colère** in anger.

efficace adj (mesure etc) effective; (personne) efficient.

efficacité f (de mesure etc) effectiveness; (de personne) efficiency.

effilocher (s') vpr to fray.

effleurer vt to skim, to touch (lightly).

effondrer (s') vpr to collapse.

efforcer (s') vpr s'e. de faire to try (hard) to do.

effort m effort; **sans e.** (réussir etc) effortlessly.

effrayant, -ante adj frightening.

effrayer vt to frighten, to scare.

effronté, -ée adj (personne) impudent.

effroyable adj dreadful.

égal, -e, aux 1 adj equal (à to); (uniforme, régulier) even; **ça m'est é.** I don't care. **2** mf (personne) equal.

également adv (aussi) also, as well.

égaler vt to equal.

égaliser vi to equalize.

égalité f equality; (régularité) evenness; **à é. (de score)** even, equal (in points).

égard m à l'é. de (envers) towards.

égarer vt (objet) to mislay.

égarer (s') vpr to lose one's way.

égayer vt (pièce) to brighten up; **é. qn** to cheer sb up.

église f church.

égoïste 1 adj selfish. **2** mf selfish person.

égorger vt to cut the throat of.

égout m sewer; **eaux d'é.** sewage.

égoutter 1 vt to drain. **2** vi, s'égoutter vpr to drain; (linge) to drip.

égouttoir m (dish) drainer.

égratigner vt to scratch.

égratignure f scratch.

eh! int hey!; **eh bien!** well!

élaborer vt (plan, idée) to develop.

élan m (vitesse) momentum; (impulsion) impulse; **prendre son é.** to get a running start.

élancer (s') vpr (bondir) to leap ou rush (forward).

élargir (s') vpr (route etc) to widen.

élastique 1 adj (objet) elastic. **2** m (lien) elastic ou rubber band.

électeur, -trice mf voter.

élection f election.

électoral, -e, -aux adj campagne électorale election campaign.

électricien m electrician.

électricité f electricity.

électrique *adj* electric.

électrocuter *vt* to electrocute.

électroménager 1 *adj m* **appareil é.** household electrical appliance. **2** *m* household appliances.

électronique *adj* electronic.

électrophone *m* record player.

élégance *f* elegance; **avec é.** elegantly.

élégant, -ante *adj* elegant.

élément *m* element; *(de meuble)* unit; **éléments** *(notions)* rudiments.

élémentaire *adj* basic; *(cours, école etc)* elementary.

éléphant *m* elephant.

élevage *m* breeding, raising.

élève *mf* pupil.

élevé, -ée *adj (haut)* high; **bien/mal é.** well-/bad-mannered.

élever *vt (prix, voix etc)* to raise; *(enfant)* to bring up, to raise; *(animal)* to breed, to raise.

élever (s') *vpr (prix, ton etc)* to rise; **s'é. à** *(prix)* to amount to.

éleveur, -euse *mf* breeder.

éliminatoire *adj & f (épreuve)* é. heat.

éliminer *vt* to eliminate.

élire* *vt* to elect (**à** to).

elle *pron (sujet)* she; *(chose, animal)* it; **elles** they. ▪ *(complément)* her; *(chose, animal)* it; **elles** them.

elle-même *pron* herself; *(chose, animal)* itself; **elles-mêmes** themselves.

éloigné, -ée *adj (lieu)* far away; *(date)* distant; **é. de** *(village etc)* far (away) from.

éloigner *vt (chose, personne)* to move *ou* go away (**de** from).

e-mail *m* e-mail; **envoyer un e.** to send an e-mail (**à** to).

émail, -aux *m* enamel.

emballage *m (action)* packing; wrapping; *(caisse)* packaging; *(papier)* wrapping (paper).

emballer *vt (dans une caisse etc)* to pack; *(dans du papier)* to wrap

(up); **e. qn** *(passionner)* Fam to thrill sb.

emballer (s') *vpr (personne)* Fam to get carried away; *(cheval)* to bolt.

embarcadère *m* quay, wharf.

embarcation *f (small)* boat.

embardée *f (sudden)* swerve.

embarquement *m (de passagers)* boarding.

embarquer 1 *vt (passagers)* to take on board; *(marchandises)* to load (up). **2** *vi,* **s'embarquer** *vpr* to (go on) board.

embarras *m (gêne)* embarrassment.

embarrassant, -ante *adj (paquet)* cumbersome; *(question)* embarrassing.

embarrasser *vt* **e. qn** to be in sb's way; *(question etc)* to embarrass sb.

embarrasser (s') *vpr* **s'e. de** to burden oneself with.

embaucher *vt (ouvrier)* to hire.

embellir 1 *vt (pièce, personne)* to make more attractive. **2** *vi (personne)* to grow more attractive.

embêtant, -ante *adj* annoying, boring.

embêtement *m* trouble.

embêter *vt (agacer)* to bother; *(ennuyer)* to bore.

embêter (s') *vpr* Fam to get bored.

emboîter *vt,* **s'emboîter** *vpr (tuyau(x))* to fit together.

embouchure *f (de fleuve)* mouth.

embourber (s') *vpr* to get bogged down.

embouteillage *m* traffic jam.

embouteillé, -ée *adj (rue)* congested.

emboutir *vt (voiture)* to crash into.

embranchement *m (de voie)* junction.

embrasser *vt (donner un baiser à)* to kiss.

embrasser (s') *vpr* to kiss (each other).

embrayage *m (de véhicule)* clutch.

embrocher *vt* to skewer.

embrouiller *vt (fils)* to tangle (up); *(papiers etc)* to mix up; **e. qn** to confuse sb.

embrouiller (s') *vpr* to get confused (**dans** in, with).

embuscade *f* ambush.

émerger *vi* to emerge (**de** from).

émerveiller *vt* to amaze, to fill with wonder.

émetteur *m* **(poste)** é. transmitter.

émettre* *vt (lumière, son etc)* to give out; *(message, radio)* to broadcast; *(timbre, monnaie)* to issue.

émeute *f* riot.

émietter *vt*, **émietter (s')** *vpr* to crumble.

émigrer *vi* to emigrate.

émission *f (de radio etc)* broadcast; *(diffusion)* transmission; *(de timbre, monnaie)* issue.

emmanchure *f* arm hole.

emmêler *vt* to tangle (up).

emménager *vi (dans un logement)* to move in; **e. dans** to move into.

emmener *vt* to take (**à** to); **e. qn en promenade** to take sb for a walk.

emmitoufler (s') *vpr* to wrap (oneself) up.

émotif, -ive *adj* emotional.

émotion *f* emotion; *(trouble)* excitement; **une é.** *(peur)* a scare.

émouvant, -ante *adj* moving.

émouvoir* *vt* to move, to touch.

empailler *vt* to stuff.

empaqueter *vt* to pack.

emparer (s') *vpr* **s'e. de** to take, to grab.

empêchement *m* **j'ai eu un e.** something's come up at the last minute.

empêcher *vt* to prevent, to stop (**de faire** (from) doing).

empêcher (s') *vpr* **s'e. de faire qch** to stop oneself from doing sth;

elle ne peut pas s'e. de rire she can't help laughing.

empereur *m* emperor.

empester 1 *vt (tabac etc)* to stink of; **e. qn** to stink sb out. **2** *vi* to stink.

empiler *vt*, **empiler (s')** *vpr* to pile up (**sur** on).

empire *m* empire.

empirer *vi* to worsen, to get worse.

emplacement *m* site; *(de stationnement)* place.

emplir *vt*, **emplir (s')** *vpr* to fill (**de** with).

emploi *m (usage)* use; *(travail)* job, employment; **e. du temps** schedule; **sans e.** *(au chômage)* unemployed.

employé, -ée *mf* employee; *(de bureau, banque)* clerk, employee.

employer *vt (utiliser)* to use; **e. qn** to employ sb.

employer (s') *vpr (expression)* to be used.

employeur, -euse *mf* employer.

empoigner *vt* to grab.

empoisonner *vt* to poison.

empoisonner (s') *vpr* to poison oneself; *(par accident)* to be poisoned.

emporter *vt (prendre)* to take (away) (**avec soi** with one); *(entraîner)* to carry away; *(par le vent)* to blow off *ou* away.

emporter (s') *vpr* to lose one's temper (**contre** with).

empreinte *f* mark; **e. (digitale)** fingerprint; **e. (de pas)** footprint.

empresser (s') *vpr* **s'e. de faire** to hasten to do.

emprisonner *vt* to jail.

emprunt *m (argent etc)* loan.

emprunter *vt (argent)* to borrow (**à** from); *(route)* to use.

ému, -ue *adj* moved; *(attristé)* upset.

en¹ *prép (lieu)* in; *(direction)* to; **être/aller en France** to be in/go to France. ▪ *(temps)* in; **en février** in February; **d'heure en heure** from hour to hour. ▪ *(moyen, état etc)* by; in; on; **en avion** by plane; **en groupe** in a group; **en congé** on leave *ou* vacation. ▪ *(matière)* in; **en bois** in wood; **chemise en nylon** nylon shirt; **c'est en or** it's (made of) gold. ▪ *(comme)* **en cadeau** as a present. ▪ *(+ participe présent)* **en mangeant**/*etc* while eating/*etc*; **en apprenant que** on hearing that; **en souriant** smiling, with a smile. ▪ *(transformation)* into; **traduire en** to translate into.

en² *pron & adv (= de là)* from there; **j'en viens** I've just come from there. ▪ *(= de ça, lui etc)* **il en est content** he's pleased with it/him/them; **en parler** to talk about it; **en mourir** to die of *ou* from it. ▪ *(partitif)* some; **j'en ai** I have some.

encadrer *vt (tableau)* to frame; *(entourer d'un trait)* to circle *(word)*.

encaisser *vt (argent, loyer etc)* to collect.

enceinte¹ *adj (femme)* pregnant; **e. de six mois** six months pregnant.

enceinte² *f* enclosure; **dans l'e. de** within; **e. (acoustique)** speaker.

encens *m* incense.

encercler *vt* to surround.

enchaîner *vt* to chain (up); *(idées etc)* to link (up).

enchaîner (s') *vpr (idées etc)* to be linked (up).

enchanté, -ée *adj (ravi)* delighted *(de* with; *que (+ subjonctif)* that); **e. (de faire votre connaissance)!** pleased to meet you!

enchantement *m* delight; **comme par e.** as if by magic.

enchanter *vt (ravir)* to delight.

enchanteur *m* magician.

enchère *f (offre)* bid; **vente aux enchères** auction; **mettre qch aux enchères** to put sth up for auction, to auction sth.

enclos *m* enclosure.

encoche *f* nick *(à* in).

encolure *f* neck; *(tour du cou)* collar (size).

encombrant, -ante *adj (paquet)* bulky.

encombrement *m (d'objets)* clutter; *(de rue)* traffic jam.

encombrer *vt (pièce etc)* to clutter up *(de* with); *(rue)* to congest *(de* with); **e. qn** to hamper sb.

encore *adv (toujours)* still; **e. là** here. ▪ *(avec négation)* yet; **pas e.** not yet. ▪ *(de nouveau)* again; **essaie e.** try again. ▪ *(de plus)* **e. un café** another coffee, one more coffee; **e. une fois** (once) again, once more; **e. un** another (one), one more; **e. du pain** (some) more bread; **e. quelque chose** something else; **qui/quoi e.?** who/what else? ▪ *(avec comparatif)* even, still; **e. mieux** even better, better still.

encourageant, -ante *adj* encouraging.

encouragement *m* encouragement.

encourager *vt* to encourage *(à* to do).

encrasser *vt* to clog up (with dirt).

encre *f* ink; **e. de Chine** India ink.

encrier *m* inkpot.

encyclopédie *f* encyclopedia.

endettement *m* debts.

endetter (s') *vpr* to get into debt.

endive *f* chicory, endive.

endommager *vt* to damage.

endormi, -ie *adj* asleep, sleeping.

endormir* *vt* to put to sleep.

endormir (s') *vpr* to fall asleep, to go to sleep.

endroit *m (lieu)* place; **à l'e.** *(vêtement)* right side out.

endurant, -ante *adj* tough.

endurcir *vt* **e. qn** to harden sb.

endurcir (s') *vpr* **s'e. à** to become hardened to *(pain etc)*.

endurer *vt* to endure.

énergie *f* energy.

énergique *adj* energetic; *(remède)* powerful; *(mesure, ton)* forceful.

énergiquement *adv* energetically.

énervé, -ée *adj* on edge.

énerver *vt* é. qn *(irriter)* to get on sb's nerves; *(rendre énervé)* to make sb nervous.

énerver (s') *vpr* to get worked up.

enfance *f* childhood.

enfant *m* child *(pl* children); **e. en bas âge** infant; **e. de chœur** altar boy.

enfantin, -ine *adj (voix, joie)* child-like; *(simple)* easy.

enfer *m* hell; **d'e.** *(bruit etc)* infernal; **à un train d'e.** at breakneck speed.

enfermer *vt* to lock up; **s'e. dans** *(chambre etc)* to lock oneself (up) in.

enfiler *vt (aiguille)* to thread; *(perles etc)* to string; *(vêtement)* to pull on.

enfin *adv (à la fin)* finally, at last; *(en dernier lieu)* lastly; **e. bref** in a word; **(mais) e.!** for heaven's sake!

enflammer *vt* to set fire to; *(allumette)* to light; *(irriter)* to inflame *(throat etc)*.

enflammer (s') *vpr* to catch on fire.

enfler *vti* to swell.

enflure *f* swelling.

enfoncer 1 *vt (clou)* to knock in, to hammer in; *(porte, voiture)* to smash in; **e. dans qch** *(couteau, mains etc)* to plunge into sth. **2** *vi*, **s'enfoncer** *vpr (s'enliser)* to sink *(dans* into).

enfouir *vt* to bury.

enfreindre* *vt* to infringe.

enfuir* (s') *vpr* to run away *ou* off *(de* from).

enfumer *vt (pièce)* to fill with smoke.

engagé, -ée *adj (écrivain)* politically committed.

engagement *m (promesse)* commitment; *(dans une compéti-*

tion) entry; **prendre l'e. de** to undertake to.

engager *vt (discussion, combat)* to start; **e. qn** *(embaucher)* to hire sb.

engager (s') *vpr (dans l'armée)* to enlist; *(sportif)* to enter **(pour** for); *(action, jeu)* to start; **s'e. à faire** to undertake to do.

engelure *f* chilblain.

engin *m* machine; **e. spatial** spaceship.

englober *vt* to include.

engloutir *vt (nourriture)* to wolf down; *(faire disparaître)* to swallow up.

engouffrer (s') *vpr* **s'e. dans** to sweep *ou* rush into.

engourdir (s') *vpr* to go numb.

engrais *m* fertilizer; *(naturel)* manure.

engraisser 1 *vt (animal)* to fatten (up). **2** *vi* to get fat.

engrenage *m* gears.

engueuler *vt* **e. qn** *Fam* to give sb hell.

énigme *f* riddle.

enivrer (s') *vpr* to get drunk **(de** on).

enjambée *f* stride.

enjamber *vt* to step over; *(pont etc)* to span *(river etc)*.

enjeu, -x *m (mise)* stake; *(de pari, de guerre)* stakes.

enjoliveur *m* hubcap.

enjoué, -ée *adj* playful.

enlaidir 1 *vt* to make ugly. **2** *vi* to grow ugly.

enlèvement *m (d'enfant)* kidnapping.

enlever *vt* to take away **(à qn** from sb); *(vêtement)* to take off; *(tache)* to take out; *(enfant etc)* to kidnap.

enlever (s') *vpr (tache)* to come out.

enliser (s') *vpr* to get bogged down **(dans** in).

enneigé, -ée *adj (montagne, route)* snow-covered; *(bloqué par la neige)* snowed in.

enneigement *m* bulletin d'e. snow report.

ennemi, -ie 1 *mf* enemy. **2** *adj* **pays/soldat e.** enemy country/soldier.

ennui *m* boredom; **un e.** *(tracas)* trouble; **l'e., c'est que** the annoying thing is that.

ennuyé, -ée *adj (air)* bored; **je suis e.** that bothers me.

ennuyer *vt (agacer, préoccuper)* to bother; *(fatiguer)* to bore.

ennuyer (s') *vpr* to get bored.

ennuyeux, -euse *adj* boring; *(contrariant)* annoying.

énoncer *vt* to state.

énorme *adj* enormous, huge.

énormément *adv* enormously; **e. de** an enormous amount of.

énormité *f (d'une demande, d'un crime, d'une somme)* enormity; *(faute)* glaring mistake.

enquête *f (de police)* investigation; *(judiciaire)* inquiry; *(sondage)* survey.

enquêter *vi* to investigate; **e. sur** to investigate.

enquêteur, -euse *mf* investigator.

enragé, -ée *adj (chien)* rabid; *(furieux)* furious.

enregistrement *m (des bagages)* check-in; *(sur bande etc)* recording.

enregistrer 1 *vt (par écrit, sur bande etc)* to record; **(faire) e.** *(bagages)* to check. **2** *vi* to record; **ça enregistre** it's recording.

enrhumer (s') *vpr* to catch a cold.

enrichir (s') *vpr* to get rich.

enrobé, -ée *adj* **e. de chocolat** chocolate-covered.

enroué, -ée *adj* hoarse.

enrouler *vt* to wind; *(tapis)* to roll up.

enrouler (s') *vpr* **s'e. dans** *(couvertures)* to wrap oneself up in.

ensanglanté, -ée *adj* bloodstained.

enseignant, -ante *mf* teacher.

enseigne *f* sign; **e. lumineuse** neon sign.

enseignement *m* education; *(action, métier)* teaching.

enseigner 1 *vt* to teach; **e. qch à qn** to teach sb sth. **2** *vi* to teach.

ensemble 1 *adv* together. **2** *m (d'objets)* set; *(vêtement féminin)* outfit; **l'e. du personnel** the whole staff; **l'e. des enseignants** all of the teachers; **dans l'e.** on the whole; **d'e.** *(vue etc)* general.

ensevelir *vt* to bury.

ensoleillé, -ée *adj* sunny.

ensuite *adv (puis)* next; *(plus tard)* afterwards.

entaille *f (fente)* notch; *(blessure)* gash.

entailler *vt (bois)* to notch; *(peau)* to gash.

entamer *vt (pain, peau etc)* to cut (into); *(bouteille etc)* to start (on).

entasser *vt,* **s'entasser** *vpr (objets)* to pile up; **(s')e. dans** *(passagers etc)* to crowd *ou* pile into.

entendre *vt* to hear; **e. parler de** to hear of; **e. dire que** to hear (it said) that.

entendre (s') *vpr (être d'accord)* to agree (**sur** on); **s'e.** *(avec qn)* to get on (with sb).

entendu, -ue *adj (convenu)* agreed; **e.!** all right!; **bien e.** of course.

entente *f (accord)* agreement; **(bonne) e.** *(amitié)* good relationship.

enterrement *m* burial; *(funérailles)* funeral.

enterrer *vt* to bury.

entêté, -ée *adj* stubborn.

entêtement *m* stubbornness; *(à faire qch)* persistence.

entêter (s') *vpr* to persist (**à faire** in doing).

enthousiasme *m* enthusiasm.

enthousiasmer *vt* to fill with enthusiasm.

enthousiasmer (s') *vpr* **s'e.**

pour to be *ou* get enthusiastic about.

enthousiaste *adj* enthusiastic.

entier, -ière 1 *adj (total)* whole; *(intact)* intact; **le pays tout e.** the whole country. **2** *m* **en e.** completely.

entièrement *adv* entirely.

entonnoir *m (ustensile)* funnel.

entorse *f* sprain.

entortiller *vt* **e. qch autour de qch** to wrap sth around sth.

entourage *m* circle of family and friends.

entourer *vt* to surround (**de** with); **entouré de** surrounded by.

entracte *m (au théâtre)* intermission.

entraide *f* mutual aid.

entraider (s') *vpr* to help each other.

entrain *m* **plein d'e.** lively.

entraînant, -ante *adj (musique)* lively.

entraînement *m (sportif)* training.

entraîner *vt* to carry away; *(causer)* to bring about; *(emmener de force)* to drag *(sb)* (away); *(athlète etc)* to train (**à** for).

entraîner (s') *vpr (sportif)* to train.

entraîneur *m (d'athlète)* coach.

entre *prép* between; **l'un d'e. vous** one of you.

entrebâillé, -ée *adj* slightly open.

entrebâiller *vt* to open slightly.

entrechoquer (s') *vpr* to chink.

entrecôte *f* (filleted) rib steak.

entrée *f (action)* entry; *(porte)* entrance; *(accès)* admission (**de** to); *(vestibule)* entrance hall; *(billet)* ticket (for admission); *(plat)* first course; *(en informatique)* input; **à son e.** as he/she came in; **'e. interdite'** 'no entry'; **'e. libre'** 'admission free'.

entreposer *vt* to store.

entrepôt *m* warehouse.

entreprendre* *vt* to undertake (**de faire** to do).

entrepreneur *m (en bâtiment)* contractor.

entreprise *f* company, firm.

entrer *vi (aux être)* to go in; *(venir)* to come in; **e. dans** *(pièce)* to come *ou* go into; *(arbre etc)* to crash into; **faire/laisser e. qn** to show/let sb in.

entre-temps *adv* meanwhile.

entretenir* *vt* to maintain; **e. sa forme** to stay in shape.

entretenir (s') *vpr* **s'e. de** to talk about (**avec** with).

entretien *m* maintenance; *(dialogue)* conversation; *(entrevue)* interview.

entrevoir* *vt (rapidement)* to catch a glimpse of; *(pressentir)* to foresee.

entrevue *f* interview.

entrouvert, -erte *adj* half-open.

énumération *f* list(ing).

énumérer *vt* to list.

envahir *vt* to invade; *(herbe etc)* to overrun *(garden)*.

envahisseur *m* invader.

enveloppe *f (pour lettre)* envelope; **e. timbrée à votre adresse** self-addressed stamped envelope.

envelopper *vt* to wrap (up) (**dans** in).

envers 1 *prép* toward(s), to. **2** *m* **à l'e.** *(chaussette)* inside out; *(pantalon)* back to front; *(la tête en bas)* upside down.

envie *f (jalousie)* envy; *(désir)* desire; **avoir e. de qch** to want sth; **j'ai e. de faire** I feel like doing.

envier *vt* to envy (**qch à qn** sb sth).

environ *adv (à peu près)* about.

environnant, -ante *adj* surrounding.

environnement *m* environment.

environner *vt* to surround.

environs *mpl* surroundings; **aux environs de** around.

envisager vt to consider (**de faire** doing).

envoi m sending; (paquet) package; **coup d'é.** Sport kick-off.

envoler (s') vpr (oiseau) to fly away; (avion) to take off; (chapeau etc) to blow away.

envoyé, -ée mf (reporter) correspondent.

envoyer* vt to send; (lancer) to throw.

épais, -aisse adj thick.

épaisseur f thickness.

épaissir vti, **s'épaissir** vpr to thicken.

épanoui, -ie adj in full bloom; (visage) beaming.

épanouir (s') vpr to blossom; (visage) to beam.

épargne f (action, vertu) saving; (sommes) savings.

épargner vt (argent) to save; (ennemi etc) to spare; **é. qch à qn** (ennuis etc) to spare sb sth.

éparpiller vt, **s'éparpiller** vpr to scatter.

épatant, -ante adj marvelous.

épaule f shoulder.

épauler vt (fusil) to raise (to one's shoulder); **é. qn** (aider) to back sb up.

épave f wreck.

épée f sword.

épeler vt (mot) to spell.

éperon m spur.

épi m (de blé etc) ear.

épice f spice.

épicé, -ée adj spicy.

épicer vt to spice.

épicerie f grocery store; (produits) groceries.

épicier, -ière mf grocer.

épidémie f epidemic.

épiler (s') vpr to remove unwanted hair; **s'é. les jambes à la cire** to wax one's legs.

épinards mpl spinach.

épine f (de plante) thorn.

épineux, -euse adj thorny.

épingle f pin; **é. de nourrice** safety pin; **é. à linge** clothes pin; **é. à cheveux** hairpin.

épisode m episode.

épithète f (adjectif) attribute.

éplucher vt (carotte, pomme etc) to peel.

épluchure f peeling.

éponge f sponge.

éponger vt to sponge.

époque f (date) time; (historique) age.

épouse f wife.

épouser vt **é. qn** to marry sb.

épousseter vt to dust.

épouvantable adj terrifying; (mauvais) appalling.

épouvantail m scarecrow.

épouvante f terror; **film d'é.** horror movie.

épouvanter vt to terrify.

époux m husband.

épreuve f (examen) test; (sportive) event; (malheur) ordeal.

éprouvant, -ante adj (pénible) trying.

éprouver vt to test; (sentiment etc) to feel.

éprouvette f test tube; **bébé-é.** test-tube baby.

épuisant, -ante adj exhausting.

épuisé, -ée adj exhausted; (marchandise) out of stock.

épuiser vt to exhaust.

épuiser (s') vpr (réserves) to run out; **s'é. à faire** to exhaust oneself doing.

équateur m equator.

équation f equation.

équerre f (pour tracer) square.

équilibre m balance; **tenir ou mettre en é.** to balance (**sur** on); **perdre l'é.** to lose one's balance.

équilibrer vt (budget) to balance.

équipage m crew.

équipe f team; (d'ouvriers) crew; **é. de secours** search party.

équipement m equipment; (de camping, ski) gear.

équiper *vt* to equip (**de** with).

équipier, -ière *mf* team member.

équitable *adj* fair.

équitation *f* (horseback) riding.

équivalent, -ente *adj & m* equivalent.

équivaloir* *vi* é. à qch to be equivalent to sth.

érafler *vt* to scrape, to scratch.

éraflure *f* scrape, scratch.

errer *vi* to wander.

erreur *f* mistake.

éruption *f* (*de boutons*) rash.

es *voir* **être**.

escabeau, -x *m* stepladder.

escadrille *f* (*groupe d'avions*) flight.

escalade *f* climbing.

escalader *vt* to climb.

escale *f* **faire e. à** (*avion*) to stop (over) at; (*navire*) to put in at.

escalier *m* stairs; **e. roulant** escalator.

escalope *f* escalope (*thin slice of meat*).

escargot *m* snail.

escarpé, -ée *adj* steep.

esclavage *m* slavery.

esclave *mf* slave.

escorte *f* escort.

escorter *vt* to escort.

escrime *f* fencing.

escrimeur, -euse *mf* fencer.

escroc *m* crook.

espace *m* space; **e. vert** garden, park.

espacer *vt* to space out.

espagnol, -ole 1 *adj* Spanish. **2** *mf* E. Spaniard. **3** *m* (*langue*) Spanish.

espèce *f* (*race*) species; (*genre*) kind, sort; **e. d'idiot!** you fool!

espèces *fpl* (*argent*) cash; **en e.** in cash.

espérance *f* hope.

espérer 1 *vt* to hope for; **e. que** to hope that; **e. faire** to hope to do. **2** *vi* to hope.

espiègle *adj* mischievous.

espion, -onne *mf* spy.

espionnage *m* spying.

espionner *vt* to spy on.

espoir *m* hope; **sans e.** (*cas etc*) hopeless.

esprit *m* spirit; (*intellect*) mind; (*humour*) wit; **venir à l'e. de qn** to cross sb's mind.

Esquimau, -de, -aux *mf* Eskimo.

esquiver *vt* to dodge.

essai *m* (*épreuve*) test; (*tentative*) try, attempt.

essaim *m* swarm (*of bees etc*).

essayage *m* (*de costume*) fitting.

essayer *vt* to try (**e. de faire** to do); (*vêtement*) to try on.

essence *f* gas.

essentiel, -ielle 1 *adj* essential. **2** *m* **l'e.** the main thing.

essentiellement *adv* essentially.

essieu, -x *m* axle.

essor *m* (*d'oiseau*) flight; (*de pays, d'entreprise*) rapid growth; **en plein e.** booming; **prendre son e.** to take off.

essorer *vt* (*dans une essoreuse*) to spin-dry; (*dans une machine à laver*) to spin.

essoufflé, -ée *adj* out of breath.

essuie-glace, *pl* **essuie-glaces** *m* windshield wiper.

essuie-mains *m inv* (hand) towel.

essuyer *vt* to wipe.

est¹ *voir* **être**.

est² *m & adj inv* east; **d'e.** (*vent*) east(erly); **de l'e.** eastern.

estime *f* regard.

estimer *vt* (*objet*) to value; (*juger*) to consider (**que** that); **e. qn** to have a high regard for sb.

estimer (s') *vpr* **s'e. heureux/***etc* to consider oneself happy/*etc*.

estivant, -ante *mf* vacationer.

estomac *m* stomach.

estrade *f* platform.

estropier *vt* to cripple.

estuaire *m* estuary.

et *conj* and; **vingt et un** twenty-one.

étable f cowshed.

établi m (work)bench.

établir vt (installer) to set up; (plan, liste) to draw up.

établir (s') vpr (habiter) to settle.

établissement m establishment; é. scolaire school.

étage m (d'immeuble) floor; à l'é. upstairs; au premier é. on the second floor.

étagère f shelf.

étais, était etc voir **être**.

étalage m (vitrine) display window.

étaler vt to lay out; (en vitrine) to display; (beurre etc) to spread.

étanche adj watertight; (montre) waterproof.

étang m pond.

étant voir **être**.

étape f stage; (lieu) stop(over).

État m (nation) State; homme d'É. statesman.

état m (condition) state; en bon é. in good condition; être en é. de faire to be up to doing.

étau, -x m vise.

été¹ pp of **être**.

été² m summer; en é. in (the) summer.

éteindre* 1 vt (feu etc) to put out; (lampe etc) to turn ou switch off. **2** vi to switch off.

éteindre (s') vpr (feu) to go out.

éteint, -einte adj (feu, bougie) out; (lampe) off.

étendre vt (nappe) to spread (out); (linge) to hang out; é. le bras/etc to stretch out one's arm/etc.

étendre (s') vpr (personne) to stretch out; (plaine) to stretch; (feu) to spread.

étendu, -ue adj (forêt etc) extensive; (personne) stretched out.

étendue f (importance) extent; (surface) area.

éterniser (s') vpr (débat) to drag on endlessly; (visiteur) Fam to stay for ever.

éternité f eternity.

éternuement m sneeze.

éternuer vi to sneeze.

êtes voir **être**.

étinceler vi to sparkle.

étincelle f spark.

étiqueter vt to label.

étiquette f label.

étirer (s') vpr to stretch (oneself).

étoffe f material.

étoile f star; à la belle é. (out) in the open.

étoilé, -ée adj (ciel) starry.

étonnant, -ante adj surprising.

étonnement m surprise.

étonner vt to surprise.

étonner (s') vpr to be surprised (de qch at sth; que (+ subjonctif) that).

étouffant, -ante adj (air) stifling.

étouffer 1 vt (tuer) to suffocate, to smother; (bruit) to muffle; (feu) to smother; é. qn (chaleur) to stifle sb. **2** vi on étouffe! it's stifling!

étouffer (s') vpr (en mangeant) to choke (sur, avec on).

étourderie f thoughtlessness; une é. a thoughtless blunder.

étourdi, -ie adj thoughtless.

étourdir vt to stun; (vertige) to make dizzy.

étourdissant, -ante adj (bruit) deafening.

étourdissement m (malaise) dizzy spell.

étrange adj strange, odd.

étranger, -ère 1 adj (d'un autre pays) foreign; (non familier) strange (à to). **2** mf foreigner; (inconnu) stranger; à l'é. abroad; de l'é. from abroad.

étrangler vt (tuer) to strangle.

étrangler (s') vpr to choke.

être* 1 vi to be; il est tailleur he's a tailor; est-ce qu'elle vient? is she coming?; il vient, n'est-ce pas? he's coming, isn't he?; est-ce qu'il aime le thé? does he like tea?; nous sommes dix there are ten of us; nous sommes le dix today is the tenth (of the month); **il a été à Paris** he has been to Paris. **2** *v aux (avec venir, partir etc)* to have; **elle est arrivée** she has arrived. **3** *m* **ê. humain** human being.

étrennes *fpl* New Year's gift.

étrier *m* stirrup.

étroit, -oite *adj* narrow; *(vêtement)* tight; **être à l'é.** to be cramped.

étroitement *adv (surveiller etc)* closely.

étude *f* study; *(salle)* study hall; **à l'é.** *(projet)* under consideration; **faire des études de** *(médecine etc)* to study.

étudiant, -ante *mf & adj* student.

étudier *vti* to study.

étui *m (à lunettes etc)* case.

eu, eue *pp of* **avoir**.

euh! *int* hem!, er!

euro *m (monnaie)* euro.

euro- *préfixe* Euro-.

européen, -enne 1 *adj* European. **2** *mf* **E.** European.

eux *pron (sujet)* they; *(complément)* them; *(réfléchi, emphase)* themselves.

eux-mêmes *pron* themselves.

évacuer *vt* to evacuate.

évadé, -ée *mf* escaped prisoner.

évader (s') *vpr* to escape (**de** from).

évaluer *vt* to estimate; *(bien)* to value.

Évangile *m* Gospel.

évanouir (s') *vpr* to faint, to pass out.

évanouissement *m* blackout.

évasion *f* escape (**de** from).

éveiller *vt (susciter)* to arouse.

événement *m* event.

éventail *m* fan; *(choix)* range.

éventrer *vt (sac, oreiller)* to rip open; *(animal)* to open up.

éventuel, -elle *adj* possible.

éventuellement *adv* possibly.

évêque *m* bishop.

évidemment *adv* obviously.

évident *adj* obvious (**que** that); *(facile) Fam* easy.

évier *m (kitchen)* sink.

éviter *vt* to avoid (**de faire** doing); **é. qch à qn** to spare sb sth.

évoluer *vi (changer)* to develop; *(société, situation)* to evolve; *(se déplacer)* to move around.

ex- *préfixe* ex-; **ex-mari** ex-husband.

exact, -e *adj (précis)* exact, accurate; *(juste, vrai)* correct.

exactement *adv* exactly.

exactitude *f (expression précise)* accuracy; *(justesse)* correctness.

ex æquo *adv* **être classés e.** to tie.

exagération *f* exaggeration.

exagéré, -ée *adj* excessive.

exagérer *vti* to exaggerate.

examen *m* examination; *(bac etc)* exam(ination).

examinateur, -trice *mf* examiner.

examiner *vt* to examine.

exaspérer *vt (personne)* to exasperate.

excédent *m* **e. de bagages** excess baggage.

excellent, -ente *adj* excellent.

excepté *prép* except.

exception *f* exception; **à l'e. de** except (for).

exceptionnel, -elle *adj* exceptional.

exceptionnellement *adv* exceptionally.

excès *m* excess; **e. de vitesse** speeding.

excessif, -ive *adj* excessive.

excitant, -ante *adj Fam* exciting.

excitation *f* excitement.

excité, -ée *adj* excited.

exciter *vt* to excite.

exclamation *f* exclamation.

exclamer (s') *vpr* to exclaim.

exclure* *vt* to exclude (**de** from).

excursion *f* trip, outing; *(à pied)* hike.

excuse *f (prétexte)* excuse; **excuses**

(regrets) apology; **faire des excuses** to apologize (**à** to).

excuser *vt* to excuse (**qn d'avoir fait, qn de faire** sb for doing).

excuser (s') *vpr* to apologize (**de** for; **auprès de** to).

exécuter *vt (travail etc)* to carry out; *(jouer)* to perform; **e. qn** *(tuer)* to execute sb.

exécution *f (mise à mort)* execution.

exemplaire *m* copy.

exemple *m* example; **par e.** for example; **donner l'e.** to set an example (**à** to).

exercer *vt (muscles, droits)* to exercise.

exercer (s') *vpr* to practice (**à qch** sth; **à faire** doing).

exercice *m* exercise; **faire de l'e.** to (take) exercise.

exigeant, -eante *adj* demanding.

exigence *f* demand.

exiger *vt* to demand (**de** from; **que** (+ *subjonctif*) that).

exiler (s') *vpr* to go into exile.

existence *f* existence.

exister *vi* to exist; **il existe** there is, *pl* there are.

exorbitant, -ante *adj* exorbitant.

expédier *vt (envoyer)* to send off.

expéditeur, -trice *mf* sender.

expédition *f (envoi)* dispatch; *(voyage)* expedition.

expérience *f (connaissance)* experience; *(scientifique)* experiment; **faire l'e. de qch** to experience sth.

expérimenté, -ée *adj* experienced.

expérimenter *vt (remède, vaccin)* to try out (**sur** on).

expert *m* expert (**en** on, in).

expirer *vi* to breathe out; *(mourir)* to pass away.

explicatif, -ive *adj* explanatory.

explication *f* explanation; *(mise au point)* discussion.

expliquer *vt* to explain (**à** to; **que** that).

expliquer (s') *vpr (discuter)* to talk things over (**avec** with).

exploit *m* feat, exploit.

exploitation *f (agricole)* farm.

exploiter *vt (champs)* to farm; *(profiter de)* to exploit.

explorateur, -trice *mf* explorer.

exploration *f* exploration.

explorer *vt* to explore.

exploser *vi* to explode.

explosif *m* explosive.

explosion *f* explosion.

exportateur, -trice 1 *mf* exporter. **2** *adj* exporting.

exportation *f* export.

exporter *vt* to export (**vers** to; **de** from).

exposé, -ée *adj* **e. au sud**/*etc* facing south/*etc*.

exposer *vt* to expose (**à** to); *(tableau etc)* to exhibit; *(vie)* to risk.

exposer (s') *vpr* **s'e. à** to expose oneself.

exposition *f (salon)* exhibition.

exprès *adv* on purpose; *(spécialement)* specially.

express *m inv (train)* express; *(café)* espresso.

expression *f (phrase, mine)* expression.

exprimer *vt* to express.

exprimer (s') *vpr* to express oneself.

expulser *vt* to expel (**de** from); *(joueur)* to send off.

exquis, -ise *adj (nourriture)* delicious.

exténué, -ée *adj* exhausted.

extérieur, -e 1 *adj* outside; *(surface)* outer, external; *(signe)* outward. **2** *m* outside; **à l'e. (de)** outside.

extérioriser *vt* to express.

externe *mf (élève)* day student.

extincteur *m* fire extinguisher.

extra- *préfixe* extra-.
extraire* *vt* to extract (**de** from).
extrait *m* extract.
extraordinaire *adj* extraordinary.
extrême *adj & m* extreme.
extrêmement *adv* extremely.
extrémité *f* end.

F

fable *f* fable.
fabricant, -ante *mf* manufacturer.
fabrication *f* manufacture.
fabriquer *vt* to make; (*en usine*) to manufacture; **qu'est-ce qu'il fabrique?** *Fam* what's he up to?
fabuleux, -euse *adj* fabulous.
fac *f abrév* (**faculté**) university.
façade *f* (*de bâtiment*) front.
face *f* face; (*de cube etc*) side; **en f.** opposite; **en f. de** opposite, facing; (*en présence de*) in front of, face to face with; **f. à un problème** faced with a problem; **regarder qn en f.** to look sb in the face; **f. à f.** face to face.
fâché, -ée *adj* (*air*) angry; (*amis*) on bad terms.
fâcher *vt* to anger.
fâcher (se) *vpr* to get angry (**contre** with); **se f. avec qn** to fall out with sb.
facile *adj* easy; **c'est f. à faire** it's easy to do; **il nous est f. de** it's easy for us to do.
facilement *adv* easily.
facilité *f* easiness; (*à faire qch*) ease.
faciliter *vt* to make easier.
façon *f* way; **la f. dont elle parle** the way (in which) she talks; **f. (d'agir)** behavior; **façons** (*manières*) manners; **de toute f.** anyway; **à ma f.** my way.
facteur *m* mailman, postal carrier.
factrice *f* postal carrier.
facture *f* bill, invoice.
facturer *vt* to bill, to invoice.
facultatif, -ive *adj* optional.
faculté *f* university; **à la f.** at the university, at school.
fade *adj* (*nourriture*) bland.
faible 1 *adj* weak; (*bruit*) faint; (*vent*) slight; **f. en anglais**/*etc* poor at English/*etc*. **2** *m* **avoir un f. pour** to have a soft spot for.
faiblement *adv* weakly; (*légèrement*) slightly; (*éclairer*) faintly.
faiblesse *f* weakness; faintness; slightness.
faiblir *vi* (*forces*) to weaken.
faïence *f* (*matière*) earthenware; **faïences** (*objets*) earthenware.
faillir* *vi* **il a failli tomber** he almost fell.
faillite *f* faire f. to go bankrupt.
faim *f* hunger; **avoir f.** to be hungry; **donner f. à qn** to make sb hungry.
fainéant, -ante *mf* lazy bones.
faire* **1** *vt* (*bruit, faute, gâteau etc*) to make; (*devoir, ménage etc*) to do; (*rêve*) to have; (*sourire*) to give; (*promenade, chute*) to take; **ça fait dix mètres/euros** (*mesure, prix*) it's *ou* that's ten metres/euros; **qu'a-t-il fait (de)?** what's he done (with)?; **que f.?** what should I/you/we/*etc* do?; **f. du tennis**/*etc* to play tennis/ *etc*; **f. l'idiot** to play the fool; **ça ne fait rien** that doesn't matter. **2** *vi* (*agir*) to do; (*paraître*) to look; **il fait vieux** he looks old; **elle ferait bien de partir** she'd do well to leave; **il fait beau/froid**/*etc* it's sunny/ cold/*etc*; **ça fait deux ans que je ne l'ai pas vu** I haven't seen him for two years; **ça fait un an que je suis là** I've been here for a year. **3** *v aux* (+ *infinitif*) **f. construire une maison** to have *ou* get a house built; **f. crier**/*etc* **qn** to make sb shout/*etc*;

se f. obéir/*etc* to be obeyed/*etc;* **se f. tuer**/*etc* to get *ou* be killed/*etc.*

faire (se) *vpr* **se f. des amis** to make friends; **se f. vieux**/*etc* to get old/*etc;* **il se fait tard** it's getting late; **se f. à** to get used to; **ne t'en fais pas!** don't worry!

faire-part *m inv* announcement.

faisable *adj* feasible.

faisan *m* pheasant.

faisceau, -x *m (rayons)* beam.

fait, faite *(pp de faire)* **1** *adj (fromage)* ripe; *(yeux)* made up; **tout f.** ready made; **c'est bien f.!** it serves you right! **2** *m* event; *(réalité)* fact; **prendre sur le f.** to catch redhanded; **f. divers** news item; **au f.** by the way; **en f.** in fact.

falaise *f* cliff.

falloir* *v i* **il faut qch/qn** I/you/we/ *etc* need sth/sb; **il lui faut un stylo** he/she needs a pen; **il faut partir** I/ you/we/*etc* have to go; **il faut que je parte** I have to go; **il faudrait qu'elle reste** she ought to stay; **il faut un jour** it takes a day (**pour faire** to do).

fameux, -euse *adj* famous; *(excellent)* first-class.

familial, -e, -aux *adj (atmosphère, ennuis)* family; *(entreprise)* family-run.

familiariser (se) *vpr* to familiarize oneself (**avec** with).

familiarité *f* familiarity (**avec** with).

familier, -ière *adj* familiar (**à** to); **f. avec qn** (over)familiar with sb; **animal f.** pet.

familièrement *adv (parler)* informally.

famille *f* family; **en f.** with one's family.

fan *m* fan.

fana *mf* **être f. de** to be crazy about.

fané, -ée *adj* faded.

faner (se) *vpr* to fade.

fanfare *f (orchestre)* brass band.

fantaisie *f (caprice)* whim; **(de) f.** *(bouton etc)* novelty.

fantastique *adj* fantastic.

fantôme *m* ghost.

faon *m* fawn.

FAQ *f abrév (foire aux questions)* FAQ.

farce¹ *f* practical joke.

farce² *f (viande)* stuffing.

farceur, -euse *mf* practical joker.

farcir *vt* to stuff.

fardeau, -x *m* burden.

farine *f* flour.

farouche *adj (animal)* easily scared; *(violent)* fierce.

fascination *f* fascination.

fasciner *vt* to fascinate.

fasse(s), fassent *etc voir* **faire.**

fatal, -e, -als *adj* fatal; *(inévitable)* inevitable.

fatalement *adv* inevitably.

fatigant, -ante *adj* tiring; *(ennuyeux)* tiresome.

fatigue *f* tiredness.

fatigué, -ée *adj* tired (**de** of).

fatiguer *vt* to tire.

fatiguer (se) *vpr* to get tired (**de** of).

fauché, -ée *adj Fam* (flat) broke.

faucher *vt (herbe)* to mow; *(blé)* to reap.

faucon *m* hawk.

faufiler (se) *vpr* to edge one's way (**dans** through, into).

fausse *voir* **faux.**

fausser *vt (réalité, résultat)* to distort.

faut *voir* **falloir.**

faute *f* mistake; *(responsabilité)* fault; *(péché)* sin; **c'est ta f.** it's your fault.

fauteuil *m* armchair; **f. roulant** wheelchair.

fautif, -ive *adj (personne)* at fault; *(erroné)* faulty.

fauve *m* wild animal, big cat.

faux, fausse 1 *adj* false; *(pas exact)* wrong; *(monnaie)* forged. **2** *adv (chanter)* out of tune.

faux f scythe.

faux-filet m sirloin.

faveur f en f. de in aid ou favor of.

favorable adj favorable (à to).

favori, -ite adj & mf favorite.

favoriser vt to favor.

fax m (appareil, message) fax.

faxer vt (message) to fax.

fée f fairy.

féerique adj fairy(-like).

feinte f (ruse) ruse.

fêler vt, **se fêler** vpr to crack.

félicitations fpl congratulations (pour on).

féliciter vt to congratulate (qn de ou sur sb on).

fêlure f crack.

femelle adj & f (animal) female.

féminin, -ine adj (prénom etc) female; (trait, pronom etc) feminine; (mode, revue etc) women's.

femme f woman (pl women); (épouse) wife; **f. médecin** woman doctor; **f. de ménage** cleaning woman.

fendre vt (bois etc) to split.

fendre (se) vpr to crack.

fenêtre f window.

fente f slit.

fer m iron; **barre de f.** iron bar; **f. forgé** wrought iron; **f. à cheval** horseshoe; **f. à repasser** iron (for clothes); **santé de f.** cast-iron constitution.

fera, ferai(t) etc voir **faire**.

fer-blanc, pl **fers-blancs** m tin.

férié adj **jour f.** holiday.

ferme¹ f farm.

ferme² **1** adj firm; (pas, voix) steady. **2** adv (travailler, boire) hard.

fermé, -ée adj (porte etc) closed, shut; (route etc) closed; (gaz etc) off.

fermement adv firmly.

fermer **1** vt to close, to shut; (gaz etc) to turn ou switch off; (vêtement) to do up; **f. (à clef)** to lock. **2** vi, **se fermer** vpr to close, to shut.

fermeté f firmness.

fermeture f closing; (heure) closing time; **f. éclair**® zipper.

fermier, -ière m farmer.

féroce adj fierce, savage.

feront voir **faire**.

ferraille f scrap metal, old iron; **mettre à la f.** to scrap.

ferrée adj f **voie f.** railroad; (rails) track.

ferroviaire adj **compagnie f.** railroad company.

fertile adj fertile.

fesse f buttock; **les fesses** one's behind.

fessée f spanking.

festin m (banquet) feast.

festival, pl **-als** m festival.

fête f (civile) holiday; (religieuse) feast (day); (entre amis) party; **f. foraine** fair, carnival; **f. de famille** family celebration; **c'est sa f.** it's his/her saint's ou feast day; **f. des Mères** Mother's Day; **jour de f.** holiday; **faire la f.** to have a good time.

fêter vt to celebrate.

feu, -x m fire; (de réchaud) burner; **feux de détresse** (hazard) warning flashers; **f. rouge** red light; (objet) traffic lights; **mettre le f. à** to set fire to; **en f.** on fire; **faire du f.** to light ou make a fire; **avez-vous du f.?** have you got a light?; **à f. doux** on low heat; **au f.!** fire!; **coup de f.** (bruit) gunshot.

feuillage m leaves.

feuille f leaf; (de papier etc) sheet; **f. d'impôt** tax form; **f. de paye** pay slip.

feuilleter vt to flip through; **pâte feuilletée** puff pastry ou paste.

feuilleton m serial.

feutre m crayon **f.** felt-tip (pen).

février m February.

fiabilité f reliability.

fiable adj reliable.

fiançailles fpl engagement.

fiancé m fiancé.

fiancée f fiancée.

fiancer (se) *vpr* to get engaged (*avec* to).

ficeler *vt* to tie up.

ficelle *f* string.

fiche *f* (*carte*) index card; (*papier*) form.

fiche(r) *vt* (*pp* fichu) *Fam* f. le camp to shove off; fiche-moi la paix! leave me alone!

fiche(r) (se) *vpr* se f. de qn to make fun of sb; je m'en fiche! I don't give a damn!

fichier *m* card index.

fichu, -ue *adj* c'est f. (*abîmé*) *Fam* it's had it.

fidèle *adj* faithful (à to); (*client*) regular.

fidélité *f* fidelity, faithfulness.

fier (se) *vpr* se f. à to trust.

fier, fière *adj* proud (de of).

fièrement *adv* proudly.

fierté *f* pride.

fièvre *f* fever; avoir de la f. to have a temperature *ou* a fever.

fiévreux, -euse *adj* feverish.

figer *vti*, **se figer** *vpr* to congeal.

figue *f* fig.

figurant, -ante *mf* (*de film*) extra.

figure *f* (*géométrique*) figure.

figurer *vi* to appear.

figurer (se) *vpr* to imagine.

fil¹ *m* thread; f. dentaire dental floss.

fil² *m* (*métallique*) wire; sans f. wireless; f. de fer wire; passer un coup de f. à qn to call sb (up).

file *f* line; (*couloir*) lane; f. d'attente line; en f. (indienne) in single file.

filer 1 *vt* f. qn (*suivre*) to shadow sb. **2** *vi* (*partir*) to rush off; (*aller vite*) to speed along.

filet *m* (*à bagages*) rack; (*d'eau*) trickle; (*de poisson*) fillet; f. (à provisions) string bag.

filiale *f* subsidiary (company).

filière *f* (*voie obligée*) channels; (*domaine d'études*) field of study; (*organisation clandestine*) network; suivre la f. normale to go through the official channels.

fille *f* girl; (*parenté*) daughter; petite f. (little *ou* young) girl; jeune f. girl, young lady.

fillette *f* little girl.

filleul *m* godson.

filleule *f* goddaughter.

film *m* movie, film; (*pellicule*) film; f. plastique plastic wrap.

filmer *vt* to film.

filtre *m* filter; (à bout) f. (*cigarette*) (filter-)tipped; (bout) f. filter tip.

filtrer *vt* to filter.

fin *f* end; mettre la f. à to put an end to; prendre f. to come to an end; sans f. endless; à la f. in the end; f. mai at the end of May.

fin, fine 1 *adj* (*pointe etc*) fine; (*peu épais*) thin; (*esprit, oreille*) sharp. **2** *adv* (*couper etc*) finely.

final, -e, -aux *ou* **-als** *adj* final.

finale *f* final.

finalement *adv* finally.

finance *f* finance.

financement *m* financing.

financer *vt* to finance.

financier, -ière *adj* financial.

finir *vt* to finish; f. de faire to finish doing; (*cesser*) to stop doing; f. par faire to end up doing; c'est fini it's over.

finlandais, -aise 1 *adj* Finnish. **2** *mf* F. Finn.

finnois *m* (*langue*) finnish.

fisc *m* = Internal Revenue.

fissure *f* crack.

fissurer (se) *vpr* to crack.

fixe *adj* fixed; idée f. obsession; regard f. stare.

fixement *adv* regarder f. to stare at.

fixer *vt* (*attacher*) to fix (à to); (*date etc*) to fix; f. (du regard) to stare at; être fixé (*décidé*) to be decided.

flacon *m* (small) bottle.

flair *m* (*d'un chien etc*) (sense of) smell; (*intuition*) insight.

flairer *vt* to smell.

flamand, -ande 1 *adj* Flemish. **2** *m (langue)* Flemish.

flamber *vi* to burn.

flamme *f* flame; **en flammes** on fire.

flan *m (dessert)* custard tart, baked custard.

flanc *m* side.

flâner *vi* to stroll.

flaque *f* puddle.

flash, *pl* **flashes** *m (de photographie)* flash(light); *(dispositif)* flash(gun); *(d'informations)* (news)-flash.

flatter *vt* to flatter.

flatterie *f* flattery.

fléau, -x *m (catastrophe)* scourge.

flèche *f* arrow; *(d'église)* spire; **monter en f.** *(prix)* to shoot up.

flécher *vt* to mark (with arrows).

fléchette *f* dart; **fléchettes** *(jeu)* darts.

fléchir 1 *vt (membre)* to flex. **2** *vi (poutre)* to sag.

flétrir *vt*, **se flétrir** *vpr* to wither.

fleur *f* flower; *(d'arbre)* blossom; **en fleur(s)** in flower; **à fleurs** *(tissu)* flowered, flowery.

fleuri, -ie *adj* in bloom; *(tissu)* flowered, flowery.

fleurir *vi* to flower; *(arbre)* to blossom.

fleuriste *mf* florist.

fleuve *m* river.

flexible *adj* pliable.

flic *m* Fam cop.

flipper *m (jeu)* pinball; *(appareil)* pinball machine.

flocon *m (de neige)* flake.

flot *m (de souvenirs etc)* flood; **à f.** afloat; **les flots** the waves.

flotte *f (de bateaux)* fleet; *(pluie)* Fam rain; *(eau)* Fam water.

flotter *vi* to float; *(drapeau)* to fly.

flotteur *m* Pêche float.

flou, -e *adj* fuzzy, blurred.

fluide *adj & m* fluid.

fluo *adj inv (couleur etc)* luminous, fluorescent.

fluorescent, -ente *adj* fluorescent.

flûte 1 *f* flute; *(verre)* champagne glass. **2** *int* heck!

foi *f* faith; **être de bonne/mauvaise f.** to be/not to be (completely) sincere.

foie *m* liver.

foin *m* hay.

foire *f* fair.

fois *f* time; **une f.** once; **deux f.** twice; **chaque f. que** whenever; **une f. qu'il sera arrivé** once he has arrived; **à la f.** at the same time; **des f.** sometimes; **une f. pour toutes** once and for all.

fol *voir* **fou**.

folie *f* madness.

folklore *m* folklore.

folklorique *adj* **musique f.** folk music.

folle *voir* **fou**.

foncé, -ée *adj (couleur)* dark.

foncer *vi (aller vite)* to tear along; **f. sur qn** to charge at sb.

fonction *f* function; **la f. publique** public *ou* civil service.

fonctionnaire *mf* civil servant.

fonctionnement *m* working.

fonctionner *vi (machine etc)* to work; **faire f.** to operate.

fond *m (de boîte, jardin etc)* bottom; *(de salle etc)* back; *(arrière-plan)* background; **au f. de** at the bottom of; at the back of; **f. de teint** foundation (makeup); **à f.** *(connaître etc)* thoroughly.

fonder *vt (ville etc)* to found.

fondre 1 *vt* to melt; *(métal)* to melt down; **faire f.** *(sucre etc)* to dissolve. **2** *vi* to melt; *(sucre etc)* to dissolve; **f. en larmes** to burst into tears.

fonds *mpl (argent)* funds.

font *voir* **faire**.

fontaine *f* fountain.

fonte *f (des neiges)* melting; *(fer)* cast iron.

football *m* soccer; **f. américain** football.

footballer, -euse *mf* soccer player.

footing *m* jogging.

force *f* force; *(physique, morale)* strength; **ses forces** one's strength; **de f.** by force; **à f. de lire/etc** through reading/etc, after much reading/etc.

forcément *adv* obviously; **pas f.** not necessarily.

forcer *vt (porte etc)* to force; **f. qn à faire** to force sb to do.

forcer (se) *vpr* to force oneself (**à faire** to do).

forêt *f* forest.

forfait *m* **déclarer f.** to withdraw from the game.

formalité *f* formality.

format *m* size.

formation *f* education, training.

forme *f (contour)* shape, form; **en f. de poire/etc** pear/etc-shaped; **en (pleine) f.** in good shape *ou* form.

formel, -elle *adj (absolu)* formal.

former *vt* to form; *(apprenti etc)* to train.

former (se) *vpr (apparaître)* to form.

formidable *adj* terrific, tremendous.

formulaire *m (feuille)* form.

formule *f* formula; *(phrase)* (set) expression; **f. de politesse** polite form of address.

fort, forte 1 *adj* strong; *(pluie, mer)* heavy; *(voix, radio)* loud; *(fièvre)* high; *(élève)* bright; **f. en (maths etc)** good at; **c'est plus f. qu'elle** she can't help it. **2** *adv (frapper, pleuvoir)* hard; *(parler)* loud(ly); *(serrer)* tight; **sentir f.** to have a strong smell.

fort *m* fort.

forteresse *f* fortress.

fortifiant *m* tonic.

fortune *f* fortune; **faire f.** to make one's fortune.

fosse *f (trou)* pit; *(tombe)* grave.

fossé *m* ditch.

fou (*or* **fol** *before vowel or mute h*), **folle 1** *adj* crazy; *(succès, temps)* tremendous; **f. de** *(musique etc)* crazy about; **f. de joie** wildly happy. **2** *mf* madman, madwoman. **3** *m* Echecs bishop; **faire le f.** to play the fool.

foudre *f* **la f.** lightning.

foudroyant, -ante *adj (succès etc)* staggering.

foudroyer *vt (tuer)* to electrocute.

fouet *m* whip; *(de cuisine)* whisk.

fouetter *vt* to whip; *(œufs)* to whisk.

fougère *f* fern.

fouiller 1 *vt (personne, maison etc)* to search. **2** *vi* **f. dans** *(tiroir etc)* to search through.

fouillis *m* jumble, mess.

foulard *m* (head)scarf.

foule *f* crowd; **une f. de** *(objets etc)* a mass of.

fouler (se) *vpr* **se f. la cheville/etc** to sprain one's ankle/etc.

foulure *f* sprain.

four *m* oven.

fourche *f (embranchement)* fork.

fourchette *f (pour manger)* fork.

fourgon *m* van; *(mortuaire)* hearse.

fourgonnette *f* (small) van.

fourmi *f* ant; **avoir des fourmis** to have pins and needles (**dans** in).

fourneau, -x *m (poêle)* stove.

fournée *f* batch.

fournir *vt* to supply; *(effort)* to make; **f. qch à qn** to supply sb with sth.

fournisseur *m (commerçant)* supplier; **f. d'accès** access provider.

fournitures *fpl* **f. de bureau** office supplies; **f. scolaires** school stationery.

fourré, -ée *adj (gant etc)* furlined.

fourrer *vt Fam (mettre)* to stick.

fourre-tout *m inv (sac)* carryall.

fourrière *f (lieu)* pound.

fourrure f fur.

foyer m (maison, famille) home; (résidence de jeunes etc) hostel.

fracas m din.

fracasser vt, **se fracasser** vpr to smash.

fraction f fraction.

fracture f fracture; **se faire une f. au bras**/etc to fracture one's arm/etc.

fracturer vt (porte etc) to break (open).

fracturer (se) vpr **se f. la jambe/** etc to fracture one's leg/etc.

fragile adj fragile.

fragment m fragment.

fraîcheur f freshness; (du temps) coolness.

frais, fraîche 1 adj fresh; (temps) cool; (boisson) cold; **servir f.** (vin etc) to serve chilled. **2** m **il fait f.** it's cool; **mettre au f.** to put in a cool place; (au frigo) to refrigerate.

frais mpl expenses; **à mes f.** at my (own) expense.

fraise f strawberry.

framboise f raspberry.

franc, franche adj (personne etc) frank; **coup f.** Football free kick; Basket-ball foul shot.

franc m (monnaie) franc.

français, -aise 1 adj French. **2** mf **F.** Frenchman, Frenchwoman; **les F.** the French. **3** m (langue) French.

franchement adv frankly; (vraiment) really.

franchir vt (fossé) to jump (over), to clear; (frontière etc) to cross; (porte) to go through; (distance) to cover.

franchise f frankness.

francophone mf French speaker.

frange f (de cheveux) bangs.

frappant, -ante adj striking.

frapper 1 vt to hit, to strike; **f. qn** (surprendre) to strike sb. **2** vi (à la porte etc) to knock (**à** at); **f. du pied** to stamp (one's foot).

fraternel, -elle adj fraternal, brotherly.

fraude f (à un examen) cheating; (crime) fraud; **passer qch en f.** to smuggle sth.

frauder vi (à un examen) to cheat (**à** on).

frayer (se) vpr **se f. un passage** to clear a way (**à travers, dans** through).

frayeur f fright.

fredonner vt to hum.

freezer m freezer.

frein m brake; **donner un coup de f.** to brake.

freinage m braking.

freiner vi to brake.

frêle adj frail.

frémir vi (trembler) to shudder (**de** with).

fréquemment adv frequently.

fréquent, -ente adj frequent.

fréquenter vt (école, église) to attend; **f. qn** to see sb.

fréquenter (se) vpr to see each other.

frère m brother.

friandises fpl candy.

fric m (argent) Fam cash.

frictionner vt to rub (down).

frigidaire® m refrigerator.

frigo m fridge.

frileux, -euse adj sensitive to cold.

frire* vti to fry; **faire f.** to fry.

frisé, -ée adj curly.

friser vti (cheveux) to curl.

frisson m (de froid) shiver; (de peur etc) shudder.

frissonner vi (de froid) to shiver; (de peur etc) to shudder (**de** with).

frit, frite (pp of **frire**) adj fried.

frites fpl French fries.

friteuse f (deep) fryer.

froid, froide 1 adj cold. **2** m cold; **avoir/prendre f.** to be/catch cold; **il fait f.** it's cold.

froisser (se) vpr (tissu) to crumple; (personne) to take offense (**de** at).

frôler vt (toucher) to brush against.

fromage m cheese; **f. blanc** soft white cheese.

fromagerie f (magasin) cheese shop.

froncer vt f. les sourcils to frown.

front m forehead, brow; (de bataille) front.

frontière f border.

frotter vti to rub; (pour nettoyer) to scrub.

frousse f Fam fear; **avoir la f.** to be scared.

fruit m fruit; **des fruits, les fruits** fruit; **fruits de mer** seafood.

fruitier adj **arbre f.** fruit tree.

frustré, -ée adj frustrated.

fuel m (fuel) oil.

fugitif, -ive mf fugitive.

fugue f **faire une f.** (enfant) to run away.

fuir* vi to run away; (gaz, robinet etc) to leak.

fuite f flight (**de** from); (de gaz etc) leak; **en f.** on the run; **prendre la f.** to run away ou off.

fulgurant, -ante adj (progrès) spectacular; (douleur) shooting.

fumé, -ée adj smoked.

fumée f smoke; (vapeur) fumes.

fumer 1 vi to smoke; (liquide brûlant) to steam. **2** vt to smoke.

fumeur, -euse mf smoker; **compartiment fumeurs** smoking compartment.

fumier m manure.

funérailles fpl funeral.

fur et à mesure (au) adv as one goes along; **au f. que** as.

fureur f fury; **faire f.** (mode etc) to be all the rage.

furie f fury.

furieux, -euse adj furious (**contre** with, at); (vent) raging.

furoncle m boil.

fuseau, -x m (pantalon) ski pants; **f. horaire** time zone.

fusée f rocket.

fusible m fuze.

fusil m rifle, gun; (de chasse) shotgun; **coup de f.** gunshot.

fusillade f (tirs) gunfire.

fusiller vt (exécuter) to shoot; **f. qn du regard** to glare at sb.

fusion f (de métal) melting; (en physique) fusion; **métal en f.** molten metal. ■ (de sociétés) merge.

fusionner vti (sociétés) to merge.

fût m (tonneau) barrel, cask.

futé, -ée adj cunning.

futile adj (personne) frivolous; (prétexte) trivial.

futur, -ure adj & m future.

G

gâcher vt to spoil; (argent etc) to waste.

gâchette f trigger.

gâchis m (gaspillage) waste.

gadget m gadget.

gaffe f Fam (maladresse) gaffe; **faire une g.** to put one's foot in it. ■ **faire g.** to be careful.

gag m gag.

gage m (garantie) security; **mettre en g.** to pawn.

gagnant, -ante 1 adj winning. **2** mf winner.

gagner 1 vt to earn; (par le jeu) to win; (atteindre) to reach; **g. une heure/etc** to save an hour/etc. **2** vi to win.

gai, -e adj cheerful.

gaiement adv cheerfully.

gaieté f cheerfulness.

gain m un **g. de temps** a saving of time; **gains** (salaire) earnings; (au jeu) winnings.

gaine f (sous-vêtement) girdle; (étui) sheath.

gala m gala.

galant, -ante adj gallant.

galerie f gallery; (porte-bagages) roof rack.

galet m pebble.

galette f (gâteau) butter cookie; (crêpe) buckwheat pancake; **g. des Rois** = Twelfth Night cake.

gallois, -oise 1 adj Welsh. **2** m f G. Welshman, Welshwoman. **3** m (langue) Welsh.

galon m (ruban) braid; (de soldat) stripe.

galop m gallop; **aller au g.** to gallop.

galoper vi to gallop.

gambade f leap.

gambader vi to leap around.

gamelle f Fam pan; (de chien) bowl; (d'ouvrier) lunch box.

gamin, -ine mf (enfant) kid.

gamme f (de notes) scale; (série) range.

gangster m gangster.

gant m glove; **g. de toilette** facecloth; **boîte à gants** glove compartment.

ganté, -ée adj (main) gloved; (personne) wearing gloves.

garage m garage.

garagiste mf garage mechanic.

garantie f guarantee; **garantie(s)** (d'assurance) cover.

garantir vt to guarantee (**contre** against); **g. à qn que** to assure ou guarantee sb that.

garçon m boy; (jeune homme) young man; **g. (de café)** waiter.

garde 1 m guard; **g. du corps** bodyguard. **2** f (d'enfants, de bagages etc) care (**de** of); **avoir la g. de** to be in charge of; **prendre g.** to pay attention (**à qch** to sth); **prendre g. de ne pas faire** to be careful not to do; **mettre en g.** to warn (**contre** against); **mise en g.** warning; **de g.** on duty; **monter la g.** to stand guard; **sur ses gardes** on one's guard; **chien de g.** watchdog.

garde-chasse, pl **gardes-chasses** m gamekeeper.

garder vt to keep; (vêtement) to keep on; (surveiller) to watch (over); (enfant) to take care of; **g. la chambre** to stay in one's room.

garder (se) vpr (aliment) to keep.

garderie f daycare center.

garde-robe, pl **garde-robes** f wardrobe.

gardien, -ienne mf (d'immeuble etc) caretaker, janitor; (de prison) (prison) guard; (de zoo, parc) keeper; (de musée) attendant, guard; **g. de but** goalkeeper.

gare f station; **g. routière** bus station.

garer vt to park; (au garage) to put in the garage.

garer (se) vpr to park.

garnement m rascal.

garnir vt (équiper) to outfit, equip (**de** with); (magasin) to stock; (orner) to trim (**de** with).

garniture f (de légumes) garnish.

gars m fellow, guy.

gas-oil m diesel (oil).

gaspillage m waste.

gaspiller vt to waste.

gâté, -ée adj (dent etc) bad.

gâteau, -x m cake; **g. de riz** rice pudding; **g. sec** cookie.

gâter vt to spoil.

gâter (se) vpr (aliment, dent) to go bad; (temps, situation) to get worse.

gâteux, -euse adj senile.

gauche 1 adj left. **2** f la g. (côté) the left (side); **à g.** (tourner) to the left; (marcher etc) on the left; **de g.** (fenêtre etc) left-hand; **à g. de** on ou to the left of.

gaucher, -ère adj & mf left-handed (person).

gaufre f waffle.

gaufrette f wafer.

Gaulois mpl les G. the Gauls.

gaver (se) vpr to stuff oneself (**de** with).

gaz m inv gas; **réchaud à g.** gas stove.

gaze f gauze.

gazeux, -euse adj (boisson, eau) fizzy, carbonated.

gazinière f gas stove.

gazole m diesel (oil).

gazon m grass, lawn.

géant, -ante adj & mf giant.

gel m frost.

gelée f frost; **g. blanche** ground frost. ▪ (de fruits) jelly.

geler vti to freeze; **il gèle** it's freezing.

gémir vi to groan.

gémissement m groan.

gênant, -ante adj (objet) cumbersome; (situation) awkward; (bruit) annoying.

gencive f gum.

gendarme m gendarme.

gendarmerie f (local) police headquarters.

gendre m son-in-law.

gêne f (trouble physique) discomfort; (confusion) embarrassment.

gêné, -ée adj (mal à l'aise) awkward.

gêner vt to bother; (troubler) to embarrass; (mouvement) to hamper; (circulation) to hold up; **g. qn** (par sa présence) to be in sb's way.

général, -e, -aux 1 adj general; **en g.** in general. **2** m (officier) general.

généralement adv generally.

généraliste mf (médecin) family doctor.

génération f generation.

généreusement adv generously.

généreux, -euse adj generous (de with).

générique m (de film) credits.

générosité f generosity.

génial, -e, -aux adj brilliant.

génie m genius.

genou, -x m knee; **à genoux** kneeling (down); **se mettre à genoux** to kneel (down); **sur ses genoux** on one's lap.

genre m (espèce) kind, sort; (d'un nom) gender.

gens mpl people; **jeunes g.** young people; (hommes) young men.

gentil, -ille adj nice; **g. avec qn** nice ou kind to sb; **sois g.** (sage) be good.

gentillesse f kindness.

gentiment adv kindly; (sagement) nicely.

géographie f geography.

géographique adj geographical.

géomètre m surveyor.

géométrie f geometry.

géométrique adj geometric(al).

gerbe f (de blé) sheaf; (de fleurs) bunch.

gercer vti, **se gercer** vpr to chap.

gerçure f avoir des gerçures aux mains/lèvres to have chapped hands/lips.

gérer vt to manage.

germe m (microbe) germ; (de plante) shoot.

germer vi (graine) to start to grow; (pomme de terre) to sprout.

geste m gesture; **ne pas faire un g.** not to make a move.

gesticuler vi to gesticulate.

gestion f (action) management.

gibier m (animaux etc) game.

giboulée f shower.

gicler vi (liquide) to spurt; **faire g.** to spurt.

gifle f slap (in the face).

gifler vt **g. qn** to slap sb.

gigantesque adj gigantic.

gigaoctet m gigabyte.

gigot m leg of mutton ou lamb.

gigoter vi to wriggle, to fidget.

gilet m cardigan; (de costume) vest; **g. de sauvetage** life jacket.

girafe f giraffe.

giratoire adj sens g. traffic circle.

girouette f weather vane.

gitan, -ane mf (Spanish) gipsy.

gîte m (abri) resting place; **g. rural** gîte = self-catering holiday cottage or apartment.

givre m frost.

givré, -ée adj frost-covered.

glace f (eau gelée) ice; (crème glacée) ice cream; (vitre) window; (miroir) mirror.

glacé, -ée *adj (eau, main etc)* icy.

glacer *vt* to chill.

glacial, -e, -aux *adj* icy.

glacier *m (vendeur)* ice-cream seller.

glacière *f* icebox.

glaçon *m* ice cube.

gland *m* acorn.

glande *f* gland.

glissant, -ante *adj* slippery.

glisser 1 *vi (involontairement)* to slip; *(volontairement) (sur la glace etc)* to slide; *(coulisser) (tiroir etc)* to slide; **ça glisse** it's slippery. **2** *vt* to slip (**dans** into).

glissière *f* **porte à g.** sliding door.

global, -e, -aux *adj* total, global.

globe *m* globe.

gloire *f* glory.

glorieux, -euse *adj* glorious.

gloussement *m* cluck(ing).

glousser *vi* to cluck.

glouton, -onne 1 *adj* greedy. **2** *mf* glutton.

gluant, -ante *adj* sticky.

goal *m* goalkeeper.

gobelet *m (de plastique, papier)* cup.

godet *m* pot.

golf *m* golf; *(terrain)* golf course.

golfe *m* gulf, bay.

golfeur, -euse *mf* golfer.

gomme *f (à effacer)* eraser.

gommer *vt (effacer)* to rub out, to erase.

gond *m* hinge.

gonflable *adj* inflatable.

gonflé, -ée *adj* swollen.

gonfler 1 *vt (pneu)* to pump up; *(en soufflant)* to blow up. **2** *vi, se gonfler vpr* to swell.

gonfleur *m (air)* pump.

gorge *f* throat; *(vallée)* gorge.

gorgée *f* mouthful *(of wine etc)*; **petite g.** sip.

gorille *m* gorilla.

gosier *m* throat.

gosse *mf (enfant) Fam* kid.

gouache *f* gouache.

goudron *m* tar.

goudronner *vt* to tar.

goulot *m (de bouteille)* neck; **boire au g.** to drink from the bottle.

gourde *f* water bottle.

gourdin *m* club, cudgel.

gourmand, -ande 1 *adj* (over)-fond of food; **g. de** fond of. **2** *mf* hearty eater.

gourmandise *f* (over)fondness for food.

gourmet *m* gourmet.

gourmette *f* identity bracelet.

gousse *f* **g. d'ail** clove of garlic.

goût *m* taste; **de bon g.** in good taste; **sans g.** tasteless.

goûter 1 *vt* to taste; **g. à qch** to taste (a little of) sth. **2** *vi* to have an afternoon snack. **3** *m* afternoon snack.

goutte *f* drop.

gouttelette *f* droplet.

goutter *vi* to drip *(de from)*.

gouttière *f (d'un toit)* gutter.

gouvernail *m* rudder; *(barre)* helm.

gouvernement *m* government.

gouverner *vti* to govern.

grâce 1 *f* grace; *(avantage)* favor. **2** *prép* **g. à** thanks to.

gracieux, -euse *adj (élégant)* graceful.

grade *m* rank.

gradin *m* tier (of seats).

graffiti *mpl* graffiti.

grain *m* grain; *(de café)* bean; *(de poussière)* speck; **g. de beauté** mole; *(sur le visage)* beauty spot.

graine *f* seed.

graisse *f* fat; *(pour machine)* grease; **graisses saturées** saturated fats.

graisser *vt* to grease.

graisseux, -euse *adj (vêtement etc)* greasy.

grammaire *f* grammar; **livre de g.** grammar (book).

gramme *m* gram.

grand, grande 1 *adj* big, large;

(en hauteur) tall; *(chaleur, découverte etc)* great; *(bruit)* loud; *(différence)* big, great; **g. frère/etc** *(plus âgé)* big brother/etc; **il est g. temps** it's high time (**que** that). **2** *adv* **g. ouvert** wide-open; **ouvrir g.** to open wide.

grand-chose *pron* **pas g.** not much.

grandeur *f (importance)* greatness; *(dimension)* size; **g. nature** life-size.

grandiose *adj* imposing.

grandir *vi* to grow.

grand-mère, *pl* **grands-mères** *f* grandmother.

grand-père, *pl* **grands-pères** *m* grandfather.

grand-route, *pl* **grands-routes** *f* main road.

grands-parents *mpl* grandparents.

grange *f* barn.

graphique *m* graph.

grappe *f* cluster; **g. de raisin** bunch of grapes.

gras, grasse 1 *adj* fat; *(aliment)* fatty; *(graisseux)* greasy; **matières grasses** fat. **2** *m (de viande)* fat.

gratin *m* **macaronis/chou-fleur au g.** macaroni and/cauliflower with cheese.

gratitude *f* gratitude.

gratte-ciel *m inv* skyscraper.

gratter *vt* to scrape; *(avec les ongles etc)* to scratch; **ça me gratte** it itches.

gratter (se) *vpr* to scratch oneself.

gratuit, -uite *adj* free.

gratuitement *adv* free (of charge).

gravats *mpl* rubble.

grave *adj* serious; *(voix)* deep; **ce n'est pas g.!** it's not important!; **accent g.** grave accent.

gravement *adv* seriously.

graver *vt (sur métal etc)* to engrave; *(sur bois)* to carve.

graveur *m* engraver.

gravier *m* gravel.

gravillons *mpl* gravel.

gravir *vt* to climb *(with effort)*.

gravité *f (de situation etc)* seriousness.

gravure *f (image)* print.

grec, grecque 1 *adj* Greek. **2** *mf* **G.** Greek. **3** *m (langue)* Greek.

greffe *f (de peau, d'arbre)* graft; *(d'organe)* transplant.

greffer *vt (peau etc)* to graft (**à** on to); *(organe)* to transplant.

grêle *f* hail.

grêler *vi* to hail.

grêlon *m* hailstone.

grelot *m (small round)* bell *(that jingles)*.

grelotter *vi* to shiver (**de** with).

grenade *f (fruit)* pomegranate; *(projectile)* grenade.

grenadine *f* pomegranate syrup, grenadine.

grenier *m* attic.

grenouille *f* frog.

grève *f* strike; **g. de la faim** hunger strike; **se mettre en g.** to go (out) on strike.

gréviste *mf* striker.

gribouiller *vti* to scribble.

gribouillis *m* scribble.

grièvement *adv* **g. blessé** seriously injured.

griffe *f (ongle)* claw; *(de couturier)* (designer) label.

griffer *vt* to scratch.

griffonner *vt* to scribble.

grignoter *vti* to nibble.

gril *m* grill.

grillade *f (viande)* grill.

grillage *m* window screen, chicken wire.

grille *f (clôture)* railing.

grille-pain *m inv* toaster.

griller 1 *vt (viande)* to grill; *(pain)* to toast; **g. un feu rouge** to run a red light. **2** *vi* **mettre à g.** to put on the grill.

grillon *m (insecte)* cricket.

grimace *f* faire des grimaces/la g. to make faces/a face.

grimacer *vi* to make faces *ou* a face.

grimpant, -ante *adj* climbing.

grimper 1 *vi* to climb (**à qch** up sth). **2** *vt* to climb.

grincement *m* creaking; *(des dents)* grinding.

grincer *vi* to creak; **g. des dents** to grind one's teeth.

grincheux, -euse *adj* grumpy.

grippe *f* flu.

grippé, -ée *adj* être g. to have (the) flu.

gris, grise 1 *adj* gray. **2** *m* gray.

grisaille *f* grayness.

grisâtre *adj* grayish.

grisonnant, -ante *adj (cheveux, personne)* graying.

grisonner *vi* to grow gray.

grognement *m* growl; *(d'un cochon)* grunt.

grogner *vi* to growl (**contre** at); *(cochon)* to grunt.

grognon, -onne *adj* grumpy.

grommeler *vti* to mutter.

grondement *m* growl; *(de tonnerre)* rumble.

gronder 1 *vi* to growl; *(tonnerre)* to rumble. **2** *vt* to scold, to tell off.

groom *m* bellboy.

gros, grosse 1 *adj* big; *(gras)* fat; *(épais)* thick; *(effort, progrès)* great; *(somme)* large; *(averse, rhume)* heavy; **g. mot** swearword. **2** *adv* **en g.** roughly; *(écrire)* in big letters; *(vendre)* wholesale.

groseille *f* (white *ou* red) currant.

grossesse *f* pregnancy.

grosseur *f* size; *(tumeur)* lump.

grossier, -ière *adj* rough; *(personne)* rude (**envers** to).

grossièrement *adv* roughly; *(répondre)* rudely.

grossièreté *f* roughness; *(insolence)* rudeness; *(mot)* rude word.

grossir *vi* to put on weight.

grossiste *mf* wholesaler.

grotte *f* cave, grotto.

grouiller *vi* to be swarming (**de** with).

groupe *m* group.

grouper *vt*, **se grouper** *vpr* to group (together).

grue *f* crane.

grumeau, -x *m* lump.

gruyère *m* gruyère (cheese).

guenilles *fpl* rags (and tatters).

guenon *f* female monkey.

guêpe *f* wasp.

guère *adv* (**ne**)...**g.** hardly; **il ne sort g.** he hardly goes out.

guéri, -ie *adj* cured, better.

guérir 1 *vt* to cure (**de** of). **2** *vi* to recover (**de** from).

guérison *f* recovery.

guerre *f* war; **en g.** at war (**avec** with).

guerrier, -ière *mf* warrior.

guet *m* faire le g. to be on the lookout.

guetter *vt* to be on the lookout for.

gueule *f* mouth.

gui *m* mistletoe.

guichet *m* ticket office; *(de banque etc)* window.

guichetier, -ière *mf (de banque etc)* teller; *(à la gare)* ticket agent.

guide *m (personne, livre)* guide.

guider *vt* to guide.

guidon *m* handlebar(s).

guignol *m (spectacle)* = Punch and Judy show.

guillemets *mpl* quotation marks; **entre g.** in quotation marks.

guirlande *f* garland.

guitare *f* guitar.

guitariste *mf* guitarist.

gymnase *m* gymnasium.

gymnastique *f* gymnastics.

gynécologue *mf* gynecologist.

H

habile *adj* skillful (**à qch** at sth; **à faire** at doing).

habileté *f* skill.

habillé, -ée *adj* dressed (**de** in; **en** as a).

habiller *vt* to dress (**de** in).

habiller (s') *vpr* to dress, to get dressed; *(avec élégance)* to dress up.

habitable *adj (maison)* fit to live in.

habitant, -ante *mf (de pays etc)* inhabitant; *(de maison)* occupant.

habitation *f* house.

habité, -ée *adj (région)* inhabited; *(maison)* occupied.

habiter 1 *vi* to live (**à, en, dans** in). **2** *vt (maison etc)* to live in.

habits *mpl (vêtements)* clothes.

habitude *f* habit; **avoir l'h. de qch/faire** to be used to sth/doing; **d'h.** usually; **comme d'h.** as usual.

habitué, -ée *mf* regular.

habituel, -elle *adj* usual.

habituellement *adv* usually.

habituer *vt* **h. qn à** to accustom sb to.

habituer (s') *vpr* to get accustomed (**à** to).

hache *f* ax.

hacher *vt* to chop (up); *(avec un appareil)* to grind.

hachis *m* ground meat.

haie *f (clôture)* hedge; **course de haies** *(coureurs)* hurdle race.

haine *f* hatred.

haïr *vt* to hate.

haleine *f* breath; **hors d'h.** out of breath.

haleter *vi* to pant.

hall *m (de gare)* main hall; *(de maison)* hall(way).

halle *f* (covered) market; **les halles** the central food market.

hallucinant, -ante *adj* extraordinary.

halte 1 *f (arrêt)* stop. **2** *int* stop!

haltères *mpl* weights.

hamac *m* hammock.

hameçon *m* (fish) hook.

hamster *m* hamster.

hanche *f* hip.

handicap *m (physique, mental)* disability, handicap.

handicapé, -ée 1 *adj* disabled, handicapped. **2** *mf* disabled person, handicapped person.

hangar *m* shed; *(pour avions)* hangar.

hanté, -ée *adj* haunted.

harassé, -ée *adj (fatigué)* exhausted.

harceler *vt (importuner)* to harass; *(insister auprès de)* to pester.

hardi, -ie *adj* bold.

hareng *m* herring.

hargneux, -euse *adj* bad-tempered.

haricot *m (blanc)* (haricot) bean; *(vert)* green bean.

harmonica *m* harmonica.

harmonie *f* harmony.

harmonieux, -euse *adj* harmonious.

harnais *m* harness.

harpe *f* harp.

hasard *m* **le h.** chance; **un h.** a coincidence; **par h.** by chance; **au h.** at random; **à tout h.** just in case.

hasardeux, -euse *adj* risky.

hâte *f* haste; **à la h.** in a hurry; **avoir h. de faire** to be eager to do.

hâter (se) *vpr* to hurry (**de faire** to do).

hausse *f* rise (**de** in); **en h.** rising.

haut, haute 1 *adj* high; *(de taille)* tall; **à haute voix** aloud; **h. de 5 mètres** 16 feet high *ou* tall. **2** *adv (voler etc)* high (up); *(parler)* loud; **tout h.** *(lire etc)* aloud; **h. placé** *(personne)* in a high position. **3** *m* top; **en h. de** at the top of; **en h.** *(loger)* upstairs; *(regarder)* up; *(mettre)* on (the) top;

avoir 5 mètres de h. to be 16 feet high ou tall.

hautain, -aine adj haughty.

hauteur f height.

haut-parleur m loudspeaker.

hayon m (porte) hatchback.

hé! int (appel) hey!

hebdomadaire adj & m weekly.

héberger vt to put up.

hectare m hectare (= 2,47 acres).

hein! int Fam eh!

hélas! int unfortunately.

hélice f propeller.

hélicoptère m helicopter.

helvétique adj Swiss.

hémorragie f hemorrhage; **h. cérébrale** stroke.

hennir vi to neigh.

hépatite f hepatitis.

herbe f grass; (pour soigner etc) herb; **mauvaise h.** weed; **fines herbes** herbs.

hérisser (se) vpr (poils) to bristle (up).

hérisson m hedgehog.

héritage m (biens) inheritance.

hériter vti to inherit (**qch de qn** sth from sb); **h. de qch** to inherit sth.

héritier m heir.

héritière f heiress.

hermétique adj airtight.

héroïne f (femme) heroine; (drogue) heroin.

héroïque adj heroic.

héros m hero.

hésitant, -ante adj hesitant; (pas, voix) unsteady.

hésitation f hesitation; **avec h.** hesitantly.

hésiter vi to hesitate (**sur** over, about; **à faire** to do).

hêtre m (arbre, bois) beech.

heu! int er!

heure f hour; (moment) time; **quelle h. est-il?** what time is it?; **il est six heures** it's six (o'clock); **six heures moins cinq** five to six; **six heures cinq** five after ou past six; **à l'h.** (arriver) on time; **dix kilomè-**

tres à l'h. six miles an hour; **de bonne h.** early; **tout à l'h.** (futur) later; (passé) a moment ago; **heures supplémentaires** overtime; **l'h. de pointe** (circulation etc) rush hour.

heureusement adv (par chance) fortunately (**pour** for).

heureux, -euse 1 adj happy; (chanceux) lucky; **h. de qch/de voir qn** happy ou glad about sth/to see sb. **2** adv (vivre etc) happily.

heurter vt to hit.

heurter (se) vpr **se h. à** to bump into, to hit.

hexagone m hexagon; **l'H.** France.

hibou, -x m owl.

hier adv & m yesterday; **h. soir** last night.

hi-fi adj inv & f inv hi-fi.

hilarant, -ante adj hilarious.

hippodrome m racetrack.

hippopotame m hippopotamus.

hirondelle f swallow.

hisser (se) vpr to heave oneself up.

histoire f history; (récit, mensonge) story; **des histoires** (ennuis) trouble; **sans histoires** (voyage etc) uneventful.

historique adj historical; (lieu, événement) historic.

hiver m winter.

HLM m ou f abrév (habitation à loyer modéré) = low-income housing.

hocher vt **h. la tête** (pour dire oui) to nod one's head; (pour dire non) to shake one's head.

hochet m (jouet) rattle.

hockey m hockey; **h. sur glace** ice hockey.

hold-up m inv (attaque) holdup.

hollandais, -aise 1 adj Dutch. **2** mf **H.** Dutchman, Dutchwoman; **les H.** the Dutch. **3** m (langue) Dutch.

homard m lobster.

homme m man (pl men); **l'h.** (espèce) man(kind); **des vête-**

ments d'h. men's clothes; **h. d'af-faires** businessman.

homosexuel, -elle *adj & mf* homosexual.

honnête *adj* honest; *(satisfaisant)* decent.

honnêtement *adv* honestly; decently.

honnêteté *f* honesty.

honneur *m* honor; **en l'h.** de in honor of; **faire h. à** *(sa famille etc)* to be a credit to; *(repas)* to do justice to.

honorable *adj* honorable; *(convenable)* respectable.

honoraires *mpl* fees.

honte *f* shame; **avoir h.** to be *ou* feel ashamed (**de qch** of sth; **de faire** to do, of doing).

honteux, -euse *adj* ashamed; *(scandaleux)* shameful.

hôpital, -aux *m* hospital; **à l'h.** in the hospital.

hoquet *m* **avoir le h.** to have (the) hiccups.

horaire *m* timetable.

horizon *m* horizon; **à l'h.** on the horizon.

horizontal, -e, -aux *adj* horizontal.

horloge *f* clock.

horreur *f* horror; **faire h. à** to disgust; **avoir h. de** to hate.

horrible *adj* horrible.

horriblement *adv* horribly.

horrifiant, -ante *adj* horrifying.

horrifié, -ée *adj* horrified.

hors *prép* **h. service** out of order; **h.** de out of.

hors-bord *m inv* speedboat.

hors-d'œuvre *m inv* *(à table)* hors d'oeuvre, appetizer.

hors-taxe *adj inv* duty-free.

hospitaliser *vt* to hospitalize.

hospitalité *f* hospitality.

hostile *adj* hostile (**à** to, towards).

hostilité *f* hostility (**envers** to, towards).

hôte 1 *m (qui reçoit)* host. **2** *mf (invité)* guest.

hôtel *m* hotel; **h. de ville** city hall.

hôtesse *f* hostess; **h. (de l'air)** flight attendant.

hotte *f* basket *(carried on back)*.

houleux, -euse *adj (mer)* rough; *(réunion)* stormy.

hourra! *int* hurray!

housse *f* *(protective)* cover.

HT *abrév (hors taxe)* before tax, exclusive of tax.

hublot *m* porthole.

huées *fpl* boos.

huile *f* oil.

huit *adj & m* eight; **h. jours** a week.

huitième *adj & mf* eighth.

huître *f* oyster.

humain, -aine *adj* human.

humanité *f* humanity.

humble *adj* humble.

humblement *adv* humbly.

humecter *vt* to moisten.

humeur *f* mood; *(caractère)* temperament; **bonne h.** *(gaieté)* good humor; **de bonne/mauvaise h.** in a good/bad mood.

humide *adj* damp.

humidité *f* humidity; *(plutôt froide)* damp(ness).

humiliation *f* humiliation.

humilier *vt* to humiliate.

humoristique *adj* humorous.

humour *m* humor; **avoir de l'h.** to have a sense of humor.

hurlement *m (d'un loup, du vent)* howl; *(d'une personne)* scream.

hurler 1 *vi (loup, vent)* to howl; *(personne)* to scream. **2** *vt* to scream.

hydrater *vt (peau)* to moisturize.

hygiène *f* hygiene.

hygiénique *adj* hygienic; **papier h.** toilet paper.

hymne *m* **h. national** national anthem.

hypermarché *m* hypermarket.

hypocrisie *f* hypocrisy.

hypocrite 1 *adj* hypocritical. **2** *mf* hypocrite.

hypothèse *f (supposition)* assumption.

I

iceberg *m* iceberg.

ici *adv* here; **par i.** *(passer)* this way; *(habiter)* around here; **jusqu'i.** *(temps)* up to now; *(lieu)* as far as this **ou** here; **d'i. peu** before long.

idéal, -e, -aux *ou* **-als** *adj & m* ideal.

idée *f* idea; **changer d'i.** to change one's mind.

identifier *vt* to identify.

identifier (s') *vpr* **s'i. à** *ou* **avec** to identify (oneself) with.

identique *adj* identical (**à** to, with).

identité *f* identity; **carte d'i.** identity card, ID card.

idiot, -ote 1 *adj* silly. **2** *mf* idiot.

idiotie *f* une i. a silly thing.

idole *m* idol.

igloo *m* igloo.

ignifugé, -ée *adj* fireproof(ed).

ignoble *adj* vile.

ignorance *f* ignorance.

ignorant, -ante *adj* ignorant (**de** of).

ignorer *vt* not to know; **i. qn** to ignore sb.

il *pron (personne)* he; *(chose, animal)* it; **il pleut** it's raining; **il y a** there is; *pl* there are; **il y a six ans** six years ago; **il y a une heure qu'il travaille** he's been working for an hour; **qu'est-ce qu'il y a?** what's the matter?

île *f* island.

illégal, -e, -aux *adj* illegal.

illettré, -ée *adj* illiterate.

illisible *adj (écriture)* illegible.

illuminer *vt*, **s'illuminer** *vpr* to light up.

illusion *f* illusion; **se faire des illusions** to delude oneself (**sur** about).

illustration *f* illustration.

illustré *m* comic.

illustrer *vt* to illustrate (**de** with).

ils *pron* they.

image *f* picture; *(dans une glace)* reflection.

imaginaire *adj* imaginary.

imagination *f* imagination.

imaginer *vt*, **s'imaginer** *vpr* to imagine (**que** that).

imbattable *adj* unbeatable.

imbécile *mf* idiot.

imbécilité *f (état)* imbecility; **une i.** *(action, parole)* an idiotic thing.

imbuvable *adj* undrinkable.

imitateur, -trice *mf (artiste)* impersonator.

imitation *f* imitation.

imiter *vt* to imitate; **i. qn** *(pour rire)* to mimic sb; *(faire comme)* to do the same as sb.

immangeable *adj* inedible.

immatriculation *f* registration.

immédiat, -ate *adj* immediate.

immédiatement *adv* immediately.

immense *adj* immense.

immeuble *m* building; *(d'habitation)* apartment building; *(de bureaux)* office building.

immigration *f* immigration.

immigré, -ée *adj & mf* immigrant.

immobile *adj* still.

immobilier, -ère 1 *adj* marché i. property market. **2** *m* l'i. real estate.

immobiliser *vt* to bring to a stop.

immobiliser (s') *vpr* to come to a stop.

immonde *adj (sale)* foul; *(ignoble, laid)* vile.

immortel, -elle *adj* immortal.

immuable *adj* immutable, unchanging.

impair, -e *adj (nombre)* odd.

impardonnable *adj* unforgivable.

imparfait *m (temps) Grammaire* imperfect.

impartial, -e, -aux *adj* fair, un-biased.

impasse *f* dead end.

impassible *adj* impassive.

impatience *f* impatience.

impatient, -ente *adj* impatient (**de faire** to do).

impatienter (s') *vpr* to get impa-tient.

impeccable *adj* (*propre*) imma-culate.

impératif *m* Grammaire imperative.

imperméable 1 *adj* (*tissu*) water-proof. **2** *m* raincoat.

impitoyable *adj* ruthless.

implanter (s') *vpr* to become established.

impoli, -ie *adj* rude.

impolitesse *f* rudeness.

importance *f* importance; **ça n'a pas d'i.** it doesn't matter.

important, -ante 1 *adj* impor-tant; (*quantité etc*) big. **2** *m* **l'i., c'est de** the important thing is to.

importateur, -trice 1 *adj* im-porting. **2** *mf* importer.

importation *f* import; **d'i.** (*arti-cle*) imported.

importer 1 *vi* **n'importe qui/ quoi/où/quand/comment** any-one/anything/anywhere/anytime/ anyhow. **2** *vt* to import (**de** from).

imposer *vt* to impose (**à** on).

impossibilité *f* impossibility.

impossible *adj* impossible (**à faire** to do); **il (nous) est i. de le faire** it is impossible (for us) to do it.

impôt *m* tax; **i. sur le revenu** in-come tax; (**service des) impôts** tax authorities.

impression *f* impression.

impressionnant, -ante *adj* im-pressive.

impressionner *vt* (*émouvoir*) to make a strong impression on.

imprévisible *adj* unforeseeable.

imprévu, -ue *adj* unexpected.

imprimante *f* (*d'ordinateur*) prin-ter.

imprimé *m* printed form.

imprimer *vt* (*livre etc*) to print.

imprimerie *f* printing plant.

improviser *vti* to improvize.

improviste (à l') *adv* unexpec-tedly.

imprudence *f* carelessness, fool-ishness; **commettre une i.** to do something foolish.

imprudent, -ente *adj* careless, foolish.

impuissant, -ante *adj* helpless.

impulsif, -ive *adj* impulsive.

inabordable *adj* (*prix*) prohibitive.

inacceptable *adj* unacceptable.

inachevé, -ée *adj* unfinished.

inadapté, -ée *adj* (*socialement*) maladjusted; (*physiquement, men-talement*) handicapped; (*matériel*) unsuitable (**à** for).

inadmissible *adj* unacceptable, inadmissible.

inanimé, -ée *adj* (*mort*) lifeless; (*évanoui*) unconscious.

inaperçu, -ue *adj* **passer i.** to go unnoticed.

inapte *adj* (*intellectuellement*) un-suited (**à** for); (*médicalement*) unfit (**à** for).

inattendu, -ue *adj* unexpected.

inattention *f* lack of attention; **un moment d'i.** a moment of distrac-tion.

inauguration *f* inauguration.

inaugurer *vt* to inaugurate.

incapable *adj* **i. de faire qch** unable to do sth.

incapacité *f* (*impossibilité*) inabili-ty (**de faire** to do); (*invalidité*) dis-ability; **être dans l'i. de faire qch** to be unable to do sth.

incarner *vt* to embody.

incassable *adj* unbreakable.

incendie *m* fire.

incendier *vt* to set fire to.

incertain, -aine *adj* uncertain; (*temps*) unsettled.

incertitude *f* uncertainty.

incessamment *adv* very soon.

incessant, -ante *adj* continual.
inchangé, -ée *adj* unchanged.
incident *m* incident.
incisive *f* incisor (tooth).
inciter *vt* to encourage (**à faire** to do).
incliner *vt* (*courber*) to bend; (*pencher*) to tilt.
incliner (s') *vpr* (*se courber*) to bow (down).
inclure *vt* to include; (*dans un courrier*) to enclose (**dans** with).
inclus, -use *adj* inclusive; **jusqu'à lundi i.** up to and including Monday.
incohérent, -ente *adj* (*propos*) incoherent; (*histoire*) inconsistent.
incolore *adj* colorless; (*vernis*) clear.
incommoder *vt* to bother.
incomparable *adj* matchless.
incompatible *adj* incompatible.
incompétent, -ente *adj* incompetent.
incomplet, -ète *adj* incomplete.
incompréhensible *adj* incomprehensible.
inconnu, -ue 1 *adj* unknown (**à** to). **2** *mf* (*étranger*) stranger.
inconscient, -ente *adj* unconscious (**de** of); (*imprudent*) thoughtless.
inconsolable *adj* heartbroken, cut up.
incontestable *adj* undeniable.
inconvenant, -ante *adj* improper.
inconvénient *m* drawback.
incorrect, -e *adj* (*grossier*) impolite.
incroyable *adj* incredible.
inculpé, -ée *mf* **l'i.** the accused.
inculper *vt* to charge (**de** with).
inculte *adj* (*terre, personne*) uncultivated.
incurable *adj* incurable.
indécis, -ise *adj* (*hésitant*) undecided.
indéfini, -ie *adj* indefinite.
indéfiniment *adv* indefinitely.

indemne *adj* unhurt.
indemnisation *f* compensation.
indemnité *f* compensation; (*allocation*) allowance.
indépendance *f* independence.
indépendant, -ante *adj* independent (**de** of).
indescriptible *adj* indescribable.
indéterminé, -ée *adj* (*date, heure*) unspecified; (*raison*) unknown.
index *m* (*doigt*) index finger, forefinger.
indicatif *m* (*à la radio*) theme song *ou* music; (*téléphonique*) area code; *Grammaire* indicative.
indication *f* (piece of) information; **indications** (*pour aller quelque part*) directions.
indice *m* (*dans une enquête*) clue.
indien, -ienne 1 *adj* Indian. **2** *mf* I. Indian.
indifférence *f* indifference (**à** to).
indifférent, -ente *adj* indifferent (**à** to).
indigestion *f* (attack of) indigestion.
indignation *f* indignation.
indigne *adj* (*personne*) unworthy; (*conduite*) shameful; **i. de qn/qch** unworthy of sb/sth.
indigner (s') *vpr* to be *ou* become indignant (**de** at).
indiquer *vt* (*montrer*) to show; (*dire*) to tell; **i. du doigt** to point to *ou* at.
indirect, -e *adj* indirect.
indirectement *adv* indirectly.
indiscipliné, -ée *adj* unruly.
indiscret, -ète *adj* inquisitive.
indiscrétion *f* indiscretion.
indispensable *adj* essential.
indisponible *adj* unavailable.
indistinct, -incte *adj* unclear.
individu *m* individual.
individuel, -elle *adj* individual.
indolore *adj* painless.
indulgent, -ente *adj* indulgent (**envers** to).

industrialisé, -ée *adj* industrialized.

industrie *f* industry.

industriel, -elle *adj* industrial.

inédit, -ite *adj (texte)* unpublished.

inefficace *adj (mesure etc)* ineffective; *(personne)* inefficient.

inégal, -e, -aux *adj (parts, lutte)* unequal; *(sol, humeur)* uneven; *(travail)* inconsistent.

inépuisable *adj* inexhaustible.

inespéré, -ée *adj* unhoped-for.

inestimable *adj* priceless.

inévitable *adj* inevitable, unavoidable.

inexact, -e *adj* inaccurate.

inexcusable *adj* inexcusable.

inexplicable *adj* inexplicable.

inexpliqué, -ée *adj* unexplained.

infaillible *adj* infallible.

infarctus *m* un i. a coronary.

infatigable *adj* tireless.

infect, -e *adj (odeur)* foul; *(café etc)* vile.

infecter (s') *vpr* to get infected.

infection *f* infection; *(odeur)* stench.

inférieur, -e *adj* lower; *(qualité etc)* inferior (à to); **l'étage i.** the floor below.

infériorité *f* inferiority.

infernal, -e, -aux *adj* infernal.

infesté, -ée *adj* i. de requins/etc shark/etc-infested.

infidèle *adj* unfaithful (à to).

infiltrer (s') *vpr (liquide)* to seep (through) (dans into).

infini, -ie 1 *adj* infinite. **2** *m* infinity.

infiniment *adv (regretter, remercier)* very much.

infinitif *m Grammaire* infinitive.

infirme *adj & mf* disabled (person).

infirmerie *f* sick room, sickbay.

infirmier *m* male nurse.

infirmière *f* nurse.

inflammable *adj* (in)flammable.

inflammation *f* inflammation.

inflation *f* inflation.

inflexible *adj* inflexible.

influence *f* influence.

influencer *vt* to influence.

informaticien, -enne *mf* computer scientist.

information *f* information; *(nouvelle)* piece of news; **les informations** the news.

informatique *f (science)* computer science, IT; *(technique)* data processing.

informatisé, -ée *adj* computerized.

informer *vt* to inform (**de** of, about; **que** that).

informer (s') *vpr* to inquire (**de** about; **si** if, whether).

infraction *f* offense.

infusion *f* herbal ou herb tea.

ingénieur *m* engineer.

ingénieux, -euse *adj* ingenious.

ingrat, -ate *adj* ungrateful (**envers** to).

ingratitude *f* ingratitude.

ingrédient *m* ingredient.

inhabitable *adj* uninhabitable.

inhabité, -ée *adj* uninhabited.

inhabituel, -elle *adj* unusual.

inhumain, -aine *adj* inhuman.

inimaginable *adj* unimaginable.

ininflammable *adj* non-flammable.

ininterrompu, -ue *adj* continuous.

initiale *f (lettre)* initial.

initier (s') *vpr* s'i. à qch to start learning sth.

injecter *vt* to inject.

injection *f* injection.

injure *f* insult.

injurier *vt* to insult.

injuste *adj (contraire à la justice)* unjust; *(non équitable)* unfair.

injustice *f* injustice.

inlassable *adj* untiring.

innocence *f* innocence.

innocent, -ente 1 *adj* innocent (**de** of). **2** *mf* innocent person.

innombrable *adj* countless.

inoccupé, -ée *adj* unoccupied.
inoffensif, -ive *adj* harmless.
inondation *f* flood.
inonder *vt* to flood.
inoubliable *adj* unforgettable.
inouï, -ïe *adj* incredible.
inox *m* stainless steel.
inoxydable *adj* acier i. stainless steel.
inqualifiable *adj* unspeakable.
inquiet, -iète *adj* worried (**de** about).
inquiétant, -ante *adj* worrying.
inquiéter *vt* to worry.
inquiéter (s') *vpr* s'i. (**de**) to worry (about).
inquiétude *f* worry.
insatisfait, -aite *adj* (*personne*) dissatisfied.
inscription *f* registration; (*sur écriteau etc*) inscription; **frais d'i.** (*à l'université*) tuition fees.
inscrire* *vt* to write *ou* put down; **i. qn** to enroll sb.
inscrire (s') *vpr* to put one's name down; **s'i. à** (*club*) to join; (*examen*) to enroll for, to register for.
insecte *m* insect.
insecticide *m* insecticide.
insécurité *f* insecurity.
insensé, -ée *adj* (*projet, idée*) crazy; (*espoir*) wild.
insensible *adj* insensitive (**à** to).
inséparable *adj* inseparable (**de** from).
insigne *m* badge.
insignifiant, -ante *adj* insignificant.
insistance *f* insistence.
insister *vt* to insist (**pour faire** to do doing); **i. sur** (*détail etc*) to stress.
insolation *f* sunstroke.
insolence *f* insolence.
insolent, -ente *adj* insolent.
insomnie *f* insomnia.
insonoriser *vt* to soundproof.
insouciant, -ante *adj* carefree.
inspecter *vt* to inspect.
inspecteur, -trice *mf* inspector.

inspection *f* inspection.
inspiration *f* inspiration.
inspirer *vt* to inspire (**qch à qn** sb with sth).
instable *adj* (*meuble*) shaky.
installation *f* putting in; (*dans une maison*) moving in.
installer *vt* (*appareil etc*) to install, to put in; (*étagère*) to put up.
installer (s') *vpr* (*s'asseoir, s'établir*) to settle (down); **s'i. dans** (*maison*) to move into.
instant *m* moment; **à l'i.** a moment ago; **pour l'i.** for the moment.
instaurer *vt* to establish.
instinct *m* instinct.
instinctif, -ive *adj* instinctive.
instituteur, -trice *mf* elementary school teacher.
institution *f* (*organisation, structure*) institution.
instructif, -ive *adj* instructive.
instruction *f* education; **instructions** (*ordres*) instructions.
instruire* *vt* to teach, to educate.
instruire (s') *vpr* to educate oneself.
instrument *m* instrument; (*outil*) implement.
insuffisant, -ante *adj* inadequate.
insulte *f* insult (**à** to).
insulter *vt* to insult.
insupportable *adj* unbearable.
intact, -e *adj* intact.
intégral, -e, -aux *adj* (*paiement*) full; (*édition*) unabridged; **version intégrale** (*de film*) uncut version.
intégralement *adv* in full.
intégrer (s') *vpr* to become integrated.
intellectuel, -elle *adj & mf* intellectual.
intelligemment *adv* intelligently.
intelligence *f* intelligence.
intelligent, -ente *adj* intelligent.
intempéries *fpl* **les i.** bad weather.

intense *adj* intense; *(circulation)* heavy.

intensifier *vt*, **s'intensifier** *vpr* to intensify.

intensité *f* intensity.

intention *f* intention; **avoir l'i. de faire** to intend to do.

interchangeable *adj* interchangeable.

interdiction *f* ban (**de** on); **'i. de fumer'** 'no smoking'.

interdire* *vt* to forbid, not to allow (**qch à qn** sb sth); **i. à qn de faire** not to allow sb to do.

interdit, -ite *adj* forbidden; **'stationnement i.'** 'no parking'.

intéressant, -ante *adj* interesting; *(prix etc)* attractive.

intéresser *vt* to interest.

intéresser (s') *vpr* **s'i. à** to take an interest in.

intérêt *m* interest; **intérêts** *(argent)* interest; **tu as i. à faire** you'd do well to do.

intérieur, -e *adj* inner; *(poche)* inside; *(politique)* domestic. **2** *m* inside (**de** of); **à l'i. (de)** inside.

intérim *m* *(travail temporaire)* temporary work; **président par i.** acting president.

intérimaire 1 *adj* *(fonction, employé)* temporary. **2** *mf* *(travailleur)* temporary worker; *(secrétaire)* temp.

interlocuteur, -trice *mf* **mon i.** the person I am/was/*etc* speaking to.

intermédiaire *mf* **par l'i. de** through (the medium of).

interminable *adj* endless.

international, -e, -aux *adj* international.

internaute *mf* Internet surfer.

interne *mf* *(élève)* boarder.

Internet *m* the Internet; **sur I.** on the Internet.

interpeller *vt* *(appeler)* to shout at.

interphone *m* intercom.

interposer (s') *vpr* to intervene (**dans** in).

interprète *mf* interpreter; *(chanteur)* singer.

interpréter *vt* *(expliquer)* to interpret; *(chanter)* to sing.

interrogatif, -ive *adj & m Grammaire* interrogative.

interrogation *f* question; *(à l'école)* test.

interrogatoire *m* interrogation.

interroger *vt* to question.

interrompre* *vt* to interrupt.

interrupteur *m* *(électrique)* switch.

interruption *f* interruption.

intersection *f* intersection.

intervalle *m* *(écart)* gap; *(temps)* interval.

intervenir* *vi* to intervene; *(survenir)* to occur.

intervention *f* intervention; **i. (chirurgicale)** operation.

interview *f* interview.

interviewer *vt* to interview.

intestin *m* bowel.

intime *adj* intimate; *(journal, mariage)* private.

intimider *vt* to intimidate.

intimité *f* *(familiarité)* intimacy; *(vie privée)* privacy; **dans l'i.** in private.

intituler (s') *vpr* to be entitled.

intolérable *adj* intolerable (**que** (+ *subjonctif*) that).

intoxication *f* *(empoisonnement)* poisoning; **i. alimentaire** food poisoning.

intraduisible *adj* impossible to translate.

intransitif, -ive *adj Grammaire* intransitive.

intrépide *adj* fearless.

intrigue *f* intrigue; *(de film, roman)* plot.

introduction *f* introduction.

introduire* *vt* *(insérer)* to put in (**dans** to); *(faire entrer)* to show in.

introduire (s') *vpr* s'**i. dans** to get into.

introuvable *adj* nowhere to be found.

intrus, -use *mf* intruder.

inusable *adj* durable.

inutile *adj* useless.

inutilement *adv* needlessly.

inutilisable *adj* unusable.

invalide 1 *adj* disabled. **2** *mf* disabled person.

invariable *adj* invariable.

invasion *f* invasion.

inventer *vt* to invent; *(imaginer)* to make up.

inventeur, -trice *mf* inventor.

invention *f* invention.

inverse *adj (sens)* opposite; *(ordre)* reverse.

inverser *vt (ordre)* to reverse.

investir *vti* to invest (**dans** in).

investissement *m* investment.

invisible *adj* invisible.

invitation *f* invitation.

invité, -ée *mf* guest.

inviter *vt* to invite.

inviter (s') *vpr* s'**i. (chez qn)** to (gate)crash (sb's house/*etc*).

involontaire *adj (geste etc)* unintentional.

invraisemblable *adj (extraordinaire)* incredible; *(alibi)* implausible.

ira, irai(t) *voir* aller[1].

irlandais, -aise 1 *adj* Irish. **2** *mf* I. Irishman, Irishwoman; **les I.** the Irish. **3** *m (langue)* Irish.

ironie *f* irony.

ironique *adj* ironic(al).

iront *voir* aller[1].

irréel, -elle *adj* unreal.

irrégulier, -ière *adj* irregular.

irremplaçable *adj* irreplaceable.

irréparable *adj (véhicule etc)* beyond repair.

irréprochable *adj* irreproachable.

irrésistible *adj* irresistible.

irriguer *vt* to irrigate.

irritable *adj* irritable.

irritation *f* irritation.

irriter *vt* to irritate.

irruption *f* **faire i. dans** to burst into.

islamique *adj* Islamic.

isolant *m* insulation (material).

isolé, -ée *adj* isolated (**de** from).

isolement *m (de personne)* isolation.

isoler *vt* to isolate (**de** from); *(du froid etc)* to insulate.

issu, -ue *adj* être i. **de** to come from.

issue *f* exit; **rue/***etc* **sans i.** dead end.

italien, -ienne 1 *adj* Italian. **2** *mf* I. Italian. **3** *m (langue)* Italian.

italique *m* italics.

itinéraire *m* route.

IUT *m abrév (institut universitaire de technologie)* = vocational higher education college.

ivoire *m* ivory.

ivre *adj* drunk.

ivresse *f* drunkenness.

ivrogne *mf* drunk, drunkard.

J

jaillir *vi (liquide)* to spurt (out); *(lumière)* to beam out, to shine (forth).

jalousie *f* jealousy.

jaloux, -ouse *adj* jealous (**de** of).

jamais *adv* never; **elle ne sort j.** she never goes out; **j. de la vie!** (absolutely) never!; **si j.** if ever.

jambe *f* leg.

jambon *m* ham.

janvier *m* January.

japonais, -aise 1 *adj* Japanese. **2** *mf* J. Japanese man, Japanese woman, Japanese *inv*; **les J.** the Japanese. **3** *m (langue)* Japanese.

jardin m garden; **j. public** park.

jardinage m gardening.

jardinier m gardener.

jardinière f (caisse à fleurs) window box.

jaune 1 adj yellow. **2** m yellow; **j. d'œuf** (egg) yolk.

jaunir vti to turn yellow.

jaunisse f jaundice.

Javel (eau de) f bleach.

jazz m jazz.

je pron (**j'** before vowel or mute h) I.

jean m (pair of) jeans.

jeep® f jeep®.

jerrycan m gasoline can; (pour l'eau) water can.

jet m (de vapeur) burst; (de tuyau d'arrosage) nozzle; **j. d'eau** fountain.

jetable adj disposable.

jetée f pier.

jeter vt to throw (**à** to; **dans** into); (à la poubelle) to throw away.

jeter (se) vpr **se j. sur** to pounce on; **le fleuve se jette dans la mer** the river flows into the sea.

jeton m (pièce) token; (de jeu) chip.

jeu, -x m game; (amusement) play; (d'argent) gambling; (série complète) set; (de cartes) deck; **j. de mots** play on words; **jeux de société** parlor ou indoor games; **j. télévisé** (television) quiz show.

jeudi m Thursday.

jeun (à) adv **être à j.** to have eaten no food.

jeune 1 adj young. **2** mf young person; **les jeunes** young people.

jeûner vi to fast.

jeunesse f youth; **la j.** (jeunes) the young.

jockey m jockey.

jogging m jogging; **faire du j.** to jog.

joie f joy.

joindre* vt to join; (envoyer avec) to enclose (**à** with); **j. qn** to get in touch with sb.

joindre (se) vpr **se j. à** (un groupe etc) to join.

joint, -ointe 1 adj **à pieds joints** with feet together; **pièces jointes** (de lettre) enclosures. **2** m joint; (d'étanchéité) seal; (de robinet) washer; **j. de culasse** gasket.

joker m Cartes joker.

joli, -ie adj nice; (femme, enfant) pretty.

jongler vi to juggle (**avec** with).

jongleur, -euse mf juggler.

jonquille f daffodil.

joue f cheek.

jouer 1 vi to play; (acteur) to act; (au tiercé etc) to gamble, to bet; **j. au tennis/aux cartes/etc** to play tennis/cards/etc; **j. du piano/etc** to play the piano/etc. **2** vt to play; (risquer) to bet (**sur** on); (pièce, film) to put on.

jouet m toy.

joueur, -euse mf player; (au tiercé etc) gambler; **bon j.** good loser.

jour m day; (lumière) (day)light; **il fait j.** it's light; **en plein j.** in broad daylight; **de nos jours** nowadays; **du j. au lendemain** overnight; **le j. de l'An** New Year's Day.

journal, -aux m (news)paper; (intime) diary; **j. (télévisé)** television news.

journaliste mf journalist.

journée f day; **toute la j.** all day (long).

joyeux, -euse adj merry, happy; **j. Noël!** merry Christmas!; **j. anniversaire!** happy birthday!

jubiler vi to be jubilant.

judo m judo.

juge m judge.

jugement m judgment; (verdict) sentence; **passer en j.** to stand trial.

juger vt to judge; (au tribunal) to try; (estimer) to consider (**que** that).

juif, juive 1 adj Jewish. **2** mf Jew.

juillet m July.

juin m June.

jumeau, -elle, pl -eaux, -elles mf & adj twin; **frère j.** twin brother;

sœur jumelle twin sister; **lits jumeaux** twin beds.

jumelles *fpl (pour regarder)* binoculars.

jument *f* mare.

jungle *f* jungle.

jupe *f* skirt.

jupon *m* slip, petticoat.

juré, -ée *mf* juror.

jurer 1 *vi (dire un gros mot)* to swear (**contre** at). **2** *vt (promettre)* to swear (**que** that; **de faire** to do).

juron *m* swearword.

jury *m* jury.

jus *m* juice; *(de viande)* gravy.

jusque 1 *prép* **jusqu'à** *(espace)* as far as; *(temps)* until; **jusqu'à cinquante euros** *(limite)* up to fifty euros; **jusqu'en mai** until May; **jusqu'où?** how far?; **jusqu'ici** *(temps)* up till now. **2** *conj* **jusqu'à ce qu'il vienne** until he comes.

juste 1 *adj (équitable)* fair; *(légitime)* just; *(exact)* right; *(étroit)* tight. **2** *adv (deviner etc)* right; *(chanter)* in tune; *(seulement)* just.

justement *adv* exactly.

justesse *f (exactitude)* accuracy; **de j.** *(éviter, gagner)* just.

justice *f* justice; *(autorités)* law.

justifier *vt* to justify.

juteux, -euse *adj* juicy.

K

kangourou *m* kangaroo.

karaoké *m* karaoke.

karaté *m* karate.

képi *m* cap, kepi.

kidnapper *vt* to kidnap.

kilo *m* kilo.

kilogramme *m* kilogram.

kilométrage *m* ≃ mileage.

kilomètre *m* kilometer.

kilo-octet, *pl* **kilo-octets** *m* kilobyte.

kinésithérapeute *mf* physical therapist.

kiosque *m (à journaux)* kiosk.

kit *m* **meuble en k.** (piece of) flat-pack furniture.

klaxon® *m* horn.

klaxonner *vi* to honk.

K.-O. *adj inv* **mettre K.** to knock out.

L

l', la *voir* **le.**

là 1 *adv (lieu)* there; *(chez soi)* in; *(temps)* then; **je reste là** I'll stay here; **c'est là que** that's where; **à cinq mètres de là** 16 feet away; **jusque-là** *(lieu)* as far as that; *(temps)* up till then. **2** *int* **oh là là!** oh my goodness!

là-bas *adv* over there.

laboratoire *m* laboratory.

labourer *vt* to plow.

labyrinthe *m* maze.

lac *m* lake.

lacet *m (shoe-)* lace; *(de route)* twist.

lâche 1 *adj* cowardly. **2** *mf* coward.

lâcher 1 *vt* to let go of; *(bombe)* to drop. **2** *vi (corde)* to give way.

lâcheté *f* cowardice.

là-dedans *adv* in there.

là-dessous *adv* underneath.

là-dessus *adv* on there.

là-haut *adv* up there; *(à l'étage)* upstairs.

laid, laide *adj* ugly.

laideur *f* ugliness.

lainage *m* woolen garment.

laine *f* wool; **en l.** woolen.

laisse *f* lead, leash.

laisser *vt* to leave; **l. qn partir/etc** to let sb go/etc; **l. qch à qn** to let sb have sth.

lait m milk.

laitier adj (produit l.) dairy product.

laitue f lettuce.

lambeau, -x m shred, bit.

lame f (de couteau etc) blade; (vague) wave.

lamentable adj (mauvais) terrible.

lamenter (se) vpr to moan.

lampadaire m floor lamp; (de rue) street lamp.

lampe f lamp; (au néon) light; **l. de poche** flashlight.

lance f spear; (extrémité de tuyau) nozzle; **l. d'incendie** fire hose.

lancement m (de fusée etc) launch(ing).

lancer vt to throw (à to); (avec force) to hurl; (fusée, produit etc) to launch; (appel etc) to issue.

lancer (se) vpr (se précipiter) to rush.

landau, pl -aus m baby carriage.

langage m language.

langouste f (spiny) lobster.

langue f tongue; (langage) language; **l. maternelle** mother tongue; **langues vivantes** modern languages.

lanière f strap.

lanterne f lantern; **lanternes** (de véhicule) parking lights.

lapin m rabbit.

laque f lacquer.

lard m (fumé) bacon; (gras) (pig's) fat.

large 1 adj wide, broad; (vêtement) loose; **l. de six mètres** 20 feet wide. 2 m breadth, width; **avoir six mètres de l.** to be 20 feet wide; **le l.** (mer) the open sea; **au l. de Cherbourg** off Cherbourg.

largement adv (ouvrir) wide; (au moins) easily; **avoir l. le temps** to have plenty of time.

largeur f width, breadth.

larme f tear; **en larmes** in tears.

laser m laser.

lasser vt, **se lasser** vpr to tire (de of).

latéral, -e, -aux adj side.

latin m (langue) Latin.

lavabo m washbasin, sink.

lave-auto, pl **lave-autos** m car wash.

lave-linge m inv washing machine.

laver vt to wash.

laver (se) vpr to wash up; **se l. les mains** to wash one's hands.

laverie f (automatique) laundromat.

lavette f dishcloth.

lave-vaisselle m inv dishwasher.

layette f baby clothes.

le, la, pl les (le and la become l' before a vowel or mute h) **1** art déf (à + le = au, à + les = aux; de + le = du, de + les = des) the. ▪ (généralisation) **la beauté** beauty; **la France** France; **les hommes** men; **aimer le café** to like coffee. ▪ (possession) **il ouvrit la bouche** he opened his mouth; **avoir les cheveux blonds** to have blond hair. ▪ (mesure) **dix dollars la livre** ten dollars a pound. ▪ (temps) **elle vient le lundi** she comes on Monday(s); **l'an prochain** next year; **une fois l'an** once a year. **2** pron (homme) him; (femme) her; (chose, animal) it; pl them; **es-tu fatigué? – je le suis** are you tired?– I am; **je le crois** I think so.

lécher vt to lick.

lécher (se) vpr **se l. les doigts** to lick one's fingers.

leçon f lesson.

lecteur, -trice mf reader; **l. de cassettes/CD/DVD** cassette/CD/DVD player.

lecture f reading; **lectures** (livres) books.

légal, -e, -aux adj legal.

légende f (histoire) legend; (de plan) key; (de photo) caption.

léger, -ère adj (bruit, fièvre etc) slight; (café, thé) weak; (bière, tabac) mild.

légèrement adv (un peu) slightly.

légèreté f lightness.

légitime *adj* être en état de l. défense to act in self-defense.

légume *m* vegetable.

lendemain *m* le l. the next day; **le l. de** the day after; **le l. matin** the next morning.

lent, lente *adj* slow.

lentement *adv* slowly.

lenteur *f* slowness.

lentille *f* (*graine*) lentil; (*verre*) lens.

léopard *m* leopard.

lequel, laquelle, *pl* **lesquels, lesquelles** (+ à = **auquel,** à **laquelle, auxquel(le)s;** + de = **duquel, de laquelle, desquel(le)s**) *pron* (*chose, animal*) which; (*personne*) who, (*indirect*) whom; (*interrogatif*) which (one); **dans l.** in which; **parmi lesquels** (*choses, animaux*) among which; (*personnes*) among whom.

les *voir* **le**.

lessive *f* (laundry) detergent; (*linge*) laundry; **faire la l.** to do the laundry.

lettre *f* letter; **en toutes lettres** (*mot*) in full.

leur 1 *adj poss* their. **2** *pron poss* **le l., la l., les leurs** theirs. **3** *pron inv* (*indirect*) (to) them; **il l. est facile de** it's easy for them to.

levé, -ée *adj* être l. (*debout*) to be up.

lever 1 *vt* to lift (up); **l. les yeux** to look up. **2** *m* **le l. du soleil** sunrise.

lever (se) *vpr* to get up; (*soleil, rideau*) to rise; (*jour*) to break.

levier *m* lever; (*pour soulever*) crowbar.

lèvre *f* lip.

lézard *m* lizard.

liaison *f* (*routière etc*) link; (*entre mots*) liaison.

liasse *f* bundle.

libération *f* freeing, release.

libérer *vt* to (set) free, to release (de from).

libérer (se) *vpr* to free oneself (de from).

liberté *f* freedom; **en l. provisoire** on bail; **mettre en l.** to free.

libraire *mf* bookseller.

librairie *f* bookshop.

libre *adj* free (**de qch** from sth; **de faire** to do); (*voie*) clear.

libre-échange *m* free trade.

librement *adv* freely.

libre-service, *pl* **libres-services** *m* self-service.

licence *f* (*diplôme*) (Bachelor's) degree; (*sportive*) license.

licencié, -ée *adj & mf* graduate; **l. ès lettres/sciences** Bachelor of Arts/Science.

licenciement *m* dismissal.

licencier *vt* (*ouvrier*) to lay off, to dismiss.

liège *m* (*matériau*) cork.

lien *m* (*rapport*) link; (*ficelle*) tie; **l. de parenté** family tie.

lier *vt* (*attacher*) to tie (up); (*relier*) to link (up).

lierre *m* ivy.

lieu, -x *m* place; (*d'un accident*) scene; **les lieux** (*locaux*) the premises; **avoir l.** to take place; **au l. de** instead of.

lièvre *m* hare.

ligne *f* line; (*belle silhouette*) figure; **(se) mettre en l.** to line up; **en l.** (*au téléphone*) connected; **grandes lignes** (*de train*) main line (services); **à la l.** new paragraph; **l. d'arrivée** finish line.

ligoter *vt* to tie up.

lilas *m* lilac.

limace *f* slug.

lime *f* file.

limer *vt* to file.

limitation *f* (*de vitesse, poids*) limit.

limite 1 *f* limit (à to); (*frontière*) boundary. **2** *adj* (*cas*) extreme; (*vitesse etc*) maximum; **date l.** latest date; **date l. de vente** sell-by date.

limiter *vt* to limit (à to).

limoger *vt* to dismiss.

limonade *f* lemon-lime soda.

limpide *adj* (*crystal*) clear.

lin *m* (*tissu*) linen.

linge *m* linen; (*à laver*) laundry.

lingerie f underwear.

lion m lion.

lionne f lioness.

liqueur f liqueur.

liquide 1 adj liquid; **argent l.** ready cash. **2** m liquid; **du l.** (argent) ready cash.

lire* vti to read.

lis m lily.

lis, lisant, lise(nt) etc voir **lire**.

lisible adj (écriture) legible.

lisse adj smooth.

lisser vt to smooth.

liste f list; **sur la l. rouge** (numéro de téléphone) unlisted.

lit¹ m bed; **l. d'enfant** crib; **lits superposés** bunk beds.

lit² voir **lire**.

literie f bedding.

litre m liter.

littéraire adj literary.

littérature f literature.

littoral m coast(line).

livraison f delivery.

livre¹ m book; **l. de poche** paperback (book).

livre² f (monnaie, poids) pound.

livrer vt to deliver (à qn); **l. qn à** (la police etc) to give sb over to.

livret m **l. scolaire** report card; **l. de caisse d'épargne** bankbook, passbook.

livreur, -euse mf delivery man, delivery woman.

local, -ale, -aux adj local.

local, -aux m room; **locaux** premises.

locataire mf tenant.

location f (de maison, voiture) rental; (par propriétaire) renting (out), letting; (loyer) rental.

locomotive f (de train) engine.

locution f phrase.

loge f (de concierge) lodge; (d'acteur) dressing room; (de spectateur) box.

logement m accommodations; (appartement) apartment; (maison) house; **le l.** housing.

loger 1 vt to accommodate; (héberger) to put up. **2** vi (à l'hôtel etc) to put up; (habiter) to live.

logiciel m software inv.

logique adj logical.

logiquement adv logically.

loi f law; (du Parlement) act; **projet de l.** bill.

loin adv far (away ou off); **Boston est l. (de Paris)** Boston is a long way away (from Paris); **plus l.** further, farther; **de l.** from a distance.

lointain, -aine adj distant.

loisirs mpl spare time, leisure (time); (distractions) leisure activities.

long, longue 1 adj long; **être l. (à faire)** to be a long time ou slow (in doing); **l. de deux mètres** seven feet long. **2** m **avoir deux mètres de l.** to be seven feet long; **(tout) le l. de** (espace) (all) along; **de l. en large** (marcher) up and down; **à la longue** in the long run.

longer vt to go along; (forêt, mer) to skirt; (mur) to hug.

longtemps adv (for) a long time; **trop l.** too long.

longuement adv (expliquer) at length; (réfléchir) for a long time.

longueur f length; **à l. de journée** all day long; **l. d'ondes** wavelength.

lors adv **l. de** at the time of.

lorsque conj when.

losange m (forme) diamond.

lot m (de loterie) prize; **gros l.** grand prize, jackpot.

loterie f lottery.

lotion f lotion.

lotissement m (habitations) housing development.

louche f ladle.

loucher vi to squint.

louer vt (prendre en location) to rent; (donner en location) to rent (out), to let; **maison à l.** house to let.

loup m wolf; **avoir une faim de l.** to be ravenous.

loupe f magnifying glass.

lourd, lourde 1 adj heavy;

(temps) close; *(faute)* gross. **2** *adv*
peser l. to be heavy.

loyal, -e, -aux *adj (honnête)* fair
(envers to).

loyauté *f* fairness.

loyer *m* rent.

lu, lue *pp of* lire.

lucarne *f(fenêtre)* skylight.

luceur *f* glimmer.

luge *f* sled, toboggan.

lui 1 *pron mf (complément indirect)*
(to) him; *(femme)* (to) her; *(chose,*
animal) (to) it; **il lui est facile de** it's
easy for him/her to. **2** *pron m (com-*
plément direct) him; *(chose, ani-*
mal) it; *(sujet emphatique)* he.

lui-même *pron* himself; *(chose,*
animal) itself.

luisant, -ante *adj* shiny.

lumière *f* light.

lumineux, -euse *adj (idée, ciel*
etc) bright.

lundi *m* Monday.

lune *f* moon; **l. de miel** honeymoon.

lunettes *fpl* glasses, spectacles;
(de protection, de plongée) goggles;
l. de soleil sunglasses.

lustre *m (éclairage)* chandelier.

lutte *f* fight, struggle; *(sport)* wrestling.

lutter *vi* to fight, to struggle.

luxe *m* luxury; **article de l.** luxury
article.

luxueux, -euse *adj* luxurious.

lycée *m* = high school.

lycéen, -enne *mf* = high school
student.

M

ma *voir* mon.

macaroni(s) *m(pl)* macaroni.

macédoine *f* **m. (de légumes)**
mixed vegetables.

mâcher *vt* to chew.

machin *m Fam (chose)* whatchamacallit.

machinalement *adv* instinctively.

machine *f* machine; **m. à coudre**
sewing machine; **m. à écrire** typewriter; **m. à laver** washing machine.

mâchoire *f* jaw.

maçon *m* bricklayer.

madame, *pl* **mesdames** *f* madam;
bonjour mesdames good morning
(ladies); **Madame** *ou* **Mme Legras**
Mrs Legras; **Madame** *(dans une let-*
tre) Dear Madam.

madeleine *f(small)* sponge cake.

mademoiselle, *pl* **mesdemoisel-**
les *f* miss; **bonjour mesdemoiselles**
good morning (ladies); **Mademoi-**
selle *ou* **Mlle Legras** Miss Legras;
Mademoiselle *(dans une lettre)*
Dear Madam.

magasin *m* store; **grand m.** department store; **en m.** in stock.

magazine *m* magazine.

magicien, -ienne *mf* magician.

magie *f* magic.

magique *adj (baguette etc)* magic;
(mystérieux) magical.

magnétophone *(Fam* magnéto*)*
m tape recorder; **m. à cassettes**
cassette recorder.

magnétoscope *m* VCR, video (recorder).

magnifique *adj* magnificent.

mai *m* May.

maigre *adj (personne)* thin;
(viande) lean.

maigrir *vi* to get thin(ner).

maille *f (de tricot)* stitch; *(de filet)*
mesh.

maillon *m (de chaîne)* link.

maillot *m (de sportif)* jersey, shirt;
m. (de corps) undershirt; **m. (de**
bain) *(de femme)* bathing costume;
(d'homme) bathing trunks.

main *f* hand; **tenir à la m.** to hold in
one's hand; **à la m.** *(faire, coudre*
etc) by hand; **haut les mains!** hands
up!; **donner un coup de m. à qn** to

lend sb a (helping) hand; **sous la m.** handy.

main-d'œuvre, *pl* **mains-d'œuvre** *f* labor.

maintenant *adv* now; **m. que** now that.

maintenir* *vt* (*conserver*) to keep; (*retenir*) to hold.

maire *m* mayor.

mairie *f* city hall.

mais *conj* but; **m. oui, m. si** yes of course; **m. non** definitely not.

maïs *m* (*céréale*) corn.

maison *f* (*bâtiment*) house; (*chez-soi*) home; (*entreprise*) firm; **à la m.** at home; **aller à la m.** to go home; **m. de la culture** arts center; **m. des jeunes** youth center.

maître *m* (*d'un chien etc*) master; **m. d'école** teacher; **m. d'hôtel** (*restaurant*) head waiter; **m. nageur** swimming instructor (and lifeguard).

maîtresse *f* mistress; **m. d'école** teacher.

maîtrise *f* (*diplôme*) Master's degree (**de** in).

maîtriser *vt* (*incendie*) to (bring under) control; **m. qn** to overpower sb.

majesté *f* **Votre M.** (*titre*) Your Majesty.

majeur, -e 1 *adj* **être m.** to be of age. **2** *m* (*doigt*) middle finger.

majorette *f* majorette.

majoritaire *adj* majority; **être m.** to be in the majority.

majorité *f* majority (**de** of); (*âge*) coming of age.

majuscule *f* capital letter.

mal, maux 1 *m* (*douleur*) pain; **dire du m. de qn** to say bad things about sb; **m. de dents** toothache; **m. de gorge** sore throat; **m. de tête** headache; **m. de ventre** stomachache; **avoir le m. de mer** to be seasick; **avoir m. à la tête/gorge/***etc* to have a headache/sore throat/*etc*; **ça (me) fait m.,** **j'ai m.** it hurts (me); **faire du m. à** to hurt; **avoir du m. à**

faire to have trouble doing; **le bien et le m.** good and evil. **2** *adv* (*travailler etc*) badly; (*entendre, comprendre*) not too well; **pas m.!** not bad!; **c'est m. de mentir** it's wrong to lie.

malade 1 *adj* ill, sick; **être m. du cœur** to have a bad heart. **2** *mf* sick person; (*d'un médecin*) patient.

maladie *f* illness.

maladresse *f* clumsiness.

maladroit, -droite *adj* clumsy.

malaise *m* **avoir un m.** to feel dizzy.

malaria *f* malaria.

malbouffe *f* *Fam* junk food.

malchance *f* bad luck.

malchanceux, -euse *adj* unlucky.

mâle *adj & m* male.

malentendant, -ante 1 *adj* hearing-impaired. **2** *mf* person who is hard of hearing.

malentendu *m* misunderstanding.

malfaiteur *m* criminal.

malgré *prép* in spite of; **m. tout** after all.

malheur *m* (*événement, malchance*) misfortune.

malheureusement *adv* unfortunately.

malheureux, -euse 1 *adj* (*triste*) miserable. **2** *mf* (*pauvre*) poor person.

malhonnête *adj* dishonest.

malice *f* mischievousness.

malicieux, -euse *adj* mischievous.

malin, -igne *adj* (*astucieux*) clever.

malle *f* (*coffre*) trunk; (*de véhicule*) trunk.

mallette *f* small suitcase; (*pour documents*) attaché case.

malmener *vt* to manhandle, to treat badly.

malpoli, -ie *adj* rude.

malsain, -saine *adj* unhealthy.

maltraiter *vt* to ill-treat.

malveillant, -ante *adj* malevolent.

maman f mom(my).

mamie f Fam grandma.

mammifère m mammal.

manche¹ f (de vêtement) sleeve; (d'un match) round; **la M.** the English Channel.

manche² m (d'outil) handle; **m. à balai** broomstick; (d'avion etc) joystick.

manchette f (de chemise) cuff.

manchot m (oiseau) penguin.

mandarine f tangerine.

mandat m (postal) money order.

manège m (à la foire) merry-go-round.

manette f lever.

mangeable adj (médiocre) eatable.

mangeoire f (feeding) trough.

manger vti to eat; **donner à m.** to feed.

maniable adj easy to handle.

maniaque 1 adj fussy. **2** mf fuss-budget.

manie f craze.

manier vt to handle.

manière f way; **de toute m.** anyway; **à ma m.** (in) my own way; **la m. dont elle parle** the way (in which) she talks; **faire des manières** (chichis) to make a fuss.

maniéré, -ée adj affected.

manifestant, -ante mf demonstrator.

manifestation f (défilé) demonstration.

manifester 1 vt (sa colère etc) to show. **2** vi (dans la rue) to demonstrate.

manifester (se) vpr (maladie) to show itself.

manipulation f (d'appareils, de produits) handling; **manipulations génétiques** genetic engineering.

manipuler vt (manier) to handle.

mannequin m (personne) (fashion) model; (statue) dummy, mannequin.

manœuvre 1 m (ouvrier) laborer.

2 f (action) maneuver.

manœuvrer vti (véhicule) to maneuver.

manque m lack (de of).

manquer vt (cible, train etc) to miss. **2** vi (faire défaut) to be short; (être absent) to be absent (à from); **m. de** (pain, argent etc) to be short of; (attention) to lack; **ça manque de sel** there isn't enough salt; **elle/cela lui manque** he misses her/that; **elle a manqué (de) tomber** she nearly fell; **il manque/il nous manque dix tasses** there are/we are ten cups short.

mansarde f attic.

manteau, -x m coat.

manuel, -elle 1 adj (travail) manual. **2** m handbook, manual; (scolaire) textbook.

mappemonde f map of the world; (sphère) globe.

maquereau, -x m (poisson) mackerel.

maquette f (scale) model.

maquillage m (fard) make-up.

maquiller vt (visage) to make up.

maquiller (se) vpr to put one's make-up on.

marais m marsh.

marathon m marathon.

marbre m marble.

marchand, -ande mf storekeeper; (de voitures, meubles) dealer; **m. de journaux** (dans un magasin) newspaper vendor; **m. de légumes** grocer.

marchander vi to haggle.

marchandise(s) f(pl) goods.

marche f (d'escalier) step; (trajet) walk; **la m.** (sport) walking; **faire m. arrière** (en voiture) to reverse; **un train en m.** a moving train; **mettre qch en m.** to start sth (up).

marché m (lieu) market; **faire son** ou **le m.** to do one's shopping (in the market); **bon m.** cheap.

marcher vi (à pied) to walk; (poser le pied) to step (**dans** in); (fonction-

ner) to work; **faire m.** *(machine)* to work; **ça marche?** *Fam* how's it going?

mardi *m* Tuesday; **M. gras** Shrove Tuesday, Mardi Gras.

mare *f (étang)* pond.

marécage *m* swamp.

marécageux, -euse *adj* swampy.

marée *f* tide; **m. noire** oil slick.

marelle *f* hopscotch.

margarine *f* margarine.

marge *f (de cahier etc)* margin.

marginal, -e, aux 1 *adj (secondaire)* marginal; *(personne)* on the fringes of society. **2** *mf* dropout.

marguerite *f* daisy.

mari *m* husband.

mariage *m* marriage; *(cérémonie)* wedding.

marié, -ée 1 *adj* married. **2** *m* (bride)groom; **les mariés** the bride and (bride)groom. **3** *f* bride.

marier *vt* **m. qn** *(prêtre etc)* to marry sb.

marier (se) *vpr* to get married (**avec qn** to sb).

marin, -ine 1 *adj* air/*etc* m. sea air/*etc*. **2** *m* sailor.

marine 1 *f* **m. (de guerre)** navy. **2** *m & adj inv (couleur) (bleu)* **m.** navy (blue).

marionnette *f* puppet.

marmelade *f* **m. (de fruits)** stewed fruit.

marmite *f* (cooking) pot.

marmonner *vti* to mutter.

maroquinerie *f (magasin)* leather goods store.

marquant, -ante *adj (remarquable)* outstanding; *(épisode)* significant.

marque *f (trace)* mark; *(de produit)* make, brand; *(points)* score; **m. de fabrique** trademark; **m. déposée** (registered) trademark.

marquer *vt* **1** *(par une marque)* to mark; *(écrire)* to note down; *(but)* to score; **m. les points** to keep (the)

score. **2** *vi (trace)* to leave a mark; *(joueur)* to score.

marqueur *m (crayon)* marker.

marraine *f* godmother.

marrant, -ante *adj Fam* funny.

marre *f* **en avoir m.** *Fam* to be fed up (**de** with).

marron 1 *m* chestnut. **2** *m & adj inv (couleur)* brown.

mars *m* March.

marteau, -x *m* hammer; **m. piqueur** jackhammer.

martien, -ienne *mf & adj* Martian.

martyriser *vt (enfant)* to batter, to abuse.

mascara *m* mascara.

mascotte *f* mascot.

masculin, -ine 1 *adj* male. **2** *adj & m Grammaire* masculine.

masque *m* mask.

massacre *m* slaughter.

massacrer *vt* to slaughter.

massage *m* massage.

masse *f (volume)* mass; **en m.** in large numbers.

masser *vt (frotter)* to massage.

masser (se) *vpr (gens)* to (form a) crowd.

masseur *m* masseur.

masseuse *f* masseuse.

massif, -ive 1 *adj (or, bois etc)* solid. **2** *m (de fleurs)* clump; *(de montagnes)* massif.

mastic *m (pour vitres)* putty.

mastiquer *vt (vitre)* to putty; *(mâcher)* to chew.

mat, mate *adj (papier, couleur)* mat(t).

mât *m (de navire)* mast; *(poteau)* pole.

match *m Sport* match, game.

matelas *m* mattress; **m. pneumatique** air mattress.

matelot *m* sailor.

matériaux *mpl* (building) materials.

matériel, -ielle 1 *adj (dégâts)* material. **2** *m (de camping etc)* equipment; *(d'ordinateur)* hardware *inv.*

maternel, -elle 1 *adj (amour, femme etc)* maternal. **2** *f (école)* **maternelle** kindergarten.

maternité *f (hôpital)* labor ward.

mathématiques *fpl* mathematics.

maths *fpl* math.

matière *f (à l'école)* subject; *(substance)* material; **m. première** raw material.

matin *m* morning; **le m.** *(chaque matin)* in the morning; **à sept heures du m.** at seven in the morning.

matinal, -e, -aux *adj* **être m.** to be an early riser.

matinée *f* morning; **faire la grasse m.** to sleep late.

matraque *f (de policier)* billy club; *(de malfaiteur)* club.

maussade *adj (personne)* bad-tempered, moody; *(temps)* gloomy.

mauvais, -aise *adj* bad; *(méchant)* wicked; *(mal choisi)* wrong; *(mer)* rough; **plus m.** worse; **le plus m.** the worst; **il fait m.** the weather's bad; **m. en** *(anglais etc)* bad at.

mauve *adj & m (couleur)* mauve.

maximal, -e *adj* maximum.

maximum *m* maximum; **le m. de** *(force etc)* the maximum (amount of); **au m.** *(tout au plus)* at most.

mayonnaise *f* mayonnaise.

mazout *m (fuel)* oil.

me (**m'** before vowel or mute *h*) *pron (complément direct)* me; *(indirect)* (to) me; *(réfléchi)* myself.

mécanicien *m* mechanic; *(de train)* engineer.

mécanique *adj* mechanical; **jouet m.** wind-up toy.

mécanisme *m* mechanism.

méchanceté *f* malice; **une m.** *(parole)* a malicious word.

méchant, -ante *adj (cruel)* wicked; *(enfant)* naughty.

mèche *f (de cheveux)* lock; *(de bougie)* wick; *(de pétard)* fuse.

méconnaissable *adj* unrecognizable.

mécontent, -ente *adj* dissatisfied (**de** with).

mécontentement *m* dissatisfaction.

mécontenter *vt* to displease.

médaille *f (décoration)* medal; *(bijou)* medallion; **être m. d'or** to be a gold medalist.

médecin *m* doctor.

médecine *f* medicine; **étudiant en m.** medical student.

médias *mpl* (mass) media.

médical, -e, -aux *adj* medical.

médicament *m* medicine.

médiéval, -e, -aux *adj* medieval.

médiocre *adj* second-rate.

médisance(s) *f(pl)* malicious gossip.

Méditerranée *f* **la M.** the Mediterranean.

méditerranéen, -enne *adj* Mediterranean.

méduse *f* jellyfish.

meeting *m* meeting.

méfiance *f* distrust.

méfiant, -ante *adj* suspicious.

méfier (se) *vpr* **se m. de** to distrust; *(faire attention à)* to watch out for; **méfie-toi!** watch out!; **je me méfie** I'm suspicious.

mégaoctet *m* megabyte.

mégarde (par) *adv* inadvertently.

mégot *m* cigarette butt.

meilleur, -e 1 *adj* better (**que** than); **le m. résultat/etc** the best result/etc. **2** *mf* **le m., la meilleure** the best (one).

mélange *m* mixture.

mélanger *vt*, **se mélanger** *vpr* *(mêler)* to mix.

mêlée *f* fight, scuffle; *Rugby* scrum.

mêler *vt* to mix (**à** with).

mêler (se) *vpr* to mix (**à** with); **se m. à** *(la foule)* to join; **mêle-toi de ce qui te regarde!** mind your own business!

mélodie f melody.

melon m (fruit) melon; (chapeau) m. derby.

membre m (bras, jambe) limb; (d'un groupe) member.

même 1 adj same; **en m. temps** at the same time (**que** as). **2** pron **le m., la m.** the same (one); **les mêmes** the same (ones). **3** adv even; **m. si** even if; **ici m.** in this very place.

mémoire f memory; **à la m. de** in memory of.

mémorable adj memorable.

menaçant, -ante adj threatening.

menace f threat.

menacer vt to threaten (**de faire** to do).

ménage m housekeeping; (couple) couple; **faire le m.** to do the housework.

ménager, -ère adj (appareil) domestic; **travaux ménagers** housework.

ménagère f housewife.

mendiant, -ante mf beggar.

mendier vti to beg (for).

mener 1 vt (personne, vie etc) to lead; (enquête etc) to carry out; **m. qn à** to take sb to. **2** vi (en sport) to lead.

menottes fpl handcuffs.

mensonge m lie.

mensuel, -elle adj monthly.

mensurations fpl measurements.

mental, -e, -aux adj mental.

menteur, -euse mf liar.

menthe f mint.

mention f (à un examen) distinction.

mentir* vi to lie (**à** to).

menton m chin.

menu m menu.

menuiserie f carpentry.

menuisier m carpenter.

mépris m contempt (**pour** for).

méprisant, -ante adj contemptuous.

méprise f mistake.

mépriser vt to despise.

mer f sea; **en m.** at sea; **aller à la m.** to go to the seaside.

mercerie f (magasin) notions store.

merci int & m thank you (**de, pour** for).

mercredi m Wednesday.

merde! int Fam shit!

mère f mother; **m. de famille** mother (of a family).

mérite m merit; (honneur) credit; **avoir du m. à faire qch** to deserve credit for doing sth.

mériter vt (être digne de) to deserve.

merle m blackbird.

merveille f wonder.

merveilleux, -euse adj wonderful.

mes voir mon.

mésaventure f slight mishap.

mesdames voir madame.

mesdemoiselles voir mademoiselle.

mesquin, -ine adj mean, petty.

message m message; **m. vocal** voicemail (message); **messages publicitaires** (e-mails) spam.

messager m messenger.

messagerie f courier company; **m. électronique** e-mail service; **m. instantanée** instant messaging; **m. vocale** voicemail (service).

messe f mass (church service).

messieurs voir monsieur.

mesure f (dimension) measurement; (action) measure, (cadence) time.

mesurer vt to measure; **m. 1 mètre 83** (personne) to be six feet tall; (objet) to measure six feet.

métal, -aux m metal.

métallique adj **échelle/etc m.** metal ladder/etc.

métallurgie f (industrie) steel industry.

météo f (bulletin) weather forecast.

météorologique *adj* **bulletin/** *etc* **m.** weather report/*etc*.

méthode *f (manière, soin)* method.

méthodique *adj* methodical.

métier *m (travail)* job.

mètre *m (mesure)* meter; *(règle)* (meter) stick; **m. carré** square meter; **m. (à ruban)** tape measure.

métrique *adj* metric.

métro *m* subway.

metteur *m* **m. en scène** *(de cinéma)* director.

mettre* *vt* to put; *(table)* to set, to lay; *(vêtement)* to put on; *(chauffage etc)* to put on, to switch on; *(réveil)* to set (à for); **j'ai mis une heure** it took me an hour; **m. en colère** to make angry.

mettre (se) *vpr* to put oneself; *(debout)* to stand; *(assis)* to sit; *(objet)* to go; **se m. en short/***etc* to put on one's shorts/*etc*; **se m. à faire** to start doing; **se m. à table** to sit (down) at the table.

meuble *m* piece of furniture; **meubles** furniture.

meublé *m* furnished apartment.

meubler *vt* to furnish.

meugler *vi (vache)* to moo.

meule *f (de foin)* haystack.

meurtre *m* murder.

meurtrier, -ière *mf* murderer.

mi- *préfixe* **la mi-mars/***etc* mid-March/*etc*.

miauler *vt* to miaow.

miche *f* round loaf.

mi-chemin (à) *adv* halfway.

mi-côte (à) *adv* halfway up *ou* down (the hill).

micro *m* microphone.

microbe *m* germ.

micro-ondes *m inv* microwave; **four à m.** microwave (oven).

micro-ordinateur, *pl* **micro-ordinateurs** *m* microcomputer.

microscope *m* microscope.

midi *m (heure)* twelve o'clock, noon; *(heure du déjeuner)* lunchtime.

mie *f* **la m.** the soft part of the bread; **pain de m.** sandwich loaf.

miel *m* honey.

mien, mienne *pron poss* **le m., la mienne, les miens, les miennes** mine; **les deux miens** my two.

miette *f (de pain)* crumb.

mieux *adv & adj inv* better (**que** than); **le m., la m., les m.** the best; *(de deux)* the better; **tu ferais m. de partir** you had better leave.

mignon, -onne *adj (joli)* cute; *(agréable)* nice.

migraine *f* headache.

mijoter 1 *vt (lentement)* to simmer. **2** *vi* to simmer.

mil *m inv (dans les dates)* **l'an deux m.** the year two thousand.

milieu, -x *m (centre)* middle; **au m. de** in the middle of.

militaire 1 *adj* military. **2** *m* soldier.

mille *adj & m inv* thousand; **m. hommes/***etc* a *ou* one thousand men/*etc*.

mille-pattes *m inv* centipede.

milliard *m* billion.

millième *adj & mf* thousandth.

millier *m* thousand; **un m. (de)** a thousand or so.

millimètre *m* millimeter.

million *m* million; **un m. d'euros/** *etc* a million euros/*etc*; **deux millions** two million.

millionnaire *mf* millionaire.

mime *mf (acteur)* mime.

mimer *vti* to mime.

minable *adj* shabby.

mince *adj* thin; *(élancé)* slim.

mincir *vi* to get thin.

mine¹ *f* appearance; **avoir bonne m.** to look well.

mine² *f (de charbon etc)* mine; *(de crayon)* lead; *(engin explosif)* mine.

miner *vt (terrain)* to mine.

minerai *m* ore.

minéral, -e, -aux *adj & m* mineral.

mineur *m (ouvrier)* miner.

miniature *adj inv (train etc)* miniature.

minimal, -e *adj* minimum.

minimum *m* minimum; **le m. de** *(force etc)* the minimum (amount of); **au (grand) m.** at the very least.

ministère *m* ministry.

ministre *m* minister.

minorité *f* minority.

minou *m (chat)* kitty.

minuit *m* midnight.

minuscule *adj (petit)* tiny.

minute *f* minute.

minuterie *f* timer *(for lighting in a stairway)*.

minuteur *m* timer.

minutieux, -euse *adj* meticulous.

miracle *m* miracle; **par m.** miraculously.

miraculeux, -euse *adj* miraculous.

miroir *m* mirror.

mis, mise *pp of* **mettre**.

mise¹ *f (action)* putting; **m. en marche** starting up; **m. en scène** *(de film)* direction.

mise² *f (argent)* stake.

misérable 1 *adj (très pauvre)* destitute. **2** *mf (personne pauvre)* pauper.

misère *f (grinding)* poverty.

missile *m (fusée)* missile.

mission *f* mission.

mite *f (clothes)* moth.

mi-temps *f (pause) (en sport)* half-time; *(période) (en sport)* half; **à m.** *(travailler)* part-time.

mitigé, -ée *adj (accueil)* lukewarm; *(sentiments, impressions)* mixed.

mitraillette *f* machinegun *(portable)*.

mitrailleuse *f* machinegun.

mi-voix (à) *adv* in a low voice.

mixe(u)r *m (pour mélanger)* (food) mixer.

mixte *adj (école)* co-educational, mixed.

mobile *adj (pièce)* moving; *(personne)* mobile.

mobilier *m* furniture.

mobylette® *f* moped.

moche *adj (laid)* ugly.

mode 1 *f* fashion; **à la m.** fashionable. **2** *m Grammaire* mood; **m. d'emploi** directions (for use).

modèle *m* model; **m. (réduit)** (scale) model.

modération *f* moderation.

modéré, -ée *adj* moderate.

modérer *vt (vitesse, chaleur etc)* to reduce.

moderne *adj* modern.

moderniser *vt,* **se moderniser** *vpr* to modernize.

modeste *adj* modest.

modestie *f* modesty.

modification *f* alteration.

modifier *vt* to alter.

moelle *f (d'os)* marrow; **m. épinière** spinal cord.

moelleux, -euse *adj (lit, tissu)* soft.

mœurs *fpl (morale)* morals; *(habitudes)* customs; **entrer dans les m.** to become part of everyday life.

moi *pron (complément direct)* me; *(indirect)* (to) me; *(sujet emphatique)* I.

moi-même *pron* myself.

moindre *adj* **la m. erreur/etc** the slightest mistake/etc; **le m.** *(de mes problèmes etc)* the least (**de** of).

moine *m* monk.

moineau, -x *m* sparrow.

moins 1 *adv* less (**que** than); **m. de** *(temps, travail)* less (**que** than); *(gens, livres)* fewer (**que** than); *(cent euros)* less than; **m. grand** not as big (**que** as); **de m. en m.** less and less; **le m.** *(travailler)* the least; **le m. grand, la m. grande, les m. grand(e)s** the smallest; **au m., du m.** at least; **de m., en m.** *(qui manque)* missing; **dix ans de m.** ten years less; **en m.** *(personne, objet)* less; *(personnes, objets)* fewer; **à**

m. que (+ *subjonctif*) unless. **2** *prép* (en calcul) minus; **deux heures m. cinq** five to two; **il fait m. dix (degrés)** it's minus ten (degrees).

mois *m* month; **au m. de juin** in (the month of) June.

moisi, -ie 1 *adj* moldy. **2** *m* mold; **sentir le m.** to smell musty.

moisir *vi* to go moldy.

moisson *f* harvest.

moissonner *vt* to harvest.

moite *adj* sticky.

moitié *f* half; **la m. de la pomme** half (of) the apple; **à m. fermé** half closed; **à m. prix** (at) half-price; **de m. by half.**

mol *voir* **mou.**

molaire *f* back tooth.

molette *f* **clé à m.** adjustable wrench.

molle *voir* **mou.**

mollet *m* (de jambe) calf.

moment *m* (instant) moment; (période) time; **en ce m.** at the moment; **par moments** at times; **au m. de partir** when just about to leave; **au m. où** just as; **du m. que** (puisque) seeing that.

momentanément *adv* (temporairement) temporarily; (brièvement) briefly.

mon, ma, *pl* **mes** (ma becomes **mon** before a vowel or mute *h*) adj poss my; **m. père** my father; **ma mère** my mother; **m. ami(e)** my friend.

monde *m* world; **du m.** (beaucoup de gens) a lot of people; **le m. entier** the whole world; **tout le m.** everybody.

mondial, -e, -aux *adj* (crise etc) worldwide; **guerre mondiale** world war.

mondialisation *f* globalization.

moniteur, -trice *mf* instructor; (de colonie de vacances) camp counselor.

monnaie *f* (devise) currency; (pièces) change; **faire de la m.** to get

change; **faire de la m. à qn** to give sb change (**sur un billet** for a bill).

monopoliser *vt* to monopolize.

monotone *adj* monotonous.

monotonie *f* monotony.

monsieur, *pl* **messieurs** *m* (homme) man, gentleman; **oui m.** yes sir; **oui messieurs** yes gentlemen; **M. Legras** Mr Legras; **Monsieur** (dans une lettre) Dear Sir.

monstre *m* monster.

monstrueux, -euse *adj* (abominable) hideous.

mont *m* (montagne) mount.

montage *m* (d'un appareil) assembling; (d'un film) editing; (image truquée) montage.

montagnard, -arde *mf* mountain dweller.

montagne *f* mountain; **la m.** (zone) the mountains.

montagneux, -euse *adj* mountainous.

montant *m* (somme) amount; (de barrière) post.

montée *f* (ascension) climb; (chemin) slope.

monter 1 *vi* (aux être) (personne) to go ou come up; (s'élever) (ballon, prix etc) to go up; (grimper) to climb (up) (**sur** onto); (marée) to come in; **m. dans un véhicule** to get in(to) a vehicle; **m. dans un train** to get on(-to) a train; **m. sur** ou **à (échelle)** to climb up; **m. en courant/etc** to run/ etc up; **m. (à cheval)** to ride (a horse). **2** *vt* (aux **avoir**) (côte) to climb (up); (objet) to bring ou take up; (cheval) to ride; (tente) to set up; **m. l'escalier** to go ou come up the stairs.

montre *f* watch.

montrer *vt* to show (**à** to); **m. du doigt** to point to.

montrer (se) *vpr* to show oneself.

monture *f* (de lunettes) frame.

monument *m* monument; **m. aux morts** war memorial.

moquer (se) *vpr* **se m. de** to make

fun of; **je m'en moque!** I couldn't care less!

moquette f wall-to-wall carpeting.

moqueur, -euse adj mocking.

moral m spirits, morale.

morale f (d'histoire) moral.

morceau, -x m piece; (de sucre) lump.

morceler vt (terrain) to divide up.

mordiller vt to nibble.

mordre vt to bite.

morne adj (temps) dismal; (silence) gloomy; (personne) glum.

morse m (animal) walrus.

morsure f bite.

mort f death.

mort, morte (pp of mourir) **1** adj (personne, plante etc) dead. **2** mf dead man, dead woman; **les morts** the dead; **de nombreux morts** (victimes) many casualties ou dead.

mortel, -elle adj (hommes, ennemi etc) mortal; (accident) fatal.

morue f cod.

mosquée f mosque.

mot m word; **envoyer un m. à** to drop a line to; **mots croisés** crossword (puzzle); **m. de passe** password.

motard m motorcyclist.

moteur (de véhicule etc) engine, motor.

motif m (raison) reason (**de** for).

motivé, -ée adj motivated.

motiver vt (inciter, causer) to motivate; (justifier) to justify.

moto f motorcycle.

motocycliste mf motorcyclist.

motte f (de terre) lump.

mou (or **mol** before vowel or mute h), **molle** adj soft; (sans énergie) feeble.

mouche f (insecte) fly.

moucher (se) vpr to blow one's nose.

moucheron m midge.

mouchoir m handkerchief; (en papier) tissue.

moudre* vt (café) to grind.

moue f long face; **faire la m.** to pull a (long) face.

mouette f (sea)gull.

moufle f mitten.

mouillé, -ée adj wet (**de** with).

mouiller vt to (make) wet; **se faire m.** to get wet.

mouiller (se) vpr to get (oneself) wet.

moulant, -ante adj (vêtement) tight-fitting.

moule¹ m mold; **m. à gâteaux** cake pan.

moule² f (animal) mussel.

mouler vt to mold; **m. qn** (vêtement) to fit sb tightly.

moulin m mill; **m. à vent** windmill; **m. à café** coffee grinder.

moulu (pp of moudre) adj (café) ground.

mourir* vi (aux être) to die (**de** of, from); **m. de froid** to die of exposure; **je meurs de faim!** I'm starving!

mousse f (plante) moss; (écume) foam; (de bière) froth; (de savon) lather; (dessert) mousse.

mousser vi (bière) to froth; (savon) to lather; (eau) to foam.

mousseux 1 adj (vin) sparkling. **2** m sparkling wine.

moustache f mustache; **moustaches** (de chat) whiskers.

moustachu, -ue adj **être m.** to have a mustache.

moustique m mosquito.

moutarde f mustard.

mouton m sheep inv; (viande) mutton.

mouvement m (geste, groupe etc) movement; (de colère) outburst.

mouvementé, -ée adj (vie, voyage etc) eventful.

moyen, -enne adj average; (format etc) medium(-sized); **classe moyenne** middle class. **2** f average; (dans un examen, un devoir) passing grade; **en moyenne** on average.

moyen m (procédé, façon) means, way (**de faire** of doing, to do); **il n'y a pas m. de faire** it's not possible to do; **je n'ai pas les moyens** (argent) I can't afford it.

MP3 f abrév (MPEG1 Audio Layer) **lecteur M.** MP3 player.

muer vi (animal) to molt; (voix) to break.

muet, -ette 1 adj (infirme) mute; (film, voyelle) silent. **2** mf mute person.

mufle m (d'animal) muzzle.

mugir vi (bœuf) to bellow.

mugissement(s) m(pl) bellow(-ing).

muguet m lily of the valley.

mule f (pantoufle) mule; (animal) (she-)mule.

multicolore adj multicolored.

multiculturel, -elle adj multicultural.

multiple m (nombre) multiple.

multiplexe m multiplex.

multiplication f multiplication.

multiplier vt to multiply.

municipal, -e, -aux adj municipal; **conseil m.** city council.

municipalité f (maires et conseillers) city council; (commune) municipality.

munir vt m. de to equip with.

munir (se) vpr se m. de to provide oneself with.

munitions fpl ammunition.

mur m wall; **m. du son** sound barrier.

mûr, mûre adj (fruit) ripe.

muraille f (high) wall.

mûre f (baie) blackberry.

mûrir vti (fruit) to ripen.

murmure m murmur.

murmurer vti to murmur.

muscle m muscle.

musclé, -ée adj (bras) muscular.

museau, -x m (de chien, chat) nose, muzzle.

musée m museum.

museler vt (animal, presse) to muzzle.

muselière f (appareil) muzzle.

musical, -e, -aux adj musical.

musicien, -ienne mf musician.

musique f music.

musulman, -ane adj & mf Muslim.

muter vt to transfer.

mutuel, -elle adj (réciproque) mutual.

myope adj & mf shortsighted (person).

myrtille f (baie) bilberry.

mystère m mystery.

mystérieux, -euse adj mysterious.

N

nage f (swimming) stroke; **traverser à la n.** to swim across; **en n.** sweating.

nageoire f (de poisson) fin.

nager 1 vi to swim. **2** vt (crawl etc) to swim.

nageur, -euse mf swimmer.

naïf, -ïve adj naïve.

nain, naine mf dwarf.

naissance f (de personne, animal) birth.

naître* vi to be born.

nappe f (sur une table) table cloth; **n. de pétrole** oil slick.

napperon m (pour vase etc) (cloth) mat, doily.

narguer vt to taunt.

narine f nostril.

naseau, -x m (de cheval) nostril.

natal, -e, -als adj (pays) native; **sa maison natale** the house where he/she was born.

natation f swimming.

nation f nation.

national, -e, -aux adj national; **(route) nationale** highway.

nationalité f nationality.

natte f (de cheveux) braid; (tapis) mat.

nature 1 f (monde naturel, caractère) nature. **2** adj inv (omelette, yaourt etc) plain; (café) black.

naturel, -elle adj natural.

naufrage m shipwreck; **faire n.** to be shipwrecked.

naufragé, -ée adj & mf shipwrecked (person).

nausée f nausea, sickness; **avoir la n.** to feel nauseous.

nautique adj **ski/etc n.** water skiing/etc.

naval, -e, -als adj naval.

navet m (plante) turnip.

navette f **faire la n.** to shuttle back and forth (**entre** between); **n. spatiale** space shuttle.

navigateur, -trice mf (marin) navigator.

navigation f (trafic de bateaux) shipping.

naviguer vi (bateau) to sail; (sur Internet) to surf.

navire m ship.

navrant, -ante adj appalling.

navré, -ée adj **je suis n.** I'm (terribly) sorry (**de faire** to do).

ne (n' before vowel or mute h; used to form negative verb with **pas, jamais, personne, rien, que** etc) adv (+ pas) not; **il ne boit pas** he doesn't drink.

né, -ée adj (pp of **naître**) born; **elle est née** she was born.

néanmoins adv nevertheless.

nécessaire 1 adj necessary. **2** m **n. de toilette** (d'homme) shaving kit; (de femme) cosmetic case; **faire le n.** to do what's necessary.

nécessité f necessity.

nécessiter vt to require.

nectarine f nectarine.

néerlandais, -aise 1 adj Dutch. **2** mf N. Dutchman, Dutchwoman; **les N.** the Dutch. **3** m (langue) Dutch.

néfaste adj harmful (**à** to).

négatif, -ive 1 adj negative. **2** m (de photo) negative.

négation f Grammaire negation; (mot) negative.

négligence f (défaut) carelessness.

négligent, -ente adj careless.

négliger vt (personne, travail etc) to neglect; **n. de faire** to neglect to do.

négociant, -ante mf merchant, dealer.

négociation f negotiation.

négocier vti to negotiate.

neige f snow; **n. fondue** sleet.

neiger vi to snow.

nénuphar m water lily.

néon m éclairage au **n.** neon lighting.

nerf m nerve; **du n.!** buck up!; **ça me tape sur les nerfs** it gets on my nerves.

nerveux, -euse adj (agité) nervous.

nescafé® m instant coffee.

n'est-ce pas? adv isn't he?/don't you?/etc; **tu l'as, n?** you've got it, haven't you?; **elle vient, n.?** she's coming, isn't she?

net, nette 1 adj (image, refus) clear; (coupure, linge) clean; (soigné) neat; (poids, prix) net. **2** adv (s'arrêter) dead; (casser, couper) clean.

nettement adv (bien plus) definitely.

nettoyage m cleaning; **n. à sec** dry cleaning.

nettoyer vt to clean (up).

neuf, neuve 1 adj new; **quoi de n.?** what's new? **2** m **remettre à n.** to make as good as new.

neuf adj & m nine.

neutre adj (pays) neutral.

neuvième adj & mf ninth.

neveu, -x m nephew.

nez m nose; **n. à n.** face to face (**avec** with).

ni conj **ni...ni** (+ ne) neither...nor; **il**

n'a ni faim ni soif he's neither hungry nor thirsty; **sans manger ni boire** without eating or drinking; **ni l'un(e) ni l'autre** neither (of them).

niche f (de chien) doghouse.

nicher vi, **se nicher** vpr (oiseau) to nest.

nid m nest.

nièce f niece.

nier vt to deny (**que** that).

niveau, -x m level; **au n. de qn** (élève etc) up to sb's standard.

noble 1 adj noble. **2** mf nobleman, noblewoman.

noce(s) f(pl) wedding.

nocif, -ive adj harmful.

Noël m Christmas; **le père N.** Santa Claus.

nœud m knot; (ruban) bow; **n. coulant** slipknot, noose; **n. papillon** bow tie.

noir, noire 1 adj black; (nuit, lunettes etc) dark; **il fait n.** it's dark. **2** m (couleur) black; (obscurité) dark; **N.** (homme) black. **3** f **Noire** (femme) black.

noircir 1 vt to make black. **2** vi, **se noircir** vpr to turn black.

noisetier m hazel (tree).

noisette f hazelnut.

noix f (du noyer) walnut; **n. de coco** coconut.

nom m name; Grammaire noun; **n. de famille** last name, surname; **n. propre** Grammaire proper noun.

nombre m number.

nombreux, -euse adj (amis, livres) numerous, many; (famille) large; **peu n.** few; **venir n.** to come in large numbers.

nombril m navel.

nommer vt (appeler) to name; **n. qn** (désigner) to appoint sb (**à un poste** to a post).

nommer (se) vpr to be called.

non adv & m inv no; **tu viens ou n.?** are you coming or not?; **n. seulement** not only; **je crois que n.** I don't

think so; **(ni) moi n. plus** neither do/am/can/etc I.

nonante adj & m (en Belgique, en Suisse) ninety.

non-fumeur, -euse mf nonsmoker.

non-voyants mpl **les n.** the unsighted.

nord m north; **au n. de** north of; **du n.** (vent) northerly; (ville) northern.

nord-africain, -aine 1 adj North African. **2** mf **N.-A.** North African.

nord-américain, -aine 1 adj North American. **2** mf **N.-A.** North American.

nord-est m & adj inv northeast.

nord-ouest m & adj inv northwest.

normal, -e, -aux adj normal.

normale f **au-dessus/au-dessous de la n.** above/below normal.

normalement adv normally.

norvégien, -ienne 1 adj Norwegian. **2** mf **N.** Norwegian. **3** m (langue) Norwegian.

nos voir **notre**.

notaire m lawyer.

notamment adv particularly.

note f (de musique, remarque) note; (à l'école) grade; (facture) bill; **prendre n. de** to make a note of.

noter vt to note; (un devoir) to grade.

notice f (mode d'emploi) instructions.

notoriété f (renom) fame; **il est de n. publique que…** it's common knowledge that…

notre, pl nos adj poss our.

nôtre pron poss **le** ou **la n., les nôtres** ours.

nouer vt (chaussure etc) to tie.

nouilles fpl noodles.

nounours m teddy bear.

nourrice f (assistante maternelle) nanny.

nourrir vt to feed.

nourrissant, -ante adj nourishing.

nourrisson m infant.

nourriture f food.

nous pron (sujet) we; (complément direct) us; (indirect) (to) us; (réfléchi) ourselves; (réciproque) each other.

nous-mêmes pron ourselves.

nouveau (or **nouvel** before vowel or mute h), **nouvelle**, pl **nouveaux, nouvelles 1** adj new. **2** mf (dans une classe) new boy, new girl. **3** m de n., à n. again.

nouveau-né, -née mf new-born baby.

nouveauté f novelty; nouveautés (livres) new books; (disques) new releases.

nouvelle f (information) nouvelle(s) news; une n. a piece of news.

novembre m November.

noyade f drowning.

noyau, -x f (fruit) pit.

noyé, -ée mf drowned person.

noyer[1] vt, se noyer vpr to drown.

noyer[2] m (arbre) walnut tree.

nu, nue adj (personne) naked; (mains) bare; **tout nu** (stark) naked; **tête nue, nu-tête** bareheaded.

nuage m cloud.

nuageux, -euse adj cloudy.

nuance f (de couleurs) shade.

nucléaire adj nuclear.

nuire vi n. à qn to harm sb.

nuisible adj harmful.

nuit f night; (obscurité) dark(ness); **il fait n.** it's dark; **la n.** (se promener etc) at night; **cette n.** (aujourd'hui) tonight; (hier) last night; **bonne n.** (au coucher) good night.

nul, nulle adj (médiocre) hopeless; **faire match n.** to tie; **nulle part** nowhere.

numérique adj numerical; (montre, clavier, données) digital.

numéro m number; (de journal) issue; (au cirque) act; **un n. de danse** a dance number; **n. vert** (au téléphone) = tollfree number.

numéroter vt (page etc) to number.

nuque f back of the neck.

nylon® m nylon; **chemise/etc en n.** nylon shirt/etc.

O

obéir vi to obey; **o. à qn** to obey sb.

obéissance f obedience.

obéissant, -ante adj obedient.

objectif m (but) objective; (d'appareil photo) lens.

objet m (chose) object; **objets trouvés** (bureau) lost and found.

obligation f obligation.

obligatoire adj compulsory.

obliger vt to force, to compel (à faire to do); **être obligé de faire** to have to do.

oblique adj oblique.

obscène adj obscene.

obscur, -e adj (noir) dark.

obscurcir vt (pièce) to make dark(er).

obscurcir (s') vpr (ciel) to get dark(er).

obscurité f dark(ness).

obséder vt to obsess.

obsèques fpl funeral.

observation f (étude) observation; (reproche) (critical) remark.

observatoire m (endroit élevé) lookout (post).

observer vt (regarder) to watch; (remarquer, respecter) to observe.

obstacle m obstacle.

obstiné, -ée adj stubborn, obstinate.

obstiner (s') vpr s'o. à faire to persist in doing.

obstruer vt to obstruct.

obtenir* vt to get, to obtain.

obus m (arme) shell.

occasion f chance (**de faire** to do); (prix avantageux) bargain; **d'o.** second-hand, used.

occasionner vt to cause.

Occident m l'O. the West.

occidental, -e, -aux adj western.

occupation f (activité etc) occupation.

occupé, -ée adj busy (**à faire** doing); (place, maison etc) occupied; (téléphone) busy; (taxi) hired.

occuper vt (maison, pays etc) to occupy; (place, temps) to take up; **o. qn** (travail, jeu) to keep sb busy.

occuper (s') vpr to keep (oneself) busy (**à faire** doing); **s'o. de** (affaire, problème) to deal with; **s'o. de qn** (malade etc) to take care of sb; **occupe-toi de tes affaires!** mind your own business!

océan m ocean.

octet m byte; **milliard d'octets** gigabyte.

octobre m October.

oculiste mf eye specialist.

odeur f smell.

odieux, -euse adj horrible.

odorat m sense of smell.

œil, pl **yeux** m eye; **lever/baisser les yeux** to look up/down; **coup d'o.** look, glance; **jeter un coup d'o. sur** to (have a) look at; **o. poché, o. au beurre noir** black eye.

œillet m (fleur) carnation.

œuf, pl **œufs** m egg; **o. sur le plat** fried egg.

œuvre f (travail, livre etc) work.

offenser vt to offend.

office m (messe) service.

officiel, -ielle adj official.

officier m (dans l'armée etc) officer.

offre f offer; **l'o. et la demande** supply and demand; **offres d'emploi** job vacancies, positions vacant.

offrir* vt to offer (**de faire** to do); (cadeau) to give.

offrir (s') vpr **s'o. qch** to treat oneself to sth.

oh! int oh!

oie f goose (pl geese).

oignon m (légume) onion; (de fleur) bulb.

oiseau, -x m bird.

oisif, -ive adj (inactif) idle.

oisiveté f idleness.

olive f olive; **huile d'o.** olive oil.

olivier m olive tree.

olympique adj (jeux) Olympic.

ombragé, -ée adj shady.

ombre f (d'arbre etc) shade; (de personne, objet) shadow; **à l'o.** in the shade.

omelette f omelet(te); **o. au fromage**/etc cheese/etc omelet(te).

omettre* vt to omit (**de faire** to do).

omnibus adj & m (train) **o.** slow ou local train.

omoplate f shoulder blade.

on pron (les gens) they, people; (nous) we; (vous) you; **on frappe** someone's knocking; **on m'a dit que** I was told that.

oncle m uncle.

onde (de radio) wave; **grandes ondes** long wave; **ondes courtes** short wave.

ondulation f (de cheveux) wave.

onduler vi (cheveux) to be wavy.

ongle m (finger) nail.

ont voir **avoir**.

ONU f abrév (Organisation des Nations Unies) UN.

onze adj & m eleven.

onzième adj & mf eleventh.

opaque adj opaque.

opéra m (musique) opera; (édifice) opera house.

opération f operation.

opérer vt (en chirurgie) to operate on (**de** for); **se faire o.** to have an operation.

opinion f opinion (**sur** about, on).

opportun, -une adj opportune, timely.

EXPRIMER SON OPINION

Qu'est-ce que tu en penses/vous en pensez ?
What do you think?

Ça me plaît beaucoup/Ça m'a beaucoup plu.
I really like it/liked it.

C'était génial/beau !
It was great/beautiful!

Ce n'était pas mal.
It was OK.

La visite du château était assez intéressant.
The tour of the castle was quite interesting.

J'adore les croissants/faire de la randonné.
I love croissants/hiking.

Je déteste la neige/faire les magasins.
I hate snow/shopping.

Je préférerais du café.
I'd rather have coffee.

Tu préfères/Vous préférez lequel/laquelle ?
Which do you prefer?

Je la trouve très sympa.
I think she's very nice.

Je suis d'accord (avec toi/vous).
I agree (with you).

Absolument !
Absolutely!

Je suis sûr(e) qu'il fera beau demain.
I'm sure it'll be nice tomorrow.

C'est vrai.
That's true.

J'ai changé d'avis.
I've changed my mind.

Je ne sais pas.
I don't know.

Ah bon ?/C'est vrai ?
Really?

Quelle surprise !
What a surprise!

Le musée d'art t'a/vous a plu ?
Did you like the art gallery?

Ça ne me plaît pas/Ça ne m'a pas plu.
I don't like it/didn't like it.

C'était un peu ennuyeux/trop touristique.
It was a bit boring/too touristy.

La nourriture n'a rien d'exceptionnel.
The food's nothing special.

On s'est éclatés !
We had a great time!

Je n'aime pas le jazz/faire du vélo.
I don't like jazz/cycling.

C'est délicieux/dégoûtant !
This is delicious/disgusting!

Je préfère les petits hôtels aux grands.
I prefer small hotels to big ones.

Je préfère le (la) plus grand(e)/le (la) plus petit(e).
I prefer the bigger/smaller one.

Je crois que c'est/Je ne crois pas que ce soit possible.
I think/I don't think it's possible.

Je ne suis pas d'accord (avec toi/vous).
I disagree (with you).

Bien sur (que non) !
Of course (not)!

Tu en es sûr(e)/Vous en êtes sûr(e) ?
Are you sure?

Je ne te/vous crois pas.
I don't believe you.

Je ne suis pas sûr(e).
I'm not sure.

Ça dépend.
It depends.

C'est étrange/bizarre !
That's strange!

Quel dommage !
What a pity!

opposé, -ée 1 adj (direction, opinion etc) opposite; (équipe) opposing; **o. à** opposed to. **2 m l'o.** the opposite (**de** of); **à l'o.** (côté) on the opposite side (**de** from, to).

opposer vt (résistance) to put up (**à** against); (équipes) to bring together; **o. qn à qn** to set sb against sb.

opposer (s') vpr (équipes) to play against each other; **s'o. à** (mesure, personne) to be opposed to, to oppose.

opposition f opposition (**à** to).

oppressant, -ante adj oppressive.

opticien, -ienne mf optician.

optimiste adj optimistic.

optique 1 adj (nerf) optic; (verre, fibres) optical. **2** f optics; **d'o.** (instrument) optical. ▪ (point de vue) perspective.

or 1 m gold; **montre/etc en or** gold watch/etc; **d'or** (règle) golden; **mine d'or** goldmine. **2** conj (cependant) now, well.

orage m (thunder)storm.

orageux, -euse adj stormy.

oral, -e, -aux 1 adj oral. **2** m (examen) oral.

orange 1 f (fruit) orange. **2** adj & m inv (couleur) orange.

orangeade f orangeade.

orbite f (d'astre) orbit; (d'œil) socket.

orchestre m (classique) orchestra; (jazz, pop) band; (places) orchestra.

ordinaire adj (habituel, normal) ordinary, regular; (médiocre) ordinary; **d'o.** usually.

ordinateur m computer.

ordonnance f (de médecin) prescription.

ordonné, -ée adj tidy.

ordonner vt to order (**que** (+ subjonctif) that); (médicament etc) to prescribe; **o. à qn de faire** to order sb to do.

ordre m (commandement, classe-

ment) order; (absence de désordre) tidiness (of room, person etc); **en o.** (chambre etc) tidy; **mettre en o., mettre de l'o. dans** to tidy (up); **jusqu'à nouvel o.** until further notice.

ordures fpl (débris) garbage.

oreille f ear; **faire la sourde o.** to take no notice, to refuse to listen.

oreiller m pillow.

oreillons mpl mumps.

organe m (de corps) organ.

organisateur, -trice mf organizer.

organisation f organization.

organiser vt to organize.

organiser (s') vpr to get organized.

organisme m (corps) body; (bureaux etc) organization.

orge f barley.

orgue 1 m (instrument) organ. **2** fpl **grandes orgues** great organ.

orgueil m pride.

orgueilleux, -euse adj proud.

oriental, -e, -aux adj (côte, pays etc) eastern; (du Japon, de la Chine) far-eastern, oriental.

orientation f direction; (de maison) orientation; **o. professionnelle** career counseling.

orienté, -ée adj (appartement etc) **o. à l'ouest** facing west.

orienter vt (lampe etc) to position; (voyageur, élève) to direct.

orienter (s') vpr to find one's bearings ou direction.

originaire adj **être o. de** (natif) to be a native of.

original, -e, -aux 1 adj (idée, artiste etc) original. **2** m (texte) original.

originalité f originality.

origine f origin; **à l'o.** originally; **d'o.** (pneu etc) original; **pays d'o.** country of origin.

ornement m ornament.

orner vt to decorate (**de** with).

orphelin, -ine mf orphan.

orphelinat *m* orphanage.
orteil *m* toe; **gros o.** big toe.
orthographe *f* spelling.
ortie *f* nettle.
os *m* bone; **trempé jusqu'aux os** soaked to the skin.
osé, -ée *adj* daring.
oser *vti* to dare; **o. faire** to dare (to) do.
osier *m* wicker; **panier d'o.** wicker basket.
otage *m* hostage; **prendre qn en o.** to take sb hostage.
OTAN *f abrév (Organisation du traité de l'Atlantique Nord)* NATO.
otarie *f (animal)* sea lion.
ôter *vt* to take away (**à qn** from sb); *(vêtement)* to take off; *(déduire)* to take away.
otite *f* ear infection.
ou *conj* or; **ou bien** or else; **ou elle ou moi** either her or me.
où *adv & pron* where; **le jour où** the day when; **la table où** the table on which; **par où?** which way?; **d'où?** where from?; **le pays d'où** the country from which.
oubli *m* **l'o. de qch** forgetting sth; **un o.** *(dans une liste etc)* an oversight.
oublier *vt* to forget (**de faire** to do).
ouest *m & adj inv* west; **d'o.** *(vent)* west(erly); **de l'o.** western.
ouf! *int (whew,)* what a relief!
oui *adv & m inv* yes; **tu viens, o. ou non?** are you coming or aren't you?; **je crois que o.** I think so.
ouïe *f* hearing.
ouïes *fpl (de poisson)* gills.
ouille! *int* ouch!
ouragan *m* hurricane.
ourlet *m* hem.
ours *m* bear; **o. blanc** polar bear.
outil *m* tool.
outillage *m* tools.
outre 1 *prép* besides. **2** *adv* **en o.** besides.
outre-mer *adv* overseas; **d'o.**

(marché) overseas; **territoires d'o.** overseas territories.
outré, -ée *adj (révolté)* outraged.
ouvert, -erte *(pp de ouvrir) adj* open; *(robinet, gaz)* on.
ouvertement *adv* openly.
ouverture *f* opening; *(trou)* hole.
ouvrage *m (travail, livre)* work; *(couture)* (needle)work; **un o.** *(travail)* a piece of work.
ouvre-boîtes *m inv* can opener.
ouvre-bouteilles *m inv* bottle opener.
ouvreuse *f* usherette.
ouvrier, -ière 1 *mf* worker; **o. qualifié/spécialisé** skilled/unskilled worker. **2** *adj (quartier)* working-class; **classe ouvrière** working class.
ouvrir* 1 *vt* to open (up); *(gaz, radio etc)* to turn on, to switch on. **2** *vi* to open; *(ouvrir la porte)* to open (up).
ouvrir (s') *vpr (porte, boîte etc)* to open (up).
ovale *adj & m* oval.
OVNI *m abrév (objet volant non identifié)* UFO.
oxygène *m* oxygen.

P

pacifique 1 *adj (manifestation etc)* peaceful; *(côte etc)* Pacific. **2** *m* **le P.** the Pacific.
pagaie *f* paddle.
pagaille *f (désordre)* mess; **en p.** in a mess.
pagayer *vi* to paddle.
page *f (de livre etc)* page; **p. web** web page.
paie *f* pay, wages.
paiement *m* payment.
paillasson *m* (door)mat.
paille *f* straw; *(pour boire)* (drink-

ing) straw; **tirer à la courte p.** to draw lots *ou* straws.

paillette *f (d'habit)* sequin; **paillettes** *(de savon)* flakes.

pain *m* bread; **un p.** a loaf (of bread); **p. grillé** toast; **p. complet** whole-wheat bread; **p. d'épice** gingerbread; **p. de seigle** rye bread; **petit p.** roll.

pair, -e *adj (numéro)* even.

paire *f* pair (**de** of).

paisible *adj (vie, endroit)* peaceful.

paître* *vi* to graze.

paix *f* peace; *(traité)* peace treaty; **en p.** in peace; **avoir la p.** to have (some) peace and quiet.

palais¹ *m (château)* palace; **P. de justice** courthouse; **p. des sports** sports stadium.

palais² *m (dans la bouche)* palate.

pâle *adj* pale.

paletot *m (knitted)* cardigan.

palette *f (de peintre)* palette.

pâleur *f* paleness.

palier *m (d'escalier)* landing; **être voisins de p.** to live on the same floor.

pâlir *vi* to turn pale (**de** with).

palissade *f* fence (*of stakes*).

palmarès *m* prize list; *(de chansons)* charts.

palme *f* palm (leaf); *(de nageur)* flipper.

palmier *m* palm (tree).

palper *vt* to feel.

palpitant, -ante *adj* thrilling.

palpiter *vi (cœur)* to throb.

pamplemousse *m* grapefruit.

pan! *int* bang!

panaché *adj & m (demi) p.** shandy *(beer and lemonade)*.

pancarte *f* sign; *(de manifestant)* placard.

pané, -ée *adj* breaded.

panier *m* basket; **p. à salade** *(ustensile)* salad basket.

panique *f* panic.

paniqué, -ée *adj* panic-stricken.

paniquer *vi* to panic.

panne *f* breakdown; **tomber en p.** to break down; **être en p.** to have broken down; **p. d'électricité** blackout, power outage.

panneau, -x *m (écriteau)* sign; *(de porte etc)* panel; **p. (de signalisation)** road sign; **p. (d'affichage)** billboard.

panoplie *f (jouet)* outfit.

panorama *m* view.

pansement *m* dressing, bandage; **p. adhésif** Band-Aid®.

panser *vt (main etc)* to dress, to bandage.

pantalon *m* (pair of) pants; **en p.** in pants.

pantin *m* puppet, jumping jack.

pantoufle *f* slipper.

paon *m* peacock.

papa *m* dad(dy).

pape *m* pope.

papeterie *f (magasin)* stationery store.

papi *m Fam* grand(d)ad.

papier *m (matière)* paper; **un p.** *(feuille)* a sheet of paper; *(formulaire)* a form; **sac/etc** paper bag/*etc*; **papiers (d'identité)** (identity) papers; **p. hygiénique** toilet paper; **p. à lettres** writing paper; **du p. journal** (some) newspaper; **p. peint** wallpaper; **p. de verre** sandpaper.

papillon *m* butterfly; **p. (de nuit)** moth.

paquebot *m* (ocean) liner.

pâquerette *f* daisy.

Pâques *m sing & fpl* Easter.

paquet *m (de bonbons etc)* packet; *(colis)* package; *(de cigarettes)* pack; *(de cartes)* pack, deck.

par *prép (agent, manière, moyen)* by; **choisi p.** chosen by; **p. le train** by train; **p. le travail** by *ou* through work; **apprendre p. un ami** to learn from *ou* through a friend; **commencer p. qch** to begin with sth. ▪ *(lieu)* through; **p. la porte** through *ou* by the door; **jeter p. la fenêtre** to throw out (of) the window; **p. ici/là** *(aller)* this/that way; *(habiter)* around here/there. ▪ *(motif)* out of, from; **p. pitié** out of *ou* from pity. ▪ *(temps)* on; **p. un jour d'hiver** on a winter day; **p. ce froid** in this cold. ▪ *(distributif)* **dix fois p. an** ten times a year; **deux p. deux** two by two.

parachute *m* parachute.

parachutisme *m* parachute jumping.

paradis *m* heaven, paradise.

paragraphe *m* paragraph.

paraître* *vi (sembler)* to seem; *(livre)* to come out; **il paraît qu'il va partir** it appears *ou* seems he's leaving.

parallèle *adj* parallel (**à** with, to).

paralyser *vt* to paralyze.

parapente *m (activité)* paragliding; **faire du p.** to go paragliding.

parapluie *m* umbrella.

parasite *m* parasite; **parasites** *(à la radio)* interference.

parasol *m* sunshade.

paravent *m* (folding) screen.

parc *m* park; *(de château)* grounds; *(de bébé)* playpen; **p. (de stationnement)** parking lot.

parce que *conj* because.

parcelle *f* fragment; *(terrain)* plot.

par-ci par-là *adv* here, there and everywhere.

parcmètre *m* parking meter.

parcourir* *vt (région)* to travel all over; *(distance)* to cover; *(texte)* to glance through.

parcours *m (itinéraire)* route; *(distance)* distance.

par-dessous *prép & adv* under(-neath).

pardessus *m* overcoat.

par-dessus *prép & adv* over (the top of); **p. tout** above all.

pardon *m* **p.!** *(excusez-moi)* sorry!; **demander p.** to apologize (**à** to).

pardonner *vt* to forgive; **p. qch à qn/à qn d'avoir fait qch** to forgive

sb for sth/for doing sth.

pare-brise *m inv* windshield.

pare-chocs *m inv* bumper.

pareil, -eille 1 *adj* similar; **p. à** the same as; **être pareils** to be the same; **un p. désordre/etc** such a mess/etc. **2** *adv Fam* the same.

parent, -ente 1 *mf* relative. **2** *mpl (père et mère)* parents. **3** *adj* related (**de** to).

parenté *f* relationship; **avoir un lien de p.** to be related.

parenthèse *f (signe)* bracket.

paresse *f* laziness.

paresseux, -euse 1 *adj* lazy. **2** *mf* lazy person.

parfait, -aite *adj* perfect; **p.!** excellent!

parfaitement *adv* perfectly; *(certainement)* certainly.

parfois *adv* sometimes.

parfum *m (odeur)* fragrance; *(goût)* flavor; *(liquide)* perfume.

parfumé, -ée *adj (savon, fleur)* scented; **p. au café/etc** coffee/etc flavored.

parfumer *vt* to perfume; *(glace, crème)* to flavor (**à** with).

parfumer (se) *vpr* to put on perfume.

parfumerie *f* perfume shop.

pari *m* bet; **p. mutuel urbain** = parimutuel.

parier *vti* to bet (**sur** on; **que** that).

parisien, -ienne 1 *adj* Parisian; **la banlieue parisienne** the outskirts of Paris. **2** *mf* **P.** Parisian.

parking *m* parking lot.

parlement *m* parliament.

parlementaire *mf* member of parliament, = Congressman.

parler 1 *vi* to talk, to speak (**de** about, of; **à** to). **2** *vt (langue)* to speak.

parler (se) *vpr (langue)* to be spoken.

parmi *prép* among(st).

paroi *f* (inside) wall; *(de rocher)* (rock) face.

paroisse f parish.

paroissial, -e, -aux adj église/etc paroissiale parish church/etc.

parole f (mot, promesse) word; **adresser la p. à** to speak to; **prendre la p.** to speak; **demander la p.** to ask to speak.

parquet m (parquet) floor.

parrain m godfather.

parrainer vt (course etc) to sponsor.

parsemé, -ée adj p. de (sol) strewn (all over) with.

part f (portion) share; (de gâteau) portion; **prendre p. à** (activité) to take part in; (la joie etc de qn) to share; **de toutes parts** from ou on all sides; **de p. et d'autre** on both sides; **d'autre p.** (d'ailleurs) moreover; **de la p. de** (provenance) from; **quelque p.** somewhere; **nulle p.** nowhere; **autre p.** somewhere else; **à p.** (mettre) aside; (excepté) apart from; (personne) different.

partage m (de gâteau, trésor etc) sharing.

partagé, -ée adj (amour) mutual; **les avis sont partagés** opinions are divided.

partager vt (repas, joie etc) to share (**avec** with).

partance (en) adj (train) about to depart; **en p. pour...** for...

partenaire mf partner.

partenariat m partnership.

parterre m (de jardin) flower bed.

parti m (politique) party.

partial, -e, -aux adj biased.

participant, -ante mf participant.

participation f participation; **p. (aux frais)** contribution (towards expenses).

participe m Grammaire participle.

participer vi p. à (jeu etc) to take part in; (frais, joie) to share (in).

particularité f peculiarity.

particulier, -ière adj (spécial) particular; (privé) private; (bizarre) peculiar; **en p.** (surtout) in particular.

particulièrement adv particularly.

partie f part; (de cartes, tennis etc) game; **en p.** partly; **faire p. de** to be a part of; (club etc) to belong to.

partiel, -elle adj partial.

partir* vi (aux être) (aller) to go; (s'en aller) to go, to leave; (coup de feu) to go off; (tache) to come out; **à p. de** (date, prix) from.

partisan m supporter; **être p. de qch/de faire** to be in favor of sth/of doing.

partition f (musique) score.

partout adv everywhere; **p. où tu vas** ou **iras** everywhere ou wherever you go.

parvenir* vi (aux être) **p. à** (lieu) to reach; **p. à faire** to manage to do.

pas¹ adv (négatif) not; (ne)...**p.** not; **je ne sais p.** I don't know; **p. de pain**/etc no bread/etc; **p. encore** not yet; **p. du tout** not at all.

pas² m step; (allure) pace; (bruit) footstep; (trace) footprint; **rouler au p.** (véhicule) to go dead slow; **au p. (cadencé)** in step; **faire les cent p.** to walk up and down, to pace; **faux p.** (en marchant) stumble; (erreur) blunder; **le p. de la porte** the doorstep.

passable adj (travail, résultat) (just) average.

passage m passing; (traversée en bateau) crossing; (extrait, couloir) passage; (droit) right of way; (chemin) path; **p. clouté** ou **pour piétons** (pedestrian) crosswalk; **p. souterrain** underground passage (for pedestrians); **p. à niveau** grade crossing; **'p. interdit'** 'no through traffic', **'cédez le p.'** (au carrefour) 'yield'.

passager, -ère mf passenger.

passant, -ante mf passer-by.

passe f Sport pass.

passé, -ée 1 adj (temps) past; (cou-

leur) faded; **la semaine passée** last week; **dix heures passées** after ten (o'clock); **être passé** *(personne)* to have been here/there; *(orage)* to be over; **avoir vingt ans passés** to be over twenty. **2** *m* past; *Grammaire* past (tense).

passe-passe *m inv* **tour de p.** magic trick.

passeport *m* passport.

passer 1 *vi (aux* **être** *ou* **avoir)** to pass (**à** to; **de** from); *(traverser)* to go through *ou* over; *(facteur)* to come; *(temps)* to pass, to go by; *(film)* to be shown; *(douleur)* to go by; *(couleur)* to fade; **p. devant** *(maison etc)* to go past, to pass (by); **p. à la boulangerie** *ou* **chez le boulanger** to go to *ou* by the bakery; **laisser p.** *(personne, lumière)* to let through; **p. prendre** to pick up; **p. voir qn** to drop in on sb; **p. pour** *(riche etc)* to be taken for; **p. en** *(seconde etc)* **(à l'école)** to advance to; *(en voiture)* to shift into. **2** *vt (aux* **avoir)** *(frontière etc)* to cross; *(donner)* to pass, to hand **(à** to); *(temps)* to spend **(à faire** doing); *(CD, chemise, film)* to put on; *(examen)* to take; *(thé)* to strain; *(café)* to filter; *(limites)* to go beyond; *(visite médicale)* to have; **p. qch à qn** *(caprice etc)* to grant sb sth; **p. un coup d'éponge/etc à qch** to go over sth with a sponge/etc.

passer (se) *vpr* to take place, to happen; *(douleur)* to go (away); **se p. de** to do *ou* go without; **ça s'est bien passé** it went off well.

passerelle *f* footbridge; *(d'avion, de bateau)* gangway.

passe-temps *m inv* pastime.

passif, -ive 1 *adj* passive. **2** *m* *Grammaire* passive.

passion *f* passion; **avoir la p. des voitures/d'écrire** to have a passion for cars/writing.

passionnant, -ante *adj* thrilling.

passionné, -ée *adj* passionate; **p.**

de qch passionately fond of sth.

passionner *vt* to thrill.

passionner (se) *vpr* **se p. pour** to have a passion for.

passoire *f (à thé)* strainer; *(à légumes)* colander.

pastèque *f* watermelon.

pasteurisé, -ée *adj* pasteurized.

pastille *f* pastille, lozenge.

patauger *vi* to wade *(in the mud etc)*; *(barboter)* to splash around.

pâte *f* paste; *(à pain)* dough; *(à tarte)* pastry; **pâtes (alimentaires)** pasta; **p. à modeler** modeling clay.

pâté *m (charcuterie)* pâté; **p. (en croûte)** meat pie; **p. (de sable)** sand castle; **p. de maisons** block of houses.

pâtée *f (pour chien, chat)* pet food.

paternel, -elle *adj* paternal.

pathétique *adj* moving.

patiemment *adv* patiently.

patience *f* patience.

patient, -ente 1 *adj* patient. **2** *mf (malade)* patient.

patienter *vi* to wait.

patin *m* **p. (à glace)** (ice) skate; **p. à roulettes** roller skate.

patinage *m* skating; **p. artistique** figure skating.

patiner *vi (en sport)* to skate; *(roue)* to spin round.

patineur, -euse *mf* skater.

patinoire *f* skating rink.

pâtisserie *f* pastry; *(magasin)* cake shop.

pâtissier, -ière *mf* pastry cook.

patrie *f* (native) country.

patrimoine *m* heritage; *(biens)* property.

patriote 1 *mf* patriot. **2** *adj* patriotic.

patriotique *adj (chant etc)* patriotic.

patron, -onne 1 *mf (chef)* boss. **2** *m (modèle de papier)* pattern.

patronat *m* employers.

patrouille *f* patrol.

patrouiller *vi* to patrol.

patte *f* leg; *(de chat, chien)* paw; **marcher à quatre pattes** to crawl.

pâturage *m* pasture.

paume *f (de main)* palm.

paupière *f* eyelid.

pause *f (arrêt)* break.

pauvre **1** *adj* poor. **2** *mf* poor person; **les pauvres** the poor.

pauvreté *f (besoin)* poverty.

pavé *m (de rue)* paving stone.

paver *vt* to pave.

pavillon *m (maison)* (detached) house; *(drapeau)* flag.

payant, -ante *adj (hôte, spectateur)* paying; *(place, entrée)* that one has to pay for.

paye *f* pay, wages.

payer **1** *vt (personne, somme)* to pay; *(service, objet)* to pay for; **p. qn pour faire** to pay sb to do *ou* for doing. **2** *vi (personne, métier)* to pay.

pays *m* country; **du p.** *(vin, gens)* local.

paysage *m* landscape.

paysan, -anne *mf* (small) farmer.

PC *m abrév (personal computer)* PC.

PCV *abrév (paiement contre vérification)* **téléphoner en P.** to call collect.

PDA *m abrév (personal digital assistant)* PDA.

PDG *m abrév (président directeur général)* CEO.

péage *m (droit)* toll; *(lieu)* tollbooth.

peau, -x *f* skin; *(de fruit)* peel, skin; *(cuir)* hide.

pêche[1] *f* fishing; *(poissons)* catch; **p. (à la ligne)** angling; **aller à la p.** to go fishing.

pêche[2] *f (fruit)* peach.

péché *m* sin.

pêcher[1] **1** *vi* to fish. **2** *vt (attraper)* to catch.

pêcher[2] *m* peach tree.

pêcheur *m* fisherman; *(à la ligne)* angler.

pédale *f* pedal; **p. de frein** footbrake (pedal).

pédaler *vi* to pedal.

pédalo *m* paddle boat.

pédiatre *mf* children's doctor.

pédicure *mf* chiropodist.

pédomètre *m* pedometer.

peigne *m* comb; **se donner un coup de p.** to give one's hair a comb.

peigner *vt (cheveux)* to comb; **p. qn** to comb sb's hair.

peigner (se) *vpr* to comb one's hair.

peignoir *m* bathrobe; **p. (de bain)** bathrobe.

peindre* *vti* to paint; **p. en bleu/** *etc* to paint blue/etc.

peine (à) *adv* hardly.

peine *f (châtiment)* **la p. de mort** the death penalty; **p. de prison** prison sentence. ▪ *(chagrin)* sorrow; **avoir de la p.** to be upset; **faire de la p. à** to upset. ▪ *(effort, difficulté)* trouble; **se donner de la p.** to go to a lot of trouble (**pour faire** to do); **avec p.** with difficulty; **ça vaut la p. d'attendre**/etc it's worth(while) waiting/etc; **ce n'est pas** *ou* **ça ne vaut pas la p.** it's not worth it.

peintre *m* painter; **p. (en bâtiment)** (house) painter.

peinture *f (tableau, activité)* painting; *(matière)* paint; **'p. fraîche'** 'wet paint'.

pelage *m (d'animal)* coat, fur.

peler **1** *vt (fruit)* to peel. **2** *vi (peau bronzée)* to peel.

pelle *f* shovel; *(d'enfant)* spade; **p. à poussière** dustpan.

pelleteuse *f* steam shovel.

pellicule *f (pour photos)* film; *(couche)* layer; **pellicules** *(dans les cheveux)* dandruff.

pelote *f (de laine)* ball.

peloton *m (cyclistes)* pack.

pelotonner (se) *vpr* to curl up (into a ball).

pelouse *f* lawn.

peluche *f* peluches *(flocons)* fluff; **jouet en p.** = stuffed animal; **chien**

en p. *(jouet)* stuffed dog; **ours en p.** teddy bear.

penalty *m Football* penalty.

penchant *m (préférence)* penchant (**pour** for); *(tendance)* propensity (**pour** for).

penché, -ée *adj* leaning.

pencher 1 *vt (objet)* to tilt; *(tête)* to lean. **2** *vi (arbre etc)* to lean (over).

pencher (se) *vpr* to lean (over *ou* forward); **se p. par** *(fenêtre)* to lean out of.

pendant *prép* during; **p. la nuit** during the night; **p. deux mois** for two months; **p. que** while.

penderie *f* closet.

pendre *vti* to hang (**à** from); **p. qn** to hang sb (**pour** for).

pendre (se) *vpr* to hang (**à** from).

pendu, -ue *adj (objet)* hanging (**à** from).

pendule *f* clock.

pénétrer *vi* **p. dans** to enter; *(profondément)* to penetrate (into).

pénible *adj* difficult; *(douloureux)* painful.

péniblement *adv* with difficulty.

péniche *f* barge.

pénicilline *f* penicillin.

pensée *f (idée)* thought.

penser 1 *vi* to think (**à** of, about); **p. à qch/à faire qch** *(ne pas oublier)* to remember sth/to do sth. **2** *vt* to think (**que** that); **je pensais rester** I was thinking of staying; **je pense réussir** I hope to succeed; **que pensez-vous de?** what do you think of *ou* about?

pensif, -ive *adj* thoughtful, pensive.

pension¹ *f* boarding school; *(somme à payer)* board; **être en p.** to board (**chez** with); **p. complète** full board.

pension² *f (de retraite etc)* pension.

pensionnaire *mf (élève)* boarder; *(d'hôtel)* resident; *(de famille)* lodger.

pensionnat *m* boarding school.

pente *f* slope; **en p.** sloping.

Pentecôte *f* Pentecost.

pénurie *f* shortage (**de** of).

pépin *m (de fruit)* seed, pit.

perçant, -ante *adj (cri, froid)* piercing; *(yeux)* sharp.

percepteur *m* tax collector.

percer 1 *vt* to pierce; *(avec une perceuse)* to drill (a hole in); *(ouverture)* to make. **2** *vi (avec un outil)* to drill.

perceuse *f (outil)* drill.

percevoir* *vt (sensation)* to perceive; *(son)* to hear. ▪ *(impôt)* to collect.

perche *f (bâton)* pole.

percher (se) *vpr (oiseau)* to perch.

perchoir *m* perch.

percuter *vt (véhicule)* to crash into.

perdant, -ante *mf* loser.

perdre 1 *vt* to lose; *(gaspiller)* to waste; **p. de vue** to lose sight of. **2** *vi* to lose.

perdre (se) *vpr (s'égarer)* to get lost; **je m'y perds** I'm lost *ou* confused.

perdrix *f* partridge.

perdu, -ue *adj* lost; *(gaspillé)* wasted; **c'est du temps p.** it's a waste of time.

père *m* father.

perfection *f* perfection; **à la p.** perfectly.

perfectionné, -ée *adj (machine)* advanced.

perfectionnement *m* improvement (**de** in; **par rapport à** on); **cours de p.** proficiency course.

perfectionner *vt* to improve.

perfectionner (se) *vpr* **se p. en anglais/etc** to improve one's English/*etc*.

perforeuse *f* (paper) punch.

performance *f* performance.

performant, -ante *adj* highly efficient.

péril *m* danger, peril.

périlleux, -euse *adj* dangerous.

périmé, -ée *adj (billet)* expired.

période *f* period.

périphérique *adj & m* **(boulevard) p.** beltway.

perle *f (bijou)* pearl; *(de bois, verre)* bead.

permanence *f (salle d'étude)* study hall; **être de p.** to be on duty; **en p.** permanently.

permanent, -ente 1 *adj* permanent; *(spectacle)* continuous. **2** *f (coiffure)* perm.

permettre* *vt* to allow; **p. à qn de faire** to allow sb to do; **vous permettez?** may I?; **je ne peux pas me p. de l'acheter** I can't afford (to buy) it.

permis, -ise 1 *adj* allowed. **2** *m* license; **p. de conduire** driver's license; **passer son p. de conduire** to take one's driving test.

permission *f* permission; *(congé de soldat)* leave; **demander la p.** to ask permission (**de faire** to do).

perpendiculaire *adj* perpendicular (**à** to).

perpétuel, -elle *adj (incessant)* continual, non-stop.

perplexe *adj* perplexed, puzzled.

perquisitionner *vi* to make a search.

perron *m (front)* steps.

perroquet *m* parrot.

perruche *f* parakeet.

perruque *f* wig.

persécuter *vt* to persecute.

persécution *f* persecution.

persévérance *f* perseverance.

persévérer *vi* to persevere (**dans** in).

persil *m* parsley.

persister *vi* to persist (**à faire** in doing; **dans qch** in sth).

personnage *m* (important) person; *(de livre, film)* character.

personnalité *f* personality.

personne 1 *f* person; **personnes** people; **grande p.** grown-up; **en p.** in person. **2** *pron (négatif)* nobody; **je ne vois p.** I don't see anybody; **mieux que p.** better than anybody.

personnel, -elle 1 *adj* personal. **2** *m* staff.

personnellement *adv* personally.

perspective *f (idée, possibilité)* prospect (**de** of).

perspicace *adj* shrewd.

persuader *vt* to persuade (**qn de faire** sb to do); **être persuadé que** to be convinced that.

persuasion *f* persuasion.

perte *f* loss; *(gaspillage)* waste (**de temps/d'argent** of time/money).

pertinent *adv* **savoir qch p.** to know sth for a fact.

perturbation *f* disruption.

perturber *vt (trafic etc)* to disrupt; *(personne)* to disturb.

pervers, -erse 1 *adj* perverse. **2** *mf* pervert.

pesant, -ante *adj* heavy.

pesanteur *f (force)* gravity.

pèse-personne, *pl* **pèse-personne(s)** *m* (bathroom) scales.

peser *vti* to weigh; **p. lourd** to be heavy.

pessimiste *adj* pessimistic.

peste *f (maladie)* plague.

pétale *m* petal.

pétanque *f* (French) bowling game.

pétard *m* firecracker.

pétillant, -ante *adj* fizzy; *(vin, yeux)* sparkling.

pétiller *vi (champagne)* to fizz; *(yeux)* to sparkle.

petit, -ite 1 *adj* small, little; *(de taille)* short; *(bruit, coup)* slight; *(jeune)* little; **tout p.** tiny; **un p. Français** a (little) French boy. **2** *mf* (little) boy/girl; *(personne)* small person; **petits** *(d'animal)* young. **3** *adv* **p. à p.** little by little.

petite-fille, *pl* **petites-filles** *f* granddaughter.

petit-fils, *pl* **petits-fils** *m* grandson.

petits-enfants *mpl* grandchildren.

petit-suisse *m* soft cheese *(for dessert)*.

pétrole *m* oil.

pétrolier *m (navire)* (oil) tanker.

peu *adv (manger etc)* not much, little; **un p.** a little, a bit; **p. de sel/de temps/***etc* not much salt/time/*etc*; **un p. de fromage/***etc* a little cheese/*etc*; **p. de gens/***etc* few people/*etc*; **un (tout) petit p.** a (tiny) little bit; **p. intéressant/***etc* not very interesting/*etc*; **p. de chose** not much; **p. à p.** little by little; **à p. près** more or less; **p. après** shortly after.

peuple *m* people.

peuplé, -ée *adj* **très/peu/***etc* **p.** highly/sparsely/*etc* populated; **p. de** populated by.

peur *f* fear; **avoir p.** to be afraid *ou* frightened *(de qch/qn* of sth/sb; *de faire* to do, of doing); **faire p. à** to frighten; **de p. que** (+ *subjonctif)* for fear that.

peureux, -euse *adj* easily frightened.

peut, peuvent, peux *voir* **pouvoir.**

peut-être *adv* perhaps, maybe; **p. qu'il viendra** perhaps *ou* maybe he'll come.

phare *m (pour bateaux)* lighthouse; *(de véhicule)* headlight; **faire un appel de phares** to flash one's lights.

pharmacie *f* drugstore, pharmacy; *(armoire)* medicine cabinet.

pharmacien, -ienne *mf* pharmacist.

philatélie *f* stamp collecting.

philatéliste *mf* stamp collector.

philosophe 1 *mf* philosopher. **2** *adj (résigné)* philosophical.

philosophie *f* philosophy.

phonétique *adj* phonetic.

phoque *m (animal)* seal.

photo *f* photo; *(art)* photography; **prendre une p. de** to take a photo of; **se faire prendre en p.** to have one's photo taken.

photocopie *f* photocopy.

photocopier *vt* to photocopy.

photocopieuse *f (machine)* photocopier.

photographe *mf* photographer.

photographier *vt* to photograph.

photographique *adj* photographic.

photomaton® *m* photo booth.

phrase *f* sentence.

physique 1 *adj* physical. **2** *m (corps, aspect)* physique; *(science)* physics.

physiquement *adv* physically.

pianiste *mf* pianist.

piano *m* piano.

pic *m (cime)* peak.

pic (à) *adv* **couler à p.** to sink to the bottom.

pichet *m* jug.

pickpocket *m* pickpocket.

picorer *vti* to peck.

picoter *vt (yeux)* to make sting; **les yeux me picotent** my eyes are stinging.

pièce *f (de maison etc)* room; *(de pantalon)* patch; **p. (de monnaie)** coin; **p. (de théâtre)** play; **p. d'identité** identity card; **pièces détachées** *(de véhicule etc)* spare parts; **cinq dollars p.** five dollars each.

pied *m* foot *(pl* feet); *(de meuble)* leg; *(de verre, lampe)* base; **à p.** on foot; **au p. de** at the foot of; **coup de p.** kick; **donner un coup de p.** to kick *(à qn* sb).

piège *m* trap.

piéger *vt (animal)* to trap; *(voiture)* to booby-trap.

piercing *m (body)* piercing.

pierre *f* stone; *(précieuse)* gem; **p. (à briquet)** flint.

piétiner 1 *vt* to trample (on). **2** *vt* to stamp (one's) feet.

piéton *m* pedestrian.

piétonne adj rue p. pedestrian street.

pieu, -x m post, stake.

pieuvre f octopus.

pigeon m pigeon.

pile 1 f (électrique) battery; (tas) pile; radio à piles battery radio; **en p.** in a pile; **p. (ou face)?** heads (or tails)? **2** adv s'arrêter **p.** to stop short; **à deux heures p.** at two o'clock sharp ou on the dot.

pilier m pillar.

pillage m looting.

piller vti to loot.

pilotage m poste de p. cockpit.

pilote m (d'avion) pilot; (de voiture) driver.

piloter vt (avion) to fly; (voiture) to drive.

pilule f pill; prendre la p. to be on the Pill.

piment m (chili) pepper.

pimenté, -ée adj spicy.

pin m (arbre) pine; pomme de p. pine cone.

pince f (outil) pliers; (de cycliste) clip; (de crabe) pincer; **p. (à linge)** (clothes) pin; **p. (à épiler)** tweezers; **p. (à sucre)** (sugar) tongs; **p. à cheveux** bobby pin.

pinceau, -x m (paint)brush.

pincée f (de sel etc) pinch (de of).

pincer vt to pinch.

pincer (se) vpr se p. le doigt to get one's finger caught (dans in).

pingouin m penguin.

ping-pong m table tennis.

pin's m inv button, lapel pin.

pintade f guinea fowl.

pioche f pick(ax).

piocher vti to dig (with a pick).

pion m (au jeu de dames) piece; Échecs pawn.

pipe f pipe; fumer la p. to smoke a pipe.

pipi m faire p. Fam to take a pee.

piquant, -ante adj (plante, barbe) prickly.

pique m (couleur) Cartes spades.

pique-nique, pl pique-niques m picnic.

pique-niquer vi to picnic.

piquer 1 vt (percer) to prick; (langue, yeux) to sting; (coudre) to (machine-)stitch; **p. qn** (abeille) to sting sb; **p. qch dans** (enfoncer) to stick sth into; **p. une colère** to fly into a rage. **2** vi (avion) to dive; (moutarde etc) to be hot.

piquet m (pieu) stake; (de tente) peg.

piqûre f (d'abeille) sting; (avec un seringue) injection, shot.

pirate m pirate; **p. de l'air** hijacker; **p. informatique** hacker.

pire 1 adj worse (que than); **le p. moment/etc** the worst moment/etc. **2** mf **le** ou **la p.** the worst.

piscine f swimming pool.

pissenlit m dandelion.

pistache f pistachio.

piste f (traces) trail; (de course) racetrack; (de cirque) ring; (de patinage) rink; **p. (d'envoi)** runway; **p. cyclable** bicycle path; **p. de danse** dance floor; **p. de ski** ski run ou slope.

pistolet m gun; **p. à eau** water pistol.

pitié f pity; j'ai p. de lui I feel sorry for him.

pitoyable adj pitiful.

pittoresque adj picturesque.

pivoter vi (personne) to swing round; (fauteuil) to swivel.

pizza f pizza.

pizzeria f pizzeria.

placard m (dans la cuisine) cupboard, cabinet; (pour linge, vêtements etc) closet.

place f (endroit, rang) place; (espace) room; (lieu public) square; (siège) seat, place; (emploi) job; **p. de parking** parking place ou space; **à la p. (de)** instead (of); **à votre p.** in your place; **sur p.** on the spot; **en p.** in place; **mettre en p.** (installer) to set up; **changer de p.** to change pla-

ces; **changer qch de p.** to move sth.
placement *m (d'argent)* investment.
placer *vt* to place; *(invité, specta-*
teur) to seat; *(argent)* to invest
(**dans** in).
placer (se) *vpr (debout)* to (go
and) stand; *(s'asseoir)* to (go and)
sit; **se p. troisième/etc (en sport)** to
come third/*etc.*
plafond *m* ceiling.
plage *f* beach; **p. arrière** *(de voi-*
ture) (back) window shelf.
plaider *vti (défendre)* to plead; **p.**
coupable to plead guilty.
plaie *f* wound; *(coupure)* cut.
plaindre* *vt* to feel sorry for.
plaindre (se) *vpr* to complain (**de**
about; **que** that); **se p. de** *(douleur)*
to complain of.
plaine *f* plain.
plainte *f* complaint; *(cri)* moan.
plaire* *vi* **p. à qn** to please sb; **elle**
lui plaît he likes her; **ça me plaît** I
like it; **s'il vous** *ou* **te plaît** please.
plaire (se) *vpr (dans un endroit)* to
like *ou* enjoy it.
plaisanter *vi* to joke (**sur** about).
plaisanterie *f* joke; **par p.** as a
joke.
plaisir *m* pleasure; **faire p. à** to
please; **pour le p.** for fun.
plan *m (projet, dessin)* plan; *(de*
ville) map; **au premier p.** in the
foreground.
planche *f* board; **p. à repasser** ironing board; **p. (à roulettes)** skate-
board; **p. (à voile)** sailboard; **faire**
de la p. (à voile) to go windsurfing.
plancher *m* floor.
planer *vi (oiseau, avion)* to glide.
planète *f* planet.
planeur *m (avion)* glider.
planifier *vt* to plan.
plante[1] *f* plant; **p. verte** house
plant.
plante[2] *f* **p. du pied** sole (of the foot).
planter *vt (fleur etc)* to plant; *(clou,*
couteau) to drive in.

planter (se) *vpr* **se p. devant** to
come *ou* go and stand in front of, to
plant oneself in front of.
plaque *f* plate; *(de verre, métal,*
verglas) sheet; *(de chocolat)* bar; **p.**
chauffante hotplate; **p. d'immatri-**
culation license plate.
plaqué, -ée *adj* **p.** or gold-plated.
plaquer *vt* Sport to tackle; *(aplatir)*
to flatten (**contre** against).
plastique *adj & m (matière)* **p.**
plastic; **en p.** *(bouteille etc)* plastic.
plat, plate 1 *adj* flat; **à p. ventre**
flat on one's face; **à p.** *(pneu, bat-*
terie) flat; **poser à p.** to put down
flat; **assiette plate** dinner plate;
eau plate still water. **2** *m (récipient,*
nourriture) dish; *(partie du repas)*
course; **'p. du jour'** 'today's special'.
platane *m* plane tree.
plateau, -x *m (pour servir)* tray; **p.**
à fromages cheeseboard.
plate-forme, *pl* **plates-formes** *f*
platform; **p. pétrolière** oil rig.
plâtre *m (matière)* plaster; **un p.** a
(plaster) cast; **dans le p.** in plaster.
plâtrer *vt (bras, jambe)* to put a
cast on.
plein, pleine 1 *adj* full (**de** of); **en**
pleine mer out at sea; **en pleine fi-**
gure right in the face. **2** *prép & adv*
des bonbons p. les poches pockets
full of candy; **du chocolat p. la fi-**
gure chocolate all over one's face;
p. de lettres/d'argent/etc Fam lots
of letters/money/*etc.* **3** *m* **faire le p.**
(d'essence) to fill up (the tank).
pleurer *vi* to cry.
pleuvoir* *vi* to rain; **il pleut** it's
raining.
pli *m (de papier)* fold; *(de jupe)*
pleat; *(de pantalon)* crease; **(faux)**
p. crease; **mise en plis** *(coiffure)*
set.
pliable *adj* foldable.
pliant, -ante *adj (chaise etc)* folding.
plier 1 *vt* to fold; *(courber)* to bend.
2 *vi (branche)* to bend.

plier (se) *vpr (lit, chaise etc)* to fold (up).

plissé, -ée *adj (tissu, jupe)* pleated.

plisser *vt (front)* to wrinkle; to crease, to fold; **p. les yeux** to squint.

plomb *m (métal)* lead; *(fusible)* fuze; **plombs** *(de chasse)* lead shot.

plombage *m (de dent)* filling.

plomber *vt (dent)* to fill.

plomberie *f* plumbing.

plombier *m* plumber.

plongée *f (sport)* diving.

plongeoir *m* diving board.

plongeon *m* dive.

plonger 1 *vi (personne)* to dive. **2** *vt (mettre)* to plunge *(dans* into).

plongeur, -euse *mf* diver.

plu *voir* **plaire, pleuvoir**.

pluie *f* rain; **sous la p.** in the rain.

plume *f (d'oiseau)* feather; *(de stylo)* (pen) nib; **stylo à p.** (fountain) pen.

plumer *vt (volaille)* to pluck.

plupart (la) *f* most; **la p. des cas** most cases; **la p. du temps** most of the time; **la p. d'entre eux** most of them; **pour la p.** mostly.

pluriel, -ielle *adj & m* plural; **au p.** in the plural.

plus¹ *adv comparatif (travailler etc)* more (**que** than); **p. d'une livre/de dix** more than a pound/ten; **p. de thé** more tea; **p. beau** more beautiful (**que** than); **p. tard** later; **p. petit** smaller; **de p. en p.** more and more; **p. ou moins** more or less; **en p.** in addition (**de** to); **de p.** more (**que** than); *(en outre)* moreover; *(âgé)* **de p. de dix ans** over ten; **j'ai dix ans de p. qu'elle** I'm ten years older than she is; **il est p. de cinq heures** it's after five. **2** *adv superlatif* **le p.** *(travailler etc)* (the) most; **le p. beau** the most beautiful (**de** in); **le p. grand** the biggest (**de** in); **j'ai le p. de livres** I have (the) most books.

plus² *adv de négation* **p. de** *(pain, argent)* no more; **il n'a p. de pain**

he has no more bread, he doesn't have any more bread; **tu n'es p. jeune** you're not young any more; **je ne la reverrai p.** I won't see her again.

plus³ *prép* plus; **deux p. deux** two plus two; **il fait p. deux (degrés)** it's two degrees above freezing.

plusieurs *adj & pron* several.

plutôt *adv* rather (**que** than).

pluvieux, -euse *adj* rainy.

pneu *m (pl -s)* tire.

pneumatique *adj* **matelas p.** air mattress; **canot p.** rubber dinghy.

poche *f* pocket; *(de kangourou)* pouch.

pocher *vt (œufs)* to poach; **p. l'œil à qn** to give sb a black eye.

pochette *f (sac)* bag; *(d'allumettes)* book; *(de disque)* sleeve; *(sac à main)* (clutch) bag.

podcast *m* podcast.

poêle 1 *m* stove. **2** *f* **p. (à frire)** frying pan.

poème *m* poem.

poésie *f (art)* poetry; *(poème)* poem.

poète *m* poet.

poétique *adj* poetic.

poids *m* weight; **au p.** by weight.

poids lourd *m* (heavy) truck.

poignard *m* dagger.

poignarder *vt* to stab.

poignée *f (quantité)* handful (**de** of); *(de porte etc)* handle; **p. de main** handshake; **donner une p. de main à** to shake hands with.

poignet *m* wrist; *(de chemise)* cuff.

poil *m* hair; *(pelage)* fur.

poilu, -ue *adj* hairy.

poinçonner *vt (billet)* to punch.

poing *m* fist; **coup de p.** punch.

point *m (lieu, score etc)* point; *(sur i, à l'horizon)* dot; *(tache)* spot; *(de couture)* stitch; **sur le p. de faire** about to do; **p. (final)** period; **p. d'exclamation** exclamation point; **p. d'interrogation** question mark; **points de suspension** ellipsis; **p.**

de vue *(opinion)* point of view; **à p.** *(steak)* medium rare; **au p. mort** *(véhicule)* in neutral; **p. de côté** *(douleur)* stitch (in one's side).

pointe *f (extrémité)* tip; *(clou)* nail; **sur la p. des pieds** on tiptoe; **en p.** pointed.

pointer 1 *vt (cocher)* to check (off); *(braquer)* to point (**sur** at). **2** *vi* **p. vers** to point (upwards) towards.

pointillé *m* dotted line.

pointu, -ue *adj (en pointe)* pointed.

pointure *f (de chaussure, gant)* size.

point-virgule, *pl* **points-virgules** *m* semicolon.

poire *f* pear.

poireau, -x *m* leek.

poirier *m* pear tree.

pois *m* pea; **petits p.** peas; **p. chiche** garbanzo, chickpea.

poison *m* poison.

poisseux, -euse *adj* sticky.

poisson *m* fish; **p. rouge** goldfish.

poissonnerie *f* fish market.

poissonnier, -ière *mf* fish merchant.

poitrine *f* chest; *(de femme)* bust.

poivre *m* pepper.

poivré, -ée *adj (piquant)* peppery.

poivrer *vt* to pepper.

poivrière *f* peppershaker.

poivron *m (légume)* pepper.

pôle *m* **p. Nord/Sud** North/South Pole.

polémique 1 *adj* polemical. **2** *f* heated debate.

poli, -ie *adj (courtois)* polite (**avec** to, with); *(lisse)* polished.

police[1] *f* police; **p. secours** police emergency services.

police[2] *f* **p. (d'assurance)** (insurance) policy.

policier, -ière 1 *adj* enquête/*etc* **policière** police investigation/*etc*; **roman p.** mystery novel. **2** *m* policeman, detective.

poliment *adv* politely.

polio 1 *f (maladie)* polio. **2** *mf (personne)* polio victim.

polir *vt* to polish.

politesse *f* politeness.

politique 1 *adj* political; **homme p.** politician. **2** *f (activité)* politics; **une p.** a policy.

pollen *m* pollen.

polluer *vt* to pollute.

pollution *f* pollution.

polo *m (chemise)* polo shirt.

polochon *m* bolster.

polonais, -aise 1 *adj* Polish. **2** *mf* **P.** Pole. **3** *m (langue)* Polish.

polycopié *m* duplicated course notes.

polyester *m* polyester; **chemise/** *etc* **en p.** polyester shirt/*etc*.

polyvalent, -ente *adj (salle)* multi-purpose; *(personne)* versatile.

pommade *f* ointment.

pomme *f* apple; **p. de terre** potato; **pommes frites** French fries; **pommes chips** potato chips.

pommier *m* apple tree.

pompe *f* pump; **p. à essence** gas station; **pompes funèbres** undertaker's; **entrepreneur de pompes funèbres** undertaker.

pomper *vt (eau)* to pump out (**de** of).

pompier *m* fireman; **voiture des pompiers** fire engine.

pompiste *mf* gas station attendant.

pompon *m* pompon.

poncer *vt* to rub down, to sand.

ponctuation *f* punctuation.

ponctuel, -elle *adj (à l'heure)* punctual.

pondre 1 *vt (œuf)* to lay. **2** *vi (poule)* to lay (eggs **ou** an egg).

poney *m* pony.

pont *m* bridge; *(de bateau)* deck.

pop *m & adj inv (musique)* pop.

populaire *adj (qui plaît)* popular; *(quartier)* working-class; *(expression)* colloquial.

population *f* population.

porc m pig; (viande) pork.
porcelaine f china.
porche m porch.
porcherie f (pig)sty.
port m port, harbor.
portable 1 adj (portatif) portable. **2** m (ordinateur) laptop; (téléphone) cellphone.
portail m (de jardin) gate(way).
portant, -ante adj bien p. in good health.
portatif, -ive adj portable.
porte f door; (de jardin) gate; (de ville) entrance; **p. (d'embarquement)** (d'aéroport) (departure) gate; **p. d'entrée** front door; **p. coulissante** sliding door; **mettre à la p.** to throw out.
porte-avions m inv aircraft carrier.
porte-bagages m inv luggage rack.
porte-bonheur m inv (lucky) charm.
porte-clefs m inv key ring.
porte-documents m inv briefcase.
portée f (de fusil etc) range; (animaux) litter; **à p. de la main** within (easy) reach; **à p. de voix** within earshot; **hors de p.** out of reach.
porte-fenêtre, pl **portes-fenêtres** f French door ou window.
portefeuille m wallet.
portemanteau, -x m coatrack; (crochet) coat hook.
porte-monnaie m inv purse.
porte-parole m inv spokesman; (femme) spokeswoman.
porter 1 vt to carry; (vêtement, lunettes, barbe etc) to wear; **p. qch à** (apporter) to take sth to; **p. bonheur/malheur** to bring good/bad luck. **2** vi (voix) to carry.
porter (se) vpr (vêtement) to be worn; **se p. bien/mal** to be well/ill; **comment te portes-tu?** how are you?
porte-revues m inv newspaper rack.

porte-savon m inv soapdish.
porte-serviettes m inv towel rack.
porteur m (à la gare) porter.
porte-voix m inv loudspeaker, megaphone.
portier m doorman.
portière f (de véhicule, train) door.
portion f (partie) portion; (de nourriture) helping.
portique m (de balançoire etc) crossbar.
portrait m portrait.
portrait-robot, pl **portraits-robots** m composite picture.
portugais, -aise 1 adj Portuguese. **2** mf P. Portuguese man, Portuguese woman, Portuguese inv; **les P.** the Portuguese. **3** m (langue) Portuguese.
pose f (installation) putting up; putting in; laying; (attitude de modèle) pose.
posé, -ée adj (calme) composed.
poser 1 vt to put (down); (papier peint, rideaux) to put up; (sonnette, chauffage) to put in; (moquette) to lay; (question) to ask (à qn sb). **2** vi (modèle) to pose (pour for).
poser (se) vpr (oiseau, avion) to land.
positif, -ive adj positive.
position f position.
posséder vt to possess; (maison etc) to own.
possessif, -ive adj & m Grammaire possessive.
possibilité f possibility.
possible 1 adj possible (à faire to do); **il (nous) est p. de le faire** it is possible (for us) to do it; **il est p. que** (+ subjonctif) it is possible that; **si p.** if possible; **le plus tôt p.** as soon as possible; **autant que p.** as far as possible; **le plus p.** as much ou as many as possible. **2** m faire son p. to do one's best (pour faire to do).
postal, -e, -aux adj postal; **boîte**

postale PO Box; **code p.** zip code.
poste 1 f (service) post; (bureau de) **p.** post office; **la P.** the Post Office; **par la p.** by post; **p. aérienne** airmail. **2** m (lieu, emploi) post; (radio, télévision) set; **p. de secours** first aid station; **p. de police** police station.

poster vt (lettre) to mail.

postier, -ière mf postal worker.

postuler vi **p. à un emploi** to apply for a job.

pot m pot; (à confiture) jar; (à lait) jug; (à bière) mug; (de crème, yaourt) carton; (de bébé) potty; **p. de fleurs** flower pot.

potable adj drinkable; **'eau p.'** 'drinking water'.

potage m soup.

potager adj & m (jardin) **p.** vegetable garden.

pot-au-feu m inv beef stew.

pot-de-vin, pl **pots-de-vin** m bribe.

poteau, -x m post; **p. indicateur** signpost; **p. d'arrivée** winning post; **p. télégraphique** telegraph pole.

poterie f (art) pottery; **une p.** a piece of pottery; **des poteries** (objets) pottery.

potier m potter.

potiron m pumpkin.

pou, -x m louse; **poux** lice.

poubelle f garbage can.

pouce m thumb; (mesure) inch.

poudre f powder; (explosif) gunpowder; **en p.** (lait) powdered; **chocolat en p.** cocoa powder.

poudrer (se) vpr (femme) to powder one's face.

poudrier m (powder) compact.

pouf m (siège) (cushioned) ottoman ou footstool.

poulailler m henhouse.

poulain m (cheval) foal.

poule f hen.

poulet m chicken.

poulie f pulley.

pouls m pulse.

poumon m lung; **à pleins poumons** (respirer) deeply; (crier) loudly.

poupée f doll.

pour 1 prép for; **p. toi/etc** for you/etc; **partir p.** (Paris, cinq ans) to leave for; **elle est p.** she's in favor; **p. faire** (in order) to do; **p. que tu saches** so (that) you know; **p. quoi faire?** what for?; **trop petit/etc p. faire** too small/etc to do; **assez grand/etc p. faire** big/etc enough to do. **2** m **le p. et le contre** the pros and cons.

pourboire m (argent) tip.

pourcentage m percentage.

pourchasser vt to pursue.

pourparlers mpl negotiations, talks.

pourquoi adv & conj why; **p. pas?** why not?

pourra, pourrai(t) etc voir **pouvoir**.

pourri, -ie adj (fruit, temps etc) rotten.

pourriel m spam e-mail; **des pourriels** spam.

pourrir vi to rot.

poursuite f chase; **se mettre à la p. de** to go after, to chase (after).

poursuivant, -ante mf pursuer.

poursuivre* vt to chase, to go after; (lecture, voyage etc) to continue (with).

poursuivre (se) vpr to continue, to go on.

pourtant adv yet.

pourvu que conj (condition) provided ou providing (that); (souhait) **p. qu'elle soit là!** I only hope (that) she's there!

pousser 1 vt to push; (cri) to utter; (soupir) to heave; **p. qn à faire** to urge sb to do. **2** vi (croître) to grow; **faire p.** (plante etc) to grow.

poussette f stroller.

poussière f dust.

poussiéreux, -euse adj dusty.

poussin m (poulet) chick.

poutre f *(en bois)* beam; *(en acier)* girder.

pouvoir* 1 v aux *(capacité)* can, be able to; *(permission, éventualité)* may, can; **je peux deviner** I can guess; **tu peux entrer** you may *ou* can come in; **il peut être sorti** he may *ou* might be out; **elle pourrait/pouvait venir** she might/could come; **j'ai pu l'obtenir** I managed to get it; **j'aurais pu l'obtenir** I could have gotten it; **je n'en peux plus** I'm utterly exhausted. **2** m *(capacité, autorité)* power; **les pouvoirs publics** the authorities; **au p.** in power.

pouvoir (se) vpr **il se peut qu'elle parte** (it's possible that) she might leave.

prairie f meadow.

pratique 1 adj practical. **2** f *(exercice, procédé)* practice; **la p. de la natation/du golf** swimming/golfing.

pratiquement adv *(presque)* practically.

pratiquer vt *(sport, art etc)* to practice.

pré m meadow.

préalable 1 adj prior, previous; **p. à** prior to. **2** m precondition, prerequisite; **au p.** beforehand.

préau, -x m *(d'école)* covered playground.

préavis m *(advance)* notice *(de* of); **p. de grève** strike notice; **p. de licenciement** notice of dismissal.

précarité f precariousness; **p. de l'emploi** lack of job security.

précaution f precaution *(de faire* of doing); *(prudence)* caution.

précédent, -ente 1 adj previous. **2** mf previous one.

précéder vti to precede.

précieux, -euse adj precious.

précipice m chasm, precipice.

précipitamment adv hastily.

précipitation f haste.

précipiter vt *(hâter)* to rush.

précipiter (se) vpr to throw one-self; *(foncer)* to rush *(à, sur* on to); *(s'accélérer)* to speed up.

précis, -ise adj precise; **à deux heures précises** at two o'clock sharp.

préciser vt to specify *(que* that).

préciser (se) vpr to become clear(er).

précision f precision; *(explication)* explanation.

précoce adj *(fruit etc)* early; *(enfant)* precocious.

prédécesseur m predecessor.

prédiction f prediction.

prédire* vt to predict *(que* that).

préfabriqué, -ée adj prefabricated.

préface f preface.

préfecture f prefecture; **la P. de police** police headquarters.

préféré, -ée adj & mf favorite.

préférence f preference *(pour* for); **de p.** preferably.

préférer vt to prefer *(à* to); **p. faire** to prefer to do.

préfet m prefect *(chief administrator in a department)*.

préfixe m prefix.

préhistorique adj prehistoric.

préjudice m *(à une cause)* prejudice; *(à une personne)* harm; **porter p. à qn** to do sb harm.

préjugé m prejudice; **être plein de préjugés** to be full of prejudice.

prélèvement m *(d'échantillon)* taking; *(de somme)* deduction; **p. automatique** automatic deduction.

premier, -ière 1 adj first; *(étage)* second; **nombre p.** prime number; **le p. rang** the front row; **P. ministre** Prime Minister. **2** mf first (one); **arriver le p.** to arrive first; **être le p. de la classe** to be (at the) head of the class. **3** m *(date)* first; *(étage)* second floor; **le p. de l'an** New Year's Day. **4** f *(wagon, billet)* first class; *(au lycée)* = junior year; *(de véhicule)* first (gear).

premièrement adv firstly.

prendre* 1 vt to take *(à qn* from

sb); *(attraper)* to catch; *(voyager par)* to take *(train etc)*; *(douche, bain)* to take, to have; *(repas)* to have; *(photo)* to take; *(temps)* to take (up); **p. qn pour** *(un autre)* to mistake sb for; *(considérer)* to take sb for; **p. feu** to catch fire; **p. de la place** to take up room; **p. du poids** to put on weight. **2** *vi (feu)* to catch; *(ciment)* to set; *(vaccin)* to take.

prendre (se) *vpr (objet)* to be taken; *(s'accrocher)* to get caught; **se p. pour un génie** to think one is a genius; **s'y p.** to go about it; **s'en p. à** to attack; *(accuser)* to blame.

prénom *m* first name.

prénommer *vt* to name.

prénommer (se) *vpr* to be called; **il se prénomme Daniel** his first name is Daniel.

préoccupation *f* worry.

préoccupé, -ée *adj* worried.

préoccuper *vt (inquiéter)* to worry.

préoccuper (se) *vpr* **se p. de** to be worried about.

préparatifs preparations **(de** for).

préparation *f* preparation.

préparer *vt* to prepare **(qch pour** sth for; **qn à** sb for); *(examen)* to prepare for.

préparer (se) *vpr* to get (oneself) ready **(à, pour qch** for sth); **se p. à faire** to prepare to do.

préposition *f* Grammaire preposition.

préretraite *f* early retirement.

près *adv* **p. de** *(qn, qch)* near (to); **p. de deux ans** */etc* nearly two years/ *etc*; **tout p.** nearby **(de qn/qch** sb/ sth); **de p.** *(lire, suivre)* closely.

presbyte *adj* long-sighted.

prescrire* *vt (médicament)* to prescribe.

présence *f* presence; *(à l'école etc)* attendance **(à** at); **feuille de p.** attendance sheet; **en p. de** in the presence of.

présent, -ente 1 *adj (non absent)*

present **(à** at; **dans** in); *(actuel)* present. **2** *m* Grammaire present (tense); **à p.** at present.

présentateur, -trice *mf* announcer.

présentation *f* presentation; *(d'une personne à une autre)* introduction.

présenter *vt* to present; **p. qn à qn** to introduce sb to sb.

présenter (se) *vpr* to introduce oneself **(à** to); **se p. à** *(examen)* to take; *(élections)* to run in.

préservatif *m* condom.

préserver *vt* to protect **(de, contre** from).

présidence *f (de nation)* presidency; *(de firme)* chairmanship.

président, -ente *mf (de nation)* president; *(de réunion, firme)* chairman, chairwoman; **p. directeur général** chief executive officer.

présidentiel, -ielle *adj* presidential.

presque *adv* almost.

presqu'île *f* peninsula.

presse *f (journaux, appareil)* press; **conférence/***etc* **de p.** press conference/*etc.*

presse-citron *m inv* lemon juicer.

pressé, -ée *adj (personne)* in a hurry; *(travail)* urgent.

pressentir* *vt* to sense **(que** that).

presser 1 *vt (serrer)* to squeeze; *(bouton)* to press; *(fruit)* to squeeze, to juice. **2** *vi (temps)* to press; **rien ne presse** there's no hurry.

presser (se) *vpr (se serrer)* to squeeze (together); *(se hâter)* to hurry **(de faire** to do).

pressing *m (magasin)* dry cleaner's.

pression *f* pressure.

prestation *f (allocation)* benefit; **prestations** *(services)* services; **prestations sociales** welfare payments. ■ *(de comédien)* performance.

prestidigitateur, -trice *mf* magician.

prestidigitation *f* tour de p. magic trick.

prêt *m (emprunt)* loan.

prêt, prête *adj (préparé)* ready (à faire to do; à qch for sth).

prêt-à-porter *m inv* ready-to-wear clothes.

prétendre *vt* to claim (que that; être to be).

prétendre (se) *vpr* elle se prétend riche she claims to be rich.

prétendu, -ue *adj* so-called.

prétentieux, -euse *adj & mf* conceited (person).

prêter *vt (argent, objet)* to lend (à to); **p. attention** to pay attention (à to).

prétexte *m* excuse; **sous p. de/ que** on the pretext of/that.

prêtre *m* priest.

preuve *f* **preuve(s)** proof, evidence; **faire p. de** to show.

prévenir *vt (avertir)* to warn (que that); *(aviser)* to inform (que that).

prévention *f* prevention; **p. routière** road safety.

prévisible *adj* foreseeable.

prévision *f* forecast.

prévoir* *vt (anticiper)* to foresee (que that); *(prédire)* to forecast (que that); *(temps)* to forecast; *(organiser)* to plan; *(préparer)* to provide, to make provision for.

prévoyant, -ante *adj* farsighted.

prévu, -ue *adj* un repas est p. a meal is provided; **au moment p.** at the appointed time; **comme p.** as expected; **p. pour** *(véhicule, appareil)* designed for.

prier 1 *vti* to pray (pour for). **2** *vt* **p. qn de faire** to ask sb to do; **je vous en prie** *(faites donc)* please; *(en réponse à 'merci')* you're welcome.

prière *f* prayer; **p. de répondre/***etc* please reply/*etc.*

primaire *adj* primary.

prime *f (d'employé)* bonus; **en p.** *(cadeau)* as a free gift; **p. (d'assurance)** (insurance) premium.

primevère *f* primrose.

primitif, -ive *adj (société etc)* primitive.

primordial, -e, -aux *adj* vital (de faire to do).

prince *m* prince.

princesse *f* princess.

principal, -e, -aux 1 *adj* main. **2** *m (de collège)* principal; **le p.** *(essentiel)* the main thing.

principe *m* principle; **en p.** theoretically; *(normalement)* as a rule.

printemps *m (saison)* spring.

prioritaire *adj* être p. to have priority; *(en voiture)* to have the right of way.

priorité *f* priority (sur over); **la p.** *(sur la route)* the right of way; **la p. à droite** right of way to traffic coming from the right; **'cédez la p.'** 'yield'.

pris, prise *(pp of* prendre*) adj (place)* taken; *(crème, ciment)* set; *(nez)* congested; **être (très)** p. to be (very) busy; **p. de** *(peur, panique)* stricken with.

prise *f (de judo etc)* hold; *(objet saisi)* catch; **p. (de courant)** *(mâle)* plug; *(femelle)* outlet, socket; **p. multiple** *(électrique)* adaptor; **p. de sang** blood test.

prison *f* prison, jail; **en p.** in prison ou jail.

prisonnier, -ière *mf* prisoner; **faire qn p.** to take sb prisoner.

privé, -ée *adj* private.

priver *vt* to deprive (de of).

priver (se) *vpr* se p. de to do without.

prix¹ *m (d'un objet etc)* price; **à tout p.** at all costs; **à aucun p.** on no account.

prix² *m (récompense)* prize.

probable *adj* likely, probable (que that); **peu p.** unlikely.

probablement *adv* probably.

problème *m* problem.

procédé *m* process.

procéder *vi (agir)* to proceed; **p. à** *(enquête, arrestation)* to carry out; **p. par élimination** to follow a process of elimination.

procès *m (criminel)* trial; *(civil)* lawsuit; **faire un p.** à to take to court.

procès-verbal, -aux *m (contravention)* (traffic) ticket.

prochain, -aine *adj* next.

prochainement *adv* shortly.

proche *adj (espace)* near, close; *(temps)* close (at hand); *(parent, ami)* close; **p. de** near (to), close to.

procuration *f* power of attorney; **par p.** by proxy.

procurer *vt* **p. qch à qn** *(personne)* to obtain sth for sb.

procurer (se) *vpr* **se p. qch** to obtain sth.

prodigieux, -euse *adj* extraordinary.

producteur, -trice 1 *mf* producer. **2** *adj* **pays p. de pétrole** oil-producing country.

production *f* production.

produire* *vt (fabriquer, causer etc)* to produce.

produire (se) *vpr (événement etc)* to happen.

produit *m (article etc)* product; *(pour la vaisselle)* liquid; **produits (de la terre)** produce; **p. (chimique)** chemical; **p. de beauté** cosmetic.

prof *mf Fam* teacher; *(à l'université)* professor.

proférer *vt* to utter.

professeur *m* teacher; *(à l'université)* professor.

profession *f* occupation; *(de médecin etc)* profession; *(manuelle)* trade.

professionnel, -elle 1 *adj* professional; *(école)* vocational. **2** *mf* professional.

profil *m* **de p.** (viewed) from the side, in profile.

profit *m* profit; **tirer p. de** to benefit from *ou* by.

profitable *adj (utile)* beneficial (à to).

profiter *vi* **p. de** to take advantage of; **p. à qn** to profit sb.

profond, -onde 1 *adj* deep; **p. de deux mètres** seven feet deep. **2** *adv (pénétrer etc)* deep.

profondément *adv* deeply; *(dormir)* soundly.

profondeur *f* depth; **à six mètres de p.** at a depth of 20 feet.

progiciel *m (software)* package.

programmateur *m (de four etc)* timer.

programme *m* program; *(scolaire)* syllabus; *(d'ordinateur)* program.

programmer *vt (ordinateur)* to program.

progrès *m & mpl* progress; **faire des p.** to make progress.

progresser *vi* to progress.

progressif, -ive *adj* gradual.

progressivement *adv* gradually.

proie *f* prey.

projecteur *m (de monument)* floodlight; *(de film etc)* projector.

projectile *m* missile.

projection *f (de film)* projection; *(séance)* showing.

projet *m* plan.

projeter *vt (lancer)* to hurl; *(film)* to project; *(voyage, fête etc)* to plan; **p. de faire** to plan to do.

prolonger *vt* to extend.

prolonger (se) *vpr (séance, rue)* to continue.

promenade *f (à pied)* walk; *(en voiture)* drive; *(en vélo, à cheval)* ride; **faire une p.** to (go for a) walk; *(en voiture)* to (go for a) drive.

promener *vt* to take for a walk *ou* drive.

promener (se) *vpr* to (go for a) walk; *(en voiture)* to (go for a) drive.

promeneur, -euse *mf* stroller.

promesse *f* promise.

promettre* vt to promise (**qch à qn** sb sth; **que** that); **p. de faire** to promise to do; **c'est promis** it's a promise.

promotion f **en p.** (produit) on (special) offer.

pronom m pronoun.

prononcer vt (articuler) to pronounce; (dire) to utter; (discours) to deliver.

prononcer (se) vpr (mot) to be pronounced.

prononciation f pronunciation.

pronostic m forecast; (d'un médecin) prognosis.

propager vt, **se propager** vpr to spread.

propice adj favorable (à to); **le moment p.** the right moment.

proportion f proportion; (rapport) ratio.

propos 1 mpl (paroles) remarks. 2 prép **à p. de** about. 3 adv **à p.!** by the way!

proposer vt to suggest, to propose (**qch à qn** sth to sb; **que** (+ subjonctif) that); (offrir) to offer (**qch à qn** sb sth; **de faire** to do); **je te propose de rester** I suggest you stay.

proposer (se) vpr **se p. pour faire** to offer to do.

proposition f Grammaire clause.

propre[1] 1 adj clean; (soigné) neat. 2 **mettre qch au p.** to make a clean copy of sth.

propre[2] adj own; **mon p. argent** my own money.

proprement adv cleanly; (avec netteté) neatly.

propreté f cleanliness; (netteté) neatness.

propriétaire mf owner; (qui loue) landlord, landlady.

propriété f (bien, maison) property.

prose f prose.

prospectus m leaflet.

prospère adj thriving.

protecteur, -trice 1 mf protector.

2 adj (geste etc) protective.

protection f protection; **de p.** (écran etc) protective.

protège-cahier, pl **protège-cahiers** m note book cover.

protéger vt to protect (**de** from; **contre** against).

protestant, -ante adj & mf Protestant.

protestataire mf protester.

protestation f protest (**contre** against).

protester vi to protest (**contre** against).

prothèse f prosthesis; **p. auditive** hearing aid; **p. dentaire** false teeth.

prouver vt to prove (**que** that).

provenance f origin; **en p. de** from.

provenir* vi **p. de** to come from.

proverbe m proverb.

province f province; **la p.** the provinces; **en p.** in the provinces; **de p.** (ville etc) provincial.

provincial, -e, -aux adj & mf provincial.

proviseur m (de lycée) principal.

provision f supply; **provisions** (achats) shopping; (nourriture) food; **sac à provisions** shopping bag; **chèque sans p.** bad check.

provisoire adj temporary.

provisoirement adv temporarily.

provoquer vt (causer) to bring (sth) about; (défier) to provoke (sb).

proximité f closeness; **à p.** close by; **à p. de** close to.

prudemment adv cautiously, carefully.

prudence f caution, care.

prudent, -ente adj cautious, careful.

prune f (fruit) plum.

pruneau, -x m prune.

prunier m plum tree.

psychiatre mf psychiatrist.

psychologique adj psychological.

psychologue mf psychologist.

PTT fpl abrév (Postes, Télégraphes, Téléphones) Post Office.

pu *voir* **pouvoir**.

puanteur *f* stink.

public, -ique 1 *adj* public. **2** *m* public; *(de spectacle)* audience; **en p.** in public.

publication *f* publication.

publicité *f* advertising, publicity; *(annonce)* advertisement; *(filmée)* commercial.

publier *vt* to publish.

puce *f* flea; *(d'ordinateur)* chip; **marché aux puces** flea market.

pudeur *f* modesty; **par p.** out of a sense of decency.

pudique *adj* modest.

puer 1 *vi* to stink. **2** *vt* to stink of.

puéricultrice *f* pediatric nurse.

puis *adv* then.

puiser *vt* to draw (**dans** from).

puisque *conj* since, as.

puissance *f* *(force, nation)* power.

puissant, -ante *adj* powerful.

puisse(s), puissent *etc voir* **pouvoir**.

puits *m* well; *(de mine)* shaft.

pull(-over) *m* sweater.

pulluler *vi* *(abonder)* to swarm.

pulvérisateur *m* spray.

pulvériser *vt* *(liquide)* to spray.

punaise *f* *(insecte)* bug; *(clou)* thumbtack.

punir *vt* to punish (**de qch** for sth; **pour avoir fait** for doing).

punition *f* punishment.

pupille *f* *(d'œil)* pupil.

pupitre *m* *(d'écolier)* desk; *(d'orateur)* lectern.

pur, -e *adj* pure.

purée *f* purée; **p. (de pommes de terre)** mashed potatoes.

pureté *f* purity.

pus *m* *(liquide)* pus.

puzzle *m* (jigsaw) puzzle.

p.-v. *m inv abrév (procès-verbal)* (traffic) ticket.

pyjama *m* pajamas; **un p.** a pair of pajamas.

pylône *m* pylon.

pyramide *f* pyramid.

Q

QI *m inv abrév (quotient intellectuel)* IQ.

quadrillé, -ée *adj* *(papier)* squared.

quai *m* *(de port) (pour passagers)* quay; *(pour marchandises)* wharf; *(de fleuve)* embankment; *(de gare)* platform.

qualifié, -ée *adj* *(équipe etc)* that has qualified; *(ouvrier)* skilled.

qualifier *vt* *(équipe)* to qualify (**pour qch** for sth; **pour faire** to do); *(décrire)* to describe (**de** as).

qualifier (se) *vpr (en sport)* to qualify (**pour** for).

qualité *f* quality.

quand *conj & adv* when; **q. je viendrai** when I come; **q. même** all the same.

quant à *prép* as for.

quantité *f* quantity; **une q.** *(beaucoup)* a lot (**de** of).

quarantaine *f* **une q. (de)** about forty.

quarante *adj & m* forty.

quarantième *adj & mf* fortieth.

quart *m* quarter; **q. (de litre)** quarter liter (= *one cup*); **q. d'heure** quarter of an hour; **une heure et q.** an hour and a quarter; **il est une heure et q.** it's a quarter after one; **une heure moins le q.** quarter to one.

quartier[1] *m* *(de ville)* neighborhood, district; *(chinois etc)* quarter; **de q.** *(cinéma etc)* local.

quartier[2] *m* *(de pomme)* quarter; *(d'orange)* segment.

quartz *m* **montre/etc à q.** quartz watch/*etc*.

quasiment *adv* almost.

quatorze *adj & m* fourteen.

quatre *adj & m* four; **q. heures**

(goûter) afternoon snack.

quatre-quatre *m* SUV.

quatre-vingt(s) *adj & m* eighty; **q.-vingts** ans eighty years; **q.-vingt-un** eighty-one; **page quatre-vingt** page eighty.

quatre-vingt-dix *adj & m* ninety.

quatrième *adj & mf* fourth.

que (qu' *before a vowel or mute h*) **1** *conj* that; **je pense qu'elle restera** I think (that) she'll stay; **qu'elle vienne ou non** whether she comes or not; **qu'il s'en aille!** let him leave! ■ **(ne)...q.** only; **tu n'as qu'un euro** you only have one euro. ■ *(comparaison)* than; *(avec aussi, même, tel, autant)* as; **plus âgé q.** older than; **aussi sage q.** as wise as; **le même q.** the same as. **2** *adv* **(ce) qu'il est bête!** how silly he is! **3** *pron rel (chose)* that, which; *(personne)* that; *(temps)* when; **le livre q. j'ai** the book (that *ou* which) I have; **l'ami q. j'ai** the friend (that) I have; **un jour q.** one day when. **4** *pron interrogatif* what; **q. fait-il?, qu'est-ce qu'il fait?** what is he doing?; **qu'est-ce qui est dans ta poche?** what's in your pocket?

quel, quelle 1 *adj interrogatif* what, which; *(qui)* who; **q. livre/acteur?** what *ou* which book/actor?; **je sais q. est ton but** I know what your aim is. **2** *pron interrogatif* which (one); **q. est le meilleur?** which (one) is the best? **3** *adj exclamatif* **q. idiot!** what a fool!

quelconque *adj* any (whatever); **une raison q.** any reason (whatever).

quelque 1 *adj* **quelques femmes/livres/etc** some *ou* a few women/books/*etc*; **les quelques amies qu'elle a** the few friends she has. **2** *pron* **q. chose** something; *(interrogation)* anything; **il a q. chose** *(un problème)* there's something the matter with him; **q. chose d'autre/de grand/etc**

something else/big/*etc*. **3** *adv* **q. part** somewhere; *(interrogation)* anywhere, somewhere.

quelquefois *adv* sometimes.

quelques-uns, -unes *pron pl* some.

quelqu'un *pron* someone; *(interrogation)* anyone, someone; **q. d'intelligent/etc** someone smart/etc.

question *f* question; *(problème)* matter; **il est q. de** there's some talk about ('faire doing); **il a été q. de vous** we/they/*etc* talked about you; **il n'en est pas q.** it's out of the question.

questionner *vt* to question (**sur** about).

quête *f (collecte)* collection; **faire la q.** to collect money.

quêter *vi* to collect money.

queue[1] *f (d'animal etc)* tail; *(de fleur)* stem; *(de fruit)* stalk; *(de poêle)* handle; *(de train)* rear; **q. de cheval** *(coiffure)* ponytail; **à la q. leu leu** in single file.

queue[2] *f (file)* line; **faire la q.** to line up.

qui *pron (personne)* who, that; *(interrogatif)* who; *(chose)* which, that; **l'homme q.** the man who *ou* that; **la maison q.** the house which *ou* that; **q. est là?** who's there?; **q. désirez-vous voir?, q. est-ce que vous désirez** voir? who do you want to see?; **la femme de q. je parle** the woman I'm talking about; **l'ami sur l'aide de q. je compte** the friend on whose help I rely; **à q. est ce livre?** whose book is this?

quiche *f* quiche.

quiconque *pron (sujet)* whoever; *(complément)* anyone.

quille *f (de jeu)* (bowling) pin; **jouer aux quilles** to bowl.

quincaillerie hardware store.

quincaillier, -ière *mf* hardware store owner.

quinzaine *f* une q. (de) about fifteen; q. (de jours) two weeks.

quinze *adj & m* fifteen; q. jours two weeks.

quinzième *adj & mf* fifteenth.

quittance *f (reçu)* receipt.

quitte *adj* even (envers with).

quitter 1 *vt* to leave; q. qn des yeux to take one's eyes off sb. **2** *vi* ne quittez pas! (au téléphone) hold on!

quitter (se) *vpr (se séparer)* to part, to say goodbye.

quoi *pron* what; *(après prép)* which; à q. penses-tu? what are you thinking about?; de q. manger something to eat; de q. couper/écrire something to cut/write with; il n'y a pas de q.! (en réponse à 'merci') don't mention it!

quoique *conj* (al)though; q. je le sache déjà (al)though I already know.

quotidien, -ienne 1 *adj* daily. **2** *m* daily (paper).

R

rabâcher 1 *vt* to repeat endlessly. **2** *vi* to say the same thing over and over again.

rabais *m* reduction, discount.

rabattre* *vt* to pull down; *(refermer)* to close (down).

rabattre (se) *vpr (barrière)* to come down; *(après avoir doublé un véhicule)* to cut in.

rabbin *m* rabbi.

rabot *m (outil)* plane.

raboter *vt* to plane.

raccommodage *m* mending; *(de chaussette)* darning.

raccommoder *vt* to mend; *(chaussette)* to darn.

raccompagner *vt* to see *ou* accompany back (home); r. à la porte to see to the door.

raccord *m (dispositif)* connection, connector; *(de papier peint)* seam.

raccourci *m (chemin)* short cut.

raccourcir 1 *vt* to shorten. **2** *vi* to get shorter.

raccrocher 1 *vt (objet tombé)* to hang back up; *(téléphone)* to put down. **2** *vi (au téléphone)* to hang up.

race *f (groupe ethnique)* race; *(d'animal)* breed.

rachat *m (de voiture, d'appartement)* repurchase; *(de firme)* buy-out.

racheter *vt* r. un manteau/une voiture/etc to buy another coat/car/etc; r. des chaussettes/du pain/etc to buy some more socks/bread/etc.

racial, -e, -aux *adj* racial.

racine *f* root; prendre r. *(plante)* to take root.

racisme *m* racism.

raciste *adj & mf* racist.

racler *vt* to scrape; *(enlever)* to scrape off.

racler (se) *vpr* se r. la gorge to clear one's throat.

racontars *mpl* gossip.

raconter *vt (histoire)* to tell; r. qch à qn *(vacances etc)* to tell sb about sth; r. à qn que to tell sb that.

radar *m* radar.

radeau, -x *m* raft.

radiateur *m* heater; *(de chauffage central, voiture)* radiator.

radieux, -euse *adj (personne, visage)* beaming; *(soleil)* brilliant; *(temps)* glorious.

radio¹ *f* radio; *(poste)* radio (set); à la r. on the radio.

radio² *f (examen, photo)* X-ray; passer une r. to have an X-ray.

radioactif, -ive *adj* radioactive.

radiodiffuser *vt* to broadcast (on the radio).

radiographier *vt* to X-ray.

radis *m* radish.

radoucir (se) *vpr (temps)* to become milder.

radoucissement *m* **r. (du temps)** milder weather.

rafale *f (vent)* gust.

raffiné, -ée *adj* refined.

raffoler *vi* **r. de** *(aimer)* to be crazy about.

rafistoler *vt Fam* to patch up.

rafraîchir *vt* to cool (down).

rafraîchir (se) *vpr (boire)* to refresh oneself; *(temps)* to get cooler.

rafraîchissant, -ante *adj* refreshing.

rafraîchissement *m (de température)* cooling; *(boisson)* cold drink; **rafraîchissements** *(glaces etc)* refreshments.

rage *f (colère)* rage; *(maladie)* rabies; **r. de dents** violent toothache.

ragoût *m* stew.

raid *m* raid.

raide *adj (rigide)* stiff; *(côte)* steep; *(cheveux)* straight; *(corde)* tight.

raidir *vt*, **se raidir** *vpr* to stiffen; *(corde)* to tighten.

raie *f (trait)* line; *(de tissu, zèbre)* stripe; *(de cheveux)* part.

rail *m (barre)* rail *(for train)*.

rainure *f* groove.

raisin *m (grain de)* **r.** grape; **du r., des raisins** grapes; **r. sec** raisin.

raison *f* reason; **la r. de/pour laquelle...** the reason for/why...; **en r. de** on account of; **avoir r.** to be right **(de faire** to do).

raisonnable *adj* reasonable.

raisonnement *m* reasoning.

raisonner 1 *vi (penser)* to reason. **2** *vt* **r. qn** to reason with.

rajeunir *vt* to make (feel *ou* look) younger.

rajouter *vt* to add **(à** to).

ralenti *m* **au r.** *(filmer)* in slow motion; **tourner au r.** *(moteur)* to turn over.

ralentir *vti* to slow down.

ralentissement *m* slowing down; *(embouteillage)* hold-up.

rallonge *f (de table)* extension; *(électrique)* extension cord.

rallonger *vti* to lengthen.

rallumer *vt (feu, pipe)* to light again; *(lampe)* to switch on again.

rallye *m (automobile)* rally.

ramassage *m (de par terre)* picking up; *(d'ordures, de copies)* collection; *(de fruits, de coquillages)* gathering; **r. scolaire** school bus service.

ramasser *vt (prendre par terre, réunir)* to pick up; *(ordures, copies)* to collect; *(fruits, coquillages)* to gather.

rame *f (aviron)* oar; *(de métro)* train.

ramener *vt* to bring *ou* take *(sb)* back.

ramer *vi* to row.

ramollir *vt*, **se ramollir** *vpr* to soften.

ramoner *vt (cheminée)* to sweep.

rampe *f (d'escalier)* banister(s); **r. (d'accès)** ramp; **r. de lancement** *(de fusées)* launching pad.

ramper *vi* to crawl.

ranch *m* ranch.

rançon *f (argent)* ransom.

rancune *f* grudge; **garder r. à qn** to bear sb a grudge.

rancunier, -ière *adj* spiteful.

randonnée *f (à pied)* hike; *(en voiture)* drive; *(en vélo)* ride.

rang *m (rangée)* row, line; *(classement)* rank; **se mettre en rang(s)** to line up **(par trois/etc** in threes/ *etc).*

rangé, -ée *adj (chambre etc)* tidy.

rangée *f* row, line.

rangements *mpl (placards)* storage space.

ranger *vt (papiers etc)* to put away; *(chambre etc)* to tidy (up); *(chiffres, mots)* to arrange; *(voiture)* to park.

ranger (se) *vpr (élèves etc)* to line

up; (*s'écarter*) to stand aside; (*voiture*) to pull over.

ranimer *vt* (*réanimer*) to revive (*sb*), (*feu*) to poke, to stir.

rapace *m* bird of prey.

râpe *f* (*à fromage etc*) grater.

râper *vt* (*fromage, carottes*) to grate.

rapetisser *vi* to get smaller.

rapide 1 *adj* fast, quick. **2** *m* (*train*) express (train).

rapidement *adv* fast, quickly.

rapidité *f* speed.

rapiécer *vt* to patch (up).

rappeler *vt* to call back; (*souvenir*) to recall; **r. qch à qn** to remind sb of sth.

rappeler (se) *vpr* to remember (**que** that).

rapport *m* (*lien*) connection; (*récit*) report; **rapports** (*entre personnes*) relations; **par r. à** compared to; **ça n'a aucun r.!** it has nothing to do with it!

rapporter 1 *vt* to bring *ou* take back; (*profit*) to bring in. **2** *vi* (*dénoncer*) *Fam* to tell tales; (*investissement*) to bring in a good return.

rapporter (se) *vpr* **se r. à** to relate to.

rapporteur, -euse 1 *mf* telltale. **2** *m* (*en géométrie*) protractor.

rapprocher *vt* to bring closer (**de** to); (*chaise*) to pull up (**de** to).

rapprocher (se) *vpr* to come *ou* get closer (**de** to).

raquette *f* (*de tennis*) racket; (*de ping-pong*) paddle.

rare *adj* rare; **il est r. que** (+ *subjonctif*) it's rare that.

rarement *adv* rarely, seldom.

ras, rase *adj* (*cheveux*) close-cropped; (*herbe, poil*) short; **en rase campagne** in the open country; **à r. bord** (*remplir*) to the brim.

rasé, -ée *adj* **être bien r.** to have shaved; **mal r.** unshaven.

raser *vt* (*menton, personne*) to shave; (*barbe, moustache*) to shave off; (*démolir*) to knock down; (*frôler*) to skim.

raser (se) *vpr* to (have a) shave.

rasoir *m* razor; (*électrique*) shaver.

rassemblement *m* gathering.

rassembler *vt* (*gens, objets*) to gather (together).

rassembler (se) *vpr* to gather.

rassis, f rassie *adj* (*pain etc*) stale.

rassurant, -ante *adj* reassuring.

rassurer *vt* to reassure; **rassure-toi** don't worry.

rat *m* rat.

ratatiner (se) *vpr* to shrivel up.

râteau, -x *m* (*outil*) rake.

rater *vt* (*bus, cible etc*) to miss; (*travail, gâteau etc*) to ruin; (*examen*) to fail.

ration *f* ration.

rationnement *m* rationing.

rationner *vt* to ration.

ratisser *vt* (*allée etc*) to rake; (*feuilles etc*) to rake up.

rattacher *vt* (*lacets etc*) to tie up again.

rattrapage *m* **cours de r.** remedial class.

rattraper *vt* to catch; (*prisonnier*) to recapture; (*temps perdu*) to make up for; **r. qn** (*rejoindre*) to catch up with sb.

rature *f* crossing out.

raturer *vt* to cross out.

rauque *adj* (*voix*) hoarse.

ravager *vt* to devastate.

ravages *mpl* havoc; **faire des r.** to cause havoc *ou* widespread damage.

ravaler *vt* (*façade etc*) to clean (and restore).

ravi, -ie *adj* delighted (**de** with; **de faire** to do).

ravin *m* ravine.

ravioli(s) *mpl* ravioli.

ravir *vt* (*plaire*) to delight.

raviser (se) *vpr* to change one's mind.

ravissant, -ante *adj* beautiful.

ravisseur, -euse mf kidnapper.

ravitaillement m supplying; (denrées) supplies.

ravitailler vt to supply (en with).

ravitailler (se) vpr to stock up (with supplies).

rayé, -ée adj scratched; (tissu) striped.

rayer vt (érafler) to scratch; (mot etc) to cross out.

rayon m (de lumière, soleil) ray; (de cercle) radius; (de roue) spoke; (planche) shelf; (de magasin) department.

rayonnant, -ante adj (visage etc) beaming (de with).

rayure f scratch; (bande) stripe; **à rayures** striped.

raz-de-marée m inv tidal wave.

re-, ré- préfixe re-.

réacteur m (d'avion) jet engine; (nucléaire) reactor.

réaction f reaction; **avion à r.** jet (aircraft).

réagir vi to react (contre against; à to).

réalisateur, -trice mf (de film) director.

réaliser vt (projet etc) to carry out; (rêve) to fulfill; (fabriquer) to make; (film) to direct.

réaliser (se) vpr (vœu) to come true; (projet) to materialize.

réaliste adj realistic.

réalité f reality; **en r.** in fact.

réanimation f **en r.** in intensive care.

réanimer vt to revive, to resuscitate.

rebond m bounce.

rebondir vi to bounce.

rebord m **r. de (la) fenêtre** windowsill.

reboucher vt (flacon) to put the top back on; (trou) to fill in again.

rébus m inv rebus (word guessing game).

récemment adv recently.

récent, -ente adj recent.

réception f (réunion, de radio etc) reception; (d'hôtel) reception (desk); **dès r. de** on receipt of.

recette f (de cuisine) recipe (de for); (argent, bénéfice) takings.

recevoir* 1 vt to receive; (accueillir) to welcome; **être reçu (à) (examen)** to pass. **2** vi to have guests.

rechange (de) adj (outil etc) spare; **vêtements de r.** a change of clothes.

recharge f (de stylo) refill.

recharger vt (fusil, appareil photo) to reload; (briquet, stylo) to refill; (batterie) to recharge.

réchaud m (portable) stove.

réchauffement m (de température) rise (de in).

réchauffer vt to warm up.

réchauffer (se) vpr **se r.** to warm oneself up; (temps) to get warmer.

recherche f **la r., des recherches** (scientifique etc) research (sur on, into); **faire des recherches** to (do) research; (enquêter) to investigate.

recherché, -ée adj **r. pour meurtre** wanted for murder.

rechercher vt (personne, objet) to search for.

rechute f relapse.

récif m reef.

récipient m container.

réciproque adj mutual.

récit m (histoire) story.

récitation f (poème) poem (learned by heart and recited aloud).

réciter vt to recite.

réclamation f complaint.

réclame f advertising; (annonce) advertisement; **en r.** on (special) offer.

réclamer 1 vt (demander) to ask for (sth) back. **2** vi to complain.

recoin m nook.

recoller vt (objet cassé) to stick back together; (enveloppe) to reseal.

récolte f (action) harvest; (produits) crop.

récolter vt to harvest.

recommandation f recommendation.

recommander vt to recommend (à to; pour for); r. à qn de faire to recommend to sb to do; lettre recommandée certified letter; en recommandé (envoyer) by certified mail.

recommencer vti to start again.

récompense f reward (pour for).

récompenser vt to reward (de, pour for).

réconciliation f reconciliation.

réconcilier (se) vpr to settle one's differences, to make it up (avec with).

reconduire* vt r. qn to see sb back.

réconfort m comfort.

réconfortant, -ante adj comforting.

réconforter vt to comfort.

reconnaissance f (gratitude) gratitude.

reconnaissant, -ante adj grateful (à qn de qch to sb for sth).

reconnaître vt to recognize (à qch by sth); (admettre) to admit (que that); reconnu coupable found guilty.

reconstruire* vt (ville) to rebuild.

reconvertir (se) vpr (personne) to retrain.

recopier vt to copy out.

record m & adj inv (en sport etc) record.

recoudre* vt (bouton) to sew (back) on; (vêtement) to stitch (up).

recourbé, -ée adj (clou etc) bent; (nez) hooked.

recourir* vi r. à (moyen, violence) to resort to; (personne) to turn to.

recours m recourse; avoir r. à (chose) to resort to; (personne) to turn to; en dernier r. as a last resort.

recouvrir* vt (livre, meuble etc) to cover.

récréation f (à l'école) recess.

recroquevillé, -ée adj (personne, papier etc) curled up.

recrue f recruit.

rectangle m rectangle.

rectangulaire adj rectangular.

rectification f correction.

rectifier vt to correct.

recto m front (of the page).

reçu, reçue 1 pp of **recevoir. 2** m (écrit) receipt.

recueil m anthology, collection (de of).

recueillir* vt to collect; (prendre chez soi) to take (sb) in.

recul m (d'armée, de négociateur, de maladie) retreat; (de canon) recoil; (déclin) decline; avoir un mouvement de r. to recoil; manquer de r. to be too closely involved; prendre du r. to stand back from things.

reculer 1 vi to move back; (véhicule) to reverse. **2** vt to push back.

reculons (à) adv backwards.

récupérer 1 vt (objet prêté) to get back. **2** vi to get one's strength back.

récurer vt (casserole etc) to scrub.

recyclage m (de matériaux) recycling; (de personne) retraining.

recycler vt (matériaux) to recycle.

rédacteur, -trice mf (de journal) editor; r. en chef editor(-in-chief).

rédaction f (devoir de français) essay, composition.

redescendre 1 vi (aux être) to come ou go back down. **2** vt (aux avoir) to bring ou take back down.

rediffusion f (de film etc) repeat, rerun.

rédiger vt to write.

redire* vt to repeat.

redonner vt (donner plus) to give more; r. un euro/etc to give another euro/etc.

redoublant, -ante mf student repeating a grade.

redoublement *m* repeating a grade.

redoubler *vti* r. (une classe) to repeat a grade.

redoutable *adj* formidable.

redouter *vt* to dread (**de faire** doing).

redresser *vt* (objet tordu etc) to straighten (out).

redresser (se) *vpr* to sit up; (debout) to stand up.

réduction *f* reduction (**de** in); (prix réduit) discount; **en r.** (copie, modèle) small-scale.

réduire* *vt* to reduce (**à** to; **de** by); **r. en cendres** to reduce to ashes.

réduit, -uite *adj* (prix, vitesse) reduced; (modèle) small-scale.

rééducation *f* (de personne) rehabilitation; **faire de la r.** to have physical therapy.

réel, -elle *adj* real.

réellement *adv* really.

réexpédier *vt* (faire suivre) to forward (letter).

refaire* *vt* (exercice, travail) to do again, to redo; (chambre etc) to redecorate.

réfectoire *m* refectory.

référence *f* reference.

refermer *vt*, **se refermer** *vpr* to close (again).

réfléchir 1 *vt* (image) to reflect; **verbe réfléchi** reflexive verb. **2** *vi* (penser) to think (**à** about).

réfléchir (se) *vpr* to be reflected.

reflet *m* (image) reflection; **reflets** (couleurs) highlights.

refléter *vt* (image etc) to reflect.

refléter (se) *vpr* to be reflected.

réflexe *m* reflex.

réflexion *f* (méditation) thought; (remarque) remark.

réforme *f* (changement) reform.

refrain *m* (de chanson) chorus.

réfrigérateur *m* refrigerator.

refroidir *vti* to cool (down).

refroidir (se) *vpr* (prendre froid) to catch cold; (temps) to get cold.

refroidissement *m* (rhume) chill; **r. de la température** fall in the temperature.

refuge *m* refuge; (pour piétons) median; (de montagne) (mountain) hut.

réfugié, -ée *mf* refugee.

réfugier (se) *vpr* to take refuge.

refus *m* refusal.

refuser 1 *vt* to refuse (**qch à qn** sb sth; **de faire** to do); (candidat) to fail. **2** *vi* to refuse.

regagner *vt* to regain, to get back; (revenir à) to get back to.

régaler (se) *vpr* to have a feast.

regard *m* look; (fixe) stare; **jeter un r. sur** to glance at.

regarder¹ *vt* to look at; (fixement) to stare at; (observer) to watch; **r. qn faire** to watch sb do. **2** *vi* to look; to stare; to watch.

regarder² *vt* (concerner) to concern; **ça ne te regarde pas!** it's none of your business!

régime¹ *m* (politique) (form of) government; (alimentaire) diet; **se mettre au r.** to go on a diet; **suivre un r.** to be on a diet.

régime² *m* (de bananes, dattes) bunch.

régiment *m* (soldats) regiment.

région *f* region, area.

régional, -e, -aux *adj* regional.

registre *m* register.

réglable *adj* (siège) adjustable.

réglage *m* adjustment; (de moteur) tuning.

règle *f* rule; (instrument) ruler; **en r. générale** as a rule; **règles** (de femme) (monthly) period.

règlement *m* (règles) regulations; (paiement) payment; **contraire au r.** against the rules.

réglementation *f* (règles) regulations.

régler 1 *vt* (problème etc) to settle; (mécanisme) to adjust; (moteur) to tune. **2** *vti* (payer) to pay; **r. qn** to settle up with sb.

réglisse f licorice.

règne m (de roi) reign.

régner vi (roi, silence) to reign (**sur** over).

regret m regret; **à r.** with regret.

regrettable adj unfortunate, regrettable.

regretter vt to regret; **r. qn** to miss sb; **r. que** (+ subjonctif) to be sorry that; **je (le) regrette** I'm sorry.

regrouper vt, **se regrouper** vpr to gather together.

régularité f regularity; (de progrès, vitesse) steadiness.

régulier, -ière adj regular; (progrès, vitesse) steady.

régulièrement adv regularly.

réhabituer (se) vpr **se r. à qch/à faire qch** to get used to sth/to doing sth again.

rein m kidney; **les reins** (dos) the (small of the) back.

reine f queen.

réinsertion f reintegration; **r. sociale** rehabilitation.

rejeter vt to throw back; (refuser) to reject.

rejoindre* vt (famille, lieu etc) to get back to; **r. qn** (rattraper) to join sb; (rattraper) to catch up with sb.

rejoindre (se) vpr (personnes, routes) to meet.

réjouir (se) vpr to be delighted (**de** at, about; **de faire** to do).

réjouissances fpl festivities.

relâcher vt (corde etc) to slacken; **r. qn** to release sb.

relais m **prendre le r.** to take over (**de** from).

relancer vt (lancer à nouveau) to throw again; (rendre) to throw back; (production) to boost; (moteur) to restart.

relatif, -ive adj relative.

relation f relation(ship); (ami) acquaintance; **entrer en relations avec** to come into contact with.

relativement adv (assez) relatively.

relayer vt to take over from (sb).

relayer (se) vpr to take (it in) turns (**pour faire** to do).

relevé m (de compteur) reading; **r. de compte** (bank) statement.

relever vt to raise; (personne tombée) to help up; (col) to turn up; (manches) to roll up; (compteur) to read.

relever (se) vpr (personne tombée) to get up.

relief m (forme) relief; **en r.** (cinéma) 3-D.

relier vt to connect (**à** to); (livre) to bind.

religieux, -euse 1 adj religious. **2** f nun.

religion f religion.

relire* vt to read again, to reread.

reliure f (de livre) binding.

reluire* vi to shine.

remarquable adj remarkable (**par** for).

remarquablement adv remarkably.

remarque f remark; (écrite) note.

remarquer vt to notice (**que** that); **faire r.** to point out (**à** to; **que** that); **se faire r.** to attract attention; **remarque!** mind you!, you know!

rembobiner vt, **se rembobiner** (bande) to rewind.

rembourré, -ée adj (fauteuil etc) padded.

remboursement m repayment; (dans un magasin etc) refund.

rembourser vt to pay back, to repay; (billet) to refund.

remède m cure, (médicament) medicine.

remédier vi **r. à qch** to remedy sth.

remémorer (se) vpr to remember.

remerciements mpl thanks.

remercier vt to thank (**de qch, pour qch** for sth); **je vous remercie d'être venu** thank you for coming.

remettre* vt to put back; (vêtement) to put back on; (donner) to hand over (**à** to); (*démission, devoir*) to hand in; (*différer*) to postpone (**à** until); **r. en question** to call into question; **r. en état** to repair.

remettre (se) *vpr* **se r. à** (*activité*) to go back to; **se r. à faire** to start to do again; **se r. de** (*chagrin, maladie*) to get over.

remise *f* (*rabais*) discount.

remonte-pente, *pl* **remonte-pentes** *m* ski lift.

remonter 1 *vi* (*aux* **être**) to come *ou* go back up; **r. dans** (*voiture*) to get back in(to); (*bus, train*) to get back on(to); **r. sur** (*cheval, vélo*) to get back on(to). **2** *vt* (*aux* **avoir**) (*escalier, pente*) to come *ou* go back up; (*porter*) to bring *ou* take back up; (*montre*) to wind; (*relever*) to raise; (*col*) to turn up; (*objet démonté*) to put back together.

remords *m & mpl* remorse; **avoir des r.** to feel remorse.

remorque *f* (*de voiture etc*) trailer; **prendre en r.** to tow; **en r.** in tow.

remorquer *vt* to tow.

remorqueur *m* tug(boat).

remplaçant, -ante *mf* (*personne*) replacement; (*enseignant*) substitute teacher; (*en sport*) reserve.

remplacement *m* replacement; **assurer le r. de qn** to stand in for sb.

remplacer *vt* to replace (**par** with, by); (*succéder*) to take over from.

rempli, -ie *adj* full (**de** of).

remplir *vt* to fill (up) (**de** with); (*fiche etc*) to fill in *ou* out.

remplir (se) *vpr* to fill (up).

remporter *vi* (*objet*) to take back; (*prix, victoire*) to win.

remuant, -ante *adj* (*enfant*) restless.

remuer 1 *vt* to move; (*café etc*) to stir; (*salade*) to toss. **2** *vi* to move; (*gigoter*) to fidget.

renard *m* fox.

rencontre *f* meeting; (*en sport*) game; **aller à la r. de qn** to go to meet sb.

rencontrer *vt* to meet; (*équipe*) to play.

rencontrer (se) *vpr* to meet.

rendez-vous *m inv* appointment; (*d'amoureux*) date; (*lieu*) meeting place; **donner r. à qn** to make an appointment with sb.

rendormir* (se) *vpr* to go back to sleep.

rendre 1 *vt* to give back; (*monnaie*) to give; (*vomir*) to bring up; **r. célèbre/plus grand/etc** to make famous/bigger/etc. **2** *vti* (*vomir*) to throw up.

rendre (se) *vpr* to surrender (**à qn** to sb); (*aller*) to go (**à** to); **se r. utile/etc** to make oneself useful/etc.

rênes *fpl* reins.

renfermé *m* **sentir le r.** (*chambre etc*) to smell stuffy.

renfermer *vt* to contain.

renflement *m* bulge.

renforcer *vt* to strengthen.

renforts *mpl* (*troupes*) reinforcements.

renier *vt* (*ami, pays*) to disown; (*foi*) to deny.

renifler *vti* to sniff.

renne *m* reindeer.

renommé, -ée *adj* famous (**pour** for).

renommée *f* fame.

renoncer *vi* **r. à qch/à faire** to give up sth/doing.

renouvelable *adj* renewable.

renouveler *vt* to renew; (*erreur, question*) to repeat.

renouveler (se) *vpr* (*incident*) to happen again.

renseignement *m* (piece of) information; **des renseignements** information; **les renseignements** (*au téléphone*) directory assistance, information.

renseigner *vt* to inform, to give some information to (**sur** about).

renseigner (se) *vpr* to find out, to inquire (**sur** about).

rentable *adj* profitable.

rentrée *f* return; **r. (des classes)** beginning of the school year.

rentrer 1 *vi* (*aux être*) to go *ou* come back; (*chez soi*) to go *ou* come (back) home; (*entrer de nouveau*) to go *ou* come back in; (*élèves*) to go back to school; **r. dans** to go *ou* come back in; (*pays*) to return to; (*heurter*) to crash into; (*s'emboîter dans*) to fit into. **2** *vt* (*aux avoir*) to bring *ou* take in; (*voiture*) to put away; (*chemise*) to tuck in; (*griffes*) to draw in.

renverse (à la) *adv* (*tomber*) backwards.

renverser *vt* (*mettre à l'envers*) to turn upside down; (*faire tomber*) to knock over; (*piéton*) to knock down; (*liquide*) to spill.

renverser (se) *vpr* (*vase etc*) to fall over; (*liquide*) to spill.

renvoi *m* (*d'un employé*) dismissal; (*rot*) burp.

renvoyer* *vt* to send back; (*employé*) to dismiss; (*élève*) to expel; (*balle etc*) to throw back.

réorganiser *vt* to reorganize.

repaire *m* den.

répandre *vt* (*liquide*) to spill; (*nouvelle*) to spread.

répandre (se) *vpr* **se r. dans** (*fumée, odeur*) to spread through.

répandu, -ue *adj* (*opinion etc*) widespread.

reparaître *vi* to reappear.

réparateur, -trice *mf* repairer.

réparation *f* repair; **en r.** under repair.

réparer *vt* to repair, to mend; (*erreur*) to correct.

repartir* *vi* (*aux être*) to set off again; (*s'en retourner*) to go back.

répartir *vt* (*partager*) to share (out).

repas *m* meal; **prendre un r.** to have a meal.

repassage *m* ironing.

repasser 1 *vi* to come *ou* go back. **2** *vt* (*traverser*) to go back over; (*leçon*) to go over; (*film*) to show again; (*linge*) to iron.

repêcher *vt* (*objet*) to fish out.

repentir* (se) *vpr* to be sorry (**de** for).

repère *m* (guide) mark; **point de r.** (*espace, temps*) landmark.

repérer *vt* to locate.

repérer (se) *vpr* to get one's bearings.

répertoire *m* **r. d'adresses** address book.

répéter *vti* to repeat; (*pièce de théâtre*) to rehearse.

répéter (se) *vpr* (*événement*) to happen again.

répétitif, -ive *adj* repetitive.

répétition *f* repetition; (*au théâtre*) rehearsal.

répit *m* rest, respite; **sans r.** ceaselessly.

replacer *vt* to put back.

repli *m* fold.

replier *vt* to fold (up); (*couverture*) to fold back; (*ailes, jambes*) to tuck in.

replier (se) *vpr* (*siège*) to fold up; (*couverture*) to fold back.

réplique *f* (sharp) reply; (*au théâtre*) lines.

répliquer 1 *vt* to reply (sharply) (**que** that). **2** *vi* to answer back.

répondeur *m* (*téléphonique*) answering machine.

répondre 1 *vi* to answer; (*être impertinent*) to answer back; (*réagir*) to respond (**à** to); **r. à qn** to answer sb; (*avec impertinence*) to answer sb back; **r. à** (*lettre, question*) to answer. **2** *vt* **r. que** to answer that.

réponse *f* answer.

reportage *m* (news) report; (*en direct*) (live) commentary.

reporter[1] *vt* to take back; (*différer*) to put off (**à** until).

reporter[2] *m* reporter.

repos *m* rest; (*tranquillité*) peace

(and quiet); **jour de r.** day off.
reposant, -ante *adj* restful.
reposer *vt* (*objet*) to put back down; (*délasser*) to relax.
reposer (se) *vpr* to rest.
repousser 1 *vt* to push back; (*écarter*) to push away; (*différer*) to put off. **2** *vi* (*cheveux, feuilles*) to grow again.
reprendre* 1 *vt* (*objet*) to take back; (*évadé*) to recapture; (*souffle, forces*) to get back; (*activité*) to take up again; (*refrain*) to take up; **r. de la viande/un œuf/**etc to take (some) more meat/another egg/ etc. **2** *vi* (*recommencer*) to start (up) (again); (*affaires*) to pick up; (*dire*) to go on.
reprendre (se) *vpr* to correct oneself; **s'y r. à deux fois** to give it another try.
représentant, -ante *mf* representative; **r. de commerce** (traveling) salesman, saleswoman.
représentation *f* (*au théâtre*) performance.
représenter *vt* to represent; (*pièce de théâtre*) to peform.
réprimander *vt* to reprimand.
reprise *f* (*d'émission de télévision*) rerun, repeat; (*de tissu*) mend; *Boxe* round; (*économique*) recovery; (*pour nouvel achat*) trade-in; **à plusieurs reprises** on several occasions.
repriser *vt* (*chaussette etc*) to mend.
reproche *m* criticism; **faire des reproches à qn** to criticize sb.
reprocher *vt* **r. qch à qn** to criticize sb for sth.
reproduction *f* breeding; (*copie*) copy.
reproduire* *vt* (*modèle etc*) to copy.
reproduire (se) *vpr* (*animaux*) to breed; (*incident etc*) to happen again.
reptile *m* reptile.

républicain, -aine *adj & mf* republican.
république *f* republic.
réputation *f* reputation; **avoir la r. d'être** to have a reputation for being.
requin *m* (*poisson*) shark.
rescapé, -ée *mf* survivor.
réseau, -x *m* network.
réservation *f* reservation, booking.
réserve *f* (*provision*) stock, reserve; (*entrepôt*) storeroom; **en r.** in reserve; **r. naturelle** nature reserve.
réservé, -ée *adj* (*personne, place*) reserved.
réserver *vt* (*garder*) to save, to reserve (**à** for); (*place, table*) to book, to reserve.
réserver (se) *vpr* **se r. pour** to save oneself for.
réservoir *m* (*citerne*) tank; **r. d'essence** gas tank.
résidence *f* residence; **r. secondaire** second home.
résidentiel, -ielle *adj* (*quartier*) residential.
résider *vi* to be resident (**à, en, dans** in).
résigner (se) *vpr* to resign oneself (**à qch** to sth; **à faire** to doing).
résistance *f* resistance (**à** to); (*électrique*) (*heating*) element; **plat de r.** main dish.
résistant, -ante *adj* tough; **r. à la chaleur** heat-resistant; **r. au choc** shockproof.
résister *vi* **r. à** to resist; (*chaleur, fatigue*) to withstand.
résolu, -ue *adj* determined (**à faire** to do).
résolution *f* (*décision*) decision.
résonner *vi* (*cris etc*) to ring out; (*salle*) to echo (**de** with).
résoudre* *vt* (*problème*) to solve; (*difficulté*) to clear up.
respect *m* respect (**pour, de** for).
respecter *vt* to respect.
respectueux, -euse *adj* respectful (**envers** to).

respiration f breathing; (haleine) breath.

respirer 1 vi to breathe; (reprendre haleine) to get one's breath back. **2** vt to breathe (in).

resplendissant, -ante adj (visage) glowing (**de** with).

responsabilité f responsibility.

responsable 1 adj responsible (**de qch** for sth; **devant qn** to sb). **2** mf (chef) person in charge; (coupable) person responsible (**de** for).

ressaisir (se) vpr to pull oneself together.

ressemblance f likeness (**avec** to).

ressembler vi **r. à** to look ou be like.

ressembler (se) vpr to look ou be alike.

ressentir* vt to feel.

resserrer vt, **se resserrer** vpr (nœud etc) to tighten.

resservir* vi (outil etc) to come in useful (again).

resservir (se) vpr **se r. de** (plat) to have another helping of.

ressort m (objet) spring.

ressortir* vi (aux être) to go ou come back out; (se voir) to stand out.

ressources fpl (moyens, argent) resources.

restaurant m restaurant.

restauration f (hôtellerie) catering; (de tableau) restoration.

restaurer vt (réparer) to restore.

reste m rest (**de** of); **restes** (de repas) leftovers; **un r. de fromage/** etc some leftover cheese/etc.

rester vi (aux être) to stay; (calme etc) to keep, to stay; (subsister) to be left; **il reste du pain/**etc there's some bread/etc left (over); **il me reste une minute** I have one minute left; **l'argent qui lui reste** the money he ou she has left.

restreindre* vt to limit (**à** to).

résultat m (score, d'examen etc) results; (conséquence) outcome, result.

résumé m summary.

résumer vt to summarize; (situation) to sum up.

rétablir vt to restore.

rétablir (se) vpr (malade) to recover.

rétablissement m (de malade) recovery.

retard m (sur un programme etc) delay; **en r.** late; **en r. dans qch** behind in sth; **en r. sur qn/qch** behind sb/sth; **rattraper son r.** to catch up; **avoir du r.** to be late; (sur un programme) to be behind; (montre) to be slow; **avoir une heure de r.** to be an hour late.

retardataire mf latecomer.

retarder 1 vt to delay; (date, montre) to put back; **r. qn** (dans une activité) to put sb behind. **2** vi (montre) to be slow; **r. de cinq minutes** to be five minutes slow.

retenir* vt (empêcher d'agir) to hold back; (souffle) to hold; (réserver) to book; (se souvenir de) to remember; (fixer) to hold (in place); (chiffre) to carry; (chaleur, odeur) to retain; **r. qn prisonnier** to keep sb prisoner.

retenir (se) vpr (se contenir) to restrain oneself; **se r. de faire** to stop oneself (from) doing; **se r. à** to cling to.

retentir vi to ring (out) (**de** with).

retenue f (punition) detention.

retirer vt (sortir) to take out; (ôter) to take off; (éloigner) to take away; **r. qch à qn** (permis etc) to take sth away from sb.

retomber vi to fall (again); (pendre) to hang (down); (après un saut etc) to land.

retouche f (de vêtement) alteration.

retoucher vt (vêtement) to alter.

retour m return; **être de r.** to be back (**de** from); **à mon r.** when I get ou got back.

retourner 1 vt (aux avoir) (matelas, steak etc) to turn over; (terre etc) to turn; (vêtement, sac etc) to turn inside out. **2** vi (aux être) to go back, to return.

retourner (se) vpr to turn around, to look around; (sur le dos) to turn over; (voiture) to overturn.

retrait m withdrawal; (de bagages, de billets) collection; (des eaux) receding; **en r.** (maison) set back; **rester en r.** to stay in the background.

retraite f (d'employé) retirement; (pension) (retirement) pension; **prendre sa r.** to retire; **à la r.** retired.

retraité, -ée 1 adj retired. **2** mf senior citizen, pensioner.

retransmettre vt to broadcast.

retransmission f broadcast.

rétrécir vi (au lavage) to shrink.

rétrécir (se) vpr (rue etc) to narrow.

rétro adj inv (personne, idée etc) old-fashioned.

rétrograder vi (automobiliste) to change down.

retrousser vt (manches) to roll up.

retrouver vt to find (again); (rejoindre) to meet (again); (forces, santé) to get back; (se rappeler) to recall.

retrouver (se) vpr to find oneself (back); (se rencontrer) to meet (again); **s'y r.** to find one's way.

rétroviseur m (de véhicule) rearview mirror.

réunion f (séance) meeting.

réunir vt (objets) to gather; (convoquer) to call together.

réunir (se) vpr to meet, to get together.

réussi, -ie adj successful.

réussir vi to succeed (**à faire** in doing); **r. à** (examen) to pass; **r. à qn** (aliment, climat) to agree with sb. **2** vt to make a success of.

réussite f success.

revanche f (en sport) rematch; **en r.** on the other hand.

rêve m dream; **faire un r.** to have a dream (**de** about); **maison/etc de r.** dream house/etc.

réveil m (pendule) alarm (clock); **à son r.** when he wakes (up)/woke (up).

réveillé, -ée adj awake.

réveiller vt, **se réveiller** vpr to wake (up).

réveillon m midnight supper (on Christmas Eve or New Year's Eve).

réveillonner vi to see in Christmas/the New Year (with a midnight supper and party).

révéler vt to reveal (**que** that).

revenant m ghost.

revendication f claim; (exigence) demand.

revendiquer vt to claim; (exiger) to demand.

revenir* vi (aux être) to come back; (coûter) to cost (**à qn** sb); **r. à** (activité, sujet) to go back to; **r. à qn** (forces, mémoire) to come back to sb; **r. à soi** to come to; **r. de** (surprise, promesse) to get over; **r. sur** (décision, promesse) to go back on.

revenu m income (**de** from).

rêver 1 vi to dream (**de** of; **de faire** of doing). **2** vt to dream (**que** that).

rêverie f daydream.

revers m (de veste) lapel; (de pantalon) cuff.

revêtement m (de route etc) surface.

rêveur, -euse mf dreamer.

revient m **prix de r.** (production) cost.

réviser vt (leçon) to revise; (machine, voiture) to service.

révision f (de leçon) revision; (de machine, voiture) service.

revoir* vt to see (again); (texte, leçon) to revise; **au r.** goodbye.

révoltant, -ante adj revolting.

révolte f rebellion, revolt.

révolté, -ée mf rebel.

révolter vt to sicken.

révolter (se) *vpr* to rebel (**contre** against).

révolution *f* revolution.

révolutionnaire *adj & mf* revolutionary.

revolver *m* gun.

revue *f (magazine)* magazine.

rez-de-chaussée *m inv* first floor.

rhabiller (se) *vpr* to get dressed again.

rhinocéros *m* rhinoceros.

rhubarbe *f* rhubarb.

rhum *m* rum.

rhumatisme *m* rheumatism; **avoir des rhumatismes** to have rheumatism.

rhume *m* cold; **r. des foins** hay fever.

ri, riant *pp & pres p of* **rire**.

ricaner *vi* to snicker.

riche 1 *adj* rich. **2** *mf* rich person; **les riches** the rich.

richesse *f* wealth; **richesses** *(trésor)* riches.

ricocher *vi* to ricochet.

ricochet *m (de pierre)* ricochet.

ride *f* wrinkle.

ridé, -ée *adj* wrinkled.

rideau, -x *m* curtain; *(de magasin)* shutter.

ridicule *adj* ridiculous.

ridiculiser (se) *vpr* to make a fool of oneself.

rien 1 *pron* nothing; **il ne sait r.** he knows nothing, he doesn't know anything; **r. du tout** nothing at all; **r. d'autre/de bon/***etc* nothing else/ good/*etc*; **de r.!** *(je vous en prie)* don't mention it!; **ça ne fait r.** it doesn't matter; **r. que** just. **2** *m (mere)* nothing.

rigide *adj* rigid; *(carton, muscle)* stiff.

rigoler *vi Fam* to laugh; *(s'amuser)* to have fun.

rigolo, -ote *adj Fam* funny.

rigoureux, -euse *adj (analyse)* rigorous; *(climat, punition)* harsh; *(personne, morale, neutralité)* strict.

rigueur *f (d'analyse)* rigor; *(de climat)* harshness; *(de personne)* strictness; **être de r.** to be the rule; **à la r.** if need be.

rillettes *fpl* potted ground pork.

rime *f* rhyme.

rimer *vi* to rhyme (**avec** with).

rinçage *m* rinsing.

rincer *vt* to rinse; *(verre)* to rinse (out).

ring *m* (boxing) ring.

ringard, -e *Fam* **1** *adj* uncool, geeky. **2** *mf* geek.

riposter 1 *vt* **r. que...** to retort that... **2** *vi* to counterattack; **r. à** *(attaque)* to counter; *(insulte)* to reply to.

rire* 1 *vi* to laugh (**de** at); *(s'amuser)* to have a good time; *(plaisanter)* to joke; **pour r.** as a joke. **2** *m* laugh; **rires** laughter; **le fou r.** the giggles.

risque *m* risk (**de faire** of doing; **à faire** in doing); **assurance tous risques** comprehensive insurance.

risqué, -ée *adj* risky.

risquer *vt* to risk; **r. de faire** to stand a good chance of doing.

rivage *m* shore.

rival, -e, -aux *adj & mf* rival.

rivaliser *vi* to compete (**avec** with; **de** in).

rive *f (de fleuve)* bank; *(de lac)* shore.

riverain, -aine *mf (près d'une rivière)* riverside resident; *(près d'un lac)* lakeside resident; *(de rue)* resident.

rivière *f* river.

riz *m* rice; **r. au lait** rice pudding.

RN *abrév* = **route nationale**.

robe *f (de femme)* dress; **r. du soir/ de mariée** evening/wedding dress; **r. de chambre** bathrobe.

robinet *m* tap, faucet; **eau du r.** tap water

robot *m* robot.

robuste *adj* sturdy.

roche *f*, **rocher** *m* rock.

rocheux, -euse *adj* rocky.

rock *m (musique)* rock.

roder *vt (moteur, voiture)* to break in.

rôder *vi* to prowl (about).

rôdeur, -euse *mf* prowler.

rognon *m (d'animal)* kidney.

roi *m* king.

rôle *m (au théâtre)* role, part; *(d'un père etc)* job; **à tour de r.** in turn.

romain, -aine *adj & mf* Roman.

roman *m* novel; **r. d'aventures** adventure story.

romancier, -ière *mf* novelist.

romantique *adj* romantic.

romarin *m* rosemary.

rompre* (se) *vpr (corde etc)* to break; *(digue)* to burst.

ronces *fpl* brambles.

ronchonner *vi Fam* to grumble.

rond, ronde 1 *adj* round; **dix euros tout r.** ten euros exactly. **2** *m (cercle)* circle, ring; **en r.** *(s'asseoir etc)* in a ring *ou* circle; **tourner en r.** to go round and round.

ronde *f (de soldat)* round; *(de policier)* beat, round.

rondelle *f (tranche)* slice.

rondin *m* log.

rond-point, *pl* **ronds-points** *m* traffic circle.

ronflement *m* snore; **ronflements** snoring.

ronfler *vi* to snore.

ronger *vt* to gnaw (at); *(ver, mer, rouille)* to eat into.

ronger (se) *vpr* **se r. les ongles** to bite one's nails.

ronronnement *m* purr(ing).

ronronner *vi* to purr.

rosbif *m* **du r.** roast beef; *(à rôtir)* (beef) roast; **un r.** (beef) roast.

rose 1 *f (fleur)* rose. **2** *adj & m (couleur)* pink.

rosé *adj & m (vin)* rosé.

roseau, -x *m (plante)* reed.

rosée *f* dew.

rosier *m* rose bush.

rossignol *m* nightingale.

rot *m Fam* burp.

roter *vi Fam* to burp.

rôti *m* **du r.** roast; *(cuit)* meat roast; **un r.** a roast; **r. de porc** pork roast.

rotin *m* cane.

rôtir *vti*, **se rôtir** *vpr* to roast; **faire r.** to roast.

roue *f* wheel.

rouge 1 *adj* red; *(fer)* red-hot. **2** *m (couleur)* red; **r. (à lèvres)** lipstick; **le feu est au r.** the (traffic) light is red.

rouge-gorge, *pl* **rouges-gorges** *m* robin.

rougeole *f* measles.

rougir *vi (de honte)* to blush; *(de colère)* to flush (**de** with).

rouille *f* rust.

rouillé, -ée *adj* rusty.

rouiller *vi*, **se rouiller** *vpr* to rust.

roulant, -ante *adj (escalier)* moving; *(meuble)* on wheels.

rouleau, -x *m (outil)* roller; *(de papier etc)* roll; **r. à pâtisserie** rolling pin; **r. compresseur** steamroller.

rouler 1 *vt* to roll; *(brouette)* to push; *(crêpe, ficelle etc)* to roll up. **2** *vi* to roll; *(train, voiture)* to go; *(conducteur)* to drive.

rouler (se) *vpr* to roll; **se r. dans** *(couverture etc)* to roll oneself (up) in.

roulette *f (de meuble)* castor; *(de dentiste)* drill.

roulotte *f (de gitan)* caravan.

round *m Boxe* round.

rouspéter *vi Fam* to complain.

rousse *voir* **roux**.

rousseur *f* **tache de r.** freckle.

roussir *vt (brûler)* to scorch.

route *f* road (**de** to); *(itinéraire)* way; **r. nationale/départementale** main/secondary road; **en r.!** let's go!; **par la r.** by road; **mettre en r.** *(voiture etc)* to start (up); **se mettre en r.** to set out *(pour* for); **une heure de r.** an hour's drive; **bonne r.!** have a good trip!

routier, -ière 1 *adj* **carte/sécurité routière** road map/safety. **2** *mf* (long-distance) truck driver.

roux, rousse 1 *adj* (*cheveux*) red; (*personne*) red-haired. **2** *mf* redhead.

royal, -e, -aux *adj* (*famille, palais*) royal.

royaume *m* kingdom.

ruban *m* ribbon; **r. adhésif** (adhesive) tape.

rubéole *f* German measles.

rubis *m* ruby; (*montre*) jewel.

rubrique *f* (*article de journal*) column; (*catégorie, titre*) heading.

ruche *f* (bee)hive.

rude *adj* (*pénible*) tough; (*hiver, voix*) harsh; (*grossier*) crude; (*rêche*) rough.

rudement *adv* (*parler, traiter*) harshly; (*très*) *Fam* awfully.

rue *f* street; **à la r.** (*sans domicile*) on the streets.

ruelle *f* alley(way).

ruer *vi* (*cheval*) to kick (out).

ruer (se) *vpr* to rush (**sur** at).

rugby *m* rugby.

rugbyman, pl -men *m* rugby player.

rugir *vi* to roar.

rugissement *m* roar.

rugueux, -euse *adj* rough.

ruine *f* ruin; **en r.** in ruins; **tomber en r.** (*bâtiment*) to become a ruin, to crumble; (*mur*) to crumble.

ruiner *vt* (*personne, santé etc*) to ruin.

ruiner (se) *vpr* **se r.** to be(come) ruined.

ruisseau, -x *m* stream.

ruisseler *vi* to stream (**de** with).

rumeur *f* (*murmure*) murmur; (*nouvelle*) rumor.

rupture *f* breaking; (*de fiançailles, de relations*) breaking off; (*de pourparlers*) breakdown (**de** in); (*dispute*) break-up; **être en r. de stock** to be out of stock.

rural, -e, -aux *adj* **vie/école/etc**

rurale country life/school/*etc*.

ruse *f* (*subterfuge*) trick; **la r.** (*habileté*) cunning.

rusé, -ée *adj & mf* cunning (person).

russe 1 *adj* Russian. **2** *mf* **R.** Russian. **3** *m* (*langue*) Russian.

rythme *m* rhythm; (*de travail*) rate; **au r. de trois par jour** at a rate of three a day.

rythmé, -ée *adj* rhythmical.

S

sa *voir* **son**.

sable *m* sand.

sabler *vt* (*rue*) to sand.

sablier *m* (*de cuisine*) egg timer.

sablonneux, -euse *adj* sandy.

sabot *m* (*de cheval etc*) hoof; (*chaussure*) clog; **s. (de Denver)** (Denver) boot.

sac *m* bag; (*grand et en toile*) sack, tote; **s. (à main)** purse; **s. à dos** backpack.

saccadé, -ée *adj* jerky.

saccager *vt* (*détruire*) to wreck.

sachant, sache(s), sachent *etc voir* **savoir**.

sachet *m* (small) bag; **s. de thé** teabag.

sacoche *f* bag; (*de vélo*) saddlebag.

sacré, -ée *adj* (*saint*) sacred; **un s. menteur/etc** *Fam* a damned liar/*etc*.

sacrifice *m* sacrifice.

sacrifier *vt* to sacrifice (**à** to; **pour** for).

sacrifier (se) *vpr* to sacrifice oneself.

sage *adj* wise; (*enfant*) good.

sage-femme, pl sages-femmes *f* midwife.

sagement *adv* wisely; (*avec calme*) quietly.

sagesse f (philosophie) wisdom; (calme) good behavior.

saignant, -ante adj (viande) rare.

saignement m bleeding; **s. de nez** nosebleed.

saigner vti to bleed.

sain, saine adj healthy; **s. et sauf** safe and sound.

saint, sainte 1 adj holy; **s. Jean** Saint John; **la Sainte Vierge** the Blessed Virgin. **2** mf saint.

Saint-Sylvestre f New Year's Eve.

sais, sait voir **savoir**.

saisir vt to grab (hold of); (occasion) to jump at; (comprendre) to understand.

saisir (se) vpr **se s. de** to grab (hold of).

saison f season.

salade f (laitue) lettuce; **s. (verte)** (green) salad; **s. de fruits/etc** fruit/etc salad.

saladier m salad bowl.

salaire m wage(s).

salarié, -ée mf wage earner.

sale adj dirty; (dégoûtant) filthy.

salé, -ée adj (goût, plat) salty; (aliment) salted.

saler vt to salt.

saleté f dirtiness; filthiness; (crasse) dirt, filth; **saletés** (détritus) garbage.

salière f saltshaker.

salir vt to (make) dirty.

salir (se) vpr to get dirty.

salissant, -ante adj dirty; (étoffe) that shows the dirt.

salive f saliva.

salle f room; (très grande) hall; (de théâtre) theater, auditorium; (de cinéma) cinema; (d'hôpital) ward; **s. à manger** dining room; **s. de bain(s)** bathroom; **s. d'opération** operating room.

salon m sitting room, lounge; (exposition) show.

salopette f (d'enfant, d'ouvrier) overalls.

saluer vt to greet; (de la main) to wave to; (de la tête) to nod to.

salut 1 m greeting; (de la main) wave; (de la tête) nod. **2** int hi!; (au revoir) bye!

samedi m Saturday.

SAMU m abrév (service d'aide médicale d'urgence) emergency medical service.

sanctionner vt (approuver) to sanction; (punir) to punish.

sandale f sandal.

sandwich m sandwich; **s. au fromage/etc** cheese/etc sandwich.

sandwicherie f sandwich shop.

sang m blood.

sang-froid m self-control; **garder son s.** to keep calm; **avec s.** calmly.

sanglant, -ante adj bloody.

sangle f strap.

sanglier m wild boar.

sanglot m sob.

sangloter vi to sob.

sanguin adj **groupe s.** blood group.

sans prép without; **s. faire** without doing; **s. qu'il le sache** without him ou his knowing; **s. cela** otherwise; **s. importance** unimportant.

sans-abri mf inv homeless person.

sans-gêne 1 adj inv ill-mannered. **2** m inv ill manners.

sans-papiers mf inv illegal immigrant.

santé f health; (à votre) **s.!** cheers!

sapeur-pompier, pl **sapeurs-pompiers** m fireman, firefighter.

sapin m (arbre, bois) fir; **s. de Noël** Christmas tree.

sardine f sardine.

satellite m satellite.

satin m satin.

satisfaction f satisfaction.

satisfaire* vt to satisfy (sb); **satisfait (de)** satisfied (with).

satisfaisant, -ante adj satisfactory.

sauce f sauce; (jus de viande) gravy; **s. tomate** tomato sauce.

saucisse *f* sausage.

saucisson *m* (cold) sausage.

sauf *prép* except (**que** that).

saule *m* willow.

saumon *m* salmon.

sauna *m* sauna.

saupoudrer *vt* to sprinkle (**de** with).

saura, saurai(t) *etc voir* **savoir**.

saut *m* jump, leap; **faire un s.** to jump, to leap; **faire un s. chez qn** to drop in on sb, to pop over to see sb.

sauter 1 *vi* to jump, to leap; **faire s.** (*détruire*) to blow up; **s. à la corde** to jump rope; **ça saute aux yeux** it's obvious. **2** *vt* to jump (over); (*mot, repas*) to skip.

sauterelle *f* grasshopper.

sauvage *adj* (*animal, plante*) wild; (*tribu, homme*) primitive.

sauvegarder *vt* to safeguard; (*fichier*) to save.

sauver *vt* to save; (*d'un danger*) to rescue (**de** from); **s. la vie à qn** to save sb's life.

sauver (se) *vpr* to run away *ou* off.

sauvetage *m* rescue.

sauveteur *m* rescuer.

sauveur *m* savior.

savant *m* scientist.

savate *f* old slipper.

saveur *f* flavor.

savoir* *vt* to know; **s. lire/nager/** *etc* to be able to read/swim/*etc*; **faire s. à qn que** to inform sb that; **je n'en sais rien** I have no idea.

savon *m* soap; (*morceau*) (bar of) soap.

savonner *vt* to wash with soap.

savonnette *f* bar of soap.

savonneux, -euse *adj* soapy.

savourer *vt* to enjoy.

savoureux, -euse *adj* tasty.

saxophone *m* saxophone.

scandale *m* scandal; **faire un s.** to make a scene.

scandaleux, -euse *adj* shocking.

scandaliser *vt* to shock.

scandinave 1 *adj* Scandinavian. **2** *mf* S. Scandinavian.

scanner *m* (*appareil*) scanner.

scarlatine *f* scarlet fever.

scénario *m* (*dialogues etc*) movie script.

scénariste *mf* scriptwriter.

scène *f* (*plateau*) stage; (*décors, partie de pièce, dispute*) scene; **mettre en s.** to direct.

sceptique 1 *adj* skeptical. **2** *mf* skeptic.

schéma *m* diagram.

scie *f* saw.

science *f* science; **étudier les sciences** to study science.

science-fiction *f* science fiction.

scientifique 1 *adj* scientific. **2** *mf* scientist.

scier *vt* to saw.

scintiller *vi* to sparkle; (*étoiles*) to twinkle.

scission *f* (*de parti*) split (**de** in).

scolaire *adj* **année/***etc* **s.** school year/*etc*.

scolarité *f* schooling; **pendant ma s.** during my school years.

score *m* (*de match*) score.

scotch® *m* (*ruban*) scotch tape®.

scrutin *m* voting, ballot.

sculpter *vt* to carve, to sculpt.

sculpteur *m* sculptor.

sculpture *f* (*art, œuvre*) sculpture.

SDF *mf abrév* (*sans domicile fixe*) homeless person.

se (**s'** before vowel or mute h) *pron* (*complément direct*) himself; (*féminin*) herself; (*non humain*) itself; (*indéfini*) oneself, *pl* themselves. ▪ (*indirect*) to himself; (*féminin*) to herself; (*non humain*) to itself; (*indéfini*) to oneself. ▪ (*réciproque*) each other, one another; (*indirect*) to each other, to one another. ▪ (*possessif*) **il se lave les mains** he washes his hands.

séance *f* (*au cinéma*) screening.

seau, -x *m* bucket.

sec, sèche 1 *adj* dry; (*légumes*)

dried; *(ton)* harsh; **coup s.** (sharp) knock, bang; **frapper un coup s.** to knock (sharply), to bang; **bruit s.** *(rupture)* snap. **2 m à s.** *(rivière)* dried up; **au s.** in a dry place.

sécateur *m* pruning shears.

sèche-cheveux *m inv* hair dryer.

sèche-linge *m inv* tumble dryer.

sécher 1 *vti* to dry. **2** *vt (cours)* to skip.

sécheresse *f (période)* drought.

séchoir *m* **s. à linge** drying rack.

second, -onde 1 *adj* second; *(étage)* third. **2** *mf* second (one) **3** *m (étage)* third floor. **4** *f (de lycée)* = sophomore year; *(vitesse)* second (gear).

secondaire *adj* secondary.

seconde *f (instant)* second.

secouer *vt* to shake.

secourir *vt* to assist.

secouriste *mf* first-aid worker.

secours *m* assistance, help; **(premiers) s.** first aid; **au s.!** help!; **sortie de s.** emergency exit; **roue de s.** spare tire.

secousse *f* jolt.

secret, -ète 1 *adj* secret. **2** *m* secret; **en s.** in secret.

secrétaire 1 *mf* secretary; *(de médecin etc)* receptionist. **2** *m (meuble)* writing desk.

secrétariat *m (bureau)* secretary's office.

secteur *m (électricité)* mains.

sectionner *vt (couper)* to sever.

sécurité *f* safety; **en s.** safe; **S. sociale** = Social security.

séduire* *vt* to charm; *(plaire à)* to appeal to; *(abuser de)* to seduce.

séduisant, -ante *adj* attractive.

segment *m* segment.

seigneur *m* lord.

sein *m* breast.

séisme *m* earthquake.

seize *adj & m* sixteen.

seizième *adj & mf* sixteenth.

séjour *m* stay; **(salle de) s.** living room.

séjourner *vi* to stay.

sel *m* salt; **sels de bain** bath salts.

sélection *f* selection.

sélectionner *vt* to select.

self(-service) *m* self-service restaurant *ou* store.

selle *f* saddle.

selon *prép* according to (**que** whether).

semaine *f* week; **en s.** during the week.

semblable *adj* similar (**à** to).

semblant *m* **faire s.** to pretend (**de faire** to do).

sembler *vi* to seem (**à** to); **il (me) semble vieux** he seems *ou* looks old (to me); **il me semble que** (+ *indicatif*) I think that, it seems to me that.

semelle *f (de chaussure)* sole.

semer *vt (graines)* to sow.

semestre *m* half(-year); *(scolaire)* semester.

semi-remorque *m* semi(-trailer).

semoule *f* semolina.

sénat *m* senate.

sens¹ *m (signification)* meaning, sense; **avoir du bon s.** to have sense, to be sensible; **avoir un s.** to make sense; **ça n'a pas de s.** that doesn't make sense.

sens² *m (direction)* direction; **s. giratoire** traffic circle; **s. interdit** *ou* **unique** *(rue)* one-way street; **'s. interdit'** 'no entry'; **s. dessus dessous** upside down; **dans le s./le s. inverse des aiguilles d'une montre** clockwise/counterclockwise.

sensation *f* feeling.

sensationnel, -elle *adj* sensational.

sensé, -ée *adj* sensible.

sensibilité *f* sensitivity.

sensible *adj* sensitive (**à** to); *(douloureux)* tender; *(progrès etc)* noticeable.

sentier *m* path.

sentiment *m* feeling.

sentimental, -e, -aux *adj* sentimental; **vie sentimentale** love life.

sentir* vt to feel; (odeur) to smell; (goût) to taste; **s. le parfum**/etc to smell of perfume/etc; **s. le poisson**/etc (avoir le goût de) to taste of fish/etc, Fam **je ne peux pas le s.** (supporter) I can't stand him.

sentir (se) vpr **se s. fatigué**/etc to feel tired/etc.

séparément adv separately.

séparer vt to separate (**de** from).

séparer (se) vpr (se quitter) to part; (couple) to separate; **se s. de** (chien etc) to part with.

sept adj & m seven.

septante adj & m (en Belgique, en Suisse) seventy.

septembre m September.

septième adj & mf seventh.

sera, serai(t) etc voir **être**.

serein, -eine adj serene.

série f series; (ensemble) set.

sérieusement adv seriously; (travailler) conscientiously.

sérieux, -euse 1 adj serious. **2** m **prendre au s.** to take seriously; **garder son s.** to keep a straight face.

seringue f syringe.

serment m oath; **faire le s. de faire** to promise to do.

sermonner vt (faire la morale à) to lecture.

séropositif, -ive adj HIV positive.

serpent m snake.

serpillière f floor cloth.

serre f greenhouse; **effet de s.** greenhouse effect.

serré, -ée adj (nœud etc) tight; (gens) packed (together).

serrer 1 vt (tenir) to grip; (presser) to squeeze; (nœud, vis) to tighten; (poing) to clench; (frein) to apply; **s. la main à qn** to shake hands with sb; **s. qn** (embrasser) to hug sb. **2** vi **s. à droite** to keep (to the) right.

serrer (se) vpr to squeeze up ou together; **se s. contre** to squeeze up against.

serrure f lock.

serveur, -euse mf waiter, waitress; (au bar) bartender, barmaid.

serviable adj helpful.

service m service; (pourboire) service (charge); (dans une entreprise) department; **un s.** (aide) a favor; **rendre s.** to be of service (**à qn** to sb); **s. (non) compris** service (not) included; **s. après-vente** aftersales service; **être de s.** to be on duty.

serviette f towel; (sac) briefcase; **s. hygiénique** sanitary napkin; **s. (de table)** napkin, serviette.

servir* 1 vt to serve (**qch à qn** sb with sth, sth to sb). **2** vi (être utile) to be useful; **s. à qch/à faire** (objet) to be used for sth/to do; **ça ne sert à rien** it's useless (**de faire** doing); **ça me sert à faire/de qch** I use it to do/as sth.

servir (se) vpr (à table) to help oneself (**de** to); **se s. de** (utiliser) to use.

ses voir **son**.

set m Tennis set; **s. (de table)** place mat.

seuil m doorstep.

seul¹, -e 1 adj alone; **tout s.** by oneself, on one's own; **se sentir s.** to feel lonely. **2** adv (tout) **s.** (rentrer, vivre etc) by oneself, on one's own, alone; (parler) to oneself.

seul², -e adj (unique) only; **la seule femme**/etc the only woman/etc; **un s. chat**/etc only one cat/etc; **pas un s. livre**/etc not a single book/etc. **2** mf **le s., la seule** the only one; **un s., une seule** only one; **pas un s.** not (a single) one.

seulement adv only.

sévère adj severe; (parents etc) strict.

sévérité f severeness, severity; (de parents etc) strictness.

sévices mpl ill-treatment; **s. à enfant** child abuse.

sexe m sex.

sexuel, -elle adj sexual; **éducation/vie sexuelle** sex education/life.

shampooing *m* shampoo; **faire un s. à qn** to shampoo sb's hair.

short *m* (pair of) shorts.

si¹ 1 (*s'* before **il, ils**) *conj* if; **je me demande si** I wonder whether *ou* if; **si on restait?** what if we stayed? **2** *adv* (*tellement*) so; **pas si riche que toi** not as rich as you; **un si bon dîner** such a good dinner; **si bien que** (+ *indicatif*) with the result that.

si² *adv* (*après négative*) yes; **tu ne viens pas? – si!** you're not coming? – yes (I am)!

SIDA *m abrév* (*syndrome immuno-déficitaire acquis*) AIDS.

sidérurgie *f* iron and steel industry.

siècle *m* century; (*époque*) age.

siège *m* seat; (*de parti etc*) headquarters; **s. (social)** head office.

sien, sienne *pron poss* **le s., la sienne, les sien(ne)s** his; (*de femme*) hers; (*de chose*) its; **les deux siens** his *ou* her two.

sieste *f* **faire la s.** to take a nap.

sifflement *m* whistling; (*de gaz, serpent*) hiss(ing).

siffler 1 *vi* to whistle; (*avec un sifflet*) to blow one's whistle; (*gaz, serpent*) to hiss. **2** *vt* (*chanson*) to whistle; (*chien*) to whistle to; (*acteur*) to boo.

sifflet *m* whistle; (**coup de**) **s.** (*son*) whistle; **sifflets** (*des spectateurs*) boos.

sigle *m* acronym.

signal, -aux *m* signal; **s. d'alarme** (*de train*) alarm.

signaler *vt* to point out (**à qn** to sb; **que** that); (*à la police etc*) to report (**à** to).

signature *f* signature.

signe *m* sign; **faire s. à qn** (*geste*) to motion (to) sb (**de faire** to do).

signer *vt* to sign.

signification *f* meaning.

signifier *vt* to mean (**que** that).

silence *m* silence; **en s.** in silence;

garder le s. to keep silent (**sur** about).

silencieusement *adv* silently.

silencieux, -euse *adj* silent.

silhouette *f* outline; (*ligne du corps*) figure.

sillonner *vt* (*parcourir*) to crisscross.

similitude *f* similarity.

simple *adj* simple.

simplement *adv* simply.

simplifier *vt* to simplify.

simultané, -ée *adj* simultaneous.

simultanément *adv* simultaneously.

sincère *adj* sincere.

sincèrement *adv* sincerely.

sincérité *f* sincerity.

singe *m* monkey, ape.

singeries *fpl* antics.

singulier, -ière *adj & m* (*non pluriel*) singular; **au s.** in the singular.

sinistre 1 *adj* sinister. **2** *m* disaster.

sinon *conj* (*autrement*) otherwise, or else.

sirène *f* (*d'usine etc*) siren.

sirop *m* syrup; **s. contre la toux** cough medicine *ou* syrup.

site *m* (*endroit*) site; (*pittoresque*) beauty spot; **s. touristique** place of interest; **s. classé** conservation area; **s. Web** website.

situation *f* situation.

situé, -ée *adj* situated, located.

situer (se) *vpr* to be situated, to be located.

six *adj & m* six.

sixième *adj & mf* sixth.

sketch, pl sketches *m* (*de théâtre*) sketch.

ski *m* ski; (*sport*) skiing; **faire du s.** to ski; **s. nautique** water skiing.

skier *vi* to ski.

skieur, -euse *mf* skier.

slip *m* (*d'homme*) briefs, underwear; (*de femme*) panties, underwear; **s. de bain** (bathing) trunks.

slogan m slogan.

SMIC m abrév (salaire minimum interprofessionnel de croissance) guaranteed minimum wage.

smoking m (veston, costume) tuxedo.

SMS m abrév (short message service) text (message); **envoyer un S. à qn** to text sb, to send sb a text.

SNCF f abrév (Société nationale des chemins de fer français) = French railroad system.

social, -e, -aux adj social.

socialiste adj & mf socialist.

société f society; (compagnie) company.

socquette f anklet.

sœur f sister.

soi pron oneself; **cela va de soi** it's evident (**que** that).

soi-disant 1 adj inv so-called. **2** adv supposedly.

soie f silk.

soient voir **être**.

soif f thirst; **avoir s.** to be thirsty; **donner s. à qn** to make sb thirsty.

soigné, -ée adj (vêtement) neat; (travail) careful.

soigner vt to look after, to take care of; (maladie) to treat; **se faire s.** to get (medical) treatment, to be treated.

soigneusement adv carefully.

soigneux, -euse adj careful (**de** with); (propre) neat.

soi-même pron oneself.

soin m care; (à un malade) treatment, care; **avec s.** carefully; **prendre s. de qch** to take care of sth; **les premiers soins** first aid.

soir m evening; **le s.** (chaque soir) in the evening; **à neuf heures du s.** at nine in the evening.

soirée f evening; (réunion) party.

sois, soit voir **être**.

soit conj **s.... s....** either... or...

soixantaine f **une s. (de)** about sixty.

soixante adj & m sixty.

soixante-dix adj & m seventy.

soixante-dixième adj & mf seventieth.

soixantième adj & mf sixtieth.

soja m (plante) soya; **germes ou pousses de s.** beanshoots.

sol m ground; (plancher) floor.

solaire adj solar; **crème/huile s.** sun(tan) lotion/oil.

soldat m soldier.

solde m (de compte) balance; **en s.** (acheter) on sale; **soldes** (marchandises) sale goods; (vente) (clearance) sale(s).

soldé, -ée adj (article etc) reduced.

solder vt (articles) to put on sale.

sole f (poisson) sole.

soleil m sun; (chaleur, lumière) sunshine; **au s.** in the sun; **il fait (du) s.** it's sunny; **coup de s.** sunburn.

solennel, -elle adj solemn.

solidarité f (de personnes) solidarity.

solide adj & m solid.

solidement adv solidly.

solitaire adj (tout seul) all alone.

solitude f **aimer la s.** to like being alone.

solliciter vt (audience) to request; (emploi) to apply for; **s. qn** (faire appel à) to appeal to sb (**de faire** to do).

sombre adj dark; **il fait s.** it's dark.

sombrer vi (bateau) to sink; **s. dans** (folie, sommeil) to sink into.

sommaire 1 adj summary; (repas) basic. **2** m (table des matières) contents.

somme 1 f sum; **faire la s. de** to add up. **2** m (sommeil) nap; **faire un s.** to take a nap.

sommeil m sleep; **avoir s.** to be ou feel sleepy.

sommes voir **être**.

sommet m top.

sommier m (de lit) base.

somnifère m sleeping pill.

somnoler *vi* to doze.

son *m (bruit)* sound.

son, sa, *pl* **ses** (*sa becomes* **son** *before a vowel or mute h*) *adj poss* his; *(de femme)* her; *(de chose)* its; *(indéfini)* one's; **s. père** his/her/ one's father; **sa mère** his/her/one's mother; **son ami(e)** his/her/one's friend; **sa durée** its duration.

sondage *m* **s. (d'opinion)** opinion poll.

songer *vi* **s. à qch/à faire** to think of sth/of doing.

songeur, -euse *adj* thoughtful, pensive.

sonner *vi* to ring; **on a sonné** *(à la porte)* someone's at the door.

sonnerie *f (son)* ring(ing); *(appareil)* bell; *(au téléphone)* ring; **s.'occupé** busy signal.

sonnette *f* bell; **coup de s.** ring.

sonore *adj (rire)* loud; *(salle)* resonant.

sont *voir* **être**.

sorcière *f* witch.

sort *m (destin, hasard)* fate; *(condition)* lot.

sorte *f* sort, kind (**de** of); **toutes sortes de** all sorts *ou* kinds of; **de (telle) s. que** (+ *subjonctif*) so that; **faire en s. que** (+ *subjonctif*) to see to it that.

sortie *f (promenade à pied)* walk; *(en voiture)* drive; *(excursion)* outing; *(porte)* exit, way out; *(de disque, film)* release; **à la s. de l'école** when the children get out of school.

sortir* 1 *vi (aux* **être)** to go out, to leave; *(venir)* to come out; *(pour s'amuser, danser etc)* to go out; *(film etc)* to come out; **s. de table** to leave the table; **s'en s.** to pull *ou* come through. **2** *vt (aux* **avoir)** to take out (**de** of).

sottise *f (action, parole)* foolish thing; **faire des sottises** *(enfant)* to misbehave.

sou *m* **sous** *(argent)* money; **elle n'a pas un s.** she doesn't have a bean;

appareil *ou* **machine à sous** slot machine.

souche *f (d'arbre)* stump.

souci *m* worry; *(préoccupation)* concern (**de** for); **se faire du s.** to worry; **ça lui donne du s.** it worries him/her.

soucier (se) *vpr* **se s. de** to be worried about.

soucieux, -euse *adj* worried (**de qch** about sth).

soucoupe *f* saucer; **s. volante** flying saucer.

soudain *adv* suddenly.

souder *vt* to weld.

souffle *m* puff; *(haleine)* breath; *(respiration)* breathing; *(de bombe etc)* blast.

souffler 1 *vi* to blow. **2** *vt (bougie)* to blow out; *(chuchoter)* to whisper.

souffrance(s) *f(pl)* suffering.

souffrant, -ante *adj* unwell.

souffrir* *vi* to suffer (**de** from); **faire s. qn** to hurt sb.

souhait *m* wish; **à vos souhaits!** *(après un éternuement)* bless you!, gesundheit!

souhaitable *adj* desirable.

souhaiter *vt* to wish for; **s. qch à qn** to wish sb sth; **s. faire** to hope to do; **s. que** (+ *subjonctif*) to hope that.

soûl, soûle *adj* drunk.

soulagement *m* relief.

soulager *vt* to relieve (**de** of).

soulever *vt* to lift (up); *(poussière, question)* to raise.

soulier *m* shoe.

souligner *vt* to underline; *(faire remarquer)* to emphasize.

soumettre *vt (pays, rebelles)* to subdue; *(rapport, demande)* to submit (**à** to); **s. qn à** *(assujettir)* to subject sb to.

soumis, -ise *adj (docile)* submissive; **s. à** subject to.

soupçon *m* suspicion.

soupçonner *vt* to suspect (**de** of); **d'avoir fait** of doing; **que** that).

soupe f soup.

souper 1 m supper. **2** vi to have supper.

soupir m sigh.

soupirer vi to sigh.

souple adj supple; (tolérant) flexible.

souplesse f suppleness; (tolérance) flexibility.

source f (point d'eau) spring; (origine) source; **eau de s.** spring water.

sourcil m eyebrow.

sourd, sourde 1 adj deaf; (douleur) dull; **bruit s.** thump. **2** mf deaf person.

sourd-muet, sourde-muette, pl **sourds-muets, sourdes-muettes** adj & mf deaf-mute.

sourire* 1 vi to smile (**à qn** at sb). **2** m smile; **faire un s. à qn** to give sb a smile.

souris f mouse (pl mice).

sournois, -oise adj sly, underhand.

sous prép (position) under(neath), beneath; **s. la pluie** in the rain; **s. Charles X** under Charles X; **s. peu** (bientôt) shortly.

sous-développé, -ée adj (pays) underdeveloped.

sous-entendre vt to imply.

sous-entendu, pl **sous-entendus** m insinuation.

sous-estimer vt to underestimate.

sous-marin, pl **sous-marins** m submarine.

sous-sol, pl **sous-sols** m (d'immeuble) basement.

sous-titre, pl **sous-titres** m subtitle.

soustraction f subtraction.

soustraire* vt (nombre) to take away, to subtract (**de** from).

sous-traitant, pl **sous-traitants** m subcontractor.

sous-vêtements mpl underwear.

soutenir* vt to support; **s. que** to maintain that.

soutenir (se) vpr (blessé etc) to hold oneself up.

souterrain, -aine 1 adj underground. **2** m underground passage.

soutien m support; (personne) supporter.

soutien-gorge, pl **soutiens-gorge** m bra.

souvenir m memory; (objet) memento; (cadeau) keepsake; (pour touristes) souvenir.

souvenir* (se) vpr se s. de to remember; **se s. que** to remember that.

souvent adv often; **peu s.** seldom; **le plus s.** usually.

soyeux, -euse adj silky.

soyez, soyons voir **être**.

spacieux, -euse adj spacious.

spaghetti(s) mpl spaghetti.

sparadrap m Band-Aid®.

speaker, speakerine mf (à la radio etc) announcer.

spécial, -e, -aux adj special.

spécialement adv specially.

spécialiste mf specialist.

spécialité f specialty.

spécimen m specimen.

spectacle m (vue) sight; (représentation) show.

spectaculaire adj spectacular.

spectateur, -trice mf spectator; (témoin) onlooker; **les spectateurs** (le public) the audience.

sphère f sphere.

spirale f spiral.

spirituel, -elle adj (amusant) witty.

splendide adj splendid.

spontané, -ée adj spontaneous.

sport m sport; **faire du s.** to play sports; **voiture/veste/terrain de s.** sports car/jacket/ground.

sportif, -ive 1 adj (personne) fond of sports. **2** mf sportsman, sportswoman, athlete.

spot m (lampe) spotlight; **s. (publicitaire)** commercial.

squash m (jeu) squash.

squelette m skeleton.

stable *adj* stable.

stade *m* stadium.

stage *m (cours)* (training) course; *(en entreprise)* internship.

stagiaire *mf* intern.

stand *m (d'exposition etc)* stand.

standard 1 *m (téléphonique)* switchboard. **2** *adj inv (modèle etc)* standard.

station *f* station; *(de ski etc)* resort; *(d'autobus)* stop; **s. de taxis** taxi stand.

stationnement *m* parking.

stationner *vi (se garer)* to park; *(être garé)* to be parked.

station-service, *pl* **stations-service** *f* service station, gas station.

statistique *f (donnée)* statistic.

statue *f* statue.

steak *m* steak.

stéréo *adj inv* stereo.

stériliser *vt* to sterilize.

stock *m* stock, supply *(de* of); **en s.** in stock.

stocker *vt (provisions etc)* to store.

stop 1 *int* stop. **2** *m (panneau)* stop sign; *(feu arrière)* brake light; **faire du s.** to hitchhike.

stopper *vti* to stop.

store *m* (window) shade.

stress *m inv* stress.

stressant, -ante *adj* stressful.

stressé, -ée *adj* stressed.

strict, -e *adj* strict.

strictement *adv* strictly.

string *m* thong.

structure *f* structure.

studieux, -euse *adj* studious; *(vacances)* devoted to study.

studio *m* studio; *(logement)* studio apartment.

stupéfaction *f* amazement.

stupéfait, -faite *adj* amazed *(de* at, by).

stupéfiant, -ante 1 *adj* amazing. **2** *m* drug, narcotic.

stupide *adj* stupid.

stupidité *f* stupidity; *(action, parole)* stupid thing.

style *m* style.

stylo *m* pen; **s. à bille** ballpoint (pen); **s.-plume** fountain pen.

su, sue *pp de* **savoir**.

subir *vt* to undergo; *(conséquences, défaite)* to suffer; *(influence)* to be under.

subit, -ite *adj* sudden.

subitement *adv* suddenly.

subjonctif *m Grammaire* subjunctive.

submergé, -ée *adj* flooded *(de* with); **s. de travail** overwhelmed with work.

substance *f* substance.

subtil, -e *adj* subtle.

subvention *f* subsidy.

succéder *vi* **s. à qch** to follow sth.

succéder (se) *vpr* to follow one another.

succès *m* success; **avoir du s.** to be successful.

successif, -ive *adj* successive.

succession *f (série)* sequence *(de* of).

succursale *f (de magasin)* branch; **magasin à succursales multiples** chain store.

sucer *vt* to suck.

sucette *f* lollipop; *(tétine)* pacifier.

sucre *m* sugar; *(morceau)* sugar lump; **s. cristallisé** granulated sugar; **s. en morceaux** lump sugar; **s. en poudre, s. semoule** fine sugar.

sucré, -ée *adj* sweet.

sucrer *vt* to sugar.

sucreries *fpl* candy.

sucrier *m* sugar bowl.

sud *m* south; **au s. de** south of; **du s.** *(vent)* southerly; *(ville)* southern.

sud-est *m & adj inv* southeast.

sud-ouest *m & adj inv* southwest.

suédois, -oise 1 *adj* Swedish. **2** *mf* **S.** Swede. **3** *m (langue)* Swedish.

suer *vi* to sweat; **faire s. qn** *Fam* to get on sb's nerves.

sueur *f* sweat; **en s.** sweating.

suffire* *vi* to be enough *(à* for); **ça suffit!** that's enough!; **il suffit**

d'une **goutte**/*etc* **pour faire** a drop/*etc* is enough to do.

suffisamment *adv* sufficiently; **s. de** enough.

suffisant, -ante *adj* sufficient.

suffocant, -ante *adj* stifling.

suggérer *vt* to suggest (**à** to; **de faire** doing; **que** (+ *subjonctif*) that).

suggestion *f* suggestion.

suicide *m* suicide.

suicider (se) *vpr* to commit suicide.

suis *voir* **être, suivre**.

suisse **1** *adj* Swiss. **2** *mf* **S.** Swiss *inv*; **les Suisses** the Swiss.

Suissesse *f* Swiss woman/girl, Swiss *inv*

suite *f* (*reste*) rest; (*de film, roman*) sequel; (*série*) series; **faire s.** (**à**) to follow; **par la s.** afterwards; **à la s.** one after another; **à la s. de** (*événement etc*) as a result of; **de s.** (*deux jours etc*) in a row.

suivant, -ante **1** *adj* next, following. **2** *mf* next (one); **au s.!** next!

suivre* **1** *vt* to follow; (*accompagner*) to go with; (*classe*) to attend, to go to; **s. (des yeux** *ou* **du regard)** to watch. **2** *vi* to follow; **faire s.** (*courrier*) to forward; **'à s.'** 'to be continued'.

suivre (se) *vpr* to follow each other.

sujet *m* (*question*), Grammaire subject; (*d'examen*) question; **au s. de** about; **à quel s.?** about what?

super **1** *adj inv* (*bon*) great. **2** *m* (*essence*) premium gas.

superbe *adj* superb.

supercherie *f* deception.

supérette *f* convenience store.

superficie *f* surface.

superficiel, -ielle *adj* superficial.

supérieur, -e *adj* upper; (*qualité etc*) superior (**à** to); (*études*) higher; **l'étage s.** the floor above.

supériorité *f* superiority.

supermarché *m* supermarket.

superposer *vt* (*objets*) to put on top of each other.

superstitieux, -euse *adj* superstitious.

superstition *f* superstition.

supplément *m* (*argent*) extra charge; **en s.** extra.

supplémentaire *adj* extra.

supplier *vt* **s. qn de faire** to beg sb to do.

support *m* support; (*d'instrument etc*) stand.

supporter¹ *vt* to bear; (*résister à*) to withstand; (*soutenir*) to support.

supporter² *m* supporter.

supposer *vti* to suppose (**que** that).

supposition *f* assumption.

suppositoire *m* suppository.

suppression *f* removal; (*de train*) cancellation.

supprimer *vt* to get rid of; (*mot*) to cut out; (*train*) to cancel.

sur *prép* on, upon; (*par-dessus*) over; (*au sujet de*) on, about; **six s. dix** six out of ten; **un jour s. deux** every other day; **six mètres s. dix** 20 by 33 feet.

sûr, sûre *adj* sure, certain (**de** of; **que** that); (*digne de confiance*) reliable; (*lieu*) safe; **c'est s. que** (+ *indicatif*) it's certain that; **s. de soi** self-assured; **bien s.!** of course!

sûrement *adv* certainly.

sûreté *f* safety; **être en s.** to be safe; **mettre en s.** to put in a safe place.

surexcité, -ée *adj* overexcited.

surf *m* surfing; **faire du s.** to go surfing.

surface *f* surface; (*dimensions*) (surface) area; (**magasin à**) **grande s.** hypermarket.

surgelé, -ée *adj* (*viande etc*) frozen.

surgelés *mpl* frozen foods.

surgir *vi* to appear suddenly (**de** from); (*problème*) to arise.

sur-le-champ *adv* immediately.

surlendemain *m* **le s.** two days

LES SUGGESTIONS, LES INVITATIONS ET LES DÉSIRS

Qu'est-ce que tu veux/vous voulez faire ?
What do you/want to do?

Tu veux/Vous voulez allez au restaurant ?
Do you want to go to a restaurant?

Et si on allait faire une promenade ?
How about going for a walk?

On se retrouve à midi/devant le cinéma ?
Let's meet at noon/outside the movie theater.

Je ne veux pas aller au musée d'art.
I don't want to go to the art gallery.

J'ai envie d'une glace.
I feel like an ice-cream.

Qu'est ce que tu préfères/vous préférez faire ?
What would you rather do?

J'aimerais apprendre le français.
I'd like to learn French.

Ça m'est égal.
I don't mind.

Avec plaisir !
I'd love to!

Je n'en ai pas envie.
I don't feel like it.

Est-ce que tu es/vous êtes libre demain soir ?
Are you free tomorrow night?

C'est très gentil.
That's very kind of you.

On va prendre un café ?
Shall we go for a coffee?

Ça te/vous dit d'aller boire un verre ?
Would you like to go for a drink?

Allons nous baigner !
Let's go for a swim!

J'aimerais aller à la plage.
I'd like to go to the beach.

Je préférerais faire les magasins.
I'd rather go shopping.

Je n'ai pas envie d'aller au marché.
I don't feel like going to the market.

Je propose qu'on parte vers six heures et demie.
I think we should leave around 6.30.

J'aimerais bien habiter ici.
I wouldn't mind living here.

C'est comme tu veux/vous voulez.
It's up to you.

C'est une bonne idée.
That's a good idea.

Je suis désolé(e), je ne peux pas.
I'm sorry, I can't.

Je regrette, j'ai déjà quelque chose de prévu.
I'm afraid I already have plans.

Merci de m'avoir invité.
Thank you for inviting me.

later; **le s. de** two days after.

surligneur *m* highlighter (pen).

surmener (se) *vpr* to overwork.

surmonter *vt* (*obstacle etc*) to get over.

surnom *m* nickname.

surnommer *vt* to nickname.

surpasser (se) *vpr* to surpass oneself.

surprenant, -ante *adj* surprising.

surprendre* *vt* (*étonner*) to surprise; (*prendre sur le fait*) to catch; (*conversation*) to overhear.

surpris, -ise *adj* surprised (**de** at; **que** (+ *subjonctif*) that); **je suis surpris de te voir** I'm surprised to see you.

surprise *f* surprise.

sursauter *vi* to jump, to start.

surtout *adv* especially; (*avant tout*) above all; **s. pas** certainly not; **s. que** especially since.

surveillant, -ante *mf* (*au lycée*) monitor; (*au prison*) (prison) guard.

surveiller *vt* to watch; (*contrôler*) to supervise.

survêtement *m* tracksuit.

survivant, -ante *mf* survivor.

survivre* *vi* to survive (**à qch** sth).

survoler *vt* to fly over.

susceptibilité *f* touchiness, sensitivity.

susceptible *adj* touchy, sensitive.

susciter *vt* (*sentiment*) to arouse; (*ennuis, obstacles*) to create.

suspect, -ecte 1 *adj* suspicious. **2** *mf* suspect.

suspendre *vt* (*accrocher*) to hang (up) (**à** on).

suspendre (se) *vpr* **se s. à** to hang from.

suspendu, -ue *adj* **s. à** hanging from.

suspense *m* suspense.

suspension *f* (*de véhicule*) suspension.

suture *f* **point de s.** stitch (*in wound*).

SVP *abrév* (*s'il vous plaît*) please.

syllabe *f* syllable.

symbole *m* symbol.

symbolique *adj* symbolic.

sympa *adj inv Fam* = **sympathique**.

sympathie *f* liking; **avoir de la s. pour qn** to be fond of sb.

sympathique *adj* nice, pleasant.

sympathiser *vi* to get along well (**avec** with).

symphonie *f* symphony.

symptôme *m* symptom.

synagogue *f* synagogue.

syndicat *m* (*d'ouvriers*) (labor) union; **s. d'initiative** tourist (information) office.

syndiqué, -ée *mf* union member.

synonyme 1 *adj* synonymous (**de** with). **2** *m* synonym.

système *m* system.

T

ta *voir* **ton**.

tabac *m* tobacco; (*magasin*) tobacco store.

table *f* table; (*d'école*) desk; **t. de nuit** bedside table; **t. basse** coffee table; **t. à repasser** ironing board; **t. roulante** (serving) cart; **t. des matières** table (of contents); **à t.** sitting at the table; **à t.!** (food's) ready!

tableau, -x *m* (*image*) picture; (*panneau*) board; (*liste*) list; (*graphique*) chart; **t. (noir)** (black) board; **t. d'affichage** bulletin board; **t. de bord** dashboard.

tablette *f* (*de chocolat*) bar; (*petite planche*) shelf.

tablier *m* apron; (*d'écolier*) smock.

tabouret *m* stool.

tache *f* spot; (*salissure*) stain.

tâche f task, job; **tâches ménagères** housework.

tacher vti, **se tacher** vpr to stain.

tâcher vi t. **de faire** to try to do.

tact m tact; **avoir du t.** to be tactful.

tactique f **la t.** tactics; **une t.** a tactic.

tag m graffiti tag.

taie d'oreiller f pillowcase.

taille f (hauteur) height; (dimension, mesure) size; (ceinture) waist; **tour de t.** waist measurement.

taille-crayon, pl **taille-crayons** m pencil sharpener.

tailler vt to cut; (haie, barbe) to trim; (arbre) to prune; (crayon) to sharpen.

tailleur m (personne) tailor; (vêtement) suit.

taire* (se) vpr (ne rien dire) to keep quiet (**sur qch** about sth); (cesser de parler) to stop talking; **tais-toi!** be quiet!

talent m talent; **avoir du t. pour** to have a talent for.

talentueux, -euse adj talented.

talon m heel; (de chèque, carnet) stub.

talus m slope, embankment.

tambour m drum; (personne) drummer.

tambourin m tambourine.

tamis m sieve.

tamiser vt (farine) to sift.

tampon m (marque, instrument) stamp; (de coton) wad; **t. hygiénique** tampon; **t. à récurer** scrubbing pad.

tamponner vt (lettre, document) to stamp; (visage) to dab; (plaie) to swab; (train, voiture) to crash into.

tandis que conj while.

tant adv (travailler etc) so much (**que** that); **t. de** (temps etc) so much (**que** that); (gens etc) so many (**que** that); **t. que** (aussi longtemps que) as long as; **t. mieux!** good!; **t. pis!** too bad!

tante f aunt.

tantôt adv t.... t.... sometimes... sometimes...

tapage m din, uproar.

tape f slap.

taper¹ 1 vt (enfant, cuisse) to slap; (table) to bang. **2** vi t. **sur qch** to bang on sth; **t. du pied** to stamp one's foot.

taper² vti t. (à la machine) to type.

tapis m carpet; **t. roulant** (pour marchandises) conveyor belt.

tapisser vt (mur) to (wall)paper.

tapisserie f (papier peint) wallpaper; (broderie) tapestry.

tapoter vt to tap; (joue) to pat.

taquiner vt to tease.

tard adv late; **plus t.** later (on); **au plus t.** at the latest.

tarder vi t. **à faire** to take one's time doing; **elle ne va pas t.** she won't be long; **sans t.** without delay.

tardif, -ive adj late; (regrets) belated.

tarif m (prix) rate; (de train) fare; (tableau) price list.

tarte f (open) pie, tart.

tartine f slice of bread; **t. (de beurre/de confiture)** slice of bread and butter/jam.

tartiner vt (beurre etc) to spread.

tas m pile, heap; **un** ou **des t. de** (beaucoup) Fam lots of; **mettre en t.** to pile ou heap up.

tasse f cup; **t. à café** coffee cup; **t. à thé** teacup.

tasser vt to pack, to squeeze (**dans** into).

tasser (se) vpr (se serrer) to squeeze together.

tâter vt to feel.

tâtonner vi to grope around.

tâtons (à) adv avancer à t. to feel one's way (along); **chercher à t.** to grope for.

tatouage m (dessin) tattoo.

tatouer vt to tattoo.

taudis m slum.

taupe f mole.

taureau, -x m bull.

taux *m* rate; **t. d'alcool** alcohol level.

taxe *f (impôt)* tax; *(de douane)* duty; **t. à la valeur ajoutée** sales tax.

taxé, -ée *adj* taxed.

taxi *m* taxi.

te (**t'** *before vowel or mute h*) *pron (complément direct)* you; *(indirect)* (to) you; *(réfléchi)* yourself.

technicien, -ienne *mf* technician.

technique 1 *adj* technical. **2** *f* technique.

technologie *f* technology.

tee-shirt *m* tee-shirt.

teindre* *vt* to dye; **t. en rouge** to dye red.

teindre (se) *vpr* to dye one's hair.

teint *m* complexion.

teinte *f* shade.

teinture *f (produit)* dye.

teinturerie *f (boutique)* (dry) cleaner's.

teinturier, -ière *mf* (dry) cleaner.

tel, telle *adj* such; **un t. livre/etc** such a book/etc; **un t. intérêt/etc** such interest/etc; **de tels mots/etc** such words/etc; **rien de t. que** (there's) nothing like.

télé *f* TV; **à la t.** on TV.

téléchargement *m* download.

télécharger *vt* to download.

télécommande *f* remote control.

télécopie *f* fax.

télécopieur *m* fax (machine).

téléfilm *m* TV movie.

télégramme *m* telegram.

téléphérique *m* cable car.

téléphone *m* (tele)phone; **coup de t.** (phone) call; **passer un coup de t. à qn** to give sb a call; **au t.** on the (tele)phone.

téléphoner *vi* to (tele)phone; **t. à qn** to (tele)phone sb.

téléphonique *adj* **appel/etc t.** (tele)phone call/etc.

télescope *m* telescope.

télésiège *m* chair lift.

téléspectateur, -trice *mf* (television) viewer.

télévisé *adj* **journal t.** television news.

téléviseur *m* television (set).

télévision *f* television; **à la t.** on (the) television; **t. en circuit fermé** CCTV.

telle *voir* **tel**.

tellement *adv (si)* so; *(tant)* so much; **t. de** *(travail etc)* so much; *(soucis etc)* so many; **pas t.!** not much!

téméraire *adj* reckless.

témoignage *m* evidence; *(récit)* account.

témoigner *vi* to give evidence (**contre** against).

témoin *m* witness; **être t. de** to witness.

température *f* temperature; **avoir de la t.** to have a fever.

tempête *f* storm; **t. de neige** snowstorm.

temple *m (romain, grec)* temple.

temporaire *adj* temporary.

temps¹ *m* time; *(de verbe)* tense; **il est t. (de faire)** it's time (to do); **ces derniers t.** lately; **de t. en t.** from time to time; **à t.** *(arriver)* in time; **à plein t.** *(travailler)* full-time; **à t. partiel** *(travailler)* part-time; **dans le t.** *(autrefois)* once.

temps² *m (climat)* weather; **quel t. fait-il?** what's the weather like?

tenailles *fpl (outil)* pincers.

tendance *f* tendency; **avoir t. à faire** to tend to do.

tendeur *m (à bagages)* bungee (cord).

tendre¹ *vt* to stretch; *(main)* to hold out (**à qn** to sb); *(bras, jambe)* to stretch out; *(piège)* to set, to lay; **t. qch à qn** to hold out sth to sb; **t. l'oreille** to prick up one's ears.

tendre² *adj (viande etc)* tender; *(personne)* affectionate (**avec** to).

tendrement *adv* tenderly.

tendresse *f* affection.

TÉLÉPHONER

Allô ?
Hello?

Allô, Alain Petit à l'appareil ?
Hello, Alain Petit speaking?

Salut Claire, c'est Alex.
Hi Claire, it's Alex.

Éditions Libro, bonjour !
Good morning/afternoon, Éditions Libro!

Bonjour, pouvez-vous me passer le service clientèle, s'il vous plaît ?
Hello, could you put me through to Customer Services, please?

Est-ce que je peux parler à Steve Brown, s'il vous plaît ? C'est Julie Rey de la part de CPS.
Can I speak to Steve Brown, please? This is Julie Rey from CPS.

C'est moi !
Speaking!

C'est de la part de qui ?
Who's calling, please?

Vous pouvez répéter/l'épeler ?
Could you repeat that/spell it?

Un instant, je vais le/la chercher.
Just a moment, I'll get him/her.

Ne quittez pas, je vous le/la passe.
Hold the line please, I'll put you through.

Je regrette, elle est en réunion/elle n'est pas là.
I'm afraid she's in a meeting/she's not here.

Ça sonne occupé, voulez-vous patienter ?
The line's busy, would you like to hold?

Ça ne répond pas.
There's no reply.

Voulez-vous laisser un message ?
Would you like to leave a message?

Veuillez laisser un message après le bip.
Please leave a message after the tone.

Non merci, je rappellerai plus tard.
No thanks, I'll call back later.

Vous pouvez lui dire que j'ai appelé ?
Could you tell him/her I called?

Pouvez-vous lui demander de me rappeler dès que possible ?
Can you ask him/her to call me back as soon as possible?

Mon numéro est le quarante-deux, trente-cinq, cinquante-neuf, zéro-un.
My number is 42-35-59-01.

Merci d'avoir appelé.
Thank you for calling.

On s'appelle !
Talk to you later!

Je peux avoir votre/ton numéro?
Can I take your number?

Vous pouvez/Tu peux me joindre sur mon portable.
You can reach me on my cell.

Je vous/t'envoie un SMS plus tard.
I'll text you later.

Je ne capte pas ici.
I can't get a signal in here.

Il ne me reste plus beaucoup de crédit.
I don't have many minutes left.

J'ai besoin de recharger mon portable.
I need to charge my cellphone.

Vous vous êtes trompé(e) de numéro.
You've got the wrong number.

Désolé(e), j'ai dû me tromper de numéro.
Sorry, I must have the wrong number.

Je vous/t'entends très mal.
I can barely hear you.

On a été coupés.
We got cut off.

Est-ce qu'il y a une cabine téléphonique par ici ?
Is there a payphone around here?

Je voudrais appeler en PCV.
I'd like to call collect.

tendu, -ue adj (corde) tight; (personne, situation, muscle) tense; (main) held out.

tenir* 1 vt to hold; (promesse, comptes, hôtel) to keep; (rôle) to play; **t. sa droite** (conducteur) to keep to the right. 2 vi to hold; (résister) to hold out; **t. à** (personne, jouet etc) to be attached to; **t. à faire** to be anxious to do; **t. dans qch** (être contenu) to fit into sth; **tenez!** (prenez) here (you are)!; **tiens!** (surprise) well!

tenir (se) vpr (avoir lieu) to be held; **se t.** (debout) to stand (up); **se t. droit** to stand up ou sit up straight; **se t. par la main** to hold hands; **se t. bien** to behave oneself.

tennis m tennis; (terrain) (tennis) court; (chaussure) sneaker; **t. de table** table tennis.

tension f tension; **t. (artérielle)** blood pressure; **avoir de la t.** to have high blood pressure.

tentant, -ante adj tempting.

tentation f temptation.

tentative f attempt.

tente f tent.

tenter[1] vt to try (**de faire** to do).

tenter[2] vt (faire envie à) to tempt.

tenue f (vêtements) clothes; (conduite) (good) behavior; **t. de soirée** evening dress.

tergal® m Dacron®.

terme m (mot) term; (fin) end; **mettre un t. à** to put an end to; **à court/long t.** (conséquences) short-/long-term; **en bons/mauvais termes** on good/bad terms (**avec** with).

terminaison f (de mot) ending.

terminal, -e, -aux 1 adj & f (classe) **terminale** = senior year. 2 m **t.** (d'ordinateur) (computer) terminal.

terminer vt to end.

terminer (se) vpr to end (**par** with; **en** in).

terne adj dull.

terrain m ground; (étendue) land; (à bâtir) plot; Football etc field; **t. de camping** campsite; **t. de jeux** (pour enfants) playground; (stade) playing field; **t. vague** vacant lot.

terrasse f terrace; (de café) sidewalk area.

terre f (matière, monde) earth; (sol) ground; (opposé à mer) land; **par t.** (poser, tomber) to the ground; (assis, couché) on the ground; **sous t.** underground.

terre-à-terre adj inv down-to-earth.

terrestre adj **la surface t.** the earth's surface; **globe t.** globe (model).

terreur f terror.

terrible adj awful, terrible; (formidable) Fam terrific.

terrifiant, -ante adj terrifying.

terrifier vt to terrify.

territoire m territory.

terroir m (sol) soil; (région) region.

terroriser vt to terrorize.

terroriste adj & mf terrorist.

tes voir **ton**.

test m test.

testament m (en droit) will.

tester vt to test.

tête f head; (visage) face; (d'arbre) top; **tenir t. à** to stand up to; **faire la t.** to sulk; **à la t. de** (entreprise) at the head of; (classe) at the top ou head of; **en t.** (sportif) in the lead.

tête-à-tête adv (en) **t.** alone together.

téter 1 vt to suck. 2 vi le bébé tète the baby is feeding; **donner à t. à** to feed.

tétine f (de biberon) nipple; (sucette) pacifier.

têtu, -ue adj stubborn.

texte m text.

textile adj & m textile.

texto m text (message); **envoyer un t. à qn** to text sb, to send sb a text.

TGV *m abrév* = **train à grande vitesse**.

thé *m* tea.

théâtre *m* theater; (*œuvres*) drama; **faire du t.** to act.

théière *f* teapot.

théorie *f* theory; **en t.** in theory.

thérapie *f* therapy.

thermomètre *m* thermometer.

thermos® *m ou f* Thermos®.

thermostat *m* thermostat.

thèse *f* (*proposition, ouvrage*) thesis.

thon *m* tuna (fish).

tibia *m* shin (bone).

ticket *m* ticket.

tiède *adj* (luke)warm.

tien, tienne *pron poss* **le t., la tienne, les tien(ne)s** yours; **les deux tiens** your two.

tiens, tient *voir* **tenir**.

tiercé *m* **jouer/gagner au t.** = to bet/win on the horses.

tiers *m* (*fraction*) third.

tiers-monde *m* **le t.** the Third World.

tige *f* (*de plante*) stem; (*barre*) rod.

tigre *m* tiger.

tilleul *m* (*arbre*) lime tree; (*infusion*) lime blossom tea.

timbre *m* stamp.

timbre-poste, *pl* **timbres-poste** *m* (postage) stamp.

timbrer *vt* (*lettre*) to stamp.

timide *adj* shy.

timidement *adv* shyly.

timidité *f* shyness.

tinter *vi* (*cloche*) to ring; (*clefs*) to jingle.

tir *m* shooting; *Sport* shot; **t. à arc** archery.

tirage *m* (*de journal*) circulation; (*de loterie*) draw; **t. au sort** drawing of lots.

tire-bouchon, *pl* **tire-bouchons** *m* corkscrew.

tirelire *f* coin bank.

tirer 1 *vt* to pull; (*langue*) to stick out; (*trait, rideaux*) to draw; (*balle,*

canon) to shoot; **t. de** (*sortir*) to pull *ou* draw out of; (*obtenir*) to get from; **t. qn de** (*danger, lit*) to get sb out of. **2** *vi* to pull (**sur** on, at); (*faire feu*) to shoot (**sur** at); *Sport* to shoot; **t. au sort** to draw lots; **t. à sa fin** to draw to a close.

tirer (se) *vpr* **se t. de** (*travail*) to cope with; (*situation*) to get out of; **se t. d'affaire** to get out of trouble.

tiret *m* (*trait*) dash.

tireur *m* (*au fusil*) gunman.

tiroir *m* drawer.

tisane *f* herbal tea.

tisonnier *m* poker.

tisser *vt* to weave.

tissu *m* material, cloth; **du t.-éponge** toweling.

titre *m* title; (**gros**) **t.** (*de journal*) headline; **à t. d'exemple** as an example; **à juste t.** rightly.

tituber *vi* to stagger.

titulaire 1 *adj* (*enseignant*) tenured; **être t. de** (*permis*) to be the holder of; (*poste*) to hold. **2** *mf* (*de permis, de poste*) holder (**de** of).

toast *m* (*pain grillé*) piece *ou* slice of toast.

toboggan *m* slide; (*pour voitures*) overpass.

toc *int* **t. t.!** knock knock!

toi *pron* (*complément, sujet*) you; (*réfléchi*) **assieds-t.** sit (yourself) down; **dépêche-t.** hurry up.

toile *f* cloth; (*à voile, sac etc*) canvas; (*tableau*) painting; **t. d'araignée** spider's web.

toilette *f* (*action*) wash(ing); (*vêtements*) clothes; **eau de t.** eau de toilette; **faire sa t.** to wash (and dress); **les toilettes** the bathroom, the men's/ladies' room; **aller aux toilettes** to go to the bathroom *ou* to the men's/ladies' room.

toi-même *pron* yourself.

toit *m* roof; **t. ouvrant** (*de voiture*) sunroof.

tôle *f* **une t.** a piece of sheet metal; **t. ondulée** corrugated iron.

tolérant, -ante *adj* tolerant (**à l'égard de** of).

tolérer *vt* to tolerate.

tomate *f* tomato.

tombe *f* grave.

tombeau, -x *m* tomb.

tombée *f* **t. de la nuit** nightfall.

tomber *vi* (*aux être*) to fall; **t. malade** to fall ill; **t. (par terre)** to fall (down); **faire t.** (*personne*) to knock over; **laisser t.** to drop; **tu tombes bien/mal** you've come at the right/wrong time; **t. sur** (*trouver*) to come across.

tombola *f* raffle.

ton, ta, *pl* **tes** (**ta** *becomes* **ton** *before a vowel or mute h*) *adj poss* your; **t. père** your father; **ta mère** your mother; **t. ami(e)** your friend.

ton *m* (*de voix etc*) tone.

tonalité *f* (*téléphonique*) dial tone.

tondeuse *f* **t. (à gazon)** (lawn-)mower.

tondre *vt* (*gazon*) to mow.

tongs *fpl* thongs, flip-flops.

tonne *f* metric ton; **des tonnes de** (*beaucoup*) *Fam* tons of.

tonneau, -x *m* barrel.

tonner *vi* **il tonne** it's thundering.

tonnerre *m* thunder; **coup de t.** clap of thunder.

tonton *m* *Fam* uncle.

top model *m* supermodel.

torche *f* (*flamme*) torch; **t. électrique** flashlight.

torchon *m* (*à vaisselle*) dish towel; (*de ménage*) dust cloth.

tordre *vt* to twist; (*linge*) to wring (out); (*barre*) to bend.

tordre (se) *vpr* to twist; (*barre*) to bend; **se t. la cheville** to twist *ou* sprain one's ankle, **se t. de douleur** to be doubled up with pain; **se t. (de rire)** to split one's sides (laughing).

tordu, -ue *adj* twisted; (*esprit*) warped.

torrent *m* (mountain) stream; **il pleut à torrents** it's pouring (down).

torse *m* chest; **t. nu** stripped to the waist.

tort *m* **avoir t.** to be wrong (**de faire** to do, in doing); **être dans son t.** to be in the wrong; **donner t. à qn** (*accuser*) to blame sb; **à t.** wrongly; **parler à t. et à travers** to talk nonsense.

torticolis *m* **avoir le t.** to have a stiff neck.

tortiller *vt* to twist, to twirl.

tortue *f* turtle.

torture *f* torture.

torturer *vt* to torture.

tôt *adv* early; **le plus t. possible** as soon as possible; **t. ou tard** sooner or later; **je n'étais pas plus t. sorti que** no sooner had I gone out than.

total, -e, -aux *adj & m* total.

totalement *adv* totally.

totaliser *vt* to total.

totalité *f* **en t.** (*détruit etc*) entirely; (*payé*) fully.

touchant, -ante *adj* moving; touching.

touche *f* (*de clavier*) key; (*de téléphone*) (push-)button; **téléphone à touches** touch-tone phone.

toucher 1 *vt* to touch; (*paie*) to draw; (*chèque*) to cash; (*cible*) to hit; (*émouvoir*) to touch, to move. **2** *vi* **t. à** to touch. **3** *m* (*sens*) touch.

toucher (se) *vpr* (*lignes, mains etc*) to touch.

touffe *f* (*de cheveux, d'herbe*) tuft.

toujours *adv* always; (*encore*) still; **pour t.** for ever.

tour¹ *f* tower; (*immeuble*) high-rise; *Echecs* castle, rook.

tour² *m* turn; (*de magie etc*) trick; **t. de poitrine/etc** chest/etc measurement; **faire le t. de** to go around; **faire un t.** to go for a walk; (*en voiture*) to go for a drive; (*voyage*) to go on a trip; **jouer un t. à qn** to play a trick on sb; **c'est mon t.** it's my turn; **à t. de rôle** in turn.

tourbillon *m* (*de vent*) whirlwind; (*d'eau*) whirlpool; (*de sable*) swirl.

tourisme m tourism; **faire du t.** to go sightseeing.

touriste mf tourist.

touristique adj guide/etc **t.** tourist guide/etc.

tourmenter (se) vpr to worry.

tournage m (de film) shooting.

tournant m (de route) bend.

tourne-disque m record player.

tournée f (de livreur, boissons) round; (de spectacle) tour.

tourner 1 vt to turn; (film) to shoot. **2** vi to turn; (tête) to spin; (moteur) to run; (lait) to go off; **t. autour de** (objet) to go around.

tourner (se) vpr to turn (**vers** to).

tournesol m sunflower.

tournevis m screwdriver.

tournoi m tournament.

Toussaint f All Saints' Day.

tousser vi to cough.

tout, toute, pl **tous, toutes 1** adj all; **tous les livres** all the books; **t. l'argent/le temps** all the money/ time; **t. le village** the whole village; **toute la nuit** all night; **tous (les) deux** both; **tous les trois** all three. ▪ (chaque) every; **tous les ans** every ou each year; **tous les cinq mois/mètres** every five months/16 feet. **2** pron pl all; **ils sont tous là** they're all there. **3** pron m sing everything; **t. ce que** everything that, all that; **en t.** (au total) in all. **4** adv (tout à fait) quite, very; **t. simplement** quite simply; **t. petit** very small; **t. neuf** brand new; **t. seul** all alone; **t. autour** all around; **t. en chantant/etc** while singing/etc; **t. à coup** suddenly; **t. à fait** completely; **t. de même** all the same; **t. de suite** at once. **5** m **le t.** everything; **pas du t.** not at all; **rien du t.** nothing at all.

toutefois adv nevertheless, however.

toux f cough.

toxique adj poisonous.

trac m **avoir le t.** to be ou become nervous.

tracasser vt, **se tracasser** vpr to worry.

trace f trace (**de** of); (marque) mark; **traces** (de bête, pneus) tracks; **traces de pas** footprints.

tracer vt (dessiner) to draw.

tracteur m tractor.

tradition f tradition.

traditionnel, -elle adj traditional.

traducteur, -trice mf translator.

traduction f translation.

traduire* vt to translate (**de** from; **en** into).

trafic m traffic.

trafiquant, -ante mf trafficker, dealer.

tragédie f tragedy.

tragique adj tragic.

trahir vt to betray.

trahir (se) vpr to give oneself away.

trahison f betrayal.

train¹ m train; **t. à grande vitesse** high-speed train; **t. couchettes** sleeper.

train² m **être en t. de faire** to be (busy) doing.

traîneau, -x m sled.

traînée f (de peinture etc) streak.

traîner 1 vt to drag. **2** vi (jouets etc) to lie around; (s'attarder) to lag behind; **t. (par terre)** (robe etc) to trail (on the ground).

traîner (se) vpr (par terre) to crawl.

train-train m routine.

traire* vt to milk.

trait m line; (en dessinant) stroke; (caractéristique) feature; **t. d'union** hyphen.

traité m (accord) treaty; (ouvrage) treatise (**sur** on); **t. de paix** peace treaty.

traitement m treatment; (salaire) salary; **t. de texte** word processing; **machine de t. de texte** word processor.

traiter 1 vt to treat; (problème) to deal with; **t. qn de lâche/etc** to call sb a coward/*etc*. **2** *vi* **t. de** (*sujet*) to deal with.

traiteur *m* **chez le t.** at the delicatessen.

traître *m* traitor.

trajectoire *f* path.

trajet *m* trip; (*distance*) distance; (*itinéraire*) route.

tramway *m* streetcar, trolley.

tranchant, -ante *adj* (*couteau, voix*) sharp.

tranche *f* (*morceau*) slice.

tranchée *f* trench.

trancher *vt* to cut.

tranquille *adj* quiet; (*mer*) calm; (*conscience*) clear; **laisser t.** to leave alone.

tranquillement *adv* calmly.

tranquillisant *m* tranquilizer.

tranquilliser *vt* to reassure.

tranquillité *f* (peace and) quiet.

transat *m* (*chaise*) deckchair.

transférer *vt* to transfer (**à** to).

transfert *m* transfer.

transformation *f* change.

transformer *vt* to change; (*maison*) to remodel; **t. en** to turn into.

transfusion *f* **t. (sanguine)** (blood) transfusion.

transgresser *vt* (*ordres*) to disobey; (*loi*) to infringe.

transistor *m* transistor (radio).

transitif, -ive *adj* Grammaire transitive.

transmettre* *vt* (*message etc*) to pass on (**à** to).

transparent, -ente *adj* clear, transparent.

transpercer *vt* to pierce.

transpiration *f* sweat.

transpirer *vi* to sweat.

transport *m* transportation (**de** of); **moyen de t.** means of transportation; **les transports en commun** public transportation.

transporter *vt* to transport; (*à la main*) to carry; **t. d'urgence à l'hôpital** to rush to the hospital.

trappe *f* trap door.

trapu, -ue *adj* (*personne*) stocky, thickset.

traquer *vt* to hunt (down).

traumatisant, -ante *adj* traumatic.

traumatisme *m* (*choc*) trauma.

travail, -aux *m* (*activité, lieu*) work; (*à effectuer*) job, task; (*emploi*) job; **travaux** (*dans la rue*) roadwork, construction; (*aménagement*) alterations; **travaux pratiques** (*à l'école etc*) practical work.

travailler *vi* to work (**à qch** at *ou* on sth).

travailleur, -euse 1 *adj* hardworking. **2** *mf* worker.

travers 1 *prép & adv* **à t.** through; **en t. (de)** across. **2** *adv* **de t.** (*chapeau etc*) crooked; (*comprendre*) badly; **j'ai avalé de t.** it went down the wrong way.

traversée *f* crossing.

traverser *vt* to cross, to go across; (*foule, période*) to go through.

traversin *m* bolster.

trébucher *vi* to stumble (**sur** over); **faire t. qn** to trip sb (up).

trèfle *m* Cartes clubs.

treize *adj & m inv* thirteen.

treizième *adj & mf* thirteenth.

tréma *m* dieresis.

tremblement *m* shaking, trembling; **t. de terre** earthquake.

trembler *vi* to shake, to tremble (**de** with).

tremper 1 *vt* to soak; (*plonger*) to dip (**dans** in). **2** *vi* to soak; **faire t. qch** to soak sth.

tremplin *m* springboard.

trentaine *f* **une t. (de)** about thirty.

trente *adj & m* thirty; **un t.-trois tours** an album.

trentième *adj & mf* thirtieth.

très *adv* very; **t. aimé**/*etc* (with past participle) much *ou* greatly liked/*etc*.

trésor *m* treasure.

tresse *f* (*cheveux*) braid.

tresser *vt* to braid.

tri *m* sorting (out); **faire le t. de** to

sort (out); **centre de t.** *(des postes)* sorting office.

triangle *m* triangle.

triangulaire *adj* triangular.

tribu *f* tribe.

tribunal, -aux *m* court.

tribune *f (de stade)* (grand)stand.

tricher *vi* to cheat.

tricheur, -euse *mf* cheater.

tricolore *adj* red, white and blue; **feu t.** traffic light.

tricot *m (activité)* knitting; *(chandail)* sweater.

tricoter *vti* to knit.

tricycle *m* tricycle.

trier *vt* to sort (out).

trimestre *m (période)* quarter; *(scolaire)* term.

trimestriel, -ielle *adj (revue)* quarterly; **bulletin t.** (quarter) report card.

tringle *f* rail, rod.

trinquer *vi* to clink glasses; **t. à la santé de qn** to drink to sb's health.

triomphe *m* triumph (**sur** over).

triompher *vi* to triumph (**de** over).

triple *m* **le t.** three times as much (**de** as).

tripler *vti* to treble, to triple.

tripoter *vt* to fiddle around with.

triste *adj* sad; *(couleur, temps)* gloomy.

tristement *adv* sadly.

tristesse *f* sadness; *(du temps)* gloom(iness).

trivial, -e, -aux *adj* coarse, vulgar.

trognon *m (de fruit)* core.

trois *adj & m* three.

troisième *adj & mf* third.

troisièmement *adv* thirdly.

trombone *m* trombone; *(agrafe)* paper clip.

trompe *f (d'éléphant)* trunk.

tromper *vt* to deceive; *(être infidèle à)* to be unfaithful to.

tromper (se) *vpr* to be mistaken; **se t. de route/etc** to take the wrong road/etc; **se t. de date/etc** to get the date/etc wrong.

trompette *f* trumpet.

trompeur, -euse *adj (apparences)* deceptive, misleading; *(personne)* deceitful.

tronc *m* trunk.

tronçonneuse *f* chain saw.

trône *m* throne.

trop *adv* too; too much; **t.** too hard/etc; **t. fatigué pour jouer** too tired to play; **boire/etc t.** to drink/etc too much; **t. de sel/etc** *(quantité)* too much salt/etc; **t. de gens/etc** *(nombre)* too many people/etc; **un euro/etc de t.** ou **en t.** one euro/etc too many.

tropical, -e, -aux *adj* tropical.

trot *m* trot; **aller au t.** to trot.

trotter *vi (cheval)* to trot.

trottinette *f (jouet)* scooter.

trottoir *m* sidewalk.

trou *m* hole; **t. de (la) serrure** keyhole; **t. (de mémoire)** lapse (of memory).

troublant, -ante *adj (détail)* disturbing, disquieting.

trouble *adj (liquide)* cloudy; *(image)* blurred; **voir t.** to see things blurred.

troubler *vt* to disturb; *(vue)* to blur.

troubles *mpl (de santé)* trouble; *(désordres)* disturbances.

trouer *vt* to make a hole ou holes in.

troupe *f (groupe)* group; *(de théâtre)* company; **troupes** *(armée)* troops.

troupeau, -x *m (vaches)* herd; *(moutons, oies)* flock.

trousse *f (étui)* case, kit; *(d'écolier)* pencil case; **t. à outils** toolkit; **t. à pharmacie** first-aid kit; **t. de toilette** *(de femme)* cosmetic case; *(d'homme)* shaving kit.

trousseau, -x *m (de clefs)* bunch.

trouver *vt* to find; **aller/venir t. qn** to go/come and see sb; **je trouve que** I think that.

trouver (se) *vpr* to be; *(être situé)* to be located; *(se sentir)* to feel; *(dans une situation)* to find oneself.

truc *m (astuce)* trick; *(moyen)* way; *(chose) Fam* thing.

truite f trout.

truquer vt (photo) to fake; (élections, match) to rig.

TTC abrév (toutes taxes comprises) inclusive of tax.

tu pron you (familiar form of address).

tu, tue voir **taire**.

tuba m (instrument de musique) tuba; (de plongée) snorkel.

tube m tube; (chanson) Fam hit.

tuberculose f TB.

tue-tête (à) adv at the top of one's voice.

tuer vti to kill.

tuer (se) vpr to kill oneself; (dans un accident) to be killed.

tuile f tile.

tulipe f tulip.

tunisien, -ienne 1 adj Tunisian. **2** mf T. Tunisian.

tunnel m tunnel.

turbulent, -ente adj (enfant) disruptive.

tutoyer vt t. qn to use the familiar tu form with sb.

tutu m tutu, ballet skirt.

tuyau, -x m pipe; t. d'arrosage hose(pipe); t. d'échappement tailpipe.

TVA f abrév (taxe à la valeur ajoutée) sales tax.

type m type; (individu) fellow, guy.

typique adj typical (de of).

tzigane 1 adj gipsy. **2** mf T. gipsy.

U

UE f abrév (Union Européenne) EU.

ulcère m ulcer.

ULM m inv abrév (ultraléger motorisé) microlight.

ultérieurement adv later (on), subsequently.

ultime adj last; (préparatifs) final.

ultramoderne adj ultramodern.

ultra-secret, -ète adj top-secret.

un, une 1 art indéf a; (devant voyelle) an; **une page** a page; **un ange** an angel. **2** adj one; **la page un** page one; **un mètre** one metre. **3** pron & mf one; **l'un** one; **les uns** some; **j'en ai un** I have one; **l'un d'eux, l'une d'elles** one of them; **la une** (de journal) the front page.

unanime adj unanimous.

unanimité f à l'u. unanimously.

uni, -ie adj united; (famille) close; (surface) smooth; (couleur) plain.

unième adj (after a number) (-)first; **trente et u.** thirty-first; **cent u.** hundred and first.

uniforme m uniform.

union f union.

Union Européenne f European Union.

unique adj (fille, espoir etc) only; (prix, marché) single; (exceptionnel) unique.

uniquement adv only.

unir vt (efforts, forces) to combine; (deux pays etc) to unite, to join together; **u. deux personnes** (amitié) to unite two people.

unir (s') vpr (étudiants etc) to unite.

unité f (mesure, élément) unit.

univers m universe.

universel, -elle adj universal.

universitaire adj ville/etc u. university town/etc.

université f university; **à l'u.** at college, at school.

urgence f (cas) emergency; (de décision etc) urgency; **faire qch d'u.** to do sth urgently; **(service des) urgences** (d'hôpital) emergency room.

urgent, -ente adj urgent.

urne f ballot box; **aller aux urnes** to go to the polls, to vote.

usage m use; (habitude) custom;

faire u. de to make use of; **hors d'u.** not in service.

usagé, -ée *adj* worn.

usager *m* user.

usé, -ée *adj (tissu etc)* worn (out).

user *vt*, **s'user** *vpr (vêtement)* to wear out.

usine *f* factory.

ustensile *m* utensil.

usuel, -elle *adj* everyday.

usure *f* wear (and tear).

utile *adj* useful (**à** to).

utilisateur, -trice *mf* user.

utilisation *f* use.

utiliser *vt* to use.

utilité *f* use(fulness); **d'une grande u.** very useful.

V

va *voir* **aller¹**.

vacances *fpl* vacation; **en v.** on vacation; **les grandes v.** the summer vacation.

vacancier, -ière *mf* vacationer.

vacarme *m* din, uproar.

vaccin *m* vaccine; **faire un v. à** to vaccinate.

vaccination *f* vaccination.

vacciner *vt* to vaccinate.

vache 1 *f (animal)* cow. **2** *adj (méchant) Fam* mean.

vachement *adv Fam (très)* damned; *(beaucoup)* a hell of a lot.

vaciller *vi* to sway; *(flamme, lumière)* to flicker.

vagabond, -onde *mf* tramp, hobo.

vague 1 *adj* vague; *(regard)* vacant. **2** *f* wave; **v. de chaleur** heat wave; **v. de froid** cold spell.

vaguement *adv* vaguely.

vain (en) *adv* in vain.

vaincre* *vt* to beat.

vaincu, -ue *mf (sportif)* loser.

vainqueur *m (sportif)* winner.

vais *voir* **aller¹**.

vaisselle *f* dishes; *(à laver)* dirty dishes; **faire la v.** to wash the dishes.

valable *adj (billet etc)* valid.

valet *m Cartes* jack.

valeur *f* value; **avoir de la v.** to be valuable; **objets de v.** valuables.

valide *adj (personne)* fit, able-bodied; *(billet)* valid.

valise *f* (suit)case; **faire ses valises** to pack (one's bags).

vallée *f* valley.

valoir* *vi* to be worth; **v. cher** to be worth a lot; **un vélo vaut bien une auto** a bicycle is just as good as a car; **il vaut mieux rester** it's better to stay; **il vaut mieux que j'attende** I'd better wait; **ça ne vaut rien** it's no good; **ça vaut le coup** it's worth it (**de faire** to do).

valoir (se) *vpr* to be as good as each other; **ça se vaut** it's all the same.

valse *f* waltz.

vandale *mf* vandal.

vanille *f* vanilla; **glace à la v.** vanilla ice cream.

vaniteux, -euse *adj* conceited.

vantard, -arde *mf* braggart.

vanter (se) *vpr* to boast (**de** about, of).

vapeur *f* v. (d'eau) steam.

vaporisateur *m (appareil)* spray.

variable *adj (humeur, temps)* changeable.

varicelle *f* chicken pox.

varié, -ée *adj* varied; *(divers)* various.

varier *vti* to vary.

variété *f* variety; **spectacle de variétés** variety show.

vas *voir* **aller¹**.

vase *m* vase.

vaste *adj* vast, huge.

vaut *voir* **valoir**.

veau, -x *m* calf; *(viande)* veal;

(cuir) calfskin, (calf) leather.

vécu, -ue *(pp of vivre) adj (histoire etc)* true.

vedette *f (de cinéma etc)* star.

végétarien, -ienne *adj & mf* vegetarian.

végétation *f* vegetation.

véhicule *m* vehicle; **v. tout terrain** all-terrain *ou* four-wheel drive vehicle.

veille *f* **la v. (de)** the day before; **la v. de Noël** Christmas Eve.

veiller *vi* to stay up; *(sentinelle)* to keep watch; **v. à qch** to see to sth; **v. sur qn** to watch over sb.

veilleur *m* **v. de nuit** night watchman.

veilleuse *f (de voiture)* parking light; *(de cuisinière)* pilot light; *(lampe allumée la nuit)* nightlight.

veine *f* vein; *(chance) Fam* luck.

vélo *m* bike, bicycle; *(activité)* cycling; **faire du v.** to cycle; **v. tout terrain** mountain bike.

vélomoteur *m* motorcycle.

velours *m* velvet; **v. côtelé** corduroy.

velu, -ue *adj* hairy.

vendange *f (récolte)* grape harvest; *(raisin récolté)* grapes (harvested); **vendanges** *(période)* grape-harvesting time; **faire les vendanges** to pick the grapes.

vendeur, -euse *mf* sales clerk; *(de voitures etc)* salesman, saleswoman.

vendre *vt* to sell (**qch à qn** sb sth, sth to sb); **à v.** for sale.

vendre (se) *vpr* to sell; **ça se vend bien** it sells well.

vendredi *m* Friday; **V. saint** Good Friday.

vénéneux, -euse *adj* poisonous.

vengeance *f* revenge.

venger (se) *vpr* to get one's revenge, to get one's own back (**de qn** on sb; **de qch** for sth).

venimeux, -euse *adj* poisonous.

venin *m* poison.

venir* *vi (aux être)* to come (**de** from); **v. faire** to come to do; **viens me voir** come and see me; **je viens/venais d'arriver** I've/I'd just arrived; **où veux-tu en v.?** what are you getting at?; **faire v.** to send for, to get.

vent *m* wind; **il y a du v.** it's windy; **coup de v.** gust of wind.

vente *f* sale; **v. (aux enchères)** auction; **en v.** on sale; **prix de v.** selling price.

ventilateur *m* fan.

ventre *m* stomach; **avoir mal au v.** to have a stomach ache.

venu, -ue *mf* **nouveau v., nouvelle venue** newcomer; **le premier v.** anyone.

ver *m* worm; *(de fruits etc)* maggot; **v. de terre** (earth)worm.

véranda *f (en verre)* sunroom *(attached to house)*.

verbe *m* verb.

verdict *m* verdict.

verdure *f (végétation)* greenery.

verger *m* orchard.

verglas *m* (black) ice.

véridique *adj* truthful.

vérification *f* check(ing).

vérifier *vt* to check.

véritable *adj* true, real; *(non imité)* real.

véritablement *adv* really.

vérité *f* truth.

vernir *vt* to varnish.

vernis *m* varnish; **v. à ongles** nail polish.

verra, verrai(t) *etc voir* **voir**.

verre *m* glass; **boire** *ou* **prendre un v.** to have a drink; **v. de bière** glass of beer; **v. à bière** beer glass.

verrou *m* bolt; **fermer au v.** to bolt.

verrouiller *vt (porte)* to bolt; *(quartier)* to seal off.

verrue *f* wart.

vers[1] *prép (direction)* toward(s).

vers[2] *m (de poème)* line.

verse (à) *adv* pleuvoir à v. to pour (down).

versement *m* payment.

verser *vt* to pour; *(larmes)* to shed; *(argent)* to pay.

version *f* (*de film, d'incident etc*) version.

verso *m* 'voir au v.' 'see over'.

vert, verte 1 *adj* green; *(pas mûr)* unripe. **2** *m* green.

vertical, -e, -aux *adj* vertical.

vertige *m* **avoir le v.** to be *ou* feel dizzy; **donner le v. à qn** to make sb (feel) dizzy.

vessie *f* bladder.

veste *f* jacket.

vestiaire *m* locker room.

veston *m* (suit) jacket.

vêtement *m* garment; **vêtements** clothes; **vêtements de sport** sportswear.

vétérinaire *f* vet.

vêtu, -ue *adj* dressed (**de** in).

vétuste *adj* dilapidated.

veuf, veuve 1 *adj* widowed. **2** *mf* widower, widow.

veuille(s), veuillent *etc voir* **vouloir.**

veulent, veut, veux *voir* **vouloir.**

vexant, -ante *adj* upsetting.

vexer *vt* to upset.

VF *f abrév* (*version française*) film **en VF** film dubbed into French.

viande *f* meat.

vibration *f* vibration.

vibrer *vi* to vibrate.

vice *m* vice.

vicieux, -euse *adj* (*pervers*) depraved; *(perfide)* underhand.

victime *f* victim; *(d'un accident)* casualty; **être v. de** to be the victim of.

victoire *f* victory; *(en sports)* win.

victorieux, -euse *adj* victorious; *(équipe)* winning.

vidange *f* (*de véhicule*) oil change.

vide 1 *adj* empty. **2** *m* emptiness; *(trou)* gap.

vidéo *adj inv* video.

vidéocassette *f* video cassette.

vide-ordures *m inv* garbage chute.

vide-poches *m inv* glove compartment.

vider *vt*, **se vider** *vpr* to empty.

vie *f* life; *(durée)* lifetime; **le coût de la v.** the cost of living; **gagner sa v.** to earn one's living; **en v.** living.

vieil *voir* **vieux.**

vieillard *m* old man.

vieille *voir* **vieux.**

vieillesse *f* old age.

vieillir 1 *vi* to get old; *(changer)* to age. **2** *vt* **v. qn** *(vêtement etc)* to make sb look old(er).

vierge 1 *adj (femme, neige)* virgin; *(feuille de papier, film)* blank; **être v.** *(femme, homme)* to be a virgin. **2** *f* virgin.

vieux (*or* **vieil** *before vowel or mute* h), **vieille,** *pl* **vieux, vieilles 1** *adj* old. **2** *m* old man; **les vieux** old people; **mon v.!** *(mon ami)* buddy!, pal! **3** *f* old woman; **ma vieille!** *(ma chère)* dear!

vif, vive *adj (enfant)* lively; *(couleur, lumière)* bright; *(froid)* biting; **brûlé v.** burned alive.

vignette *f* (*de véhicule*) road tax sticker.

vignoble *m* vineyard.

vilain, -aine *adj (laid)* ugly; *(enfant)* bad; *(impoli)* rude.

villa *f* (detached) house.

village *m* village.

villageois, -oise *mf* villager.

ville *f* town; *(grande)* city; **aller/ être en v.** to go (in)to/be in town.

vin *m* wine.

vinaigre *m* vinegar.

vinaigrette *f* oil-and-vinegar dressing, vinaigrette.

vingt *adj & m* twenty; **v. et un** twenty-one.

vingtaine *f* **une v. (de)** about twenty.

vingtième *adj & mf* twentieth.

viol *m* rape.

violemment *adv* violently.

violence f violence.

violent, -ente adj violent.

violer vt to rape.

violet, -ette adj & m purple.

violeur m rapist.

violon m violin.

violoncelle m cello.

vipère f adder.

virage m (de route) bend; (de véhicule) turn.

virement m transfer.

virgule f comma; (de nombre) (decimal) point; **2 v. 5** 2 point 5.

virus m virus.

vis¹ voir **vivre, voir**.

vis² f screw.

visa m (de passeport) visa.

visage m face.

viser 1 vi to aim (**à** to). **2** vt (cible) to aim at.

visible adj visible.

visite f visit; **rendre v. à** to visit; **v. (médicale)** medical examination; **v. guidée** guided tour.

visiter vt to visit.

visiteur, -euse mf visitor.

visser vt to screw on.

vit voir **vivre, voir**.

vitamine f vitamin.

vite adv quickly.

vitesse f speed; (sur un véhicule) gear; **boîte de vitesses** transmission; **à toute v.** at full speed.

viticulteur, -trice mf wine grower.

vitrail, -aux m stained-glass window.

vitre f (window)pane; (de véhicule, train) window.

vitrine f (shop) window; (meuble) display cabinet.

vivace adj (plante) perennial; (tradition, sentiment) deep-rooted; (souvenir) vivid.

vivant, -ante adj living; (récit, rue) lively.

vive int **v. le roi**/etc! long live the king/etc!; **v. les vacances!** bring on the vacation!

vivement adv quickly; (répliquer) sharply; (regretter) deeply.

vivre* 1 vi to live; **v. vieux** to live to be old; **v. de** (fruits etc) to live on; (travail etc) to live by. **2** vt (vie) to live; (aventure) to live through.

VO f abrév (version originale) **film en VO** film in the original language.

vocabulaire m vocabulary.

vodka f vodka.

vœu, -x m wish.

voici prép here is, this is, pl here are, these are; **me v.** here I am; **v. dix ans que** it's ten years since.

voie f road; (rails) track; (partie de route) lane; (chemin) way; (de gare) platform; **v. sans issue** dead end; **sur la bonne v.** on the right track.

voilà prép there is, that is, pl there are, those are; **les v.** there they are; **v., j'arrive!** all right, I'm coming!; **v. dix ans que** it's ten years since.

voile¹ m (tissu) veil.

voile² f (de bateau) sail; (sport) sailing; **faire de la v.** to sail.

voilier m (de plaisance) sailboat.

voir* vti to see; **faire v. qch** to show sth; **fais v.** let me see; **v. qn faire** to see sb do ou doing; **je ne peux pas la v.** Fam I can't stand (the sight of) her; **ça n'a rien à v. avec** that's got nothing to do with.

voir (se) vpr (se fréquenter) to see each other; **ça se voit** that's obvious.

voisin, -ine 1 adj neighboring; (maison, pièce) next (**de** to). **2** mf neighbor.

voisinage m neighborhood.

voiture f car.

voix f voice; (d'électeur) vote; **à v. basse** in a whisper.

vol¹ m (d'avion, d'oiseau) flight.

vol² m (délit) theft; (hold-up) robbery; **v. d'identité** identity theft.

volaille f une **v.** a fowl.

volant m (steering) wheel.

volcan *m* volcano.

voler[1] *vi (oiseau, avion etc)* to fly.

voler[2] *vti (prendre)* to steal (**à** from).

volet *m (de fenêtre)* shutter.

voleur, -euse *mf* thief; **au v.!** stop thief!

volontaire 1 *adj (voulu) (geste etc)* deliberate. **2** *mf* volunteer.

volontairement *adv (exprès)* deliberately.

volontariat *m* voluntary work.

volonté *f* will; **bonne v.** goodwill; **mauvaise v.** ill will.

volontiers *adv* gladly.

volume *m (de boîte, de son, livre)* volume.

volumineux, -euse *adj* bulky.

vomir 1 *vt* to bring up. **2** *vi* to be sick, to vomit.

vomissements *mpl* **avoir des v.** to vomit.

vont *voir* **aller**[1].

vos *voir* **votre**.

vote *m* vote; *(de loi)* passing; **bureau de v.** polling place.

voter 1 *vi* to vote. **2** *vt (loi)* to pass.

votre, *pl* **vos** *adj poss* your.

vôtre *pron poss* **le** *ou* **la v., les vôtres** yours; **à la v.!** cheers!

voudra, voudrai(t) *etc voir* **vouloir**.

vouloir* *vt* to want (**faire** to do); **je veux qu'il parte** I want him to go; **v. dire** to mean (**que** that); **je voudrais rester** I'd like to stay; **je voudrais un pain** I'd like a loaf of bread; **voulez-vous me suivre** will you follow me; **si tu veux** if you like *ou* wish; **en v. à qn d'avoir fait qch** to be angry with sb for doing sth; **je veux bien (attendre)** I don't mind (waiting); **sans le v.** unintentionally.

vous *pron (sujet, complément direct)* you; *(complément indirect)* (to) you; *(réfléchi)* yourself, *pl* yourselves; *(réciproque)* each other.

vous-même *pron* yourself.

vous-mêmes *pron pl* yourselves.

vouvoyer *vt* **v. qn** to use the formal *vous* form with sb.

voyage *m* trip, journey; **aimer les voyages** to like traveling; **faire un v., partir en v.** to go on a trip; **bon v.!** have a good trip!; **v. organisé** (package) tour; **agent/agence de voyages** travel agent/agency.

voyager *vi* to travel.

voyageur, -euse *mf* traveler; *(passager)* passenger.

voyant, -ante 1 *adj (couleur)* gaudy, loud. **2** *m (signal)* (warning) light; *(d'appareil électrique)* pilot light.

voyelle *f* vowel.

voyou *m* hooligan.

vrac (en) *adv (en désordre)* in a muddle, haphazardly; *(non emballé)* loose.

vrai, -e *adj* true; *(réel)* real; *(authentique)* genuine.

vraiment *adv* really.

vraisemblable *adj (probable)* likely.

VTT *m inv abrév (vélo tout terrain)* mountain bike.

vu, vue *pp of* **voir**.

vue *f (spectacle)* sight; *(sens)* (eye)sight; *(panorama, photo)* view; **en v. (proche)** in sight; **de v. (connaître)** by sight.

vulgaire *adj* vulgar.

W

wagon *m (de voyageurs)* car; *(de marchandises)* freight car.

wagon-lit, *pl* **wagons-lits** *m* sleeping car.

wagon-restaurant, *pl* **wagons-restaurants** *m* dining car.

WAP *m abbr (Wireless Application Protocol)* WAP.

waters *mpl* bathroom, men's/ladies' room.

w-c *mpl* bathroom, men's/ladies' room.

Web *m* le W. the Web.

webcam *m* webcam.

week-end *m* weekend.

western *m (film)* western.

whisky, *pl* **-ies** *m* whiskey.

pron (= à cela) je m'y attendais I was expecting it; **ça y est!** that's it!

yacht *m* yacht.

yaourt *m* yogurt.

yeux *voir* œil.

Y

y 1 *adv* there; **allons-y** let's go; **j'y suis!** now I get it!; **je n'y suis pour rien** I have nothing to do with it. **2**

Z

zèbre *m* zebra.

zéro *m* zero; **deux buts à z.** two zero.

zeste *m* **un z. de citron** a piece of lemon peel.

zigzag *m* zigzag; **en z.** *(route etc)* zigzag(ging).

zigzaguer *vi* to zigzag.

zone *f* zone, area; **z. bleue** restricted parking area; **z. industrielle** industrial park.

zoo *m* zoo.

zut! *int* oh dear!